FUZZY SYSTEMS TO QUANTUM MECHANICS

SERIES IN MACHINE PERCEPTION AND ARTIFICIAL INTELLIGENCE*

ISSN: 1793-0839

This book series addresses all aspects of machine perception and artificial intelligence. Of particular interest are the areas of pattern recognition, image processing, computer vision, natural language understanding, speech processing, neural computing, machine learning, hardware architectures, software tools, and others. The series includes publications of various types, for example, textbooks, monographs, edited volumes, conference and workshop proceedings, PhD theses with significant impact, and special issues of the International Journal of Pattern Recognition and Artificial Intelligence.

Published

Vol. 87: *Fuzzy Systems to Quantum Mechanics*
by Hong-Xing Li

Vol. 86: *Graph-Based Keyword Spotting*
edited by Michael Stauffer, Andreas Fischerand Kaspar Riesen

Vol. 85: *Ensemble Learning: Pattern Classification Using Ensemble Methods (Second Edition)*
by L. Rokach

Vol. 84: *Hybrid Metaheuristics: Research and Applications*
by Siddhartha Bhattacharyya

Vol. 83: *Data Mining in Time Series and Streaming Databases*
edited by Mark Last, Horst Bunke and Abraham Kandel

Vol. 82: *Document Analysis and Text Recognition: Benchmarking State-of-the-Art Systems*
edited by Volker Märgner, Umapada Pal and Apostolos Antonacopoulos

Vol. 81: *Data Mining with Decision Trees: Theory and Applications (Second Edition)*
by L. Rokach and O. Maimon

Vol. 80: *Multimodal Interactive Handwritten Text Transcription*
by V. Romero, A. H. Toselli and E. Vidal

Vol. 79: *Document Analysis and Recognition with Wavelet and Fractal Theories*
by Y. Y. Tang

Vol. 78: *Integration of Swarm Intelligence and Artificial Neural Network*
edited by S. Dehuri, S. Ghosh and S.-B. Cho

Vol. 77: *Graph Classification and Clustering Based on Vector Space Embedding*
by K. Riesen and H. Bunke

*The complete list of the published volumes in the series can be found at
https://www.worldscientific.com/series/smpai

Series in Machine Perception and Artificial Intelligence – Vol. 87

FUZZY SYSTEMS TO QUANTUM MECHANICS

Hong-Xing Li
Beijing Normal University at Zhuhai, China

World Scientific

NEW JERSEY • LONDON • SINGAPORE • BEIJING • SHANGHAI • HONG KONG • TAIPEI • CHENNAI • TOKYO

Published by

World Scientific Publishing Co. Pte. Ltd.
5 Toh Tuck Link, Singapore 596224
USA office: 27 Warren Street, Suite 401-402, Hackensack, NJ 07601
UK office: 57 Shelton Street, Covent Garden, London WC2H 9HE

British Library Cataloguing-in-Publication Data
A catalogue record for this book is available from the British Library.

Series in Machine Perception and Artificial Intelligence — Vol. 87
FUZZY SYSTEMS TO QUANTUM MECHANICS

ISBN 978-981-121-118-8 (hardcover)
ISBN 978-981-121-119-5 (ebook for institutions)
ISBN 978-981-121-120-1 (ebook for individuals)

For any available supplementary material, please visit
https://www.worldscientific.com/worldscibooks/10.1142/11577#t=suppl

Preface

Fuzzy sets theory has been more than five decades of development and applications since the finding of it by L. A. Zadeh in 1965. The scope of development and applications ranges from theoretical basis to practical foundation and from natural science and engineering to humanity, medicine, and artificial intelligence. The broad array of applications demonstrates the value of the theory.

I have researched fuzzy sets, fuzzy systems and fuzzy neural network theories and their applications almost four decades since 1981. Since around 1999, I have been thinking an important question which I think that it is important and interesting: To where in science ocean can fuzzy sets theory lead us? Why I always consider this question? Because I regard Prof. Zadeh as one Columbus in Science Ocean and I am a diligent Chinese sailor in his ship, I really want to know where I can go and what I can discover on Zadeh's research ship.

Although fuzzy sets theory has been more than fifty years since it was founded, people still think it as a new subject in Science Ocean. Of course, we all have known many other similar new subjects such as neural networks, machine learning, deep learning, soft computing, data mining, big data, granular computing, rough sets, and the like.

For any one of these new subjects, it must be in the face of a strict test question: Can it solve an important problem which cannot be solved by using any methods or theories coming from any other subjects?

For example, probability theory had ever not admitted by a lot of mathematicians in its early development stage partly on account of its coming from gambles. Later on, a mathematician, Kolmogorov, built the mathematical theory for it by means of measure theory. More importantly, a lot of successful applications of probability theory made its case improved. As we all know, without probability theory, we even do not know how to do weather forecast nowadays. Without probability theory, we do not know what statistic mechanics is. Without probability theory, quantum mechanics does not have today's situation, because Schrodinger Equation is one of backbones of quantum mechanics, and the solutions of Schrodinger Equation have been given their statistical interpretation by M. Born, a German physicist, the solutions are called de Broglie waves. This means that, without probability theory, basically there is no today's quantum mechanics; therefore basically there is no today's modern physics.

For any one new subject in science, considering some important open problem, I think that there are four cases:

Case 1: the new subject cannot solve the open problem, and any other subjects cannot solve the open problem, too;

Case 2: the new subject cannot solve the open problem, but there is one of other subjects can solve the open problem, which means that the new subject is of little science worth;

Case 3: the new subject can solve the open problem, but there are some of other subjects can also solve the open problem, which means that the new subject is just of a little science worth;

Case 4: the new subject can solve the open problem very well, but all other subjects cannot solve the open problem, which means that the new subject is of a great science worth in no doubt.

Now I return to talk about fuzzy sets theory and fuzzy systems. Whether there exists at least one important problem in science or in real practice application such that fuzzy sets theory and fuzzy systems can effectively solve it but just this problem cannot be solved by using any methods or theories coming from any other subjects? Maybe there is only one answer: no.

Why I use the word "maybe"? I should tell a science story coming from 2002 to explain this question. Dr. Li H. X. with his fuzzy sets theory research group successfully achieved the stable control experiment of four-stage inverted pendulum in 2002, which is real hardware equipment not a simulation and was the first experiment in the world (see Photo. f.1). This four-stage inverted pendulum can be called linear four-stage inverted pendulum because its cart or slider bearing four rods moves along a linear sliding rail, while the four rods move around a plane. This problem belongs to fuzzy control theory while I do not involve this issue in this book. I want to write another book to focus on my own control theory with fuzzy sets theory and introduce the stable control experiment of four-stage inverted pendulum in details.

As we all know, the experiment of three-stage inverted pendulum has been a very difficult thing and a few of people can do this experiment. As far as I can see, from 2002 to now, I have not learned that second experiment of four-stage inverted pendulum appears.

Photo. f.1. linear four-stage inverted pendulum

Much more difficult about the stable control experiment of four-stage inverted pendulum is on the spherical four-stage inverted pendulum. “Spherical” means that its cart or slider bearing four rods moves around plane, while the four rods move around in three-dimension space. From 2002 to 2010, after going through a lot of control method exploring and stable control experiments, Dr. Li H. X. with his fuzzy sets theory research group successfully achieved the stable control experiment of spherical four-stage inverted pendulum in 2010, which is also real hardware equipment not a simulation and was the first experiment in the world (see Photo. f.2).

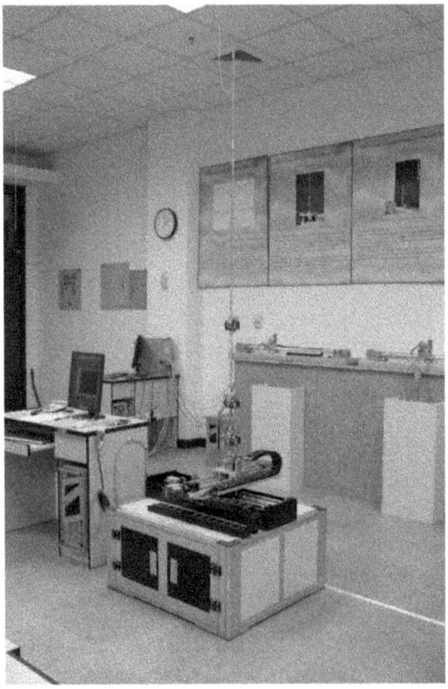

Photo. f.2. spherical four-stage inverted pendulum

Around 2012 to 2013, my student Dr. Hu Dan was a visiting scholar at San Jose State University and Prof. T. Y. Lin was her supervisor. Dr. Hu had a chance to tell the four-stage inverted pendulum story to Prof. Lin, and then Prof. Lin told the story to Prof. Zadeh. And Prof. Zadeh invited me to UC Berkeley with carrying my linear four-stage inverted pendulum (my spherical four-stage inverted pendulum is too big and heavy to carry to USA) to give a talk and to do demonstration in front of Prof. Zadeh. Of course I also visited San Jose State University invited by Prof. T. Y. Lin and discussed some interesting problems on fuzzy sets theory with Prof. Lin. The following photos can show the situations of my visiting Prof. Zadeh in April, 2013.

Photo. f.3. Prof. Zadeh and Prof. Li

Photo. f.4. stable linear four-stage inverted pendulum in UC Berkeley

Photo. f.5. Prof. Zadeh and Prof. Li

Photo. f.6. (from left to right) Dr. D. G. Wang, Prof. Y. Zheng, Dr. D. Hu, Prof. T. Y. Lin, Prof. L. A. Zadeh, Prof. H. X. Li and Dr. J. Y. Wang

After I came back from UC Berkeley to China, Prof. Zadeh sent me a thank note. In order to make readers to learn how to exchange academic viewpoints for two scholars on some academic problems, I would better copy the note as following:

Dear Professor Li:

Many thanks for coming to Berkeley to make a presentation of your work on the four-stage inverted pendulum. The system which you described is a remarkable achievement. I believe that what you achieved is worthy of a major prize. I was highly impressed by the sophisticated mathematics which you employed to stabilize the pendulum. I was also highly impressed by the two-stage self-learning pendulum. Please accept my compliments and congratulations on your path-breaking achievement.

With my thanks and warm regards
Sincerely,
Lotfi Zadeh
Professor Emeritus
Director, Berkeley Initiative in Soft Computing (BISC)

In my answer letter, I explained my idea on the relationship between the variable universe adaptive fuzzy control and type-2 fuzzy sets, which is as follows:

Dear Professor Zadeh,

I just came back to China from USA yesterday and I have blessedly received your "thank note". Many thanks for you giving me such a good opportunity to have my talk in Berkeley.

I view that the idea on the fuzzy sets defined on variable universe is essentially a kind of type-2 fuzzy sets or a kind of generating method of type-2 fuzzy sets. In other words, some finite type-1 fuzzy sets can generate a type-2 fuzzy set. By the use of my experiments, I think that type-2 fuzzy sets are much more powerful than type-1 fuzzy sets.

I regard you as another Columbus leading us to discover many new lands or continents in science world. I am a Chinese diligent sailor on your ship continuing to do hard work on fuzzy sets. When I obtain some new good work, I will visit you again in the future.

Sincerely yours,
H. X. Li

To make me very sad is that our well-beloved mentor Prof. L. A. Zadeh passed away in 2017 so that I have not any chance to visit him.

Prof. Zadeh had ever been a well-known control theory expert and did many important contributions on control theory. Since 1965, he had devoted himself to develop his fuzzy sets theory. As I mentioned four Cases above for any new subjects, particularly Case 4 is the most important. I think that the stable control of the four-stage inverted pendulum should strong enough support Zadeh's fuzzy sets theory, which means that the Case 4 has been realized for fuzzy sets theory.

I need to think another question calmly: the stable control of the four-stage inverted pendulum is of strong application background. Can fuzzy sets theory and fuzzy systems lead us into main fields of science such as physics and mathematics to solve some important and interesting problems?

Since I came back from UC Berkeley in 2013, I have been doing some research on quantum mechanics by using fuzzy sets theory and fuzzy systems. Fortunately, I have got some important and interesting research results so that I have this book to be published to show these research conclusions not only in quantum mechanics but in mathematics as well. These conclusions are as the following.

On physics, I have pointed that the motion of a mass point in classic mechanics has also waviness in Section 8.3. The wave function of the motion of a mass point has surely no uncertainty. On the other hand, although the motion of a particle has surely uncertainty, the wave function of the particle must have no uncertainty. Thus, we can consider the relation between the wave function of a mass point in classic mechanics and the wave functions of some particles in quantum mechanics. As I discussed in Section 8.2, I have revealed the relation by means of Theorem 8.2.1. In other words, by using wave functions of both classic mechanics and quantum mechanics, classic mechanics and quantum mechanics are unified, which is the significance of our unified theory about the two kinds of mechanics.

I need to emphasize my new and important and interesting conclusion: The motion of a mass point has also so-called duality: wave-mass-point duality, which is very similar to the case of the motion of a particle in quantum mechanics and is an important support to our unified theory on classic mechanics and quantum mechanics. It is not difficult to understand that Theorem 8.2.1 should be the most important in physics.

On mathematics, another new and important and interesting conclusion of me is coming from Theorem 8.4.1 which means that, for any a continuous function, there must be a sequence of probability spaces and a sequence of random vectors defined on the sequence of probability spaces, such that the sequence of conditional mathematical expectations of the sequence of random vectors uniformly converges to the continuous function. This conclusion can establish a new bridge between real analysis and probability theory.

It is worth noting that, Prigogine had ever pointed out his conclusion by many experiments: world is random not certain (see [20]). In fact, Theorem 8.4.1 just prove his idea, because, as we all know, a large part of physical phenomenon can be described by some kind of continuous functions, and based on Theorem 8.4.1, any one of these continuous functions must be the limit of the sequence of conditional mathematical expectations of a sequence of random vectors.

Besides, in Section 8.5, approximation theory significance of Theorem 8.2.1 is discussed in detail and its main conclusion is expressed by Theorem 8.5.1. This undoubtedly gives a new kind of new method to function approximation theory.

Another important thing is worth noting that, in this book, I give the definition of wave-set duality which its idea is coming from the wave-particle dualism in quantum mechanics (see Section 1.2).

In this book, there are three unifications problems and their solution schemes: One is just the unification between classic mechanics and quantum mechanics (see Chapter 8); second is the unification between fuzzy systems and stochastic systems (see Chapter 5 and Chapter 6); third is the unification between Riemann integral and Lebesgue integral (see Chapter 9).

At last, I want to say, Zadeh's one of the most basic contributions for fuzzy sets theory is that he extended characteristic functions of Cantor's sets to membership functions of fuzzy sets. I regard this thing as Extension Principle. Why this Extension Principle? Because a principle is a principle and a theorem is a theorem, a principle needs not to be proved but a theorem must be proved. As I pointed out in Section 2.10, Zadeh's extension principle can be proved by this Extension Principle which I suggested in Section 2.10. This means that Zadeh's extension principle is not a principle but a theorem or a proposition.

Li Hong-Xing

Contents

Chapter 1

Fuzzy Sets

1.1 Cantor's Sets

Set theory was found in 1874 by G. Cantor, a German mathematician. One of the important methods used by Cantor in creating sets is the **comprehension principle**, which means that for any P, a property, all the objects with P and only with P can be included together to form a set denoted by the symbol as follows:

$$A = \{a | P(a)\}$$

where A expresses the set and "a" means an object in A. Generally, "a" is referred to as an element or a member of A. The symbol $P(a)$ represents the fact that the element "a" satisfies P, and "$\{\}$" means that all the elements satisfying P are collected to form a set. In logic, the comprehension principle is stated as the following:

$$(\forall a)(a \in A \Leftrightarrow P(a)).$$

People routinely use the word "concept", for example, the word "man" is a concept. A concept has its intension and extension; by intension we mean attributes of "man", and by extension we mean all of the objects defined by the concept. That is, sets can be used to express concepts. Since set operations and transformations can express judging and reasoning, modern mathematics based on set theory becomes a formal language for describing and expressing certain areas of knowledge.

In a practical problem, a set is always regarded as an extension of a concept so that a topic under discussion may be limited to the same "scope". For example, if the topic of discussion is the concept "man", then the scope is limited to "people", and it is not necessary to consider other objects that have no relation to the concept. Let all people be denoted by U, and all men selected from U form a set A in U, in fact it is a subset of U, which is just the extension of the concept "man".

All objects of a "concept" under discussion form a **universe** which is also called universal set or total set. We prefer to use universe. A universe is often denoted by capital letters, e.g. by $U, V, \cdots, X, Y$. Each object in the universe is called an element, denoted by corresponding lower letters $u, v, \cdots, x, y$. A number of elements in U is a set on U, denoted by capital letters $A, B, C, \cdots$.

A universe U may be imaged as a "rectangle" and the elements of U are abstract "points" without mass and size. A set on U may be represented by a "circular ring" or "oval" in the "rectangle". The relationship between the elements of U and a set A on U is depicted as a Venn diagram in Figure 1.1.1.

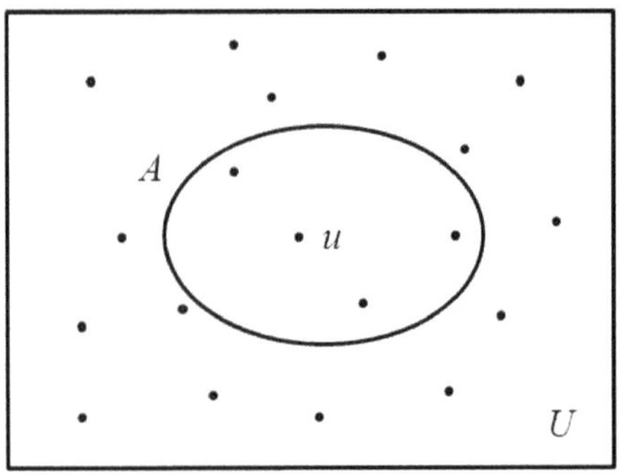

Fig. 1.1.1. A Venn diagram containing a universe, a set and its elements

For any element u in U and a set A on U, u either belongs to A (denoted by $u \in A$) or does not belongs to A (denoted by $u \notin A$). If $u \in A$, i.e. u lies inside of the oval, then the relationship between u and A is denoted by 1; If $u \notin A$, i.e. u lies outside of the oval, then the relationship between u and A is denoted by 0. This means we can in fact get a mapping based on A as follows:

$$\chi_A : U \to \{0,1\}, \quad u \mapsto \chi_A(u) = \begin{cases} 1, & u \in A, \\ 0, & u \notin A \end{cases}$$

The mapping χ_A is called **characteristic function** of the set A, which clearly indicates membership between an element u and a set A.

Let A and B be any two sets on U. If A and B satisfy the following condition:

$$(\forall u \in U)(u \in A \Rightarrow u \in B),$$

we call A being a subset of B or A being included by B or B including A, denoted by $A \subset B$ or $B \supset A$. So when we say that A is a set on U, this just means A is a subset of U, i.e. $A \subset U$.

We all well know that this class of sets, $\mathcal{P}(U) = \{A | A \subset U\}$, is called power set of U. In U, we define two binary algebraic operations $\bigcup, \bigcap$ and one unitary algebraic operations "c" as follows

$$\begin{aligned}&\bigcup : \mathcal{P}(U) \times \mathcal{P}(U) \to \mathcal{P}(U)\\&(A, B) \mapsto A \bigcup B = \bigcup(A, B) = \{u \in U | (u \in A) \vee (u \in B)\},\end{aligned}$$

$$\begin{aligned}&\bigcap : \mathcal{P}(U) \times \mathcal{P}(U) \to \mathcal{P}(U)\\&(A, B) \mapsto A \bigcap B = \bigcap(A, B) = \{u \in U | (u \in A) \wedge (u \in B)\},\end{aligned}$$

$$\begin{aligned}&c : \mathcal{P}(U) \to \mathcal{P}(U)\\&A \mapsto A^c = c(A) = U \setminus A = \{u \in U | u \notin A\}.\end{aligned}$$

This algebraic system $(\mathcal{P}(U), \bigcup, \bigcap, c)$ is called **set algebra**, where $\vee$ is logic symbol: extraction, meaning "or", and $\wedge$ is conjunction, meaning "and".

It is easy to prove the following results: for any two sets $A, B \in \mathcal{P}(U)$, we have

$$\begin{aligned}&(\forall u \in U)(\chi_{A \cup B}(u) = \chi_A(u) \vee \chi_B(u)),\\&(\forall u \in U)(\chi_{A \cap B}(u) = \chi_A(u) \wedge \chi_B(u)),\\&(\forall u \in U)(\chi_{A^c}(u) = 1 - \chi_A(u)),\end{aligned}$$

where $\vee$ is of another meaning: $\vee = \max$, i.e.

$$(\forall a,b\in\mathbb{R})(a\vee b=\max\{a,b\})$$

and $\wedge=\min$, i.e.

$$(\forall a,b\in\mathbb{R})(a\wedge b=\min\{a,b\}).$$

In addition, let V be another universe and for any a set $B\in\mathcal{P}(V)$, we well know the symbol:

$$A\times B=\{(a,b)|a\in A,b\in B\}$$

which is called the **direct product** of A and B, especially we have

$$U\times V=\{(u,v)|u\in U,v\in V\}$$

and we easy know the fact: $\forall(u,v)\in U\times V$,

$$\chi_{A\times B}(u,v)=\chi_A(u)\wedge\chi_B(v)=\chi_A(u)\cdot\chi_B(v). \tag{1.1.1}$$

Now we use the following symbol to express the set of such mappings:

$$\mathrm{Ch}(U)=\{\chi|\chi:U\to[0,1]\},$$

and define two binary algebraic operations $\vee,\wedge$ and one unitary algebraic operation "c" as follows:

$$\begin{aligned}&\vee:\mathrm{Ch}(U)\times\mathrm{Ch}(U)\to\mathrm{Ch}(U)\\&(\chi_1,\chi_2)\mapsto\chi_1\vee\chi_2=\vee(\chi_1,\chi_2),\\&(\forall u\in U)((\chi_1\vee\chi_2)(u)=\chi_1(u)\vee\chi_2(u))\end{aligned}$$

$$\begin{aligned}&\wedge:\mathrm{Ch}(U)\times\mathrm{Ch}(U)\to\mathrm{Ch}(U)\\&(\chi_1,\chi_2)\mapsto\chi_1\wedge\chi_2=\wedge(\chi_1,\chi_2),\\&(\forall u\in U)((\chi_1\wedge\chi_2)(u)=\chi_1(u)\wedge\chi_2(u))\end{aligned}$$

$$\begin{aligned}&c:\mathrm{Ch}(U)\to\mathrm{Ch}(U)\\&\chi\mapsto\chi^c=c(\chi),\\&(\forall u\in U)(\chi^c(u)=1-\chi(u))\end{aligned}$$

It is easy to prove that this algebraic system $(\mathcal{P}(U),\bigcup,\bigcap,c)$ must be isomorphic with the algebraic system $(\text{Ch}(U),\vee,\wedge,c)$, i.e.

$$(\mathcal{P}(U),\bigcup,\bigcap,c)\cong(\text{Ch}(U),\vee,\wedge,c). \tag{1.1.2}$$

Thus we will regard $\text{Ch}(U)$ and $\mathcal{P}(U)$ as the same thing.

Now we prove (1.1.2). In fact, consider the following mapping:

$$f:\mathcal{P}(U)\to\text{Ch}(U)$$
$$A\mapsto f(A)=\chi_A$$

For any $A,B\in\mathcal{P}(U)$, if $A\neq B$, then

$$(\exists u\in U)\{[(u\in A)\wedge(u\notin B)]\vee[(u\notin A)\wedge(u\in B)]\}.$$

Assume that $(u\in A)\wedge(u\notin B)$ is true, and then we have

$$(\chi_A(u)=1)\wedge(\chi_B(u)=0),$$

thus $\chi_A\neq\chi_B$. This means that f is an injection. For any $\chi\in\text{Ch}(U)$, by it we can form a set $A\in\mathcal{P}(U)$ as follows

$$A=\{u\in U\,|\,\chi(u)=1\}.$$

Then by using A, we can get another $\chi_A\in\text{Ch}(U)$ as well, i.e.

$$\chi_A:U\to\{0,1\}$$
$$u\mapsto\chi_A(u)=\begin{cases}1, & u\in A,\\ 0, & u\notin A\end{cases}$$

Now we can prove the fact that $\chi_A=\chi$. In the matter of fact, for any an element $u\in U$, we have the following expression:

$$\chi_A(u)=1\Leftrightarrow u\in A\Leftrightarrow \chi(u)=1.$$

So we have the fact that $\chi_A=\chi$, which means that $f(A)=\chi_A=\chi$, i.e. f is a surjection. Therefore f is a bijection.

Now for any two sets $A,B\in\mathcal{P}(U)$, we can easily have the following expressions:

$$f(A\bigcup B)=\chi_{A\cup B},\quad f(A\bigcap B)=\chi_{A\cap B},\quad f(A^c)=\chi_{A^c}$$

In fact, by noticing the following facts

$$[f(A\cup B)](u)=\chi_{A\cup B}(u)=\chi_A(u)\vee\chi_B(u)$$
$$=[f(A)](u)\vee[f(B)](u)=\{[f(A)]\vee[f(B)]\}(u),$$

$$[f(A\cap B)](u)=\chi_{A\cap B}(u)=\chi_A(u)\wedge\chi_B(u)$$
$$=[f(A)](u)\wedge[f(B)](u)=\{[f(A)]\wedge[f(B)]\}(u),$$

$$\left[f\left(A^c\right)\right](u)=\chi_{A^c}(u)=1-\chi_A(u)=1-[f(A)](u)$$
$$=[f(A)]^c(u)$$

we know that f keeps algebra operations. This proves that (1.1.2) is true.

1.2 Physical Significance for Cantor's Sets

In this section, we consider physical significance for Cantor's sets with interest. For any a nonempty universe U, since it has nothing to do with time t, U can be regarded as a static system. For any an element $u\in U$, it is an element in U. However, if we put a "dress" on it, i.e. put $A=\{u\}$, it becomes a set $A=\{u\}\in\mathcal{P}(U)$. So we get its characteristic function as follows:

$$\chi_A(x)=\chi_{\{u\}}(x)=\begin{cases}1, & x=u,\\ 0, & x\neq u\end{cases}$$

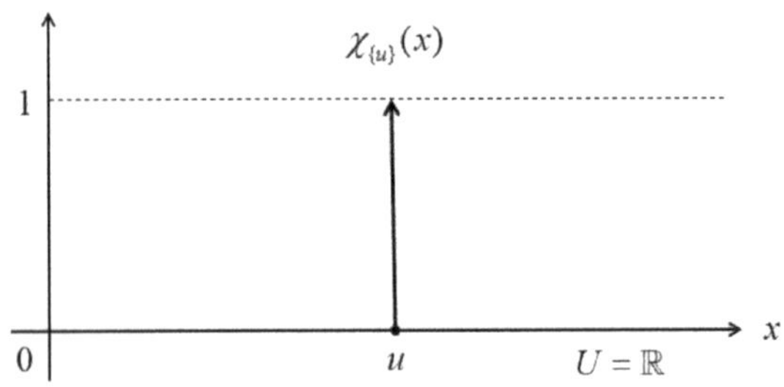

Fig. 1.2.1. Unit impulse wave of u

For convenience, we take $U = \mathbb{R}$ (the set of all real numbers). Then the graph of the characteristic function $\chi_{\{u\}}(x)$ is drawn as Figure 1.2.1.

This clearly is a **unit impulse wave** corresponding to the set $A = \{u\}$ or the element u. We can regard this fact as **wave-element duality**. This reveals that every element in U must have its unit impulse wave, which is very important phenomenon.

And then, for any nonempty set $A \in \mathcal{P}(U)$, corresponding to it, we have its characteristic function χ_A; particularly, if we take the universe $U = \mathbb{R}$ and $A = [a,b] \subset \mathbb{R}$, then the graph of the characteristic function $\chi_A(x)$ is drawn as Figure 1.2.2.

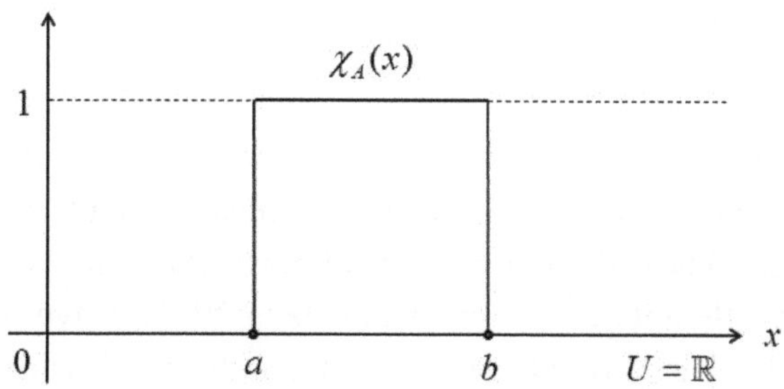

Fig. 1.2.2. Unit rectangle wave of $A = [a,b]$

This clearly is a **unit rectangle wave** corresponding to the set $A = [a,b]$. As having known the fact that

$$\left(\mathcal{P}(U), \bigcup, \bigcap, c\right) \cong \left(\mathrm{Ch}(U), \vee, \wedge, c\right),$$

we have some reason to regard this fact as **wave-set duality**. This reveals that every set in $\mathcal{P}(U)$ must have its unit rectangle wave, which is also very important phenomenon.

By taking notice the following fact:

$$A = \bigcup_{x \in A} \{x\},$$

we clearly know that a set in $\mathcal{P}(U)$ must be made up of some elements in U. From a physical point of view, if we regard elements in U as **microscopic particles**, then any set in $\mathcal{P}(U)$ can be regarded as a **macroscopical**

mass point; it is easy to imagine that the mass point is composed of a group of elements in U. We can prove the following fact:

$$(\forall u \in U)\left(\chi_A(u) = \sum_{x \in A} \chi_{\{x\}}(u)\right). \tag{1.2.1}$$

In the matter of fact, for any $u \in U$, we have that

$$\chi_A(u) = 1 \Leftrightarrow u \in A \Leftrightarrow$$

$$\sum_{x \in A} \chi_{\{x\}}(u) = \chi_{\{u\}}(u) + \sum_{x \in A \setminus \{u\}} \chi_{\{x\}}(u) = 1 + 0 = 1$$

We want to know that this fact can give us what new idea. In fact, we all know that any object in real macroscopical physical world can be regarded as a mass point and the object must be made up of a lot of microscopic particles. If a macroscopical mass point movement is also of wave property, then its wave must be made up of the waves of the microscopic particles based on (1.2.1). Unfortunately, in classical mechanics, there is no the idea that a macroscopical mass point movement is of wave property.

1.3 Background of Fuzzy Sets

We start this section from a kind of open loop system with one-input and one-output shown as Figure 1.3.1, where S stands for a system, x for input variable taking values in the universe $X = [a,b] \subset \mathbb{R}$ and y for output variable taking values in the universe $Y = [c,d] \subset \mathbb{R}$.

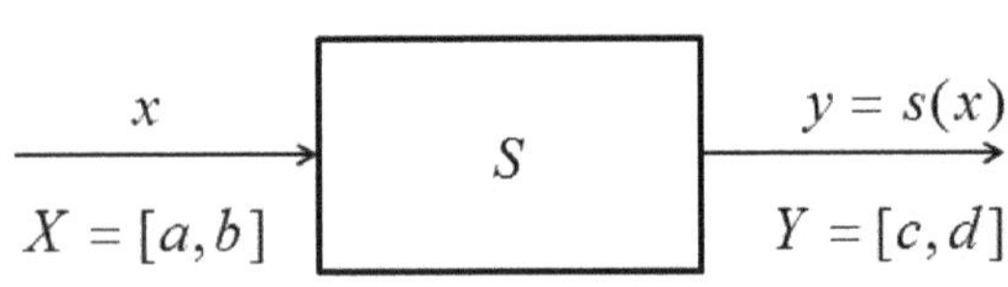

Fig. 1.3.1. One-input one-output open loop system

If S is a complicated uncertainty system, then it is hard to model the system by mechanism modeling method. Thus we often use some experiments to get a group of discrete data which usually describe the relationship between input and output of the system.

The data set is denoted by IOD, Input and Output Data, as the following

$$\text{IOD} \triangleq \{(x_i, y_i) | i = 0, 1, \cdots, n\} \subset X \times Y$$

where " $\triangleq$ " means "be defined as". And the input data and the out data are also respectively written by

$$X_0 \triangleq \{x_i | i = 0, 1, \cdots, n\}, \quad Y_0 \triangleq \{y_i | i = 0, 1, \cdots, n\},$$

in which we can assume that

$$a = x_0 < x_1 < \cdots < x_n = b, \quad c = \min_{0 \le i \le n} y_i, \quad d = \max_{0 \le i \le n} y_i$$

Actually data set IOD can be viewed as a mapping:

$$g_0 : X_0 \to Y_0, \quad x_i \mapsto g(x_i) \triangleq y_i, \quad i = 0, 1, \cdots, n.$$

From the view of systems, for every number $i \in \{0, 1, \cdots, n\}$, $g_0(x_i) = y_i$ is regarded as a response of the system to input x_i. However the mapping g_0 has no definition in $X_0^c = X \setminus X_0$, which means that S does not respond to any element in X_0^c. The mapping g_0 can be shown as Figure 1.3.2.

Now we expand the mapping $g_0 : X_0 \to Y_0$ as the following mapping:

$$g : X \to Y, \quad x \mapsto y = g(x) = \sum_{i=0}^{n} \chi_{\{x_i\}}(x) y_i$$

Now we expand the mapping $g_0 : X_0 \to Y_0$ as the following mapping:

$$g : X \to Y$$

$$x \mapsto y = g(x) = \sum_{i=0}^{n} \chi_{\{x_i\}}(x) y_i$$

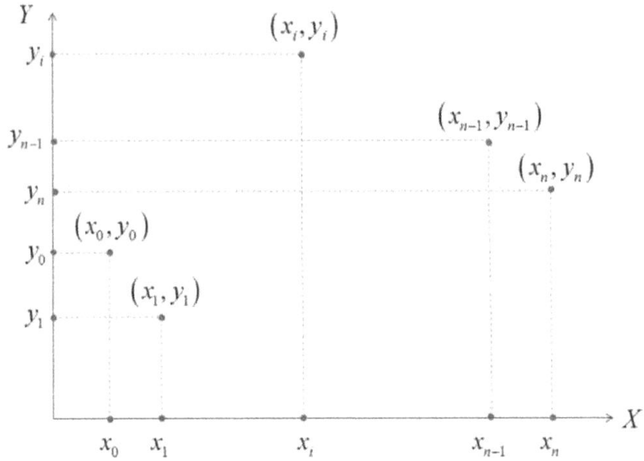

Fig. 1.3.2. Discrete response of the system by $g_0 : X_0 \to Y_0$

Now we expand the mapping $g_0 : X_0 \to Y_0$ as the following mapping:

$$g : X \to Y, \quad x \mapsto y = g(x) = \sum_{i=0}^{n} \chi_{\{x_i\}}(x) y_i$$

Although the mapping $g : X \to Y$ makes the system S having response on every $x \in X$, i.e.,

$$g(x) = \begin{cases} y_i, & x = x_i, \\ 0, & x \in X - X_0 \end{cases}$$
$$\forall x \in X, \quad i = 0, 1, \cdots, n$$

if we notice that $(\forall x \in X \setminus X_0)(g(x) = 0)$, we know the fact that the responses of S in $X \setminus X_0$ are almost useless.

Then we consider a Problem: How to get a practical mapping $f : X \to Y$ by using of the discrete mapping $g_0 : X_0 \to Y_0$ such that S has useful response to every element in X and satisfies the natural condition:

$$(\forall i \in \{0, 1, \cdots, n\})(f(x_i) = g_0(x_i)).$$

Of course, as we all know, interpolation is one of methods for solving the problem, but this method is without system view and also without meanings of operations of sets, logic and inference.

We will consider a new schedule to solve the problem by adequately using sets, logic and inference.

We all know well that the data $x_i, y_i, i = 0,1,\cdots,n$ have their errors, thus we have the following expressions:

$$x_i \pm \delta_i, \quad y_i \pm \varepsilon_i, \quad \delta_i \geq 0, \quad \varepsilon_i \geq 0, \quad i = 0,1,\cdots,n$$

Or we can write above expression as the following:

$$x_i \in [x_i - \delta_i, x_i + \delta_i], \quad y_i \in [y_i - \varepsilon_i, y_i + \varepsilon_i], \quad i = 0,1,\cdots,n$$

This implies that our data is extended step by step as follows

$$\text{IOD} = \{(x_i, y_i) | i = 0,1,\cdots,n\} \Rightarrow \{(\{x_i\},\{y_i\}) | i = 0,1,\cdots,n\}$$
$$\Rightarrow \{([x_i - \delta_i, x_i + \delta_i],[y_i - \varepsilon_i, y_i + \varepsilon_i]) | i = 0,1,\cdots,n\}$$

By noticing the characteristic function of every error interval as follows

$$\chi_{[x_i-\delta_i,x_i+\delta_i]}(x) = \begin{cases} 1, & x \in [x_i - \delta_i, x_i + \delta_i], \\ 0, & x \in X - [x_i - \delta_i, x_i + \delta_i] \end{cases}$$
$$i = 0,1,\cdots,n$$

based on wave-element duality and wave-set duality, every unit impulse wave $\chi_{\{x_i\}}(x)$ has turned into an unit rectangle wave $\chi_{[x_i-\delta_i,x_i+\delta_i]}(x)$ shown as Figure 1.3.3. From unit impulse waves $\chi_{\{x_i\}}(x)$ to unit rectangle waves $\chi_{[x_i-\delta_i,x_i+\delta_i]}(x)$, we actually gain more information quantity by using errors of the data. Now we calculate a kind of information quantity from $[x_i - \delta_i, x_i + \delta_i]$ as follows:

$$\int_a^b \chi_{[x_i-\delta_i,x_i+\delta_i]}(x)dx = 2\delta_i, \quad i = 0,1,\cdots,n. \tag{1.3.1}$$

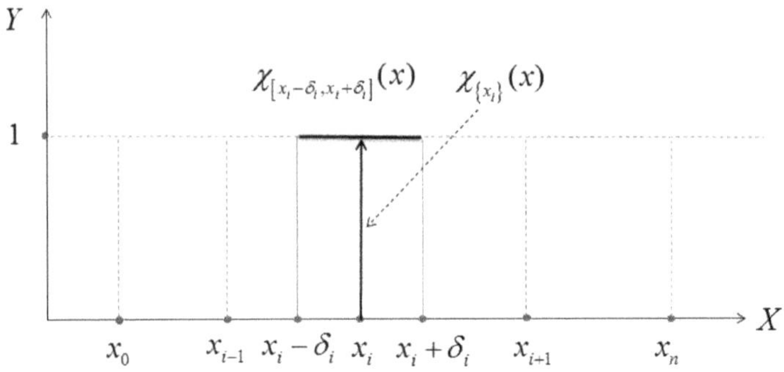

Fig. 1.3.3. Unit rectangle waves $\chi_{[x_i-\delta_i,x_i+\delta_i]}(x)$

As shown in Figure 1.3.4, it is easy to learn that the system does not respond for the inputs in these interspaces.

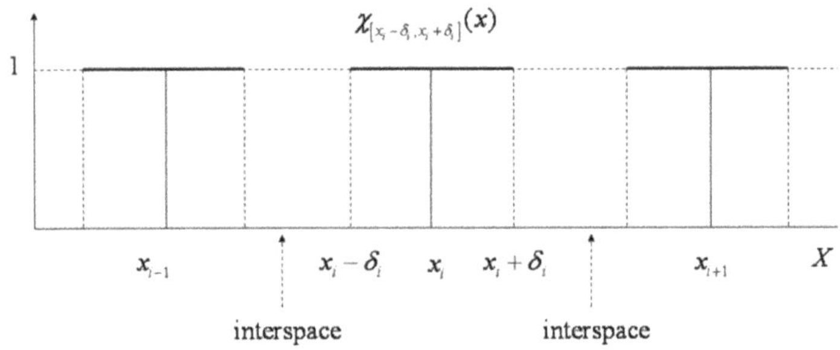

Fig. 1.3.4. The system does not respond for the inputs in these interspaces

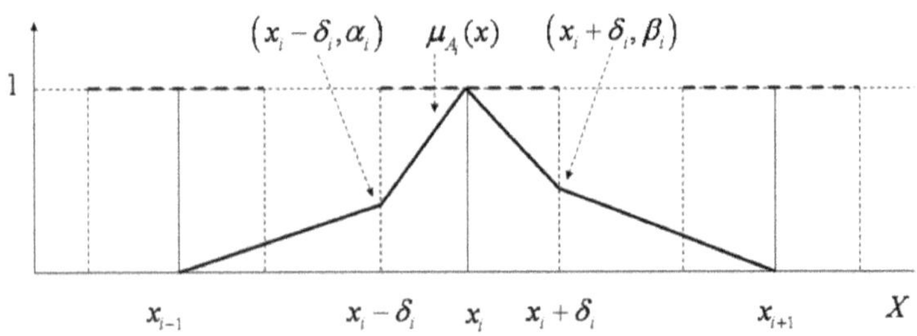

Fig. 1.3.5. Another type of waves $\mu_{A_i}(x)$ of "some sets A_i"

In order to solve this problem, our idea is that, under keeping the information quantity obtained by the definite integrals (1.3.1), we consider another type of waves $\mu_{A_i}(x)$ of "some kind of sets A_i" as shown as Figure 1.3.5. In order to keep the condition as follows:

$$(\forall i \in \{0,1,\cdots,n\})\left(\int_a^b \mu_{A_i}(x)dx = 2\delta_i\right),$$

if we take the following two numbers:

$$\alpha_i = \frac{\delta_i}{x_i - x_{i-1}}, \quad \beta_i = \frac{\delta_i}{x_{i+1} - x_i}$$

then we can get the following wave functions:

$$\mu_{A_i}(x) = \begin{cases} 0, & x \in [a, x_{i-1}), \\ \dfrac{\delta_i(x - x_{i-1})}{(x_i - x_{i-1})(x_i - x_{i-1} - \delta_i)}, & x \in [x_{i-1}, x_i - \delta_i), \\ \dfrac{(x_i - x_{i-1} - \delta_i)(x - x_i + \delta_i) + \delta_i^2}{(x_i - x_{i-1})\delta_i}, & x \in [x_{i-1}, x_i - \delta_i), \\ 1 - \dfrac{(x_{i+1} - x_i - \delta_i)(x - x_i)}{\delta_i(x_{i+1} - x_i)}, & x \in [x_{i-1}, x_i - \delta_i), \\ \dfrac{\delta_i(x - x_{i+1})}{(x_{i+1} - x_i)(x_i - x_{i+1} + \delta_i)}, & x \in [x_{i-1}, x_i - \delta_i), \\ 0, & x \in [x_{i+1}, b] \end{cases} \tag{1.3.2}$$

And then we have already kept the condition:

$$(\forall i \in \{0,1,\cdots,n\})\left(\int_a^b \mu_{A_i}(x)dx = 2\delta_i\right).$$

It is easy to learn that the wave functions are of a property:

$$(\forall i \in \{0,1,\cdots,n\})(\mu_{A_i}(X) = [0,1]),$$

where $\mu_{A_i}(X)$ is the image set of the universe X under the mapping μ_{A_i}, which is quite different from $\chi_{[x_i-\delta_i,x_i+\delta_i]}(X)=\{0,1\}$, the image set of the universe X under the mapping $\chi_{[x_i-\delta_i,x_i+\delta_i]}$.

Based on wave-set duality stated in the Section 1.2, we may guess or image a possible fact that the wave functions $\mu_{A_i}(x)$ should be corresponding to a new type of sets that will be called "fuzzy sets". In the next section, we will give its definition.

1.4 Definition and Operations of Fuzzy Sets

From above section, we have learned the fact that

$$(\forall i\in\{0,1,\cdots,n\})\left(\mu_{A_i}(X)=[0,1]\right).$$

So naturally we give the following definition.

Definition 1.4.1 A **fuzzy set** A on a given universe U is that, for any $u\in U$, there is one and only one corresponding real number $\mu_A(u)\in[0,1]$ to u, where $\mu_A(u)$ is called the **grade of membership** of u belonging to A. This means that we get a mapping:

$$\mu_A:U\to[0,1],\quad u\mapsto\mu_A(u),$$

and this mapping is called the **membership function** of A. The set of all fuzzy sets on U is denoted by $\mathcal{F}(U)$ which can be called fuzzy power set of U. □

We can illustrate fuzzy sets by using a graphing method similar to Venn diagrams. First, universe U is taken to be a rectangle in a Euclidean plane. Then elements of U are regarded as line segments with unit length 1, and a fuzzy set A is regarded as a "circular ring" or "oval" in the rectangle as well as Figure 1.1.1, which is shown as Figure 1.4.1, and the diagrammatic sketch of Figure 1.4.1 is called **pan-Venn-diagram**.

From Figure 1.4.1, we easy to learn the fact that

$$\mu_A(u_1)=1,\quad\mu_A(u_2)=0,\quad\mu_A(u_3)=0.3,\quad\mu_A(u_4)=0.6.$$

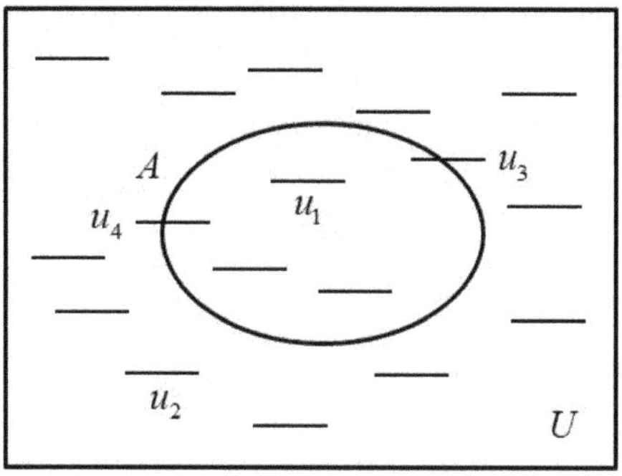

Fig. 1.4.1. Pan-Venn-diagram on fuzzy sets

Clearly $\mathcal{F}(U) \supset \mathcal{P}(U)$ where $\mathcal{P}(U)$ is just the power set of U. Just as Cantor's sets can be completely described by characteristic functions, fuzzy sets can also be completely described by membership functions. If the range of μ_A admits only two values 0 and 1, that is, $\mu_A(U) = \{0,1\}$, then this membership function degenerates to a characteristic function, which means the result as the following:

$$A = \{u \in U \mid \mu_A(u) = 1\}.$$

Therefore, Cantor's sets are special cases of fuzzy sets. Clearly it is true that $\mathcal{F}(U) \setminus \mathcal{P}(U) \neq \varnothing$, and if $A \in \mathcal{F}(U) \setminus \mathcal{P}(U)$, then A is called a **proper fuzzy set** because $(\exists u_0 \in U)(\mu_A(u_0) \in (0,1))$ where (0,1) is an open interval. These $\mu_{A_i}(x), i = 0,1,\cdots,n$, shown by (1.3.2), are proper fuzzy sets which are useful examples of fuzzy sets.

Example 1.4.1 Zadeh has defined two fuzzy sets "young" and "old", denoted by Y and O, respectively, on the universe $U = [0,100]$ as the following:

$$\mu_Y(u) = \begin{cases} 1, & u \in [0,25], \\ \dfrac{1}{1 + \left(\dfrac{u-25}{5}\right)^2}, & u \in (25,100] \end{cases}$$

$$\mu_O(u)=\begin{cases}0, & u\in[0,50],\\ \dfrac{1}{1+\left(\dfrac{u-50}{5}\right)^{-2}}, & u\in(50,100]\end{cases}$$

□

Recalling algebraic system $(\mathrm{Ch}(U),\vee,\wedge,c)$, let

$$\mathrm{Meb}(U)=\{\mu|\mu:U\to[0,1]\},$$

and define two binary algebraic operations $\vee,\wedge$ and one unitary algebraic operation "c" as follows

$$\begin{aligned}&\vee:\mathrm{Meb}(U)\times\mathrm{Meb}(U)\to\mathrm{Meb}(U)\\&(\mu_1,\mu_2)\mapsto\mu_1\vee\mu_2=\vee(\mu_1,\mu_2),\\&(\forall u\in U)((\mu_1\vee\mu_2)(u)=\mu_1(u)\vee\mu_2(u));\end{aligned}$$

$$\begin{aligned}&\wedge:\mathrm{Meb}(U)\times\mathrm{Meb}(U)\to\mathrm{Meb}(U)\\&(\mu_1,\mu_2)\mapsto\mu_1\wedge\mu_2=\wedge(\mu_1,\mu_2),\\&(\forall u\in U)((\mu_1\wedge\mu_2)(u)=\mu_1(u)\wedge\mu_2(u));\end{aligned}$$

$$\begin{aligned}&c:\mathrm{Meb}(U)\to\mathrm{Meb}(U)\\&\mu\mapsto\mu^c=c(\mu),\\&(\forall u\in U)(\mu^c(u)=1-\mu(u))\end{aligned}$$

Then we get an algebraic system $(\mathrm{Meb}(U),\vee,\wedge,c)$. It is very important idea to define two binary algebraic operations $\cup,\cap$ and one unitary algebraic operation "c" on $\mathcal{F}(U)$ such that

$$(\mathcal{F}(U),\cup,\cap,c)\cong(\mathrm{Meb}(U),\vee,\wedge,c). \tag{1.4.1}$$

It is important to indicate that the extension from the following:

$$(\mathcal{P}(U), \bigcup, \bigcap, c) \cong (\mathrm{Ch}(U), \vee, \wedge, c)$$

to Expression (1.4.1) should be called **extension principle**.

In the matter of fact, for any two fuzzy sets $A, B \in \mathcal{F}(U)$, we define basic fuzzy set operations such as inclusion, equality, union, intersection and complement as follows:

$$A \supset B \Leftrightarrow (\forall u \in U)(\mu_A(u) \geq \mu_B(u));$$

$$A = B \Leftrightarrow (A \supset B) \wedge (B \supset A) \Leftrightarrow (\forall u \in U)(\mu_A(u) = \mu_B(u));$$

$$C = A \bigcup B \Leftrightarrow (\forall u \in U)(\mu_C(u) = \mu_A(u) \vee \mu_B(u));$$

$$C = A \bigcap B \Leftrightarrow (\forall u \in U)(\mu_C(u) = \mu_A(u) \wedge \mu_B(u));$$

$$C = A^c \Leftrightarrow (\forall u \in U)(\mu_C(u) = 1 - \mu_A(u))$$

In addition, let V another universe. For any $A \in \mathcal{F}(U)$ and $B \in \mathcal{F}(V)$, based on (1.1.1), we define the direct product $A \times B \in \mathcal{F}(U \times V)$ of fuzzy sets A and B as follows

$$(\forall (u,v) \in U \times V)(\mu_{A \times B}(u,v) = \mu_A(u) \wedge \mu_B(v)) \tag{1.4.2}$$

Remark 1.4.1 Based on (1.1.1), we also define $A \times B \in \mathcal{F}(U \times V)$ as the follows:

$$(\forall (u,v) \in U \times V)(\mu_{A \times B}(u,v) = \mu_A(u) \cdot \mu_B(v)) \tag{1.4.3}$$

□

Under above the operations on fuzzy sets just defined by us, it is easy to know the fact that

$$(\mathcal{F}(U), \bigcup, \bigcap, c) \cong (\mathrm{Meb}(U), \vee, \wedge, c).$$

Because $(\mathcal{F}(U), \bigcup, \bigcap, c)$ and $(\text{Meb}(U), \vee, \wedge, c)$ are isomorphic, we need not differentiate $\mathcal{F}(U)$ and $\text{Meb}(U)$, which should be regarded as **wave-fuzzy-set duality**.

It is easy to prove that the union, intersection and complement operations of fuzzy sets have the following properties: for any $A, B, C \in \mathcal{F}(U)$, we have the following operation laws:

(1) Idempotency.

$$A \bigcup A = A, \quad A \bigcap A = A$$

(2) Commutativity.

$$A \bigcup B = B \bigcup A, \quad A \bigcap B = B \bigcap A$$

(3) Associativity.

$$(A \bigcup B) \bigcup C = A \bigcup (B \bigcup C),$$
$$(A \bigcap B) \bigcap C = A \bigcap (B \bigcap C)$$

(4) Absorption.

$$(A \bigcap B) \bigcup A = A, \quad (A \bigcup B) \bigcap A = A$$

(5) Distributive law.

$$A \bigcap (B \bigcap C) = (A \bigcap B) \bigcup (A \bigcap C),$$
$$A \bigcup (B \bigcap C) = (A \bigcup B) \bigcap (A \bigcup C)$$

(6) Bipolarity.

$$A \bigcup U = U, \quad A \bigcap U = A, \quad A \bigcup \varnothing = A, \quad A \bigcap \varnothing = \varnothing$$

(7) Reflexivity.

$$(A^c)^c = A$$

(8) De Morgan's Law.

$$(A \cup B)^c = A^c \cap B^c, \quad (A \cap B)^c = A^c \cup B^c$$

Note that the complementary law of Cantor sets does not apply to fuzzy sets, that is,

$$(\forall A \in \mathcal{F}(U) \setminus \mathcal{P}(U))\left[\left(A \cup A^c \neq U\right) \wedge \left(A \cap A^c \neq \varnothing\right)\right]. \qquad (1.4.4)$$

As a matter of fact, for any $A \in \mathcal{F}(U) \setminus \mathcal{P}(U)$, since there exists $u_0 \in U$ such that $0 < \mu_A(u_0) < 1$, we have

$$\left(\mu_A(u_0) \vee (1 - \mu_A(u_0)) < 1\right) \wedge \left(\mu_A(u_0) \wedge (1 - \mu_A(u_0)) > 0\right)$$
$$\Rightarrow \left(\mu_{A \cup A^c}(u_0) < 1\right) \wedge \left(\mu_{A \cap A^c}(u_0) > 0\right)$$

So (1.4.1) is true because of $\left(\mu_U(u) \equiv 1\right) \wedge \left(\mu_{\varnothing}(u) \equiv 0\right)$.

Example 1.4.2 Based on Example 1.4.1, we can get fuzzy sets "young or old" $Y \cup O$, "young and "not young" Y^c and old" $Y \cap O$ shown as the following:

$$\mu_{Y \cup O}(u) = \begin{cases} 1, & 0 \le u \le 25 \\ \left[1 + \left(\dfrac{u - 25}{5}\right)^2\right]^{-1}, & 25 < u \le 51 \\ \left[1 + \left(\dfrac{u - 50}{5}\right)^{-2}\right]^{-1}, & 51 < u \le 100 \end{cases}$$

$$\mu_{Y^c}(u) = \begin{cases} 0, & 0 \le u \le 25 \\ 1 - \left[1 + \left(\dfrac{u - 25}{5}\right)^2\right]^{-1}, & 25 < u \le 100 \end{cases}$$

$$\mu_{Y\cap O}(u)=\begin{cases}0, & 0\le u\le 50\\ \left[1+\left(\dfrac{u-50}{5}\right)^{-2}\right]^{-1}, & 50<u\le 51\\ \left[1+\left(\dfrac{u-25}{5}\right)^{2}\right]^{-1}, & 51<u\le 100\end{cases}$$

□

References

1. Bellman, R. and Giertz, M. (1973). On the analytic formalism of the theory of fuzzy sets, Information Sciences, 5, pp. 149-156.
2. Dubois, D. and Prade, H. (1980) *Fuzzy Sets and Systems*, (Academic Press, New York).
3. Li, H. X., Wang, P. Z., and Xu, H. Q. (1987) *Interesting Talks on Fuzzy Mathematics*, (Sichuan Education Press, China, in Chinese).
4. Li, H. X. (1993) *Fuzzy Mathematics Methods in Engineering and Its Applications*, (Tianjin Science and Technical Press, China, in Chinese).
5. Li, H. X. and Wang, P. Z. (1994) *Fuzzy Mathematics*, (National Defense Press, China, in Chinese).
6. Li, H. X. and Yen V. C. (1995) *Fuzzy Sets and Fuzzy Decision-Making*, (CRC Press, Boca Raton).
7. Wang, P. Z. (1983) *Fuzzy Set Theory and Its Applications*, (Shanghai Science and Technical Press, China, in Chinese).
8. Wang, P. Z. (1983) *Fuzzy Sets and Falling Shadow of Random Sets*, (Beijing Normal Press, China, in Chinese).
9. Zadeh, L. A. (1965). Fuzzy sets, Information and Control, 8, pp. 338-353.
10. Zadeh, L. A. (1978). Fuzzy sets as a basic for a theory of possibility, Fuzzy Sets and Systems, 1, pp. 3-28.
11. Zimmermann, H. J. (1984) *Fuzzy Sets Theory and Its Applications*, (Kluwer Academic Publications, Hingham).

Chapter 2

Fuzzy Relations

2.1 Cantor's Relations

Again we consider $\text{IOD} = \{(x_i, y_i) | i = 0, 1, \cdots, n\}$ coming from the system S shown as Figure 1.1.1. If we put $(\forall i \in \{0, 1, \cdots, n\})(R_i \triangleq \{(x_i, y_i)\})$ and $R = \bigcup_{i=0}^{n} R_i$, then R makes input universe X and output universe Y to have some kind of relation. Unfortunately, this "relation" is discrete or incomplete. However, if we can find a curve through every binary point (x_i, y_i), just like $y = f(x)$ in Figure 2.1.1, this new kind of relation should be complete.

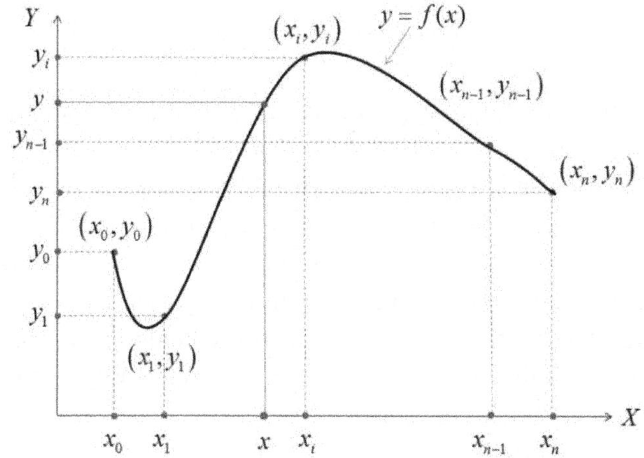

Fig. 2.1.1. The curve as a relation

In a matter of fact, it is very hard to find a reasoning curve to meet the need for the system response. Our idea is that, first of all, every single-point relation $\{(x_i, y_i)\}$ should be extended as a non-single-point relation R_i just like the one shown in Figure 2.1.2. Then the relation $R = \bigcup_{i=0}^{n} R_i$ may be complete.

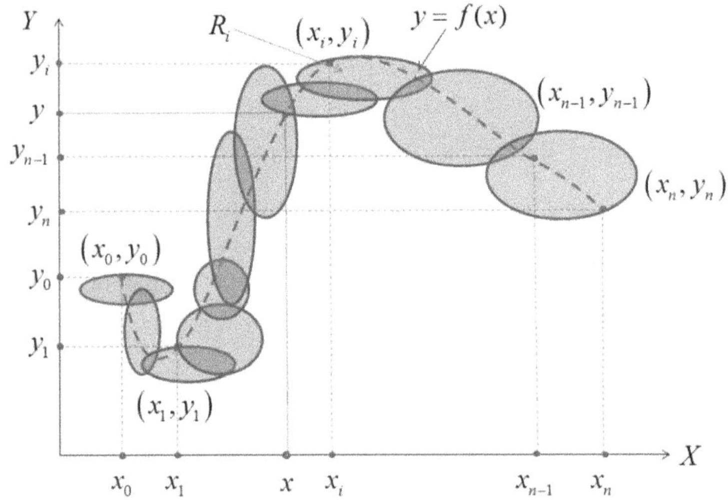

Fig. 2.1.2. Every single-point relation is extended as R_i

Though $R = \bigcup_{i=0}^{n} R_i$ may be complete, the response of the system based on it will not be single value, which is shown as Figure 2.1.3. For example, for input x^*, the system gives a set value to response B^*. But do not worry about this case, because we will have a very good method to handle it by using centroid method coming from physics.

Now we start to learn so called relations being with what kind of mathematical significance. Let U and V be two nonempty universes. Any one subset as the following:

$$R \subset U \times V = \{(u, v) | u \in U, v \in V\}$$

is called a **binary relation** between U and V, simply called a **relation**. In order to differ from fuzzy relation coming from next section, sometimes we call relations here to be Cantor's relations.

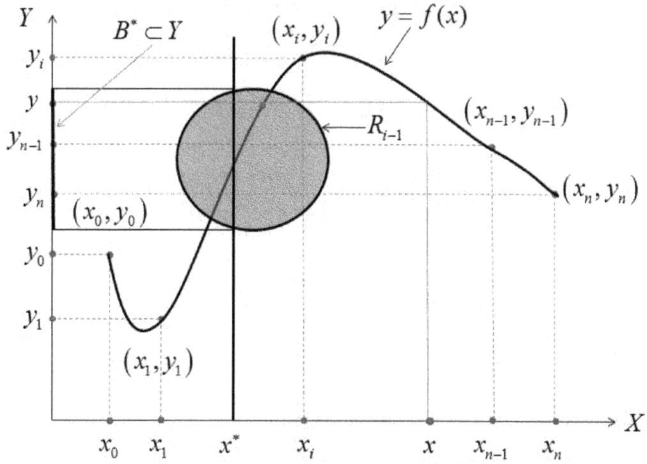

Fig. 2.1.3. Set value response B^* for input x^*

For any $(u,v) \in U \times V$, if $(u,v) \in R$, then u and v are called being are of relation R, denoted by uRv, or else, i.e. $(u,v) \notin R$, called being not of relation R, denoted by $u\not{R}v$, shown as Figure 2.1.4.

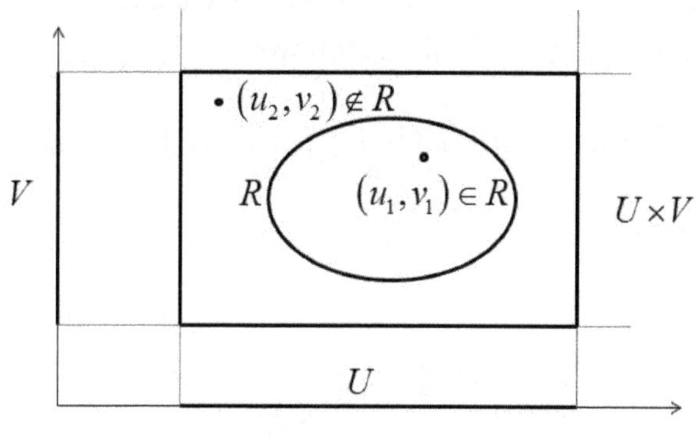

Fig. 2.1.4. Relation R between U and V

If one relation $f \subset U \times V$ satisfies such condition

$$(\forall u \in U)(\exists! v \in V)(u f v)$$

where "!" means "one and only one", then this relation f actually defines a mapping as follows

$$f : U \to V, \quad u \mapsto f(u) = v .$$

This fact means that mappings or functions are special cases of relations. The image of this mapping, denoted by G_f, is as follows

$$G_f = \{(u,v) \in U \times V \mid v = f(u)\} = f .$$

This means that the image G_f is just the relation f regarded as a mapping. For example, a function defined as

$$f : [0, 2\pi] \to [-1,1], x \mapsto f(x) = \sin x$$

just gives the following relation:

$$f = \{(x, y) \in [0, 2\pi] \times [-1,1] \mid y = \sin x\} \subset [0, 2\pi] \times [-1,1]$$

Let U, V and W be three nonempty universes; and we take a relation $P \subset U \times V$ and another relation $Q \subset V \times W$. By using P and Q, we can get a new relation $P \circ Q \subset U \times W$ as follows

$$P \circ Q = \{(u,w) \in U \times W \mid (\exists v \in V)(((u,v) \in P) \wedge ((v,w) \in Q))\}$$

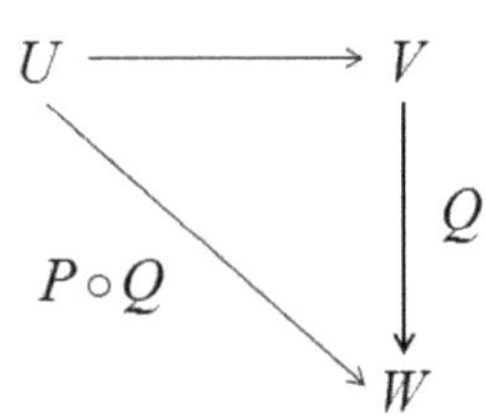

Fig. 2.1.5. Interchange graph for $P \circ Q$

This relation $P \circ Q$ is called the composition (or composition relation) of P and Q, which we can use an interchange graph as shown as Figure 2.1.5 to express $P \circ Q$.

For composition relation $P \circ Q$, we can prove the following result:

$$\left(\forall (u,w) \in U \times W\right)\left(\chi_{P \circ Q}(u,w) = \bigvee_{v \in V}\left(\chi_P(u,v) \wedge \chi_Q(v,w)\right)\right). \quad (2.1.1)$$

Proof. For any $(u,w) \in U \times W$, we have

$$\begin{aligned}
&\chi_{P \circ Q}(u,w) = 1 \Leftrightarrow (u,w) \in U \times W \\
&\Leftrightarrow \left(\exists v \in V\right)\left(\left((u,v) \in P\right) \wedge \left((v,w) \in Q\right)\right) \\
&\Leftrightarrow \left(\exists v \in V\right)\left(\left(\chi_P(u,v) = 1\right) \wedge \left(\chi_Q(v,w) = 1\right)\right) \\
&\Leftrightarrow \left(\exists v \in V\right)\left(\chi_P(u,v) \wedge \chi_Q(v,w) = 1\right) \\
&\Leftrightarrow \bigvee_{v \in V}\left(\chi_P(u,v) \wedge \chi_Q(v,w)\right) = 1
\end{aligned}$$

So (2.1.1) is true. □

Example 2.1.1 For three finite universes as follows

$$U = \{u_1, u_2, \cdots, u_n\}, \quad V = \{v_1, v_2, \cdots, v_l\}, \quad W = \{w_1, w_2, \cdots, w_m\},$$

we take two relations $P \subset U \times V$ and $Q \subset V \times W$, where the two relation can be expressed by so-called **Boolean matrixes** as the following

$$P = \left(\chi_P(u_i, v_k)\right)_{n \times l} = \left(p_{ik}\right)_{n \times l} = \begin{pmatrix} p_{11} & p_{12} & \cdots & p_{1l} \\ p_{21} & p_{22} & \cdots & p_{2l} \\ \vdots & \vdots & & \vdots \\ p_{n1} & p_{n2} & \cdots & p_{nl} \end{pmatrix}$$

$$Q = \left(\chi_Q(v_k, w_j)\right)_{l \times m} = \left(q_{lm}\right)_{l \times m} = \begin{pmatrix} q_{11} & q_{12} & \cdots & q_{1m} \\ q_{21} & q_{22} & \cdots & q_{2m} \\ \vdots & \vdots & & \vdots \\ q_{l1} & q_{l2} & \cdots & q_{lm} \end{pmatrix},$$

$$Q=\left(\chi_Q\left(v_k,w_j\right)\right)_{l\times m}=\left(q_{lm}\right)_{l\times m}=\begin{pmatrix} q_{11} & q_{12} & \cdots & q_{1m} \\ q_{21} & q_{22} & \cdots & q_{2m} \\ \vdots & \vdots & & \vdots \\ q_{l1} & q_{l2} & \cdots & q_{lm} \end{pmatrix},$$

$$p_{ik}\triangleq\chi_P\left(u_i,v_k\right),\quad q_{lm}\triangleq\chi_Q\left(v_k,w_j\right),$$
$$i=1,2,\cdots,n;\quad k=1,2,\cdots,l;\quad j=1,2,\cdots,m$$

Based on (2.1.1), if we write $R\triangleq P\circ Q$, then we have the following result:

$$P\circ Q=R=\left(\chi_R\left(u_i,w_j\right)\right)_{n\times m}=\begin{pmatrix} r_{11} & r_{12} & \cdots & r_{1m} \\ r_{21} & r_{22} & \cdots & r_{2m} \\ \vdots & \vdots & & \vdots \\ r_{n1} & r_{n2} & \cdots & r_{nm} \end{pmatrix},$$

$$r_{ij}\triangleq\chi_R\left(u_i,w_j\right),\quad r_{ij}=\bigvee_{k=1}^{l}\left(p_{ik}\wedge q_{kj}\right),$$
$$i=1,2,\cdots,n,\quad j=1,2,\cdots,m$$

□

Example 2.1.2 In Example 2.1.1, when $n=4,k=3,m=5$, we have

$$U=\{u_1,u_2,u_3,u_4\},\quad V=\{v_1,v_2,v_3\},\quad W=\{w_1,w_2,w_3,w_4,w_5\}.$$

We take two relations $P\subset U\times V$ and $Q\subset V\times W$ as follows

$$P=\{(u_1,v_2),(u_1,v_3),(u_2,v_1),(u_3,v_1)\},$$
$$Q=\{(v_1,w_1),(v_1,w_2),(v_2,w_3),(v_3,w_5)\},$$
$$P\circ Q=\{(u_1,w_3),(u_1,w_5),(u_2,w_1),(u_2,w_2),(u_3,w_1),(u_3,w_2)\}$$

Then we can clearly draw a relation graph very like a neural network shown as Figure 2.1.6.

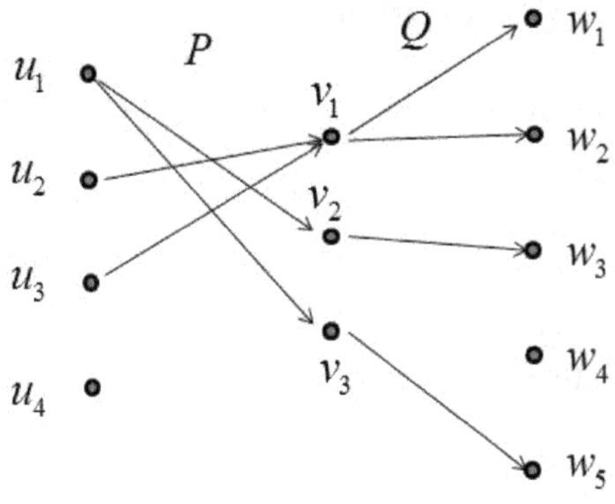

Fig. 2.1.6. Relation graph like a neural network

We can also use Boolean matrixes to express them as the following:

$$P=\begin{pmatrix}\chi_P(u_1,v_1) & \chi_P(u_1,v_2) & \chi_P(u_1,v_3)\\ \chi_P(u_2,v_1) & \chi_P(u_2,v_2) & \chi_P(u_2,v_3)\\ \chi_P(u_3,v_1) & \chi_P(u_3,v_2) & \chi_P(u_3,v_3)\\ \chi_P(u_4,v_1) & \chi_P(u_4,v_2) & \chi_P(u_4,v_3)\end{pmatrix}=\begin{pmatrix}0&1&1\\1&0&0\\1&0&0\\0&0&0\end{pmatrix},$$

$$Q=\begin{pmatrix}\chi_Q(v_1,w_1) & \chi_Q(v_1,w_2) & \chi_Q(v_1,w_3) & \chi_Q(v_1,w_4) & \chi_Q(v_1,w_5)\\ \chi_Q(v_2,w_1) & \chi_Q(v_2,w_2) & \chi_Q(v_2,w_3) & \chi_Q(v_2,w_4) & \chi_Q(v_2,w_5)\\ \chi_Q(v_3,w_1) & \chi_Q(v_3,w_2) & \chi_Q(v_3,w_3) & \chi_Q(v_3,w_4) & \chi_Q(v_3,w_5)\end{pmatrix}$$

$$=\begin{pmatrix}1&1&0&0&0\\0&0&1&0&0\\0&0&0&0&1\end{pmatrix},$$

$$P\circ Q=\begin{pmatrix}0&1&1\\1&0&0\\1&0&0\\0&0&0\end{pmatrix}\circ\begin{pmatrix}1&1&0&0&0\\0&0&1&0&0\\0&0&0&0&1\end{pmatrix}=\begin{pmatrix}0&0&1&0&1\\1&1&0&0&0\\1&1&0&0&0\\0&0&0&0&0\end{pmatrix}$$

□

2.2 Definition of Fuzzy Relations

Based on the preparation from Section 2.1, we start to consider fuzzy relations.

Definition 2.2.1 Let U and V be two nonempty universes and make a new universe $U \times V$ by U and V. Any one fuzzy set $R \in \mathcal{F}(U \times V)$ is called a **fuzzy relation** between U and V, where the membership function of the fuzzy relation R is as the following

$$\mu_R : U \times V \to [0,1], \quad (u,v) \mapsto \mu_R(u,v).$$

And $\mu_R(u,v)$ is called relationship strength between u and v. Especially, when $U = V$, i.e.,

$$R \in \mathcal{F}(U \times U) = \mathcal{F}(U^2),$$

R is called a fuzzy relation on U. □

Example 2.2.1 Let $U = V = \mathbb{R}$, and define a fuzzy relation $\gg \in \mathcal{F}(\mathbb{R}^2)$, where "$\gg$" means "far more greater than", as follows

$$\mu_{\gg} : \mathbb{R}^2 \to [0,1]$$

$$(x,y) \mapsto \mu_{\gg}(x,y) = \begin{cases} 0, & x \le y \\ \left(1 + \dfrac{100}{(x-y)^2}\right)^{-1}, & x > y \end{cases}$$

It is easy to calculate the following situations:

$$(x,y) = (1000,100) \Rightarrow \mu_{\gg}(x,y) \approx 0.9999;$$
$$(x,y) = (20,10) \Rightarrow \mu_{\gg}(x,y) \approx 0.5000;$$
$$(x,y) = (20,18) \Rightarrow \mu_{\gg}(x,y) \approx 0.0385.$$

□

For the situation about finite universes as the following:

$$U=\{u_1,u_2,\cdots,u_n\},\quad V=\{v_1,v_2,\cdots,v_m\},$$

a fuzzy relation $R\in\mathcal{F}(U\times V)$ can be expressed by a fuzzy matrix as follows

$$R=(r_{ij})_{n\times m},\quad r_{ij}\triangleq\mu_R(u_i,v_j),$$
$$i=1,2,\cdots,n,\quad j=1,2,\cdots,m.$$

Definition 2.2.2 Let U,V and W be three nonempty universes. We take one fuzzy relation $P\in\mathcal{F}(U\times V)$ and another fuzzy relation $Q\in\mathcal{F}(V\times W)$. By using P and Q, we can get a new fuzzy relation between U and W as being $R=P\circ Q\in\mathcal{F}(U\times W)$, and it is called the **composition** (or composition fuzzy relation) of P and Q, where its membership function is defined based on Extension Principle coming from Section 1.4 as follows, for any $(u,w)\in U\times W$,

$$\mu_R(u,w)=\mu_{P\circ Q}(u,w)=\bigvee_{v\in V}\left(\mu_P(u,v)\wedge\mu_Q(v,w)\right) \tag{2.2.1}$$

□

Remark 2.2.1 When $U=V=W$, for any $R\in\mathcal{F}(U^2)$, we have

$$R^2\triangleq R\circ R\in\mathcal{F}(U^2),$$

then we have $R^3\triangleq R^2\circ R\in\mathcal{F}(U^2)$, and so on, we have

$$R^n\triangleq R^{n-1}\circ R\in\mathcal{F}(U^2),\quad n=2,3,\cdots$$

□

Remark 2.2.2 For three finite universes as follows

$$U=\{u_1,u_2,\cdots,u_n\},\quad V=\{v_1,v_2,\cdots,v_l\},\quad W=\{w_1,w_2,\cdots,w_m\},$$

we take two fuzzy relations $P\in\mathcal{F}(U\times V)$ and $Q\in\mathcal{F}(V\times W)$. Then P,Q and $R=P\circ Q$ can be expressed by fuzzy matrixes as the following:

$$
\begin{aligned}
&P=\left(p_{ik}\right)_{n\times l}, \quad Q=\left(q_{kj}\right)_{l\times m}, \quad R=\left(r_{ij}\right)_{n\times m}, \\
&p_{ik} \triangleq \mu_P\left(u_i, v_k\right), \quad q_{kj} \triangleq \mu_Q\left(v_k, w_j\right), \\
&r_{ij} \triangleq \mu_R\left(u_i, w_j\right)=\bigvee_{k=1}^{l}\left(p_{ik} \wedge q_{kj}\right), \\
&i=1,2,\cdots,n, \quad j=1,2,\cdots,m, \quad k=1,2,\cdots,l
\end{aligned}
$$

□

Example 2.2.2 Let $U=\{u_1,u_2,u_3,u_4\}, V=\{v_1,v_2,v_3\}, W=\{w_1,w_2\}$, and

$$
P=\begin{bmatrix} 0.3 & 0.7 & 0.2 \\ 1 & 0 & 0.4 \\ 0 & 0.5 & 1 \\ 0.6 & 0.7 & 0.8 \end{bmatrix} \in \mathcal{F}(U\times V), \quad Q=\begin{bmatrix} 0.1 & 0.9 \\ 0.9 & 0.1 \\ 0.6 & 0.4 \end{bmatrix} \in \mathcal{F}(V\times W).
$$

Then we have the following result:

$$
R=P\circ Q=\begin{bmatrix} 0.3 & 0.7 & 0.2 \\ 1 & 0 & 0.4 \\ 0 & 0.5 & 1 \\ 0.6 & 0.7 & 0.8 \end{bmatrix} \circ \begin{bmatrix} 0.1 & 0.9 \\ 0.9 & 0.1 \\ 0.6 & 0.4 \end{bmatrix} = \begin{bmatrix} 0.7 & 0.3 \\ 0.4 & 0.9 \\ 0.6 & 0.4 \\ 0.7 & 0.6 \end{bmatrix}.
$$

□

Remark 2.2.3 Because a fuzzy relation $R\in\mathcal{F}(U\times V)$ is a fuzzy set on $U\times V$, the operations on fuzzy sets are also valid for fuzzy relations. For example, for any two fuzzy relations $P,R\in\mathcal{F}(U\times V)$, we have the results:

$$
\begin{aligned}
&P\subset R \Leftrightarrow \left(\forall u,v\in U\times V\right)\left(\mu_P(u,v)\le \mu_R(u,v)\right), \\
&P=R \Leftrightarrow \left(\forall u,v\in U\times V\right)\left(\mu_P(u,v)=\mu_R(u,v)\right) \\
&Q=P\bigcup R \Leftrightarrow \left(\forall u,v\in U\times V\right)\left(\mu_Q(u,v)=\mu_P(u,v)\vee \mu_R(u,v)\right), \\
&Q=P\bigcap R \Leftrightarrow \left(\forall u,v\in U\times V\right)\left(\mu_Q(u,v)=\mu_P(u,v)\wedge \mu_R(u,v)\right), \\
&Q=R^c \Leftrightarrow \left(\forall u,v\in U\times V\right)\left(\mu_Q(u,v)=1-\mu_R(u,v)\right).
\end{aligned}
$$

□

2.3 Projections and Cross-section' Projections of Relations

In order to make a fuzzy system, it is necessary to know some knowledge projections and cross-section' projections of relations and fuzzy relations. But we start it from Cantor's relations.

Definition 2.3.1 Let X and Y be two nonempty universes and the set $R \subset X \times Y$ is a relation between X and Y. By using the following symbols:

$$R_X = \{x \in X \mid (\exists y \in Y)((x, y) \in R)\},$$
$$R_Y = \{y \in Y \mid (\exists x \in X)((x, y) \in R)\}$$

we call R_X and R_Y to be projection of R on X and on Y, respectively; they are shown as Figure 2.3.1.

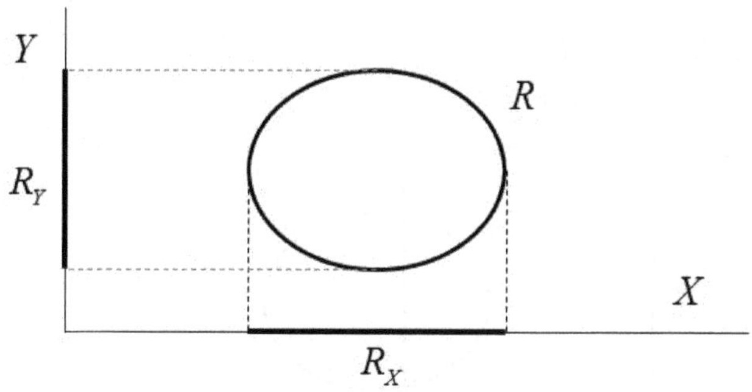

Fig. 2.3.1. Projections R_X and R_Y of relation R on X and on Y

Clearly, we have $R_X \subset X$ and $R_Y \subset Y$. □

Proposition 2.3.1 Let X and Y be two nonempty universes and take a relation between X and Y as $R \subset X \times Y$. We have the following results:

$$(\forall x \in X)\left(\chi_{R_X}(x) = \bigvee_{y \in Y} \chi_R(x, y)\right),$$
$$(\forall y \in Y)\left(\chi_{R_Y}(y) = \bigvee_{x \in X} \chi_R(x, y)\right).$$

Proof. For any a point $x \in X$, it is not difficult to understand the fact that

$$\chi_{R_X}(x)=1 \Leftrightarrow x \in R_X \Leftrightarrow (\exists y \in Y)((x,y)\in R)$$
$$\Leftrightarrow (\exists y \in Y)(\chi_R(x,y)=1) \Leftrightarrow \bigvee_{y\in Y} \chi_R(x,y)=1$$

So the first expression is true. Similarly, the second is also true. □

Definition 2.3.2 Let X and Y be two nonempty universes and $R \subset X \times Y$ is a relation between X and Y. For any $x \in X$ and any $y \in Y$, by using the following symbols:

$$R\big|_x = \{y \in Y \mid (x,y)\in R\}, \quad R\big|_y = \{x \in X \mid (x,y)\in R\}$$

we call $R\big|_x$ and $R\big|_y$ to be cross-section' projection of R at x and at y, respectively, where $R\big|_x$ is shown as Figure 2.3.2 and the situation about $R\big|_y$ is quite similar as $R\big|_x$. □

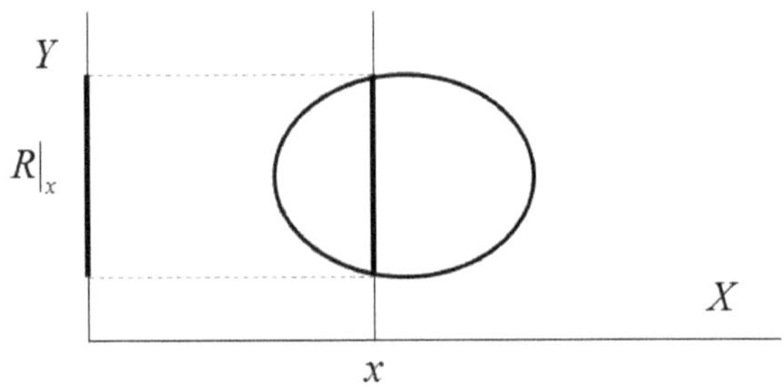

Fig. 2.3.2. Cross-section' projections $R\big|_x$ of relation R at x

Proposition 2.3.2 Let X and Y be two nonempty universes and take a relation between X and Y as being $R \subset X \times Y$. We have the results:

$$(\forall y \in Y)\left(\chi_{R|_x}(y) = \chi_R(x,y)\right), \quad (\forall x \in X)\left(\chi_{R|_y}(x) = \chi_R(x,y)\right).$$

Proof. For any a point $y \in Y$, by noticing the fact as the following

$$\chi_{R|_x}(y)=1 \Leftrightarrow y\in R|_x \Leftrightarrow (x,y)\in R \Leftrightarrow \chi_R(x,y)=1,$$

we know that the first expression is true. Similarly the second expression is also true. □

Proposition 2.3.3 Let X and Y be two nonempty universes and take a relation between X and Y as being $R\subset X\times Y$. We have the following results:

$$R_X=\bigcup_{y\in Y} R|_y, \quad R_Y=\bigcup_{x\in X} R|_x$$

Proof. For any $y\in Y$, by using of Proposition 2.3.1 and Proposition 2.3.2, we have the following results:

$$\chi_{R_Y}(y)=\bigvee_{x\in X}\chi_R(x,y)=\bigvee_{x\in X}\chi_{R|_x}(y)=\chi_{\bigcup_{x\in X}R|_x}(y).$$

Thus the second expression is true. Similarly the first is also true. □

Proposition 2.3.4 Let X and Y be two nonempty universes and take a relation between X and Y as $R\subset X\times Y$. We have the following results:

$$R=\bigcup_{x\in X}\left(\{x\}\times R|_x\right), \quad R=\bigcup_{y\in Y}\left(R|_y\times\{y\}\right)$$

Proof. For any $(u,v)\in X\times Y$, by using Proposition 2.3.2, we have

$$\begin{aligned}\chi_{\bigcup_{x\in X}(\{x\}\times R|_x)}(u,v)&=\bigvee_{x\in X}\chi_{\{x\}\times R|_x}(u,v)\\ &=\bigvee_{x\in X}\left(\chi_{\{x\}}(u)\wedge\chi_{R|_x}(v)\right)=\chi_{\{u\}}(u)\wedge\chi_{R|_u}(v)\\ &=1\wedge\chi_{R|_u}(v)=\chi_{R|_u}(v)=\chi_R(u,v)\end{aligned}$$

So the first expression is true. Similarly, we can get the second expression as well. □

Remark 2.3.1 From Figure 2.3.3, Proposition 2.3.4 is obvious, where cross-section of relation R at x is just $\{x\}\times R|_x=(\{x\}\times Y)\bigcap R$. □

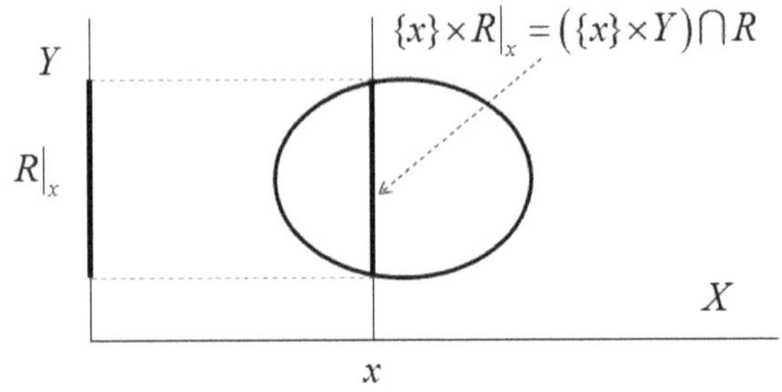

Fig. 2.3.3. Cross-section of relation R at x is just $\{x\}\times R|_x$

Proposition 2.3.5 Let X and Y be two nonempty universes and take a relation between X and Y as being $R \subset X \times Y$. We have the following results:

$$(\forall x \in X)\left(R|_x = \left[(\{x\}\times Y)\cap R\right]_Y\right),$$
$$(\forall y \in Y)\left(R|_y = \left[(X\times\{y\})\cap R\right]_X\right)$$

Proof. For any $(x, y) \in X \times Y$, by using Proposition 2.3.1 and Proposition 2.3.2, we have

$$\begin{aligned}
\chi_{[(\{x\}\times Y)\cap R]_Y}(y) &= \bigvee_{u\in X} \chi_{(\{x\}\times Y)\cap R}(u, y) \\
&= \bigvee_{u\in X}\left(\chi_{\{x\}\times Y}(u, y) \wedge \chi_R(u, y)\right) \\
&= \bigvee_{u\in X}\left(\chi_{\{x\}}(u) \wedge \chi_Y(y) \wedge \chi_R(u, y)\right) \\
&= \bigvee_{u\in X}\left(\chi_{\{x\}}(u) \wedge \chi_R(u, y)\right) \\
&= \chi_{\{x\}}(x) \wedge \chi_R(x, y) = \chi_{R|_x}(y)
\end{aligned}$$

So the first expression is true. Similarly, we can get the second expression as well. □

Remark 2.3.2 From Figure 2.3.3, Proposition 2.3.5 is obvious as well. □

Proposition 2.3.6 Let X and Y be two nonempty universes and take two relations $P,Q \subset X \times Y$. If $P \supset Q$, then we have the following results:

$$P_X \supset Q_X, \quad P_Y \supset Q_Y, \quad (\forall x \in X)\left(P|_x \supset Q|_x\right), \quad (\forall y \in Y)\left(P|_y \supset Q|_y\right)$$

It is not necessary to prove them for they are obvious. □

2.4 Projections and Cross-section' Projections of Fuzzy Relations

Based on the discussion in Section 2.3 and by using Extension Principle coming from Section 1.4, we can consider the same subjects on fuzzy relations.

Definition 2.4.1 Let X and Y be two nonempty universes and take a fuzzy relation $R \in \mathcal{F}(X \times Y)$. A fuzzy set $R_X \in \mathcal{F}(X)$ is called projection of R on X, if its membership function is defined by the following condition:

$$(\forall x \in X)\left(\mu_{R_X}(x) = \bigvee_{y \in Y} \mu_R(x, y)\right).$$

Another fuzzy set $R_Y \in \mathcal{F}(Y)$ is called projection of R on Y, if its membership function is defined by the following

$$(\forall y \in X)\left(\mu_{R_Y}(y) = \bigvee_{x \in X} \mu_R(x, y)\right).$$ □

Definition 2.4.2 Let X and Y be two nonempty universes and take a fuzzy relation between X and Y as $R \in \mathcal{F}(X \times Y)$. For any $x \in X$, a fuzzy set $R|_x \in \mathcal{F}(Y)$ is called cross-section' projection of R at x, if its membership function is defined by the following

$$(\forall y \in Y)\left(\mu_{R|_x}(y) = \mu_R(x, y)\right).$$

For any a point $y \in Y$, another fuzzy set $R|_y \in \mathcal{F}(X)$ is called cross-section' projection of R at y, if its membership function is defined by the following

$$(\forall x \in X)\left(\mu_{R|_y}(x) = \mu_R(x, y)\right). \qquad \square$$

Proposition 2.4.1 Let X and Y be two nonempty universes and take a fuzzy relation $R \in \mathcal{F}(X \times Y)$. We have the following results:

$$R_X = \bigcup_{y \in Y} R|_y, \quad R_Y = \bigcup_{x \in X} R|_x$$

Proof. For any a point $x \in X$, by using Definition 2.4.1 and Definition 2.4.2, we have

$$\mu_{R_X}(x) = \bigvee_{y \in Y} \mu_R(x, y) = \bigvee_{y \in Y} \mu_{R|_y}(x) = \mu_{\bigcup_{y \in Y} R|_y}(x).$$

Thus the first expression is true. Similarly the second is also true. $\square$

Proposition 2.4.2 Let X and Y be two nonempty universes and take a fuzzy relation as being $R \in \mathcal{F}(X \times Y)$. We have the following results:

$$R = \bigcup_{x \in X} \left(\{x\} \times R|_x\right), \quad R = \bigcup_{y \in Y} \left(R|_y \times \{y\}\right)$$

Proof. For any $(u, v) \in X \times Y$, by using Definition 2.4.2, we have

$$\begin{aligned} &\mu_{\bigcup_{x \in X}(\{x\} \times R|_x)}(u, v) = \bigvee_{x \in X} \mu_{\{x\} \times R|_x}(u, v) \\ &= \bigvee_{x \in X} \left(\mu_{\{x\}}(u) \wedge \mu_{R|_x}(v)\right) = \mu_{\{u\}}(u) \wedge \mu_{R|_u}(v) \\ &= 1 \wedge \mu_{R|_u}(v) = \mu_{R|_u}(v) = \mu_R(u, v) \end{aligned}$$

So the first expression is true. Similarly, we can get the second expression as well. $\square$

Proposition 2.4.3 Let X and Y be two nonempty universes and take a fuzzy relation as being $R \in \mathcal{F}(X \times Y)$. We have the following results:

$$(\forall x \in X)\left(R|_x = \left[(\{x\} \times Y) \cap R\right]_Y\right),$$
$$(\forall y \in Y)\left(R|_y = \left[(X \times \{y\}) \cap R\right]_X\right)$$

Proof. For any $(x,y) \in X \times Y$, by using Definition 2.4.1 and Definition 2.4.2, we have

$$\mu_{\left[(\{x\}\times Y)\cap R\right]_Y}(y) = \bigvee_{u \in X} \mu_{(\{x\}\times Y)\cap R}(u,y)$$

$$\begin{aligned}
&= \bigvee_{u \in X}\left(\mu_{\{x\}\times Y}(u,y) \wedge \mu_R(u,y)\right) \\
&= \bigvee_{u \in X}\left(\mu_{\{x\}}(u) \wedge \mu_Y(y) \wedge \mu_R(u,y)\right) \\
&= \bigvee_{u \in X}\left(\mu_{\{x\}}(u) \wedge \mu_R(u,y)\right) \\
&= \mu_{\{x\}}(x) \wedge \mu_R(x,y) = \mu_R(x,y) \\
&= \mu_{R|_x}(y)
\end{aligned}$$

So the first expression is true. Similarly, we can get the second expression as well. □

Proposition 2.4.4 Let X and Y be two nonempty universes and take two fuzzy relations $P, Q \in \mathcal{F}(X \times Y)$. If $P \supset Q$, then we have the following results:

$$P_X \supset Q_X, \quad P_Y \supset Q_Y, \quad (\forall x \in X)\left(P|_x \supset Q|_x\right), \quad (\forall y \in Y)\left(P|_y \supset Q|_y\right)$$

It is not necessary to prove them for they are obvious. □

Example 2.4.1 Let $X = \{x_1, x_2, \cdots, x_n\}$ and $Y = \{y_1, y_2, \cdots, y_m\}$ be two finite universes and a fuzzy relation as being the following:

$$R = \left(\mu_R\left(x_i, y_j\right)\right)_{n\times m} = \left(r_{ij}\right)_{n\times m} \in \mathcal{F}(X \times Y),$$

where

$$r_{ij} = \mu_R\left(x_i, y_j\right), \quad i = 1,2,\cdots,n,\ j = 1,2,\cdots,m.$$

We can calculate projections and cross-section' projections of R as follows:

$$R_X = \begin{pmatrix} a_1 \\ a_2 \\ \vdots \\ a_n \end{pmatrix}, \quad R_Y = \left(b_1, b_2, \cdots, b_m\right),$$

$$a_i = \mu_{R_X}\left(x_i\right) = \bigvee_{j=1}^{m} \mu_R\left(x_i, y_j\right) = \bigvee_{j=1}^{m} r_{ij},$$

$$b_j = \mu_{R_Y}\left(y_j\right) = \bigvee_{i=1}^{n} \mu_R\left(x_i, y_j\right) = \bigvee_{i=1}^{n} r_{ij},$$

$$\mu_{R|_{x_i}}\left(y_j\right) = \mu_R\left(x_i, y_j\right),$$

$$\mu_{R|_{y_j}}\left(x_i\right) = \mu_R\left(x_i, y_j\right),$$

$$i = 1,2,\cdots,n, \quad j = 1,2,\cdots,m$$

□

Example 2.4.2 Let $X = \{x_1, x_2, x_3\}$ and $Y = \{y_1, y_2, y_3, y_4\}$ be two finite universes and we take a fuzzy relation as

$$R = \left(\mu_R\left(x_i, y_j\right)\right)_{n\times m} = \left(r_{ij}\right)_{n\times m} \in \mathcal{F}\left(X \times Y\right)$$

as the following:

$$R = \left(\mu_R\left(x_i, y_j\right)\right)_{3\times 4} = \left(r_{ij}\right)_{3\times 4} = \begin{pmatrix} 0.3 & 0.5 & 0.7 & 0.9 \\ 0.4 & 1 & 0.2 & 0.7 \\ 0.8 & 0.6 & 0.9 & 0 \end{pmatrix}.$$

We can calculate projections and cross-section' projections of R as the following:

$$R_X = \begin{pmatrix} a_1 \\ a_2 \\ a_3 \end{pmatrix} = \begin{pmatrix} 0.9 \\ 1 \\ 0.9 \end{pmatrix}, \quad R_Y = (b_1, b_2, b_3, b_4) = (0.8, 1, 0.9, 0.9),$$

$$\mu_{R|_{x_i}}(y_j) = \mu_R(x_i, y_j), \quad i = 1,2,3, \quad j = 1,2,3,4,$$

$$\mu_{R|_{y_j}}(x_i) = \mu_R(x_i, y_j), \quad i = 1,2,3, \quad j = 1,2,3,4,$$

$$R|_{x_1} = (0.3, 0.5, 0.7, 0.9), \quad R|_{x_2} = (0.4, 1, 0.2, 0.7),$$

$$R|_{x_3} = (0.8, 0.5, 0.9, 0),$$

$$R|_{y_1} = \begin{pmatrix} 0.3 \\ 0.4 \\ 0.8 \end{pmatrix}, \quad R|_{y_2} = \begin{pmatrix} 0.5 \\ 0.1 \\ 0.6 \end{pmatrix}, \quad R|_{y_3} = \begin{pmatrix} 0.7 \\ 0.2 \\ 0.9 \end{pmatrix}, \quad R|_{y_4} = \begin{pmatrix} 0.9 \\ 0.7 \\ 0 \end{pmatrix}$$

□

2.5 Cantor's Set Transformations

Let X and Y be two nonempty universes. Any mapping as the following

$$T: \mathcal{P}(X) \to \mathcal{P}(Y), \quad A \mapsto B = T(A)$$

is called a **set transformation** from X to Y.

Definition 2.5.1 Let X and Y be two nonempty universes and $R \subset X \times Y$. The following mapping

$$\begin{aligned} &T: \mathcal{P}(X) \to \mathcal{P}(Y) \\ &A \mapsto B = T(A) \triangleq [(A \times Y) \cap R]_Y \end{aligned} \tag{2.5.1}$$

is called a **set transformation induced by relation** R from X to Y, denoted by

$$B = T(A) = A \circ R. \tag{2.5.2}$$

□

In expression (2.5.1), the relation R can be regarded as a transformer or a convertor from $\mathcal{P}(X)$ to $\mathcal{P}(Y)$, which is shown as Figure 2.5.1.

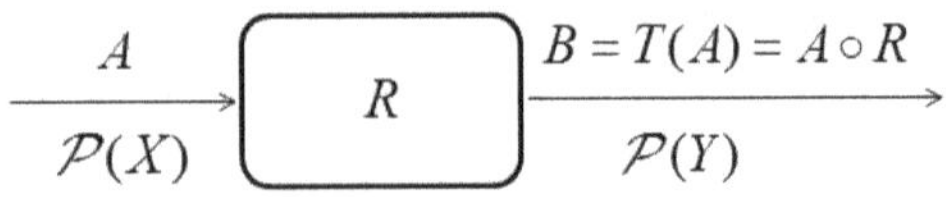

Fig. 2.5.1. R is regarded as a transformer from $\mathcal{P}(X)$ to $\mathcal{P}(Y)$

Proposition 2.5.1 Let X and Y be two nonempty universes and take a relation $R \subset X \times Y$. About (2.5.1), for any a point $y \in Y$, we have

$$\chi_B(y) = \bigvee_{x \in X} \left(\chi_A(x) \wedge \chi_R(x, y)\right). \tag{2.5.3}$$

Proof. For any an element $y \in Y$, by using Proposition 2.3.1, we have the following equation:

$$\begin{aligned}
&\chi_B(y) = \chi_{T(A)}(y) = \chi_{[(A \times Y) \cap R]_Y}(y) \\
&= \bigvee_{x \in X} \chi_{(A \times Y) \cap R}(y) \\
&= \bigvee_{x \in X} \left[\chi_{A \times Y}(x, y) \wedge \chi_R(x, y)\right] \\
&= \bigvee_{x \in X} \left[\chi_A(x) \wedge \chi_Y(y) \wedge \chi_R(x, y)\right] \\
&= \bigvee_{x \in X} \left(\chi_A(x) \wedge \chi_R(x, y)\right)
\end{aligned}$$

So (2.5.3) is true. □

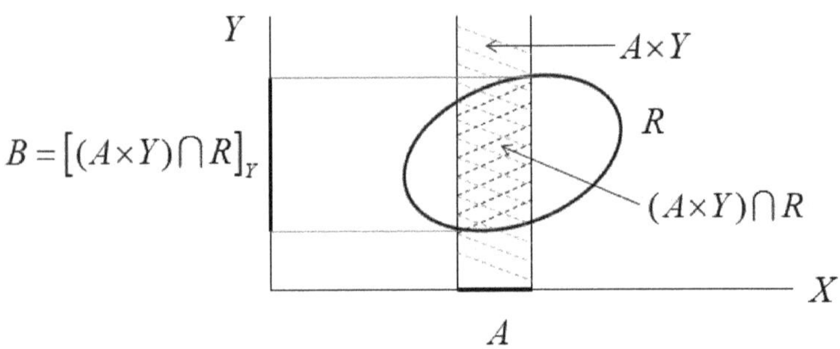

Fig. 2.5.2. $A \mapsto T(A) = [(A \times Y) \cap R]_Y$

Remark 2.5.1 In fact, it is easy to understand (2.5.3) by Figure 2.5.2. Besides, the mapping:

$$\begin{aligned} &T : \mathcal{F}(X) \to \mathcal{F}(Y) \\ &A \mapsto B \triangleq T(A) = [(A \times Y) \cap R]_Y \end{aligned}$$

is obtained by the following three steps:

(1) By use of A, we make the cylinder expansion $A \times Y$.

(2) Get $(A \times Y) \cap R$ by intersection operation between $A \times Y$ and R.

(3) We obtain $[(A \times Y) \cap R]_Y$ by the projection of $(A \times Y) \cap R$ on Y. □

Remark 2.5.2 For any $x \in X$, if we regard x as a single point set as to be $A = \{x\}$, by (2.5.1), we can get another mapping

$$\begin{aligned} &T : X \to \mathcal{P}(Y) \\ &x \mapsto B_x = T(x) \triangleq [(\{x\} \times Y) \cap R]_Y \end{aligned} \tag{2.5.4}$$

This is a point-set mapping. By using (2.5.3), for any $y \in Y$, we have

$$\begin{aligned} \chi_{B_x}(y) &= \bigvee_{u \in X} (\chi_A(u) \wedge \chi_R(u, y)) \\ &= \bigvee_{u \in X} \left(\chi_{\{x\}}(u) \wedge \chi_R(u, y)\right) \\ &= \chi_{\{x\}}(x) \wedge \chi_R(x, y) = \chi_R(x, y) = \chi_{R|_x}(y) \end{aligned}$$

This means the following expression:

$$(\forall x \in X)\left(B_x = R|_x\right) \tag{2.5.5}$$

□

Example 2.5.1 Let $X = \{x_1, x_2, \cdots, x_n\}$ and $Y = \{y_1, y_2, \cdots, y_m\}$ be two finite universes and $R \subset X \times Y$ and $A \subset X$, where

$$R = \left(\chi_R\left(x_i, y_j\right)\right)_{n \times m} = \left(r_{ij}\right)_{n \times m},$$

and then we have the following results:

$$\chi_B(y_j) = \bigvee_{i=1}^{n} (\chi_A(x_i) \wedge \chi_R(x_i, y_j)),$$
$$a_i = \chi_A(x_i), \quad r_{ij} = \chi_R(x_i, y_j),$$
$$b_j = \chi_B(y_j) = \bigvee_{i=1}^{n} (a_i \wedge r_{ij}),$$
$$i = 1, 2, \cdots, n, \quad j = 1, 2, \cdots, m,$$
$$(b_1, b_2, \cdots, b_m) = (a_1, a_2, \cdots, a_n) \circ \begin{pmatrix} r_{11} & r_{12} & \cdots & r_{1m} \\ r_{21} & r_{22} & \cdots & r_{2m} \\ \vdots & \vdots & & \vdots \\ r_{n1} & r_{n2} & \cdots & r_{nm} \end{pmatrix}$$

□

2.6 Fuzzy Set Transformations

Let X and Y be two nonempty universes. Any one mapping as the following

$$T : \mathcal{F}(X) \to \mathcal{F}(Y), \quad A \mapsto B = T(A)$$

is called a **fuzzy set transformation** from X to Y.

Definition 2.6.1 Let X and Y be two nonempty universes and for any a fuzzy relation $R \in \mathcal{F}(X \times Y)$. The following mapping

$$\begin{aligned} &T : \mathcal{F}(X) \to \mathcal{F}(Y) \\ &A \mapsto B = T(A) \triangleq [(A \times Y) \cap R]_Y \end{aligned} \tag{2.6.1}$$

is called a **fuzzy set transformation induced by relation** R from X to Y, denoted by

$$B = T(A) = A \circ R. \tag{2.6.2}$$

□

In expression (2.6.1), the relation R can also be regarded as a transformer or a convertor from $\mathcal{F}(X)$ to $\mathcal{F}(Y)$, which is shown as Figure 2.5.1.

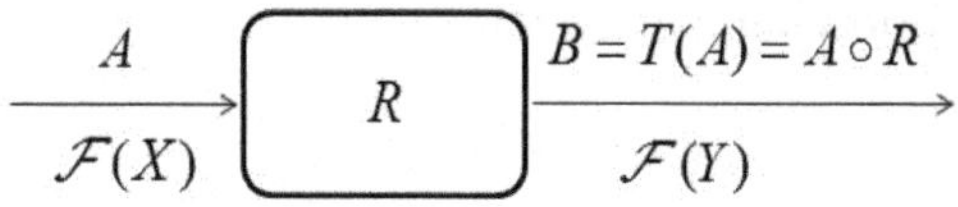

Fig. 2.6.1. R is regarded as a transformer from $\mathcal{F}(X)$ to $\mathcal{F}(Y)$

Proposition 2.6.1 Let X and Y be two nonempty universes and take one fuzzy relation $R \in \mathcal{F}(X \times Y)$. About (2.6.1), for any a point $y \in Y$, we have the following equation:

$$\mu_B(y) = \underset{x \in X}{\vee} \left(\mu_A(x) \wedge \mu_R(x,y)\right). \tag{2.6.3}$$

Proof. For any a point $y \in Y$, by using Definition 2.4.1, we have

$$\begin{aligned}
&\mu_B(y) = \mu_{T(A)}(y) = \mu_{[(A\times Y)\cap R]_Y}(y) \\
&= \underset{x \in X}{\vee} \mu_{(A\times Y)\cap R}(y) = \underset{x \in X}{\vee} \left[\mu_{A\times Y}(x,y) \wedge \mu_R(x,y)\right] \\
&= \underset{x \in X}{\vee} \left[\mu_A(x) \wedge \mu_Y(y) \wedge \mu_R(x,y)\right] \\
&= \underset{x \in X}{\vee} \left(\mu_A(x) \wedge \mu_R(x,y)\right)
\end{aligned}$$

So (2.6.3) is true. □

Remark 2.6.1 It is necessary to state that Remark 2.5.1 is also effective in the use. □

Remark 2.6.2 For any a point $x \in X$, if we regard x as a single point set as to be $A = \{x\}$, by (2.6.1), we can get another mapping:

$$T : X \to \mathcal{P}(Y), \quad x \mapsto B_x = T(x) \triangleq \left[(\{x\} \times Y) \cap R\right]_Y \tag{2.6.4}$$

This is a point-fuzzy-set mapping. By using (2.6.3), for any a point $y \in Y$, we have the following result:

$$\begin{aligned}
&\mu_{B_x}(y) = \underset{u \in X}{\vee} \left(\mu_A(u) \wedge \mu_R(u,y)\right) \\
&= \underset{u \in X}{\vee} \left(\mu_{\{x\}}(u) \wedge \mu_R(u,y)\right) \\
&= \mu_{\{x\}}(x) \wedge \mu_R(x,y) = \mu_R(x,y) = \mu_{R|_x}(y)
\end{aligned}$$

This means the following expression:

$$\left(\forall x \in X\right)\left(B_x = R\big|_x\right) \tag{2.6.5}$$

□

Example 2.6.1 Let $X = \{x_1, x_2, \cdots, x_n\}$ and $Y = \{y_1, y_2, \cdots, y_m\}$ be two finite universes and $R \in \mathcal{F}(X \times Y), A \in \mathcal{F}(X)$, where

$$R = \left(\mu_R\left(x_i, y_j\right)\right)_{n\times m} = \left(r_{ij}\right)_{n\times m},$$

and then we have the following results:

$$\mu_B\left(y_j\right) = \bigvee_{i=1}^{n}\left(\mu_A\left(x_i\right) \wedge \mu_R\left(x_i, y_j\right)\right),$$

$$a_i = \mu_A\left(x_i\right), \quad r_{ij} = \mu_R\left(x_i, y_j\right), \quad b_j = \mu_B\left(y_j\right) = \bigvee_{i=1}^{n}\left(a_i \wedge r_{ij}\right),$$

$$i = 1, 2, \cdots, n, \quad j = 1, 2, \cdots, m,$$

$$\left(b_1, b_2, \cdots, b_m\right) = \left(a_1, a_2, \cdots, a_n\right) \circ \begin{pmatrix} r_{11} & r_{12} & \cdots & r_{1m} \\ r_{21} & r_{22} & \cdots & r_{2m} \\ \vdots & \vdots & & \vdots \\ r_{n1} & r_{n2} & \cdots & r_{nm} \end{pmatrix}$$

□

Example 2.6.2 We now consider a fuzzy relation between height and weight for male young person. Let $X = \{40, 50, 60, 70, 80\}$ (kg) be weight universe and $Y = \{1.4, 1.5, 1.6, 1.7, 1.8\}$ (meter) be height universe. We have known the fuzzy relation between height and weight for male young person as follows:

$$R = \begin{pmatrix} 1 & 0.8 & 0.2 & 0.1 & 0 \\ 0.8 & 1 & 0.8 & 0.2 & 0.1 \\ 0.2 & 0.8 & 1 & 0.8 & 0.2 \\ 0.1 & 0.2 & 0.8 & 1 & 0.8 \\ 0 & 0.1 & 0.2 & 0.8 & 1 \end{pmatrix} \in \mathcal{F}(X \times Y)$$

Let β be a "male young person" and he has an expression on X as a fuzzy set as the following:

$$A = (0.8, 0.9, 0.6, 0.2, 0) \in \mathcal{F}(X).$$

Then we can get an expression on Y as the following fuzzy set:

$$B = A \circ R = (0.8, 0.9, 0.6, 0.2, 0) \circ \begin{pmatrix} 1 & 0.8 & 0.2 & 0.1 & 0 \\ 0.8 & 1 & 0.8 & 0.2 & 0.1 \\ 0.2 & 0.8 & 1 & 0.8 & 0.2 \\ 0.1 & 0.2 & 0.8 & 1 & 0.8 \\ 0 & 0.1 & 0.2 & 0.8 & 1 \end{pmatrix}$$
$$= (0.8, 0.9, 0.8, 0.6, 0.2) \in \mathcal{F}(Y).$$

□

2.7 Ternary Relations and Their Projections and Cross-section' Projections

In order to make a fuzzy multi-input system, it is necessary to know some knowledge for projections and cross-section' projections of Cantor's ternary relations and fuzzy ternary relations. But we start it from Cantor's ternary relations.

Let X, Y and Z be three nonempty universes. Any one subset of the set $X \times Y \times Z$ as the following:

$$R \subset X \times Y \times Z = \{(x, y, z) | x \in X, y \in Y, z \in Z\}$$

is called a **ternary relation** among X, Y and Z. In order to differ from fuzzy ternary relation coming from next section, sometimes we call ternary relations here to be Cantor's ternary relations.

Definition 2.7.1 Let X, Y and Z be three nonempty universes and $R \subset X \times Y \times Z$ is a ternary relation among X, Y and Y. Let

$$R_X = \{x \in X | (\exists (y, z) \in Y \times Z)((x, y, z) \in R)\},$$

$$R_Y = \{y \in X \mid (\exists (x,z) \in X \times Z)((x,y,z) \in R)\},$$
$$R_Z = \{z \in Z \mid (\exists (x,y) \in X \times Y)((x,y,z) \in R)\}.$$

We call R_X, R_Y and R_Z projection of R on X, Y and on Z, respectively. Clearly we have $R_X \subset X, R_Y \subset Y$ and $R_Z \subset Z$. □

Proposition 2.7.1 Let X, Y and Z be three nonempty universes and $R \subset X \times Y \times Z$. We have

$$(\forall x \in X)\Big(\chi_{R_X}(x) = \bigvee_{(y,z)\in Y\times Z} \chi_R(x,y,z)\Big),$$
$$(\forall y \in Y)\Big(\chi_{R_Y}(y) = \bigvee_{(x,z)\in X\times Z} \chi_R(x,y,z)\Big),$$
$$(\forall z \in Z)\Big(\chi_{R_Z}(z) = \bigvee_{(x,y)\in X\times Y} \chi_R(x,y,z)\Big)$$

Proof. For any a point $x \in X$, it is not difficult to understand the following equivalence expression:

$$\chi_{R_X}(x) = 1 \Leftrightarrow x \in R_X$$
$$\Leftrightarrow (\exists (y,z) \in Y \times Z)((x,y,z) \in R)$$
$$\Leftrightarrow (\exists (y,z) \in Y \times Z)(\chi_R(x,y) = 1)$$
$$\Leftrightarrow \bigvee_{(y,z)\in Y\times Z} \chi_R(x,y,z) = 1$$

So the first expression is true. Similarly the other two expressions are also true. □

Definition 2.7.2 Let X, Y and Z be three nonempty universes and the set $R \subset X \times Y \times Z$ is a ternary relation among X, Y and Y. For any $x \in X$, any $y \in Y$ and any $z \in Z$, let

$$R|_x = \{(y,z) \in Y \times Z \mid (x,y,z) \in R\},$$
$$R|_y = \{(x,z) \in X \times Z \mid (x,y,z) \in R\},$$
$$R|_z = \{(x,y) \in X \times Y \mid (x,y,z) \in R\}.$$

We call $R|_x, R|_y$ and $R|_z$ to be cross-section' projection of R at x, at y and at z, respectively. And for any $(x,y)\in X\times Y$, any $(y,z)\in Y\times Z$ and any $(x,z)\in X\times Z$, let

$$R|_{(x,y)}=\{z\in Z|(x,y,z)\in R\},$$
$$R|_{(y,z)}=\{x\in X|(x,y,z)\in R\},$$
$$R|_{(x,z)}=\{y\in Y|(x,y,z)\in R\}.$$

We call $R|_{(x,y)}, R|_{(y,z)}$ and $R|_{(x,z)}$ to be cross-section' projection to R at (x,y), at (y,z) and at (x,z), respectively. □

Proposition 2.7.2 Let X, Y and Z be three nonempty universes and we take $R\subset X\times Y\times Z$. We have the following results:

$$(\forall(y,z)\in Y\times Z)\left(\chi_{R|_x}(y,z)=\chi_R(x,y,z)\right),$$
$$(\forall(x,z)\in X\times Z)\left(\chi_{R|_y}(x,z)=\chi_R(x,y,z)\right),$$
$$(\forall(x,y)\in X\times Y)\left(\chi_{R|_z}(x,y)=\chi_R(x,y,z)\right);$$
$$(\forall z\in Z)\left(\chi_{R|_{(x,y)}}(z)=\chi_R(x,y,z)\right),$$
$$(\forall x\in X)\left(\chi_{R|_{(y,z)}}(x)=\chi_R(x,y,z)\right),$$
$$(\forall y\in Y)\left(\chi_{R|_{(x,z)}}(y)=\chi_R(x,y,z)\right)$$

Proof. For any $(y,z)\in Y\times Z$, by noticing the following expression:

$$\chi_{R|_x}(y,z)=1\Leftrightarrow(y,z)\in R|_x\Leftrightarrow(x,y,z)\in R\Leftrightarrow\chi_R(x,y,z)=1,$$

we know that the first expression is true. Similarly the other two expressions are also true.

And for any an element $z\in Z$, by noticing the following

$$\chi_{R|_{(x,y)}}(z)=1\Leftrightarrow z\in R|_{(x,y)}\Leftrightarrow(x,y,z)\in R\Leftrightarrow\chi_R(x,y,z)=1$$

we know that the fourth expression is true. Similarly the other two expressions are also true. □

Proposition 2.7.3 Let X, Y and Z be two nonempty universes and take $R \subset X \times Y \times Z$. We have

$$R_X = \bigcup_{(y,z)\in Y\times Z} R\big|_{(y,z)},$$
$$R_Y = \bigcup_{(x,z)\in X\times Z} R\big|_{(x,z)},$$
$$R_Z = \bigcup_{(x,y)\in X\times Y} R\big|_{(x,y)}$$

Proof. For any an element $z \in Z$, by using of Proposition 2.7.1 and Proposition 2.7.2, we have the following result:

$$\chi_{R_Z}(z) = \bigvee_{(x,y)\in X\times Y} \chi_R(x,y,z) = \bigvee_{(x,y)\in X\times Y} \chi_{R|_{(x,y)}}(z) = \chi_{\bigcup_{(x,y)\in X\times Y} R|_{(x,y)}}(z).$$

Thus the third expression is true. Similarly the other two expressions are also true. □

Proposition 2.7.4 Let X, Y and Z be three nonempty universes and take $R \subset X \times Y \times Z$. We have the following expressions:

$$R = \bigcup_{(x,y)\in X\times Y} \left(\{(x,y)\} \times R\big|_{(x,y)}\right)$$
$$= \bigcup_{(x,y)\in X\times Y} \left(\{x\} \times \{y\} \times R\big|_{(x,y)}\right),$$
$$R = \bigcup_{(y,z)\in Y\times Z} \left(R\big|_{(y,z)} \times \{(y,z)\}\right)$$
$$= \bigcup_{(y,z)\in Y\times Z} \left(R\big|_{(y,z)} \times \{y\} \times \{z\}\right),$$
$$R = \bigcup_{(x,z)\in X\times Z} \left(\{x\} \times R\big|_{(x,z)} \times \{z\}\right),$$
$$R = \bigcup_{x\in X} \left(\{x\} \times R\big|_{x}\right), \quad R = \bigcup_{z\in Z} \left(R\big|_{z} \times \{z\}\right)$$

Proof. For any $(u,v,w)\in X\times Y\times Z$, by using Proposition 2.7.2, we have the following equations:

$$\chi_{\bigcup\limits_{(x,y)\in X\times Y}\left(\{(x,y)\}\times R|_{(x,y)}\right)}(u,v,w)=\bigvee_{(x,y)\in X\times Y}\chi_{\{(x,y)\}\times R|_{(x,y)}}(u,v,w)$$

$$=\bigvee_{(x,y)\in X\times Y}\left(\chi_{\{(x,y)\}}(u,v)\wedge\chi_{R|_{(x,y)}}(w)\right)$$

$$=\chi_{\{(u,v)\}}(u,v)\wedge\chi_{R|_{(u,v)}}(w)=\chi_{R|_{(u,v)}}(w)=\chi_R(u,v,w);$$

$$\chi_{\bigcup\limits_{x\in X}\left(\{x\}\times R|_x\right)}(u,v,w)=\bigvee_{x\in X}\chi_{\{x\}\times R|_x}(u,v,w)=\bigvee_{x\in X}\left(\chi_{\{x\}}(u)\wedge\chi_{R|_x}(v,w)\right)$$

$$=\chi_{\{u\}}(u)\wedge\chi_{R|_u}(v,w)=\chi_{R|_u}(v,w)=\chi_R(u,v,w)$$

So the first expression and the fourth expression are true. Similarly, we can know that the other expressions are also true. □

Proposition 2.7.5 Let X,Y and Z be three nonempty universes and take relation $R\subset X\times Y\times Z$. We have the following results:

$$(\forall(x,y)\in X\times Y)\left(R|_{(x,y)}=\left[\left(\{(x,y)\}\times Z\right)\cap R\right]_Z\right),$$

$$(\forall(y,z)\in Y\times Z)\left(R|_{(y,z)}=\left[\left(X\times\{(y,z)\}\right)\cap R\right]_X\right),$$

$$(\forall(x,z)\in X\times Z)\left(R|_{(x,z)}=\left[\left(\{x\}\times Y\times\{z\}\right)\cap R\right]_Y\right)$$

Proof. For any $(x,y,z)\in X\times Y\times Z$, by using Proposition 2.7.1 and Proposition 2.7.2, we have the following result:

$$\chi_{[(\{(x,y)\}\times Z)\cap R]_Z}(z)=\bigvee_{(u,v)\in X\times Y}\chi_{(\{(x,y)\}\times Z)\cap R}(u,v,z)$$

$$=\bigvee_{(u,v)\in X\times Y}\left(\chi_{\{(x,y)\}\times Z}(u,v,z)\wedge\chi_R(u,v,z)\right)$$

$$=\bigvee_{(u,v)\in X\times Y}\left(\chi_{\{(x,y)\}}(u,v)\wedge\chi_Z(z)\wedge\chi_R(u,v,z)\right)$$

$$=\bigvee_{(u,v)\in X\times Y}\left(\chi_{\{(x,y)\}}(u,v)\wedge 1\wedge\chi_R(u,v,z)\right)$$

$$=\chi_{\{(x,y)\}}(x,y)\wedge\chi_R(x,y,z)=\chi_R(x,y,z)=\chi_{R|_{(x,y)}}(z)$$

So the first expression is true. Similarly, we can get the other expressions as well. □

Proposition 2.7.6 Let X, Y and Z be three nonempty universes and take two ternary relations $P, Q \subset X \times Y \times Z$. If $P \supset Q$, then we have the following results:

$$P_X \supset Q_X, \quad P_Y \supset Q_Y, \quad P_Z \supset Q_Z,$$
$$(\forall x \in X)\left(P|_x \supset Q|_x\right),$$
$$(\forall y \in Y)\left(P|_y \supset Q|_y\right),$$
$$(\forall z \in Y)\left(P|_z \supset Q|_z\right),$$
$$(\forall (x,y) \in X \times Y)\left(P|_{(x,y)} \supset Q|_{(x,y)}\right),$$
$$(\forall (y,z) \in Y \times Z)\left(P|_{(y,z)} \supset Q|_{(y,z)}\right),$$
$$(\forall (x,z) \in X \times Z)\left(P|_{(x,z)} \supset Q|_{(x,z)}\right)$$

It is not necessary to prove them for they are obvious. □

2.8 Fuzzy Ternary Relations and Its Projections and Cross- section' Projections

Let X, Y and Z be three nonempty universes. Any one fuzzy set as being $R \in \mathcal{F}(X \times Y \times Z)$ is called a **fuzzy ternary relation** among X, Y and Z.

Definition 2.8.1 Let X, Y and Z be three nonempty universes and take one fuzzy ternary relation as being $R \in \mathcal{F}(X \times Y \times Z)$ among X, Y and Y. Three fuzzy sets $R_X \in \mathcal{F}(X), R_Y \in \mathcal{F}(Y)$ and $R_Z \in \mathcal{F}(Z)$ are respectively called to be projection of R on X, Y and Z, if their membership functions are defined by the following

$$(\forall x \in X)\left(\mu_{R_X}(x) = \bigvee_{(y,z) \in Y \times Z} \mu_R(x,y,z)\right),$$
$$(\forall y \in Y)\left(\mu_{R_Y}(y) = \bigvee_{(x,z) \in X \times Z} \mu_R(x,y,z)\right),$$

$$\left(\forall z \in Z\right)\left(\mu_{R_Z}(z) = \bigvee_{(x,y)\in X\times Y} \mu_R(x,y,z)\right)$$

□

Definition 2.8.2 Let X, Y and Z be three nonempty universes and take a fuzzy ternary relation as being $R \in \mathcal{F}(X \times Y \times Z)$ among X, Y and Y. For any $x \in X$, any $y \in Y$ and any $z \in Z$, three fuzzy sets as follows:

$$R\big|_x \in \mathcal{F}(Y \times Z), \quad R\big|_y \in \mathcal{F}(X \times Z), \quad R\big|_z \in \mathcal{F}(X \times Y)$$

are respectively called to be cross-section' projection of R at x, y and z, if their membership functions are defined by the following:

$$\left(\forall (y,z) \in Y \times Z\right)\left(\mu_{R|_x}(y,z) = \mu_R(x,y,z)\right),$$

$$\left(\forall (y,z) \in X \times Z\right)\left(\mu_{R|_y}(x,z) = \mu_R(x,y,z)\right),$$

$$\left(\forall (x,y) \in X \times Y\right)\left(\mu_{R|_z}(x,y) = \mu_R(x,y,z)\right)$$

And for any $(x,y) \in X \times Y$, any $(y,z) \in Y \times Z$ and $(x,z) \in X \times Z$, three fuzzy sets $R\big|_{(x,y)} \in \mathcal{F}(Z), R\big|_{(y,z)} \in \mathcal{F}(X)$ and $R\big|_{(x,z)} \in \mathcal{F}(Y)$ are respectively called to be cross-section' projection of R at (x,y), at (y,z) and at (x,z), if their membership functions are defined by the following:

$$\left(\forall z \in Z\right)\left(\mu_{R|_{(x,y)}}(z) = \mu_R(x,y,z)\right),$$

$$\left(\forall x \in X\right)\left(\mu_{R|_{(y,z)}}(x) = \mu_R(x,y,z)\right),$$

$$\left(\forall y \in Y\right)\left(\mu_{R|_{(x,z)}}(y) = \mu_R(x,y,z)\right)$$

□

Proposition 2.8.1 Let X, Y and Z be three nonempty universes and take a fuzzy ternary relation as being $R \in \mathcal{F}(X \times Y \times Z)$. We have the following results:

$$R_X = \bigcup_{(y,z)\in Y\times Z} R\big|_{(y,z)}, \quad R_Y = \bigcup_{(x,z)\in X\times Z} R\big|_{(x,z)}, \quad R_Z = \bigcup_{(x,y)\in X\times Y} R\big|_{(x,y)}$$

Proof. For any $z \in Z$, by using of Definition 2.8.1 and Definition 2.8.2, we have the following expression:

$$\mu_{R_Z}(z) = \bigvee_{(x,y)\in X\times Y} \chi_R(x,y,z) = \bigvee_{(x,y)\in X\times Y} \mu_{R|_{(x,y)}}(z) = \mu_{\bigcup_{(x,y)\in X\times Y} R|_{(x,y)}}(z).$$

Thus the third expression is true. Similarly the other two expressions are also true. □

Proposition 2.8.2 Let X, Y and Z be three nonempty universes and take a fuzzy ternary relation as being $R \in \mathcal{F}(X\times Y\times Z)$. We have the following results:

$$R = \bigcup_{(x,y)\in X\times Y} \left(\{(x,y)\}\times R|_{(x,y)}\right)$$
$$= \bigcup_{(x,y)\in X\times Y} \left(\{x\}\times\{y\}\times R|_{(x,y)}\right),$$
$$R = \bigcup_{(y,z)\in Y\times Z} \left(R|_{(y,z)}\times\{(y,z)\}\right)$$
$$= \bigcup_{(y,z)\in Y\times Z} \left(R|_{(y,z)}\times\{y\}\times\{z\}\right),$$
$$R = \bigcup_{(x,z)\in X\times Z} \left(\{x\}\times R|_{(x,z)}\times\{z\}\right),$$
$$R = \bigcup_{x\in X}\left(\{x\}\times R|_x\right), \quad R = \bigcup_{z\in Z}\left(R|_z\times\{z\}\right)$$

Proof. For any $(u,v,w)\in X\times Y\times Z$, by using Definition 2.8.1 and Definition 2.8.2 and Proposition 2.8.1, we have the following results:

$$\mu_{\bigcup_{(x,y)\in X\times Y}\left(\{(x,y)\}\times R|_{(x,y)}\right)}(u,v,w)$$
$$= \bigvee_{(x,y)\in X\times Y} \mu_{\{(x,y)\}\times R|_{(x,y)}}(u,v,w)$$
$$= \bigvee_{(x,y)\in X\times Y} \left(\chi_{\{(x,y)\}}(u,v) \wedge \mu_{R|_{(x,y)}}(w)\right)$$
$$= \chi_{\{(u,v)\}}(u,v) \wedge \mu_{R|_{(u,v)}}(w)$$
$$= \mu_{R|_{(u,v)}}(w) = \mu_R(u,v,w);$$

$$\mu_{\bigcup_{x\in X}(\{x\}\times R|_x)}(u,v,w) = \vee_{x\in X}\mu_{\{x\}\times R|_x}(u,v,w)$$
$$= \vee_{x\in X}\left(\chi_{\{x\}}(u)\wedge\mu_{R|_x}(v,w)\right)$$
$$= \chi_{\{u\}}(u)\wedge\mu_{R|_u}(v,w)$$
$$= \mu_{R|_u}(v,w) = \mu_R(u,v,w)$$

So the first expression and fourth expression are true. Similarly we can know that the second expression and fourth expression are also true. □

Proposition 2.8.3 Let X,Y and Z be three nonempty universes and take a fuzzy ternary relation as being $R\in\mathcal{F}(X\times Y\times Z)$. We have the following results:

$$(\forall(x,y)\in X\times Y)\left(R|_{(x,y)} = \left[(\{(x,y)\}\times Z)\cap R\right]_Z\right),$$
$$(\forall(y,z)\in Y\times Z)\left(R|_{(y,z)} = \left[(X\times\{(y,z)\})\cap R\right]_X\right),$$
$$(\forall(x,z)\in X\times Z)\left(R|_{(x,z)} = \left[(\{x\}\times Y\times\{z\})\cap R\right]_Y\right)$$

Proof. For any $(x,y,z)\in X\times Y\times Z$, by using Proposition 2.8.1 and Proposition 2.8.2, we have the following results:

$$\mu_{[(\{(x,y)\}\times Z)\cap R]_Z}(z) = \vee_{(u,v)\in X\times Y}\mu_{(\{(x,y)\}\times Z)\cap R}(u,v,z)$$
$$= \vee_{(u,v)\in X\times Y}\left(\chi_{\{(x,y)\}\times Z}(u,v,z)\wedge\mu_R(u,v,z)\right)$$
$$= \vee_{(u,v)\in X\times Y}\left(\chi_{\{(x,y)\}}(u,v)\wedge\chi_Z(z)\wedge\mu_R(u,v,z)\right)$$
$$= \vee_{(u,v)\in X\times Y}\left(\chi_{\{(x,y)\}}(u,v)\wedge 1\wedge\mu_R(u,v,z)\right)$$
$$= \chi_{\{(x,y)\}}(x,y)\wedge\mu_R(x,y,z)$$
$$= \mu_R(x,y,z) = \mu_{R|_{(x,y)}}(z)$$

So the first expression is true. Similarly, we can get the other expressions as well. □

Proposition 2.8.4 Let X,Y and Z be three nonempty universes and take two fuzzy ternary relations $P,Q\in\mathcal{F}(X\times Y\times Z)$. If $P\supset Q$, then we have the following results:

$$
\begin{aligned}
&P_X\supset Q_X,\quad P_Y\supset Q_Y,\quad P_Z\supset Q_Z,\\
&(\forall x\in X)\left(P|_x\supset Q|_x\right),\\
&(\forall y\in Y)\left(P|_y\supset Q|_y\right),\\
&(\forall z\in Z)\left(P|_z\supset Q|_z\right),\\
&(\forall (x,y)\in X\times Y)\left(P|_{(x,y)}\supset Q|_{(x,y)}\right),\\
&(\forall (y,z)\in Y\times Z)\left(P|_{(y,z)}\supset Q|_{(y,z)}\right),\\
&(\forall (x,z)\in X\times Z)\left(P|_{(x,z)}\supset Q|_{(x,z)}\right)
\end{aligned}
$$

It is not necessary to prove them for they are obvious. □

2.9 Fuzzy Set Transformations Based on Fuzzy Ternary Fuzzy Relations

First of all, we consider Cantor's set transformations based on ternary relations.

Definition 2.9.1 Let X,Y and Z be three nonempty universes and take a relation $R\subset X\times Y\times Z$. The following mapping

$$
\begin{aligned}
&T:\mathcal{P}(X)\times\mathcal{P}(Y)\to\mathcal{P}(Z)\\
&(A,B)\mapsto C=T(A,B)\triangleq\left[((A\times B)\times Z)\cap R\right]_Z
\end{aligned}
\tag{2.9.1}
$$

is called a **set transformation induced by ternary relation** R among X, Y and Z, denoted by the following equation:

$$C=T(A,B)=(A\times B)\circ R. \tag{2.9.2}$$

□

Proposition 2.9.1 Let X,Y and Z be three nonempty universes and take a relation $R \subset X \times Y \times Z$. About (2.9.1), for any $z \in Z$, we have

$$\chi_C(z) = \bigvee_{(x,y)\in X\times Y} \left(\chi_A(x) \wedge \chi_B(y) \wedge \chi_R(x,y,z)\right). \qquad (2.9.3)$$

Proof. For any $z \in Z$, by using Proposition 2.7.1, we have

$$\begin{aligned}
\chi_C(z) &= \chi_{T(A)}(z) = \chi_{[(A\times Y)\cap R]_Z}(z) \\
&= \bigvee_{(x,y)\in X\times Y} \chi_{((A\times B)\times Z)\cap R}(x,y,z) \\
&= \bigvee_{(x,y)\in X\times Y} \left[\chi_{(A\times B)\times Z}(x,y,z) \wedge \chi_R(x,y,z)\right] \\
&= \bigvee_{(x,y)\in X\times Y} \left[\chi_{A\times B}(x,y) \wedge \chi_Z(z) \wedge \chi_R(x,y,z)\right] \\
&= \bigvee_{(x,y)\in X\times Y} \left(\chi_{A\times B}(x,y) \wedge \chi_R(x,y)\right) \\
&= \bigvee_{(x,y)\in X\times Y} \left(\chi_A(x) \wedge \chi_B(y) \wedge \chi_R(x,y)\right)
\end{aligned}$$

So (2.9.3) is true. □

Remark 2.9.1 The set transformation as the following:

$$(A,B) \mapsto T(A,B) = \left[((A\times B)\times Z)\cap R\right]_Z$$

is obtained by the following three steps:

Step 1. By use of (A,B), we make the cylinder expansion $(A\times B)\times Z$.

Step 2. Get $((A\times B)\times Z)\cap R$ by intersection operation between the two relations $(A\times B)\times Z$ and R.

Step 3. We obtain the set what we want as being $\left[((A\times B)\times Z)\cap R\right]_Z$, by the projection of $((A\times B)\times Z)\cap R$ on Z. □

Remark 2.9.2 For any one point $(x,y)\in X\times Y$, if we regard x,y as two single point sets by (2.9.1) as following:

$$A = \{x\} \subset X, \quad B = \{y\} \subset Y,$$

we can get another mapping as follows:

$$\begin{aligned} &T: X \times Y \to \mathcal{P}(Z) \\ &(x,y) \mapsto C_{(x,y)} = T(x,y) \triangleq \left[\left((\{x\} \times \{y\}) \times Z \right) \cap R \right]_Z \end{aligned} \tag{2.9.4}$$

This is a point-set mapping. By using (2.9.3), for any $(x,y) \in X \times Y$, we have the following equation:

$$\begin{aligned} &\chi_{C_{(x,y)}}(z) = \bigvee_{(u,v)\in X\times Y} \left(\chi_A(u) \wedge \chi_B(v) \wedge \chi_R(u,v,z) \right) \\ &= \bigvee_{(u,v)\in X\times Y} \left(\chi_{\{x\}}(u) \wedge \chi_{\{y\}}(v) \wedge \chi_R(u,v,z) \right) \\ &= \chi_{\{x\}}(x) \wedge \chi_{\{y\}}(y) \wedge \chi_R(x,y,z) = \chi_R(x,y,z) \\ &= \chi_{R|_{(x,y)}}(z) \end{aligned}$$

This means that

$$\left(\forall (x,y) \in X \times Y \right) \left(C_{(x,y)} = T(x,y) = R|_{(x,y)} \right) \tag{2.9.5}$$

□

Now we turn to consider fuzzy set transformations based on fuzzy ternary relations.

Definition 2.9.2 Let X, Y and Z be three nonempty universes and $R \in \mathcal{F}(X \times Y \times Z)$. The following mapping

$$\begin{aligned} &T: \mathcal{F}(X) \times \mathcal{F}(Y) \to \mathcal{F}(Z) \\ &(A,B) \mapsto C = T(A,B) \triangleq \left[\left((A \times B) \times Z \right) \cap R \right]_Z \end{aligned} \tag{2.9.6}$$

is called a **fuzzy set transformation induced by fuzzy ternary relation** R among X, Y and Z, denoted by

$$C = T(A,B) = (A \times B) \circ R\,. \tag{2.9.7}$$

□

Proposition 2.9.2 Let X, Y and Z be three nonempty universes and $R \in \mathcal{F}(X \times Y \times Z)$. About (2.9.1), for any $z \in Z$, we have

$$\mu_C(z) = \bigvee_{(x,y)\in X\times Y} \left(\mu_A(x) \wedge \mu_B(y) \wedge \mu_R(x,y,z) \right). \tag{2.9.8}$$

Proof. For any an element $z \in Z$, by using Definition 2.4.1, we can have the following equation:

$$\begin{aligned}
\mu_C(z) &= \mu_{T(A)}(z) = \mu_{[(A\times Y)\cap R]_Y}(z) \\
&= \bigvee_{(x,y)\in X\times Y} \mu_{((A\times B)\times Z)\cap R}(x,y,z) \\
&= \bigvee_{(x,y)\in X\times Y} \left[\mu_{(A\times B)\times Z}(x,y,z) \wedge \mu_R(x,y,z)\right] \\
&= \bigvee_{(x,y)\in X\times Y} \left[\mu_{A\times B}(x,y) \wedge \chi_Z(z) \wedge \mu_R(x,y,z)\right] \\
&= \bigvee_{(x,y)\in X\times Y} \left(\mu_{A\times B}(x,y) \wedge \mu_R(x,y)\right) \\
&= \bigvee_{(x,y)\in X\times Y} \left(\mu_A(x) \wedge \mu_B(y) \wedge \mu_R(x,y)\right)
\end{aligned}$$

So (2.9.8) is true. □

Remark 2.9.3 The fuzzy set transformation as the following:

$$(A,B) \mapsto T(A,B) = \left[\left((A\times B)\times Z\right)\cap R\right]_Z$$

is also obtained by the following three steps:

Step 1. By use of (A,B), we make the cylinder expansion $(A\times B)\times Z$.

Step 2. Get $\left((A\times B)\times Z\right)\cap R$ by intersection operation between two fuzzy relations $(A\times B)\times Z$ and R.

Step 3. We obtain the fuzzy set as being $\left[\left((A\times B)\times Z\right)\cap R\right]_Z$ by the projection of $\left((A\times B)\times Z\right)\cap R$ on Z. □

Remark 2.9.4 For any $(x,y)\in X\times Y$, if we regard x,y as two single point sets by (2.9.6) as the following:

$$A=\{x\}\subset X, \quad B=\{y\}\subset Y,$$

we can get another mapping

$$\begin{aligned}
&T: X\times Y \to \mathcal{F}(Z) \\
&(x,y) \mapsto C_{(x,y)} = T(x,y) \triangleq \left[\left((\{x\}\times\{y\})\times Z\right)\cap R\right]_Z
\end{aligned} \tag{2.9.9}$$

This is a point-fuzzy-set mapping. By (2.9.8), for any $(x, y) \in X \times Y$, we have the following expression:

$$\mu_{C_{(x,y)}}(z) = \bigvee_{(u,v)\in X\times Y} \left(\mu_A(u) \wedge \mu_B(v) \wedge \mu_R(u,v,z)\right)$$
$$= \bigvee_{(u,v)\in X\times Y} \left(\chi_{\{x\}}(u) \wedge \chi_{\{y\}}(v) \wedge \mu_R(u,v,z)\right)$$
$$= \chi_{\{x\}}(x) \wedge \chi_{\{y\}}(y) \wedge \mu_R(x,y,z) = \mu_R(x,y,z) = \mu_{R|_{(x,y)}}(z)$$

This means that

$$\left(\forall (x,y) \in X \times Y\right)\left(C_{(x,y)} = T(x,y) = R\big|_{(x,y)}\right) \tag{2.9.10}$$

□

2.10 On Zadeh's Extension Principle

Let X and Y be two nonempty universes and consider a mapping:

$$f : X \to Y, \quad x \mapsto y = f(x)$$

Zadeh's extension principle describes such a principle which expresses how to extend the mapping $f : X \to Y$ to a following mapping:

$$f^* : \mathcal{F}(X) \to \mathcal{F}(Y), \quad A \mapsto B = f^*(A)$$

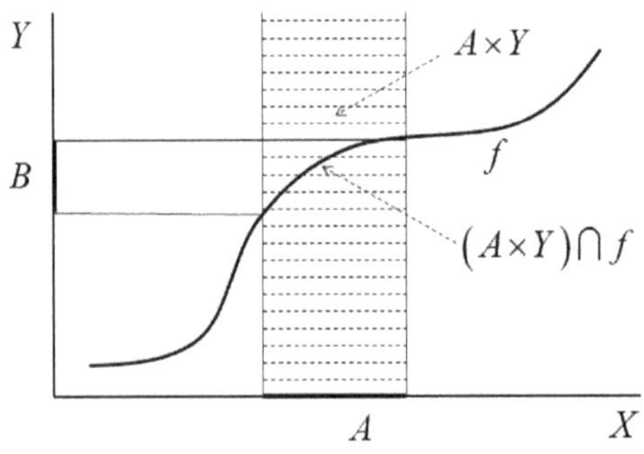

Fig. 2.10.1. The set transformation as (2.10.1)

First of all, we consider a special case about Zadeh's extension principle that how to extend the mapping $f: X \to Y$ to such a following mapping:

$$f^{\circ}: \mathcal{P}(X) \to \mathcal{P}(Y), \quad A \mapsto B = f^{\circ}(A)$$

We have known the fact that $f \subset X \times Y$, i.e., the mapping f is regarded as a Cantor's relation between X and Y. Based on Definition 2.5.1, we can get a set transformation like the following form (see Figure 2.10.1):

$$\begin{aligned} &f^{\circ}: \mathcal{P}(X) \to \mathcal{P}(Y) \\ &A \mapsto B = f^{\circ}(A) = \left[(A \times Y) \cap f\right]_Y \end{aligned} \tag{2.10.1}$$

And then by using Proposition 2.5.1, we have such a proposition:

Proposition 2.10.1 About the set transformation as (2.10.1), we have

$$\chi_B(y) = \bigvee_{y=f(x)} \chi_A(x), \quad y \in Y. \tag{2.10.2}$$

Proof. For any $y \in Y$, based on Proposition 2.5.1, we have the following result:

$$\begin{aligned} \chi_B(y) &= \chi_{f^{\circ}(A)}(y) = \chi_{[(A\times Y)\cap f]_Y}(y) \\ &= \bigvee_{x\in X} \chi_{(A\times Y)\cap f}(x, y) \\ &= \bigvee_{x\in X} \left(\chi_{A\times Y}(x, y) \wedge \chi_f(x, y)\right) \\ &= \bigvee_{x\in X} \left(\left(\chi_A(x) \wedge \chi_Y(y)\right) \wedge \chi_f(x, y)\right) \\ &= \bigvee_{x\in X} \left(\chi_A(x) \wedge \chi_f(x, y)\right) \\ &= \bigvee_{x\in\{t\in X | y=f(t)\}} \left(\chi_A(x) \wedge \chi_f(x, y)\right) \\ &= \bigvee_{x\in\{t\in X | y=f(t)\}} \left(\chi_A(x) \wedge \chi_f(x, f(x))\right) \\ &= \bigvee_{x\in\{t\in X | y=f(t)\}} \left(\chi_A(x) \wedge 1\right) = \bigvee_{x\in\{t\in X | y=f(t)\}} \chi_A(x) \end{aligned}$$

If we denote $\bigvee_{x\in\{t\in X | y=f(t)\}} \chi_A(x)$ as $\bigvee_{y=f(x)} \chi_A(x)$, we have the following form:

$$\chi_B(y) = \bigvee_{y=f(x)} \chi_A(x), \quad y \in Y .$$

Thus (2.10.2) is true. See Figure 2.10.1. □

Now we turn to consider how to extend the mapping $f : X \to Y$ to a following mapping:

$$f^* : \mathcal{F}(X) \to \mathcal{F}(Y), \quad A \mapsto B = f^*(A)$$

Based on Definition 2.6.1, we can get a set transformation like the following form:

$$\begin{aligned} &f^* : \mathcal{F}(X) \to \mathcal{F}(Y) \\ &A \mapsto B = f^*(A) = [(A \times Y) \cap f]_Y \end{aligned} \tag{2.10.3}$$

And then by using Proposition 2.6.1, we have such a proposition as follows.

Proposition 2.10.2 About the set transformation as (2.10.3), we have

$$\mu_B(y) = \bigvee_{y=f(x)} \mu_A(x), \quad y \in Y . \tag{2.10.4}$$

Proof. For any $y \in Y$, based on Proposition 2.6.1, we have the following expression:

$$\begin{aligned}
\mu_B(y) &= \mu_{f^*(A)}(y) = \mu_{[(A\times Y)\cap f]_Y}(y) \\
&= \bigvee_{x\in X} \mu_{(A\times Y)\cap f}(x,y) \\
&= \bigvee_{x\in X} \left(\mu_{A\times Y}(x,y) \wedge \chi_f(x,y)\right) \\
&= \bigvee_{x\in X} \left(\left(\mu_A(x) \wedge \chi_Y(y)\right) \wedge \chi_f(x,y)\right) \\
&= \bigvee_{x\in X} \left(\mu_A(x) \wedge \chi_f(x,y)\right) \\
&= \bigvee_{x\in\{t\in X | y=f(t)\}} \left(\mu_A(x) \wedge \chi_f(x,y)\right) \\
&= \bigvee_{x\in\{t\in X | y=f(t)\}} \left(\mu_A(x) \wedge \chi_f(x,f(x))\right) \\
&= \bigvee_{x\in\{t\in X | y=f(t)\}} \left(\mu_A(x) \wedge 1\right) = \bigvee_{x\in\{t\in X | y=f(t)\}} \mu_A(x)
\end{aligned}$$

If we denote $\bigvee_{x\in\{t\in X | y=f(t)\}} \mu_A(x)$ as $\bigvee_{y=f(x)} \mu_A(x)$, we have the following form:

$$\mu_B(y) = \bigvee_{y=f(x)} \mu_A(x), \quad y \in Y.$$

Thus (2.10.4) is true. □

Remark 2.10.1 The Equation (2.10.4) is just Zadeh's extension principle. Because Zadeh's extension principle has not proved before, it is called extension principle. In fact, it is not a principle, but should be a proposition or theorem like Proposition 2.10.2 which can be proved based on the extension principle defined by (1.4.1) in Section 1.4. □

The Equation (2.10.4) is clearly the extension principle on unary functions or functions of one variable. Of course, we should consider how to establish the extension principle on functions of many variables.

Let X, Y and Z be three nonempty universes and consider a mapping as follows:

$$f: X\times Y \to Z, \quad (x,y) \mapsto z = f(x,y)$$

We first extend the mapping $f: X\times Y \to Z$ to a following mapping:

$$f^*:\mathcal{F}(X\times Y)\to\mathcal{F}(Z),\quad R\mapsto C=f^*(R)$$

Based on Definition 2.6.1, we can get a set transformation like the following form:

$$\begin{aligned}&f^*:\mathcal{F}(X\times Y)\to\mathcal{F}(Z)\\&R\mapsto C=f^*(R)=\left[(R\times Z)\cap f\right]_Z\end{aligned}\tag{2.10.5}$$

And then by using Proposition 2.6.1, we have such a proposition.

Proposition 2.10.2 About the fuzzy set transformation as (2.10.5), we have

$$\mu_C(z)=\bigvee_{z=f(x,y)}\mu_R(x,y),\quad z\in Z\,.\tag{2.10.6}$$

Proof. For any $z\in Z$, based on Proposition 2.6.1, by noticing the fact that $f\subset X\times Y\times Z$, we have the following expression:

$$\begin{aligned}\mu_C(z)&=\mu_{f^*(R)}(z)=\mu_{[(R\times Z)\cap f]_Z}(z)\\&=\bigvee_{(x,y)\in X\times Y}\mu_{(R\times Z)\cap f}(x,y,z)\\&=\bigvee_{(x,y)\in X\times Y}\left(\mu_{R\times Z}(x,y,z)\wedge\chi_f(x,y,z)\right)\\&=\bigvee_{(x,y)\in X\times Y}\left(\left(\mu_R(x,y)\wedge\chi_Z(z)\right)\wedge\chi_f(x,y,z)\right)\\&=\bigvee_{(x,y)\in X\times Y}\left(\mu_R(x,y)\wedge\chi_f(x,y,z)\right)\\&=\bigvee_{(x,y)\in\{(u,v)\in X\times Y|z=f(u,v)\}}\left(\mu_R(x,y)\wedge\chi_f(x,y,z)\right)\\&=\bigvee_{(x,y)\in\{(u,v)\in X\times Y|z=f(u,v)\}}\left(\mu_R(x,y)\wedge\chi_f\left(x,y,f(x,y)\right)\right)\\&=\bigvee_{(x,y)\in\{(u,v)\in X\times Y|z=f(u,v)\}}\left(\mu_R(x,y)\wedge 1\right)\\&=\bigvee_{(x,y)\in\{(u,v)\in X\times Y|z=f(u,v)\}}\mu_R(x,y)\end{aligned}$$

If we denote $\bigvee_{(x,y)\in\{(u,v)\in X\times Y|z=f(u,v)\}}\mu_R(x,y)$ as $\bigvee_{z=f(x,y)}\mu_R(x,y)$, we have the following form:

$$\mu_C(z) = \bigvee_{z=f(x,y)} \mu_R(x,y), \quad z \in Z .$$

Thus (2.10.6) is true. □

Then we extend the mapping $f: X \times Y \to Z$ to a following mapping:

$$f^*: \mathcal{F}(X) \times \mathcal{F}(Y) \to \mathcal{F}(Z)$$
$$(A, B) \mapsto C = f^*(A, B)$$

In order to use Equation (2.10.5), take $R = A \times B \in \mathcal{F}(X \times Y)$, and then we have a set transformation like the following form:

$$\begin{aligned} &f^*: \mathcal{F}(X) \times \mathcal{F}(Y) \to \mathcal{F}(Z) \\ &(A, B) \mapsto C = f^*(A, B) = \left[((A \times B) \times Z) \cap f \right]_Z \end{aligned} \tag{2.10.6}$$

Based on Proposition 2.10.2, for any $z \in Z$, we have the following fact:

$$\mu_C(z) = \bigvee_{z=f(x,y)} \mu_R(x,y) = \bigvee_{z=f(x,y)} \left(\mu_A(x) \wedge \mu_B(y) \right). \tag{2.10.7}$$

Remark 2.10.2 For the fuzzy relation $R = A \times B \in \mathcal{F}(X \times Y)$, for any $(x, y) \in X \times Y$, we have known the fact that

$$\mu_R(x,y) = \mu_{A \times B}(x,y) = \mu_A(x) \cdot \mu_B(y) .$$

Hence, (2.10.6) can be also written by membership function as follows

$$\mu_C(z) = \bigvee_{z=f(x,y)} \left(\mu_A(x) \cdot \mu_B(y) \right), \quad z \in Z . \tag{2.10.8}$$

□

At the last of this section, we consider another problem. Let X and Y be two nonempty universes and consider a mapping:

$$f: X \to Y, x \mapsto y = f(x)$$

We have known that Zadeh's extension principle means that based on the mapping $f: X \to Y$, we can get the following mapping:

$$\begin{aligned} f^*: \mathcal{F}(X) &\to \mathcal{F}(Y) \\ A &\mapsto B = f^*(A), \end{aligned}$$

$$(\forall y \in Y)\left(\mu_B(y) = \bigvee_{y=f(x)} \mu_A(x)\right)$$

On the other hand, based on the mapping $f: X \to Y$, we should another mapping:

$$\begin{aligned} \left(f^{-1}\right)^*: \mathcal{F}(Y) &\to \mathcal{F}(X) \\ B &\mapsto A = \left(f^{-1}\right)^*(B) \end{aligned}$$

In order to know what is the membership function of the fuzzy set as being $\left(f^{-1}\right)^*(B)$, we also consider a special case that how to extend the mapping $f: X \to Y$ to such a following mapping:

$$\left(f^{-1}\right)^\circ: \mathcal{P}(Y) \to \mathcal{P}(X), \quad B \mapsto A = \left(f^{-1}\right)^\circ(B)$$

In fact, it is well-known that $\left(f^{-1}\right)^\circ(B) = \{x \in X \mid f(x) \in B\}$, and then we have the following expression:

$$(\forall x \in X)\left(\chi_{\left(f^{-1}\right)^\circ(B)}(x) = \chi_{\{x \in X \mid f(x) \in B\}}(x)\right).$$

Proposition 2.10.3 $(\forall x \in X)\left(\chi_{\{x \in X \mid f(x) \in B\}}(x) = \chi_B(f(x))\right)$

Proof. For any $x \in X$, we have the following equivalence expression:

$$\begin{aligned} &\chi_{\{t \in X \mid f(t) \in B\}}(x) = 1 \Leftrightarrow x \in \{t \in X \mid f(t) \in B\} \\ &\Leftrightarrow f(x) \in B \Leftrightarrow \chi_B(f(x)) = 1 \end{aligned}$$

Therefor the proposition is true. □

By means of Proposition 2.10.3, based on the extension principle defined by (1.4.1) in Section 1.4, we have the following result:

$$(\forall x \in X)\left(\mu_{\left(f^{-1}\right)^{*}(B)}(x)=\mu_B\left(f(x)\right)\right). \tag{2.10.9}$$

References

1. Bellman, R. and Giertz, M. (1973). On the analytic formalism of the theory of fuzzy sets, Information Sciences, 5, pp. 149-156.
2. Dubois, D. and Prade, H. (1980) *Fuzzy Sets and Systems*, (Academic Press, New York).
3. Li, H. X., Wang, P. Z., and Xu, H. Q. (1987) *Interesting Talks on Fuzzy Mathematics*, (Sichuan Education Press, China, in Chinese).
4. Li, H. X. (1993) *Fuzzy Mathematics Methods in Engineering and Its Applications*, (Tianjin Science and Technical Press, China, in Chinese).
5. Li, H. X. and Wang, P. Z. (1994) *Fuzzy Mathematics*, (National Defense Press, China, in Chinese).
6. Li, H. -X. and Yen V. C. (1995) *Fuzzy Sets and Fuzzy Decision-Making*, (CRC Press, Boca Raton).
7. Terano, T, Asai, K., and Sugeno, M. (1992) *Fuzzy Systems Theory and Its Applications*, (Academic Press, San Diego).
8. Wang, P. Z. (1983) *Fuzzy Set Theory and Its Applications*, (Shanghai Science and Technical Press, China, in Chinese).
9. Wang, P. Z. (1983) *Fuzzy Sets and Falling Shadow of Random Sets*, (Beijing Normal Press, China, in Chinese).
10. Zadeh, L. A. (1965). Fuzzy sets, Information and Control, 8, pp. 338-353.
11. Zadeh, L. A. (1978). Fuzzy sets as a basic for a theory of possibility, Fuzzy Sets and Systems, 1, pp. 3-28.
12. Zimmermann, H. J. (1984) *Fuzzy Sets Theory and Its Applications*, (Kluwer Academic Publications, Hingham).

Chapter 3

Fuzzy Systems

3.1 Structure of One-input One-output Fuzzy Systems

We now return to consider fuzzy systems and begin with one-input one-output open loop system shown as Figure 1.3.1. Suppose that we have got the input output data set IOD by using a kind of experiment to get the system response, as follows

$$\begin{aligned}
&\text{IOD} = \{(x_i, y_i) | i = 0, 1, \cdots, n\} \subset X \times Y, \\
&a = x_0 < x_1 < \cdots < x_n = b, \\
&X = [a, b] = [x_0, x_n], \quad Y = [c, d], \\
&c = \min\{y_0, y_1, \cdots, y_n\}, \\
&d = \max\{y_0, y_1, \cdots, y_n\}.
\end{aligned}$$

We can build a fuzzy system based on IOD through the following steps.

Step 1. First of all, IOD should be regarded as

$$\text{IOD}^* \triangleq \{(\{x_i\}, \{y_i\}) | i = 0, 1, \cdots, n\} \subset \mathcal{P}(X) \times \mathcal{P}(Y).$$

In this step, we want to extend every single point set pair $(\{x_i\}, \{y_i\})$ to a fuzzy set pair (A_i, B_i) where $A_i \in \mathcal{F}(X)$ and $B_i \in \mathcal{F}(Y)$. We can denote it by "fuzzy input output data set" as the following

$$\text{FIOD} = \{(A_i, B_i) | i = 0, 1, \cdots, n\} \subset \mathcal{F}(X) \times \mathcal{F}(Y).$$

Case 1. Suppose $Y_0 = \{y_0, y_1, \cdots, y_n\}$ be with strict monotonicity, in a manner of speaking, strictly monotonic increasing as the following:

$$c = y_0 < y_1 < \cdots < y_n = d\ ,$$

for the situation of strictly monotonic decreasing, i.e.

$$d = y_0 > y_1 > \cdots > y_n = c\,,$$

it is very similar to deal with it. For example, we may define every fuzzy set $A_i \in \mathcal{F}(X)$ as the following, which are shown as Figure 3.1.1.

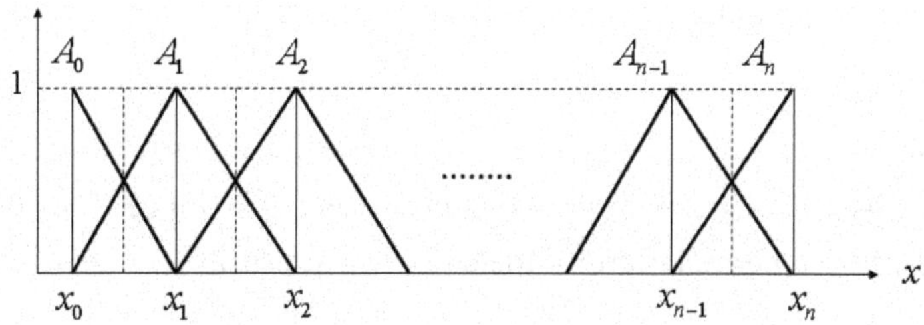

Fig. 3.1.1. Fuzzy sets $A_i \in \mathcal{F}(X)$

$$\mu_{A_0}(x) = \begin{cases} (x - x_1)/(x_0 - x_1), & x \in [x_0, x_1]; \\ 0\,, & \text{otherwise,} \end{cases}$$

$$\mu_{A_i}(x) = \begin{cases} (x - x_{i-1})/(x_i - x_{i-1}), & x \in (x_{i-1}, x_i]; \\ (x - x_{i+1})/(x_i - x_{i+1}), & x \in (x_i, x_{i+1}]; \\ 0, & \text{otherwise;} \end{cases}$$
$$i = 1, 2, \cdots, n-1,$$

$$\mu_{A_n}(x) = \begin{cases} (x - x_{n-1})/(x_n - x_{n-1}), & x \in (x_{n-1}, x_n]; \\ 0, & \text{otherwise,} \end{cases}$$

Similarly, we can get every fuzzy set $B_i \in \mathcal{F}(y)$ as follows

$$\mu_{B_0}(y)=\begin{cases}(y-y_1)/(y_0-y_1), & y\in[y_0,y_1];\\ 0, & \text{otherwise,}\end{cases}$$

$$\mu_{B_i}(y)=\begin{cases}(y-y_{i-1})/(y_i-y_{i-1}), & y\in(y_{i-1},y_i];\\ (y-y_{i+1})/(y_i-y_{i+1}), & y\in(y_i,y_{i+1}];\\ 0, & \text{otherwise;}\end{cases}$$
$$i=1,2,\cdots,n-1,$$

$$\mu_{B_n}(y)=\begin{cases}(y-y_{n-1})/(y_n-y_{n-1}), & y\in(y_{n-1},y_n];\\ 0, & \text{otherwise,}\end{cases}$$

Case 2. Suppose $Y_0=\{y_0,y_1,\cdots,y_n\}$ be not with strict monotonicity. In this case, it is hard to build those fuzzy sets $B_i\in\mathcal{F}(y)$. For this case, we can make a permutation for the subscript set $\{0,1,\cdots,n\}$ as follows

$$\sigma=\begin{pmatrix}0 & 1 & \cdots & n\\ k_0 & k_1 & \cdots & k_n\end{pmatrix}$$

such that

$$c=y_{k_0}\le y_{k_1}\le\cdots\le y_{k_k}=d\,. \tag{3.1.1}$$

It is well-known that this permutation is just a bijection as the following

$$\sigma:\{0,1,\cdots,n\}\to\{0,1,\cdots,n\}$$
$$i\mapsto k_i\triangleq\sigma(i),\quad i=0,1,\cdots,n$$

In addition, it is not difficult to understand the fact that

$$Y_0=\{y_0,y_1,\cdots,y_n\}=\{y_{k_0},y_{k_1},\cdots,y_{k_n}\}.$$

Here we also consider two situations as the following.

Situation 1. The set $Y_0 = \left\{ y_{k_0}, y_{k_1}, \cdots, y_{k_n} \right\}$ is with strict monotonicity as the following form:

$$c = y_{k_0} < y_{k_1} < \cdots < y_{k_n} = d \,. \tag{3.1.2}$$

So we easily obtain the following fuzzy sets:

$$\mu_{B_{k_0}}(y) = \begin{cases} \left(y - y_{k_1}\right) \big/ \left(y_{k_0} - y_{k_1}\right), & y \in \left[y_{k_0}, y_{k_1} \right]; \\ 0\,, & \text{otherwise,} \end{cases}$$

$$\mu_{B_{k_j}}(y) = \begin{cases} \left(y - y_{k_{j-1}}\right) \big/ \left(y_{k_j} - y_{k_{j-1}}\right), & y \in \left(y_{k_{j-1}}, y_{k_j} \right]; \\ \left(y - y_{k_{j+1}}\right) \big/ \left(y_{k_j} - y_{k_{j+1}}\right), & y \in \left(y_{k_j}, y_{k_{j+1}} \right]; \\ 0, & \text{otherwise;} \end{cases}$$

$$j = 1, 2, \cdots, n-1,$$

$$\mu_{B_{k_n}}(y) = \begin{cases} \left(y - y_{k_{n-1}}\right) \big/ \left(y_{k_n} - y_{k_{n-1}}\right), & y \in \left(y_{k_{n-1}}, y_{k_n} \right]; \\ 0, & \text{otherwise,} \end{cases}$$

Situation 2. The set $Y_0 = \left\{ y_{k_0}, y_{k_1}, \cdots, y_{k_n} \right\}$ is not with strict monotonicity like (3.1.2) but only with (3.1.1). Now for the subscript set as the following:

$$K = \left\{ k_{j_0}, k_{j_1}, \cdots, k_{j_n} \right\},$$

we make an equivalence relation "$\sim$" as the following:

$$(\forall s, t \in \{0, 1, \cdots, n\}) \left(k_s \sim k_t \Leftrightarrow y_{k_s} = y_{k_t} \right).$$

Thus we get the quotient set of "$\sim$" as follows

$$K(n) \big/ \sim \, = \left\{ \left[k_j \right] \middle| \, j = 0, 1, \cdots, n \right\},$$

where every $\left[k_j\right]$ is the equivalence class which the representative element k_j locates in.

Let different elements each other of $K(n)/_{\sim}$ be the following forms:

$$\left[k_{j_0}\right], \left[k_{j_1}\right], \cdots, \left[k_{j_{q(n)}}\right],$$

where $0 \le q(n) \le n$ and we stipulate that $k_{j_s} = \min\left[k_{j_s}\right]$. And then we can have the following result:

$$c = y_{k_{j_0}} < y_{k_{j_1}} < \cdots < y_{k_{j_{q(n)}}} = d\,. \tag{3.1.3}$$

By using the set $\left\{y_{k_{j_0}}, y_{k_{j_1}}, \cdots, y_{k_{j_{q(n)}}}\right\}$, we build some fuzzy sets as the following forms:

$$\mu_{B_{k_{j_0}}}(y) = \begin{cases} \left(y - y_{k_{j_1}}\right) / \left(y_{k_{j_0}} - y_{k_{j_1}}\right), & y \in \left[y_{k_{j_0}}, y_{k_{j_1}}\right]; \\ 0\,, & \text{otherwise,} \end{cases}$$

$$\mu_{B_{k_{j_s}}}(y) = \begin{cases} \left(y - y_{k_{j_{s-1}}}\right) / \left(y_{k_{j_s}} - y_{k_{j_{s-1}}}\right), & y \in \left(y_{k_{j_{s-1}}}, y_{k_{j_s}}\right]; \\ \left(y - y_{k_{j_{s+1}}}\right) / \left(y_{k_{j_s}} - y_{k_{j_{s+1}}}\right), & y \in \left(y_{k_{j_s}}, y_{k_{j_{s+1}}}\right]; \\ 0, & \text{otherwise;} \end{cases}$$

$$s = 1, 2, \cdots, q(n) - 1,$$

$$\mu_{B_{k_{j_{q(n)}}}}(y) = \begin{cases} \left(y - y_{k_{j_{q(n)-1}}}\right) / \left(y_{k_{j_{q(n)}}} - y_{k_{j_{q(n)-1}}}\right), & y \in \left(y_{k_{j_{q(n)-1}}}, y_{k_{j_{q(n)}}}\right]; \\ 0, & \text{otherwise} \end{cases}$$

Now we stipulate that, for any $s \in \left[k_{j_s}\right]$, we take fuzzy set

$$B_s(y) \equiv B_{k_{j_s}}(y)\,.$$

Thus, we get all fuzzy sets $B_{k_0}, B_{k_1}, \cdots, B_{k_n}$. So we got FIOD as follows:

$$\text{Case1:}\quad \text{FIOD} = \{(A_i, B_i) \,|\, i = 0,1,\cdots,n\}$$

$$\text{Case2:}\quad \text{FIOD} = \left\{\left(A_{k_j}, B_{k_j}\right) \,\middle|\, j = 0,1,\cdots,n\right\}$$

Step 2. Build a fuzzy relation $R \in \mathcal{F}(X \times Y)$. Firstly, we take

$$\text{Case1:}\quad (\forall i \in \{0,1,\cdots,n\})\left(R_i \triangleq A_i \times B_i\right)$$

$$\text{Case2:}\quad (\forall j \in \{0,1,\cdots,n\})\left(R_{k_j} \triangleq A_{k_j} \times B_{k_j}\right)$$

Then let $R \triangleq \bigcup_{i=0}^{n} R_i$ (in case 1) or $R \triangleq \bigcup_{j=0}^{n} R_{k_j}$ (in case 2). Clearly for any $(x, y) \in X \times Y$ we can know that

$$\text{Case1:}\quad \mu_R(x,y) = \mu_{\bigcup_{i=0}^{n}(A_i \times B_i)}(x,y) = \bigvee_{i=0}^{n}\left(\mu_{A_i}(x) \wedge \mu_{B_i}(y)\right),$$

$$\text{Case2:}\quad \mu_R(x,y) = \mu_{\bigcup_{j=0}^{n}\left(A_{k_j} \times B_{k_j}\right)}(x,y) = \bigvee_{j=0}^{n}\left(\mu_{A_{k_j}}(x) \wedge \mu_{B_{k_j}}(y)\right)$$

Step 3. We form a fuzzy set transformation by Definition 2.6.1 as the following:

$$\begin{aligned}
&T : \mathcal{F}(X) \to \mathcal{F}(Y) \\
&A \mapsto B = T(A) = [(A \times Y) \cap R]_Y, \\
&\mu_B(y) = \mu_{T(A)}(y) = \mu_{[(A\times Y)\cap R]_Y}(y) \\
&= \bigvee_{x \in X}\left(\mu_A(x) \wedge \mu_R(x,y)\right), \quad \forall y \in Y, \\
&= \begin{cases} \bigvee_{x\in X}\left[\mu_A(x) \wedge \left(\bigvee_{i=0}^{n}\left(\mu_{A_i}(x) \wedge \mu_{B_i}(y)\right)\right)\right], & \text{case 1,} \\ \bigvee_{x\in X}\left[\mu_A(x) \wedge \left(\bigvee_{j=0}^{n}\left(\mu_{A_{k_j}}(x) \wedge \mu_{B_{k_j}}(y)\right)\right)\right], & \text{case 2} \end{cases}
\end{aligned}$$

Step 4. Single point set input: for any $x \in X$, let $A = \{x\}$, and we have the following expression:

$$\begin{aligned}
&\mu_B(y) = \mu_{T(A)}(y) = \mu_{[(A\times Y)\cap R]_Y}(y) \\
&= \bigvee_{u\in X}\left(\mu_A(u) \wedge \mu_R(x,y)\right) \\
&= \bigvee_{u\in X}\left(\mu_{\{x\}}(u) \wedge \mu_R(x,y)\right) \\
&= \mu_R(x,y) \\
&= \begin{cases} \bigvee_{i=0}^{n}\left(\mu_{A_i}(x) \wedge \mu_{B_i}(y)\right), & \text{case 1,} \\ \bigvee_{j=0}^{n}\left(\mu_{A_{k_j}}(x) \wedge \mu_{B_{k_j}}(y)\right), & \text{case 2} \end{cases}
\end{aligned}$$

Step 5. Defuzzification: by using centroid method coming from physics, for any $y \in Y$, we have

$$\text{case 1:} \quad y = \frac{\int_c^d y\mu_B(y)dy}{\int_c^d \mu_B(y)dy} = \frac{\int_c^d y\left[\bigvee_{i=0}^{n}\left(\mu_{A_i}(x) \wedge \mu_{B_i}(y)\right)\right]dy}{\int_c^d \left[\bigvee_{i=0}^{n}\left(\mu_{A_i}(x) \wedge \mu_{B_i}(y)\right)\right]dy},$$

$$\text{case 2:} \quad y = \frac{\int_c^d y\mu_B(y)dy}{\int_c^d \mu_B(y)dy} = \frac{\int_c^d y\left[\bigvee_{j=0}^{n}\left(\mu_{A_{k_j}}(x) \wedge \mu_{B_{k_j}}(y)\right)\right]dy}{\int_c^d \left[\bigvee_{j=0}^{n}\left(\mu_{A_{k_j}}(x) \wedge \mu_{B_{k_j}}(y)\right)\right]dy}$$

This means that we have gotten the mapping of representing the response for the system as the following:

$$s: X \to Y, \quad x \mapsto y = s(x) = \frac{\int_c^d y\mu_B(y)dy}{\int_c^d \mu_B(y)dy}$$

Because $B = T(A) = T(\{x\})$, we had better denote $B = T(A) = T(\{x\})$ as the following:

$$B_x \triangleq B = T(A) = T(\{x\}).$$

So we have

$$\begin{aligned}\mu_{B_x}(y) &= \mu_{T(\{x\})}(y) = \mu_{[(\{x\}\times Y)\cap R]_Y}(y)\\ &= \bigvee_{u\in X}\left(\mu_{\{x\}}(u)\wedge\mu_R(x,y)\right) = \mu_R(x,y)\\ &= \begin{cases}\bigvee_{i=0}^{n}\left(\mu_{A_i}(x)\wedge\mu_{B_i}(y)\right), & \text{case 1,}\\ \bigvee_{j=0}^{n}\left(\mu_{A_{k_j}}(x)\wedge\mu_{B_{k_j}}(y)\right), & \text{case 2}\end{cases}\end{aligned}$$

And then

$$s: X\to Y,\quad x\mapsto y = s(x) = \frac{\int_c^d y\mu_{B_x}(y)dy}{\int_c^d \mu_{B_x}(y)dy} \tag{3.1.4}$$

This mapping should be called a **fuzzy system.**

Step 6. Simplification of (3.1.4). For avoiding the computing of the two integrals in (3.1.4), we use definition of definite integral to deal with it.

Case 1. Suppose $Y_0 = \{y_0, y_1, \cdots, y_n\}$ be with strict monotonicity, in a manner of speaking, strictly monotonic increasing as the following

$$c = y_0 < y_1 < \cdots < y_n = d\ ,$$

for the situation of strictly monotonic decreasing, i.e.

$$d = y_0 > y_1 > \cdots > y_n = c\,,$$

it is very similar to deal with it. If that

$$\Delta: c = y_0 < y_1 < \cdots < y_n = d$$

is regarded as a partition of interval $[c,d]$, then we have

$$\int_c^d \mu_{B_x}(y)dy = \lim_{\|\Delta\|\to 0}\sum_{i=1}^{n}\mu_{B_x}(\eta_i)\Delta y_i \approx \sum_{i=1}^{n}\mu_{B_x}(\eta_i)\Delta y_i,$$

$$\int_c^d y\mu_{B_x}(y)dy = \lim_{\|\Delta\|\to 0}\sum_{i=1}^{n}\eta_i\mu_{B_x}(\eta_i)\Delta y_i$$

$$\approx \sum_{i=1}^{n}\eta_i\mu_{B_x}(\eta_i)\Delta y_i,$$

$$\eta_i \triangleq y_i \in \Delta_i \triangleq [y_{i-1}, y_i], \quad \Delta y_i \triangleq y_i - y_{i-1},$$

$$i = 1, 2, \cdots, n, \quad \|\Delta\| \triangleq \max_{1\le i\le n}\{\Delta y_i\}$$

From this we obtain the following approximation form:

$$y = s(x) = \frac{\int_c^d y\mu_{B_x}(y)dy}{\int_c^d \mu_{B_x}(y)dy} \approx \frac{\sum_{j=1}^{n}\eta_j\mu_{B_x}(\eta_j)\Delta y_j}{\sum_{k=1}^{n}\mu_{B_x}(\eta_k)\Delta y_k}$$

$$= \frac{\sum_{j=1}^{n} y_j\mu_{B_x}(y_j)\Delta y_j}{\sum_{k=1}^{n}\mu_{B_x}(y_k)\Delta y_k} = \frac{\sum_{j=1}^{n} y_j\left[\bigvee_{i=0}^{n}\left(\mu_{A_i}(x)\wedge\mu_{B_i}(y_j)\right)\right]\Delta y_j}{\sum_{k=1}^{n}\left[\bigvee_{i=0}^{n}\left(\mu_{A_i}(x)\wedge\mu_{B_i}(y_k)\right)\right]\Delta y_k}$$

$$= \sum_{j=1}^{n}\left(\frac{\left[\bigvee_{i=0}^{n}\left(\mu_{A_i}(x)\wedge\mu_{B_i}(y_j)\right)\right]\Delta y_j}{\sum_{k=1}^{n}\left[\bigvee_{i=0}^{n}\left(\mu_{A_i}(x)\wedge\mu_{B_i}(y_k)\right)\right]\Delta y_k}\right)y_j$$

Now we put that

$$\varphi_j(x) \triangleq \frac{\left[\bigvee_{i=0}^{n}\left(\mu_{A_i}(x)\wedge\mu_{B_i}(y_j)\right)\right]\Delta y_j}{\sum_{k=1}^{n}\left[\bigvee_{i=0}^{n}\left(\mu_{A_i}(x)\wedge\mu_{B_i}(y_k)\right)\right]\Delta y_k}, \tag{3.1.5}$$

$$j = 1, 2, \cdots, n$$

Then we have the following result:

$$y = s(x) \approx \sum_{j=1}^{n} \varphi_j(x) y_j \ . \tag{3.1.6}$$

If let $h(x) \triangleq \sum_{j=1}^{n} \varphi_j(x) y_j, x \in X$, then function $h(x) = \sum_{j=1}^{n} \varphi_j(x) y_j$ is an kind of approximation to the mapping $y = s(x)$.

Case 2. Suppose $Y_0 = \{y_0, y_1, \cdots, y_n\}$ be not with strict monotonicity. In this case, by a permutation, we get (3.1.1), i.e.,

$$c = y_{k_0} \le y_{k_1} \le \cdots \le y_{k_k} = d \ .$$

We have known the following result:

$$\mu_{B_x}(y) = \mu_{T(\{x\})}(y) = \bigvee_{j=0}^{n} \left(\mu_{A_{k_j}}(x) \wedge \mu_{B_{k_j}}(y) \right).$$

From this we also have the following approximation form:

$$y = s(x) = \frac{\int_c^d y \mu_{B_x}(y) dy}{\int_c^d \mu_{B_x}(y) dy} \approx \frac{\sum_{j=1}^{n} y_j \mu_{B_x}(y_j) \Delta y_j}{\sum_{k=1}^{n} \mu_{B_x}(y_k) \Delta y_k}$$

$$= \sum_{j=1}^{n} \left(\frac{\left[\bigvee_{j=0}^{n} \left(\mu_{A_{k_j}}(x) \wedge \mu_{B_{k_j}}(y) \right) \right] \Delta y_{k_j}}{\sum_{k=1}^{n} \left[\bigvee_{j=0}^{n} \left(\mu_{A_{k_j}}(x) \wedge \mu_{B_{k_j}}(y) \right) \right] \Delta y_{k_j}} \right) y_j,$$

$$\Delta y_{k_j} \triangleq y_{k_j} - y_{k_{j-1}}, \quad j = 1, 2, \cdots, n$$

Now we put that

$$\varphi_j(x) \triangleq \frac{\left[\bigvee_{j=0}^{n} \left(\mu_{A_{k_j}}(x) \wedge \mu_{B_{k_j}}(y) \right) \right] \Delta y_{k_j}}{\sum_{k=1}^{n} \left[\bigvee_{j=0}^{n} \left(\mu_{A_{k_j}}(x) \wedge \mu_{B_{k_j}}(y) \right) \right] \Delta y_{k_j}}, \tag{3.1.7}$$

$$j = 1, 2, \cdots, n$$

Then we have the same expression:

$$y = s(x) \approx \sum_{j=1}^{n} \varphi_j(x) y_j \ .$$

And then, by noticing the following fact:

$$\text{case 1}: \quad (\forall i, j \in \{0,1,\cdots,n\}) \left(\mu_{B_i}\left(y_j\right) = \delta_{ij} = \begin{cases} 1, & i = j, \\ 0, & i \neq j \end{cases} \right),$$

$$\text{case 2}: \quad (\forall i, j \in \{0,1,\cdots,n\}) \left(\mu_{B_{k_i}}\left(y_{k_j}\right) = \delta_{ij} = \begin{cases} 1, & i = j, \\ 0, & i \neq j \end{cases} \right)$$

We can turn (3.1.5) and (3.1.7) into the following:

$$\varphi_j(x) = \begin{cases} \dfrac{\mu_{A_j}(x)\Delta y_j}{\sum_{k=1}^{n} \mu_{A_k}(x)\Delta y_k}, & \text{case 1}, \\ \dfrac{\mu_{A_{k_j}}(x)\Delta y_{k_j}}{\sum_{i=1}^{n} \mu_{A_{k_i}}(x)\Delta y_{k_i}}, & \text{case 2}, \end{cases} \tag{3.1.8}$$

$$j = 1, 2, \cdots, n$$

Remark 3.1.1 The fuzzy input output data set as the following

$$\text{FIOD} = \left\{ \left(A_i, B_i\right) \middle| i = 0,1,\cdots,n \right\}$$

can be regarded as a group of fuzzy inference rules:

$$\left.\begin{array}{l} \text{If } x \text{ is } A_0 \text{ then } y \text{ is } B_0 \\ \text{If } x \text{ is } A_1 \text{ then } y \text{ is } B_1 \\ \cdots\cdots \\ \text{If } x \text{ is } A_n \text{ then } y \text{ is } B_n \end{array}\right\} \tag{3.1.9}$$

□

3.2 Structure of Two-Input One-Output Fuzzy Systems

Now we consider an open loop uncertain system with two-input one-output shown as Figure 3.2.1.

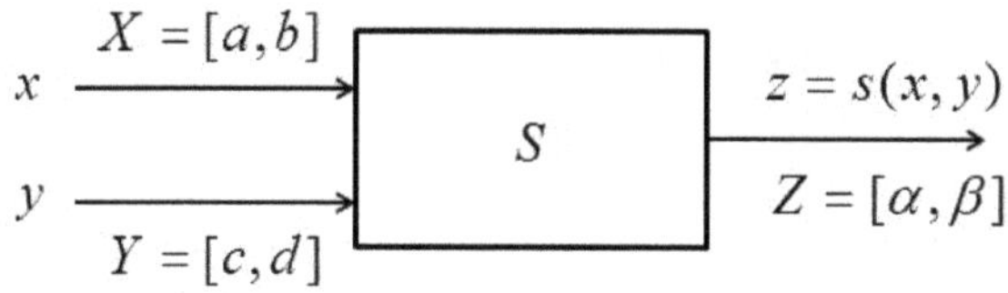

Fig. 3.2.1. An open loop system with two-input one-output

First of all, we make the partitions of the two input universes $X = [a,b]$ and $Y = [c,d]$ as the following:

$$a = x_0 < x_1 < \cdots < x_n = b,$$
$$c = y_0 < y_1 < \cdots < y_m = d$$

So we obtain an input data set

$$(X \times Y)_0 = \left\{ (x_i, y_j) \middle| i = 0,1,\cdots,n, j = 0,1,\cdots,m \right\}.$$

Very similar to the case for one-input one-output, we can get the response set of the system S for the input data set $(X \times Y)_0$ as follows

$$Z_0 = \left\{ z_{ij} \middle| i = 0,1,\cdots,n, j = 0,1,\cdots,m \right\}.$$

If we put $\alpha = \min Z_0, \beta = \max Z_0$, then we get the output universe as being $Z = [\alpha, \beta]$. So we have built a two-input one-output data set IOD:

$$\text{IOD} = \left\{ \left((x_i, y_j), z_{ij} \right) \middle| i = 0,1,\cdots,n, j = 0,1,\cdots,m \right\}.$$

Now we are going to turn IOD into FIOD:

$$\text{FIOD} = \left\{ \left((A_i, B_j), C_{ij} \right) \middle| i = 0,1,\cdots,n, j = 0,1,\cdots,m \right\},$$

$$A_i \in \mathcal{F}(X), \quad B_j \in \mathcal{F}(Y), \quad C_{ij} \in \mathcal{F}(Z),$$
$$i = 0,1,\cdots,n, \quad j = 0,1,\cdots,m$$

First we can easily to get A_i, B_j as the following

$$\mu_{A_0}(x) = \begin{cases} (x - x_1)/(x_0 - x_1), & x \in [x_0, x_1]; \\ 0, & \text{otherwise}, \end{cases}$$

$$\mu_{A_i}(x) = \begin{cases} (x - x_{i-1})/(x_i - x_{i-1}), & x \in (x_{i-1}, x_i]; \\ (x - x_{i+1})/(x_i - x_{i+1}), & x \in (x_i, x_{i+1}]; \\ 0, & \text{otherwise}; \end{cases}$$

$$i = 1,2,\cdots,n-1,$$

$$\mu_{A_n}(x) = \begin{cases} (x - x_{n-1})/(x_n - x_{n-1}), & x \in (x_{n-1}, x_n]; \\ 0, & \text{otherwise}, \end{cases}$$

$$\mu_{B_0}(y) = \begin{cases} (y - y_1)/(y_0 - y_1), & y \in [y_0, y_1]; \\ 0, & \text{otherwise}, \end{cases}$$

$$\mu_{B_j}(y) = \begin{cases} (y - y_{j-1})/(y_j - y_{j-1}), & y \in (y_{j-1}, y_j]; \\ (y - y_{i+1})/(y_i - y_{i+1}), & y \in (y_j, y_{j+1}]; \\ 0, & \text{otherwise}; \end{cases}$$

$$i = 1,2,\cdots,m-1,$$

$$\mu_{B_m}(y) = \begin{cases} (y - y_{m-1})/(y_m - y_{m-1}), & y \in (y_{m-1}, y_m]; \\ 0, & \text{otherwise}, \end{cases}$$

In order to build fuzzy sets C_{ij}, we need to change binary subscripts (i, j) into unitary subscripts written by $k\,(k = 0,1,\cdots,(n+1)\times(m+1)-1)$ which satisfy the following condition:

$$\alpha = z_0 \le z_1 \le z_2 \le \cdots \le z_{(n+1)\times(m+1)-1} = \beta\,. \tag{3.2.1}$$

We can get (3.2.1) by the following steps.

Step 1. Make a mapping:

$$\begin{aligned} g : \{0,1,\cdots,n\} \times \{0,1,\cdots,m\} &\to \{0,1,\cdots,(n+1)\times(m+1)-1\} \\ (i,j) \mapsto \tau &\triangleq g(i,j) = i(m+1)+j \end{aligned} \tag{3.2.2}$$

Denote $u_\tau = z_{ij}$, and we have the following expression:

$$\begin{aligned} &\{u_\tau \mid \tau = 0,1,2,\cdots,(n+1)\times(m+1)-1\} \\ &= \{z_{ij} \mid i = 0,1,\cdots,n, j = 0,1,\cdots,m\} \end{aligned}.$$

In a general way, the set $\{u_\tau \mid \tau = 0,1,2,\cdots,(n+1)\times(m+1)-1\}$ does not meet monotonicity on τ as follows

$$u_0 \le u_1 \le \cdots \le u_{(n+1)\times(m+1)-1}.$$

Step 2. Make a permutation:

$$\sigma = \begin{pmatrix} 0 & 1 & \cdots & (n+1)\times(m+1)-1 \\ \sigma(0) & \sigma(1) & \cdots & \sigma\big((n+1)\times(m+1)-1\big) \end{pmatrix}$$

such that

$$u_0 \le u_1 \le \cdots \le u_{(n+1)\times(m+1)-1}.$$

Denote $z_k = u_{\sigma(k)}$ $\big(k = 0,1,\cdots,(n+1)\times(m+1)-1\big)$ and we have

$$z_0 \le z_1 \le \cdots \le z_{(n+1)\times(m+1)-1}.$$

This is just (3.2.1). We turn to build fuzzy sets on Z.

Now we turn to build fuzzy sets as follows:

$$C_k \in \mathcal{F}(Z), \quad k = 0,1,\cdots,(n+1)\times(m+1)-1.$$

Situation 1. The set $Z_0 = \{z_0, z_1, \cdots, z_{(n+1)\times(m+1)-1}\}$ is with strict monotonicity as the following:

$$\alpha = z_0 < z_1 < \cdots < z_{(n+1)\times(m+1)-1} = \beta . \tag{3.2.3}$$

So we can easily obtain the following fuzzy sets:

$$\mu_{C_0}(z) = \begin{cases} (z - z_1)/(z_0 - z_1), & z \in [z_0, z_1]; \\ 0, & \text{otherwise}, \end{cases}$$

$$\mu_{C_k}(z) = \begin{cases} (z - z_{k-1})/(z_k - z_{k-1}), & z \in [z_{k-1}, z_k); \\ (z - z_{k+1})/(z_k - z_{k+1}), & z \in [z_k, z_{k+1}]; \\ 0, & \text{otherwise}; \end{cases}$$

$$k = 1, 2, \cdots, (n+1)\times(m+1) - 2, \tag{3.2.4}$$

$$\mu_{C_{(n+1)(m+1)-1}}(z) =$$

$$\begin{cases} \dfrac{z - z_{(n+1)\times(m+1)-2}}{z_{(n+1)\times(m+1)-1} - z_{(n+1)\times(m+1)-2}}, & z \in \left[z_{(n+1)\times(m+1)-2}, z_{(n+1)\times(m+1)-1} \right]; \\ 0, & \text{otherwise}, \end{cases}$$

Situation 2. The set $Z_0 = \{z_0, z_1, \cdots, z_{(n+1)\times(m+1)-1}\}$ is not with strict monotonicity like (3.2.3) but only with (3.2.1). Now for the subscript set

$$K = \{0, 1, \cdots, (n+1)\times(m+1) - 1\},$$

we make an equivalence relation " $\sim$ " as the following

$$(\forall s, t \in \{0, 1, \cdots, (n+1)\times(m+1) - 1\})(s \sim t \Leftrightarrow z_s = z_t).$$

Thus we get the quotient set of " $\sim$ " as follows

$$K(n)/_{\sim} = \{[k_j] \mid j = 0, 1, \cdots, (n+1)\times(m+1) - 1\},$$

where every $[k_j]$ is the equivalence class which the representative element k_j locates in. Let different elements each other of $K(n)/_{\sim}$ be the following:

$$\left[k_{j_0}\right],\left[k_{j_1}\right],\cdots,\left[k_{j_{q(n,m)}}\right]$$

where $0 \le q(n,m) \le (n+1)\times(m+1)-1$, and we stipulate that

$$k_{j_s} = \min\left[k_{j_s}\right].$$

And then we have the following result:

$$\alpha = z_{k_{j0}} < z_{k_{j1}} < \cdots < z_{k_{jq(n,m)}} = \beta . \tag{3.2.5}$$

By using the set $\left\{z_{k_{j0}}, z_{k_{j1}}, \cdots, z_{k_{jq(n,m)}}\right\}$, we build some fuzzy sets as the following

$$\mu_{C_{k_{j0}}}(z) = \begin{cases} \left(z - z_{k_{j1}}\right)/\left(z_{k_{j0}} - z_{k_{j1}}\right), & z \in \left[z_{k_{j0}}, z_{k_{j1}}\right]; \\ 0, & \text{otherwise}, \end{cases}$$

$$\mu_{C_{k_{j_s}}}(z) = \begin{cases} \left(z - z_{k_{j_{s-1}}}\right)/\left(z_{k_{j_s}} - z_{k_{j_{s-1}}}\right), & z \in \left(z_{k_{j_{s-1}}}, z_{k_{j_s}}\right]; \\ \left(z - z_{k_{j_{s+1}}}\right)/\left(z_{k_{j_s}} - z_{k_{j_{s+1}}}\right), & z \in \left(z_{k_{j_s}}, z_{k_{j_{s+1}}}\right]; \\ 0, & \text{otherwise}; \end{cases} \tag{3.2.6}$$

$$s = 1, 2, \cdots, q(n,m)-1,$$

$$\mu_{C_{k_{jq(n,m)}}}(z) = \begin{cases} \dfrac{z - z_{k_{jq(n,m)-1}}}{z_{k_{jq(n,m)}} - z_{k_{jq(n,m)-1}}}, & y \in \left(z_{k_{jq(n,m)-1}}, z_{k_{jq(n,m)}}\right]; \\ 0, & \text{otherwise} \end{cases}$$

Now we stipulate that, for any $s \in \left[k_{j_s}\right]$, we take fuzzy set

$$C_s(z) \equiv C_{k_{j_s}}(z).$$

Thus, we get all fuzzy sets $C_{k_0}, C_{k_1}, \cdots, C_{k_{(n+1)\times(m+1)-1}}$.

It is easy prove that the mapping:

$$g : \{0,1,\cdots,n\} \times \{0,1,\cdots,m\} \to \{0,1,\cdots,(n+1)\times(m+1)-1\}$$

defined by (3.2.2) is a bijection. So we can rewrite the following single-subscript fuzzy sets as follows:

$$C_\tau, \quad \tau = 0, 1, \cdots, (n+1)\times(m+1)-1$$

as double-subscript fuzzy sets as follows:

$$C_{ij}, \quad i = 0, 1, \cdots, n, j = 0, 1, \cdots, m.$$

Based on above two situations, we have got FIOD as follows:

$$\begin{aligned}
&\text{FIOD} = \left\{\left(\left(A_i, B_j\right), C_{ij}\right) \middle| i = 0, 1, \cdots, n, j = 0, 1, \cdots, m\right\},\\
&A_i \in \mathcal{F}(X), \quad B_j \in \mathcal{F}(Y), \quad C_{ij} \in \mathcal{F}(Z),\\
&i = 0, 1, \cdots, n, \quad j = 0, 1, \cdots, m
\end{aligned}$$

Similar to Remark 3.1.1, the fuzzy data set

$$\text{FIOD} = \left\{\left(\left(A_i, B_j\right), C_{ij}\right) \middle| i = 0, 1, \cdots, n, j = 0, 1, \cdots, m\right\}$$

can be regarded as a group of fuzzy inference rules:

$$\left.\begin{array}{l}\text{If } x \text{ is } A_i \text{ and } y \text{ is } B_j \text{ then } z \text{ is } C_{ij},\\ i = 0, 1, \cdots, n, j = 0, 1, \cdots, m\end{array}\right\} \tag{3.2.7}$$

We can also rewrite (3.2.5) as the following

$$\left.\begin{array}{l}\text{If } (x, y) \text{ is } \left(A_i, B_j\right) \text{ then } z \text{ is } C_{ij},\\ i = 0, 1, \cdots, n, j = 0, 1, \cdots, m\end{array}\right\} \tag{3.2.8}$$

Here we can use $A_i \times B_j$ to implement $\left(A_i, B_j\right)$, where $A_i \times B_j$ is the direct product between fuzzy sets A_i and B_j. By using $A_i \times B_j$ and C_{ij}, we can get a group of fuzzy relations between input universe $X \times Y$ and output universe Z as follows:

$$R_{ij} \triangleq \left(A_i \times B_j\right) \times C_{ij} \in \mathcal{F}\left((X \times Y) \times Z\right), \tag{3.2.9}$$

where

$$\mu_{R_{ij}}(x,y,z)=\left(\mu_{A_i}(x)\wedge\mu_{B_j}(y)\right)\wedge\mu_{C_{ij}}(z)$$
$$i=0,1,\cdots,n,\quad j=0,1,\cdots,m$$

Clearly $R_{ij}=\left(A_i\times B_j\right)\times C_{ij}=A_i\times B_j\times C_{ij}$ and we can have the equation:

$$\mathcal{F}((X\times Y)\times Z)=\mathcal{F}(X\times Y\times Z).$$

So R_{ij} are ternary fuzzy relations. By means of these R_{ij}, we can easily obtain an entire ternary fuzzy relation as the following

$$R=\bigcup_{i=0}^{n}\bigcup_{j=0}^{m}R_{ij}\in\mathcal{F}(X\times Y\times Z),$$
$$\mu_R(x,y,z)=\bigvee_{i=0}^{n}\bigvee_{j=0}^{m}\left(\mu_{A_i}(x)\wedge\mu_{B_j}(y)\wedge\mu_{C_{ij}}(z)\right) \tag{3.2.10}$$

It is a main procedure to build the ternary fuzzy relation expressed by (3.2.10) for us to obtain our fuzzy systems with two-input and one-output. Now based on (3.2.10), by using Definition 2.9.2, we can have a fuzzy set transformation induced by the fuzzy ternary relation R as the follows

$$T:\mathcal{F}(X)\times\mathcal{F}(Y)\to\mathcal{F}(Z)$$
$$(A,B)\mapsto C=T(A,B)=\left[((A\times B)\times Z)\cap R\right]_Z$$

Considering (2.9.8), for any $z\in Z$, we have

$$\begin{aligned}\mu_C(z)&=\mu_{T(A,B)}(z)=\bigvee_{(x,y)\in X\times Y}\left(\mu_A(x)\wedge\mu_B(y)\wedge\mu_R(x,y,z)\right)\\&=\bigvee_{(x,y)\in X\times Y}\left(\mu_A(x)\wedge\mu_B(y)\wedge\left(\bigvee_{i=0}^{n}\bigvee_{j=0}^{m}\left(\mu_{A_i}(x)\wedge\mu_{B_j}(y)\wedge\mu_{C_{ij}}(z)\right)\right)\right)\end{aligned} \tag{3.2.11}$$

And then, by use of Remark 2.9.4, we get another mapping:

$$T:X\times Y\to\mathcal{F}(Z)$$
$$(x,y)\mapsto C_{(x,y)}=T(x,y)=\left[((\{x\}\times\{y\})\times Z)\cap R\right]_Z \tag{3.2.12}$$

This is a point-fuzzy-set mapping. By using (3.2.10), for any an element $(x,y)\in X\times Y$ and for any an element $z\in Z$, we can have the following equation:

$$\begin{aligned}\mu_{C_{(x,y)}}(z) &= \mu_{R|_{(x,y)}}(z)=\mu_R(x,y,z)\\ &=\mathop{\vee}_{i=0}^{n}\mathop{\vee}_{j=0}^{m}\left(\mu_{A_i}(x)\wedge\mu_{B_j}(y)\wedge\mu_{C_{ij}}(z)\right)\end{aligned}\tag{3.2.13}$$

By using centroid method which we have already used in section 3.1, for any an element $z\in Z$, we have the expression:

$$\begin{aligned}z &= \frac{\int_\alpha^\beta z\mu_{C_{(x,y)}}(z)\mathrm{d}z}{\int_\alpha^\beta \mu_{C_{(x,y)}}(z)\mathrm{d}z}\\ &=\frac{\int_\alpha^\beta z\left[\mathop{\vee}_{i=0}^{n}\mathop{\vee}_{j=0}^{m}\left(\mu_{A_i}(x)\wedge\mu_{B_j}(y)\wedge\mu_{C_{ij}}(z)\right)\right]\mathrm{d}z}{\int_\alpha^\beta \left[\mathop{\vee}_{i=0}^{n}\mathop{\vee}_{j=0}^{m}\left(\mu_{A_i}(x)\wedge\mu_{B_j}(y)\wedge\mu_{C_{ij}}(z)\right)\right]\mathrm{d}z}\end{aligned}\tag{3.2.14}$$

This means that we have gotten the mapping of representing the response for the system as the following:

$$\begin{aligned}&s: X\times Y\to Z\\ &(x,y)\mapsto z=s(x,y)=\frac{\int_\alpha^\beta z\mu_{C_{(x,y)}}(z)dz}{\int_\alpha^\beta \mu_{C_{(x,y)}}(z)dz}\end{aligned}\tag{3.2.15}$$

The mapping expressed by (3.2.13) is just the fuzzy system with two-input and one-output we want to build.

At last, we consider the simplification of (3.2.13). For avoiding the computing of the two integrals in (3.2.13), we also use definition of definite integral to deal with it.

For above Situation 1, because the set $Z_0=\left\{z_0,z_1,\cdots,z_{(n+1)\times(m+1)-1}\right\}$ is with strict monotonicity, i.e.,

$$\alpha=z_0<z_1<\cdots<z_{(n+1)\times(m+1)-1}=\beta,$$

if that $\Delta:\alpha = z_0 < z_1 < \cdots < z_{(n+1)\times(m+1)-1} = \beta$ is regarded as a partition of interval $[\alpha, \beta]$, then we have the following expressions:

$$\begin{aligned}
\int_\alpha^\beta z\mu_{C_{(x,y)}}(z)dz &= \lim_{\|\Delta\|\to 0} \sum_{\tau=1}^{(n+1)(m+1)-1} \zeta_\tau \mu_{C_{(x,y)}}(\zeta_\tau)\Delta z_\tau \\
&\approx \sum_{\tau=1}^{(n+1)(m+1)-1} \zeta_\tau \mu_{C_{(x,y)}}(\zeta_\tau)\Delta z_\tau, \\
\int_\alpha^\beta \mu_{C_{(x,y)}}(z)dz &= \lim_{\|\Delta\|\to 0} \sum_{\tau=1}^{(n+1)(m+1)-1} \mu_{C_{(x,y)}}(\zeta_\tau)\Delta z_\tau \\
&\approx \sum_{\tau=1}^{(n+1)(m+1)-1} \mu_{C_{(x,y)}}(\zeta_\tau)\Delta z_\tau,
\end{aligned}$$

$$\zeta_\tau \triangleq z_\tau \in \Delta_\tau = [z_{\tau-1}, z_\tau], \quad \Delta z_\tau = z_\tau - z_{\tau-1},$$

$$\tau = 1, 2, \cdots, (n+1)(m+1)-1,$$

$$\|\Delta\| \triangleq \max_{1\le\tau\le(n+1)(m+1)-1} \{\Delta z_\tau\}$$

From this we obtain the following approximation form:

$$z = s(x,y) = \frac{\int_\alpha^\beta z\mu_{C_{(x,y)}}(z)dz}{\int_\alpha^\beta \mu_{C_{(x,y)}}(z)dz} \approx \frac{\sum_{\tau=1}^{(n+1)(m+1)-1} \zeta_\tau \mu_{C_{(x,y)}}(\zeta_\tau)\Delta z_\tau}{\sum_{\tau=1}^{(n+1)(m+1)-1} \mu_{C_{(x,y)}}(\zeta_\tau)\Delta z_\tau}$$

$$= \frac{\sum_{\tau=1}^{(n+1)(m+1)-1} z_\tau \mu_{C_{(x,y)}}(z_\tau)\Delta z_\tau}{\sum_{\tau=1}^{(n+1)(m+1)-1} \mu_{C_{(x,y)}}(z_\tau)\Delta z_\tau} = \sum_{\tau=1}^{(n+1)(m+1)-1} \left(\frac{\mu_{C_{(x,y)}}(z_\tau)\Delta z_\tau}{\sum_{p=1}^{(n+1)(m+1)-1} \mu_{C_{(x,y)}}(z_p)\Delta z_p} \right) z_\tau$$

Now we put the symbol as follows:

$$\psi_\tau(x,y) \triangleq \frac{\mu_{C_{(x,y)}}(z_\tau)\Delta z_\tau}{\sum_{p=1}^{(n+1)(m+1)-1} \mu_{C_{(x,y)}}(z_p)\Delta z_p}, \tag{3.2.16}$$

$$\tau = 1, 2, \cdots, (n+1)(m+1)-1$$

Then we have the following expression:

$$z = s(x,y) \approx \sum_{\tau=1}^{(n+1)(m+1)-1} \psi_\tau(x,y) z_\tau . \tag{3.2.17}$$

Based on (3.2.4), it is easy to know the following fact:

$$\left(\forall p,q \in \{0,1,\cdots,(n+1)(m+1)-1\}\right)\left(\mu_{C_p}\left(z_q\right) = \delta_{pq} = \begin{cases} 1, & p=q, \\ 0, & p \neq q \end{cases}\right)$$

So we can learn that, for any $i \in \{0,1,\cdots,n\}$ and for any $j \in \{0,1,\cdots,m\}$, we have the following equation:

$$\mu_{C_{(x,y)}}\left(z_{ij}\right) = \mu_{A_i}(x) \wedge \mu_{B_j}(y) \tag{3.2.18}$$

And then by noticing (3.2.2), if we denote $\Delta z_{ij} \triangleq \Delta z_\tau$, then we have the following result:

$$\psi_{ij}(x,y) \triangleq \psi_\tau(x,y) = \frac{\mu_{C_{(x,y)}}\left(z_\tau\right)\Delta z_\tau}{\sum_{p=1}^{(n+1)(m+1)-1} \mu_{C_{(x,y)}}\left(z_p\right)\Delta z_p}$$

$$= \frac{\left(\mu_{A_i}(x) \wedge \mu_{B_j}(y)\right)\Delta z_{ij}}{\sum_{i=1}^{n}\sum_{j=1}^{m}\left(\mu_{A_i}(x) \wedge \mu_{B_j}(y)\right)\Delta z_{ij}},$$

$$i = 1,2,\cdots,n; \quad j = 1,2,\cdots,m$$

By using (3.2.17), we have the following expression:

$$z = s(x,y) \approx \sum_{\tau=1}^{(n+1)(m+1)-1} \psi_\tau(x,y) z_\tau = \sum_{i=1}^{n}\sum_{j=1}^{m} \psi_{ij}(x,y) z_{ij}$$

$$= \sum_{i=1}^{n}\sum_{j=1}^{m}\left(\frac{\left(\mu_{A_i}(x) \wedge \mu_{B_j}(y)\right)\Delta z_{ij}}{\sum_{p=1}^{n}\sum_{q=1}^{m}\left(\mu_{A_p}(x) \wedge \mu_{B_q}(y)\right)\Delta z_{pq}} \right) z_{ij} \tag{3.2.19}$$

Remark 3.2.1 For Situation 2, as we have got all fuzzy sets as follows:

$$C_{k_0}, C_{k_1}, \cdots, C_{k_{(n+1)\times(m+1)-1}},$$

it is easy to show that (3.2.19) is also true, but we should know that there are some $\Delta z_{ij} = 0$. □

Remark 3.2.2 Because the membership function of the direct product $A_i \times B_j$ can be also defined as being $\mu_{A_i \times B_j}(x, y) = \mu_{A_i}(x) \cdot \mu_{B_j}(y)$ based on Remark 1.4.1, (3.2.14) and (3.2.19) can be written as the following

$$z = \frac{\int_\alpha^\beta z\mu_{C_{(x,y)}}(z)dz}{\int_\alpha^\beta \mu_{C_{(x,y)}}(z)dz} = \frac{\int_\alpha^\beta z\left[\bigvee_{i=0}^{n}\bigvee_{j=0}^{m}\left(\mu_{A_i}(x)\cdot\mu_{B_j}(y)\cdot\mu_{C_{ij}}(z)\right)\right]dz}{\int_\alpha^\beta \left[\bigvee_{i=0}^{n}\bigvee_{j=0}^{m}\left(\mu_{A_i}(x)\cdot\mu_{B_j}(y)\cdot\mu_{C_{ij}}(z)\right)\right]dz} \tag{3.2.20}$$

$$z = s(x,y) \approx \sum_{i=1}^{n}\sum_{j=1}^{m}\left(\frac{\left(\mu_{A_i}(x)\cdot\mu_{B_j}(y)\right)\Delta z_{ij}}{\sum_{p=1}^{n}\sum_{q=1}^{m}\left(\mu_{A_p}(x)\cdot\mu_{B_q}(y)\right)\Delta z_{pq}}\right)z_{ij} \tag{3.2.21}$$

□

Remark 3.2.3 Let $\Gamma \triangleq \left\{\Delta z_{ij} \middle| \Delta z_{ij} \neq 0\right\}$ and $h \triangleq \mathrm{mean}(\Gamma)$ which means the mean value of the elements in set Γ. If we use h to replace Δz_{ij}, then it is not difficult to know the following results:

$$z = s(x,y) \approx \sum_{i=1}^{n}\sum_{j=1}^{m}\left(\frac{\left(\mu_{A_i}(x)\wedge\mu_{B_j}(y)\right)\Delta z_{ij}}{\sum_{p=1}^{n}\sum_{q=1}^{m}\left(\mu_{A_p}(x)\wedge\mu_{B_q}(y)\right)\Delta z_{pq}}\right)z_{ij}$$

$$\approx \sum_{i=1}^{n}\sum_{j=1}^{m}\left(\frac{\left(\mu_{A_i}(x)\wedge\mu_{B_j}(y)\right)h}{\sum_{p=1}^{n}\sum_{q=1}^{m}\left(\mu_{A_p}(x)\wedge\mu_{B_q}(y)\right)h}\right)z_{ij}$$

$$= \sum_{i=1}^{n}\sum_{j=1}^{m}\left(\frac{\mu_{A_i}(x)\wedge\mu_{B_j}(y)}{\sum_{p=1}^{n}\sum_{q=1}^{m}\left(\mu_{A_p}(x)\wedge\mu_{B_q}(y)\right)}\right)z_{ij} \tag{3.2.22}$$

$$z = s(x,y) \approx \sum_{i=1}^{n}\sum_{j=1}^{m}\left(\frac{\mu_{A_i}(x)\cdot\mu_{B_j}(y)}{\sum_{p=1}^{n}\sum_{q=1}^{m}\left(\mu_{A_p}(x)\cdot\mu_{B_q}(y)\right)}\right)z_{ij} \tag{3.2.23}$$

Based on the structure of fuzzy sets as being A_i, B_j, it is not difficult to prove the following fact:

$$\sum_{p=1}^{n}\sum_{q=1}^{m}\left(\mu_{A_p}(x)\cdot\mu_{B_q}(y)\right)\equiv 1,$$

and then we have a very simple expression of (3.2.23) as the following:

$$z = s(x,y) \approx \sum_{i=1}^{n}\sum_{j=1}^{m}\left(\mu_{A_i}(x)\cdot\mu_{B_j}(y)\right)z_{ij} \tag{3.2.24}$$

□

3.3 Interpolation Mechanism of Fuzzy Systems

Based on the conclusions of above sections, we consider interpolation mechanism of fuzzy systems. From (3.1.6), we know that a fuzzy system can be approximately expressed by the following equation:

$$y = s(x) \approx \sum_{j=1}^{n}\varphi_j(x)y_j$$

If the note set $\{y_1, y_2, \cdots, y_n\}$ satisfies the following well-known interpolation condition:

$$(\forall i \in \{1,2,\cdots,n\})(s(x_i) = y_i),$$

where $\{x_1, x_2, \cdots, x_n\} \subset [a,b]$ and $x_1 < x_2 < \cdots < x_n$, then above equation, i.e. (3.1.6), is just an interpolation about function $s(x) \in C[a,b]$. This is so-called interpolation mechanism of fuzzy systems. We know that these base functions $\varphi_i(x)$ are shown as (3.1.8) and they are linearly independent in function space $C[a,b]$; so they can generate a linear subspace with n dimension of $C[a,b]$ as follows

$$\text{span}\{\varphi_1(x), \varphi_2(x), \cdots, \varphi_n(x)\}.$$

It is easy to understand the following expression:

$$\sum_{j=1}^{n} \varphi_j(x) y_j \in \text{span}\{\varphi_1(x), \varphi_2(x), \cdots, \varphi_n(x)\}.$$

This means that a fuzzy system can be regarded as the fact that we use an element in $\text{span}\{\varphi_1(x), \varphi_2(x), \cdots, \varphi_n(x)\}$ to approximate the given element $s(x) \in C[a,b]$. If we define a norm:

$$\begin{aligned} \|\cdot\| &: C[a,b] \to [0,+\infty) \\ f &\mapsto \|f\| = \max_{x \in [a,b]} |f(x)|, \end{aligned}$$

then $(C[a,b], \|\cdot\|)$ is a linear normed space. Then we define a metric:

$$\begin{aligned} d &: C[a,b] \times C[a,b] \to [0,+\infty) \\ (f,g) &\mapsto d(f,g) = \|f - g\| \end{aligned}$$

We can know that $(C[a,b], d)$ is a complete metric space, i.e., it is a Banach space. This means that the research of fuzzy systems is essentially an approximation problem in a kind of Banach space.

Furthermore, from (3.2.19), we know that a fuzzy system with two inputs one output can be approximately expressed by the following equation:

$$z = s(x,y) \approx \sum_{\tau=1}^{(n+1)(m+1)-1} \psi_\tau(x,y) z_\tau$$

$$= \sum_{i=1}^{n}\sum_{j=1}^{m} \psi_{ij}(x,y) z_{ij}$$

$$= \sum_{i=1}^{n}\sum_{j=1}^{m} \left(\frac{\left(\mu_{A_i}(x) \wedge \mu_{B_j}(y)\right)\Delta z_{ij}}{\sum_{p=1}^{n}\sum_{q=1}^{m}\left(\mu_{A_p}(x) \wedge \mu_{B_q}(y)\right)\Delta z_{pq}} \right) z_{ij}$$

If the note set $\left\{ z_{ij} \middle| i = 1,2,\cdots,n, j = 1,2,\cdots,m \right\}$ satisfies the following well-known interpolation condition:

$$\begin{aligned} & s\left(x_i, y_j\right) = z_{ij}, \\ & \left(x_i, y_j\right) \in [a,b]\times[c,d], \\ & (i,j) \in \{1,2,\cdots,n\}\times\{1,2,\cdots,m\} \\ & x_1 < x_2 < \cdots < x_n; \\ & y_1 < y_2 < \cdots < y_m, \end{aligned}$$

then above equation, i.e. (3.2.19), is just an interpolation about the function of two variables $s(x,y) \in C\left([a,b]\times[c,d]\right)$.

In the same way, since the base functions $\psi_{ij}(x,y)$ are linearly independent, they can generate a linear subspace with $n \times m$ dimension of the infinite dimension function space $C\left([a,b]\times[c,d]\right)$ as follows:

$$\mathrm{span}\left\{ \psi_{ij}(x,y) \middle| i = 1,2,\cdots,n, j = 1,2,\cdots,m \right\}.$$

It is easy to understand the following expression:

$$\sum_{i=1}^{n}\sum_{j=1}^{m} \psi_{ij}(x,y) z_{ij} \in \mathrm{span}\left\{ \psi_{ij}(x,y) \middle| i = 1,2,\cdots,n, j = 1,2,\cdots,m \right\}.$$

This means that a fuzzy system with two inputs one output can be regarded as the fact that we use an element in $\text{span}\{\psi_{ij}(x,y)\}$ to approximate the given an element $s(x,y)\in C([a,b]\times[c,d])$. If we define a norm:

$$\begin{aligned}\|\cdot\| : C([a,b]\times[c,d]) &\to [0,+\infty)\\ f \mapsto \|f\| &= \max_{(x,y)\in[a,b]\times[c,d]} |f(x,y)|,\end{aligned}$$

then $(C([a,b]\times[c,d]),\|\cdot\|)$ is also a linear normed space. Then we define a metric:

$$\begin{aligned}\rho : C([a,b]\times[c,d])\times C([a,b]\times[c,d]) &\to [0,+\infty)\\ (f,g)\mapsto \rho(f,g) &= \|f-g\|\end{aligned}$$

We can know that $(C([a,b]\times[c,d]),\rho)$ is a complete metric space, i.e., it is a Banach space. This means that the research of fuzzy systems with two input one output is also essentially an approximation problem in a kind of Banach space.

Remark 3.3.1 Based on above discussion, we should form a viewpoint coming from mathematics: so-called fuzzy systems are essentially belonging to function approximation theory which is a very important aspect of applied mathematics. □

References

1. Li, H. X. (1998). Interpolation mechanism of fuzzy control, Science in China (Series E), 41(3), pp. 312-320.
2. Li, H. X., You, F. and Peng, J. Y. (2004). Fuzzy controllers based on some fuzzy implication operators and their response functions, Progress in Nature Science, 14(1), pp. 15-20.
3. Li, H. X., Yuan, X. H., Wang, J. Y. and Li, Y. C. (2010). The normal numbers of the fuzzy systems and their classes, Science China (Series F), 53(11), pp. 2215-2229.
4. Li, H. X. (1993) *Fuzzy Mathematics Methods in Engineering and Its Applications*, (Tianjin Science and Technical Press, China, in Chinese).
5. Li, H. X. and Wang, P. Z. (1994) *Fuzzy Mathematics*, (National Defense Press, China, in Chinese).

6. Li, H. X. and Yen, V. C. (1995) *Fuzzy Sets and Fuzzy Decision-Making*, (CRC Press, Boca Raton).
7. Li. H. X. and C.L. Philip Chen. (2000). The equivalence between fuzzy logic systems and feedforward neural networks, IEEE Transactions on Neural Networks, 11(2), pp. 356-365.
8. Li, H. X. (2006). Probability representations of fuzzy systems, Science in China (Series F), 49(3), pp. 339-363.
9. Zadeh, L. A. (1965). Fuzzy sets, Information and Control, 8, pp. 338-353.
10. Zadeh, L. A. (1978). Fuzzy sets as a basic for a theory of possibility, Fuzzy Sets and Systems, 1, pp. 3-28.
11. Zimmermann, H. J. (1984) *Fuzzy Sets Theory and Its Applications*, (Kluwer Academic Publications, Hingham).

Chapter 4

Function Approximation Properties of Fuzzy Systems and Its Error Analysis

4.1 Introduction

Since fuzzy sets was proposed by L. A. Zadeh, fuzzy systems theory has been successfully used in many fields. In practical applications, based on a given approximation accuracy we can usually establish a fuzzy system to approximate a predetermined model or control process. Therefore, the research of function approximation property of fuzzy systems has become an important direction. The so-called function approximation of fuzzy systems means that we consider whether the fuzzy system can approximate any continuous function on a compact set in any degree of accuracy (by some sort of norm). From the mathematical view, a fuzzy system is regarded as a mapping from the input universe to the output universe; especially it is an interpolator. Literature [3] reveals the probability meaning of center of gravity method, and shows that the center of gravity method is reasonable. The function approximation properties of fuzzy systems constructed by the center of gravity defuzzification method are focused on in this paper, where the approximation error and the remainder expression are regarded as very important and interesting. At last, the remainder expressions of error upper bound estimate are proved.

4.2 Structures of Fuzzy Systems

We first consider a static open-loop system with one input one output, i.e.

SISO, shown as Figure 1.3.1. The value of input variable x taking its values from input universe X and the value of output variable y taking its values from output universe Y. If the system S is a deterministic system, we can use conventional methods to establish the mathematical model of the system (for example, using method of mechanism to establish differential equation model), and then the solution of the model is obtained by using analytical methods or numerical methods. So we have basically mastered the system (more depth problem is the qualitative problem of the system: controllability, observability, stability, etc.). Then, the system can be simply expressed as a function, denoted by s, that is

$$s : X \to Y,\quad x \mapsto y \triangleq s(x) \tag{4.2.1}$$

However, facing an uncertain system, we cannot use conventional methods to establish the "exact" mathematical model of the system (usually mean that the differential equation model), so it's difficult to obtain a function of (4.2.1).

For the uncertain system, we usually do some tests to gain a group of input-output data of the system, denoted by

$$\text{IOD} \triangleq \left\{ (x_i, y_i) \in X \times Y \middle| i = 0, 1, \cdots, n \right\},$$

which is called as the based data sets of the system. By means of IOD we can get a function:

$$\begin{aligned} &s_1 : X^0 \to Y^0,\quad x_i \mapsto s_1(x_i) = y_i, \\ &i = 0, 1, \cdots, n \end{aligned}$$

where $X^0 = \{x_0, x_1, \cdots, x_n\}$ and also we can write $Y^0 = \{y_0, y_1, \cdots, y_n\}$. Clearly, the data sets IOD of the system is exactly the graph of the function s_1.

In general, we cannot obtain accurate mapping $y = s(x)$ only through the data sets IOD. But we can use the data set IOD to construct a function to indicate the input-output relation of the system, as the following:

$$\overline{s}_n : X \to Y,\ x \mapsto y \triangleq \overline{s}_n(x) \tag{4.2.2}$$

We try to make the mapping $\overline{s}_n : X \to Y$ being close to our goal function $s : X \to Y$ such that it satisfies the condition $\|s - \overline{s}_n\| < \varepsilon$, where $\varepsilon > 0$ is a function approximation error which is able to meet our requirements, and $\|\cdot\|$ is a kind of norm defined in the continuous function space $C(X)$, usually the norm defined as the following:

$$\left(\forall s \in C(X)\right)\left(\|s\| \triangleq \|s\|_\infty \triangleq \max\left\{|s(x)| \,\middle|\, x \in X\right\}\right).$$

Let $X = [a, b] \subset \mathbb{R}$ be the input universe, where $\mathbb{R}$ is the real number field and $Y = [c, d] \subset \mathbb{R}$ be the output universe; without loss of generality, we can assume that the input-output data set IOD meets the following condition:

$$\begin{aligned} a = x_0 < x_1 < \cdots < x_n = b, \\ c = y_{k_0} \le y_{k_1} \le \cdots \le y_{k_n} = d \end{aligned}$$

where $k_i = \sigma(i)$, and σ is a substitution, i.e. a bijection as follows

$$\begin{aligned} \sigma : \{0, 1, \cdots, n\} &\to \{0, 1, \cdots, n\} \\ i &\mapsto \sigma(i) = k_i, \end{aligned} \tag{4.2.3}$$

$$\sigma = \begin{pmatrix} 0 & 1 & \cdots & n \\ k_0 & k_1 & \cdots & k_n \end{pmatrix}$$

If it is without substitution, the output data set $Y^0 = \left\{y_i \,\middle|\, i = 0, 1, \cdots, n\right\}$ does not meet strict order relationship:

$$c = y_1 < y_2 < \cdots < y_n = d$$

This strict order relationship is important in the construction of fuzzy sets:

$$B_i \in \mathcal{F}(Y), \quad i = 0, 1, \cdots, n.$$

We can get a group of fuzzy sets $\mathcal{A} \triangleq \{A_i \mid i = 0,1,\cdots,n\}$ by using input data set X^0, and similarly, can get a group of fuzzy sets:

$$\mathcal{B} \triangleq \{B_{k_i} \mid i = 0,1,\cdots,n\}$$

by using output data set Y^0. These fuzzy sets A_i, B_i can be defined as a kind of triangular wave functions.

Noticing that $\sigma\sigma^{-1}(i) = i$, so $k_{\sigma^{-1}(i)} = i$, and then $B_i = B_{k_{\sigma^{-1}(i)}}$, as a result, B_i is easily defined, that is $\mathcal{B} = \{B_i \mid i = 0,1,\cdots,n\}$.

According to the data set IOD, we can get a group of fuzzy inference rules of the system:

$$\text{If } x \text{ is } A_i \text{ then } y \text{ is } B_i, \quad i = 0,1,\cdots,n, \tag{4.2.4}$$

where A_i and B_i are respectively the fuzzy sets defined on the universes X and Y, i.e., $A_i \in \mathcal{F}(X)$ and $B_i \in \mathcal{F}(Y)$, $i = 0,1,\cdots,n$. Every of the inference rules can determine a fuzzy relation $R_i \in \mathcal{F}(X \times Y)$ as the following:

$$\mu_{R_i}(x,y) \triangleq \theta(\mu_A(x), \mu_B(y)), \quad (x,y) \in X \times Y,$$

where $\theta : [0,1] \times [0,1] \to [0,1]$ is a fuzzy implication operator. Usually θ can be taken as the following forms: $\theta = \wedge$ or $\theta = \cdot$, i.e.,

$$\begin{aligned} &\wedge : [0,1] \times [0,1] \to [0,1] \\ &(a,b) \mapsto \wedge(a,b) = a \wedge b, \\ &\cdot : [0,1] \times [0,1] \to [0,1] \\ &(a,b) \mapsto \cdot(a,b) = a \cdot b \end{aligned}$$

We all know that fuzzy implication operator $\theta = \cdot$ is called Larsen implication operator. In this paper we often use Larsen implication operator. Now the group of inference rules (4.2.4) can be regarded as a function as follows:

$$s^*:\mathcal{A}\to\mathcal{B},\quad A_i\mapsto s^*(A_i)\triangleq B_i,$$
$$i=0,1,\cdots,n$$

Based on these fuzzy relations $R_i, i=0,1,\cdots,n$, we can get a whole fuzzy relation $R\in\mathcal{F}(X\times Y)$, where $R=\bigcup_{i=0}^{n}R_i$ and

$$\mu_R(x,y)=\bigvee_{i=0}^{n}\mu_{R_i}(x,y),\quad (x,y)=X\times Y.$$

By using R, we can make a function as the following:

$$\begin{aligned}
&s^{**}:\mathcal{F}(X)\to\mathcal{F}(Y)\\
&A\mapsto B=s^{**}(A)\triangleq A\circ R,\\
&\mu_B(y)=\bigvee_{x\in X}\left(\mu_A(x)\wedge\mu_R(x,y)\right)\\
&=\bigvee_{x\in X}\left[\mu_A(x)\wedge\left(\bigvee_{i=0}^{n}\mu_{R_i}(x,y)\right)\right]
\end{aligned}$$

Then, in order to obtain the mapping $\overline{s}_n:X\to Y,\ x\mapsto y=\overline{s}_n(x)$, we can do it by two steps from the "set-set" mapping $s^{**}:\mathcal{F}(X)\to\mathcal{F}(Y)$ to obtain the "point-point" mapping $\overline{s}_n:X\to Y$.

Step 1. Transform "set-set" mapping into a "point-set" mapping:

$$s_1:X\to\mathcal{F}(Y),\quad x\mapsto s_1(x)\triangleq s^{**}(\{x\}),\tag{4.2.5}$$

where its membership function form is as the following: for any binary point $(x,y)\in X\times Y$,

$$\begin{aligned}
&\mu_{s_1(x)}(y)=\mu_{s^{**}(\{x\})}(y)\\
&=\bigvee_{\xi\in X}\left[\mu_{\{x\}}(\xi)\cdot\mu_R(\xi,y)\right]\\
&=\mu_R(x,y)=\bigvee_{i=0}^{n}\left(\mu_{A_i}(x)\cdot\mu_{B_i}(y)\right)
\end{aligned}\tag{4.2.6}$$

Because $(\forall x \in X)(s_1(x) \in \mathcal{F}(Y))$, we should write the symbol as the following:

$$(\forall x \in X)\big(B(\xi = x) \triangleq s_1(x)\big),$$

where ξ is regarded as a random variable taking its value in X; so for any binary point $(x, y) \in X \times Y$, $B(\xi = x)$ is shown as the following:

$$\mu_{B(\xi=x)}(y) = \mu_{s_1(x)}(y) = \bigvee_{i=0}^{n}\left(\mu_{A_i}(x) \cdot \mu_{B_i}(y)\right) \tag{4.2.7}$$

Step 2. We can turn the fuzzy set $B(\xi = x) = s_1(x) \in \mathcal{F}(Y)$ into a point as being $y = \big(y(\xi)\big)_{\xi=x} = y(x)$ in Y which corresponding to $\xi = x$.

Literature [3] has proved that the physical center of gravity of plane rigid body is reasonable and is an optimal method in the sense of least squares. Suppose that

$$\int_Y \left|y\mu_{B(\xi=x)}(y)\right| \mathrm{d}y < \infty, \quad 0 < \int_Y \mu_{B(\xi=x)}(y)\mathrm{d}y < \infty$$

by using the gravity method, we have

$$y = \big(y(\xi)\big)_{\xi=x} = y(x) = \frac{\int_Y y\mu_{B(\xi=x)}(y)\mathrm{d}y}{\int_Y \mu_{B(\xi=x)}(y)\mathrm{d}y} \tag{4.2.8}$$

This means that we have got the mapping as the following:

$$\overline{s}_n : X \to Y$$

$$x \mapsto \overline{s}_n(x) \triangleq y(x) = \frac{\int_Y y\mu_{B(\xi=x)}(y)\mathrm{d}y}{\int_Y \mu_{B(\xi=x)}(y)\mathrm{d}y} \tag{4.2.9}$$

And then substituting (4.2.7) into the equation (4.2.9), we can get the following equation:

$$\overline{s}_n(x) = \frac{\int_Y y\mu_{B(\xi=x)}(y)\mathrm{d}y}{\int_Y \mu_{B(\xi=x)}(y)\mathrm{d}y} = \frac{\int_Y y\left[\bigvee_{i=0}^{n}\left(\mu_{A_i}(x)\cdot\mu_{B_i}(y)\right)\right]\mathrm{d}y}{\int_Y \left[\bigvee_{i=0}^{n}\left(\mu_{A_i}(x)\cdot\mu_{B_i}(y)\right)\right]\mathrm{d}y} \tag{4.2.10}$$

Remark 4.2.1 Because of the following expression:

$$\left(\forall(x,y)\in X\times Y\right)\left(\mu_{B(\xi=x)}(y)=\mu_R(x,y)\right),$$

Equation (4.2.10) can be written as a more general form:

$$\overline{s}_n(x) = \frac{\int_Y y\mu_R(x,y)\mathrm{d}y}{\int_Y \mu_R(x,y)\mathrm{d}y}, \quad x\in X \tag{4.2.11}$$

And since $R=\bigcup_{i=0}^{n} R_i$, the fuzzy relation R is also regarded as obtaining from R_{k_i} $(i=0,1,\cdots,n)$ by the operation "$\bigcup$". In addition to the use of operation "$\bigcup$", many ways can be used. Therefore, (4.2.11) has a broader meaning. □

The function (4.2.11) $\overline{s}_n : X\to Y$ is called fuzzy system based on the operating process from Data to Formula by above method.

From the data set $\text{IOD}=\left\{(x_i,y_i)\in X\times Y \middle| i=0,1,\cdots,n\right\}$, we have already obtained an approximate function $\overline{s}_n : X\to Y$ which can approximate the input-output function $s: X\to Y$ of the system. However, in (4.2.11), the numerator and denominator are integral expressions; while in general, these two integrals have almost not analytical solution. To facilitate application purposes, we can use the definition of Riemann integral to simplify our method. In fact, we let

$$\left.\begin{aligned}\Delta y_{k_i} &= y_{k_{i+1}} - y_{k_i},\ i = 0,1,\cdots,n-1,\\ \Delta y_{k_n} &= \frac{\sum_{i=0}^{n-1}\Delta y_{k_i}}{n} = \frac{d-c}{n},\end{aligned}\right\}$$

Since $\Delta y_i = \Delta y_{k_{\sigma^{-1}(i)}}$, as a result, Δy_i are all defined. Then, according to the meaning of Riemann sum in the definite integration, we have the following result:

$$\begin{aligned}\bar{s}_n(x) &= \frac{\int_Y y\mu_{B(\xi=x)}(y)\mathrm{d}y}{\int_Y \mu_{B(\xi=x)}(y)\mathrm{d}y} \approx \frac{\sum_{i=0}^{n}\mu_{B(\xi=x)}(y_i)y_i\Delta y_i}{\sum_{i=0}^{n}\mu_{B(\xi=x)}(y_i)\Delta y_i}\\ &= \frac{\sum_{i=0}^{n}\left[\bigvee_{j=0}^{n}\left(\mu_{A_j}(x)\cdot\mu_{B_j}(y_i)\right)\right]y_i\Delta y_i}{\sum_{i=0}^{n}\left[\bigvee_{j=0}^{n}\left(\mu_{A_j}(x)\cdot\mu_{B_j}(y_i)\right)\right]\Delta y_i}\\ &= \frac{\sum_{i=0}^{n}\mu_{A_i}(x)y_i\Delta y_i}{\sum_{i=0}^{n}\mu_{A_i}(x)\Delta y_i} = \sum_{i=0}^{n}\frac{\mu_{A_i}(x)\Delta y_i}{\sum_{j=0}^{n}\mu_{A_j}(x)\Delta y_j}y_i = \sum_{i=0}^{n}\mu_{A_i^*}(x)y_i\end{aligned} \tag{4.2.12}$$

where we have been set the following symbol:

$$\mu_{A_i^*}(x) \triangleq \frac{A_i(x)\Delta y_i}{\sum_{j=0}^{n}\mu_{A_j}(x)\Delta y_j},\quad i = 0,1,\cdots,n. \tag{4.2.13}$$

It's not difficult to verify that the function group as being $\left\{\mu_{A_i^*}(x)\right\}_{i=0}^{n}$ is linear independent in the function space $C(X)$, and every base function $\mu_{A_i^*}(x)$ has Kronecker property:

$$\mu_{A_i^*}\left(x_j\right)=\begin{cases}1, & i=j,\\ 0, & i\neq j,\end{cases}$$

$$i,j\in\{0,1,\cdots,n\}.$$

Now we let the following function:

$$f_n(x)\triangleq\sum_{i=0}^{n}\mu_{A_i^*}(x)y_i \tag{4.2.14}$$

Then the function $f_n(x)\triangleq\sum_{i=0}^{n}\mu_{A_i^*}(x)y_i$ happens to be an interpolation function, which the function group $\left\{\mu_{A_i^*}(x)\right\}_{i=0}^{n}$ is just regarded its base functions.

In particular, when $\Delta y_i=h\ (i=0,1,\cdots,n)$, i.e. the set

$$Y^0=\left\{y_i \,\middle|\, i=0,1,\cdots,n\right\}$$

is an equidistant partition data set, which its common interval is $h>0$, and it's not difficult to verify that $\sum_{i=0}^{n}\mu_{A_i}(x)\equiv 1$, then

$$\mu_{A_i^*}(x)=\frac{\mu_{A_i}(x)\Delta y_i}{\sum_{j=0}^{n}\mu_{A_j}(x)\Delta y_j}=\frac{\mu_{A_i}(x)}{\sum_{j=0}^{n}\mu_{A_j}(x)}=\mu_{A_i}(x), \tag{4.2.15}$$

$$i=0,1,\cdots,n$$

And then the equations (4.2.12) and (4.2.14) will be simplified as: for any $x\in X$

$$s(x)\approx\overline{s}_n(x)\approx f_n(x)=\sum_{i=0}^{n}\mu_{A_i}(x)y_i \tag{4.2.16}$$

This means that $\overline{s}_n(x)$ is approximately a piecewise linear interpolation function as the following:

$$f_n(x)=\sum_{i=0}^{n}\mu_{A_i}(x)y_i$$

So $s(x)$ can be approximately regarded as a piecewise linear interpolation function $f_n(x)=\sum_{i=0}^{n}\mu_{A_i}(x)y_i$.

From the data set IOD, we write the following symbol:

$$\text{FIOD}\triangleq\left\{(A_i,B_i)\in\mathcal{F}(X)\times\mathcal{F}(Y)\,\middle|\,i=0,1,\cdots,n\right\}.$$

If it satisfies the condition:

$$(i=0,1,\cdots,n)\left(\mu_{A_i}(x)\in C(X),\ \mu_{B_i}(y)\in C(Y)\right),$$

then FIOD is called continuous fuzzy data set. We call FIOD being with two-phase property, if it satisfies the condition:

$$\sum_{i=0}^{n}\mu_{A_i}(x)\equiv 1,\ \sum_{i=0}^{n}\mu_{B_i}(x)\equiv 1,$$
$$(\forall x\in X)(\exists i\in\{0,1,\cdots,n-1\})\left(\mu_{A_i}(x)+\mu_{A_{i+1}}(x)=1\right)$$
$$(\forall y\in X)(\exists j\in\{0,1,\cdots,n-1\})\left(\mu_{B_j}(x)+\mu_{B_{j+1}}(x)=1\right)$$

Clearly, the two-phase fuzzy data set satisfies the Kronecker properties:

$$A_i(x_j)=\begin{cases}1, & i=j,\\ 0, & i\neq j,\end{cases}\quad B_i(y_j)=\begin{cases}1, & i=j,\\ 0, & i\neq j,\end{cases}$$
$$i,j\in\{0,1,\cdots,n\}.$$

Remark 4.2.2 It's not difficult to verify, when the FIOD is with two-phase property, the conclusions derived above remain valid. □

4.3 Function Approximation Properties of Fuzzy Systems

For the data set $\text{IOD} = \{(x_i, y_i) \in X \times Y \mid i = 0,1,\cdots,n\}$, write

$$\Delta x_i \triangleq x_{i+1} - x_i, \quad i = 0,1,\cdots,n-1.$$

Obviously, $\max\limits_{0 \le i \le n-1} \{\Delta x_i\} \to 0 \Rightarrow n \to \infty$; on the contrary, the following implication:

$$n \to \infty \Rightarrow \max_{0 \le i \le n-1} \{\Delta x_i\} \to 0$$

is not true. And if that $n \to \infty \Rightarrow \max\limits_{0 \le i \le n-1} \Delta x_i \to 0$ is true, then data set IOD is called coordinated. That is, IOD is coordinated if and only if

$$n \to \infty \Leftrightarrow \max_{0 \le i \le n-1} \{\Delta x_i\} \to 0.$$

We always assume that the following data sets IOD is coordinated.

In addition, for a continuous function $s \in C[a,b]$, if the data set IOD to meet the interpolation condition about s i.e.,

$$(\forall i \in \{0,1,\cdots,n\})(y_i = s(x_i)),$$

then it's not difficult to understand that IOD is coordinated implies the following equivalence expression:

$$n \to \infty \Leftrightarrow \max_{0 \le i \le n} \{\Delta y_{k_i}\} \to 0.$$

For a given data set IOD, we can get its FIOD with two-phase property as follows

$$\text{FIOD} = \{(A_i, B_i) \in \mathcal{F}(X) \times \mathcal{F}(Y) \mid i = 0,1,\cdots,n\}.$$

Suppose the fuzzy system $\overline{s}_n$ like (2.11) to be constructed by IOD and IODF, that is, we have got the equation as the following:

$$\overline{s}_n(x) = \frac{\int_Y y\mu_R(x,y)\mathrm{d}y}{\int_Y \mu_R(x,y)\mathrm{d}y}, \quad x \in X \tag{4.3.1}$$

And we also suppose that it satisfies condition:

$$0 < \int_Y \mu_R(x,y)\mathrm{d}y < \infty, \quad \int_Y |\mu_R R(x,y)|\mathrm{d}y < \infty .$$

We call the fuzzy system $\overline{s}_n$ has function approximation property in the universe $X = [a,b]$, if for any function $s \in C[a,b]$, as long as the data set IOD satisfies interpolation condition:

$$(\forall i \in \{0,1,\cdots,n\})\left(y_i = s\left(x_i\right)\right),$$

then $\overline{s}_n$ converges s according to the norm of normed linear space, that is, for any $\varepsilon > 0$, $\exists N \in \mathbb{N}^+$, such that

$$\left(\forall n \in \mathbb{N}^+\right)\left(n > N \Rightarrow \|s - \overline{s}_n\|_\infty < \varepsilon\right) \tag{4.3.2}$$

where $\mathbb{N}^+ = \mathbb{N} \setminus \{0\}$, while $\mathbb{N}$ is the set of all natural numbers; in other words, the function sequence $\left\{\overline{s}_n\right\}_{n=1}^{\infty}$ uniformly converges to a continuous function s in $X = [a,b]$.

Lemma 4.3.1 Let $f(x,y)$ be a binary continuous function on $X \times Y$, where $X = [a,b]$ and $Y = [c,d]$ are two real number closed intervals, for the integral $I(x) = \int_c^d f(x,y)\mathrm{d}y$ with parameter x, we must have this result: for any $\varepsilon > 0$, there is always $\delta > 0$ which has nothing to do with the parameter x, for any partition of Y:

$$c = y_0 < y_1 < \cdots < y_n = d ,$$

if $\lambda \triangleq \max\limits_{0 \le i \le n-1} \left\{\Delta y_i\right\} < \delta$, then for all $x \in X$, the Riemann integral sum

$\sum_{i=0}^{n-1} f(x,\xi_i)\Delta y_i$ of $I(x)$ must uniformly meet the following strict inequality:

$$\left|I(x)-\sum_{i=0}^{n-1} f(x,\xi_i)\Delta y_i\right|<\varepsilon \tag{4.3.3}$$

Proof. For any $\varepsilon>0$, take $\delta_k=1/k, k=1,2,\cdots$. It's can be proved that there must be one k, such that $\delta=\delta_k$ satisfies the conclusion of the lemma. Otherwise, for every k, there must exist a point $x_k\in X$ and a partition of Y:

$$c=y_0^{(k)}<y_1^{(k)}<\cdots<y_{n_k}^{(k)}=d,$$

and also there must exist a point $\xi_i^{(k)}\in\left[y_i^{(k)},y_{i+1}^{(k)}\right], i=0,1,\cdots,n-1$, although we have that $\lambda_k=\max_{0\le i\le n_k-1}\left\{\Delta y_i^{(k)}\right\}<\delta_k$, but

$$\left|I\left(x_k\right)-\sum_{i=0}^{n_k-1} f\left(x_k,\xi_i^{(k)}\right)\Delta y_i^{(k)}\right|\ge\varepsilon.$$

Attention to that $\{x_k\}$ is bounded point sequence, there must be a convergent subsequence $\left\{x_{k_j}\right\}$ of $\{x_k\}$, such that $x_{k_j}\xrightarrow{j\to\infty}x_*\in X$. Noticing that $\delta_{k_j}\xrightarrow{j\to\infty}0$, we have the following limit expression:

$$0<\varepsilon\le\lim_{j\to\infty}\left|I\left(x_{k_j}\right)-\sum_{i=0}^{n_{k_j}-1} f\left(x_{k_j},\xi_i^{(k_j)}\right)\Delta y_i^{(k_j)}\right|$$

$$=\left|I(x_*)-\int_c^d f(x_*,y)\mathrm{d}y\right|=0$$

This is a clear contradiction and proves the lemma. □

Lemma 4.3.2 Let $f(x,y)$ be a binary continuous function on $X \times Y$, where $X=[a,b]$ and $Y=[c,d]$ are two real number closed intervals, for the integral $I(x)=\int_c^d f(x,y)\mathrm{d}y$ with parameter x, if the following condition is satisfied

$$(\forall x \in X)(I(x)>0),$$

then there must be $\delta > 0$, such that for any partition of Y:

$$c = y_0 < y_1 < \cdots < y_n = d,$$

and any $\xi_i \in [y_i, y_{i+1}]$, the Riemann integral sum $\sum_{i=0}^{n-1} f(x,\xi_i)\Delta y_i$ of $I(x)$ must satisfy the implication: if $\lambda \triangleq \max_{0\le i\le n-1}\{\Delta y_i\} < \delta$, then

$$(\forall x \in X)\left(\sum_{i=0}^{n-1} f(x,\xi_i)\Delta y_i > 0\right) \tag{4.3.4}$$

Proof. It is easy to know that $I(x)=\int_c^d f(x,y)\mathrm{d}y \in C[a,b]$; therefore, there must be the minimal point $x_0 \in X$ of $I(x)$, such that

$$(\forall x \in X)(I(x) \ge I(x_0)).$$

Take $\varepsilon = I(x_0)$, according to Lemma 4.3.1, there exists $\delta > 0$, for any partition of Y:

$$c = y_0 < y_1 < \cdots < y_n = d,$$

and any $\xi_i \in [y_i, y_{i+1}]$, the Riemann integral sum $\sum_{i=0}^{n-1} f(x,\xi_i)\Delta y_i$ of the integral $I(x)$ must satisfy such result: if $\lambda \triangleq \max_{0\le i\le n-1}\{\Delta y_i\} < \delta$, then we can have the following expression:

$$(\forall x \in X)\left(\left|I(x)-\sum_{i=0}^{n-1} f(x,\xi_i)\Delta y_i\right| < \varepsilon\right).$$

So $\sum_{i=0}^{n-1} f(x,\xi_i)\Delta y_i > I(x)-\varepsilon \geq I(x_0)-\varepsilon = 0$ is true for all $x \in X$, therefore the conclusion of the lemma is true. □

Lemma 4.3.3 Let $f(x,y)$ and $g(x,y)$ are two binary continuous functions on $X \times Y$, where $X=[a,b]$ and $Y=[c,d]$ are two real number closed intervals, satisfying the condition:

$$(\forall x \in X)\left(\int_c^d g(x,y)\mathrm{d}y > 0\right).$$

For any $\varepsilon > 0$, there is always $\delta > 0$ which has nothing to do with parameter x, for any partition:

$$c = y_0 < y_1 < \cdots < y_n = d,$$

If $\lambda \triangleq \max_{0\leq i\leq n-1}\{\Delta y_i\} < \delta$, then for all $x \in X$, we uniformly have

$$\left|\frac{\int_c^d f(x,y)\mathrm{d}y}{\int_c^d g(x,y)\mathrm{d}y} - \frac{\sum_{i=0}^{n-1} f(x,\xi_i)\Delta y_i}{\sum_{i=0}^{n-1} g(x,\xi_i)\Delta y_i}\right| < \varepsilon \tag{4.3.5}$$

where $\xi_i \in [y_i, y_{i+1}]$, $i = 0,1,\cdots,n-1$.

Proof. According to Lemma 3.2, we know the fact that

$$1\Big/\sum_{i=0}^{n-1} g(x,\xi_i)\Delta y_i$$

is with sense for the bigger $n \in \mathbb{N}^+$. According to the limit operation rules, namely "the limit of quotient is equal to the quotient of limits", and then by Lemma 4.3.1, we can know that the conclusion of Lemma 4.3.3 is true. □

Theorem 4.3.1 With respect to the data set IOD, the fuzzy data set with two-phase property is as follows:

$$\text{FIOD} = \{(A_i, B_i) \in \mathcal{F}(X) \times \mathcal{F}(Y) \mid i = 0, 1, \cdots, n\}.$$

Suppose that the fuzzy system $\bar{s}_n$ as (4.2.11) constructed by IOD and FIOD as follows

$$\bar{s}_n(x) = \frac{\int_Y y\mu_R(x,y)\mathrm{d}y}{\int_Y \mu_R(x,y)\mathrm{d}y}, \quad x \in X$$

If the following conditions are satisfied:

$$0 < \int_Y \mu_R(x,y)\mathrm{d}y < \infty, \quad \int_Y |y\mu_R(x,y)|\mathrm{d}y < \infty,$$

then the fuzzy system $\bar{s}_n$ has function approximation property.

Proof. For any given function $s \in C[a,b]$, suppose that the data set IOD satisfies the interpolation condition:

$$(\forall i \in \{0, 1, \cdots, n\})(y_i = s(x_i)).$$

We want to prove that $\bar{s}_n$ converge to s according to the norm of normed linear space $(C[a,b], \|\cdot\|)$, that is, for any $\varepsilon > 0$, $\exists N \in \mathbb{N}^+$, such that

$$(\forall n \in \mathbb{N}^+)(n > N \Rightarrow \|s - \bar{s}_n\|_\infty < \varepsilon).$$

In fact, for any $\varepsilon > 0$, according to equation (2.14), we easily know the fact that, $\exists N_1 \in \mathbb{N}^+$, such that

$$\left(\forall n \in \mathbb{N}^+\right)\left(n > N_1 \Rightarrow \left\|f_n - \overline{s}_n\right\|_\infty < \frac{\varepsilon}{2}\right).$$

Then, when $n > N_1$, we have that

$$\left\|s - \overline{s}_n\right\|_\infty \le \left\|s - f_n\right\|_\infty + \left\|f_n - \overline{s}_n\right\|_\infty < \left\|s - f_n\right\|_\infty + \frac{\varepsilon}{2}.$$

So we only consider the estimation of $\left\|s - f_n\right\|_\infty$.

In fact, it's easy to test that $\left\{\mu_{A_i^*}(x)\right\}_{i=0}^{n}$ satisfies the two-phase property, and for any given $x \in [a,b]$, there must be $i \in \{0,1,\cdots,n-1\}$, such that $x \in \left[x_i, x_{i+1}\right]$, then

$$f_n(x) = \mu_{A_i^*}(x) y_i + \mu_{A_{i+1}^*}(x) y_{i+1}.$$

By using of the following fact:

$$\mu_{A_i^*}(x) + \mu_{A_{i+1}^*}(x) = \sum_{i=0}^{n} \mu_{A_i^*}(x) \equiv 1,$$

we have the following result:

$$\begin{aligned}
\left|s(x) - f_n(x)\right| &= \left|s(x) - \left(\mu_{A_i^*}(x) y_i + \mu_{A_{i+1}^*}(x) y_{i+1}\right)\right| \\
&= \left|s(x)\left(\mu_{A_i^*}(x) + \mu_{A_{i+1}^*}(x)\right) - \left(\mu_{A_i^*}(x) s\left(x_i\right) + \mu_{A_{i+1}^*}(x) s\left(x_{i+1}\right)\right)\right| \\
&\le \mu_{A_i^*}(x)\left|s(x) - s\left(x_i\right)\right| + \mu_{A_{i+1}^*}(x)\left|s(x) - s\left(x_{i+1}\right)\right| \\
&\le \left|s(x) - s\left(x_i\right)\right| + \left|s(x) - s\left(x_{i+1}\right)\right| \\
&\le 2 \max_{i \le m \le i+1}\left\{\left|s(x) - s\left(x_m\right)\right|\right\}.
\end{aligned}$$

Because of $s \in C[a,b]$, so $s(x)$ is uniform continuous on $[a,b]$, then for the above $\varepsilon > 0$, there must be $\delta > 0$, such that

$$(\forall x', x'' \in [a,b])\left(|x' - x''| < \delta \Rightarrow |s(x') - s(x'')| < \varepsilon/4\right)$$

By using of the coordination of IOD, we have that, $\exists N_2 \in \mathbb{N}^+$, such that

$$(\forall n \in \mathbb{N}^+)\left(n > N_2 \Rightarrow \lambda = \max_{0 \le i \le n-1}\{\Delta x_i\} < \delta\right).$$

Noticing that $x \in [x_i, x_{i+1}]$, we can easily know that

$$\max_{i \le m \le i+1}\{|x - x_m|\} \le \max_{i \le m \le i+1}\{\Delta x_m\} \le \max_{0 \le i \le n-1}\{\Delta x_i\} < \delta .$$

Therefore we have

$$|s(x) - f_n(x)| \le 2 \max_{i \le m \le i+1}\{|s(x) - s(x_m)|\} < 2\frac{\varepsilon}{4} = \frac{\varepsilon}{2}.$$

Because x is arbitrary in $[a,b]$, we have $\max_{x \in [a,b]}\{|s(x) - f_n(x)|\} \le \frac{\varepsilon}{2}$, namely $\|s - f_n\| \le \frac{\varepsilon}{2}$.

Finally, we get the result that, $\exists N \triangleq \max\{N_1, N_2\} \in \mathbb{N}^+$, such that

$$(\forall n \in \mathbb{N}^+)\left(n > N \Rightarrow \|s - \overline{s}_n\|_\infty < \frac{\varepsilon}{2} + \frac{\varepsilon}{2} = \varepsilon\right)$$

This means that the fuzzy system $\overline{s}_n$ must have the function approximation property. □

4.4 The approximation Remainder Estimation

Theorem 4.4.1 In the condition of Theorem 4.3.1, for any $s \in C^2[a,b]$, suppose that

$$(\forall i \in \{0, 1, \cdots, n-1\})\left(\mu_{A_i}, \mu_{A_{i+1}} \in C^2[x_i, x_{i+1}]\right);$$

for the function s, if the data set IOD satisfies interpolation conditions:

$$(\forall i \in \{0,1,\cdots,n\})\left(y_i = s\left(x_i\right)\right),$$

then we have the following results:

1) The approximate remainder of $f_n(x)$ to the continuous function $s(x)$ is of the following equation:

$$\begin{aligned} r_n(x) &= s(x) - f_n(x) \\ &= \frac{\left(x-x_i\right)\left(x-x_{i+1}\right)}{2q_i(x)}\left(\varphi''_{i1}\left(\xi_i\right) - \varphi''_{i2}\left(\xi_i\right)\right), \end{aligned} \tag{4.4.1}$$

where $(\forall i \in \{0,1,\cdots,n-1\})\left(x \in \left[x_i, x_{i+1}\right], \xi_i \in \left(x_i, x_{i+1}\right)\right)$ and

$$\begin{aligned} q_i(x) &= \mu_{A_i}(x)\Delta y_i + \mu_{A_{i+1}}(x)\Delta y_{i+1}, \\ \varphi''_{i1}\left(\xi_i\right) &= s''\left(\xi_i\right)\left(\mu_{A_i}\left(\xi_i\right)\Delta y_i + \mu_{A_{i+1}}\left(\xi_i\right)\Delta y_{i+1}\right) \\ &\quad + 2s'\left(\xi_i\right)\left(\mu'_{A_i}\left(\xi_i\right)\Delta y_i + \mu'_{A_{i+1}}\left(\xi_i\right)\Delta y_{i+1}\right) \\ &\quad + s\left(\xi_i\right)\left(\mu''_{A_i}\left(\xi_i\right)\Delta y_i + \mu''_{A_{i+1}}\left(\xi_i\right)\Delta y_{i+1}\right), \\ \varphi''_{i2}(t) &= \mu''_{A_i}\left(\xi_i\right)s\left(x_i\right)\Delta y_i + \mu''_{A_{i+1}}\left(\xi_i\right)s\left(x_{i+1}\right)\Delta y_{i+1}. \end{aligned}$$

2) The approximate error estimate formula of $f_n(x)$ to the continuous function $s(x)$ is as the following inequality:

$$\left\|r_n\right\|_\infty = \left\|s(x) - f_n(x)\right\|_\infty \le M\Delta_1^3 \tag{4.4.2}$$

where $\Delta_1 \triangleq \max\limits_{0\le j\le n-1}\left\{\Delta x_j\right\}$, $\Delta_{2i} \triangleq \max\limits_{0\le i\le n-1}\left\{\Delta y_i, \Delta y_{i+1}\right\}$, and

$$\begin{aligned} C_i &\triangleq \min\left\{q_i(x) \middle| x \in \left[x_i, x_{i+1}\right]\right\}, \\ M_i &\triangleq \frac{1}{8C_i}\left(M_{2i} + 4M_{1i}L_{1i} + 4M_0L_{2i}\right), \end{aligned}$$

$$M_0 \triangleq \max_{t\in[a,b]}\{|s(t)|\}, \quad M \triangleq \max_{0\le i\le n-1}\{M_i \cdot N\}$$
$$M_{1i} \triangleq \max_{t\in[x_i,x_{i+1}]}\{|s'(t)|\}, \quad M_{2i} \triangleq \max_{t\in[x_i,x_{i+1}]}\{|s''(t)|\},$$
$$L_{1i} \triangleq \max\left\{\max_{t\in[x_i,x_{i+1}]}\{|\mu'_{A_i}(t)|\}, \max_{t\in[x_i,x_{i+1}]}\{|\mu'_{A_{i+1}}(t)|\}\right\},$$
$$L_{2i} \triangleq \max\left\{\max_{t\in[x_i,x_{i+1}]}\{|\mu''_{A_i}(t)|\}, \max_{t\in[x_i,x_{i+1}]}\{|\mu''_{A_{i+1}}(t)|\}\right\}.$$

Proof. 1) For any $x \in [a,b]$, when $x = x_i$ $(i = 0,1,\cdots,n)$, the conclusion is clearly true; so we only consider the following situation:

$$(\forall i \in \{0,1,\cdots,n\})(x \neq x_i).$$

First, it is easy to know that there must exist $i \in \{0,1,\cdots,n-1\}$, such that $x \in (x_i, x_{i+1})$, according to the two-phase property of A_i $(i = 0,1,\cdots,n)$, we have

$$\begin{aligned} f_n(x) &= \sum_{j=0}^{n} \mu_{A_j^*}(x) s(x_j) \\ &= \mu_{A_i^*}(x) s(x_i) + \mu_{A_{i+1}^*}(x) s(x_{i+1}) \\ &= \frac{\mu_{A_i}(x) s(x_i) \Delta y_i + \mu_{A_{i+1}}(x) s(x_{i+1}) \Delta y_{i+1}}{\mu_{A_i}(x)\Delta y_i + \mu_{A_{i+1}}(x)\Delta y_{i+1}} \\ &= \frac{p_i(x)}{q_i(x)} \end{aligned} \tag{4.4.3}$$

in which we have set the following expressions:

$$p_i(x) \triangleq \mu_{A_i}(x) s(x_i) \Delta y_i + \mu_{A_{i+1}}(x) s(x_{i+1}) \Delta y_{i+1} \tag{4.4.4}$$

$$q_i(x) \triangleq \mu_{A_i}(x)\Delta y_i + \mu_{A_{i+1}}(x)\Delta y_{i+1}. \tag{4.4.5}$$

As a result, $f_n(x)$ is actually a rational fraction, that is $f_n(x) = \dfrac{p_i(x)}{q_i(x)}$

and thus the approximation of $f_n(x)$ to $s(x)$ is a rational fraction approximate problem.

Because $f_n(x)$ makes sense, we know the fact as the following:

$$(\forall x \in X)(q_i(x) > 0).$$

And then, we proceed to consider the representation of the following approximate item:

$$r_n(x) = s(x) - f_n(x) = s(x) - \frac{p_i(x)}{q_i(x)}$$

Reform it into the following form:

$$\begin{aligned} r_n(x)q_i(x) &= s(x)q_i(x) - f_n(x)q_i(x) \\ &= s(x)q_i(x) - p_i(x) \end{aligned} \tag{4.4.6}$$

According to the well-known interpolation conditions, we can know the fact that $r_n(x_j) = 0, j = i, i+1$, or

$$s(x_j)q_i(x_j) - p_i(x_j) = 0, \quad j = i, i+1.$$

Assume that $r_n(x)q_i(x)$ has the following form

$$r_n(x)q_i(x) = k(x)(x - x_i)(x - x_{i+1}) \tag{4.4.7}$$

That is,

$$\begin{aligned} r_n(x)q_i(x) &= k(x)(x - x_i)(x - x_{i+1}) \\ &= s(x)q_i(x) - p_i(x) \end{aligned},$$

in which the function $k(x)$ is a undetermined. Now we start to consider how to solve out $k(x)$.

In fact, let x be a fixed point, and do an auxiliary function:

$$\varphi_i(t) = s(t)q_i(t) - p_i(t) - k(x)(t - x_i)(t - x_{i+1}). \tag{4.4.8}$$

Obviously we know the fact that $\varphi_i \in C^2\left[x_i, x_{i+1}\right]$. According to (4.4.8), we learn the fact as following:

$$\varphi_i\left(x_j\right)=0, \quad j=i,i+1;$$

also, it's not hard to see $\varphi_i(x)=0$. This means that, in the closed interval $\varphi_i(t)$ has three zero points: $x_i < x < x_{i+1}$.

According to Rolle differential intermediate value theorem, the derivate function $\varphi_i'(t)$ of $\varphi_i(t)$ in the open intervals $\left(x_i, x\right)$ and $\left(x, x_{i+1}\right)$ has a zero point respectively, denoted by $\xi_{i1}=\xi_{i1}(x)$ and $\xi_{i2}=\xi_{i2}(x)$, which all rely on x.

We can continue to use Rolle differential intermediate value theorem, the derivate function $\varphi_i''(t)$ of $\varphi_i'(t)$ in the open interval $\left(\xi_{i1}, \xi_{i2}\right)$ must have a zero point, denoted by $\xi_i=\xi_i(x)$ (certainly, they also rely on x), that is $\varphi_i''\left(\xi_i\right)=0$.

In order to be more convenience, we write the following symbols:

$$\begin{aligned}
&\varphi_i(t)=\varphi_{i1}(t)-\varphi_{i2}(t)-\varphi_{i3}(t),\\
&\varphi_{i1}(t)\triangleq s(t)q_i(t),\ \ \varphi_{i2}(t)\triangleq p_i(t),\\
&\varphi_{i3}(t)\triangleq k(x)\left(t-x_i\right)\left(t-x_{i+1}\right).
\end{aligned}$$

Then we have the following equations:

$$\begin{aligned}
\varphi_{i1}''(t)=&\,s''(t)\left(\mu_{A_i}(t)\Delta y_i+\mu_{A_{i+1}}(t)\Delta y_{i+1}\right)\\
&+2s'(t)\left(\mu_{A_i}'(t)\Delta y_i+\mu_{A_{i+1}}'(t)\Delta y_{i+1}\right)\\
&+s(t)\left(\mu_{A_i}''(t)\Delta y_i+\Delta y_{i+1}\right),\\
\varphi_{i2}''(t)=&\left(\mu_{A_i}''(t)s\left(x_i\right)\Delta y_i+\mu_{A_{i+1}}''(t)s\left(x_{i+1}\right)\Delta y_{i+1}\right),\\
\varphi_{i3}''(t)=&\,2k(x).
\end{aligned}$$

Now substituting $\varphi''_{i1}(\xi_i(x)), \varphi''_{i2}(\xi_i(x)), \varphi''_{i3}(\xi_i(x))$ into $\varphi''_i(\xi_i(x)) = 0$, we have the following equation:

$$k(x) = \frac{1}{2}\left(\varphi''_{i1}(\xi_i(x)) - \varphi''_{i2}(\xi_i(x))\right).$$

And then substituting $k(x)$ into (4.4.7), we have the following equation:

$$\begin{aligned}
r_n(x) &= s(x) - f_n(x) = s(x) - \frac{p_i(x)}{q_i(x)} \\
&= \frac{(x - x_i)(x - x_{i+1})}{2q_i(x)}\left(\varphi''_{i1}(\xi_i(x)) - \varphi''_{i2}(\xi_i(x))\right), \\
i &= 0, 1, \cdots, n-1.
\end{aligned}$$

2) For any $x \in [x_i, x_{i+1}]$, it's easy to learn the following inequality:

$$\begin{aligned}
&\left|(x - x_i)(x - x_{i+1})\right| \\
&\le \left|\left(\frac{x_i + x_{i+1}}{2} - x_i\right)\left(\frac{x_i + x_{i+1}}{2} - x_{i+1}\right)\right| \le \frac{1}{4}\Delta x_i^2.
\end{aligned}$$

Because $q_i(x) > 0$ and $q_i(x)$ is continuous in closed interval $[x_i, x_{i+1}]$, there is a minimal value as the following:

$$C_i = \min\left\{q_i(x) \,\middle|\, x \in [x_i, x_{i+1}]\right\}.$$

Let $C \triangleq \min_{1 \le i \le n-1}\{C_i\}$, and then, we have the following inequalities:

$$\begin{aligned}
&\left|\varphi''_{i1}(\xi_i(x))\right| \le \Delta_{2i}\left(M_2 + 4M_1L_1 + 2M_0L_2\right), \\
&\left|\varphi''_{i2}(\xi_i(x))\right| \le 2M_0L_2\Delta_{2i}.
\end{aligned}$$

Finally, according to the remainder expression, we have the following inequality:

$$
\begin{aligned}
r_i &\triangleq \max_{x\in[x_i,x_{i+1}]}\{|r_n(x)|\} \\
&= \max_{x\in[x_i,x_{i+1}]}\left\{\left|\frac{(x-x_i)(x-x_{i+1})}{2q_i(x)}\left(\varphi''_{i1}(\xi_i(x))-\varphi''_{i2}(\xi_i(x))\right)\right|\right\} \\
&\le \max_{x\in[x_i,x_{i+1}]}\left\{\frac{|(x-x_i)(x-x_{i+1})|}{2q_i(x)}\left(|\varphi''_{i1}(\xi_i(x))|+|\varphi''_{i2}(\xi_i(x))|\right)\right\} \\
&\le \Delta x_i^2\frac{\Delta_{2i}}{8C_i}\left(M_{2i}+4M_{1i}L_{1i}+4M_0L_{2i}\right).
\end{aligned}
$$

Also, because $s(x)$ is continuous function, so we have $\Delta y_i = s'(\xi_i)\Delta x_i$, that is, $\Delta y_i \Leftrightarrow c\cdot\Delta x_i$, where c is a constant. Therefore, we get

$$\|r_n\|_\infty = \max_{0\le i\le n-1}\{r_i\} \le M\Delta_1^3.$$

This is the end of the proof. □

Corollary 4.4.1 In Theorem 4.4.1, if all A_i $(i=0,1,\cdots,n)$ are triangular wave functions, then

1) The approximate remainder representation of $f_n(x)$ to the function $s(x)$ is shown as follows

$$r_n(x) = s(x) - f_n(x) = \varphi''_{i1}(\xi_i(x))\frac{(x-x_i)(x-x_{i+1})}{2q_i(x)} \tag{4.4.9}$$

where $i=0,1,\cdots,n-1$, $x\in[x_i,x_{i+1}]$, $\xi_i\in(x_i,x_{i+1})$, and

$$
\begin{aligned}
&q_i(x) = A_i(x)\Delta y_i + A_{i+1}(x)\Delta y_{i+1}, \\
&\varphi''_{i1}(\xi_i(x)) = s''(\xi_i(x))\left((\xi_i(x)-x_i)\frac{\Delta y_{i+1}}{\Delta x_i}-(\xi_i(x)-x_{i+1})\frac{\Delta y_i}{\Delta x_i}\right) \\
&\qquad\qquad + 2s'(\xi_i(x))\left(\frac{\Delta y_{i+1}}{\Delta x_i}-\frac{\Delta y_i}{\Delta x_i}\right).
\end{aligned}
$$

2) The approximate error estimate expression of $f_n(x)$ to the continuous function $s(x)$ is shown as follows

$$\|r_n\|_\infty \le \frac{\Delta x_i \Delta_{2i}}{8C_i}\left(M_{2i}\Delta x_i + 4M_{1i}\right). \tag{4.4.10}$$

Proof. Firstly, it's easy to understand that, for any $i \in \{0,1,\cdots,n-1\}$, we have the following equations:

$$\mu'_{A_i}(x) = -\frac{1}{\Delta x_i}, \quad \mu'_{A_{i+1}}(x) = \frac{1}{\Delta x_i}, \quad \mu''_{A_i}(x) = 0 = \mu''_{A_{i+1}}(x)$$

Substituting them into the expression of $\varphi''_{i1}\left(\xi_i(x)\right)$ and $\varphi''_{i2}\left(\xi_i(x)\right)$, we get the following inequality:

$$\left|\varphi''_{i1}\left(\xi_i(x)\right)\right| \le \Delta_{2i}\left(M_{2i} + 4M_{1i}\frac{1}{\Delta x_i}\right).$$

And then we have the fact that

$$\begin{aligned} r_i &= \max_{x\in[x_i,x_{i+1}]}\left\{\left|r_n(x)\right|\right\} \\ &= \max_{x\in[x_i,x_{i+1}]}\left|\varphi''_{i1}\left(\xi_i(x)\right)\frac{(x-x_i)(x-x_{i+1})}{2q_i(x)}\right|. \\ &\le \frac{\Delta x_i \Delta_{2i}}{8C_i}\left(M_{2i}\Delta x_i + 4M_{1i}\right). \end{aligned}$$

Finally, we have the inequality: $\|r_n\|_\infty = \max_{0\le i\le n-1} r_i \le M_s \Delta_1^2$, where

$$M_s \triangleq \max_{0\le i\le n-1}\left\{\frac{N}{8C_i}\left(M_{2i}\Delta x_i + 4M_{1i}\right)\right\}.$$

This is the end of the proof. □

4.5 Error Estimation between Fuzzy Systems $\overline{s}_n(x)$ and $f_n(x)$

Now we consider the error estimation problem between fuzzy system $\overline{s}_n(x)$ and $f_n(x)$.

Theorem 4.5.1 Under the conditions of Theorem 4.3.1, for any continuous function $s \in C[a,b]$, write $\overline{r}_n(x) \triangleq f_n(x) - \overline{s}_n(x)$. Suppose that the following condition is satisfied

$$(\forall i \in \{0,1,\cdots,n-1\})\left(\mu_{B_i}(y), \mu_{B_{i+1}}(y) \in C^1\left[y_i, y_{i+1}\right]\right),$$

and $A_i, B_{i+1}, i = 0,1,\cdots,n$ are fuzzy numbers. If the data set IOD satisfies the interpolation condition:

$$(\forall i \in \{0,1,\cdots,n\})\left(y_i = s\left(x_i\right)\right),$$

then we have the following result:

$$\|\overline{r}_n\|_\infty = \|f_n - \overline{s}_n\|_\infty \leq \Gamma \Delta_1^2 \tag{4.5.1}$$

where

$$\Gamma \triangleq 4\frac{2M_0 + 2M_0K_1N + N}{D^2}, \quad P_n(x) \triangleq \sum_{i=0}^{n} \mu_{A_i}(x) y_i \Delta y_i,$$

$$Q_n(x) \triangleq \sum_{i=0}^{n} \mu_{A_i}(x) \Delta y_i, \quad \overline{P} \triangleq \max_{x \in X} \{|P_n(x)|\} \leq 2M_0 \Delta_2,$$

$$\overline{Q} \triangleq \max_{x \in X} \{|Q_n(x)|\} \leq 2\Delta_2,$$

$$D \triangleq \min\left\{\min_{x \in X} \{|Q_n(x)|\}, \min_{x \in X} \int_c^d \mu_R(x,y) \mathrm{d}y\right\},$$

$$K_1 \triangleq \max_{0 \leq i \leq n-1}\left\{\max_{y \in \left[y_{k_i}, y_{k_{i+1}}\right]}\left\{\left|\mu'_{B_{k_i}}(y)\right|\right\}, \max_{y \in \left[y_{k_i}, y_{k_{i+1}}\right]}\left\{\left|\mu'_{B_{k_{i+1}}}(y)\right|\right\}\right\}.$$

Proof. For any $x \in X = [a,b]$, we have the following inequality:

$$|f_n(x)-\overline{s}_n(x)| = \left|\sum_{i=0}^{n}\mu_{A_{k_i}^*}(x)y_{k_i} - \frac{\int_c^d y\mu_R(x,y)\mathrm{d}y}{\int_c^d \mu_R(x,y)\mathrm{d}y}\right|$$

$$= \left|\frac{\sum_{i=0}^{n}\mu_{A_{k_i}}(x)y_{k_i}\Delta y_{k_i}}{\sum_{i=0}^{n}\mu_{A_{k_i}}(x)\Delta y_{k_i}} - \frac{\int_c^d y\mu_R(x,y)\mathrm{d}y}{\int_c^d \mu_R(x,y)\mathrm{d}y}\right| = \left|\frac{P_n(x)}{Q_n(x)} - \frac{\int_c^d y\mu_R(x,y)\mathrm{d}y}{\int_c^d \mu_R(x,y)\mathrm{d}y}\right|$$

$$= \left|\frac{Q_n(x)\left(\int_c^d y\mu_R(x,y)\mathrm{d}y - P_n(x)\right) + P_n(x)\left(Q_n(x) - \int_c^d \mu_R(x,y)\mathrm{d}y\right)}{Q_n(x)\int_c^d \mu_R(x,y)\mathrm{d}y}\right|$$

$$\le \frac{|Q_n(x)|\left|\int_c^d y\mu_R(x,y)\mathrm{d}y - P_n(x)\right| + |P_n(x)|\left|\int_c^d \mu_R(x,y)\mathrm{d}y - Q_n(x)\right|}{|Q_n(x)|\int_c^d \mu_R(x,y)\mathrm{d}y}$$

$$\le \frac{\overline{Q}\left|\int_c^d y\mu_R(x,y)\mathrm{d}y - P_n(x)\right| + \overline{P}\left|\int_c^d \mu_R(x,y)\mathrm{d}y - Q_n(x)\right|}{D^2}$$

Now we separately consider the estimations of the following two absolute values:

$$\left|\int_c^d y\mu_R(x,y)\mathrm{d}y - P_n(x)\right|,\quad \left|\int_c^d \mu_R(x,y)\mathrm{d}y - Q_n(x)\right|$$

1) First we consider the estimation of $\left|\int_c^d y\mu_R(x,y)\mathrm{d}y - P_n(x)\right|$.

By using of the two-phase property of A_{k_i} $(i=0,1,\cdots,n)$, for $x\in X$, we can easily to know the fact: $\exists s,t\in\{0,1,\cdots,n\}$, such that

$$\left(\mu_{A_{k_s}}(x)+\mu_{A_{k_t}}(x)=1\right)\wedge\left(\forall i\notin\{s,t\}\right)\left(\mu_{A_{k_i}}(x)\equiv 0\right),$$

where $\wedge$ means "and". Then we have the following expression:

$$\left|\int_c^d y\mu_R(x,y)\mathrm{d}y - P_n(x)\right|$$
$$= \left|\int_c^d y\left(\bigvee_{j=0}^{n}\left(\mu_{A_{k_j}}(x)\cdot\mu_{B_{k_j}}(y)\right)\right)\mathrm{d}y - \sum_{i=0}^{n}\mu_{A_{k_i}}(x)y_{k_i}\Delta y_{k_i}\right|$$
$$= \left|\int_c^d y\left(\left(\mu_{A_{k_s}}(x)\cdot\mu_{B_{k_s}}(y)\right)\vee\left(\mu_{A_{k_t}}(x)\cdot\mu_{B_{k_t}}(y)\right)\right)\mathrm{d}y\right.$$
$$\left. -\mu_{A_{k_s}}(x)y_{k_s}\Delta y_{k_s} - \mu_{A_{k_t}}(x)y_{k_t}\Delta y_{k_t}\right|.$$

Case 1. $|s-t|=0$, that is $s=t$. At this time, there must be $x=x_{k_s}$, that is, x just in the node x_{k_s}, then $\mu_{A_{k_s}}(x)=1$. We can process the variable y by using Taylor expansion based on three kinds of situations.

Situation 1. $0<s<n$. Refer to Figure 4.5.1, where

$$(\forall y\in Y)\left(B_{k_s}(y)\triangleq\mu_{B_{k_s}}(y)\right).$$

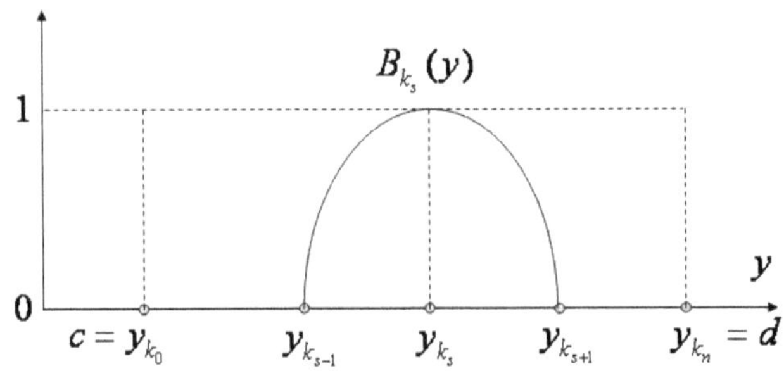

Fig. 4.5.1. The situation of $s=t$ and $0<s<n$

At this situation, there must exist $\eta_{s-1}\in\left(y_{k_{s-1}},y_{k_s}\right)$ and $\eta_s\in\left(y_{k_s},y_{k_{s+1}}\right)$, such that

$$\left|\int_c^d y\mu_R(x,y)\mathrm{d}y - P_n(x)\right| = \left|\int_c^d y\mu_{B_{k_s}}(y)\mathrm{d}y - y_{k_s}\Delta y_{k_s}\right|$$

$$=\left|\int_{y_{k_{s-1}}}^{y_{k_s}} y\mu_{B_{k_s}}(y)\mathrm{d}y+\int_{y_{k_s}}^{y_{k_{s+1}}} y\mu_{B_{k_s}}(y)\mathrm{d}y-y_{k_s}\Delta y_{k_s}\right|$$

$$=\left|\int_{y_{k_{s-1}}}^{y_{k_s}}\left(y_{k_{s-1}}\mu_{B_{k_s}}\left(y_{k_{s-1}}\right)+\left(y\mu_{B_{k_s}}(y)\right)'_{\eta_{s-1}}\left(y-y_{k_{s-1}}\right)\right)\mathrm{d}y\right.$$

$$\left.+\int_{y_{k_s}}^{y_{k_{s+1}}}\left(y_{k_s}\mu_{B_{k_s}}\left(y_{k_s}\right)+\left(y\mu_{B_{k_s}}(y)\right)'_{\eta_s}\left(y-y_{k_s}\right)\right)\mathrm{d}y-y_{k_s}\Delta y_{k_s}\right|$$

$$=\left|\int_{y_{k_{s-1}}}^{y_{k_s}}\left(y\mu_{B_{k_s}}(y)\right)'_{\eta_{s-1}}\left(y-y_{k_{s-1}}\right)\mathrm{d}y+\int_{y_{k_s}}^{y_{k_{s+1}}}\left(y\mu_{B_{k_s}}(y)\right)'_{\eta_s}\left(y-y_{k_s}\right)\mathrm{d}y\right|$$

$$\le\int_{y_{k_{s-1}}}^{y_{k_s}}\left|\left(y\mu_{B_{k_s}}(y)\right)'_{\eta_{s-1}}\left(y-y_{k_{s-1}}\right)\right|\mathrm{d}y+\int_{y_{k_s}}^{y_{k_{s+1}}}\left|\left(y\mu_{B_{k_s}}(y)\right)'_{\eta_s}\left(y-y_{k_s}\right)\right|\mathrm{d}y$$

$$\le\Delta_2^2\max\left\{\left|\left(y\mu_{B_{k_s}}(y)\right)'_{\eta_{s-1}}\right|,\left|\left(y\mu_{B_{k_s}}(y)\right)'_{\eta_s}\right|\right\}\le\Delta_2^2\left(1+M_0K_1\right)$$

Situation 2. $s=0$. Refer to Figure 4.5.2, where $B_{k_0}(y)\triangleq\mu_{B_{k_0}}(y)$. At this situation, there exists $\eta_s\in\left(y_{k_s},y_{k_{s+1}}\right)$, such that

$$\left|\int_c^d y\mu_R(x,y)\mathrm{d}y-P_n(x)\right|=\left|\int_{y_{k_s}}^{y_{k_{s+1}}} y\mu_{B_{k_s}}(y)\mathrm{d}y-y_{k_s}\Delta y_{k_s}\right|\le\frac{\Delta_2^2}{2}\left(1+M_0K_1\right)$$

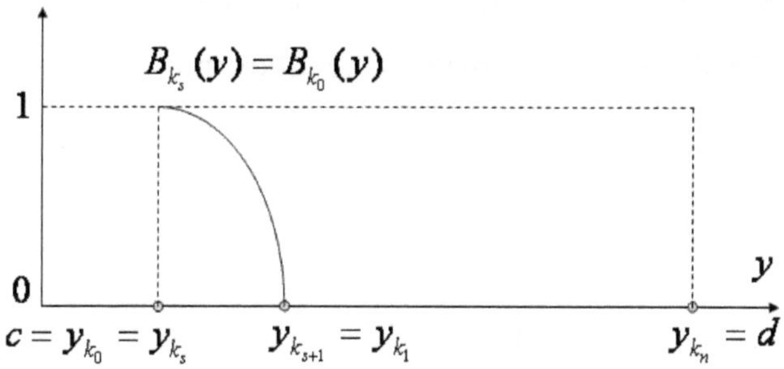

Fig. 4.5.2. The situation of $s=t$ and $s=0$

Situation 3. $s = n$. Refer to Figure 4.5.3, where $B_{k_n}(y) \triangleq \mu_{B_{k_n}}(y)$, and so on in the following figures. Similarly, we have

$$\left|\int_c^d yR(x,y)\mathrm{d}y - P_n(x)\right| \leq \frac{\Delta_2^2}{2}\left(1 + M_0 K_1\right).$$

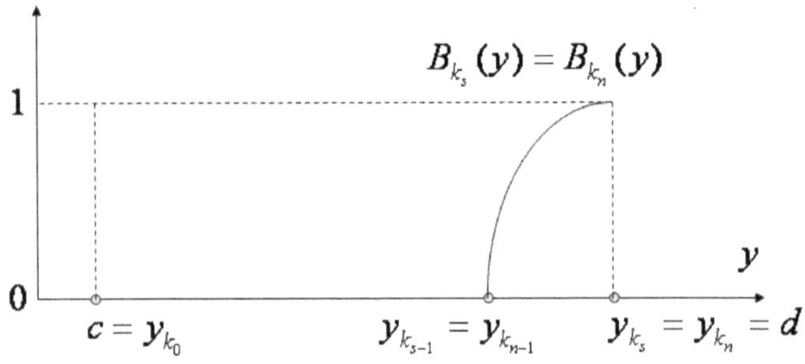

Fig. 4.5.3. The situation of $s = t$ and $s = n$

Case 2. $|s - t| = 1$. We only consider $s < t$, because we can get the same result with $s < t$ or $s < t$. We still process the variable y by using Taylor expansion on three kinds of situations.

a) $0 < s < t < n$. Refer to Figure 4.5.4. Because B_{k_i} $(i = 0, 1, \cdots, n)$ are fuzzy number, there must be a cross point $y^* \in \left(y_{k_s}, y_{k_t}\right)$ between the membership functions $\mu_{A_{k_s}}(x)\mu_{B_{k_s}}(y)$ and $\mu_{A_{k_t}}(x)\mu_{B_{k_t}}(y)$ of fuzzy sets, and then there are four points as the following:

$$\eta_{s-1} \in \left(y_{k_{s-1}}, y_{k_s}\right), \eta_1^* \in \left(y_{k_s}, y^*\right), \eta_2^* \in \left(y^*, y_{k_t}\right), \eta_t \in \left(y_{k_t}, y_{k_{t+1}}\right)$$

such that

$$\left|\int_c^d y\mu_R(x,y)\mathrm{d}y - P_n(x)\right| =$$

$$\left|\int_c^d y\left(\left(\mu_{A_{k_s}}(x)\mu_{B_{k_s}}(y)\right) \vee \left(\mu_{A_{k_t}}(x)\mu_{B_{k_t}}(y)\right)\right)\mathrm{d}y\right.$$

$$-\mu_{A_{k_s}}(x)y_{k_s}\Delta y_{k_s}-\mu_{A_{k_t}}(x)y_{k_t}\Delta y_{k_t}\Big|$$

$$=\Big|\int_{y_{k_{s-1}}}^{y_{k_s}} y\left(\mu_{A_{k_s}}(x)\mu_{B_{k_s}}(y)\right)dy+\int_{y_{k_s}}^{y^*} y\left(\mu_{A_{k_s}}(x)\mu_{B_{k_s}}(y)\right)dy$$

$$+\int_{y^*}^{y_{k_t}} y\left(\mu_{A_{k_t}}(x)\mu_{B_{k_t}}(y)\right)dy+\int_{y_{k_t}}^{y_{k_{t+1}}} y\left(A_{k_t}(x)\mu_{B_{k_t}}(y)\right)dy$$

$$-\mu_{A_{k_s}}(x)y_{k_s}\Delta y_{k_s}-\mu_{A_{k_t}}(x)y_{k_t}\Delta y_{k_t}\Big|$$

$$=\Big|\int_{y_{k_{s-1}}}^{y_{k_s}} \mu_{A_{k_s}}(x)\left(y\mu_{B_{k_s}}(y)\right)'_{\eta_{s-1}}\left(y-y_{k_{s-1}}\right)dy$$

$$+\mu_{A_{k_s}}(x)y_{k_s}\left(y^*-y_{k_s}\right)+\int_{y_{k_s}}^{y^*} \mu_{A_{k_s}}(x)\left(y\mu_{B_{k_s}}(y)\right)'_{\eta_1^*}\left(y-y_{k_{s-1}}\right)dy$$

$$+\mu_{A_{k_t}}(x)y_{k_t}\left(y_{k_t}-y^*\right)+\int_{y^*}^{y_{k_t}} \mu_{A_{k_t}}(x)\left(y\mu_{B_{k_t}}(y)\right)'_{\eta_2^*}\left(y-y^*\right)dy$$

$$+\int_{y_{k_t}}^{y_{k_{t+1}}} \mu_{A_{k_t}}(x)\left(y\mu_{B_{k_t}}(y)\right)'_{\eta_t}\left(y-y_{k_t}\right)dy$$

$$-\mu_{A_{k_s}}(x)y_{k_s}\left(y_{k_{s+1}}-y^*+y^*-y_{k_s}\right)\Big|$$

$$\le 2\Delta_2^2\left(1+M_0K_1\right)+2M_0\Delta_2$$

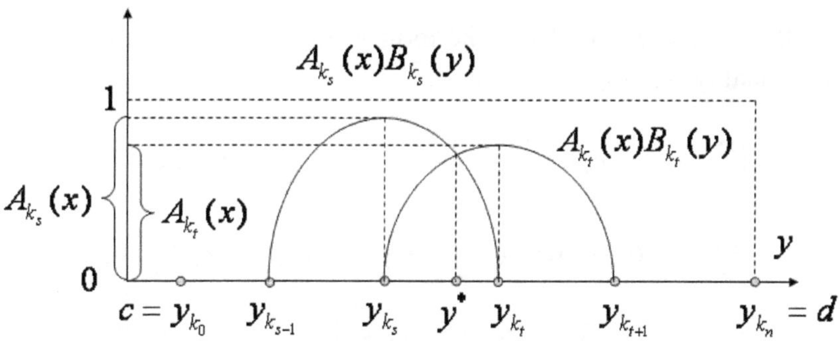

Fig. 4.5.4. The situation of $0<s<t<n$

b) $0 = s < t < n$. Similarly, we can have the following inequality (see Figure 4.5.5):

$$\left|\int_c^d y\mu_R(x,y)\mathrm{d}y - P_n(x)\right| = \left|\int_{y_{k_s}}^{y^*} y\left(\mu_{A_{k_s}}(x)\cdot\mu_{B_{k_s}}(y)\right)\mathrm{d}y\right.$$
$$+\int_{y^*}^{y_{k_t}} y\left(\mu_{A_{k_t}}(x)\cdot\mu_{B_{k_t}}(y)\right)\mathrm{d}y + \int_{y_{k_t}}^{y_{k_{t+1}}} y\left(\mu_{A_{k_t}}(x)\cdot\mu_{B_{k_t}}(y)\right)\mathrm{d}y$$
$$\left.-\mu_{A_{k_s}}(x)y_{k_s}\Delta y_{k_s} - \mu_{A_{k_t}}(x)y_{k_t}\Delta y_{k_t}\right|$$
$$\le \frac{3}{2}\Delta_2^2\left(1+M_0K_1\right)+2M_0\Delta_2$$

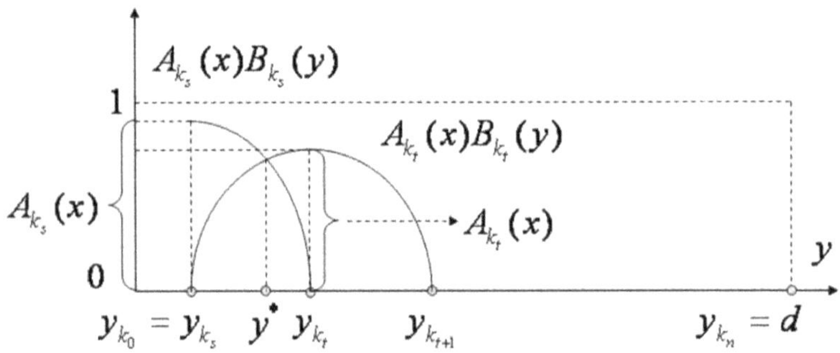

Fig. 4.5.5. The situation of $0 = s < t < n$

c) $0 < s < t = n$. Similar to the former situation, we have the following inequality (see Figure 4.5.6):

$$\left|\int_c^d y\mu_R(x,y)\mathrm{d}y - P_n(x)\right| = \left|\int_{y_{k_{s-1}}}^{y_{k_s}} y\left(\mu_{A_{k_s}}(x)\mu_{B_{k_s}}(y)\right)\mathrm{d}y\right.$$
$$+\int_{y_{k_s}}^{y^*} y\left(\mu_{A_{k_s}}(x)\mu_{B_{k_s}}(y)\right)\mathrm{d}y + \int_{y^*}^{y_{k_t}} y\left(\mu_{A_{k_t}}(x)\mu_{B_{k_t}}(y)\right)\mathrm{d}y$$
$$\left.-\mu_{A_{k_s}}(x)y_{k_s}\Delta y_{k_s} - \mu_{A_{k_t}}(x)y_{k_t}\Delta y_{k_t}\right|$$
$$\le \frac{3}{2}\Delta_2^2\left(1+M_0K_1\right)+2M_0\Delta_2$$

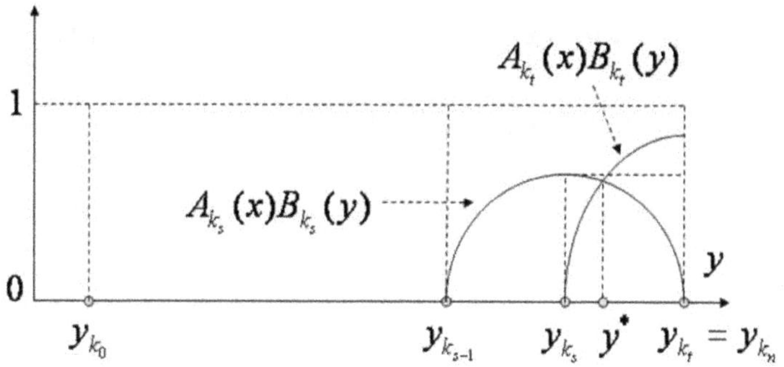

Fig. 4.5.6. The situation of $0 < s < t = n$

Case 3. $|s-t| > 1$. Assume that $s < t$, and the situation for $s > t$ is the same. We can process the variable y by using Taylor expansion on four kinds of situation.

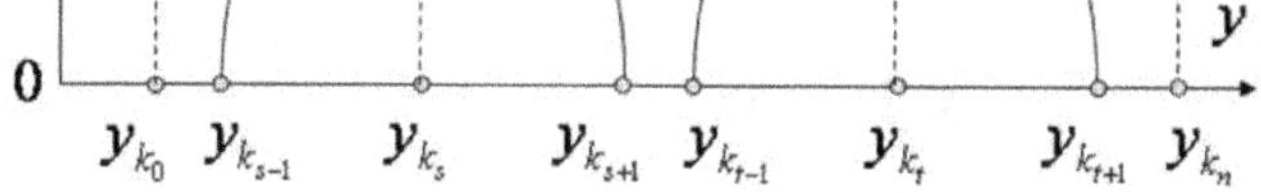

Fig. 4.5.7. The situation of $|s-t| > 1$ and $0 < s < t < n$

a) $0 < s < t < n$. For this situation, we have the following inequality (see Figure 4.5.7):

$$\left|\int_c^d y\mu_R(x,y)\mathrm{d}y - P_n(x)\right| = \left|\int_{y_{k_{s-1}}}^{y_{k_s}} y\mu_{A_{k_s}}(x)\mu_{B_{k_s}}(y)\mathrm{d}y\right.$$

$$+\int_{y_{k_s}}^{y_{k_{s+1}}} y\mu_{A_{k_s}}(x)\mu_{B_{k_s}}(y)\mathrm{d}y - \mu_{A_{k_s}}(x)y_{k_s}\Delta y_{k_s}$$

$$+\int_{y_{k_{t-1}}}^{y_{k_t}} y\mu_{A_{k_t}}(x)\mu_{B_{k_t}}(y)\mathrm{d}y+\int_{y_{k_t}}^{y_{k_{t+1}}} y\mu_{A_{k_t}}(x)\mu_{B_{k_t}}(y)\mathrm{d}y$$

$$-\mu_{A_{k_t}}(x)y_{k_t}\Delta y_{k_t}\Big|\le 2\Delta_2^2\left(1+M_0K_1\right)$$

b) $0=s<t<n$. It is easy to know the following inequality (see Figure 4.5.8):

$$\left|\int_c^d y\mu_R(x,y)\mathrm{d}y-P_n(x)\right|=\left|\int_{y_{k_s}}^{y_{k_{s+1}}} y\mu_{A_{k_s}}(x)\mu_{B_{k_s}}(y)\mathrm{d}y\right.$$

$$+\int_{y_{k_{t-1}}}^{y_{k_t}} y\mu_{A_{k_t}}(x)\mu_{B_{k_t}}(y)\mathrm{d}y+\int_{y_{k_t}}^{y_{k_{t+1}}} y\mu_{A_{k_t}}(x)\mu_{B_{k_t}}(y)\mathrm{d}y$$

$$\left.-\mu_{A_{k_s}}(x)y_{k_s}\Delta y_{k_s}-\mu_{A_{k_t}}(x)y_{k_t}\Delta y_{k_t}\right|\le\frac{3\Delta_2^2}{2}\left(1+M_0K_1\right)$$

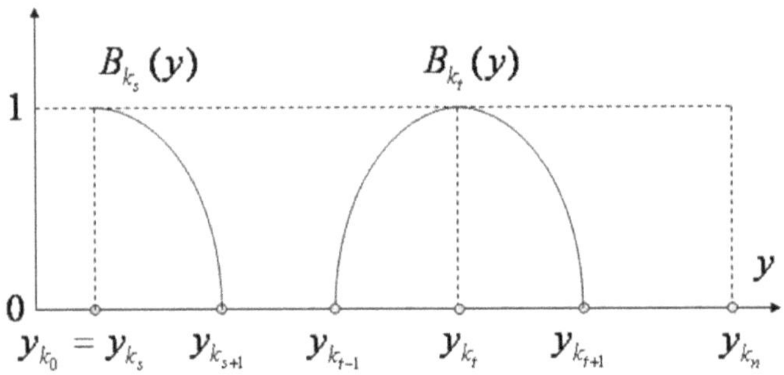

Fig. 4.5.8. The situation of $|s-t|>1$ and $0=s<t<n$

c) $0<s<t=n$. Also we can easily know the following inequality (see Figure 4.5.9):

$$\left|\int_c^d y\mu_R(x,y)\mathrm{d}y-P_n(x)\right|=\left|\int_{y_{k_{s-1}}}^{y_{k_s}} y\mu_{A_{k_s}}(x)\mu_{B_{k_s}}(y)\mathrm{d}y\right.$$

$$+\int_{y_{k_s}}^{y_{k_{s+1}}} y\mu_{A_{k_s}}(x)\mu_{B_{k_s}}(y)\mathrm{d}y+\int_{y_{k_{t-1}}}^{y_{k_t}} y\mu_{A_{k_t}}(x)\mu_{B_{k_t}}(y)\mathrm{d}y$$

$$-\mu_{A_{k_s}}(x)y_{k_s}\Delta y_{k_s}-\mu_{A_{k_t}}(x)y_{k_t}\Delta y_{k_t}\Big|\le\frac{3\Delta_2^2}{2}(1+M_0K_1)$$

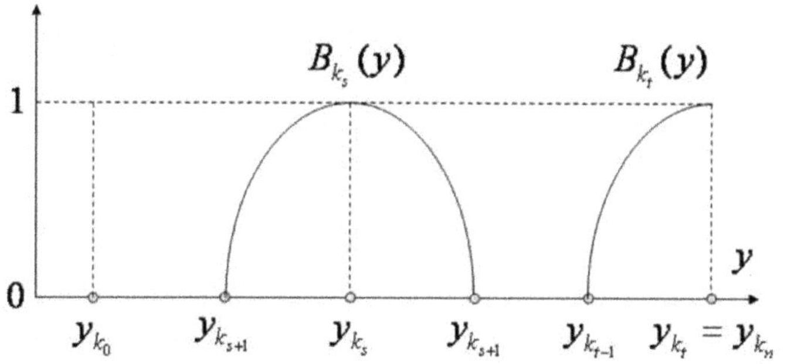

Fig. 4.5.9. The situation of $|s-t|>1$ and $0<s<t=n$

d) $0=s<t=n$. At last, we can know the following inequality:

$$\left|\int_c^d y\mu_R(x,y)\mathrm{d}y-P_n(x)\right|=\left|\int_{y_{k_s}}^{y_{k_{s+1}}} y\mu_{A_{k_s}}(x)\mu_{B_{k_s}}(y)\mathrm{d}y\right.$$

$$\left.+\int_{y_{k_{t-1}}}^{y_{k_t}} y\mu_{A_{k_t}}(x)\mu_{B_{k_t}}(y)\mathrm{d}y-\mu_{A_{k_s}}(x)y_{k_s}\Delta y_{k_s}-\mu_{A_{k_t}}(x)y_{k_t}\Delta y_{k_t}\right|$$

$$\le\Delta_2^2(1+M_0K_1)$$

For all three kinds of cases, we get the inequality:

$$\left|\int_c^d \mu_R(x,y)\mathrm{d}y-Q_n(x)\right|\le 2\Delta_2^2(1+M_0K_1)+2M_0\Delta_2.$$

2) Now, we turn to the estimation of $\left|\int_c^d \mu_R(x,y)\mathrm{d}y-Q_n(x)\right|$.

In fact, we also use the two phase property on $A_i\ (i=0,1,\cdots,n)$. For a given point $x\in X$, we know the following fact:

$$(\exists s,t\in\{0,1,\cdots,n\})\left(\mu_{A_{k_s}}(x)+\mu_{A_{k_t}}(x)=1\right).$$

Then we have the following equation:

$$\left|\int_c^d \mu_R(x,y)\mathrm{d}y - Q_n(x)\right|$$
$$=\left|\int_c^d \left(\bigvee_{j=0}^{n}\left(\mu_{A_{k_j}}(x)\mu_{B_{k_j}}(y)\right)\right)\mathrm{d}y - \sum_{i=0}^{n}\mu_{A_{k_i}}(x)\Delta y_{k_i}\right|$$
$$=\left|\int_c^d \left(\left(\mu_{A_{k_s}}(x)\mu_{B_{k_s}}(y)\right)\vee\left(\mu_{A_{k_t}}(x)\mu_{B_{k_t}}(y)\right)\right)\mathrm{d}y\right.$$
$$\left. - \mu_{A_{k_s}}(x)\Delta y_{k_s} - \mu_{A_{k_t}}(x)\Delta y_{k_t}\right|$$

Case 1. $|s-t|=0$, that is $s=t$. Similarly, we process the variable y by using Taylor expansion on three kinds of situation, and get the following results:

a) $0<s<n \Rightarrow \left|\int_c^d \mu_R(x,y)\mathrm{d}y - Q_n(x)\right| \le K_1\Delta_2^2$.

b) $s=0 \Rightarrow \left|\int_c^d \mu_R(x,y)\mathrm{d}y - Q_n(x)\right| \le \frac{\Delta_2^2}{2}K_1$.

c) $s=n \Rightarrow \left|\int_c^d \mu_R(x,y)\mathrm{d}y - Q_n(x)\right| \le \frac{\Delta_2^2}{2}K_1$.

Case 2. $|s-t|=1$. Assume that $s<t$ and for $s>t$, the situation is the same. We still process the variable y by using Taylor expansion on three kinds of situation.

a) $0<s<t<n \Rightarrow \left|\int_c^d \mu_R(x,y)\mathrm{d}y - Q_n(x)\right| \le 2\Delta_2^2K_1 + 2\Delta_2$.

b) $0=s<t<n \Rightarrow \left|\int_c^d \mu_R(x,y)\mathrm{d}y - Q_n(x)\right| \le \frac{3}{2}\Delta_2^2K_1 + 2\Delta_2$.

c) $0<s<t=n \Rightarrow \left|\int_c^d R(x,y)\mathrm{d}y - Q_n(x)\right| \le \frac{3}{2}\Delta_2^2K_1 + 2\Delta_2$.

Case 3. $|s-t|>1$. Assume that $s<t$ and for $s>t$, the situation is the same. We can process the variable y by using Taylor expansion on four kinds of situations as the following:

a) $0 < s < t < n \Rightarrow \left|\int_c^d \mu_R(x, y)\mathrm{d}y - Q_n(x)\right| \le 2\Delta_2^2 K_1.$

b) $0 = s < t < n \Rightarrow \left|\int_c^d y\mu_R(x, y)\mathrm{d}y - P_n(x)\right| \le \frac{3\Delta_2^2}{2} K_1.$

c) $0 < s < t = n \Rightarrow \left|\int_c^d \mu_R(x, y)\mathrm{d}y - Q_n(x)\right| \le \frac{3\Delta_2^2}{2} K_1.$

d) $0 = s < t = n \Rightarrow \left|\int_c^d \mu_R(x, y)\mathrm{d}y - Q_n(x)\right| \le \Delta_2^2 K_1.$

For all three kinds of cases, we get the following inequality:

$$\left|\int_c^d \mu_R(x, y)\mathrm{d}y - Q_n(x)\right| \le 2\Delta_2^2 K_1 + 2\Delta_2 .$$

In the end, according to the results of 1) and 2), we have

$$\begin{aligned}
&\left|\overline{s}_n(x) - f_n(x)\right| \\
&\le \frac{\overline{Q}\left|\int_c^d y\mu_R(x, y)\mathrm{d}y - P_n(x)\right| + \overline{P}\left|\int_c^d \mu_R(x, y)\mathrm{d}y - Q_n(x)\right|}{D^2} \\
&\le 2\frac{2\Delta_2\left(\Delta_2^2\left(1 + M_0K_1\right) + M_0\Delta_2\right) + 2M_0\Delta_2\left(\Delta_2^2K_1 + \Delta_2\right)}{D^2} \\
&= 4\frac{2M_0 + 2M_0K_1\Delta_2 + \Delta_2}{D^2}\Delta_2^2
\end{aligned}$$

Because of $\Delta_2 \Leftrightarrow c\Delta_1$, we can write $\Gamma \triangleq 4\frac{2M_0 + 2M_0K_1N + N}{D^2}$, therefore we have the result:

$$\left\|\overline{r}_n\right\|_\infty = \left\|\overline{s}_n - f_n\right\|_\infty = \max_{x\in X}\left\{\left|\overline{s}_n(x) - f_n(x)\right|\right\} \le \Gamma\Delta_1^2$$

The theorem is completely proved. □

Corollary 4.5.1 In Theorem 4.5.1, when all B_i $(i = 0,1,\cdots,n)$ are triangular fuzzy sets, then Γ in (5.1) turn into the following equation:

$$\Gamma = 4\frac{2M_0 + 2M_0 N_0 + N}{D^2} \tag{4.5.2}$$

where $N_0 = \max_{0 \le i \le n-1} \left\{ \frac{\Delta_2}{\Delta y_i} \right\}$. □

According to the results of Theorem 4.4.1 and Theorem 4.5.1, we can get the conclusion that we need and is shown as the following theorem.

Theorem 4.5.2 In the conclusion of Theorem 4.4.1 and Theorem 4.5.1, if we write $r_n^*(x) \triangleq s(x) - \overline{s}_n(x)$, then we have the following inequality:

$$\begin{aligned} \|r_n^*\|_\infty &= \|s - \overline{s}_n\|_\infty \le \|s - f_n\|_\infty + \|f_n - \overline{s}_n\|_\infty \\ &= \|r_n\|_\infty + \|\overline{r}_n\|_\infty \le (M\Delta_1 + \Gamma)\Delta_1^2 \end{aligned} \tag{4.5.3}$$

where the meanings of symbols M, Γ, Δ_1 have been provided in Theorem 4.4.1 and Theorem 4.5.1. □

4.7 Conclusions

In this section, function approximation effect analysis of fuzzy systems is researched in details. First, the structures of fuzzy systems are discussed where a kind of important structure formed by so-called CRI method and the gravity method defuzzification and Larsen implication operator. Second, it is proved that this kind of fuzzy systems can approximate any real continuous function to arbitrary accuracy in a general sense. Third, the error estimate of the function approximation is given.

Function approximation property and approximation effect analysis of fuzzy systems are essentially belonging to function approximation theory in real analysis or mathematical analysis. So we should adequately use classical tools of real analysis or mathematical analysis to study fuzzy systems.

References

1. Zadeh, L. A. (1973). Outline of a new approach to the analysis of complex systems and decision processes, IEEE Trans. SMC, 3, pp. 28–44.
2. Li, H. X. (1998). Interpolation mechanism of fuzzy control. Science in China (Series E), 41(3), pp. 312-320.
3. Li, H. X. (2006). Probability representations of fuzzy systems, China Science (F Series), 49(3), pp. 339-363.
4. Castro, J. L. (1995). Fuzzy logic controllers are universal approximators, IEEE Trans. SMC, 25, pp. 629–635.
5. Buckley, J. J. (1993). Sugeno type controllers are universal controllers, Fuzzy Sets Syst., 53, pp. 299–304.
6. Liu, P. Y. and Li, H. X. (2005). Approximation of stochastic processes by T–S fuzzy systems, Fuzzy sets and systems, Fuzzy Sets and Systems, 155, pp. 215–235.
7. Li, H. X. and C.L. Philip Chen. (2000). The equivalence between fuzzy logic systems and feedforward neural networks, IEEE Transactions on Neural Networks, 11(2), pp. 356-365.
8. Liu, P. Y. and Li, H. X. (2001). Analyses for $L_p(\mu)$-norm approximation capability of Mamdani fuzzy systems, Information Science, 138, pp. 195-210.
9. Li, Y. M., Shi, Z. K., and Li, Z. H. (2002). Approximation theory of fuzzy systems based upon genuine many-valued implications—SISO cases, Fuzzy Sets Syst., 130, pp. 147–157.
10. Zadeh, L. A. (1978). Fuzzy sets as a basic for a theory of possibility, Fuzzy Sets and Systems, 1, pp. 3-28.
11. Li, Y. M., Shi, Z. K., and Li, Z. H. (2002). Approximation theory of fuzzy systems based upon genuine many-valued implications—MIMO cases, Fuzzy Sets Syst., 130, pp. 159–174.
12. Tikk, D., Koczy, L. T. and Gedeon, T. D. (2003). A survey on universal approximation and its limits in soft computing techniques, International Journal of Approximate Reasoning, 33, pp. 185–202
13. Zeng, X. J. and Singh, M. G. (2000). Approximation accuracy analysis of fuzzy systems as function approximators. IEEE Trans. Fuzzy Systems, 4(1), pp. 44-59.

Chapter 5

Probability Representations of Fuzzy Systems

5.1 Background of Birth of Fuzzy Systems

In this Chapter, the probability-theoretical meaning of fuzzy systems is opened out and it is pointed out that COG method that is a defuzzification technique used commonly in fuzzy systems is reasonable and is optimal method in the sense of average square. Based on different fuzzy implication operators, several typical probability distributions such as Zadeh distribution, Mamdani distribution, Lukasiewicz distribution, etc. are given. They act as "inner kernels" of fuzzy systems. Furthermore, by some properties of probability distributions of fuzzy systems, it is also demonstrated that CRI method, proposed by Zadeh, for construction of fuzzy systems is logical basically and effective. Besides, the special action of uniform probability distributions in fuzzy systems is characterized. Finally, the relation between CRI method and triple I method is discussed. In the sense of construction of fuzzy systems, when restricting three fuzzy implication operators in triple I method to same one operator, for relation between CRI method and triple I method, the following three basic situations happen: 1) Two methods are equivalent; 2) The latter is degeneration of the former; 3) The latter is ordinary whereas the former is not ordinary. When three fuzzy implication operators in triple I method are not restricted to same one operator, CRI method is a special example of triple I method, that is, triple I method is a more comprehensive algorithm. Since triple I method has good logical foundation and comprises an idea of optimization of reasoning, triple I method shall possess beautiful foreground of application.

It is well-known that just due to consideration of abundant uncertain systems Zadeh put forward the notion of fuzzy sets and formed the fuzzy reasoning by means of fuzzy sets, thereby could express a system approximately [1]. Such systems constructed on the basis of fuzzy reasoning are called fuzzy systems in general [2–4]. The research that takes fuzzy systems as object has engaged broad attention of scholars [5–7]. For instance, universal approximation property of fuzzy systems is an aspect which the researchers take pleasure in studying [8,9]. If a fuzzy system serves as a controller then it also shapes fuzzy control theory that is a research discipline having extremely strong applicability [10,11]. However, one must pay attention to difference between fuzzy systems and fuzzy controllers. The fuzzy systems are distinguished to open-loop systems and closed-loop systems, and the universal approximation property of fuzzy systems is discussed for open-loop fuzzy systems as a rule. Meanwhile, fuzzy controllers are a kind of closed-loop fuzzy systems. In particular, for the fuzzy controller with adaptive function (like the variable universe adaptive fuzzy controller), one should be careful in the study of its universal approximation properties, since there does not exist a fixed and invariant function to be approximated and the object it need to approximate is a stochastic process.

We first of all talk about the background of birth of fuzzy systems. Figure 1.3.1 has shown a single-input single-output open-loop system. The input variable x takes values in the input universe X and the output variable y takes values in the output universe Y. If this system S is a deterministic system then one may use the conventional method to make a mathematical model of the system S (for example, one can use the mechanism modeling approach to establish a differential equation model) and find a solution $y(x)$ of the model by analytic or numerical methods. In this way, one think that this system has been mastered basically (the more in-depth questions are of qualitative problems, i.e., controllability, observability, stability, etc.). Then the system S may be simply understood by a functional relationship, denoted by s, i.e.,

$$s: X \to Y, \quad x \mapsto y = s(x). \tag{5.1.1}$$

However, for an uncertain system, we cannot use the conventional method to make an "accurate" mathematical model of the system S (we usually indicate the differential equation model), and so it is very difficult to obtain the functional relationship like (5.1.1). This shows that it is the too high request for an uncertain system S to directly obtain the correspondence relationship between crisp points $x \in X$ and crisp points $y \in Y$.

Without more ado, decreasing the request, we first try to obtain a correspondence relationship, denoted by the following mapping s^*, between the "rough" points as being $A \in \mathcal{A} \subset \mathcal{F}(X)$ and "rough" points as being $B \in \mathcal{B} \subset \mathcal{F}(Y)$, i.e.,

$$s^* : \mathcal{A} \to \mathcal{B}, \quad A \mapsto B \triangleq s^*(A), \tag{5.1.2}$$

where $\mathcal{F}(X)$ and $\mathcal{F}(Y)$ are the set of all fuzzy sets on X and the set of all fuzzy sets on Y, respectively, and $\mathcal{A}$ and $\mathcal{B}$ are a subset of $\mathcal{F}(X)$ and a subset of $\mathcal{F}(Y)$, respectively. How many elements should $\mathcal{A}$ and $\mathcal{B}$ contain in $\mathcal{F}(X)$ and $\mathcal{F}(Y)$, respectively?

The fundamental principle to answer this question is to consider whether the numbers of elements in $\mathcal{A}$ and $\mathcal{B}$ are enough to employ. For brevity, we customarily choose the finite sets for $\mathcal{A}$ and $\mathcal{B}$.

Obviously, the function s^* is just a correspondence relationship between some "sparsely distributed" representative points in $\mathcal{F}(X)$ and some "sparsely distributed" representative points in $\mathcal{F}(Y)$, and is not enough for the requirement to be satisfied (from the viewpoint of systems, this indicates that under the certain inputs there shall happen the phenomena such that the system has not responses). Hence, after obtaining of s^* we again extend s^* to a correspondence relationship, denoted by s^{**}, from $\mathcal{F}(X)$ to $\mathcal{F}(Y)$, i.e.,

$$s^{**} : \mathcal{F}(X) \to \mathcal{F}(Y), \quad A \mapsto B \triangleq s^{**}(A). \tag{5.1.3}$$

And then, we have to brain storm to transform s^{**} to a correspondence relationship, denoted by $\overline{s}$, between crisp points $x \in X$ and crisp points

$y \in Y$, i.e.,

$$\bar{s} : X \to Y, \quad x \mapsto y \triangleq \bar{s}(x). \tag{5.1.4}$$

If this method is "felicitous" then we regard the function $\bar{s}(x)$ as an approximation of function $s(x)$.

In this way, we think that the uncertain system S has been mastered basically.

For the uncertain system S, although we could not obtain the functional relationship $s(x)$ expressing the system through conventional method, we went around a big bend: Letting the clear functional relationship $s(x)$ be the pre-assumed target, we first attempted to obtain a "rough" functional relationship $s^*(x)$, next expanded it to $s^{**}(x)$, and finally arrived at a clear functional relationship $\bar{s}(x)$. From the viewpoint of result of construction of fuzzy systems, it is nothing but to obtain the clear functional relationship. Henceforth, we shall not distinguish the word of fuzzy system from the functional relationship $\bar{s}$. Of course, this is an understanding in narrow sense about the fuzzy system [12,13].

If we have a certain method that can realize the above transformation process from $s^*(x)$ to $\bar{s}(x)$, then it is naturally asked whether our method is felicitous or not, in other words, whether or not $\bar{s}(x)$ can approximate $s(x)$ commendably. This is the headstream of study of universal approximation property of fuzzy systems. A fuzzy system $\bar{s}(x)$ is said to have universal approximation property if for a given function $s(x)$ satisfying some conditions and for any $\varepsilon > 0$ there exists a construction of $\bar{s}$ such that $\|\bar{s} - s\|$, where $\|\cdot\|$ denotes the norm in a normed linear space where $s(x)$ and $\bar{s}(x)$ are defined.

5.2 Sketch of Fuzzy Systems

We first discuss the construction of function s^*. For convenience, restrict the input universe X and the output universe Y into a one-dimensional real space $\mathbb{R}$, i.e., $X, Y \in \mathcal{B}^1$, where $\mathcal{B}^1$ is one-dimensional Borel σ-field. Select the following fuzzy set classes:

$$\mathcal{A} = \{A_i | 1 \le i \le n\} \subset \mathcal{F}(X),$$
$$\mathcal{B} = \{B_i | 1 \le i \le n\} \subset \mathcal{F}(Y)$$

The fuzzy sets A_i and B_i are called the linguistic values. $\mathcal{A}$ and $\mathcal{B}$ are regarded as linguistic variables and take values A_i and B_i in their "abdomens", respectively. With them, we form n rules of fuzzy reasoning:

$$\text{If } x \text{ is } A_i \text{ then } y \text{ is } B_i, \quad i = 1, 2, \cdots, n. \tag{5.2.1}$$

Relative to linguistic variables $\mathcal{A}$ and $\mathcal{B}$, $x \in X$ and $y \in Y$ are called basic underlying variables. Thus we obtain the following functional relationship:

$$s^* : \mathcal{A} \to \mathcal{B}, \quad A_i \mapsto s^*(A_i) \triangleq B_i, \quad i = 1, \cdots, n. \tag{5.2.2}$$

We next consider how to gained function s^{**}. In (5.2.1), the ith rule of reasoning forms a fuzzy relation $R_i \in \mathcal{F}(X \times Y)$ (called also a truth domain) related to this rule. That is determined by a certain implication operator[14-17] $\theta : [0,1]^2 \to [0,1]$, i.e.,

$$\mu_{R_i}(x, y) \triangleq \theta\left(\mu_{A_i}(x), \mu_{B_i}(y)\right), \quad i = 1, 2, \cdots, n.$$

Doing coupling between these n rules by "OR" (it corresponds to set operation "join") naturally, we can form the total fuzzy relation of the fuzzy reasoning $R \triangleq \bigcup_{i=1}^{n} R_i$, i.e.,

$$\mu_R(x, y) = \bigvee_{i=1}^{n} \mu_{R_i}(x, y) = \bigvee_{i=1}^{n} \theta\left(\mu_{A_i}(x), \mu_{B_i}(y)\right). \tag{5.2.3}$$

The handling process to form total fuzzy relation of fuzzy reasoning R through all "partial relations of reasoning" R_i is called the "relation synthesis".

Remark 5.2.1 Due to (5.2.3), we easily see that the tool of realization of relation synthesis is binary operation on $[0,1]$, e.g.,

$$\begin{aligned} &\vee:[0,1]^2 \to [0,1] \\ &(a,b) \mapsto \vee(a,b) = a \vee b \triangleq \max(a,b) \end{aligned}$$

which we take pleasure in use. In general, we may use triangular conorm, denoted by ∇. For instance, $\nabla = \oplus$, called the bounded sum operator, is also usually considered internally:

$$\begin{aligned} &\oplus:[0,1]^2 \to [0,1] \\ &(a,b) \mapsto \oplus(a,b) = a \oplus b \triangleq (a+b) \wedge 1 \end{aligned} \tag{5.2.4}$$

For any a given fuzzy set $A \in \mathcal{F}(X)$, we can obtain a result of fuzzy reasoning $B \in \mathcal{F}(Y)$ through total fuzzy relation of fuzzy reasoning R. This corresponds to deriving a fuzzy transformation, denoted as "$\circ$", from $\mathcal{F}(X)$ to $\mathcal{F}(Y)$ in terms of the fuzzy relation R, i.e.,

$$\begin{aligned} &\circ: \mathcal{F}(X) \to \mathcal{F}(Y) \\ &A \to B = \circ(A) \triangleq A \circ R \end{aligned} \tag{5.2.5}$$

How to realize $A \circ R$? This is a quite dainty problem and is worthy of discussion. As a rule, $B \triangleq A \circ R$ is stated as the following:

$$\mu_B(y) = \bigvee_{x \in X} (\mu_A(x) \wedge \mu_R(x,y)), \quad y \in Y. \tag{5.2.6}$$

This implies that we have constructed a kind of functional relationship $s^{**} = \circ$, i.e.,

$$\begin{aligned} &s^{**}: \mathcal{F}(X) \to \mathcal{F}(Y) \\ &A \mapsto B = s^{**}(A) \triangleq A \circ R \end{aligned} \tag{5.2.7}$$

□

Remark 5.2.2 One may see that realization of fuzzy transformation $A \circ R$ needs a pair of binary operations on $[0,1]$, e.g., $(\wedge, \vee)$ used in (5.2.6). In general, one should adopt a pair (Δ, ∇) of triangular norm and triangular conorm, where Δ denotes a triangular norm. For example, multiplication and bounded sum constitute a pair of operators $(\cdot, \oplus)$ that has wonderful analytical properties. □

Remark 5.2.3 The handling process from s^* to s^{**} is just CRI (**Compositional Rule of Inference**) algorithm, proposed by Zadeh, that is widely used and extensively employed[1–4,18,19]. However, it is still disputed whether CRI method is reasonable or not[20–23]. The latter result in the present paper will show that CRI method is reasonable on the whole case. □

We finally consider the construction of function $\overline{s}$. For any a given point $x' \in X$, in order to use (5.2.6), it needs to make fuzzification to x'. How to do the fuzzification? The approaches vary and the singleton fuzzification is used mostly at present. Namely, define a singleton fuzzy set A' as follows:

$$\chi_{A'}(x) = \begin{cases} 1, & x = x' \\ 0, & x \neq x'. \end{cases} \tag{5.2.8}$$

Substituting A' into (5.2.6), we obtain result of reasoning $B' \in \mathcal{F}(Y)$ as follows:

$$\mu_{B'}(y) = \mu_R(x', y) = \bigvee_{i=1}^{n} \theta\left(\mu_{A_i}(x'), \mu_{B_i}(y)\right). \tag{5.2.9}$$

Since B' is a fuzzy set, we have to obtain exact quantity $y' \in Y$ by a defuzzification technique. If we are of the following condition:

$$\int_Y |y| B'(y)\mathrm{d}y < +\infty, \quad 0 < \int_Y B'(y)\mathrm{d}y < +\infty$$

then we often use "COG (center of gravity) method" to obtain y', i.e.,

$$y' = \frac{\int_Y y\mu_{B'}(y)\mathrm{d}y}{\int_Y \mu_{B'}(y)\mathrm{d}y}. \tag{5.2.10}$$

Noticing that notations x' and y' have been made simply for clarity when deriving (5.2.10), we gained the following functional relationship by rewriting x' as x and by replacing y' with $\overline{s}(x)$:

$$\overline{s} : X \to Y, \quad x \mapsto \overline{s}(x) \triangleq \frac{\int_Y y\mu_{B'}(y)\mathrm{d}y}{\int_Y \mu_{B'}(y)\mathrm{d}y} \tag{5.2.11}$$

As shown in Figure 5.2.1, consider how to transform a "rough quantity" $B' \in \mathcal{F}(Y)$ on Y to an exact quantity y' in Y. Starting from physical intuitive concept, COG method is a technique that is most easily accepted by persons. But, physical intuitive thing cannot replace rational mathematical expression. Then, whether or not COG method is assuredly reasonable? Whether there is any potential mathematical law in the back-side of COG method? This is an important problem worthy of discussion.

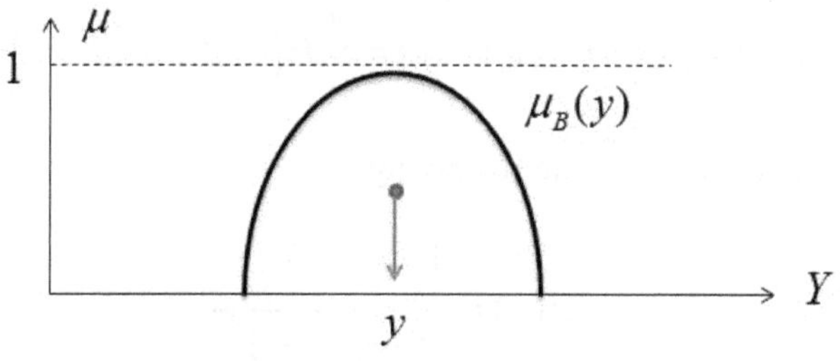

Fig. 5.2.1. Center of gravity

5.3 Probability Significance of Fuzzy Systems

A new discovery scientific researches is sometimes such a process: first carefully observe something of which it is worthy to get to the bottom, and then obtain some feeling through comparison and association, thereby produce a light of new idea and even set a piece of prairie ablaze.

Herein, we consider (5.2.10) carefully and look at that this thing been from physics and which well-known expression in mathematics are alike eventually. For clarity, we note that $\mu_{B'}(y)$ in (5.2.10) is related to input x'. With this understanding, we should denote $B' \triangleq B(x=x')$ and denote $\mu_{B'}(y)$ by the following symbol:

$$\mu_{B'(x=x')}(y) \triangleq \mu_{B'}(y), \tag{5.3.1}$$

which implies that we obtain "rough" output $B' \in \mathcal{F}(Y)$ under condition $x=x'$. Noticing arbitrariness of $x' \in X$, we rewrite $\mu_{B'(x=x')}(y)$ as the form of a bivariate function $p: X \times Y \to \mathbb{R}$ without more ado:

$$\begin{aligned} p(x',y) &\triangleq \mu_{B'(x=x')}(y) = \mu_{B'}(y) \\ &= \mu_R(x',y) = \mathop{\vee}_{i=1}^{n} \theta\left(\mu_{A_i}(x'), \mu_{B_i}(y)\right) \end{aligned}$$

Because point $x = x' \in X$ is arbitrarily chosen in X, we can rewrite above equation as the following:

$$p(x,y) = \mu_B(y) = \mu_R(x,y) = \mathop{\vee}_{i=1}^{n} \theta\left(\mu_{A_i}(x), \mu_{B_i}(y)\right) \tag{5.3.2}$$

Then, (5.2.11) changes to the following:

$$\overline{s}(x) = \frac{\int_Y y p(x,y) \mathrm{d}y}{\int_Y p(x,y) \mathrm{d}y}. \tag{5.3.3}$$

For the sake of more clarity, we expand $p(x,y)$ to a function, denoted by $q(x,y)$, on $\mathbb{R}^2$, as the follows:

$$\begin{aligned} q(x,y) &\triangleq p(x,y)\chi_{X\times Y} \triangleq p(x,y)\chi_{X\times Y}(x,y) \\ &\triangleq \begin{cases} p(x,y), & (x,y) \in X \times Y \\ 0, & (x,y) \notin X \times Y, \end{cases} \end{aligned} \tag{5.3.4}$$

where $\chi_{X\times Y}(x,y)$ is characteristic function of set $X\times Y$ and $p(x,y)\chi_{X\times Y}$ is a shortening of $p(x,y)\chi_{X\times Y}(x,y)$, and henceforth we shall write expressions according to these notations.

Notice that in (5.3.3) if replace $p(x,y)$ with $q(x,y)$ then it corresponds to extending of function $\overline{s}(x)$ to a function, denoted by $\overline{\overline{s}}(x)$ for example, on $\mathbb{R}$, and so we apparently define $\overline{\overline{s}}(x)\triangleq\overline{s}(x)\chi_X$. But, for briefness, we still denote $\overline{\overline{s}}(x)$ by $\overline{s}(x)$. This promise shall be valid for all of below similar situations as well. Thus (5.3.3) can be written as the following:

$$\overline{s}(x)=\frac{\int_{-\infty}^{+\infty} yq(x,y)\mathrm{d}y}{\int_{-\infty}^{+\infty} q(x,y)\mathrm{d}y}. \tag{5.3.5}$$

For a little of further handling, we put

$$H(2,n,\theta,\vee)\triangleq\int_{-\infty}^{+\infty}\int_{-\infty}^{+\infty} q(x,y)\mathrm{d}x\mathrm{d}y. \tag{5.3.6}$$

and call $H(2,n,\theta,\vee)$ an H-function with parameter $(2,n,\theta,\vee)$, where parameter 2 denotes that integral kernel $q(x,y)$ in (5.3.5) is bivariate function, parameter n represents the number of rules of reasoning in (5.2.1) used in process of construction of $q(x,y)$, parameter θ depends on fuzzy implication operator and parameter $\vee$ denotes a triangular conorm used in relation synthesis. It is evident that

$$H(2,n,\theta,\vee)=\int_X\int_Y\left[\bigvee_{i=1}^{n}\theta\left(\mu_{A_i}(x),\mu_{B_i}(y)\right)\right]\mathrm{d}x\mathrm{d}y. \tag{5.3.7}$$

When X and Y are all intervals, e.g., $X=[a,b]$ and $Y=[c,d]$, for distinct fuzzy implication operators θ [1,5,14-17,20,21], it is an interesting problem of mathematical analysis how to resolve and find the integral

$$H(2,n,\theta,\vee)=\int_a^b\int_c^d\left[\bigvee_{i=1}^{n}\theta\left(\mu_{A_i}(x),\mu_{B_i}(y)\right)\right]\mathrm{d}x\mathrm{d}y.$$

This is similar to the well-known special functions such as Γ function and B function, etc., as the following:

$$\Gamma(\alpha)=\int_0^{+\infty} x^{\alpha-1}\mathrm{e}^{-x}\mathrm{d}x,\quad \mathrm{B}(\alpha,\beta)=\int_0^1 x^{\alpha-1}(1-x)^{\beta-1}\mathrm{d}x$$

Remark 5.3.1 In (5.3.7), replacing operator of relation synthesis with general triangular co-norm ∇, we obtain a general expression of H-functions:

$$H(2,n,\theta,\nabla)=\int_X\int_Y\left[\mathop{\nabla}_{i=1}^{n}\theta\left(\mu_{A_i}(x),\mu_{B_i}(y)\right)\right]\mathrm{d}x\mathrm{d}y\,. \tag{5.3.8}$$

In particular, when $\nabla=\oplus$, $X=[a,b]$ and $Y=[c,d]$, and

$$\theta\triangleq\cdot:[0,1]^2\to[0,1],\quad (u,v)\mapsto\cdot(u,v)\triangleq u\cdot v,$$

we have the following expression:

$$H(2,n,\cdot,\oplus)=\int_a^b\int_c^d\left[\mathop{\oplus}_{i=1}^{n}\theta\left(\mu_{A_i}(x),\mu_{B_i}(y)\right)\right]\mathrm{d}x\mathrm{d}y\,. \tag{5.3.9}$$

This has some good analytical properties and it is easy to find its integral quantity. Notice that "$\oplus$" in (5.3.9) is a binary operation and so the binary function $\mathop{\oplus}_{i=1}^{n}\theta\left(\mu_{A_i}(x),\mu_{B_i}(y)\right)$ must be calculated one by one, but it does not need to add brackets, since the associative law is satisfied. Knowing "normalization" handling of integral kernel $q(x,y)$ that will be made below, it is not difficult to understand the farther broadening of bounded sum "$\oplus$" to ordinary sum "+", i.e.,

$$H(2,n,\cdot,+)=\int_a^b\int_c^d\left[\sum_{i=1}^{n}\left(\mu_{A_i}(x),\mu_{B_i}(y)\right)\right]\mathrm{d}x\mathrm{d}y\,. \tag{5.3.10}$$

This has better analytical properties naturally. □

The purpose of introduction of H functions is no more than normalization. If $H(2,n,\theta,\vee)>0$, then we can put

$$f(x,y) \triangleq q(x,y)/H(2,n,\theta,\vee) \tag{5.3.11}$$

It is easy to see that (5.3.5) changes again to the following:

$$\overline{s}(x) = \frac{\int_{-\infty}^{+\infty} yf(x,y)\mathrm{d}y}{\int_{-\infty}^{+\infty} f(x,y)\mathrm{d}y}. \tag{5.3.12}$$

Then any careful reader can find that (5.3.12) is awfully similar to conditional mathematical expectation in probability theory, and the real circumstance is so indeed.

Theorem 5.3.1 Given a single-input single-output fuzzy system, the related notations are same as described above. Select and fix a fuzzy implication operator θ. If the following conditions are satisfied

$$\int_Y |y| p(x,y)\mathrm{d}y < +\infty, \quad 0 < \int_Y p(x,y)\mathrm{d}y < +\infty$$

then there must exist a probability space $(\Omega, \mathcal{F}, P)$ and a random vector (ξ, η) defined on it such that

$$E(\eta \mid \xi = x) = \overline{s}(x), \tag{5.3.13}$$

i.e., functional value $\overline{s}(x)$ of function $\overline{s}$ at x equals to conditional mathematical expectation $E(\eta \mid \xi = x)$ of random variable η under condition of random variable $\xi = x$.

Proof. With input universe X and output universe Y for basic sets, we construct two probability spaces $(X, \mathcal{B}_1, P_1)$ and $(Y, \mathcal{B}_2, P_2)$, where $\mathcal{B}_1$ and $\mathcal{B}_2$ are two Borel σ-fields on X and Y, respectively, and P_1 and P_2 are probability measures on $\mathcal{B}_1$ and $\mathcal{B}_2$, respectively. Suppose that ξ and η are random variables defined on X and Y, respectively. Below, we confirm probability distribution of random vector (ξ, η).

Actually, put $\Omega \triangleq X \times Y$, $\mathcal{F} \triangleq \mathcal{B}_1 \times \mathcal{B}_2$ and $P \triangleq P_1 \times P_2$, where $\mathcal{F}$ indicates Borel σ-field generated by Cartesian product of Borel σ-

fields $\mathcal{B}_1$ and $\mathcal{B}_2$, and P is well-known product probability measure. Then we obtain joint probability space $(\Omega,\mathcal{F},P)$. With same notations, redefine ξ and η as random variables on Ω:

$$\xi:\Omega\to\mathbb{R},\quad (x,y)\mapsto\xi(x,y)\triangleq\xi(x),$$
$$\eta:\Omega\to\mathbb{R},\quad (x,y)\mapsto\eta(x,y)\triangleq\eta(y)$$

Thus (ξ,η) turns into a two-dimensional random vector on joint probability space $(\Omega,\mathcal{F},P)$. By hypothetic condition, the function

$$f(x,y)=q(x,y)/H(2,n,\theta,\vee)$$

defined by (5.3.11) satisfies condition to be a probability density function of two-dimensional random vector. Hence we choose $f(x,y)$ for probability density function of random vector (ξ,η), and so (5.3.12) just becomes to conditional mathematical expectation of random variable η under condition of random variable $\xi=x$, i.e.,

$$E(\eta\mid\xi=x)=\frac{\int_{-\infty}^{+\infty}yf(x,y)\mathrm{d}y}{\int_{-\infty}^{+\infty}f(x,y)\mathrm{d}y},\tag{5.3.14}$$

This shows that $E(\eta\mid\xi=x)=\overline{s}(x)$. □

Remark 5.3.2 By (5.3.3), we can see that for practical computation of $E(\eta\mid\xi=x)$ it suffices to use the following expression:

$$E(\eta\mid\xi=x)=\frac{\int_Y yp(x,y)\mathrm{d}y}{\int_Y p(x,y)\mathrm{d}y}.\tag{5.3.15}$$

□

Remark 5.3.3 For convenience, we make up marginal probability density functions, i.e., density function $f_\xi(x)$ of ξ and density function $f_\eta(y)$ of η by using probability density function $f(x,y)$:

$$f_\xi(x) = \int_{-\infty}^{+\infty} f(x,y)\mathrm{d}y\,, \tag{5.3.16}$$

$$f_\eta(y) = \int_{-\infty}^{+\infty} f(x,y)\mathrm{d}x\,. \tag{5.3.17}$$

When $f_\xi(x) > 0$, we can also obtain conditional probability density function $f_{\eta|\xi=x}(y\,|\,x)$ of η under $\xi = x$ as the following:

$$f_{\eta|\xi=x}(y\,|\,x) = f(x,y)/f_\xi(x)\,. \tag{5.3.18}$$

Thus (5.3.15) is simply represented as follows:

$$E(\eta\,|\,\xi = x) = \int_{-\infty}^{+\infty} y f_{\eta|\xi=x}(y\,|\,x)\mathrm{d}y\,. \tag{5.3.19}$$

□

Remark 5.3.4 Using $f(x,y)$, we immediately obtain probability distribution function of random vector (ξ,η):

$$F(x,y) \triangleq P(\xi < x, \eta < y) = \int_{-\infty}^{x}\int_{-\infty}^{y} f(u,v)\mathrm{d}u\mathrm{d}v\,. \tag{5.3.20}$$

Hereby we can also obtain marginal probability distribution functions, i.e., distribution function $F_\xi(x)$ of ξ and distribution function $F_\eta(y)$ of η:

$$\begin{aligned} F_\xi(x) &= F(x,+\infty) \\ &= \int_{-\infty}^{x}\left(\int_{-\infty}^{+\infty} f(u,v)\mathrm{d}v\right)\mathrm{d}u = \int_{-\infty}^{x} f_\xi(u)\mathrm{d}u, \end{aligned} \tag{5.3.21}$$

$$\begin{aligned} F_\eta(y) &= F(y,+\infty) \\ &= \int_{-\infty}^{y}\left(\int_{-\infty}^{+\infty} f(u,v)\mathrm{d}u\right)\mathrm{d}v = \int_{-\infty}^{y} f_\eta(v)\mathrm{d}v. \end{aligned} \qquad 5.3.22)$$

This implies that if only have probability density function $f(x,y)$ we can easily understand the whole probabilistic information of random vector (ξ,η) or the fuzzy system. □

Remark 5.3.5 For the below demands, we need the tool of conditional variance, denoted by $D(\eta \mid \xi = x)$, as well, that is

$$D(\eta \mid \xi = x) \triangleq \int_{-\infty}^{+\infty} [y - E(\eta \mid \xi = x)]^2 f_{\eta|\xi=x}(y \mid x) \mathrm{d}y . \quad (5.3.23)$$

□

Remark 5.3.6 Using $E(\eta \mid \xi = x)$, we make a function, denoted by $g(\xi)$, of random variable ξ that is determined as the following:

$$g(\xi) \triangleq E(\eta \mid \xi), \quad (5.3.24)$$

Of course, $g(\xi)$ is also a random variable, but it must satisfy the following two conditions:

1) If $\omega \in \{\omega \in \Omega \mid \xi(\omega) = x\}$, then we have

$$g(\xi) \triangleq E(\eta \mid \xi) = E(\eta \mid \xi = x);$$

2) $(\forall A \in \mathcal{B})\Big(E\big(\{E(\eta \mid \xi) \mid \xi(\omega) \in A\}\big) = E(\eta \mid \xi(\omega) \in A)\Big)$,

where $\mathcal{B}$ is one-dimensional Borel σ-field. In fact, $E(\eta \mid \xi)$ is the unified expression of $E(\eta \mid \xi = x)$ for all $x \in X$ and we call it conditional mathematical expectation of η with respect to ξ. Observe that for any a given point $x \in X$, if $\omega \in \{\omega \in \Omega \mid \xi = x\}$, then we have

$$\overline{s}(x) = E(\eta \mid \xi = x) = E(\eta \mid \xi) = g(\xi) = g(x). \quad (5.3.25)$$

This implies that two functions $\overline{s}$ and g coincide, i.e., $\overline{s} = g$. Besides, for random vector (ξ, η), if $E(\eta^2 \mid \xi)$ exists, then we may use $E(\eta \mid \xi)$ to give the unified expression of conditional variance:

$$D(\eta \mid \xi) \triangleq E\Big([\eta - E(\eta \mid \xi)]^2 \Big| \xi\Big).$$

We call it conditional variance of η with respect to ξ. Obviously,

$$D(\eta \mid \xi)=E\left(\eta^2 \middle| \xi\right)-[E(\eta \mid \xi)]^2 . \qquad \square$$

With explanations in Remarks 5.3.2 to 5.3.6, we can give a more fine and detailed probability interpretation related to fuzzy systems by means of $E(\eta \mid \xi)$. For an uncertain system, input quantity $x \in X$ and output quantity $y \in Y$ should be considered as two random variables ξ and η that depend on each other. To find functional relationship $s(x)$ between x and y corresponds to searching a Borel measurable function in which ξ and η depend on each other, and this function ought to coincide with $y=s(x)$, i.e., $\eta=s(\xi)$. We want to determine a Borel measurable function $\bar{s}(\xi)$ so that η and $\bar{s}(\xi)$ are closed up to the best, and $\bar{s}$ may be approximation to s, where the existence of $E\left(\eta^2\right)$ and $E\left[(\bar{s}(\xi))^2\right]$ are assumed. The "closeness" herein needs a criterion, and the most commonly used one is "least squares method". Then we have to demand

$$E\left[(\eta-\bar{s}(\xi))^2\right]=\inf_{\varphi}\left\{E\left[(\eta-\varphi(\xi))^2\right]\right\}, \tag{5.3.26}$$

where φ varies in a kind of space of Borel measurable functions. To prove (5.3.26) is equivalent to proving that for any above-described Borel measurable function φ it holds that

$$E\left[(\eta-\bar{s}(\xi))^2\right] \leq E\left[(\eta-\varphi(\xi))^2\right].$$

In fact, we easily understand the following equation:

$$\begin{aligned}
& E\left[(\eta-\varphi(\xi))^2\right] \\
& =E\left\{\left[(\eta-E(\eta \mid \xi))+(E(\eta \mid \xi)-\varphi(\xi))\right]^2\right\} \\
& =E\left[(\eta-E(\eta \mid \xi))^2\right]+E\left[(E(\eta \mid \xi)-\varphi(\xi))^2\right] \\
& \quad +2E\left[(\eta-E(\eta \mid \xi))(E(\eta \mid \xi)-\varphi(\xi))\right].
\end{aligned}$$

Obviously, we have the following equation:

$$E\left[\left(\eta - E(\eta \mid \xi)\right)\left(E(\eta \mid \xi) - \varphi(\xi)\right)\right] = 0,$$

and so we get the following inequality:

$$E\left[\left(\eta - \varphi(\xi)\right)^2\right] = E\left[\left(\eta - E(\eta \mid \xi)\right)^2\right] + E\left[\left(E(\eta \mid \xi) - \varphi(\xi)\right)^2\right]$$
$$\geq E\left[\left(\eta - E(\eta \mid \xi)\right)^2\right] = E\left[\left(\eta - \overline{s}(\xi)\right)^2\right].$$

This shows that random variable $\overline{s}(\xi)$ is the optimal approximation in mean square to random variable η.

Remark 5.3.7 We can also use conditional variance $D(\eta \mid \xi = x)$ to interpret that $\overline{s}(\xi)$ is the optimal approximation in mean square to η. Actually, there is a property about mathematical expectation and variance in probability theory: For any random variable η, it is certain that

$$(\forall c \in \mathbb{R})\left(c \neq E\eta \Rightarrow \left(D\eta < E[\eta - c]^2\right)\right),$$

i.e., function $f(c) \triangleq E[\eta - c]^2$ takes the least value at $c = E\eta$ as the following:

$$f(E\eta) = E[\eta - E\eta]^2 = D\eta.$$

And then for any above-described Borel measurable function φ,

$$E[(\eta - \varphi(\xi))^2] = \int_{-\infty}^{+\infty}\int_{-\infty}^{+\infty}\left(y - \varphi(x)\right)^2 f(x, y)\mathrm{d}x\mathrm{d}y$$
$$= \int_{-\infty}^{+\infty} f_\xi(x)\left[\int_{-\infty}^{+\infty}\left(y - \varphi(x)\right)^2 f_{\eta \mid \xi = x}(y \mid x)\mathrm{d}y\right]\mathrm{d}x.$$

When $\varphi(x) = E(\eta \mid \xi = x)$, we have the following expression:

$$\int_{-\infty}^{+\infty}[y-\varphi(x)]^2 f_{\eta|\xi=x}(y\mid x)\mathrm{d}y$$
$$=\int_{-\infty}^{+\infty}[y-E(\eta\mid\xi=x)]^2 f_{\eta|\xi=x}(y\mid x)\mathrm{d}y = D(\eta\mid\xi=x).$$

So $\int_{-\infty}^{+\infty}(y-\varphi(x))^2 f_{\eta|\xi=x}(y\mid x)\mathrm{d}y$ reaches the least value $D(\eta\mid\xi=x)$ here. Again, since $f_\xi(x)\ge 0$, $\overline{s}(x)=E(\eta\mid\xi=x)$ also brings about that $E\left[(\eta-\varphi(\xi))^2\right]$ arrives at the least value $\int_{-\infty}^{+\infty} f_\xi(x)D(\eta\mid\xi=x)\mathrm{d}x$. □

Based on the above discussions, we get hold of a conclusion: The function $\overline{s}(x)$ obtained by COG method is optimal approximation to $s(x)$ in the sense of least squares, accordingly COG method is reasonable.

Besides, just with COG method, we have communicated relation between fuzzy systems and probability theory. From the viewpoint of methodology, in a certain bound, we may use the method of probability theory to investigate fuzzy systems. This is good certainly. From the viewpoint of philosophy, uncertainty originally contains randomness as well as fuzziness, and randomness and fuzziness are often interwoven, so it is very difficult to divide up them.

5.4 Several Typical Probability Distributions

We return to and consider (5.3.11) again. It is expanded as

$$f(x,y)=\frac{p(x,y)}{H(2,n,\theta,\vee)}=\frac{p(x,y)\chi_{X\times Y}}{H(2,n,\theta,\vee)}$$
$$=\frac{\left[\bigvee_{i=1}^{n}\theta\left(\mu_{A_i}(x),\mu_{B_i}(y)\right)\right]\chi_{X\times Y}}{\int_X\int_Y\left[\bigvee_{i=1}^{n}\theta\left(\mu_{A_i}(x),\mu_{B_i}(y)\right)\right]\mathrm{d}x\mathrm{d}y}. \quad (5.4.1)$$

We can discover two aspects of phenomena or contexts or meanings:

1) From the viewpoint of probability theory, the probability density function $f(x,y)$ is the core of fuzzy system and serves as "inner kernel of system". This shows that a fuzzy system is a stochastic system in nature, and this is the rational thinking. Certainly, there is also no lack of worth of handling. For instance, for an uncertain system, if one predominates probability distribution function $F(x,y)$ or probability density function $f(x,y)$ of random vector (ξ,η) by method of probabilistic statistics then one can obtain $\overline{s}(x)=E(\eta\,|\,\xi=x)$, namely, understand system.

2) From the viewpoint of constructivity based on fuzzy reasoning, the above-described process of construction of fuzzy system, more precisely, from (5.2.1) to (5.2.11), has determined probability distribution of an uncertain system. In (5.4.1), choosing different fuzzy implication operators, we obtain distinct probability density functions and consequently produce diverse probability distributions. Thereby, we can also enrich capability of uncertain systems.

References [14-17] have carried through detailed textual research toward construction of fuzzy implication operators. Below, with several typical implication operators for examples, we obtain some typical probability distributions that are used commonly in fuzzy systems.

Example 5.4.1 In (5.4.1), putting $\theta=\theta_{13}$[14−17], i.e.,

$$\left(\forall(a,b)\in[0,1]^2\right)\left(\theta_{13}(a,b)\triangleq a\wedge b\right),$$

we have the following expression:

$$\begin{aligned} p(x,y) &= \bigvee_{i=1}^{n}\theta_{13}\left(\mu_{A_i}(x),\mu_{B_i}(y)\right) \\ &= \bigvee_{i=1}^{n}\left(\mu_{A_i}(x)\wedge\mu_{B_i}(y)\right) \end{aligned} \tag{5.4.2}$$

If $H\left(2,n,\theta_{13},\vee\right)>0$, then we can let

$$f(x,y) \triangleq \frac{p(x,y)\chi_{X\times Y}}{H(2,n,\theta_{13},\vee)} = \frac{\left[\bigvee_{i=1}^{n}\left(\mu_{A_i}(x)\wedge\mu_{B_i}(y)\right)\right]\chi_{X\times Y}}{\int_X\int_Y\left[\bigvee_{i=1}^{n}\left(\mu_{A_i}(x)\wedge\mu_{B_i}(y)\right)\right]\mathrm{d}x\mathrm{d}y} \tag{5.4.3}$$

Since θ_{13} is called Mamdani operator, the probability distribution with (5.4.3) for probability density function is called Mamdani distribution with parameter $(2,n,\vee)$ and denoted by $\mathrm{Mam}(2,n,\vee)$, in other words, we use $(\xi,\eta)\sim\mathrm{Mam}(2,n,\vee)$, i.e. random vector (ξ,η) obeys $\mathrm{Mam}(2,n,\vee)$. Its marginal probability density functions are as follows:

$$f_\xi(x) = \int_{-\infty}^{+\infty} f(x,y)\mathrm{d}y = \frac{\int_Y\left[\bigvee_{i=1}^{n}\left(\mu_{A_i}(x)\wedge\mu_{B_i}(y)\right)\right]\chi_X\mathrm{d}y}{\int_X\int_Y\left[\bigvee_{i=1}^{n}\left(\mu_{A_i}(x)\wedge\mu_{B_i}(y)\right)\right]\mathrm{d}x\mathrm{d}y}, \tag{5.4.4}$$

$$f_\eta(y) = \int_{-\infty}^{+\infty} f(x,y)\mathrm{d}x = \frac{\int_X\left[\bigvee_{i=1}^{n}\left(\mu_{A_i}(x)\wedge\mu_{B_i}(y)\right)\right]\chi_Y\mathrm{d}x}{\int_X\int_Y\left[\bigvee_{i=1}^{n}\left(\mu_{A_i}(x)\wedge\mu_{B_i}(y)\right)\right]\mathrm{d}x\mathrm{d}y}, \tag{5.4.5}$$

respectively. When $f_\xi(x)>0$ and $f_\eta(y)>0$, the conditional probability density functions are as the following:

$$f_{\eta|\xi=x}(y\mid x)\triangleq\frac{f(x,y)}{f_\xi(x)}=\frac{p(x,y)\chi_{X\times Y}}{\int_Y p(x,y)\chi_X\mathrm{d}y}$$

$$=\frac{\left[\bigvee_{i=1}^{n}\left(\mu_{A_i}(x)\wedge\mu_{B_i}(y)\right)\right]\chi_{X\times Y}}{\int_Y\left[\bigvee_{i=1}^{n}\left(\mu_{A_i}(x)\wedge\mu_{B_i}(y)\right)\right]\chi_X\mathrm{d}y},\qquad(5.4.6)$$

$$f_{\xi|\eta=y}(x\mid y)\triangleq\frac{f(x,y)}{f_\eta(y)}=\frac{p(x,y)\chi_{X\times Y}}{\int_X p(x,y)\chi_Y\mathrm{d}x}$$

$$=\frac{\left[\bigvee_{i=1}^{n}\left(\mu_{A_i}(x)\wedge\mu_{B_i}(y)\right)\right]\chi_{X\times Y}}{\int_X\left[\bigvee_{i=1}^{n}\left(\mu_{A_i}(x)\wedge\mu_{B_i}(y)\right)\right]\chi_Y\mathrm{d}x},\qquad(5.4.7)$$

respectively.

By these probability density functions, we immediately obtain distribution function, marginal distribution function, conditional mathematical expectation and conditional variance:

$$F(x,y)=\int_{-\infty}^{x}\int_{-\infty}^{y}f(u,v)\mathrm{d}u\mathrm{d}v$$

$$=\frac{\int_{-\infty}^{x}\int_{-\infty}^{y}p(u,v)\chi_{X\times Y}\mathrm{d}u\mathrm{d}v}{\int_{-\infty}^{+\infty}\int_{-\infty}^{+\infty}p(x,y)\chi_{X\times Y}\mathrm{d}x\mathrm{d}y}\qquad(5.4.8)$$

$$=\frac{\int_{-\infty}^{x}\int_{-\infty}^{y}\left[\bigvee_{i=1}^{n}\left(\mu_{A_i}(u)\wedge\mu_{B_i}(v)\right)\right]\chi_{X\times Y}\mathrm{d}u\mathrm{d}v}{\int_X\int_Y\left[\bigvee_{i=1}^{n}\left(\mu_{A_i}(x)\wedge\mu_{B_i}(y)\right)\right]\mathrm{d}x\mathrm{d}y},$$

$$F_\xi(x)=\int_{-\infty}^{x} f_\xi(u)\mathrm{d}u$$
$$=\frac{\int_{-\infty}^{x}\int_{-\infty}^{+\infty}\left[\bigvee_{i=1}^{n}\left(\mu_{A_i}(u)\wedge\mu_{B_i}(v)\right)\right]\chi_{X\times Y}\mathrm{d}u\mathrm{d}v}{\int_X\int_Y\left[\bigvee_{i=1}^{n}\left(\mu_{A_i}(x)\wedge\mu_{B_i}(y)\right)\right]\mathrm{d}x\mathrm{d}y}, \tag{5.4.9}$$

$$F_\eta(y)=\int_{-\infty}^{y} f_\eta(v)\mathrm{d}v$$
$$=\frac{\int_{-\infty}^{+\infty}\int_{-\infty}^{y}\left[\bigvee_{i=1}^{n}\left(\mu_{A_i}(u)\wedge\mu_{B_i}(v)\right)\right]\chi_{X\times Y}\mathrm{d}u\mathrm{d}v}{\int_X\int_Y\left[\bigvee_{i=1}^{n}\left(\mu_{A_i}(x)\wedge\mu_{B_i}(y)\right)\right]\mathrm{d}x\mathrm{d}y}, \tag{5.4.10}$$

$$E(\eta\mid\xi=x)=\overline{s}(x)$$
$$=\int_{-\infty}^{+\infty} y f_{\eta|\xi=x}(y\mid x)\mathrm{d}y \tag{5.4.11}$$
$$=\frac{\int_Y y\left[\bigvee_{i=1}^{n}\left(\mu_{A_i}(x)\wedge\mu_{B_i}(y)\right)\right]\chi_X\mathrm{d}y}{\int_Y\left[\bigvee_{i=1}^{n}\left(\mu_{A_i}(x)\wedge\mu_{B_i}(y)\right)\right]\chi_X\mathrm{d}y},$$

$$D(\eta\mid\xi=x)=\int_{-\infty}^{+\infty}\left[y-E(\eta\mid\xi=x)\right]^2 f_{\eta|\xi=x}(y\mid x)\mathrm{d}y. \tag{5.4.12}$$

Above equations are very useful. □

Example 5.4.2 In (5.4.1), putting $\theta=\theta_8$[14–17], i.e.,

$$\left(\forall(a,b)\in[0,1]^2\right)\left(\theta_8(a,b)\triangleq(1-a)\vee(a\wedge b)\right),$$

we have the following results:

$$\begin{aligned} p(x,y) &= \overset{n}{\underset{i=1}{\vee}} \theta_8\left(\mu_{A_i}(x), \mu_{B_i}(y)\right) \\ &= \overset{n}{\underset{i=1}{\vee}} \left[\left(1-\mu_{A_i}(x)\right) \vee \left(\mu_{A_i}(x) \wedge \mu_{B_i}(y)\right)\right], \end{aligned} \tag{5.4.13}$$

$$\begin{aligned} f(x,y) &= \frac{p(x,y)\chi_{X\times Y}}{H\left(2,n,\theta_8,\vee\right)} \\ &= \frac{\left\{\overset{n}{\underset{i=1}{\vee}} \left[\left(1-\mu_{A_i}(x)\right) \vee \left(\mu_{A_i}(x) \wedge \mu_{B_i}(y)\right)\right]\right\} \chi_{X\times Y}}{\int_X \int_Y \left\{\overset{n}{\underset{i=1}{\vee}} \left[\left(1-\mu_{A_i}(x)\right) \vee \left(\mu_{A_i}(x) \wedge \mu_{B_i}(y)\right)\right]\right\} \mathrm{d}x\mathrm{d}y}, \end{aligned} \tag{5.4.14}$$

where $H\left(2,n,\theta_8,\vee\right) > 0$ is assumed.

Since θ_8 is called Zadeh operator, the probability distribution with (5.4.14) for probability density function is called Zadeh distribution with parameter $(2,n,\vee)$ and denoted by $\mathrm{Zad}(2,n,\vee)$, in other words, we can use the following symbol:

$$(\xi,\eta) \sim \mathrm{Zad}(2,n,\vee),$$

i.e., random vector (ξ,η) obeys $\mathrm{Zad}(2,n,\vee)$. Similarly to Example 5.4.1, we can give its distribution function, marginal distribution function, conditional mathematical expectation and conditional variance. □

Example 5.4.3 In (5.4.1), putting $\theta = \theta_3$[14–17], i.e.,

$$\left(\forall (a,b) \in [0,1]^2\right)\left(\theta_3(a,b) \triangleq \begin{cases} 1, & a \le b \\ 1-a+b, & a > b \end{cases}\right)$$

we have the following results:

$$\begin{aligned} p(x,y) &= \overset{n}{\underset{i=1}{\vee}} \theta_3\left(\mu_{A_i}(x), \mu_{B_i}(y)\right) \\ &= \begin{cases} 1, & (\exists i)\left(\mu_{A_i}(x) \le \mu_{B_i}(y)\right), \\ \overset{n}{\underset{i=1}{\vee}} \left[1-\mu_{A_i}(x)+\mu_{B_i}(y)\right], & \text{otherwise}, \end{cases} \end{aligned} \tag{5.4.15}$$

$$f(x,y) = \frac{p(x,y)\chi_{X\times Y}}{H(2,n,\theta_3,\vee)}$$
$$= \frac{1}{\int_X\int_Y p(x,y)\mathrm{d}x\mathrm{d}y}\chi_{\{(\exists i)\,(\mu_{A_i}(x)\le\mu_{B_i}(y))\}}(x,y) \tag{5.4.16}$$
$$+\frac{\bigvee_{i=1}^{n}\left[1-\mu_{A_i}(x)+\mu_{B_i}(y)\right]}{\int_X\int_Y p(x,y)\mathrm{d}x\mathrm{d}y}\chi_{X\times Y\setminus\{(\exists i)\,(\mu_{A_i}(x)\le\mu_{B_i}(y))\}},$$

where $H(2,n,\theta_3,\vee)>0$ is assumed.

Since θ_3 is called Lukasiewicz operator, the probability distribution with (5.4.16) for probability density function is called Lukasiewicz distribution with parameter $(2,n,\vee)$ and denoted by $\mathrm{Luk}(2,n,\vee)$, in other words, we have the following form:

$$(\xi,\eta)\sim\mathrm{Luk}(2,n,\vee),$$

i.e., random vector (ξ,η) obeys $\mathrm{Luk}(2,n,\vee)$. Moreover, we can see from (5.4.16) that Lukasiewicz distribution has property of uniform distribution on the local region as the following:

$$\left\{\omega=(x,y)\in\Omega\,\middle|\,(\exists i)\left(\mu_{A_i}(x)\le\mu_{B_i}(y)\right)\right\}. \qquad \square$$

Example 5.4.4 In (5.4.1), putting $\theta=\theta_5$[14–17], i.e.,

$$\left(\forall(a,b)\in[0,1]^2\right)\left(\theta_5(a,b)\triangleq\begin{cases}1, & a\le b\\ b, & a>b\end{cases}\right)$$

we have the following expressions:

$$p(x,y)=\overset{n}{\underset{i=1}{\vee}}\theta_5\left(\mu_{A_i}(x),\mu_{B_i}(y)\right)$$

$$=\begin{cases}1, & (\exists i)\left(\mu_{A_i}(x)\le\mu_{B_i}(y)\right),\\ \overset{n}{\underset{i=1}{\vee}}\mu_{B_i}(y), & \text{otherwise,}\end{cases}\tag{5.4.17}$$

$$f(x,y)=\frac{p(x,y)\chi_{X\times Y}}{H(2,n,\theta_5,\vee)}$$

$$=\frac{1}{\int_X\int_Y p(x,y)\mathrm{d}x\mathrm{d}y}\chi_{\{(\exists i)\,(\mu_{A_i}(x)\le\mu_{B_i}(y))\}}(x,y)\tag{5.4.18}$$

$$+\frac{\overset{n}{\underset{i=1}{\vee}}\mu_{B_i}(y)}{\int_X\int_Y p(x,y)\mathrm{d}x\mathrm{d}y}\chi_{X\times Y\setminus\{(\exists i)\,(\mu_{A_i}(x)\le\mu_{B_i}(y))\}},$$

where $H(2,n,\theta_5,\vee)>0$ is assumed. Since θ_5 is called Gödel operator, the probability distribution with (5.4.18) for probability density function is called Gödel distribution with parameter $(2,n,\vee)$ and denoted by $\mathrm{God}(2,n,\vee)$, in other words, $(\xi,\eta)\sim\mathrm{God}(2,n,\vee)$, i.e., random vector (ξ,η) obeys $\mathrm{God}(2,n,\vee)$. Moreover, we can see from (5.4.18) that Gödel distribution has property of uniform distribution on the local region:

$$\left\{\omega=(x,y)\in\Omega\,\middle|\,(\exists i)\left(\mu_{A_i}(x)\le\mu_{B_i}(y)\right)\right\}.$$ □

Example 5.4.5 In (5.4.1), putting $\theta=\theta_6$[14–17], i.e.,

$$\left(\forall(a,b)\in[0,1]^2\right)\left(\theta_6(a,b)\triangleq\begin{cases}(1-a)\vee b, & (1-a)\wedge b=0\\ 1, & \text{otherwise}\end{cases}\right)$$

we have the following expressions:

$$p(x,y)=\bigvee_{i=1}^{n}\theta_6\left(\mu_{A_i}(x),\mu_{B_i}(y)\right)$$
$$=\begin{cases}1, & (\exists i)\left(\left(1-\mu_{A_i}(x)\right)\wedge\mu_{B_i}(y)\neq 0\right),\\ \bigvee_{i=1}^{n}\left[\left(1-\mu_{A_i}(x)\right)\vee\mu_{B_i}(y)\right], & \text{otherwise.}\end{cases} \tag{5.4.19}$$

$$f(x,y)=\frac{p(x,y)\chi_{X\times Y}}{H\left(2,n,\theta_6,\vee\right)}$$
$$=\frac{1}{\int_X\int_Y p(x,y)\mathrm{d}x\mathrm{d}y}\chi_{\left\{(\exists i)\left(\left(1-\mu_{A_i}(x)\right)\wedge\mu_{B_i}(y)\neq 0\right)\right\}}(x,y), \tag{5.4.20}$$
$$+\frac{\bigvee_{i=1}^{n}\left[\left(1-\mu_{A_i}(x)\right)\vee\mu_{B_i}(y)\right]}{\int_X\int_Y p(x,y)\mathrm{d}x\mathrm{d}y}I_{X\times Y\setminus\left\{(\exists i)\left(\left(1-\mu_{A_i}(x)\right)\wedge\mu_{B_i}(y)\neq 0\right)\right\}}$$

where $H\left(2,n,\theta_6,\vee\right)>0$ is assumed.

Since θ_6 is called Dubois-Prade operator, the probability distribution with (5.4.20) for probability density function is called Dubois-Prade distribution with parameter $(2,n,\vee)$ and denoted by $\mathrm{DP}(2,n,\vee)$, in other words, $(\xi,\eta)\sim\mathrm{DP}(2,n,\vee)$, that is, the random vector (ξ,η) must obey $\mathrm{DP}(2,n,\vee)$. Moreover, we can see from (5.4.20) that Dubois-Prade distribution has property of uniform distribution on the local region:

$$\left\{\omega=(x,y)\in\Omega\,\middle|\,(\exists i)\left(\left(1-\mu_{A_i}(x)\right)\wedge\mu_{B_i}(y)\neq 0\right)\right\}.$$ □

Example 5.4.6 In (5.4.1), putting $\theta=\theta_4$[14–17], i.e.,

$$\left(\forall(a,b)\in[0,1]^2\right)\left(\theta_4(a,b)\triangleq\begin{cases}1, & a=0\\ (b/a)\wedge 1, & a>0\end{cases}\right)$$

we have the following results:

$$p(x,y)=\overset{n}{\underset{i=1}{\vee}}\theta_4\left(\mu_{A_i}(x),\mu_{B_i}(y)\right)$$
$$=\begin{cases}1, & (\exists i)\left(\mu_{A_i}(x)=0\right),\\ \overset{n}{\underset{i=1}{\vee}}\left(\dfrac{\mu_{B_i}(y)}{\mu_{A_i}(x)}\wedge 1\right), & \text{otherwise,}\end{cases} \tag{5.4.21}$$

$$f(x,y)=\frac{p(x,y)\chi_{X\times Y}}{H\left(2,n,\theta_4,\vee\right)}$$
$$=\frac{1}{\int_X\int_Y p(x,y)\mathrm{d}x\mathrm{d}y}\chi_{\{(\exists i)\left(\mu_{A_i}(x)=0\right)\}}(x,y) \tag{5.4.22}$$
$$+\frac{\overset{n}{\underset{i=1}{\vee}}\left(\dfrac{\mu_{B_i}(y)}{\mu_{A_i}(x)}\wedge 1\right)}{\int_X\int_Y p(x,y)\mathrm{d}x\mathrm{d}y}\chi_{X\times Y\setminus\{(\exists i)\left(\mu_{A_i}(x)=0\right)\}},$$

where $H\left(2,n,\theta_4,\vee\right)>0$ is assumed.

Since θ_4 is called Goguen operator, the probability distribution with (5.4.22) for probability density function is called Goguen distribution with parameter $(2,n,\vee)$ and denoted by $\mathrm{Gog}(2,n,\vee)$, in other words, random vector (ξ,η) obeys $\mathrm{Gog}(2,n,\vee)$, i.e., $(\xi,\eta)\sim\mathrm{Gog}(2,n,\vee)$. Moreover, we can easily see from (5.4.22) that Goguen distribution has property of uniform distribution on the local region as the following:

$$\left\{\omega=(x,y)\in\Omega\,\middle|\,(\exists i)\left(\mu_{A_i}(x)=0\right)\right\}. \qquad \square$$

Example 5.4.7 In (5.4.1), putting $\theta=\theta_0$ [14–17,20,21], i.e.,

$$\left(\forall(a,b)\in[0,1]^2\right)\left(\theta_0(a,b)\triangleq\begin{cases}1, & a\le b\\ (1-a)\vee b, & a>b\end{cases}\right),$$

we have the following expressions:

$$p(x,y)=\bigvee_{i=1}^{n}\theta_0\left(\mu_{A_i}(x),\mu_{B_i}(y)\right)$$

$$=\begin{cases}1, & (\exists i)\left(\mu_{A_i}(x)\le\mu_{B_i}(y)\right),\\ \bigvee_{i=1}^{n}\left[\left(1-\mu_{A_i}(x)\right)\vee\mu_{B_i}(y)\right], & \text{otherwise,}\end{cases}\tag{5.4.23}$$

$$f(x,y)=\frac{p(x,y)\chi_{X\times Y}}{H\left(2,n,\theta_0,\vee\right)}$$

$$=\frac{1}{\int_X\int_Y p(x,y)\mathrm{d}x\mathrm{d}y}\chi_{\left\{(\exists i)\left(\mu_{A_i}(x)\le\mu_{B_i}(y)\right)\right\}}(x,y)\tag{5.4.24}$$

$$+\frac{\bigvee_{i=1}^{n}\left[\left(1-\mu_{A_i}(x)\right)\vee\mu_{B_i}(y)\right]}{\int_X\int_Y p(x,y)\mathrm{d}x\mathrm{d}y}\chi_{X\times Y\setminus\left\{(\exists i)\left(\mu_{A_i}(x)\le\mu_{B_i}(y)\right)\right\}},$$

where $H\left(2,n,\theta_0,\vee\right)>0$ is assumed.

Since θ_0 was proposed by G. J. Wang in [20,21], we call θ_0 the Wang operator. And probability distribution with (5.4.24) for probability density function is called Wang distribution with parameter $(2,n,\vee)$ and denoted by $\mathrm{Wang}(2,n,\vee)$, in other words, $(\xi,\eta)\sim\mathrm{Wang}(2,n,\vee)$, i.e., random vector (ξ,η) obeys the probability distribution $\mathrm{Wang}(2,n,\vee)$. Moreover, we can easily see from (5.4.24) that Wang distribution has property of uniform distribution on the local region as the following:

$$\left\{\omega=(x,y)\in\Omega\,\middle|\,(\exists i)\left(\mu_{A_i}(x)\le\mu_{B_i}(y)\right)\right\}.$$ □

Example 5.4.8 In (5.4.1), putting $\theta=\theta_{27}$ and $\theta=\theta_{28}$ [14–17], i.e.,

$$\left(\forall(a,b)\in[0,1]^2\right)\left(\theta_{27}(a,b)\triangleq\frac{ab}{1+(1-a)(1-b)}\right),$$

$$\left(\forall(a,b)\in[0,1]^2\right)\left(\theta_{28}(a,b)\triangleq\frac{a+b}{1+ab}\right)$$

we have the following results:

$$\begin{aligned} p(x,y) &= \overset{n}{\underset{i=1}{\vee}} \theta_{27}\left(\mu_{A_i}(x), \mu_{B_i}(y)\right) \\ &= \overset{n}{\underset{i=1}{\vee}} \frac{\mu_{A_i}(x)\mu_{B_i}(y)}{1+\left(1-\mu_{A_i}(x)\right)\left(1-\mu_{B_i}(x)\right)}, \end{aligned} \tag{5.4.25}$$

$$\begin{aligned} p(x,y) &= \overset{n}{\underset{i=1}{\vee}} \theta_{28}\left(\mu_{A_i}(x), \mu_{B_i}(y)\right) \\ &= \overset{n}{\underset{i=1}{\vee}} \frac{\mu_{A_i}(x)+\mu_{B_i}(y)}{1+\mu_{A_i}(x)\mu_{B_i}(y)}, \end{aligned} \tag{5.4.26}$$

$$\begin{aligned} f(x,y) &= \frac{p(x,y)\chi_{X\times Y}}{H\left(2,n,\theta_{27},\vee\right)} \\ &= \frac{\left[\overset{n}{\underset{i=1}{\vee}} \frac{\mu_{A_i}(x)\mu_{B_i}(y)}{1+\left(1-\mu_{A_i}(x)\right)\left(1-\mu_{B_i}(x)\right)}\right]\chi_{X\times Y}}{\int_X\int_Y p(x,y)\mathrm{d}x\mathrm{d}y}, \end{aligned} \tag{5.4.27}$$

$$\begin{aligned} f(x,y) &= \frac{p(x,y)\chi_{X\times Y}}{H\left(2,n,\theta_{28},\vee\right)} \\ &= \frac{\left[\overset{n}{\underset{i=1}{\vee}} \frac{\mu_{A_i}(x)+\mu_{B_i}(y)}{1+\mu_{A_i}(x)\mu_{B_i}(y)}\right]\chi_{X\times Y}}{\int_X\int_Y p(x,y)\mathrm{d}x\mathrm{d}y}, \end{aligned} \tag{5.4.28}$$

where $H(2,n,\theta_{27},\vee)>0$ and $H(2,n,\theta_{28},\vee)>0$ are assumed.

Since θ_{27} and θ_{28} are called Einstein meet operator and Einstein union operator, respectively, the probability distributions with (5.4.27) and (5.4.28) for probability density functions are called Einstein meet distribution and Einstein union distribution with parameter $(2,n,\vee)$ and denoted by $\mathrm{Einm}(2,n,\vee)$ and $\mathrm{Einu}(2,n,\vee)$, respectively; in other words, we have that $(\xi,\eta) \sim \mathrm{Einm}(2,n,\vee)$ or $(\xi,\eta) \sim \mathrm{Einu}(2,n,\vee)$, i.e., random vector (ξ,η) obeys $\mathrm{Einm}(2,n,\vee)$ or $\mathrm{Einu}(2,n,\vee)$. □

Example 5.4.9 In (5.4.1), putting $\theta = \theta_{14}$ [14–17], i.e.,

$$\left(\forall (a,b) \in [0,1]^2\right)\left(\theta_{14}(a,b) \triangleq a \cdot b\right),$$

we have the following expression:

$$p(x,y) = \bigvee_{i=1}^{n} \theta_{14}\left(\mu_{A_i}(x), \mu_{B_i}(y)\right) = \bigvee_{i=1}^{n}\left(\mu_{A_i}(x) \cdot \mu_{B_i}(y)\right). \quad (5.4.29)$$

If $H(2,n,\theta_{14},\vee) > 0$, then we let

$$f(x,y) \triangleq \frac{p(x,y)\chi_{X\times Y}}{H(2,n,\theta_{14},\vee)} = \frac{\left[\bigvee_{i=1}^{n}\left(\mu_{A_i}(x)\cdot \mu_{B_i}(y)\right)\right]\chi_{X\times Y}}{\int_X \int_Y \left[\bigvee_{i=1}^{n}\left(\mu_{A_i}(x)\cdot \mu_{B_i}(y)\right)\right] \mathrm{d}x\mathrm{d}y}, \quad (5.4.30)$$

Since θ_{14} is called Larsen operator, the probability distribution with (5.4.30) for probability density function is called Larsen distribution with parameter $(2,n,\vee)$ and denoted by $\mathrm{Lar}(2,n,\vee)$, in other words, we have the following expression:

$$(\xi,\eta) \sim \mathrm{Lar}(2,n,\vee),$$

i.e., random vector (ξ,η) obeys $\mathrm{Lar}(2,n,\vee)$. □

5.5 Probability Representations of Double-input and Single-output Fuzzy Systems

Suppose that $X,Y \in \mathcal{B}^1$ are the universes of input variables and $Z \in \mathcal{B}^1$ is universe of output variable, where $\mathcal{B}^1$ is one-dimensional Borel σ-field. And we let

$$\mathcal{A} = \{A_i | 1 \le i \le n\}, \quad \mathcal{B} = \{B_i | 1 \le i \le n\}, \quad \mathcal{C} = \{C_i | 1 \le i \le n\}$$

be the classes of fuzzy sets on X, Y, Z, respectively. Considering $\mathcal{A}$, $\mathcal{B}$ and $\mathcal{C}$ as linguistic variables, we form n rules of fuzzy reasoning:

$$\text{If } x \text{ is } A_i \text{ and } y \text{ is } B_i \text{ then } z \text{ is } C_i, \quad i = 1, \cdots, n. \tag{5.5.1}$$

Putting the following expression:

$$\mathcal{D} \triangleq \{(A_i, B_i) | 1 \le i \le n\} \subset \mathcal{A} \times \mathcal{B},$$

we can make a mapping s^* as follows:

$$s^* : \mathcal{D} \to \mathcal{C}, \quad (A_i, B_i) \mapsto s^*(A_i, B_i) \triangleq C_i, \quad i = 1, 2, \cdots, n. \tag{5.5.2}$$

Remark 5.5.1 At the first time, it is apparent that group (5.5.1) of rules of fuzzy reasoning is not "completed" and so-called "completed" expression must be shown as follows:

$$\text{If } x \text{ is } A_i \text{ and } y \text{ is } B_j \text{ then } z \text{ is } C_{ij}, \quad i = 1, 2, \cdots, n, \quad j = 12, \cdots, m$$

However, two expression methods of this expression and (5.5.1) are equivalent, i.e., they are translatable into each other. For detailed proof, see [6]. Since the expression method of (5.5.1) is simple and convenient to handle, we always use it to write group of rules of multi-input multi-output fuzzy reasoning. □

In (5.5.1), fuzzy relation of reasoning $R_i \in \mathcal{F}((X \times Y) \times Z)$ formed by and related to the $i-$th rule is also determined by a certain implication operator $\theta : [0,1]^2 \to [0,1]$ as follows:

$$\mu_{R_i}(x, y, z) \triangleq \theta\left(\mu_{A_i}(x) \wedge \mu_{B_i}(y), \mu_{C_i}(z)\right), \tag{5.5.3}$$

where $\mu_{A_i}(x) \wedge \mu_{B_i}(y)$ is a logical expression of "x is A_i and y is B_i" in (5.5.1). Thus total relation of reasoning for group (5.5.1) of rules of reasoning is $R = \bigcup_{i=1}^{n} R_i$. We use "$\vee$" for a while to realize "$\bigcup$", i.e.,

$$\begin{aligned} \mu_R(x, y, z) &= \bigvee_{i=1}^{n} \mu_{R_i}(x, y, z) \\ &= \bigvee_{i=1}^{n} \theta\left(\mu_{A_i}(x) \wedge \mu_{B_i}(y), \mu_{C_i}(z)\right) \end{aligned} \tag{5.5.4}$$

For any given $(A, B) \in \mathcal{F}(X) \times \mathcal{F}(Y)$, we can obtain result of reasoning $C \in \mathcal{F}(Z)$ through R. This can be yet realized by use of a fuzzy transformation "$\circ$":

$$\begin{aligned} &\circ : \mathcal{F}(X) \times \mathcal{F}(Y) \to \mathcal{F}(Z) \\ &(A, B) \mapsto C = \circ(A, B) \triangleq (A \times B) \circ R, \end{aligned} \tag{5.5.5}$$

where the fuzzy set $A \times B$ denotes the Cartesian product of the fuzzy sets A and B, i.e., $A \times B \in \mathcal{F}(X \times Y)$ and is defined by the follows:

$$\left(\forall (x, y) \in X \times Y\right)\left(\mu_{A \times B}(x, y) \triangleq \mu_A(x) \wedge \mu_B(y)\right). \tag{5.5.6}$$

It is not difficult to understand that $\mu_{A \times B}(x, y)$ is just the set representation of logical sentence "x is A_i and y is B_i". Here we also use basic operations $(\wedge, \vee)$ to state the form of membership function of (5.5.5):

$$\mu_C(z) = \bigvee_{(x,y) \in X \times Y} \left[\left(\mu_A(x) \wedge \mu_B(y)\right) \wedge \mu_R(x, y, z)\right]. \tag{5.5.7}$$

Thus we obtain a function s^{**} as follows:

$$\begin{aligned} &s^{**} : \mathcal{F}(X) \times \mathcal{F}(Y) \to \mathcal{F}(Z) \\ &(A, B) \mapsto C = s^{**}(A, B) \triangleq (A \times B) \circ R. \end{aligned} \tag{5.5.8}$$

For any given $(x',y')\in X\times Y$, in order to use (5.5.7), we first do the fuzzification on (x',y'), i.e., make singleton fuzzy sets A' and B' of x' and y', respectively (refer to (5.2.8)). And substituting them into (5.5.8), we obtain result of reasoning $C'\in\mathcal{F}(Z)$ as follows:

$$\begin{aligned}\mu_{C'}(z)&=\mu_R(x',y',z)\\&=\mathop{\vee}_{i=1}^{n}\theta\left(\mu_{A_i}(x')\wedge\mu_{B_i}(y'),\mu_{C_i}(z)\right).\end{aligned}\tag{5.5.9}$$

If the following conditions are satisfied

$$\int_Z |z|\,\mu_{C'}(z)\mathrm{d}z<+\infty,\quad 0<\int_Z\mu_{C'}(z)\mathrm{d}z<+\infty,$$

then to do the defuzzification on C' by COG method, we can obtain exact output z' as follows:

$$z'=\frac{\int_Z z\mu_{C'}(z)\mathrm{d}z}{\int_Z\mu_{C'}(z)\mathrm{d}z}.$$

In this way, we have a function $\overline{s}:X\times Y\to Z$, where

$$\overline{s}(x,y)=\frac{\int_Z z\mu_{C'}(z)\mathrm{d}z}{\int_Z\mu_{C'}(z)\mathrm{d}z}.\tag{5.5.10}$$

As preceding analysis, $\mu_{C'}(z)$ and (x',y') depend on each other. Actually we should give the following symbol:

$$C'(x=x',y=y')\triangleq C'.$$

Because (x',y') is arbitrarily chosen in $X\times Y$, we can use (x,y) instead of (x',y'). Therefore, we can also write it as form of a ternary function as being $p:X\times Y\times Z\to\mathbb{R}$, without further ado:

$$p(x,y,z) \triangleq \mu_C(z) = \mu_R(x,y,z)$$
$$= \bigvee_{i=1}^{n} \theta\left(\mu_{A_i}(x) \wedge \mu_{B_i}(y), \mu_{C_i}(z)\right) \tag{5.5.11}$$

And then (5.5.10) can change to the following equation:

$$\bar{s}(x,y) = \frac{\int_Z zp(x,y,z)\mathrm{d}z}{\int_Z p(x,y,z)\mathrm{d}z}. \tag{5.5.12}$$

Similarly to (5.3.4), expand domain of definition of p onto $\mathbb{R}^3$ and denote $q(x,y,z) \triangleq p(x,y,z)\chi_{X\times Y\times Z}$. Then (5.5.12) also changes to

$$\bar{s}(x,y) = \frac{\int_{-\infty}^{+\infty} zq(x,y,z)\mathrm{d}z}{\int_{-\infty}^{+\infty} q(x,y,z)\mathrm{d}z}. \tag{5.5.13}$$

Note that, according to preceding explanation, the function $\bar{s}(x,y)$ and the function $\bar{s}(x,y)\chi_{X\times Y}(x,y)$ are the same. For normalization, let

$$H(3,n,\theta,\vee) \triangleq \int_X \int_Y \int_Z p(x,y,z)\mathrm{d}x\mathrm{d}y\mathrm{d}z. \tag{5.5.14}$$

If $H(3,n,\theta,\vee) > 0$, then put again

$$f(x,y,z) \triangleq \frac{p(x,y,z)\chi_{X\times Y\times Z}(x,y,z)}{H(3,n,\theta,\vee)} \tag{5.5.15}$$

By (5.5.13), it is evident that

$$\bar{s}(x,y) = \frac{\int_{-\infty}^{+\infty} zf(x,y,z)\mathrm{d}z}{\int_{-\infty}^{+\infty} f(x,y,z)\mathrm{d}z}. \tag{5.5.16}$$

Theorem 5.5.1 Given a double-input single-output fuzzy system, the related notations are same as described above. Select and fix a fuzzy implication operator θ. If the following conditions are satisfied

$$\int_Z |z| p(x,y,z)\mathrm{d}z < +\infty, \quad 0 < \int_Z p(x,y,z)\mathrm{d}z < +\infty,$$

then there must exist a probability space $(\Omega, \mathcal{F}, P)$ and a random vector (ξ, η, ζ) defined on it such that

$$E(\zeta \mid \xi = x, \eta = y) = \overline{s}(x,y), \tag{5.5.17}$$

i.e., functional value $\overline{s}(x,y)$ of the function $\overline{s}$ at (x,y) equals to conditional mathematical expectation $E(\zeta \mid \xi = x, \eta = y)$ of random variable ζ under condition of random vector $(\xi, \eta) = (x,y)$.

Proof. Let $(X, \mathcal{B}_1, P_1), (Y, \mathcal{B}_2, P_2)$ and $(Z, \mathcal{B}_3, P_3)$ be three probability spaces, where $\mathcal{B}_1$, $\mathcal{B}_2$ and $\mathcal{B}_3$ are Borel σ-fields on X, Y and Z, respectively, and P_1, P_2 and P_3 are probability measures on $\mathcal{B}_1$, $\mathcal{B}_2$ and $\mathcal{B}_3$, respectively. Suppose that ξ, η and ζ are random variables defined on X, Y and Z, respectively.

Taking $\Omega \triangleq X \times Y \times Z$, $\mathcal{F} \triangleq \mathcal{B}_1 \times \mathcal{B}_2 \times \mathcal{B}_3$ and $P \triangleq P_1 \times P_2 \times P_3$, we obtain joint probability space $(\Omega, \mathcal{F}, P)$. With same notations, we can redefine ξ, η and ζ as random variables on Ω:

$$\begin{aligned}
&\xi : \Omega \to \mathbb{R}, \quad (u,v,w) \mapsto \xi(u,v,w) \triangleq \xi(u), \\
&\eta : \Omega \to \mathbb{R}, \quad (u,v,w) \mapsto \eta(u,v,w) \triangleq \eta(v), \\
&\zeta : \Omega \to \mathbb{R}, \quad (u,v,w) \mapsto \zeta(u,v,w) \triangleq \zeta(w).
\end{aligned}$$

Then we obtain a three-dimensional random vector (ξ, η, ζ) defined on $(\Omega, \mathcal{F}, P)$. We can consider $f(x,y,z)$ as the probability density function of (ξ, η, ζ). By definition of conditional mathematical expectation, we see that (5.5.16) just becomes to conditional mathematical expectation of random variable ζ under the condition $(\xi, \eta) = (x,y)$, i.e.,

$$E(\zeta \mid \xi = x, \eta = y) = \frac{\int_{-\infty}^{+\infty} z f(x,y,z)\mathrm{d}z}{\int_{-\infty}^{+\infty} f(x,y,z)\mathrm{d}z}. \tag{5.5.18}$$

This shows that $E(\zeta \mid \xi = x, \eta = y) = \overline{s}(x, y)$. □

Remark 5.5.2 By probability density function $f(x, y, z)$, we can make up conditional probability density function as follows:

$$\begin{aligned} f_{\zeta|(\xi,\eta)=(x,y)}(z \mid x, y) &\triangleq \frac{f(x, y, z)}{\int_{-\infty}^{+\infty} f(x, y, z)\mathrm{d}z} \\ &= \frac{p(x, y, z)\chi_{X\times Y\times Z}}{\int_Z p(x, y, z)\chi_{X\times Y}\mathrm{d}z}. \end{aligned} \tag{5.5.19}$$

Then (5.5.18) and conditional variance can be shortened as

$$\begin{aligned} E(\zeta \mid \xi = x, \eta = y) &= \overline{s}(x, y) \\ &= \int_{-\infty}^{+\infty} z f_{\zeta|(\xi,\eta)=(x,y)}(z \mid x, y)\mathrm{d}z \\ &= \frac{\int_{-\infty}^{+\infty} z p(x, y, z)\chi_{X\times Y\times Z}\mathrm{d}z}{\int_Z p(x, y, z)\chi_{X\times Y}\mathrm{d}z}, \end{aligned} \tag{5.5.20}$$

$$\begin{aligned} & D(\zeta \mid \xi = x, \eta = y) \\ & \triangleq \int_{-\infty}^{+\infty} [z - E(\zeta \mid \xi = x, \eta = y)]^2 f_{\zeta|(\xi,\eta)=(x,y)}(z \mid x, y)\mathrm{d}z \\ & = \frac{\int_{-\infty}^{+\infty} [z - E(\zeta \mid \xi = x, \eta = y)]^2 p(x, y, z)\chi_{X\times Y\times Z}\mathrm{d}z}{\int_Z p(x, y, z)\chi_{X\times Y}\mathrm{d}z} \end{aligned} \tag{5.5.21}$$

Clearly the probability distribution function of random vector (ξ, η, ζ) is as the following expression:

$$\begin{aligned} F(x, y, z) &\triangleq P(\xi < x, \eta < y, \zeta < z) \\ &= \int_{-\infty}^{x}\int_{-\infty}^{y}\int_{-\infty}^{z} f(u, v, w)\mathrm{d}u\mathrm{d}v\mathrm{d}w. \end{aligned} \tag{5.5.22}$$

Besides, it is not difficult to write out every marginal density function and marginal distribution function. □

Example 5.5.1 In (5.5.12), taking θ being Mamdani operator, Zadeh operator, Lukasiewicz operator, Gödel operator, Dubois-Prade operator, Goguen operator, Wang operator, Einstein meet operator, Einstein union operator and Larsen operator, respectively, we immediately obtain various typical probability distributions of concerned double-input single-output fuzzy systems, i.e., Mamdani distribution, Zadeh distribution, Lukasiewicz distribution, Gödel distribution, Dubois-Prade distribution, Goguen distribution, Wang distribution, Einstein meet distribution, Einstein union distribution and Larsen distribution. In order to give a demonstration, put again $\theta = \theta_2$[14–17], that is Reichenbach operator as follows:

$$\left(\forall (a,b)\in[0,1]^2\right)\left(\theta_2(a,b)\triangleq 1-a+ab\right).$$

Then we have the following expressions:

$$\begin{aligned} p(x,y,z) &= \bigvee_{i=1}^{n} \theta_2\left(\mu_{A_i}(x)\wedge\mu_{B_i}(y),\mu_{C_i}(z)\right) \\ &= \bigvee_{i=1}^{n}\left[1-\left(\mu_{A_i}(x)\wedge\mu_{B_i}(y)\right)+\left(\mu_{A_i}(x)\wedge\mu_{B_i}(y)\right)\mu_{C_i}(z)\right], \end{aligned} \tag{5.5.23}$$

$$f(x,y,z)=\frac{p(x,y,z)\chi_{X\times Y\times Z}}{H\left(3,n,\theta_2,\vee\right)}, \tag{5.5.24}$$

where $H(3,n,\theta_2,\vee)>0$ is assumed. The probability distribution with (5.5.24) for probability density function is called Reichenbach distribution with parameter $(3,n,\vee)$ and denoted by $\mathrm{Rei}(3,n,\vee)$, in other words, $(\xi,\eta,\zeta)\sim\mathrm{Rei}(3,n,\vee)$, i.e., the random vector (ξ,η,ζ) obeys the probability distribution $\mathrm{Rei}(3,n,\vee)$. □

5.6 The Probability Representations of Multi-input Multi-output Fuzzy Systems

Consider a fuzzy system with p inputs and q outputs. Suppose that the sets $X_i\in\mathcal{B}^1$ are universes of input variables and $Y_j\in\mathcal{B}^1$ are universes of output variables where $i=1,2,\cdots,p, j=1,2,\cdots,q$. And let

$$\mathcal{A}_i=\{A_{ki}|1\le k\le n\},\quad i=1,2,\cdots,p,$$
$$\mathcal{B}_j=\{B_{kj}|1\le k\le n\},\quad j=1,2,\cdots,q$$

be classes of fuzzy sets on $X_i\ (i=1,2,\cdots,p)$ and $Y_j\ (j=1,2,\cdots,q)$, respectively. Considering $\mathcal{A}_i$ and $\mathcal{B}_j$ as linguistic variables, we form n rules of fuzzy reasoning as follows:

$$\text{If } x_1 \text{ is } A_{k1} \text{ and } x_2 \text{ is } A_{k2} \text{ and } \cdots \text{ and } x_p \text{ is } A_{kp}$$
$$\text{then } y_1 \text{ is } B_{k1} \text{ and } y_2 \text{ is } B_{k2} \text{ and } \cdots \text{ and } y_q \text{ is } B_{kq}, \qquad (5.6.1)$$

where $k=1,2,\cdots,n$. If we put

$$\mathcal{D}\triangleq\{(A_{k1},A_{k2},\cdots,A_{kp})|1\le k\le n\}\subset\prod_{i=1}^{p}\mathcal{A}_i,$$

then we can make the mappings $s_j^*\ (j=1,2,\cdots,q)$ as follows:

$$\begin{aligned} &s_j^*:\mathcal{D}\to\mathcal{B}_j\\ &(A_{k1},A_{k2},\cdots,A_{kp})\mapsto s_j^*(A_{k1},A_{k2},\cdots,A_{kp})\triangleq B_{kj}\end{aligned} \qquad (5.6.2)$$

Remark 5.6.1 Here the group (5.6.1) of rules of fuzzy reasoning is also simple expression as described in Remark 5.5.1. See Remark 5.5.1 and [6] for the reason. □

In (5.6.1), the $k-$th rule can form q fuzzy relations of fuzzy reasoning are expressed by the following:

$$R_{kj}\in\mathcal{F}\left(\left(\prod_{i=1}^{p}X_i\right)\times Y_j\right),$$
$$j=1,2,\cdots,q$$

by means of a certain fuzzy implication operator θ:

$$\mu_{R_{kj}}\left(x_1,x_2,\cdots,x_p,y_j\right)\triangleq\theta\left(\overset{p}{\underset{i=1}{\wedge}}\mu_{A_{ki}}\left(x_i\right),\ \mu_{B_{kj}}\left(y_j\right)\right) \qquad (5.6.3)$$

Then we can obtain the total fuzzy relation of the fuzzy reasoning as the equation $R_j=\bigcup_{k=1}^{n}R_{kj}$ about (5.6.1) for every index j $(j=1,2,\cdots,q)$, i.e.,

$$\mu_{R_j}\left(x_1,x_2,\cdots,x_p,y_j\right)=\overset{n}{\underset{k=1}{\vee}}\theta\left(\overset{p}{\underset{i=1}{\wedge}}\mu_{A_{ki}}\left(x_i\right),\ \mu_{B_{kj}}\left(y_j\right)\right) \qquad (5.6.4)$$

If we denote the following set and mapping:

$$\mathcal{C}\triangleq\left\{\left(B_{k1},B_{k2},\cdots,B_{kq}\right)\middle|1\le k\le n\right\},$$
$$s^*\triangleq\left(s_1^*,s_2^*,\cdots,s_q^*\right),$$

then s^* is a mapping from $\mathcal{D}$ to $\mathcal{C}$, i.e.,

$$\begin{aligned}&s^*:\mathcal{D}\to\mathcal{C}\\&\left(A_{k1},\cdots,A_{kp}\right)\mapsto s^*\left(A_{k1},\cdots,A_{kp}\right)=\left(B_{k1},\cdots,B_{kq}\right),\\&k=1,2,\cdots,n.\end{aligned} \qquad (5.6.5)$$

For arbitrarily given $\left(A_1,A_2,\cdots,A_p\right)\in\prod_{i=1}^{p}\mathcal{F}(X_i)$, we can obtain result of reasoning $B_j\in\mathcal{F}\left(Y_j\right)$ through R_j. This is also realized by fuzzy transformation "$\circ$" as follows:

$$\begin{aligned}\circ:\ &\prod_{i=1}^{p}\mathcal{F}(X_i)\to\mathcal{F}\left(Y_j\right)\\&\left(A_1,\cdots,A_p\right)\mapsto B_j=\circ\left(A_1,\cdots,A_p\right)\\&\qquad\qquad\triangleq\left(\prod_{i=1}^{p}A_i\right)\circ R_j,\end{aligned} \qquad (5.6.6)$$

where $\prod_{i=1}^{p} A_i$ denotes Cartesian product of $A_1, A_2, \cdots, A_p$, i.e.,

$$\prod_{i=1}^{p} A_i \in \mathcal{F}\left(\prod_{i=1}^{p} X_i\right),$$
$$\mu_{\prod_{i=1}^{p} A_i}\left(x_1, x_2, \cdots, x_p\right) = \bigwedge_{i=1}^{p} \mu_{A_i}\left(x_i\right), \tag{5.6.7}$$

which has such logical meaning as described before. The form of membership function of (5.6.6) becomes to the following equations:

$$\mu_{B_j}\left(y_j\right) = \bigvee_{\left(x_1,\cdots,x_p\right)\in\prod_{i=1}^{p} A_i} \left[\left(\bigwedge_{i=1}^{p} \mu_{A_i}\left(x_i\right)\right) \wedge \mu_{R_j}\left(x_1, \cdots, x_p, y_j\right)\right] \tag{5.6.8}$$

Thus we obtain functions s_j^{**} $(j = 1, 2, \cdots, q)$ as follows:

$$s_j^{**} : \prod_{i=1}^{p} \mathcal{F}(X_i) \to \mathcal{F}\left(Y_j\right)$$
$$\left(A_1, \cdots, A_p\right) \mapsto B_j = s_j^{**}\left(A_1, \cdots, A_p\right) \approx \left(\prod_{i=1}^{p} A_i\right) \circ R_j \tag{5.6.9}$$

Putting $s^{**} \triangleq \left(s_1^{**}, s_2^{**}, \cdots, s_q^{**}\right)$, we obtain a vector-valued function as the following:

$$s^{**} : \prod_{i=1}^{p} \mathcal{F}(X_i) \to \prod_{j=1}^{q} \mathcal{F}\left(Y_j\right)$$
$$\left(A_1, \cdots, A_p\right) \mapsto \left(B_1, \cdots, B_q\right) = s^{**}\left(A_1, \cdots, A_p\right) \tag{5.6.10}$$
$$\triangleq \left(s_1^{**}\left(A_1, \cdots, A_p\right), \cdots, s_q^{**}\left(A_1, \cdots, A_p\right)\right)$$

For any given $\left(x_1', x_2', \cdots, x_p'\right) \in \prod_{i=1}^{p} X_i$, considering x_i' $(i = 1, 2, \cdots, p)$ as singleton fuzzy sets A_i' $(i = 1, 2, \cdots, p)$, respectively (refer to (5.2.8)), and substituting them into (5.6.8), we can obtain the results of the fuzzy reasoning $B_j' \in \mathcal{F}\left(Y_j\right)$ $(j = 1, 2, \cdots, q)$ as follows:

$$\begin{aligned} \mu_{B_j'}\left(y_j\right) &= \mu_{R_j}\left(x_1', x_2', \cdots, x_p', y_j\right) \\ &= \bigvee_{k=1}^{n} \theta\left(\bigwedge_{i=1}^{p} \mu_{A_{ki}}\left(x'\right), \mu_{B_{kj}}\left(y_j\right)\right) \end{aligned} \tag{5.6.11}$$

If the following conditions are satisfied

$$\int_{Y_j} |\, y_j \,|\, \mu_{B_j'}\left(y_j\right) \mathrm{d}y_j < +\infty, \quad 0 < \int_{Y_j} \mu_{B_j'}\left(y_j\right) \mathrm{d}y_j < +\infty$$

then we can obtain exact outputs y_j' by doing defuzzification to B_j' by COG method as the following:

$$y_j' = \frac{\int_{Y_j} y_j \mu_{B_j'}\left(y_j\right) \mathrm{d}y_j}{\int_{Y_j} \mu_{B_j'}\left(y_j\right) \mathrm{d}y_j}, \quad j = 1, 2, \cdots, q \tag{5.6.12}$$

In this way, for every index j we have a function $\overline{s}_j : \prod_{i=1}^{p} X_i \to Y_j$, where

$$\overline{s}_j\left(x_1, x_2, \cdots, x_p\right) = \frac{\int_{Y_j} y_j \mu_{B_j'}\left(y_j\right) \mathrm{d}y_j}{\int_{Y_j} \mu_{B_j'}\left(y_j\right) \mathrm{d}y_j} \tag{5.6.13}$$

Again let $\overline{s} \triangleq \left(\overline{s}_1, \overline{s}_2, \cdots, \overline{s}_q\right)$. Then $\overline{s}$ is a vector-valued function from $\prod_{i=1}^{p} X_i$ to $\prod_{j=1}^{q} Y_j$ as the follows:

$$\overline{s}\left(x_1,\cdots,x_p\right)=\left(\overline{s}_1\left(x_1,\cdots,x_p\right),\cdots,\overline{s}_q\left(x_1,\cdots,x_p\right)\right) \tag{5.6.14}$$

As known very well, since $\mu_{B'_j}\left(y_j\right)$ and $\left(x'_1,\cdots,x'_p\right)$ depend on each other, we should denote

$$B'_j\left(x_1=x'_1,\cdots,x_p=x'_p\right)\triangleq B'_j,$$
$$\mu_{B'_j\left(x_1=x'_1,\cdots,x_p=x'_p\right)}\left(y_j\right)=\mu_{B'}\left(y_j\right),$$

and can write it as a $(p+1)$-ary function alike as described before:

$$p_j:\left(\prod_{i=1}^{p}X_i\right)\times Y_j\to\mathbb{R}$$
$$p_j\left(x_1,\cdots,x_p,y_j\right)\triangleq\mu_{B'}\left(y_j\right)=\mu_{R_j}\left(x_1,\cdots,x_p,y_j\right) \tag{5.6.15}$$
$$=\bigvee_{k=1}^{n}\theta\left(\bigwedge_{i=1}^{p}\mu_{A_{ki}},\mu_{B_{kj}}\left(y_j\right)\right)$$

Then (5.6.13) can be written as the following:

$$\overline{s}_j\left(x_1,\cdots,x_p\right)=\frac{\int_{Y_j}y_jp_j\left(x_1,\cdots,x_p,y_j\right)\mathrm{d}y_j}{\int_{Y_j}p_j\left(x_1,\cdots,x_p,y_j\right)\mathrm{d}y_j} \tag{5.6.16}$$

Again expand domain of definition of p_j onto $\mathbb{R}^{p+1}$ and denote

$$q_j\left(x_1,\cdots,x_p,y_j\right)\triangleq p_j\left(x_1,\cdots,x_p,y_j\right)\chi_{\left(\prod_{i=1}^{p}X_i\right)\times Y_j}$$

Then (5.6.16) becomes to the following equation:

$$\overline{s}_j\left(x_1,\cdots,x_p\right)=\frac{\int_{-\infty}^{+\infty}y_jq_j\left(x_1,\cdots,x_p,y_j\right)\mathrm{d}y_j}{\int_{-\infty}^{+\infty}q_j\left(x_1,\cdots,x_p,y_j\right)\mathrm{d}y_j} \tag{5.6.17}$$

Also notice that $\overline{s}_j\left(x_1,\cdots,x_p\right)$ and $\overline{s}_j\left(x_1,\cdots,x_p\right)\chi_{\prod_{i=1}^{p}X_i}$ are the same.

Similarly to preceding analysis, although all of $p_j\left(x_1,\cdots,x_p,y_j\right)$ satisfy non-negativity, they do not necessarily possess normality and so need to handle. Now let

$$H(p+1,n,\theta,\vee) \triangleq \int_{X_1}\cdots\int_{X_p}\int_{Y_j} p_j\left(x_1,\cdots,x_p,y_j\right)\mathrm{d}x_1\cdots\mathrm{d}x_p\mathrm{d}y_j \tag{5.6.18}$$

If $H(p+1,n,\theta,\vee)>0$, then we can put

$$f_j\left(x_1,\cdots,x_p,y_j\right) \triangleq \frac{p_j\left(x_1,\cdots,x_p,y_j\right)\chi_{\left(\prod_{i=1}^{p}X_i\right)\times Y_j}}{H(p+1,n,\theta,\vee)}. \tag{5.6.19}$$

In (5.6.17), to replace $q_j\left(x_1,\cdots,x_p,y_j\right)$ with $f_j\left(x_1,\cdots,x_p,y_j\right)$ does not change (5.6.17}), i.e.,

$$\overline{s}_j\left(x_1,\cdots,x_p\right) = \frac{\int_{-\infty}^{+\infty} y_j f_j\left(x_1,\cdots,x_p,y_j\right)\mathrm{d}y_j}{\int_{-\infty}^{+\infty} f_j\left(x_1,\cdots,x_p,y_j\right)\mathrm{d}y_j}. \tag{5.6.20}$$

Theorem 5.6.1 Given a multi-input multi-output fuzzy system, the related notations are same as described above. Select and fix a fuzzy implication operator θ. If the following conditions are satisfied as follows:

$$\int_{Y_j}\left|y_j\right| p_j\left(x_1,x_2,\cdots,x_p,y_j\right)\mathrm{d}y_j < +\infty,$$
$$0<\int_{Y_j} p_j\left(x_1,x_2,\cdots,x_p,y_j\right)\mathrm{d}y_j < +\infty,$$

where $j=1,2,\cdots,q$, then there must exist a probability space $(\Omega,\mathcal{F},P)$ and a vector-valued random vector (ξ,η) defined on it such that

$$\xi:\Omega\to\mathbb{R}^p,\quad \eta:\Omega\to\mathbb{R}^q$$

and vector-valued conditional mathematical expectation $E(\eta\,|\,\xi)$ and $\overline{s}(\xi)$ are the same, i.e., $E(\eta\,|\,\xi)=\overline{s}(\xi)$, in other words, we have the following expression:

$$\forall\left(x_1,\cdots,x_p\right)\in\prod_{i=1}^{p}X_i,$$
$$E\left(\eta\middle|\xi_1=x_1,\cdots,\xi_p=x_p\right)=\overline{s}\left(x_1,\cdots,x_p\right),$$

where $\xi\triangleq\left(\xi_1,\xi_2,\cdots,\xi_p\right),\eta\triangleq\left(\eta_1,\eta_2,\cdots,\eta_q\right)$ and

$$E(\eta\,|\,\xi)\triangleq\left(E\left(\eta_1\middle|\xi_1,\cdots,\xi_p\right),\cdots,E\left(\eta_q\middle|\xi_1,\cdots,\xi_p\right)\right) \tag{5.6.21}$$

And $\overline{s}(\xi)$ is unified expression of (6.14), i.e.,

$$\overline{s}\left(\xi_1,\cdots,\xi_p\right)=\left(\overline{s_1}\left(\xi_1,\cdots,\xi_p\right),\cdots,\overline{s}_q\left(\xi_1,\cdots,\xi_p\right)\right). \tag{5.6.22}$$

In more detail, for every $j\in\{1,\cdots,q\}$, it holds that

$$E\left(\eta_j\middle|\xi_1=x_1,\cdots,\xi_p=x_p\right)=\overline{s}_j\left(x_1,\cdots,x_p\right), \tag{5.6.23}$$

i.e., functional value $\overline{s}_j\left(x_1,\cdots,x_p\right)$ of function $\overline{s}_j$ at $\left(x_1,\cdots,x_p\right)$ equals to conditional mathematical expectation $E\left(\eta_j\middle|\xi_1=x_1,\cdots,\xi_p=x_p\right)$ of random variable η_j under the condition of random vector as follows:

$$\left(\xi_1,\xi_2,\cdots,\xi_p\right)=\left(x_1,x_2,\cdots,x_p\right).$$

Proof. Based on the input universes X_i $(i=1,\cdots,p)$ and the output universes Y_j $(j=1,\cdots,q)$, construct $p+q$ probability spaces as follows:

$$\left(X_i, \mathcal{B}_i^x, P_i^x\right), \quad i = 1, 2, \cdots, p,$$
$$\left(Y_j, \mathcal{B}_j^y, P_j^y\right), \quad j = 1, 2, \cdots, q,$$

where $\mathcal{B}_i^x$ is Borel σ-field on X_i, and $\mathcal{B}_j^y$ is Borel σ-field on Y_j, and P_i^x is probability measure on $\mathcal{B}_i^x$, and P_j^y is probability measure on $\mathcal{B}_j^y$. Suppose that ξ_i and η_j are random variables defined on X_i and Y_j, respectively. Taking

$$\Omega_j \triangleq \left(\prod_{i=1}^{p} X_i\right) \times Y_j, \mathcal{F}_j \triangleq \left(\prod_{i=1}^{p} \mathcal{B}_i^x\right) \times \mathcal{B}_j^y, P_j \triangleq \left(\prod_{i=1}^{p} P_i^x\right) \times P_j^y,$$

we can obtain q joint probability spaces as the following:

$$\left(\Omega_j, \mathcal{F}_j, P_j\right), \quad j = 1, 2, \cdots, q.$$

With same notations, we redefine ξ_i $(i = 1, 2, \cdots, p)$ as random variables on every space Ω_j $(j = 1, 2, \cdots, q)$ as follows:

$$\begin{aligned}
&\xi_i : \Omega_j \to \mathbb{R} \\
&\left(u_1, \cdots, u_p, v_j\right) \mapsto \xi_i\left(u_1, \cdots, u_p, v_j\right) \triangleq \xi_i\left(u_i\right),
\end{aligned}$$

and we also redefine η_j on only Ω_j that has the same subscript j as follows:

$$\begin{aligned}
&\eta_j : \Omega_j \to \mathbb{R} \\
&\left(u_1, \cdots, u_p, v_j\right) \mapsto \eta_j\left(u_1, \cdots, u_p, v_j\right) \triangleq \eta_j\left(v_j\right)
\end{aligned}$$

Thus we obtain $p+1$ dimensional random vector $\left(\xi_1, \cdots, \xi_p, \eta_j\right)$ defined on $\left(\Omega_j, \mathcal{F}_j, P_j\right)(j = 1, \cdots, q)$. Now we consider $f_j\left(x_1, \cdots, x_p, y_j\right)$ in the equation (5.6.19) as a probability density function of the random vector $\left(\xi_1,\cdots,\xi_p,\eta_j\right)$. By definition of conditional mathematical expectation, we can see that (5.6.20) is just conditional mathematical expectation of random vector $\left(\xi_1,\cdots,\xi_p,\eta_j\right)$:

$$E\left(\eta_j \middle| \xi_1 = x_1,\cdots,\xi_p = x_p\right) = \frac{\int_{-\infty}^{+\infty} y_j f_j\left(x_1,\cdots,x_p,y_j\right)\mathrm{d}y_j}{\int_{-\infty}^{+\infty} f_j\left(x_1,\cdots,x_p,y_j\right)\mathrm{d}y_j},$$

which means the following equation:

$$E\left(\eta_j \middle| \xi_1 = x_1,\cdots,\xi_p = x_p\right) = \overline{s}_j\left(x_1,\cdots,x_p\right).$$

Again using unified expression of conditional mathematical expectation, we have the following expression:

$$E\left(\eta_j \middle| \xi_1,\cdots,\xi_p\right) = \overline{s}_j\left(\xi_1,\cdots,\xi_p\right). \tag{5.6.24}$$

Finally, we define $\Omega,\mathcal{F},P$ respectively as the following:

$$\Omega \triangleq \left(\prod_{i=1}^{p} X_i\right) \times \left(\prod_{j=1}^{q} Y_j\right),$$

$$\mathcal{F} \triangleq \left(\prod_{i=1}^{p} \mathcal{B}_i^x\right) \times \left(\prod_{j=1}^{q} \mathcal{B}_j^y\right),$$

$$P \triangleq \left(\prod_{i=1}^{p} P_i^x\right) \times \left(\prod_{j=1}^{q} P_j^y\right).$$

Then we obtain the total probability space $(\Omega,\mathcal{F},P)$. By this, we can define a vector-valued random vector $(\xi,\eta):\Omega \to \mathbb{R}^{p+q}$ as follows:

$$\begin{aligned} &\xi:\Omega \to \mathbb{R}^p \\ &\omega = \left(u_1,\cdots,u_p,v_1,\cdots,v_q\right) \mapsto \xi(\omega) \triangleq \left(\xi_1\left(u_1\right),\cdots,\xi_p\left(u_p\right)\right) \end{aligned} \tag{5.6.25}$$

$$\begin{aligned}&\eta:\Omega\to\mathbb{R}^q\\&\omega=\left(u_1,\cdots,u_p,v_1,\cdots,v_q\right)\mapsto\eta(\omega)\triangleq\left(\eta_1\left(v_1\right),\cdots,\eta_q\left(v_q\right)\right)\end{aligned}\tag{5.6.26}$$

If we set the following symbol:

$$E(\eta\mid\xi)\triangleq\left(E\left(\eta_1\left|\xi_1,\cdots,\xi_p\right.\right),\cdots,E\left(\eta_q\left|\xi_1,\cdots,\xi_p\right.\right)\right)$$

and notice Equation (5.6.22), it follows from (5.6.24) that

$$\begin{aligned}&E(\eta\mid\xi)=E\left(\eta\left|\xi_1,\cdots,\xi_p\right.\right)\\&=\left(E\left(\eta_1\left|\xi_1,\cdots,\xi_p\right.\right),\cdots,E\left(\eta_q\left|\xi_1,\cdots,\xi_p\right.\right)\right)\\&=\left(\overline{s}_1\left(\xi_1,\cdots,\xi_p\right),\cdots,\overline{s}_q\left(\xi_1,\cdots,\xi_p\right)\right)\\&=\left(\overline{s}_1(\xi),\cdots,\overline{s}_q(\xi)\right)=\overline{s}(\xi)\end{aligned}$$

This completes the proof. □

Remark 5.6.2 For every $j\in\{1,2,\cdots,q\}$, we take the conditional probability density function as follows:

$$\begin{aligned}f_j\left(y_j\left|x_1,\cdots,x_p\right.\right)&\triangleq\frac{f_j\left(x_1,\cdots,x_p,y_j\right)}{\int_{-\infty}^{+\infty}f_j\left(x_1,\cdots,x_p,y_j\right)\mathrm{d}y_j}\\&=\frac{p_j\left(x_1,\cdots,x_p,y_j\right)\chi_{\left(\prod_{i=1}^{p}X_i\right)\times Y_j}}{\int_{Y_j}p_j\left(x_1,\cdots,x_p,y_j\right)\mathrm{d}y_j}\end{aligned}\tag{5.6.27}$$

Then (5.6.20) and conditional variance can be shortened as

$$\begin{aligned}&E\left(\eta_j\left|\xi_1=x_1,\cdots,\xi_p=x_p\right.\right)\\&=\overline{s}_j\left(x_1,\cdots,x_p\right)=\int_{-\infty}^{+\infty}y_jf_j\left(y_j\left|x_1,\cdots,x_p\right.\right)\mathrm{d}y_j\end{aligned}\tag{5.6.28}$$

$$D\left(\eta_j \middle| \xi_1 = x_1, \cdots, \xi_p = x_p\right) = \int_{-\infty}^{+\infty}\left[y_j - E\left(\eta_j \middle| \xi_1 = x_1, \cdots, \xi_p = x_p\right)\right]^2 f_j\left(y_j \middle| x_1, \cdots, x_p\right)\mathrm{d}y_j \tag{5.6.29}$$

respectively. We should also put

$$\begin{aligned} &D\left(\eta_j \middle| \xi_1 = x_1, \cdots, \xi_p = x_p\right) \\ &\triangleq \left(D\left(\eta_1 \middle| \xi_1 = x_1, \cdots, \xi_p = x_p\right), \cdots, D\left(\eta_q \middle| \xi_1 = x_1, \cdots, \xi_p = x_p\right)\right) \end{aligned} \tag{5.6.30}$$

This is a vector-valued conditional variance. Noticing the following equation

$$D(\eta \mid \xi(\omega)) = D\left(\eta \middle| \xi_1 = x_1, \cdots, \xi_p = x_p\right),$$

its unified expression is as follows:

$$D(\eta \mid \xi) = \left(D(\eta_1 \mid \xi), \cdots, D(\eta_q \mid \xi)\right). \tag{5.6.31}$$

Moreover, the probability distribution function of the random vector as the form $\left(\xi_1, \cdots, \xi_p, \eta_j\right)$ can be expressed as the following:

$$\begin{aligned} F_j\left(x_1, \cdots, x_p, y_j\right) &\triangleq P_j\left(\xi_1 < x_1, \cdots, \xi_p < x_p, \eta_j < y_j\right) \\ &= \int_{-\infty}^{x_1} \cdots \int_{-\infty}^{x_p} \int_{-\infty}^{y_j} f_j\left(u_1, \cdots, u_p, v_j\right)\mathrm{d}u_1 \cdots \mathrm{d}u_p \mathrm{d}v_j. \end{aligned} \tag{5.6.32}$$

Besides, it is not difficult to write out every marginal probability density function and marginal probability distribution function. □

Remark 5.6.3 For the more tight expression, let

$$\begin{aligned} F(x, y) &\triangleq F\left(x_1, \cdots, x_p, y_1, \cdots, y_q\right) \\ &\triangleq \left(F_1\left(x_1, \cdots, x_p, y_1\right), \cdots, F_q\left(x_1, \cdots, x_p, y_q\right)\right) \end{aligned} \tag{5.6.33}$$

for any $x=\left(x_1,\cdots,x_p\right)\in\mathbb{R}^p$ and $y=\left(y_1,\cdots,y_q\right)\in\mathbb{R}^q$. Then we see from (5.6.32) that $F(x,y)$ is just the probability distribution function of the random vector (ξ,η). Similarly, putting

$$
\begin{aligned}
&f(x,y)\triangleq f\left(x_1,\cdots,x_p,y_1,\cdots,y_q\right)\\
&\triangleq\left(f_1\left(x_1,\cdots,x_p,y_1\right),\cdots,f_q\left(x_1,\cdots,x_p,y_q\right)\right)
\end{aligned}
\tag{5.6.34}
$$

we may also formally consider that $f(x,y)$ is the probability density function of the random vector (ξ,η). □

Example 5.6.1 In (5.6.19), taking θ being Mamdani operator, Zadeh operator, Lukasiewicz operator, Gödel operator, Dubois-Prade operator, Goguen operator, Wang operator, Einstein meet operator, Einstein union operator and Larsen operator, respectively, we immediately obtain various typical probability distributions of concerned p input and q output fuzzy systems, that is, Mamdani distribution, Zadeh distribution, Lukasiewicz distribution, Gödel distribution, Dubois-Prade distribution, Goguen distribution, Wang distribution, Einstein meet distribution, Einstein union distribution and Larsen distribution. In order to give a demonstration, put $\theta=\theta_{11}$ [14–17] that is Gaines-Rescher operator as the following:

$$
\left(\forall(a,b)\in[0,1]^2\right)\left(\theta_{11}(a,b)\triangleq\begin{cases}1, & a\le b\\ 0, & a>b\end{cases}\right).
$$

Then we have the following expression:

$$
\begin{aligned}
&p_j\left(x_1,\cdots,x_p,y_j\right)=\bigvee_{k=1}^{n}\theta_{11}\left(\bigwedge_{i=1}^{p}\mu_{A_{ki}}\left(x_i\right),\mu_{B_{kj}}\left(y_j\right)\right)\\
&=\begin{cases}1, & (\exists k)\left(\bigwedge_{i=1}^{p}\mu_{A_{ki}}\left(x_i\right)\le\mu_{B_{kj}}\left(y_j\right)\right),\\ 0, & \text{otherwise,}\end{cases}
\end{aligned}
\tag{5.6.35}
$$

and suppose that following condition is satisfied:

$$\mu^{p+1}\left(\left\{(\exists k)\left(\bigwedge_{i=1}^{p}\mu_{A_{ki}}(x_i)\le\mu_{B_{kj}}(y_j)\right)\right\}\right)>0,$$

we also have the expression as follows:

$$f_j(x_1,\cdots,x_p,y_j)=\frac{\chi_{\left\{(\exists k)\left(\bigwedge_{i=1}^{p}\mu_{A_{ki}}(x_i)\le\mu_{B_{kj}}(y_j)\right)\right\}}}{\mu^{p+1}\left(\left\{(\exists k)\left(\bigwedge_{i=1}^{p}\mu_{A_{ki}}(x_i)\le\mu_{B_{kj}}(y_j)\right)\right\}\right)} \tag{5.6.36}$$

where μ^{p+1} is Lebesgue measure on Borel σ-field $\mathcal{B}^{p+1}$ in $\mathbb{R}^{p+1}$. The probability distribution with (5.6.36) for probability density function is called Gaines-Rescher distribution with parameter $(p+1,n,\vee)$ and denoted by $\mathrm{GR}(p+1,n,\vee)$, in other words,

$$(\xi_1,\cdots,\xi_p,\eta_j)\sim\mathrm{GR}(p+1,n,\vee),$$

i.e., the random vector $(\xi_1,\cdots,\xi_p,\eta_j)$ obeys $\mathrm{GR}(p+1,n,\vee)$. □

Remark 5.6.4 By (5.6.36), we can see that Gaines-Rescher distribution is a uniform distribution. It is not good that a fuzzy system possesses uniform distribution, since output of such a system is no more than a step function. In the next section, we will discuss this problem. □

5.7 A Conclusion on Uniform Distributions in Fuzzy Systems

For brevity, the discussion in this section shall be restricted to single-input single-output fuzzy system and $(\Omega,\mathcal{F},P)$ will denote probability space related to such a system. Considering probability distributions given in Examples 5.4.3 to 5.4.7, i.e., Lukasiewicz distribution, Gödel distribution, Dubois-Prade distribution, Goguen distribution and Wang distribution, we can find out that they have a common attribute that is local uniformity. In probability theory, uniform distribution is one of familiar probability distributions of continuous type and actually reflects rather simple or rather ordinary uncertainty problems. However, local uniformity that acts as inner kernel of fuzzy system and even its extreme case, i.e., global uniformity (uniformity, for short) reflects an important property of fuzzy system: From the viewpoint of active meaning, local uniformity may be understood as a kind of robustness. $\overline{s}(x) = E(\eta \mid \xi = x)$ takes a constant value in a certain locally measurable set $D \in \mathcal{F}$, i.e., for any $\omega = (x, y) \in D$, we have

$$E(\eta \mid \xi)(\omega) = E(\eta \mid \xi = x) = \overline{s}(x) = \text{const}. \tag{5.7.1}$$

From the viewpoint of passive meaning, local uniformity embodies a kind of slowness. Output of the system is a step function on this region as being D.

When considering a certain characteristic of something, it is an efficient method to let this characteristic be in the extreme on purpose. We now let the local uniformity be in the extreme, say turn to study global uniformity, and look at what output response the fuzzy system makes here.

Theorem 5.7.1 Given a single-input single-output fuzzy system, the related notations are same as described before, and $(\Omega, \mathcal{F}, P)$ is probability space related to it, where $\Omega = X \times Y$. If probability distribution of this fuzzy system is uniform distribution (global uniformity) and its probability density function is

$$f(x, y) = \frac{1}{\mu^2(X \times Y)} \chi_{X \times Y}(x, y), \tag{5.7.2}$$

where μ^2 is two-dimensional Lebesgue measure and $\mu^2(X \times Y) > 0$ is assumed, then output of the system is a step function, i.e., $\overline{s}(x) \equiv \text{const}$.

Proof. By the condition $\mu^2(X \times Y) > 0$, we can see that $\mu^1(Y) > 0$, where μ^1 is one-dimensional Lebesgue measure. According to the results discussed before, we have that for any $x \in X$, it holds that

$$\overline{s}(x) = E(\eta \mid \xi = x) = \frac{\int_{-\infty}^{+\infty} yf(x,y)\mathrm{d}y}{\int_{-\infty}^{+\infty} f(x,y)\mathrm{d}y} = \frac{\int_Y y\mathrm{d}y}{\int_Y \mathrm{d}y} = \frac{c}{\mu^1(Y)} = \mathrm{const} \tag{5.7.3}$$

where $c \triangleq \int_Y y\mathrm{d}y$. Thus $\overline{s}(x) \equiv \mathrm{const}$. □

In general, for any one system, whether it is deterministic system or uncertain system (including fuzzy system), if output of this system is a step function, then this system is undoubtedly an ordinary system and has no applicable worth but only certain theoretical signification. This enlightens us on proposing one important problem: For a non-ordinary uncertain system S, when constructing a function $\overline{s}(x)$ that represents this system, either if select an unapt fuzzy implication operator θ or if adopt an unapt algorithm for construction of system (for example, CRI method is an algorithm for construction of system and triple I method can also serves as an algorithm for construction of system), then shall it happen that representation $\overline{s}(x)$ of system, obtained in conclusion, is only a step function, i.e., $\overline{s}(x) \equiv \mathrm{const}$? Obviously, the answer is positive. However, the further problem is much more significant: If an algorithm for construction of system results in $\overline{s}(x) \equiv \mathrm{const}$ for many fuzzy implication operators θ, then is it yet feasible to use such an algorithm to construct system?

5.8 Probability Representations of Fuzzy Systems Constructed by Triple I Method

We turn to survey CRI method again. This algorithm first needs group of rules of fuzzy reasoning (refer to (5.2.1)) that is equivalent to functional relationship s^*, next forms fuzzy relation R_i of reasoning related to every rule by some fuzzy implication operator θ, where $i = 1, 2, \cdots, n$, and finally these fuzzy relations are synthesized to be a total relation by means of $R = \bigcup_{i=1}^{n} R_i$ which is with the reasoning meaning by logical "union". Then the action of logic has been over. How to realize s^{**} ? Zadeh's CRI method relies to fuzzy transformation (called relation composition as well) "$\circ$", i.e., for every $A \in \mathcal{F}(X)$, it obtains the following reasoning result by means of the operation "$\circ$":

$$B \triangleq A \circ R \in \mathcal{F}(Y).$$

We may say that this is entire content of CRI method.

In [20, 21], Wang has thought that CRI method is outcome of mixed use of implication operator and relation composition (so as to come down to a simple interpolation problem [6,7,13,20,21]), and it is not proper from the viewpoint of logic. For this reason, he has proposed triple I method where all of steps have logical action [20,21,24–27].

The triple I method is as follows [20,21]: Suppose that $A \in \mathcal{F}(X)$ and $B \in \mathcal{F}(Y)$ are known. Given one $A^* \in \mathcal{F}(X)$, find the "least" $B^* \in \mathcal{F}(Y)$ so that the following implication expression:

$$\left(\mu_A(x) \to \mu_B(y)\right) \to \left(\mu_{A^*}(x) \to \mu_{B^*}(y)\right) \tag{5.8.1}$$

takes the greatest possible value for all $x \in X$ and all $y \in Y$.

Note that finding the "least" $B^* \in \mathcal{F}(Y)$ mentioned above can gained rather good treatment just in semi-ordered Banach space in general and certainly needs to use variational method in addition. In order to clarify idea, we herein do not touch upon tool of nonlinear functional analysis briefly. In fact, for some special situations, the use of elementary method can accomplish to resolve the problem.

For requirement below, we make a little of formal change of (5.8.1). Noticing that implication expression $\left(\mu_A(x) \to \mu_B(y)\right)$ is actually a binary relation, we can naturally denote it by the following form:

$$\mu_R(x, y) \triangleq \left(\mu_A(x) \to \mu_B(y)\right)$$

according to conventional notation of binary relation. Then (5.8.1) changes to the following form:

$$\mu_R(x,y) \to \left(\mu_{A^*}(x) \to \mu_{B^*}(y)\right). \tag{5.8.2}$$

How to use triple I method in construction of fuzzy system $\overline{s}(x)$? Obviously, all of steps in process of formation from s^* to total relation R of reasoning have logical action. The process of production from R to s^{**} alone has used relation composition (also called fuzzy transformation) "$\circ$", i.e.,

$$\circ : \mathcal{F}(X) \to \mathcal{F}(Y), \quad A \mapsto B = \circ(A) \triangleq A \circ R.$$

Now we use triple I method to replace this step, i.e., for any $A \in \mathcal{F}(X)$, the result of reasoning $B \in \mathcal{F}(Y)$ obtained by triple I method should be the least fuzzy set so that the following implication expression:

$$\mu_R(x,y) \to \left(\mu_A(x) \to \mu_B(y)\right) \tag{5.8.3}$$

takes the greatest truth value for all $(x,y) \in X \times Y$. It is trivial that (5.8.3) and (5.8.2) coincide essentially.

Remark 5.8.1 We have known that there are three implication operators "$\to$" in (5.8.1) from left to right. Usually, they are taken as a kind of implication operator. We can easily understand (5.8.3) analogously. $\mu_R(x,y)$ in (5.8.3) apparently has no symbol "$\to$" of implication operator, but as a matter of fact "$\to$" is involved in $\mu_R(x,y)$ in hidden form. As a matter of fact, writing out $\mu_R(x,y)$, we have

$$\mu_R(x,y) = \bigvee_{i=1}^{n} \mu_{R_i}(x,y) = \bigvee_{i=1}^{n} \theta\left(\mu_{A_i}(x), \mu_{B_i}(y)\right).$$

Replacing symbol "θ" of implication operator with "$\to$", we have the following equation:

$$\mu_R(x,y) = \mathop{\vee}_{i=1}^{n} \mu_{R_i}(x,y) = \mathop{\vee}_{i=1}^{n} \left(\mu_{A_i}(x) \to \mu_{B_i}(y)\right).$$

Note that for any given $(x,y) \in X \times Y$ there must exist $i_0 \in \{1,2,\cdots,n\}$ such that

$$\mu_R(x,y) = \mu_{R_{i_0}}(x,y) = \left(\mu_{A_{i_0}}(x) \to \mu_{B_{i_0}}(y)\right).$$

Substituting this into (8.3), we obtain the following expression:

$$\left(\mu_{A_{i_0}}(x) \to \mu_{B_{i_0}}(y)\right) \to \left(\mu_{A^*}(x) \to \mu_{B^*}(y)\right).$$

If we ignore subscript "i_0", then this expression and (5.8.1) coincide completely. □

Theorem 5.8.1 Given a single-input single-output fuzzy system, the related notations are same as described before. If take fuzzy implication operator $\theta = \theta_{13}$ (i.e., Mamdani operator) then fuzzy system constructed by triple I method and fuzzy system constructed by CRI method have same probability distributions. In other words, fuzzy systems constructed by two methods described above are equivalent under condition of Mamdani implication operator.

Proof. We obtain total relation of reasoning by Mamdani implication operator θ_{13} and according to (5.2.1) to (5.2.3), i.e.,

$$\mu_R(x,y) = \mathop{\vee}_{i=1}^{n} \theta_{13}\left(\mu_{A_i}(x), \mu_{B_i}(y)\right) = \mathop{\vee}_{i=1}^{n} \left(\mu_{A_i}(x) \wedge \mu_{B_i}(y)\right)$$

For any given $A \in \mathcal{F}(X)$, result of reasoning $B \in \mathcal{F}(Y)$ that will be found by triple I method should be the least fuzzy set so that the following implication expression

$$\mu_R(x,y) \wedge \left(\mu_A(x) \wedge \mu_B(y)\right) = \left(\mu_R(x,y) \wedge \mu_A(x)\right) \wedge \mu_B(y)$$

takes the greatest truth value for all $(x, y) \in X \times Y$. It is not difficult to verify that such a B should be

$$\mu_B(y) = \sup\{\mu_R(x, y) \wedge \mu_A(x) | x \in X\}$$
$$= \bigvee_{x \in X} [\mu_A(x) \wedge \mu_R(x, y)], \quad y \in Y$$

Notice that this expression is just (5.2.6). Then, by (5.2.8) to (5.2.11) and (5.3.1) to (5.3.2), we have

$$p(x, y) = \bigvee_{i=1}^{n} \left(\mu_{A_i}(x) \wedge \mu_{B_i}(y)\right),$$

which is (5.4.2). Taking probability density function as follows

$$f(x, y) \triangleq \frac{p(x, y)\chi_{X \times Y}}{H(2, n, \theta_{13}, \vee)},$$

we can see from Example 5.4.1 that random vector of representing the system $(\xi, \eta) \sim \mathrm{Mam}(2, n, \vee)$. Therefore, fuzzy system constructed by triple I method and fuzzy system constructed by CRI method are equivalent. □

For requirement of below discussion, we introduce the concept of a degenerated fuzzy system and recommend the thinking of a restriction of fuzzy system onto a certain measurable set.

Definition 5.8.1 Let two fuzzy systems S_1 and S_2 be related to same one probability space $(\Omega, \mathcal{F}, P)$ and let $f_1(x, y)$ and $f_2(x, y)$ be probability density functions of S_1 and S_2, respectively. If there exist a set as the following:

$$D \in \mathcal{B}^2 \cap (X \times Y) \triangleq \{B \cap (X \times Y) | B \in \mathcal{B}^2\}$$

and a constant $c \in [0, +\infty)$ such that

$$\left.\begin{array}{l}\big(\forall(x,y)\in D\big)\big(f_1(x,y)=cf_2(x,y)\big)\\ \big(\forall(x,y)\in D^c\big)\big(f_1(x,y)=0\big)\end{array}\right\} \tag{5.8.4}$$

then S_1 is called a degenerated fuzzy system of S_2, or a degeneration of S_2, for short. □

Definition 5.8.2 Let a fuzzy system S be related to probability space $(\Omega,\mathcal{F},P)$ and let $f(x,y)$ be probability density function of S. For every $B\in\mathcal{B}_2$, if the following conditions are satisfied

$$0<\int_B f(x,y)\mathrm{d}y<+\infty,\quad \int_B |y|\, f(x,y)\mathrm{d}y<+\infty$$

then we put the following expression:

$$\overline{s}\,|_B\,(x)\triangleq\frac{\int_B yf(x,y)\mathrm{d}y}{\int_B f(x,y)\mathrm{d}y}, \tag{5.8.5}$$

and we call $\overline{s}\,|_B\,(x)$ a restriction of system $\overline{s}(x)$ onto the measurable set B. □

Theorem 5.8.2 Suppose that two fuzzy systems S_1 and S_2 are related to same one probability space $(\Omega,\mathcal{F},P)$, $f_1(x,y)$ and $f_2(x,y)$ are probability density functions of S_1 and S_2, respectively, and S_1 is a degeneration of S_2. Let $x\in X$ and $B\in\mathcal{B}_2$ be any given, where $\mathcal{B}_2$ is Borel σ-field in Y. If $\int_B f_1(x,y)\mathrm{d}y>0$, then there exists a set as the following:

$$B^*\in\mathcal{B}_2\cap B\triangleq\{A\cap B\,|\,A\in\mathcal{B}\}$$

such that $\overline{s}_1\,|_{B^*}\,(x)=\overline{s}_2\,|_{B^*}\,(x)$. Especially, $\overline{s}_1(x)=\overline{s}_2(x)$ when $B^*=Y$.

Proof. Take $x\in X$ and $B\in\mathcal{B}_2$ arbitrarily. Since S_1 is degeneration of

S_2, there exist a measurable set $D \in \mathcal{B}^2 \cap (X \times Y)$ and a constant $c \in [0, +\infty)$ such that $f_1(x, y)$ and $f_2(x, y)$ satisfy (5.8.4). If $c = 0$, then $f_1(x, y) = 0$ for all $(x, y) \in X \times Y$ and $\int_B f_1(x, y)\mathrm{d}y > 0$ does not hold, i.e., the assumption does not hold. Hence, $c \neq 0$.

Then it is not difficult to see that $\left(\{x\} \times B\right) \cap D \neq \varnothing$. Take a set as the following:

$$B^* \triangleq \{y \in B \mid (x, y) \in D\}.$$

Below, we verify that B^* is measurable. In fact, since B is measurable, so is $\{x\} \times B$. Again since D is measurable, so is $(\{x\} \times B) \cap D$. And B^* is a projected image of $\left(\{x\} \times B\right) \cap D$ onto B. It is well known that projection is measurable transformation. So B^* is measurable too. This shows that $B^* \in \mathcal{B}_2 \cap B$. And noticing the following fact:

$$\int_{B^*} f_1(x, y)\mathrm{d}y = \int_B f_1(x, y)\mathrm{d}y > 0,$$

we have the following result:

$$\begin{aligned}\overline{s}_1 |_{B^*} (x) &= \frac{\int_{B^*} y f_1(x, y)\mathrm{d}y}{\int_{B^*} f_1(x, y)\mathrm{d}y} = \frac{\int_{B^*} y c f_2(x, y)\mathrm{d}y}{\int_{B^*} c f_2(x, y)\mathrm{d}y} \\ &= \frac{\int_{B^*} y f_2(x, y)\mathrm{d}y}{\int_{B^*} f_2(x, y)\mathrm{d}y} = \overline{s}_2 |_{B^*} (x)\end{aligned}$$

This proves the first conclusion $\overline{s}_1 |_{B^*} (x) = \overline{s}_2 |_{B^*} (x)$. The second conclusion is trivial. □

Theorem 5.8.3 Given a single-input single-output fuzzy system, the related notations are same as described before. If take fuzzy implication operator $\theta = \theta_0$ (i.e., Wang operator), then fuzzy system constructed by triple I method and fuzzy system constructed by CRI method have same probability distributions. In other words, fuzzy systems constructed by two algorithms described above are equivalent under condition of Wang implication operator.

Proof. We obtain total relation of reasoning by Wang implication operator θ_0 and according to steps (5.2.1) to (5.2.3), i.e.,

$$\mu_R(x,y) = \bigvee_{i=1}^{n} \theta_0\left(\mu_{A_i}(x), \mu_{B_i}(y)\right)$$
$$= \begin{cases} 1, & (\exists i)\left(\mu_{A_i}(x) \le \mu_{B_i}(y)\right), \\ \bigvee_{i=1}^{n}\left[\left(1-\mu_{A_i}(x)\right) \vee \mu_{B_i}(y)\right], & \text{otherwise.} \end{cases}$$

For any given $A \in \mathcal{F}(X)$, result of reasoning $B \in \mathcal{F}(Y)$ that will be found by triple I method should satisfy the following expression[20,21]:

$$\mu_B(y) = \sup\left\{\mu_R(x,y) \wedge \mu_A(x) \middle| x \in E_y\right\}$$
$$= \bigvee_{x\in E_y} \left[\mu_A(x) \wedge \mu_R(x,y)\right], \quad y \in Y, \tag{5.8.6}$$
$$E_y = \left\{x \in X \middle| 1-\mu_A(x) < \mu_R(x,y)\right\}$$

Now for any given a point as an input $x' \in X$, we make a fuzzification on x', i.e., we can define a singleton fuzzy set: $A' = \{x'\}$ which is as the form: $\mu_{A'}(x) = \begin{cases} 1, & x = x', \\ 0, & x \ne x'. \end{cases}$ Substitute A' into (5.8.6) and distinguish the following two cases.

Case 1. If $x' \in E_y$, then $E_y = \{x'\}$ is a set with one element, so that

$$\mu_{B'}(y) = \bigvee_{x\in E_y} \left[\mu_{A'}(x) \wedge \mu_R(x,y)\right] = \mu_R(x', y)$$
$$= \begin{cases} 1, & (\exists i)\left(\mu_{A_i}(x') \le \mu_{B_i}(y)\right), \\ \bigvee_{i=1}^{n}\left[\left(1-\mu_{A_i}(x')\right) \vee \mu_{B_i}(y)\right], & \text{otherwise} \end{cases}$$

Case 2. If $x' \notin E_y$, then $E_y = \varnothing$, and so we have the equation:

$$\mu_{B'}(y) = \bigvee_{x\in\varnothing}\left[\mu_{A'}(x) \wedge \mu_R(x,y)\right] = 0 .$$

In all, we have the following inference result:

$$\mu_{B'}(y) = \begin{cases} 1, & x' \in E_y, (\exists i)\left(\mu_{A_i}(x') \le \mu_{B_i}(y)\right), \\ \bigvee_{i=1}^{n}\left[\left(1-\mu_{A_i}(x')\right) \vee \mu_{B_i}(y)\right], & x' \in E_y, (\exists i)\left(\mu_{A_i}(x') > \mu_{B_i}(y)\right), \\ 0, & \text{otherwise.} \end{cases}$$

Thereby, if we learn that the point $x' \in X$ is arbitrarily chosen, we immediately obtain the following binary function:

$$p(x,y) = \begin{cases} 1, & x \in E_y, (\exists i)\left(\mu_{A_i}(x) \le \mu_{B_i}(y)\right), \\ \bigvee_{i=1}^{n}\left[\left(1-\mu_{A_i}(x)\right) \vee \mu_{B_i}(y)\right], & x \in E_y, (\exists i)\left(\mu_{A_i}(x) > \mu_{B_i}(y)\right), \\ 0, & \text{otherwise.} \end{cases}$$

Let

$$H\left(2,n,\theta_0,\vee,3\mathrm{I}\right) \triangleq \int_X \int_Y p(x,y)\mathrm{d}x\mathrm{d}y .$$

If $H\left(2,n,\theta_0,\vee,3\mathrm{I}\right) > 0$, then we obtain the probability density function as follows:

$$f_1(x,y) = \frac{p(x,y)\chi_{X\times Y}}{H\left(2,n,\theta_0,\vee,3\mathrm{I}\right)} .$$

And then we denote the following two sets:

$$D_1 \triangleq \left\{(x,y)\in X\times Y \middle| x\in E_y, (\exists i)\left(\mu_{A_i}(x)\le \mu_{B_i}(y)\right)\right\},$$
$$D_2 \triangleq \left\{(x,y)\in X\times Y \middle| x\in E_y, (\exists i)\left(\mu_{A_i}(x)> \mu_{B_i}(y)\right)\right\}.$$

We easily see that D_1 and D_2 are set expressions of the first two conditions of piecewise function $p(x,y)$, respectively, and $D_1 \cap D_2 = \varnothing$.

If we put $D \triangleq D_1 \cup D_2$, then the probability density function is also expressed as the following:

$$f_1(x,y) = \frac{1}{H\left(2,n,\theta_0,\vee,3\mathrm{I}\right)}\chi_{D_1}(x,y) + \frac{\bigvee_{i=1}^{n}\left[\left(1-\mu_{A_i}(x)\right)\vee \mu_{B_i}(y)\right]}{H\left(2,n,\theta_0,\vee,3\mathrm{I}\right)}\chi_{D_2} \tag{5.8.7}$$

In order to compare result of triple I method with result of CRI method, we rewrite the probability density function in Example 5.4.7 as being $f_2(x,y)$. When $x' \notin E_y$, by definition of E_y we have the following inequality:

$$0 = 1-\mu_A(x') \ge \mu_R(x',y),$$

and so $\mu_R(x',y)=0$, i.e., $\mu_{B'}(y)=0$. Thus it is not difficult to see that $f_2(x,y)=0$ for all $(x,y)\in D^c$. It is also obvious that

$$H\left(2,n,\theta_0,\vee,3\mathrm{I}\right) = H\left(2,n,\theta_0,\vee\right),$$
$$\left(\forall (x,y)\in D\right)\left(f_1(x,y)=f_2(x,y)\right)$$

Therefore, fuzzy systems constructed by two algorithms above are equivalent under condition of Wang implication operator. □

The following shows that result of the above theorem can be extended to quite general situations.

Theorem 5.8.4 Given a single-input single-output fuzzy system, the related notations are same as described before. If fuzzy implication operator θ satisfies the following conditions[14–17]:

P_6) $\theta(0,b)=1$,

P_7) $\theta(1,b)=b$,

P_{11}) $\theta(a,b)=1 \Leftrightarrow a \le b$,

then fuzzy system constructed by triple I method and fuzzy system constructed by CRI method have same probability distributions. In other words, fuzzy systems constructed by two algorithms described above are equivalent under condition of this implication operator θ.

Proof. We obtain total relation of reasoning by this fuzzy implication operator θ and according to steps (5.2.1) to (5.2.3), i.e.,

$$\mu_R(x,y) = \mathop{\vee}_{i=1}^{n} \theta\left(\mu_{A_i}(x), \mu_{B_i}(y)\right).$$

For any given input $x' \in X$, first fuzzifying x' and then substituting the obtained singleton fuzzy set A' into implication expression of triple I method, we have

$$\mu_R(x,y)(x,y) \to \left(\mu_{A'}(x) \to \mu_{B'}(y)\right). \tag{5.8.8}$$

When $x = x'$, by condition P_7, it is easy to learn the following implication expression:

$$\left(\mu_{A'}(x) \to \mu_{B'}(y)\right) = \left(\mu_{A'}(x') \to \mu_{B'}(y)\right) = \theta\left(1, \mu_{B'}(y)\right) = \mu_{B'}(y),$$

and so (5.8.8) turns to $\mu_R\left(x',y\right) \to \mu_{B'}(y)$. Then, by condition P_{11}, the necessary condition for implication expression $\mu_R\left(x',y\right) \to \mu_{B'}(y)$ to reach the greatest value 1 is $\mu_R\left(x',y\right) \le \mu_{B'}(y)$.

According to the basic demand of minimum for the membership function $\mu_{B'}(y)$, we should take $\mu_{B'}(y) = \mu_R\left(x',y\right)$. When $x \ne x'$, by condition P_6, we see the fact that

$$\left(\mu_{A'}(x) \to \mu_{B'}(y)\right) = \theta\left(0, \mu_{B'}(y)\right) = 1,$$

which implies that implication expression $\mu_R(x,y) \to \mu_{B'}(y)$ reaches the greatest value 1 independently of $\mu_{B'}(y)$. In all, we have

$$\mu_{B'}(y) = \mu_R\left(x', y\right).$$

This coincides with result obtained by CRI method. Thus it can be easily seen that fuzzy system constructed by triple I method and fuzzy system constructed by CRI method have same probability distributions under condition of implication operator θ. □

Corollary 5.8.1 Given a single-input single-output fuzzy system, the related notations are same as described before. If fuzzy implication operator θ is one of the following operators:

$$\theta_3(a,b) = (1-a+b) \wedge 1 \quad \text{(Lukasiewicz operator)},$$

$$\theta_4(a,b) = \begin{cases} 1, & a = 0 \\ (b/a) \wedge 1, & a > 0 \end{cases} \quad \text{(Goguen operator)},$$

$$\theta_5(a,b) = \begin{cases} 1, & a \le b \\ b, & a > b \end{cases} \quad \text{(Gödel operator)},$$

$$\theta_{24}(a,b) = \left[\left(1 - a^p + b^p\right)^{\frac{1}{p}}\right] \wedge 1, \quad p > 0$$

(generalized Lukasiewicz operator),

$$\theta_{29}(a,b) = \begin{cases} 1, & a \le b \\ 1 - a + ab, & a > b \end{cases}$$

then fuzzy system constructed by triple I method and fuzzy system constructed by CRI method have same probability distributions, that is, fuzzy systems constructed by two algorithms described above are equivalent under condition of this implication operator θ.

Proof. It is easy to verify all of these fuzzy implication operators θ satisfy conditions P_6, P_7 and P_{11}. Hence the conclusion is true. □

Remark 5.8.2 The conditions P_6, P_7 and P_{11} described in Theorem 5.8.4 are only sufficient conditions but not necessary conditions. For instance, Mamdani operator considered in Theorem 5.8.1 does not satisfy conditions P_6 and P_{11}, but it also leads to the same conclusion as that described in Theorem 5.8.4. □

Theorem 5.8.5 Given a single-input single-output fuzzy system, the related notations are same as described before. If take fuzzy implication operator $\theta = \theta_8$ (i.e., Zadeh operator), then fuzzy system constructed by triple I method is degeneration of fuzzy system constructed by CRI method.

Proof. We obtain total relation of reasoning by Zadeh implication operator θ_8 and according to steps (5.2.1) to (5.2.3), i.e.,

$$\begin{aligned}\mu_R(x,y) &= \bigvee_{i=1}^{n} \theta_8\left(\mu_{A_i}(x), \mu_{B_i}(y)\right)\\ &= \bigvee_{i=1}^{n}\left[\left(1-\mu_{A_i}(x)\right)\vee\left(\mu_{A_i}(x)\wedge\mu_{B_i}(y)\right)\right]\end{aligned}$$

For any given $A \in \mathcal{F}(X)$, the result of reasoning $B \in \mathcal{F}(Y)$ that will be found by triple I method should satisfy the following expression[20,21]:

$$\mu_B(y) = \sup\left\{\mu_A(x)\wedge\mu_R(x,y)\,\middle|\, x\in E_y,\ \mu_R(x,y) > \frac{1}{2}\right\}, \quad (5.8.9)$$

where

$$E_y = \sup\left\{x \in X \,\middle|\, 1-\mu_A(x) < \mu_R(x,y)\right\}, \quad y \in Y$$

For any given input $x' \in X$, we make the fuzzification on x', i.e., we define a singleton fuzzy set:

$$\mu_{A'}(x) = \begin{cases} 1, & x = x' \\ 0, & x \neq x' \end{cases}$$

Substitute A' into (5.8.9) and distinguish the following three cases:

Case 1: If $x' \in E_y$ and $\mu_R(x', y) > \frac{1}{2}$, then it is obvious that

$$\mu_{B'}(y) = \mu_R(x', y)$$
$$= \bigvee_{i=1}^{n} \left[\left(1 - \mu_{A_i}(x')\right) \vee \left(\mu_{A_i}(x') \wedge \mu_{B_i}(y)\right) \right]$$

Case 2: If $x' \notin E_y$ and $\mu_R(x', y) > \frac{1}{2}$, then we have $\mu_{B'}(y) = 0$ similarly to handling in proof of Theorem 5.8.3.

Case 3: When $\mu_R(x', y) \leq \frac{1}{2}$, the conditional set in (5.8.9) is empty, and so $B'(y) = 0$.

Summarizing the above three cases, we have

$$p(x, y) = \begin{cases} \bigvee_{i=1}^{n} \left[\left(1 - \mu_{A_i}(x)\right) \vee \left(\mu_{A_i}(x) \wedge \mu_{B_i}(y)\right) \right], & x \in E_y, \mu_R(x, y) > \frac{1}{2}, \\ 0, & \text{otherwise.} \end{cases} \quad (5.8.10)$$

Put the following symbol:

$$D \triangleq \left\{ (x, y) \in X \times Y \,\middle|\, x \in E_y, \mu_R(x, y) > \frac{1}{2} \right\},$$

And we let

$$H\left(2, n, \theta_8, \vee, 3\mathrm{I}\right) = \iint_D p(x, y) \mathrm{d}x \mathrm{d}y .$$

If $H\left(2, n, \theta_8, \vee, 3\mathrm{I}\right) > 0$, then we can take

$$f_1(x,y)=\frac{p(x,y)\chi_D}{H\left(2,n,\theta_8,\vee,3\mathrm{I}\right)}$$
$$=\frac{\left\{\bigvee_{i=1}^{n}\left[\left(1-\mu_{A_i}(x)\right)\vee\left(\mu_{A_i}(x)\wedge\mu_{B_i}(y)\right)\right]\right\}\chi_D}{H(2,n,\theta_8,\vee,3\mathrm{I})} \tag{5.8.11}$$

Regard $f_1(x,y)$ as the probability density function that the random vector (ξ,η) of this system obeys. Noticing (5.4.14) in Example 5.4.2, we here rewrite it as $f_2(x,y)$, i.e.,

$$f_2(x,y)=\frac{\left\{\bigvee_{i=1}^{n}\left[\left(1-\mu_{A_i}(x)\right)\vee\left(\mu_{A_i}(x)\wedge\mu_{B_i}(y)\right)\right]\right\}\chi_{X\times Y}}{H(2,n,\theta_8,\vee)}.$$

Putting the following constant:

$$c\triangleq\frac{H\left(2,n,\theta_8,\vee\right)}{H\left(2,n,\theta_8,\vee,3\mathrm{I}\right)},$$

we have that the following equation:

$$f_1(x,y)=\begin{cases}cf_2(x,y), & (x,y)\in D,\\ 0, & (x,y)\in D^c\end{cases}$$

This implies that fuzzy system constructed by triple I method is degeneration of fuzzy system constructed by CRI method. □

Remark 5.8.3 Here it is necessary to say a few words about sup operation and inf operation. For example, we consider $\sup\limits_{x\in E} f(x)$, where E is a conditional set. With regard to conditional set, when $x\in E$ always does not hold, $\sup\limits_{x\in E} f(x)$ is regarded as $\sup\limits_{x\in\varnothing} f(x)$. As well known, $\sup\limits_{x\in\varnothing} f(x)=0$, and so $\sup\limits_{x\in E} f(x)=0$. Besides, by $\inf\limits_{x\in\varnothing} f(x)=1$, we can similarly understand the case of $\inf_{x\in E} f(x)$. According to this, in the case 3 in proof of Theorem 5.8.5, since $\mu_R(x',y)\le\frac{1}{2}$, conditional set on "sup" of (5.8.9) must be regarded as empty set, and then

$$\mu_{B'}(y)=\sup\{\mu_{A'}(x)\wedge\mu_R(x,y)\,|\,x\in\varnothing\}=0\,. \qquad \square$$

Theorem 5.8.6 Given a single-input single-output fuzzy system, the related notations are same as described before. If take fuzzy implication operator $\theta=\theta_{14}$ (i.e., Larsen operator), then fuzzy system constructed by triple I method obeys uniform distribution, in other words, output of such a fuzzy system is a step function, scilicet, this system is ordinary fuzzy system.

Proof. We obtain total relation of reasoning by Larsen implication operator θ_{14} and according to steps (5.2.1) to (5.2.3), i.e.,

$$\mu_R(x,y)=\bigvee_{i=1}^{n}\theta_{14}\left(\mu_{A_i}(x),\mu_{B_i}(y)\right)=\bigvee_{i=1}^{n}\left(\mu_{A_i}(x)\cdot\mu_{B_i}(y)\right).$$

For any given $A\in\mathcal{F}(X)$, result of reasoning $B\in\mathcal{F}(Y)$ that will be found by triple I method should be the least fuzzy set so that the following implication expression

$$\begin{aligned}&\left(\mu_R(x,y)\to\left(\mu_A(x)\to\mu_B(y)\right)\right)\\&=\left[\bigvee_{i=1}^{n}\left(\mu_{A_i}(x)\cdot\mu_{B_i}(y)\right)\right]\cdot\left(\mu_A(x)\cdot\mu_B(y)\right)\end{aligned}$$

takes the greatest truth value for all $(x,y)\in X\times Y$. Let

$$E\triangleq\left\{y\in Y\,\middle|\,\sup_{x\in X}\left\{\left[\bigvee_{i=1}^{n}\left(\mu_{A_i}(x)\cdot\mu_{B_i}(y)\right)\right]\cdot\mu_A(x)\right\}>0\right\}. \qquad (5.8.12)$$

It is not difficult to verify that such a B is only as follows:

$$\mu_B(y)=\begin{cases}1, & y\in E\\ 0, & y\in Y\setminus E\end{cases}$$

Again put $D=X\times E$. Then we have

$$p(x,y)=\begin{cases}1, & (x,y)\in D\\ 0, & (x,y)\notin D\end{cases}$$

Let μ^2 be two-dimensional Lebesgue measure and put

$$H(2,n,\theta_{14},\vee,3\mathrm{I})\triangleq\int_X\int_Y p(x,y)\mathrm{d}x\mathrm{d}y=\mu^2(D)$$

If $H(2,n,\theta_{14},\vee,3\mathrm{I})>0$, then we can take

$$f(x,y)\triangleq\frac{1}{H(2,n,\theta_{14},\vee,3\mathrm{I})}\chi_D(x,y).$$

Regard $f(x,y)$ as probability density function of random vector (ξ,η) of this system. Then fuzzy system constructed by triple I method obeys uniform distribution. □

Theorem 5.8.7 Given a single-input single-output fuzzy system, the related notations are same as described before. If, in CRI method, "$\circ$" in operation $B=A\circ R$ of relation composition is realized by $(\wedge,\vee)$ and if, in triple I method, three implication operators "$\to$" in (5.8.1) are not restricted to be same one fuzzy implication operator, then CRI method can be considered as a kind of triple I method under appropriate choice of implication operators.

Proof. Suppose that, in $\mu_R(x,y)\to(\mu_A(x)\to\mu_B(y))$ of (5.8.3), the first implication operator, i.e., implication operator "$\to_1$" involved in $\mu_R(x,y)$ takes arbitrary fuzzy implication operator "θ", and the second implication operator "$\to_2$" and the third implication operator "$\to_3$" take Mamdani operator, i.e., $\to_2=\to_3\triangleq\wedge$. Then (5.8.3) becomes to the following expression:

$$\mu_R(x,y) \wedge \left(\mu_A(x) \wedge \mu_B(y)\right).$$

By triple I method, we induce the following equation:

$$\mu_B(y) = \bigvee_{i=1}^{n} \left(\mu_A(x) \wedge \mu_R(x,y)\right).$$

This is just the result of CRI method. □

Remark 5.8.4 The step of "relation composition" in CRI method apparently seems to be in defect of logical action. Actually, implication action of logic is hidden in "relation composition". Just as explicit function and implicit function in mathematical analysis, triple I method is a kind of explicit implication action and CRI method is a kind of implicit implication action that can appear explicitly under certain condition as in Theorem 5.8.7. However, note that explicitness for CRI method in Theorem 5.8.7 is quite simple one, and there are also various forms of explicitness. Besides, if three implication operators "$\rightarrow$" in triple I method are not restricted to same one fuzzy implication operator, then CRI method can be regarded as a special example of triple I method. In this sense, triple I method is more general than CRI method. Since triple I method has good logical foundation and contains an idea of optimization of reasoning, it shall possess beautiful foreground of application. □

Remark 5.8.5 By comparing two algorithms for construction of fuzzy systems, i.e., CRI method and triple I method, through consideration of examples, we have discovered that if three implication operators "$\rightarrow$" in triple I method are prescribed as same one fuzzy implication operator, then for fuzzy systems constructed by CRI method and triple I method in terms of same one fuzzy implication operator the following three basic situations happen:

1) Fuzzy system constructed by CRI method and fuzzy system constructed by triple I method are equivalent;

2) Fuzzy system constructed by triple I method is degeneration of fuzzy system constructed by CRI method;

3) Fuzzy system constructed by triple I method is uniformly distri-

buted, but for same one fuzzy implication operator, fuzzy system constructed by CRI method is not uniformly distributed. □

5.9 Conclusions

This chapter has discussed probability representation problem of fuzzy systems in detail and opened out that there exists close relation between fuzzy systems and probability theory. The main results are as follows:

1) It has been pointed out that COG method that is a defuzzification technique commonly used in fuzzy systems is reasonable and is optimal method in the sense of average square.

2) Based on different fuzzy implication operators, several typical probability distributions such as Zadeh distribution, Mamdani distribution, Lukasiewicz distribution, etc. have been given. They act as "inner kernels" of fuzzy systems.

3) Based on some properties of probability distributions of fuzzy systems, it has been explained that CRI method, proposed by Zadeh, for construction of fuzzy systems is logical basically and effective.

4) The special action of uniform probability distributions in fuzzy systems has been characterized. In general, for any one system, whether it is deterministic system or uncertain system (including fuzzy system), if this system has only step output, then it is undoubtedly an ordinary system and has no applicable worth but only certain theoretical significance.

5) The step of "relation composition" in CRI method apparently seems to be in defect of logical action. Actually, implication action of logic is hidden in "relation composition". Just as explicit function and implicit function in mathematical analysis, triple I method is a kind of explicit implication action while CRI method is a kind of implicit implication action that can appear explicitly under certain condition as in Theorem 8.7. However, note that explicitness for CRI method in Theorem 8.7 is quite simple one, and there are also various forms of explicitness.

6) By comparing two algorithms for construction of fuzzy systems, i.e., CRI method and triple I method, through consideration of examples, it has been discovered that if three implication operators "$\rightarrow$" in triple I method are prescribed as same one fuzzy implication operator, then for

fuzzy systems constructed by CRI method and triple I method in terms of same one fuzzy implication operator the following three basic situations happen: a) Fuzzy system constructed by CRI method and fuzzy system constructed by triple I method are equivalent; b) Fuzzy system constructed by triple I method is degeneration of fuzzy system constructed by CRI method; c) Fuzzy system constructed by triple I method is uniformly distributed, but for same one fuzzy implication operator, fuzzy system constructed by CRI method is not uniformly distributed.

7) If three implication operators " $\rightarrow$ " in triple I method are not restricted to same one fuzzy implication operator, then CRI method can be regarded as a special example of triple I method. In this sense, triple I method is more general than CRI method. Besides, triple I method introduced an idea of optimization into reasoning, that is a much important innovation. Thereby, the theory of support degree was also proposed, that has deep theoretical significance as well as beautiful foreground of application and is worthy to lucubrate and to apply experimentally.

8) Just with COG method, the relation between fuzzy systems and probability theory has been communicated. From the viewpoint of methodology, in a certain bound, one may use method of probability theory to investigate fuzzy systems. From the viewpoint of philosophy, uncertainty originally contains randomness as well as fuzziness. Randomness and fuzziness are often interwoven, so that it is very difficult to divide up them.

References

1. Zadeh, L.A. (1973). Outline of a new approach to the analysis of complex systems and decision processes, IEEE Trans. SMC, 3, pp. 28-44.
2. Zadeh, L. A. (1974). The concept of a linguistic variable and its applications to approximate reasoning (I), Information Sciences, 8(2), pp. 199-249.
3. Zadeh, L. A. (1974). The concept of a linguistic variable and its applications to approximate reasoning (II), Information Sciences, 8(3), pp. 301-357.
4. Zadeh, L. A. (1975). The concept of a linguistic variable and its applications to approximate reasoning (III), Information Sciences, 9(1), pp. 43-80.
5. Wu, W. M. (1994). *Principle and Methods of Fuzzy Reasoning*, (Guizhou Science and Technology Press, Guiyang, in Chinese).
6. Li, H. X. (1998). Interpolation mechanism of fuzzy control, Science in China (Series E), 41(3), pp. 312-320.

7. Li, H. X. (1995). To see the success of fuzzy logic from mathematical essence of fuzzy control, Fuzzy Systems and Mathematics, 9(4), pp. 1-14 (in Chinese).
8. Hou, J., You, F. and Li, H. X. (2005). Some fuzzy controllers constructed by triple I method and their response capability, Progress in Natural Science, 15(1), pp. 29-37 (in Chinese).
9. Li, H. X., You, F. and Peng, J. Y. (2004). Fuzzy controllers based on some fuzzy implication operators and their response functions, Progress in Natural Science, 14(1), pp. 15-20.
10. Wang, P. Z. and Li, H. X. (1995) *Fuzzy Systems Theory and Fuzzy Computers.* (Science Press, Beijing, in Chinese)
11. Zhang, W. X. and Liang, G. X. (1998) *Fuzzy Control and Systems*, (Xi'an Jiaotong University Press, Xi'an, in Chinese).
12. Wang, G. J. (1999). A new method for fuzzy reasoning, Fuzzy Systems and Mathematics (in Chinese), 13(3), pp. 1-10.
13. Wang, G. J. (1997). A formal deductive system of fuzzy propositional calculus, Chinese Science Bulletin, 42(10), pp. 1041-1045 (in Chinese).
14. You, F., Feng, Y. B. and Li, H. X. (2003). Fuzzy implication operators and their construction (I), Journal of Beijing Normal University, 39(5), pp. 606-611 (in Chinese).
15. You, F., Feng, Y. B., Wang, J. Y. and Li, H. X. (2004). Fuzzy implication operators and their construction (II), Journal of Beijing Normal University, 40(2), pp. 168-176 (in Chinese).
16. You, F., Yang, X. Y. and Li, H. X. (2004). Fuzzy implication operators and their construction (III), Journal of Beijing Normal University, 40(4), pp. 427-432 (in Chinese).
17. You, F. and Li, H. X. (2004). Fuzzy implication operators and their construction (IV), Journal of Beijing Normal University, 40(5), pp. 588-599 (in Chinese).
18. Dubois, D. and Prade, H. (1991). Fuzzy sets in approximate reasoning, Part 1: Inference with possibility distributions, Fuzzy Sets and Systems, 40(1), pp. 143-202.
19. Dubois, D. and Prade, H. (1991). Fuzzy sets in approximate reasoning, Part 2: Logical approaches, Fuzzy Sets and Systems, 40(1), pp. 203-244.
20. Wang, G. J. (2000) *Non-classical Mathematical Logic and Approximate Reasoning*, (Science Press, Beijing, in Chinese).
21. Wang, G. J. (1999). Full implication triple I method for fuzzy reasoning, Science in China (Series E), 29(1), pp. 43-53 (in Chinese).
22. Pei, D. W. (2001). Two triple I methods for FMT problem and their reductivity, Fuzzy Systems and Mathematics, 15(4), pp. 1-7 (in Chinese).
23. Wang, G. J. and Song, Q. Y. (2003). A new kind of triple I method and its logical foundation, Progress in Natural Science, 13(6), pp. 575-581 (in Chinese).
24. Guo, F. F., Chen, T. Y. and Xia, Z. Q. (2003). Triple I methods for fuzzy reasoning based on maximum fuzzy entropy principle, Fuzzy Systems and Mathematics, 17(4), pp. 55-59 (in Chinese).

25. Song, S. J. and Wu, C. (2002). Reverse triple I method of fuzzy reasoning, Science in China (Series F), 45(5), pp. 344-364.
26. Song, S. J. and Wu, C. (2002). Reverse triple I method with restrictions of fuzzy reasoning, Progress in Natural Science, 12(1), pp. 95-100 (in Chinese).
27. Song, S. J., Feng, C. B. and Wu, C. X. (2001). Theory of restriction degree of triple I method with total inference rules of fuzzy reasoning, Progress in Natural Science, 11(1), pp. 58-66.
28. Li, H. X. (2006). Probability representations of fuzzy systems, Science in China (Series F), 49(3), pp. 339-363.

Chapter 6

Fuzzy System Representations of Stochastic Systems

6.1 Introduction

Uncertainty systems have played more and more important role in many areas such as control theory, system engineering, artificial intelligence, behavior science, social science, etc. As we all know, uncertainty of systems are usually with respect to randomness or fuzziness. So if people focus on randomness of an uncertainty system, they must use probability theory or stochastic process to describe the system, which uncertainty system is called a stochastic system; if people pay attention to fuzziness of an uncertainty system, they often treat the system by using fuzzy set theory, which uncertainty system is called a fuzzy system. Clearly, it is interesting to communicate the relationship between probability theory and fuzzy set theory with respect to uncertainty systems. This paper will research the relationship between probability theory and fuzzy set theory when they are used to deal with un-certainty systems.

6.2 Sketch of Fuzzy Systems

We consider Figure 6.2.1 that shows a single-input single-output open-loop system S . We have known that if this system S is a deterministic system then one may use the conventional method to make a mathematical model of the system and find a solution $y(x)$ of the model by analytic or numerical methods. In this way, this system shall be regarded as having been mastered basically. Then the system S may be simply understood by a function, denoted by a mapping as follows, where the set X is the input universe and the set Y is the output universe:

$$s: X \to Y,\ x \mapsto y \triangleq s(x).$$

The system is formally denoted by $s = S(X, Y)$.

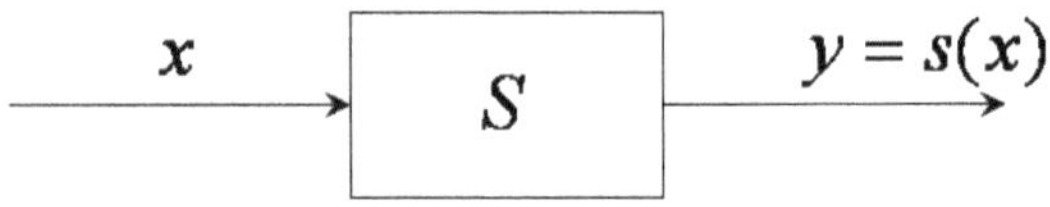

Fig. 6.2.1. Single-input single-output open-loop system

However, for an uncertain system, we cannot use the conventional method to get a “crisp” or “accurate” the function s. Having to reduce the request, we try to obtain an approximate function $\underline{s}$ as follows:

$$\underline{s}: X \to Y,\ \ x \mapsto y \triangleq \underline{s}(x), \tag{6.2.1}$$

such that $\underline{s}(x)$ approximates $s(x)$ as close as possible. With stochastic viewpoint to understand above problem there is such meaning: randomly take a point x in X and put into the input channel of system S, and after enter S there exists an output point $y(x)$ in the output channel of system S to correspond the input point x. However, what point in Y should be taken as $y(x)$ is unknown beforehand. This means that for system S there are two random variables ξ and η that are defined respectively in probability spaces $(X, \mathcal{B}_1, P_1)$ and $(Y, \mathcal{B}_2, P_2)$, where $\mathcal{B}_1$ and $\mathcal{B}_2$ are σ-fields on X and Y respectively, and P_1 and P_2 are probability measures on $\mathcal{B}_1$ and $\mathcal{B}_2$ respectively.

For convenience, we always assume that X and Y are measurable sets on real number space $\mathbb{R}$. Evidently η and ξ depend on each other, that is, there is a Borel measurable function g such that $\eta = g(\xi)$ which ought to coincide with $y = s(x)$, i.e., $\eta = s(\xi)$. We want to determine a Borel measurable function $\overline{s}(\xi)$ so that η and $\overline{s}(\xi)$ are closed up to the best, and then $\overline{s}$ may be regarded as an approximation of s, where the existence of $E\left(\eta^2\right)$ and $E\left[\left(s(\xi)\right)^2\right]$ are assumed. The "closeness" herein needs a criterion, and the most commonly used one is "least squares method". Then we have to demand that

$$E\left[\left(\eta-\underline{s}(\xi)\right)^2\right]=\inf_{\varphi}\left\{E\left[\left(\eta-\varphi(\xi)\right)^2\right]\right\},$$

where φ varies in a kind of space of Borel measurable functions. We have known that conditional mathematical expectation should meet the demand; so we can put $\underline{s}(\xi)\triangleq E\left(\eta|\xi\right)$. This shows that random variable $\overline{s}(\xi)$ is the optimal approximation in mean square to random variable η. But, it is only of formal meaning as we have not got any probability information about random vector (ξ,η). Now we start to do the work.

Taking $\Omega\triangleq X\times Y, \mathcal{F}\triangleq\mathcal{B}_1\times\mathcal{B}_2$, and $P\triangleq P_1\times P_2$, where $\mathcal{F}$ is Borel σ-field generated by Cartesian product of Borel σ-fields $\mathcal{B}_1$ and $\mathcal{B}_2$, and P is product probability measure. Then we obtain joint probability space $(\Omega,\mathcal{F},P)$. With same notations, redefine ξ and η as random variables on Ω:

$$\xi:\Omega\to\mathbb{R},\quad (x,y)\mapsto\xi(x,y)\triangleq\xi(x),$$
$$\eta:\Omega\to\mathbb{R},\quad (x,y)\mapsto\eta(x,y)\triangleq\eta(y).$$

Thus (ξ,η) turns into a two-dimensional random vector on joint probability space $(\Omega,\mathcal{F},P)$. For any $x\in X$, when $\omega\in\left\{\omega\in\Omega\middle|\xi=x\right\}$, we have

$$\underline{s}(x)=E\left(\eta|\xi=x\right). \tag{6.2.2}$$

This means that $\underline{s}(x)$ becomes the conditional mathematical expectation of random variable η under condition of random variable $\xi=x$.

If we master whole probability information on (ξ,η), especially know continuous probability density $f(x,y)$ of (ξ,η), then (6.2.2) turns into the following equation which is easy handled:

$$\underline{s}(x) = E(\eta \mid \xi = x) = \frac{\int_{-\infty}^{+\infty} f(x,y)y\mathrm{d}y}{\int_{-\infty}^{+\infty} f(x,y)\mathrm{d}y}, \tag{6.2.3}$$

where the demands need that, for any $x \in X$,

$$\int_{-\infty}^{+\infty} |y| f(x,y)\mathrm{d}y < +\infty, \quad 0 < \int_{-\infty}^{+\infty} f(x,y)\mathrm{d}y < +\infty.$$

Clearly in actual computing, (6.2.3) should be the following:

$$\underline{s}(x) = \frac{\int_Y f(x,y)y\mathrm{d}y}{\int_Y f(x,y)\mathrm{d}y}. \tag{6.2.4}$$

For an uncertainty system S, if we can know the continuous probability density $f(x,y)$ on the system, $\underline{s}$ defined by (6.2.4) is called **a continuous stochastic approximation system** of S, or **a continuous stochastic system** of S. But in our mind, we should know that the **continuous stochastic system** $\underline{s}$ is with regard to an uncertainty system S. So after time when we say a continuous stochastic system $\underline{s}$, it always has above meaning. Besides for convenience, a continuous stochastic system $\underline{s}$ is also denoted as the following:

$$\underline{s} = S(X, Y, f(x,y)). \tag{6.2.5}$$

Be careful that (6.2.4) and (6.2.5) use the same symbol $\underline{s}$, which means that $\underline{s}$ has two meanings: it not only abstractly expresses a continuous stochastic approximation system, but also indicates correspondence relationship between X and Y.

6.3 Fuzzy Reasoning Meaning of Stochastic Systems

For convenience, we need to introduce some concepts. Given a universe X, $\mathcal{A} = \{A_i \mid 1 \le i \le n\}$ is a family of normal fuzzy sets on X, i.e.,

$$(\forall i \in \{1,2,\cdots,n\})(\exists x_i \in X)(\mu_{A_i}(x_i)=1),$$

where x_i is called peak point of A_i; of course, the peak point is not unique. $\mathcal{A}$ is called a fuzzy partition of X, if it meets the condition:

$$(\forall x \in X)\left(\sum_{i=1}^{n} \mu_{A_i}(x)=1\right). \qquad (6.3.1)$$

It is not difficult to verify that such fuzzy sets have Kronecker property:

$$\mu_{A_i}(x_j)=\delta_{ij}=\begin{cases}1, & i=j,\\ 0, & i\neq j.\end{cases}$$

Besides for proving the following main theorem, we have to give two lemmas. These two lemmas are with respect to integral with parameter.

Lemma 6.3.1 Let $f(x,y)$ be a binary continuous function on $X\times Y$, where $X=[a_1,b_1]$ and $Y=[a_2,b_2]$ are finite real number intervals. For the integral with parameter $I(x)=\int_{a_2}^{b_2} f(x,y)\mathrm{d}y$, we have such a result: for arbitrarily given $\varepsilon>0$, there is always a common $\delta>0$ without dependent of parameter x such that, for any partition:

$$a_2=y_0<y_1<\cdots<y_n=b_2,$$

as long as $\lambda=\max\{\Delta y_i \mid i=1,2,\cdots,n\}<\delta$, then the Riemann sum of $I(x)$, i.e. $\sum_{i=1}^{n} f(x,\xi_i)\Delta y_i$, uniformly holds the condition that

$$(\forall x \in X)\left(\left|I(x)-\sum_{i=1}^{n} f(x,\xi_i)\Delta y_i\right|<\varepsilon\right)$$

where $\Delta y_i=y_i-y_{i-1}$ $(i=1,2,\cdots,n)$ and ξ_i takes its value in $[y_{i-1},y_i]$ arbitrarily.

Proof. For arbitrarily given $\varepsilon > 0$, let $\delta_k = \frac{1}{k}, k = 1, 2, \cdots$. We can prove that there must exist a k such that that $\delta = \delta_k$ meets the conclusion of the lemma. If it is not, then for every k, exist $x_k \in X$ and a partition:

$$a_2 = y_0^{(k)} < y_1^{(k)} < \cdots < y_{n_k}^{(k)} = b_2$$

of Y and a kind of taking value way of $\xi_i^{(k)} \in \left[y_{i-1}^{(k)}, y_i^{(k)} \right]$, although

$$\lambda_k = \max\left\{ \Delta y_i^{(k)} \middle| i = 1, 2, \cdots, n_k \right\} < \delta_k,$$

we have $\left| I(x_k) - \sum_{i=1}^{n_k} f\left(x_k, \xi_i^{(k)}\right) \Delta y_i^{(k)} \right| \geq \varepsilon$. As $\{x_k\}$ is a bounded sequence, it has a convergent subsequence $\left\{x_{k_j}\right\}$ such that $x_{k_j} \xrightarrow{j \to \infty} x_*$. Noticing $\delta_{k_j} \xrightarrow{j \to \infty} 0$, so we have the following inequality:

$$\begin{aligned} 0 < \varepsilon &\leq \lim_{j \to \infty} \left| I\left(x_{k_j}\right) - \sum_{i=1}^{n_{k_j}} f\left(x_{k_j}, \xi_i^{(k_j)}\right) \Delta y_i^{(k_j)} \right| \\ &= \left| I(x_*) - \int_{a_2}^{b_2} f(x_*, y) \mathrm{d}y \right| = 0. \end{aligned}$$

This is a clear contradiction. □

Lemma 6.3.2 Let $f(x, y)$ be a binary continuous function on $X \times Y$, where $X = [a_1, b_1]$ and $Y = [a_2, b_2]$ are finite real number intervals. For the integral with parameters follows:

$$I(x) = \int_{a_2}^{b_2} f(x, y) \mathrm{d}y,$$

if the condition $(\forall x \in X)(I(x) > 0)$ holds, then there exists a $\delta > 0$, such that for any partition:

$$a_2 = y_0 < y_1 < \cdots < y_n = b_2$$

of Y and any kind of taking value way of ξ_i in $[y_{i-1}, y_i]$, the Riemann sum $\sum_{i=1}^{n} f(x, \xi_i)\Delta y_i$ of $I(x)$ must satisfy the following implication:

$$\lambda \triangleq \max\{\Delta y_i | i = 1, 2, \cdots, n\} < \delta$$
$$\Rightarrow (x \in X)\left(\sum_{i=1}^{n} f(x, \xi_i)\Delta y_i > 0\right)$$

Proof. Firstly, it is easy to know the following fact:

$$I(x) = \int_{a_2}^{b_2} f(x, y)\mathrm{d}y \in C[a_1, b_1].$$

Thus there exists the least point of $x_0 \in X$ for $I(x)$ in X such that the condition $(\forall x \in X)(I(x) \geq I(x_0))$ holds. Taking $\varepsilon = I(x_0)$, from lemma 6.3.1 we know the fact that there exists a $\delta > 0$ such that for any partition of Y, we have

$$a_2 = y_0 < y_1 < \cdots < y_n = b_2$$

and for any kind of taking value ways of ξ_i in the subinterval $[y_{i-1}, y_i]$, the Riemann sum $\sum_{i=1}^{n} f(x, \xi_i)\Delta y_i$ of $I(x)$ must meet the implication:

$$\lambda < \delta \Rightarrow (x \in X)\left(\left|I(x) - \sum_{i=1}^{n} f(x, \xi_i)\Delta y_i\right| < \varepsilon\right).$$

Then we have the following inequality:

$$\sum_{i=1}^{n} f(x, \xi_i)\Delta y_i > I(x) - \varepsilon \geq I(x_0) - \varepsilon = 0.$$

This is uniformly true for all $x \in X$. □

Based on Lemma 6.3.2 and by using the way in the proof of Lemma 6.3.1, we can easily prove the following lemma.

Lemma 6.3.3 Let $f(x, y)$ be a binary continuous function on the universe $X \times Y$, where $X = [a_1, b_1]$ and $Y = [a_2, b_2]$ are finite real number intervals, and it is with the condition:

$$(\forall x \in X)\left(\int_{a_2}^{b_2} f(x, y)\mathrm{d}y > 0\right).$$

For arbitrarily given $\varepsilon > 0$, there is always a common $\delta > 0$ without dependent of parameter x such that, for any partition:

$$a_2 = y_0 < y_1 < \cdots < y_n = b_2,$$

as long as $\lambda = \max\{\Delta y_i | i = 1, 2, \cdots, n\} < \delta$, then

$$\left| \frac{\int_{a_2}^{b_2} f(x, y)\, y\mathrm{d}y}{\int_{a_2}^{b_2} f(x, y)\mathrm{d}y} - \frac{\sum_{i=1}^{n} f(x, \xi_i)\xi_i \Delta y_i}{\sum_{i=1}^{n} f(x, \xi_i)\Delta y_i} \right| < \varepsilon$$

is uniformly true for all $x \in X$, where $\Delta y_i = y_i - y_{i-1}$ $(i = 1, \cdots, n)$ and ξ_i takes its value in $[y_{i-1}, y_i]$ arbitrarily. □

Theorem 6.3.1 Given a continuous stochastic system as the following:

$$\underline{s} = S(X, Y, f(x, y)),$$

where $X = [a_1, b_1]$ and $Y = [a_2, b_2]$ are finite real number intervals. If the following condition is satisfied

$$(\forall x \in X)\left(\int_{a_2}^{b_2} f(x, y)\mathrm{d}y > 0\right),$$

then there exists a group of fuzzy inference rules:

$$\text{If } x \text{ is } A_i \text{ then } y \text{ is } B_i,\ i=1,2,\cdots,n, \tag{6.3.2}$$

where $A_i \in \mathcal{F}(X)$ and $B_i \in \mathcal{F}(Y)$ such that the fuzzy system $\overline{s}$ constructed by the group of fuzzy inference rules can approximate the continuous stochastic system $\underline{s}$ to arbitrarily given precision.

Proof. Noticing (6.2.4), we make a partition of interval Y as the follows:

$$a_2 = y_0 < y_1 < \cdots < y_n = b_2,$$

and write $\gamma \triangleq (y_1, y_2, \cdots, y_n)$, $\Delta y_i = y_i - y_{i-1}$, $i=1,2,\cdots,n$, and

$$\lambda = \max\left\{\Delta y_i \,\middle|\, i=1,2,\cdots,n\right\}.$$

Then we make two Riemann sums of $f(x,y)y$ and $f(x,y)$ on Y respectively, with respect to the partition and the node group γ, as the follows:

$$\sum_{i=1}^{n} f(x,y_i)\, y_i \Delta y_i,\quad \sum_{i=1}^{n} f(x,y_i)\Delta y_i.$$

From the condition of the theorem and Lemma 6.3.2, we have the fact that, $\exists \delta_1 > 0$, if $\lambda < \delta_1$, then $(x \in X)\left(\sum_{i=1}^{n} f(x,y_i)\Delta y_i > 0\right)$. So we have the following expression:

$$\underline{s}(x) = E(\eta \mid \xi = x) = \frac{\int_{a_2}^{b_2} f(x,y)\, y\mathrm{d}y}{\int_{a_2}^{b_2} f(x,y)\mathrm{d}y}$$

$$\approx \frac{\sum_{i=1}^{n} f(x,y_i)\, y_i \Delta y_i}{\sum_{i=1}^{n} f(x,y_i)\Delta y_i} = \sum_{i=1}^{n}\left(\frac{f(x,y_i)\Delta y_i}{\sum_{j=1}^{n} f(x,y_j)\Delta y_j}\right) y_i = \sum_{i=1}^{n} \mu_{A_i^*}(x) y_i,$$

where we have made a definition:

$$\mu_{A_i^*}(x) \triangleq \frac{f(x, y_i)\Delta y_i}{\sum_{j=1}^{n} f(x, y_j)\Delta y_j}, \quad i = 1, 2, \cdots, n,$$

and clearly $A_i^* \in \mathcal{F}(X)$. Now for any given an approximation precision $\varepsilon > 0$, because $f(x, y)$ is continuous, by using Lemma 6.3.3, $\exists \delta_2 > 0$ and $\delta_2 < \delta_1$, when $\lambda < \delta_2$, for all $x \in X$ the following holds uniformly:

$$\left| \underline{s}(x) - \sum_{i=1}^{n} \mu_{A_i^*}(x) y_i \right| < \frac{\varepsilon}{2}. \tag{6.3.3}$$

Based on the nodes $y_j (j = 0, 1, \cdots, n)$, we can make $n+1$ fuzzy sets $B_j (j = 0, 1, \cdots, n)$ on Y, with demand of B_j being a fuzzy partition on Y and continuous on Y, which is regarded as a kind of fuzziness of y_j $(j = 0, 1, \cdots, n)$; for example, B_j can be taken as "triangle waves" membership functions:

$$\mu_{B_0}(y) = \begin{cases} (y - y_1)/(y_0 - y_1), & y_0 \le y \le y_1, \\ 0, & \text{otherwise}; \end{cases}$$

$$\mu_{B_j}(y) = \begin{cases} (y - y_{j-1})/(y_j - y_{j-1}), & y_{j-1} \le y \le y_j, \\ (y - y_{j+1})/(y_j - y_{j+1}), & y_j < y \le y_{j+1}, \\ 0, & \text{otherwise}, \end{cases}$$

$j = 1, 2, \cdots, n-1$;

$$\mu_{B_n}(y) = \begin{cases} (y - y_{n-1})/(y_n - y_{n-1}), & y_{n-1} \le y \le y_n, \\ 0, & \text{otherwise}. \end{cases}$$

And make fuzzy sets A_i $(i = 1, \cdots, n)$ as the following:

$$\mu_{A_i}(x) \triangleq \frac{f(x, y_i)}{\sum_{j=1}^{n} f(x, y_j)}, \quad i = 1, 2, \cdots, n. \tag{6.3.4}$$

Let $\mathcal{A} \triangleq \{A_i | 1 \le i \le n\}$ and $\mathcal{B} \triangleq \{B_i | 1 \le i \le n\}$. Regarding $\mathcal{A}$ and $\mathcal{B}$ as linguistic variables that take their values in themselves, we form a group of fuzzy inference rules as the same as (6.3.2):

$$\text{If } x \text{ is } A_i \text{ then } y \text{ is } B_i, \ i = 1, 2, \cdots, n.$$

Now we construct a fuzzy system by means of CRI method as follows.

Firstly, coming from i-th fuzzy inference rule of (6.3.2), every fuzzy relation $R_i \triangleq A_i \times B_i$ on $X \times Y$ is formed, where its membership function is

$$(\forall (x, y) \in X \times Y)\left(\mu_{R_i}(x, y) = \mu_{A_i}(x) \wedge \mu_{B_i}(y)\right).$$

Since the n fuzzy inference rules should be combined by logical "or", a whole fuzzy inference relation $R = \bigcup_{i=1}^{n} R_i$ is obtained, i.e., for any binary point $(x, y) \in X \times Y$, we have

$$\mu_R(x, y) = \bigvee_{i=1}^{n} \mu_{R_i}(x, y) = \bigvee_{i=1}^{n} \left(\mu_{A_i}(x) \wedge \mu_{B_i}(y)\right).$$

For any a fuzzy set $A \in \mathcal{F}(X)$, a fuzzy inference result $B \in \mathcal{F}(Y)$ should be got by R, which is equivalent to a fuzzy transformation from $\mathcal{F}(X)$ to $\mathcal{F}(Y)$ being introduced by R, denoted by "$\circ$", i.e.,

$$\circ : \mathcal{F}(X) \to \mathcal{F}(Y), \quad A \to B = \circ(A) \triangleq A \circ R,$$

where its membership function is as follows

$$\mu_B(y) = \bigvee_{x \in X} (\mu_A(x) \wedge \mu_R(x, y)), \quad y \in Y. \tag{6.3.5}$$

For arbitrarily given an input $x' \in X$, for we may use (6.3.5), x' should be turned into a fuzzy set $A' \in \mathcal{F}(X)$ as $\mu_{A'}(x) \triangleq \chi_{\{x'\}}(x)$, where χ_D is the characteristic function of a set D. Substituting A' into (6.3.5), we obtain a result of reasoning $B' \in \mathcal{F}(Y)$ as follows

$$\mu_{B'}(y) = \mu_R(x', y) = \bigvee_{i=1}^{n} \left(\mu_{A_i}(x') \wedge \mu_{B_i}(y)\right), \quad y \in Y. \qquad (6.3.6)$$

Since B' is a fuzzy set, we have to obtain exact quantity $y' \in Y$ by a kind of defuzzification technique. From (6.3.6) we know that $\mu_{B'}(y)$ is piecewise continuous on Y. So we have that

$$\int_{a_2}^{b_2} |y| \mu_{B'}(y) \mathrm{d}y < +\infty, \quad \int_{a_2}^{b_2} \mu_{B'}(y) \mathrm{d}y < +\infty.$$

Now we can prove the fact that $\int_{a_2}^{b_2} \mu_{B'}(y) \mathrm{d}y > 0$. In fact, if it not true, i.e., $\int_{a_2}^{b_2} \mu_{B'}(y) \mathrm{d}y = 0$, then since $\mu_{B'}(y)$ is piecewise continuous on Y and non-negative, we have the fact that $\mu_{B'}(y) = 0$ a.e. Y.

Because $\sum_{i=1}^{n} f(x', y_i) > 0$, there must exist a $i_0 \in \{1, 2, \cdots, n\}$, such that $\mu_{A_{i_0}}(x') > 0$. Noticing (6.3.6), we know that $\mu_{B'}(y) = 0$, a.e. Y, which is contrary with the definition of all B_j being continuous normal fuzzy sets. Thus we can put the following symbol:

$$y' = \frac{\int_{a_2}^{b_2} y \mu_{B'}(y) \mathrm{d}y}{\int_{a_2}^{b_2} \mu_{B'}(y) \mathrm{d}y}.$$

Then we get the correspondence point y' in Y of x'. By the arbitrariness of x', x' can be replaced by a general point x in X, and y' is replaced by $\overline{s}(x)$. And we obtain a function $\overline{s} : X \to Y$ as follows:

$$\overline{s}(x) \triangleq \frac{\int_{a_2}^{b_2} \left[\bigvee_{i=1}^{n} \left(\mu_{A_i}(x) \wedge \mu_{B_i}(y) \right) \right] y \mathrm{d}y}{\int_{a_2}^{b_2} \left[\bigvee_{i=1}^{n} \left(\mu_{A_i}(x) \wedge \mu_{B_i}(y) \right) \right] \mathrm{d}y}. \tag{6.3.7}$$

$\overline{s}$ is a fuzzy approximation system with respect to the uncertainty system S, denoted by $\overline{s} \triangleq S(X, Y, \mathcal{A}, \mathcal{B})$. Besides it is not difficult to understand the following expression:

$$(\forall x \in X)\left(\int_{a_2}^{b_2} \left[\bigvee_{i=1}^{n} \left(\mu_{A_i}(x) \wedge \mu_{B_i}(y) \right) \right] \mathrm{d}y > 0 \right).$$

By Lemma 6.3.2, we have that, $\exists \delta_3 > 0$, such that when $\lambda < \delta_3$, for any appoint $x \in X$, we have the following inequality:

$$\sum_{j=1}^{n} \left[\bigvee_{i=1}^{n} \left(\mu_{A_i}(x) \wedge \mu_{B_i}(y_j) \right) \right] \Delta y_j > 0.$$

Noticing the Riemann sun of (6.3.7) and B_i being with Kronecker property, we have the following result:

$$\overline{s}(x) \approx \frac{\sum_{j=1}^{n} \left[\bigvee_{i=1}^{n} \left(\mu_{A_i}(x) \wedge \mu_{B_i}(y_j) \right) \right] y_j \Delta y_j}{\sum_{j=1}^{n} \left[\bigvee_{i=1}^{n} \left(\mu_{A_i}(x) \wedge \mu_{B_i}(y_j) \right) \right] \Delta y_j}$$

$$= \frac{\sum_{j=1}^{n} \mu_{A_j}(x) y_j \Delta y_j}{\sum_{j=1}^{n} \mu_{A_j}(x) \Delta y_j} = \frac{\sum_{j=1}^{n} f(x, y_j) y_j \Delta y_j}{\sum_{j=1}^{n} f(x, y_j) \Delta y_j} \tag{6.3.8}$$

$$= \sum_{i=1}^{n} \frac{f(x, y_i) \Delta y_i}{\sum_{j=1}^{n} f(x, y_j) \Delta y_j} y_i = \sum_{i=1}^{n} \mu_{A_i^*}(x) y_i,$$

where we have put that

$$\mu_{A_i^*}(x) \triangleq \frac{f(x, y_i)\Delta y_i}{\sum_{j=1}^{n} f(x, y_j)\Delta y_j}.$$

From (6.3.8) and Lemma 6.3.3, we know that $\exists \delta_4 > 0$ and $\delta_4 < \delta_3$, when $\lambda < \delta_4$, for all $x \in X$, the following holds uniformly:

$$\left| \overline{s}(x) - \sum_{i=1}^{n} \mu_{A_i^*}(x) y_i \right| < \frac{\varepsilon}{2}.$$

At last, take $\delta = \min\{\delta_2, \delta_4\}$. When $\lambda < \delta$, for all $x \in X$, the following holds uniformly:

$$\begin{aligned} \left| \overline{s}(x) - \underline{s}(x) \right| &= \left| \overline{s}(x) - \sum_{i=1}^{n} \mu_{A_i^*}(x) y_i + \sum_{i=1}^{n} \mu_{A_i^*}(x) y_i - \underline{s}(x) \right| \\ &\le \left| \overline{s}(x) - \sum_{i=1}^{n} \mu_{A_i^*}(x) y_i \right| + \left| \sum_{i=1}^{n} \mu_{A_i^*}(x) y_i - \underline{s}(x) \right| < \frac{\varepsilon}{2} + \frac{\varepsilon}{2} = \varepsilon. \end{aligned}$$

This means that fuzzy system $\overline{s}$ can approximate continuous stochastic system $\underline{s}$ to arbitrarily given precision ε. □

Example 6.3.1 Given a continuous stochastic system, where we take $X = Y = (-\infty, \infty)$ and $f(x, y)$ is a binary normal probability density as being $N\left(a_1, a_2, \sigma_1{}^2, \sigma_2{}^2, r\right)$, i.e.

$$f(x, y) = \frac{1}{2\pi\sigma_1\sigma_2\sqrt{1-r^2}} \cdot e^{-\frac{1}{2(1-r^2)}\left[\frac{(x-a_1)^2}{\sigma_1^2} - \frac{2r(x-a_1)(y-a_2)}{\sigma_1\sigma_2} + \frac{(y-a_2)^2}{\sigma_2^2}\right]}$$

If we take $r^2 = 0.5, a_1 = 0, a_2 = 0, \sigma_1 = 0.5$, and $\sigma_2 = 1.5$, then above equation is as the following:

$$f(x, y) = \frac{2\sqrt{2}}{3\pi} e^{-\left(4x^2 - \frac{4\sqrt{2}}{3}xy + \frac{4}{9}y^2\right)}$$

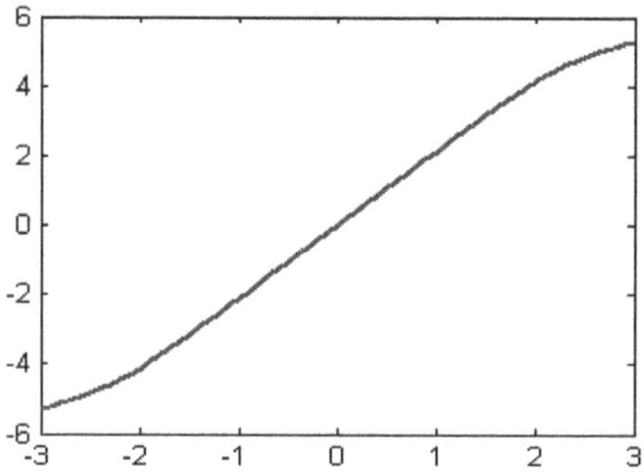

Fig. 6.3.1. Input cure of continuous stochastic system $\underline{s}(x)$

Based on 3σ principle, X and Y can be approximately taken as finite intervals. For example, X is taken as $[-3,3]$ by $6\sigma_1$, and Y is taken as $[-6,6]$ by $4\sigma_2$. By Theorem 6.3.1, we have the following equation and its image can refer to Figure 6.3.1.

$$\underline{s}(x) = E(\eta | \xi = x) = \frac{\int_{-6}^{6} y e^{-\left(4x^2 - \frac{4\sqrt{2}}{3}xy + \frac{4}{9}y^2\right)} \mathrm{dy}}{\int_{-6}^{6} e^{-\left(4x^2 - \frac{4\sqrt{2}}{3}xy + \frac{4}{9}y^2\right)} \mathrm{dy}}$$

Now we consider the fuzzy approximation system $\overline{s}$. First make a partition of Y:

$$y_0 = -6, y_1 = -5, y_2 = -4, \cdots, y_{11} = 5, y_{12} = 6;$$

then make fuzzy sets B_j $(j = 0,1,\cdots,12)$ as Figure 6.3.2. $\mu_{A_i}(x)$ are defined as the following equation (see (6.3.4)), their images refer to Figure 6.3.2.

$$\mu_{A_i}(x) = \frac{f(x, y_i)}{\sum_{j=1}^{12} f(x, y_j)} = \frac{e^{-\left(4x^2 - \frac{4\sqrt{2}}{3}xy_i + \frac{4}{9}y_i^2\right)}}{\sum_{j=1}^{12} e^{-\left(4x^2 - \frac{4\sqrt{2}}{3}xy_j + \frac{4}{9}y_j^2\right)}}$$

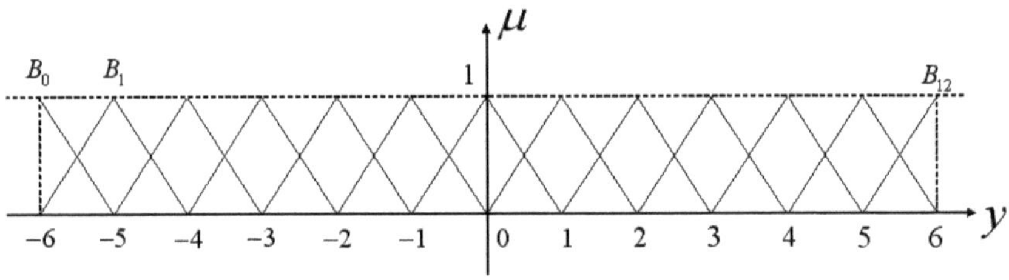

Fig. 6.3.2. Membership functions of B_j

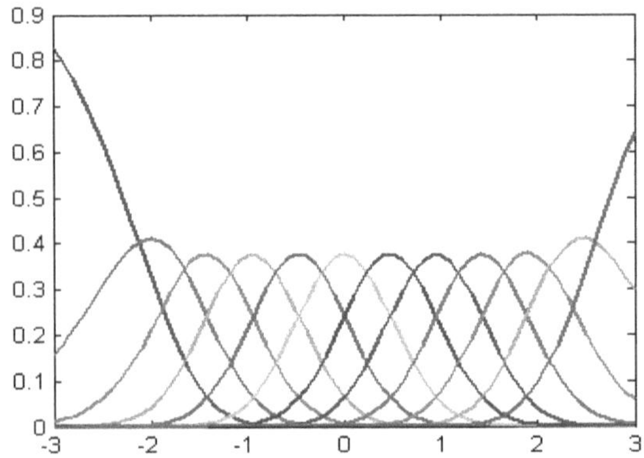

Fig. 6.3.3. Membership functions of A_i

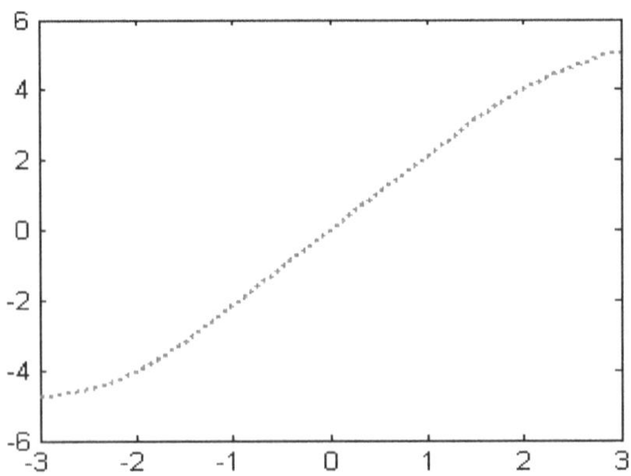

Fig. 6.3.4. Output cure of fuzzy system $\overline{s}$

We now calculate the following integral:

$$\overline{s}(x) = \frac{\int_{-6}^{6}\left[\bigvee_{i=1}^{12}\left(\mu_{A_i}(x) \wedge \mu_{B_i}(y)\right)\right] y\mathrm{d}y}{\int_{-6}^{6}\left[\bigvee_{i=1}^{12}\left(\mu_{A_i}(x) \wedge \mu_{B_i}(y)\right)\right] \mathrm{d}y},$$

which image refers to Figure 6.3.4. And the images of $\overline{s}(x)$ and $\underline{s}(x)$ refer to Figure 6.3.5.

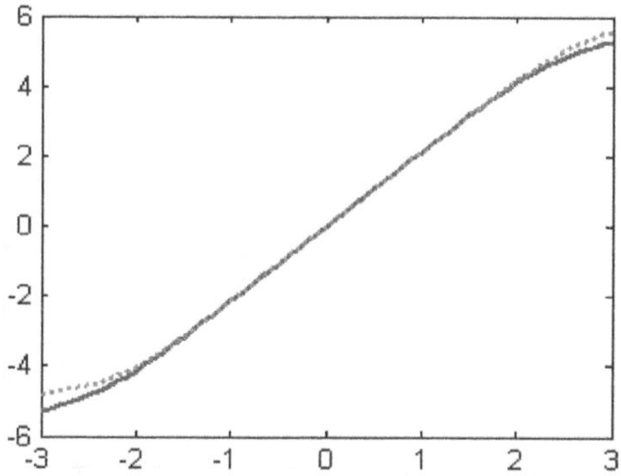

Fig. 6.3.5. The comparison cures of $\overline{s}(x)$ and $\underline{s}(x)$ when $\lambda = 1$, where "···" indicates the cure of $\overline{s}(x)$ and "—" represents the cure of $\underline{s}(x)$.

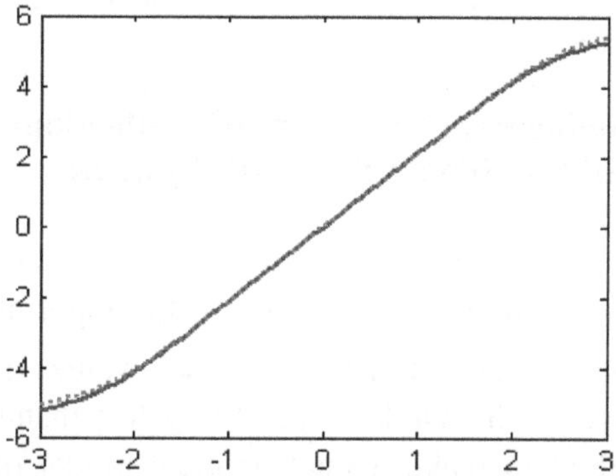

Fig. 6.3.6. The comparison cures of $\overline{s}(x)$ and $\underline{s}(x)$ when $\lambda = 0.5$, where "···" indicates the cure of $\overline{s}(x)$ and "—" represents the cure of $\underline{s}(x)$.

If the partition nodes $\{y_j\}$ are increased of double number, i.e.,

$$y_0 = -6,\ y_1 = -5.5,\ y_2 = -5, \cdots,\ y_{24} = 6,$$

then the approximation precision increases better, where the comparison cures of $\overline{s}(x)$ and $\underline{s}(x)$ refer to Figure 6.3.6. And if the partition nodes $\{y_j\}$ are increased, then the cures of $\overline{s}(x)$ and $\underline{s}(x)$ are basically coincident from Figure 6.3.7.

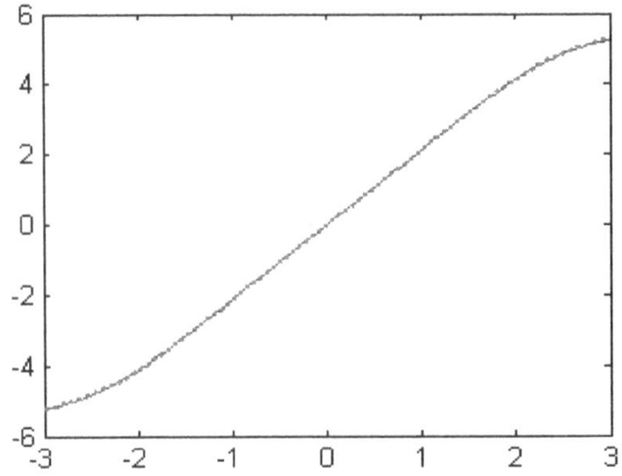

Fig. 6.3.7. The comparison cures of $\overline{s}(x)$ and $\underline{s}(x)$ when $\lambda = 0.1$, where "$\cdots$" indicates the cure of $\overline{s}(x)$ and "—" represents the cure of $\underline{s}(x)$.

6.4 Fuzzy Reasoning Representations of Double-inputs Single-output Continuous Stochastic Systems

Figure 6.4.1 shows a double-input single-output open-loop system S. The input variables x and y take values in the input universes X and Y respectively, and the output variable z takes values in the output universe Z. If this system S is a deterministic system then one may use the conventional method to make a mathematical model of the system S (for example, one can use the mechanism modeling approach to establish a partial differential equation model) and find a solution $z(x, y)$ of the model by analytic or numerical methods. In this way, this system shall be regarded as having been mastered basically.

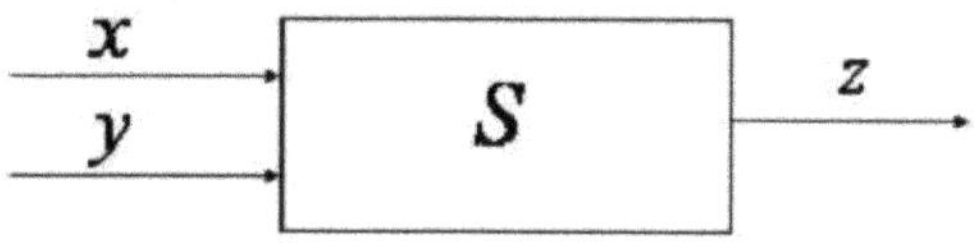

Fig. 6.4.1. A double-input single-output open-loop system

Then the system S may be simply understood by a binary function, also denoted by s, i.e.,

$$s: X \times Y \to Z, \ (x, y) \mapsto z \triangleq s(x, y). \tag{6.4.1}$$

When S is an uncertainty system, although it is hard to get a precise function as (6.4.1), we may often obtain an approximate function as follows

$$\underline{s}: X \times Y \to Z, \ (x, y) \mapsto z \triangleq \underline{s}(x, y), \tag{6.4.2}$$

such that $\underline{s}(x, y)$ and $s(x, y)$ are very close. Just as stating in section 6.2, we still consider to realize above approximation thought by using conditional mathematical expectation.

Let X, Y and Z be three measurable sets on real number space $\mathbb{R}$, and ξ, η and ζ be three random variables defined on the probability spaces $(X, \mathcal{B}_1, P_1), (Y, \mathcal{B}_2, P_2)$ and $(Z, \mathcal{B}_3, P_3)$ respectively, where $\mathcal{B}_1$, $\mathcal{B}_2$ and $\mathcal{B}_3$ are three Borel σ-fields on X, Y and Z respectively, and P_1, P_2 and P_3 are the probability measure on $\mathcal{B}_1$, $\mathcal{B}_2$ and $\mathcal{B}_3$ respectively.

Taking $\Omega \triangleq X \times Y \times Z$, $\mathcal{F} \triangleq \mathcal{B}_1 \times \mathcal{B}_2 \times \mathcal{B}_3$ and $P \triangleq P_1 \times P_2 \times P_3$, we obtain joint probability space $(\Omega, \mathcal{F}, P)$, where $\mathcal{F}$ is the Borel σ-field generated by Cartesian product of Borel σ-fields $\mathcal{B}_1, \mathcal{B}_2$ and $\mathcal{B}_3$, and P is the product probability measure. With same notations, redefine ξ, η and ζ as random variables on Ω:

$$\xi:\Omega\to\mathbb{R},\ (u,v,w)\mapsto\xi(u,v,w)\triangleq\xi(u),$$
$$\eta:\Omega\to\mathbb{R},\ (u,v,w)\mapsto\eta(u,v,w)\triangleq\eta(v),$$
$$\zeta:\Omega\to\mathbb{R},\ (u,v,w)\mapsto\zeta(u,v,w)\triangleq\zeta(w).$$

Then a three-dimensional random vector (ξ,η,ζ) defined on $(\Omega,\mathcal{F},P)$ is got. For any $(x,y)\in X\times Y$, when $\omega\in\{\omega\in\Omega|\xi=x,\eta=y\}$, let

$$\underline{s}(x,y)\triangleq E(\zeta|\xi=x,\eta=y). \tag{6.4.3}$$

As stated in section 6.2, (6.4.3) is the optimal approximation in mean square to $s(x,y)$.

Suppose that we have known the continuous probability density function $f(x,y,z)$ of the random vector (ξ,η,ζ). Then the conditional mathematical expectation (6.4.3) can be written as follows:

$$\underline{s}(x,y)=\frac{\int_Z f(x,y,z)z\mathrm{d}z}{\int_Z f(x,y,z)\mathrm{d}z}, \tag{6.4.4}$$

where there is a demand: for any $(x,y)\in X\times Y$,

$$\int_Z |z|f(x,y,z)\mathrm{d}z<+\infty,\quad 0<\int_Z f(x,y,z)\mathrm{d}z<+\infty.$$

When the continuous probability density function $f(x,y,z)$ of the uncertainty system is known, $\underline{s}$ defined by (6.4.4) is called a double-input single-output continuous approximation stochastic system or simply a double-input single-output continuous approximation stochastic system, denoted by

$$\underline{s}=S(X\times Y,Z,f(x,y,z)). \tag{6.4.5}$$

For proving the following main theorem, we still need two lemmas.

Lemma 6.4.1 Let $f(x,y,z)$ be a ternary continuous function defined on the universe $X\times Y\times Z$, where

$$X=[a_1,b_1],\quad Y=[a_2,b_2],\quad Z=[a_3,b_3],$$

are three finite real number intervals. For the integral with parameter as follows:

$$I(x,y)=\int_{a_3}^{b_3} f(x,y,z)\mathrm{d}z,$$

we have such a result: for arbitrarily given $\varepsilon>0$, there is always a common $\delta>0$ without dependent of parameter (x,y) such that, for any partition of Z as the following:

$$a_3=z_0<z_1<\cdots<z_n=b_3,$$

as long as $\lambda=\max\{\Delta z_i \mid i=1,2,\cdots,n\}<\delta$, then the Riemann sum of the integral $I(x,y)$, $\sum_{i=1}^{n} f(x,y,\xi_i)\Delta z_i$, must meet the condition that

$$\left|I(x,y)-\sum_{i=1}^{n} f(x,y,\xi_i)\Delta z_i\right|<\varepsilon$$

is uniformly true for all $(x,y)\in X\times Y$, where

$$\Delta z_i=z_i-z_{i-1},\quad i=1,2,\cdots,n,$$

and ξ_i takes its value in $[z_{i-1},z_i]$ arbitrarily.

Proof. For arbitrarily given $\varepsilon>0$, let $\delta_k=\dfrac{1}{k}, k=1,2,\cdots$. We can prove that there must exist one k such that $\delta=\delta_k$ meets the conclusion of the lemma. If it is not, then for every k, exist $(x_k,y_k)\in X\times Y$ and a partition of Z as follows

$$a_3=z_0^{(k)}<z_1^{(k)}<\cdots<z_{n_k}^{(k)}=b_3$$

and a kind of taking value way of $\xi_i^{(k)}$ in $\left[z_{i-1}^{(k)},z_i^{(k)}\right]$, although

$$\lambda_k = \max\left\{\Delta z_i^{(k)} \middle| i = 1, 2, \cdots, n_k\right\} < \delta_k,$$

we have the following inequality:

$$\left| I(x_k, y_k) - \sum_{i=1}^{n_k} f\left(x_k, y_k, \xi_i^{(k)}\right)\Delta z_i^{(k)} \right| \geq \varepsilon. \qquad (6.4.6)$$

As a matter of fact, notice that $\{x_k\}$ in binary sequence $\{(x_k, y_k)\}$ are all bounded sequences and so it has a convergent subsequence $\{x_{k_j}\}$ such that $x_{k_j} \xrightarrow{j\to\infty} x_* \in X$.

In the same way, for the subsequence $\{y_{k_j}\}$, there is also a convergent subsequence $\{y_{k_{j_p}}\}$ such that $y_{k_{j_p}} \xrightarrow{p\to\infty} y_* \in Y$. And noticing the limit expression $\delta_{k_{j_p}} \xrightarrow{p\to\infty} 0$, we can have the following result:

$$0 < \varepsilon \leq \lim_{p\to\infty} \left| I\left(x_{k_{j_p}}, y_{k_{j_p}}\right) - \sum_{i=1}^{n_{k_{j_p}}} f\left(x_{k_{j_p}}, y_{k_{j_p}}, \xi_i^{\left(k_{j_p}\right)}\right)\Delta z_i^{\left(k_{j_p}\right)} \right|$$

$$= \left| I(x_*, y_*) - \int_{a_3}^{b_3} f(x_*, y_*, z)\mathrm{d}z \right| = 0.$$

This is a clear contradiction. □

Lemma 6.4.2 Let $f(x, y, z)$ be a ternary continuous function defined in the set $X \times Y \times Z$, where $X = [a_1, b_1]$, $Y = [a_2, b_2]$ and $Z = [a_3, b_3]$ are finite real number intervals. For the integral with parameter as follows

$$I(x, y) = \int_{a_3}^{b_3} f(x, y, z)\mathrm{d}z,$$

if the following condition $(\forall (x, y) \in X \times Y)(I(x, y) > 0)$ is satisfied, then there must exist a $\delta > 0$, such that for any partition of Z as follows

$$a_3 = z_0 < z_1 < \cdots < z_n = b_3$$

and any kind of taking value ways of ξ_i in $[z_{i-1}, z_i]$, the Riemann sum of the integral $I(x, y)$, $\sum_{i=1}^{n} f(x, y, \xi_i)\Delta z_i$, must meet the following implication:

$$\lambda = \max\{\Delta z_i | i = 1, 2, \cdots, n\} < \delta \Rightarrow$$

$$(\forall (x, y) \in X \times Y)\left(\sum_{i=1}^{n} f(x, y, \xi_i)\Delta z_i > 0\right)$$

Because the way of the proof is the same as the proof of Lemma 6.4.1, it is omitted. □

Besides, we have the following lemma just like Lemma 6.3.3.

Lemma 6.4.3 Let $f(x, y, z)$ be a ternary continuous function defined in the set $X \times Y \times Z$, where $X = [a_1, b_1], Y = [a_2, b_2], Z = [a_3, b_3]$ are finite real number intervals, and meet the condition:

$$(\forall (x, y) \in X \times Y)\left(\int_{a_3}^{b_3} f(x, y, z)\mathrm{d}z > 0\right).$$

For arbitrarily given $\varepsilon > 0$, there is always a common $\delta > 0$ without dependent of parameter (x, y) such that, for any partition of the set Z as being : $a_3 = z_0 < z_1 < \cdots < z_n = b_3$, the following implication:

$$\lambda = \max\{\Delta z_i | i = 1, 2, \cdots, n\} < \delta \Rightarrow$$

$$\left| \frac{\int_{a_3}^{b_3} f(x, y, z)z\mathrm{d}z}{\int_{a_3}^{b_3} f(x, y, z)\mathrm{d}z} - \frac{\sum_{i=1}^{n} f(x, y, \xi_i)\xi_i\Delta z_i}{\sum_{i=1}^{n} f(x, y, \xi_i)\Delta z_i} \right| < \varepsilon$$

is uniformly true for all $(x, y) \in X \times Y$, where

$$\Delta z_i \triangleq z_i - z_{i-1}, \quad i = 1, 2, \cdots, n,$$

and ξ_i takes its value in $[z_{i-1}, z_i]$ arbitrarily. □

Theorem 6.4.1 Given a double-input single-output continuous stochastic system: $\underline{s} = S(X \times Y, Z, f(x, y, z))$, where

$$X = [a_1, b_1], \quad Y = [a_2, b_2], \quad Z = [a_3, b_3]$$

are finite real number intervals. If the following condition is satisfied:

$$(\forall (x, y) \in X \times Y)\left(\int_{a_3}^{b_3} f(x, y, z) \mathrm{d}z > 0\right),$$

then there must exist a group of fuzzy inference rules as follows:

$$\text{If } (x, y) \text{ is } D_i \text{ then } z \text{ is } C_i, \; i = 1, 2, \cdots, n, \tag{6.4.7}$$

where $D_i \in \mathcal{F}(X \times Y)$ and $C_i \in \mathcal{F}(Z)$, such that the fuzzy system $\overline{s}$ constructed by the group of fuzzy inference rules can approximate the continuous stochastic system $\underline{s}$ to arbitrarily given precision.

Proof. We make a partition of interval $Z = [a_3, b_3]$ as the following:

$$a_3 = z_0 < z_1 < \cdots < z_n = b_3.$$

Write $\Delta z_i = z_i - z_{i-1}$ $(i = 1, 2, \cdots, n)$ and put the following symbol:

$$\lambda = \max\{\Delta z_i \,|\, i = 1, 2, \cdots, n\}.$$

Then we can get two Riemann sums as following:

$$\sum_{i=1}^{n} f(x, y, z_i) z_i \Delta z_i, \quad \sum_{i=1}^{n} f(x, y, z_i) \Delta z_i.$$

From the condition of the theorem and Lemma 6.4.2, the following result is true: there exists a $\delta_1 > 0$, when the real number $\lambda < \delta_1$, then we have the following inequality:

$$(\forall (x,y) \in X \times Y)\left(\sum_{i=1}^{n} f(x,y,z_i)\Delta z_i > 0 \right).$$

So we have the following result:

$$\underline{s}(x,y) = E(\zeta \mid \xi = x, \eta = y) = \frac{\int_{a_3}^{b_3} f(x,y,z) z \mathrm{d}z}{\int_{a_3}^{b_3} f(x,y,z) \mathrm{d}z}$$

$$\approx \frac{\sum_{i=1}^{n} f(x,y,z_i) z_i \Delta z_i}{\sum_{i=1}^{n} f(x,y,z_i)\Delta z_i} = \sum_{i=1}^{n} \left(\frac{f(x,y,z_i)\Delta z_i}{\sum_{j=1}^{n} f(x,y,z_j)\Delta z_j} \right) z_i$$

$$= \sum_{i=1}^{n} \left(\frac{\mu_{D_i}(x,y)\Delta z_i}{\sum_{j=1}^{n} \mu_{D_j}(x,y)\Delta z_j} \right) z_i = \sum_{i=1}^{n} \mu_{D_i^*}(x,y) z_i,$$

where we have given the definitions as follows:

$$\left.\begin{array}{l} \mu_{D_i}(x,y) \triangleq f(x,y,z_i)/M, \\ \mu_{D_i^*}(x,y) \triangleq \dfrac{\mu_{D_i}(x,y)\Delta z_i}{\sum_{j=1}^{n} \mu_{D_j}(x,y)\Delta z_j}, \\ i = 0,1,\cdots,n, \\ M \triangleq \max\{ f(x,y,z) \mid (x,y,z) \in X \times Y \times Z \} \end{array}\right\} \tag{6.4.8}$$

Clearly $D_i, D_i^* \in \mathcal{F}(X \times Y)$.

For any given approximation precision $\varepsilon > 0$, since $f(x,y,z)$ is continuous, from Lemma 6.4.3, $\exists \delta_2 > 0$ and $\delta_2 < \delta_1$, when $\lambda < \delta_2$, for all $(x,y) \in X \times Y$, that the following inequality:

$$\left| \underline{s}(x, y) - \sum_{i=1}^{n} \mu_{D_i^*}(x, y) z_i \right| < \frac{\varepsilon}{2}$$

holds uniformly.

By using the partition nodes $z_j (j = 0, 1, \cdots, n)$, construct $n+1$ fuzzy sets $C_j (j = 0, 1, \cdots, n)$ on Z, which form a fuzzy partition of Z, i.e. make a kind of fuzziness of the nodes $z_j (j = 0, 1, \cdots, n)$. And we put

$$\mathcal{D} = \{ D_i | 1 \le i \le n \}, \quad \mathcal{C} = \{ C_i | 1 \le i \le n \}.$$

Regarding $\mathcal{D}$ and $\mathcal{C}$ as linguistic variables, a group of fuzzy inference rules can be formed as follows:

$$\text{If } (x, y) \text{ is } D_i \text{ then } z \text{ is } C_i, \; i = 1, 2, \cdots, n. \tag{6.4.9}$$

We still use CRI method to make a fuzzy system $\overline{s}$. First, from i-th fuzzy inference rule of (6.4.9), a fuzzy relation $R_i \triangleq D_i \times C_i$ on the universe $X \times Y \times Z$ is formed, where its membership function is the following:

$$\mu_{R_i}(x, y, z) = \mu_{D_i}(x, y) \wedge \mu_{C_i}(z).$$

Then a whole fuzzy inference relation $R \triangleq \bigcup_{i=1}^{n} R_i$ is obtained as follows

$$\mu_R(x, y, z) = \bigvee_{i=1}^{n} \mu_{R_i}(x, y, z) = \bigvee_{i=1}^{n} \left(\mu_{D_i}(x, y) \wedge \mu_{C_i}(z) \right)$$

For any $D \in \mathcal{F}(X \times Y)$, a fuzzy inference result $C \in \mathcal{F}(Z)$ should be got by R, where $C \triangleq D \circ R$, i.e.

$$\mu_C(z) = \bigvee_{(x,y) \in X \times Y} \left(\mu_D(x, y) \wedge \mu_R(x, y, z) \right), \quad z \in Z. \tag{6.4.10}$$

For arbitrarily given an input $(x', y') \in X \times Y$, the point (x', y')

should be turned into a fuzzy set:

$$\mu_{D'}(x,y) \triangleq \chi_{\{(x',y')\}}(x,y).$$

Substituting D' into (6.4.10), we obtain result of reasoning $C' \in \mathcal{F}(Z)$ as follows:

$$\mu_{C'}(z) = \mu_R(x',y',z) = \bigvee_{i=1}^{n} \left(\mu_{D_i}(x',y') \wedge \mu_{C_i}(z)\right), \quad z \in Z$$

It is easy to know that $\mu_{C'}(z) > 0$. Let

$$z' = \frac{\int_{a_3}^{b_3} z\mu_{C'}(z)\mathrm{d}z}{\int_{a_3}^{b_3} \mu_{C'}(z)\mathrm{d}z}.$$

And (x',y') is replaced by general point (x,y) in $X \times Y$ and z' by $\overline{s}(x,y)$. So we get a function $\overline{s}: X \times Y \to Z$ as follows:

$$\overline{s}(x,y) \triangleq \frac{\int_{a_3}^{b_3} \left[\bigvee_{i=1}^{n} \left(\mu_{D_i}(x,y) \wedge \mu_{C_i}(z)\right)\right] z\mathrm{d}z}{\int_{a_3}^{b_3} \left[\bigvee_{i=1}^{n} \left(\mu_{D_i}(x,y) \wedge \mu_{C_i}(z)\right)\right] \mathrm{d}z}, \tag{6.4.11}$$

which is still called a fuzzy approximation system of S, or called a double-input single fuzzy system, denoted by $\overline{s} = S(X \times Y, Z, \mathcal{D}, \mathcal{C})$. Because for any $(x,y) \in X \times Y$, we have

$$\int_{a_3}^{b_3} \left[\bigvee_{i=1}^{n} \left(\mu_{D_i}(x,y) \wedge \mu_{C_i}(z)\right)\right] \mathrm{d}z > 0,$$

and by using Lemma 6.4.2, $\exists \delta_3 > 0$, when $\lambda < \delta_3$, we have that, for any binary point $(x,y) \in X \times Y$, the following inequality is true:

$$\sum_{j=1}^{n}\left[\bigvee_{i=1}^{n}\left(\mu_{D_i}(x,y)\wedge\mu_{C_i}\left(z_j\right)\right)\right]\Delta z_j>0.$$

Noticing the Riemann sum of (6.4.11) and C_i being with Kronecker property, we have the following result:

$$\overline{s}(x,y)\approx\frac{\sum_{j=1}^{n}\left[\bigvee_{i=1}^{n}\left(\mu_{D_i}(x,y)\wedge\mu_{C_i}\left(z_j\right)\right)\right]z_j\Delta z_j}{\sum_{j=1}^{n}\left[\bigvee_{i=1}^{n}\left(\mu_{D_i}(x,y)\wedge\mu_{C_i}\left(z_j\right)\right)\right]\Delta z_j}$$

$$=\frac{\sum_{j=1}^{n}\mu_{D_j}(x,y)z_j\Delta z_j}{\sum_{j=1}^{n}\mu_{D_j}(x,y)\Delta z_j}=\sum_{i=1}^{n}\frac{\mu_{D_i}(x,y)\Delta z_i}{\sum_{j=1}^{n}\mu_{D_j}(x,y)\Delta z_j}z_i$$

$$=\sum_{i=1}^{n}\mu_{D_i^*}(x,y)z_i,$$

where

$$\mu_{D_i^*}(x,y)\triangleq\frac{\mu_{D_i}(x,y)\Delta z_i}{\sum_{j=1}^{n}\mu_{D_j}(x,y)\Delta z_j},\quad i=1,2,\cdots,n.$$

From Lemma 6.4.3, $\exists\delta_4>0$ and $\delta_4<\delta_3$, when $\lambda<\delta_4$, for all binary points $(x,y)\in X\times Y$, it uniformly holds that

$$\left|\overline{s}(x,y)-\sum_{i=1}^{n}\mu_{D_i^*}(x,y)z_i\right|<\frac{\varepsilon}{2}.$$

At last, if we take $\delta=\min\{\delta_2,\delta_4\}$, then when $\lambda<\delta$, we have the following result:

$$\left(\forall(x,y)\in X\times Y\right)\left(\left|\overline{s}(x,y)-\underline{s}(x,y)\right|<\varepsilon\right)$$

This means that fuzzy system $\overline{s}$ can approximate continuous stochastic system $\underline{s}$ to arbitrarily given ε. □

Remark 6.4.1 In the proof of the theorem, fuzzy sets D_i are formed by (6.4.8). In fact, we can also make them as follows:

$$\mu_{D_i}(x, y) \triangleq \frac{f(x, y, z_i)}{\sum_{j=1}^{n} f(x, y, z_j)}, \tag{6.4.12}$$

Based on (6.4.12), we can also prove the theorem. Here omits it. However, Theorem 6.4.1 is proved in such way. □

Example 6.4.1 Given a continuous stochastic system as the following:

$$\underline{s} = S(X \times Y, Z, f(x, y, z)),$$
$$X = Y = Z = [0, 2\pi],$$
$$f(x, y, z) = \frac{1 - \sin x \sin y \sin z}{8\pi^3}$$

Based on Theorem 6.4.1, we have the following equation and its image refers to Figure 6.4.2.

$$\underline{s}(x, y) = E(\zeta \mid \xi = x, \eta = y)$$
$$= \frac{\int_0^{2\pi} f(x, y, z) z \mathrm{d}z}{\int_0^{2\pi} f(x, y, z) \mathrm{d}z} = \pi + \sin x \sin y.$$

Now we consider constructing a fuzzy approximation system $\overline{s}$. First make a partition of Z:

$$z_0 = 0,\ z_1 = 0.2\pi,\ z_2 = 0.4\pi, \cdots, z_9 = 1.8\pi,\ z_{10} = 2\pi;$$

then fuzzy sets $C_j (j = 0, 1, \cdots, 10)$ are formed as Figure 6.4.3. The fuzzy sets $\mu_{D_i}(x, y)$ are defined as the following equation (see (6.4.8)) where $M = \dfrac{1}{4\pi^3}$, which images refer to Figure 6.4.4.

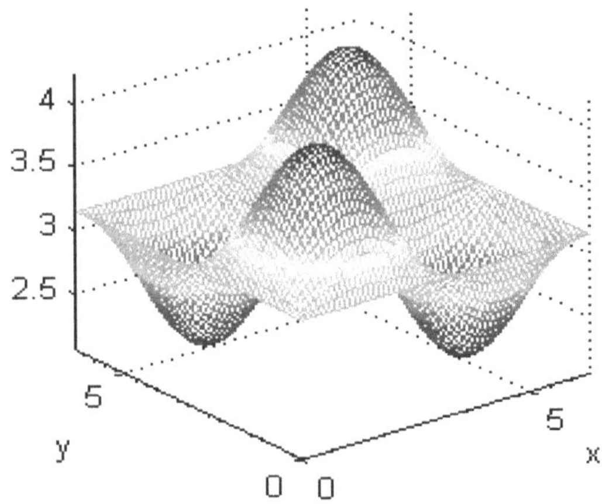

Fig. 6.4.2. Output surface of the continuous stochastic system $\underline{S}$

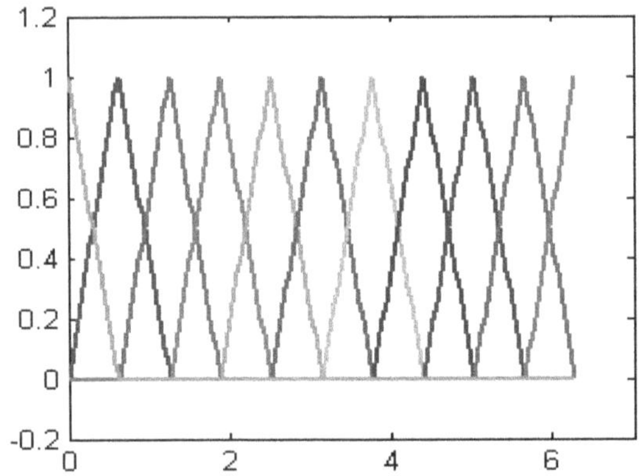

Fig. 6.4.3. Membership function curves of fuzzy sets C_j

$$\mu_{D_i}(x, y) = \frac{f(x, y, z_i)}{M} = \frac{1}{2}\left(1 - \sin x \sin y \sin \frac{i\pi}{5}\right)$$

We calculate the following binary function:

$$\overline{s}(x,y)=\frac{\int_0^{2\pi}\left[\bigvee_{i=1}^{10}\left(\mu_{D_i}(x,y)\wedge\mu_{C_i}(z)\right)\right]z\mathrm{d}z}{\int_0^{2\pi}\left[\bigvee_{i=1}^{10}\left(\mu_{D_i}(x,y)\wedge\mu_{C_i}(z)\right)\right]\mathrm{d}z}$$

which its function image refers to Figure 6.4.5, and the surface of the error $\overline{s}(x,y)-\underline{s}(x,y)$ refers to Figure 6.4.6.

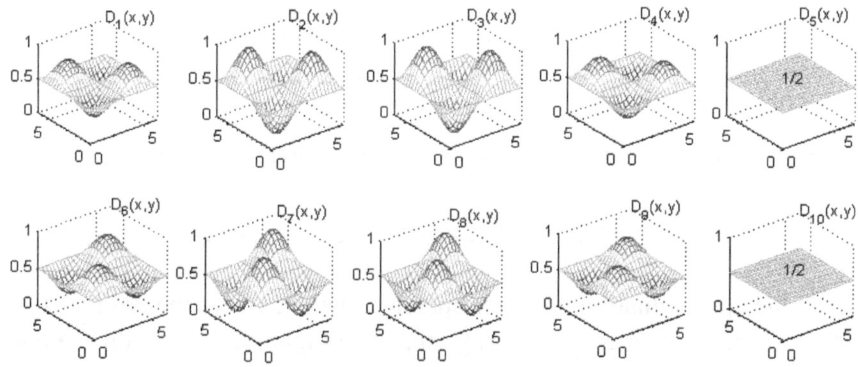

Fig. 6.4.4. Membership function surfaces of fuzzy sets D_i

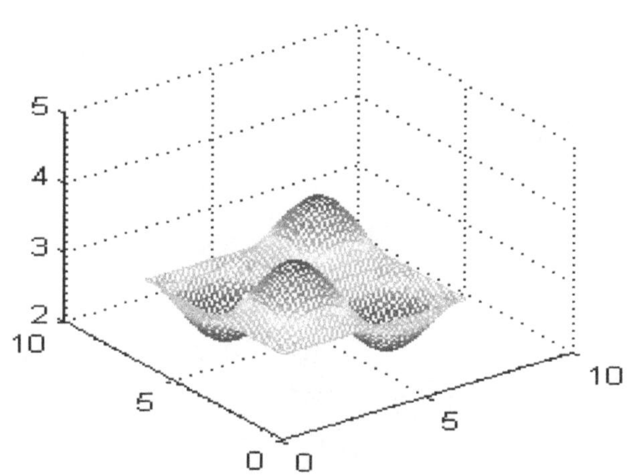

Fig. 6.4.5. Output surface of fuzzy system $\overline{s}$

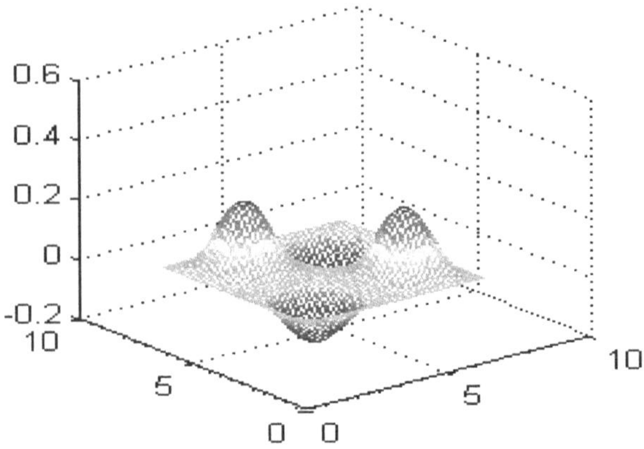

Fig. 6.4.6. The error surface when $\lambda = 0.2\pi$

If the partition nodes $\{z_j\}$ are increased of double number, i.e.,

$$z_0 = 0,\ z_1 = 0.1\pi,\ z_2 = 0.2\pi, \cdots, z_{20} = 2\pi\,,$$

then the approximation precision increases better, where the error surface of error function $\overline{s}(x, y) - \underline{s}(x, y)$ refers to Figure 6.4.7. And if the partition nodes $\{z_j\}$ are increased more, then we can see that the error between $\overline{s}(x, y)$ and $\underline{s}(x, y)$ is very small from Figure 6.4.8.

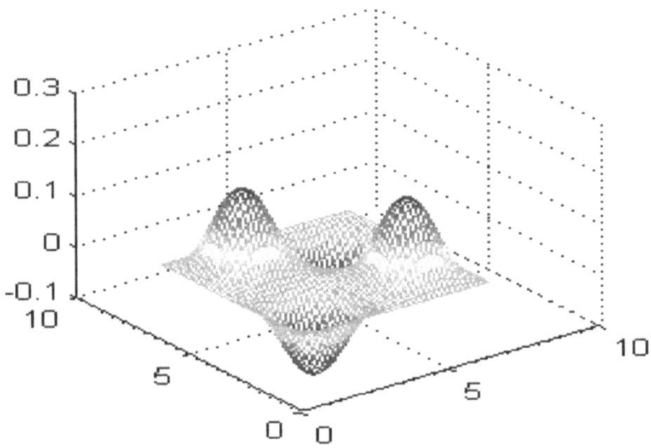

Fig. 6.4.7. The error surface when $\lambda = 0.1\pi$

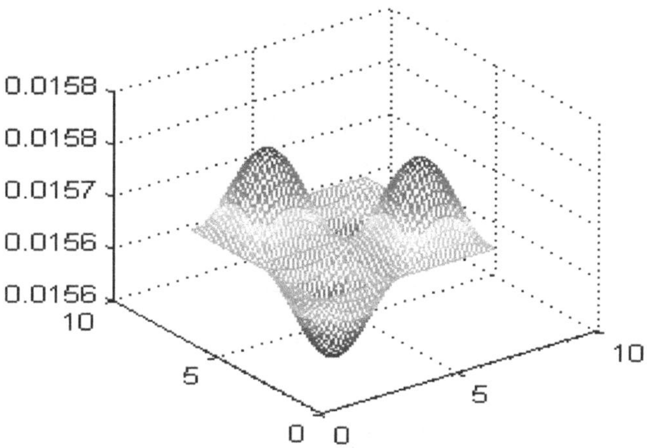

Fig. 6.4.8. The error surface when $\lambda = 0.01\pi$

6.5 Fuzzy Reasoning Representations of Discrete Stochastic Systems

First we consider the single-input and single-output uncertainty system as $s = S(X,Y)$. Suppose that we have known some probability information about the system S. And we should be seeing about the system from stochastic viewpoint.

Let X and Y be measurable sets in real number space $\mathbb{R}$, and input random variable ξ and output random variable η be defined in probability spaces $(X, \mathcal{B}_1, P_1)$ and $(Y, \mathcal{B}_2, P_2)$ respectively, where $\mathcal{B}_1$ and $\mathcal{B}_2$ are Borel σ-fields on X and Y, respectively, and P_1 and P_2 be probability measures on $\mathcal{B}_1$ and $\mathcal{B}_2$, respectively. As doing in section 6.1, we can construct a joint probability space $(\Omega, \mathcal{F}, P)$. Then (ξ, η) is a random vector on $(\Omega, \mathcal{F}, P)$.

Suppose that we have mastered the discrete probability distribution of the system as the following:

$$\left\{P\left(x_i, y_j\right) \middle| 1 \le i \le n, 1 \le j \le m\right\},$$

where $X = [a_1, b_1], Y = [a_2, b_2]$, and $a_1 \le x_1 < \cdots < x_n \le b_1$, and

$$y_0 \triangleq a_2 < y_1 < \cdots < y_m = b_2.$$

Assume that $(\forall i \in \{1,2,\cdots,n\})\left(\sum_{j=1}^{m} P(x_i, y_j) > 0\right)$. Write

$$\underline{s}(x_i) \triangleq E(\eta \mid \xi = x_i) = \frac{\sum_{j=1}^{m} P(x_i, y_j)\, y_j}{\sum_{j=1}^{m} P(x_i, y_j)}. \tag{6.5.1}$$

This is regarded as the response of S after x_i is input. So, if we write the system as the following:

$$\underline{s} = S\left(X, Y, \left\{P(x_i, y_j) \middle| 1 \le i \le n, 1 \le j \le m\right\}\right),$$

Then $\underline{s}$ defined as (6.5.1) is called a discrete stochastic approximation system of the uncertainty S or simply called a discrete stochastic system.

Theorem 6.5.1 Given arbitrarily a discrete stochastic system as follows:

$$\underline{s} = S\left(X, Y, \left\{P(x_i, y_j) \middle| 1 \le i \le n, 1 \le j \le m\right\}\right)$$

where $X = [a_1, b_1]$ and $Y = [a_2, b_2]$ are finite real number intervals, then there exists a group of fuzzy inference rules:

$$\text{If } x \text{ is } A_j \text{ then } y \text{ is } B_j,\ j = 1, 2, \cdots, m, \tag{6.5.2}$$

where $A_j \in \mathcal{F}(X)$ and $B_j \in \mathcal{F}(Y)$, such that the fuzzy system $\overline{s}$ constructed by the group of fuzzy inference rules can approximate the discrete stochastic system $\underline{s}$ to some precision $\varepsilon > 0$, i.e.,

$$(\forall i \in \{1,2,\cdots,n\})\left(\left|\overline{s}(x_i) - \underline{s}(x_i)\right| \le \varepsilon\right),$$

and the smaller is $\lambda = \max\limits_{1\le j\le m}\{\Delta y_j\}$, the higher is precision, where

$$\Delta y_j = y_j - y_{j-1}, \quad j = 1, 2, \cdots, m.$$

Proof. First of all, we consider how to make a group of fuzzy inference rules (6.5.2). One side, $B_j \in \mathcal{F}(Y)$ are easy to get. In fact, as the same as Figure 6.3.2 we can form "triangle waves" membership functions of the fuzzy sets, where subscript n should be replaced by m. So the linguistic variable $\mathcal{B}=\{B_j \mid 1\le j\le m\}$ is obtained. Other side, we have to make fuzzy sets $A_j \in \mathcal{F}(X)$. For every $j \in \{1, 2, \cdots, m\}$, we construct a group of fuzzy sets $\alpha_i \in \mathcal{F}(X)$ $(i = 1, 2, \cdots, n)$ as base functions as follows:

$$\mu_{\alpha_1}(x) = \begin{cases} (x - x_2)/(x_1 - x_2), & x_1 \le x \le x_2, \\ 0, & \text{otherwise}; \end{cases}$$

$$\mu_{\alpha_i}(x) = \begin{cases} (x - x_{i-1})/(x_i - x_{i-1}), & x_{i-1} \le x \le x_i, \\ (x - x_{i+1})/(x_i - x_{i+1}), & x_i < x \le x_{i+1}, \\ 0, & \text{otherwise}, \end{cases}$$

$$i = 2, 3, \cdots, n-1;$$

$$\mu_{\alpha_n}(x) = \begin{cases} (x - x_{n-1})/(x_n - x_{n-1}), & x_{n-1} \le x \le x_n, \\ 0, & \text{otherwise}. \end{cases}$$

Secondly, (6.5.1) is turned into the following:

$$\underline{s}(x_i) = \frac{\sum_{j=1}^{m} P(x_i, y_j)\, y_j}{\sum_{j=1}^{m} P(x_i, y_j)} = \sum_{j=1}^{m} \left(\frac{P(x_i, y_j)}{\sum_{j=1}^{m} P(x_i, y_j)} \right) y_j = \sum_{j=1}^{m} a_{ij} y_j,$$

where

$$a_{ij} \triangleq \frac{P(x_i, y_j)}{\sum_{j=1}^{m} P(x_i, y_j)}.$$

And then by means of above the weighted mean of those fuzzy sets as being α_i $(i=1,2,\cdots,n)$, we form fuzzy sets A_j as follows:

$$\mu_{A_j}(x) \triangleq \sum_{i=1}^{n} a_{ij}\mu_{\alpha_i}(x), \quad j=1,\cdots,m, \tag{6.5.3}$$

where the group of weight vector as follows:

$$\left\{(a_{1j}, a_{2j}, \cdots, a_{nj}) \middle| 1 \le j \le m\right\}$$

will be determined. Thus another linguistic variable set as follows:

$$\mathcal{A} = \left\{A_j \middle| 1 \le j \le m\right\}$$

is regarded as being obtained, and we have got a group of fuzzy inference rules as (6.5.2) as follows

$$\text{If } x \text{ is } A_j \text{ then } y \text{ is } B_j, \quad j=1,2,\cdots,m.$$

As in the proof of Theorem 6.4.1, by CRI method, we can make a fuzzy system $\overline{s}$:

$$\overline{s}(x) \triangleq \frac{\int_{a_2}^{b_2}\left[\bigvee_{k=1}^{m}\left(\mu_{A_k}(x) \wedge \mu_{B_k}(y_j)\right)\right] y\mathrm{d}y}{\int_{a_2}^{b_2}\left[\bigvee_{k=1}^{m}\left(\mu_{A_k}(x) \wedge \mu_{B_k}(y_j)\right)\right] \mathrm{d}y}. \tag{6.5.4}$$

This means that we get a fuzzy approximation system of the uncertainty system S as the follows:

$$\overline{s} = S(X, Y, \mathcal{A}, \mathcal{B})$$

Noticing the Riemann sum of (6.5.4) and B_j with Kronecker property, we have the following expression:

$$\overline{s}(x) \approx \frac{\sum_{j=1}^{m}\left[\bigvee_{k=1}^{m}\left(\mu_{A_k}(x) \wedge \mu_{B_k}\left(y_j\right)\right)\right] y_j \Delta y_j}{\sum_{j=1}^{m}\left[\bigvee_{k=1}^{m}\left(\mu_{A_k}(x) \wedge \mu_{B_k}\left(y_j\right)\right)\right] \Delta y_j}$$

$$= \frac{\sum_{j=1}^{m} \mu_{A_j}(x) y_j \Delta y_j}{\sum_{j=1}^{m} \mu_{A_j}(x) \Delta y_j}$$

Since $\left(\forall (i, j) \in \{1, \cdots, n\} \times \{1, \cdots, m\}\right)\left(\mu_{A_j}\left(x_i\right) = a_{ij}\right)$, we have the following equation:

$$\overline{s}\left(x_i\right) \approx \frac{\sum_{j=1}^{m} \mu_{A_j}(x) y_j \Delta y_j}{\sum_{j=1}^{m} \mu_{A_j}(x) \Delta y_j} = \frac{\sum_{j=1}^{m}\left(a_{ij} \Delta y_j\right) y_j}{\sum_{j=1}^{m} a_{ij} \Delta y_j}. \tag{6.5.5}$$

After comparing (6.5.1) and (6.5.5), we take $a_{ij} = P\left(x_i, y_j\right) M \big/ \Delta y_j$, where $M \triangleq \min\limits_{(i,j)}\left\{\Delta y_j \big/ P\left(x_i, y_j\right)\right\}$. Let

$$\varepsilon \triangleq \max\left\{\left|\overline{s}\left(x_i\right) - \underline{s}\left(x_i\right)\right| \middle| i = 1, 2, \cdots, n\right\}.$$

Then we at last get the following result:

$$\left(\forall i \in \{1, 2, \cdots, n\}\right)\left(\left|\overline{s}\left(x_i\right) - \underline{s}\left(x_i\right)\right| \le \varepsilon\right).$$

Besides, for any given $\varepsilon > 0$, from the equation (6.5.5), $\exists \delta > 0$, when $\lambda < \delta$, for all $x_i \, (i = 1, 2, \cdots, n)$, we have $\left|\overline{s}\left(x_i\right) - \underline{s}\left(x_i\right)\right| < \varepsilon$. Clearly, the more is λ, the higher is precision. □

We now turn to consider double-input single-output uncertainty system $s = S(X \times Y, Z)$. Let X, Y and Z be measurable sets in real number space $\mathbb{R}$ and input random variables ξ and η and output random variable ζ be defined respectively in the probability spaces as the following:

$$(X, \mathcal{B}_1, P_1),\quad (Y, \mathcal{B}_2, P_2),\quad (Z, \mathcal{B}_3, P_3),$$

where $\mathcal{B}_1, \mathcal{B}_2$ and $\mathcal{B}_3$ are Borel $\sigma-$fields on X, Y and Z, and P_1, P_2 and P_3 are probability measures on $\mathcal{B}_1$, $\mathcal{B}_2$ and $\mathcal{B}_3$, respectively. We can also get the joint probability space $(\Omega, \mathcal{F}, P)$ in the same.

So (ξ, η, ζ) becomes a random vector on $(\Omega, \mathcal{F}, P)$. Suppose that we have known a discrete probability distribution:

$$\left\{P\left(x_i, y_j, z_k\right) \middle| 1 \le i \le n, 1 \le j \le m, 1 \le k \le p\right\},$$

where $X = [a_1, b_1], Y = [a_2, b_2], Z = [a_2, b_2]$, and

$$\begin{aligned} &a_1 \le x_1 < \cdots < x_n \le b_1, \\ &a_2 \le y_1 < \cdots < y_m \le b_2, \\ &z_0 \triangleq a_3 < z_1 < \cdots < z_p = b_3 \end{aligned}$$

Assume $(\forall (i, j) \in \{1, \cdots, n\} \times \{1, \cdots, m\}) \left(\sum_{k=1}^{p} P\left(x_i, y_j, z_k\right) > 0 \right)$. Write

$$\underline{s}\left(x_i, y_j\right) \triangleq E\left(\zeta \middle| \xi = x_i, \eta = y_j\right) = \frac{\sum_{k=1}^{p} P\left(x_i, y_j, z_k\right) z_k}{\sum_{k=1}^{p} P\left(x_i, y_j, z_k\right)} \tag{6.5.6}$$

It is regarded as a response quantity after a input $\left(x_i, y_j\right)$ is input into the system S. Put

$$\underline{s} = S\left(X \times Y, Z, \left\{P\left(x_i, y_j, z_k\right) \middle| 1 \le i \le n, 1 \le j \le m, 1 \le k \le p\right\}\right)$$

Then $\underline{s}$ defined by above expression is called a double-input single-output discrete stochastic approximation system of S or simply a double-input single-output discrete stochastic system.

Theorem 6.5.2 Given a discrete stochastic system (6.5.7), where

$$X = [a_1, b_1], \quad Y = [a_2, b_2], \quad Z = [a_2, b_2]$$

are finite real number intervals, then there exists a group of fuzzy inference rules:

$$\text{If } (x, y) \text{ is } D_k \text{ then } z \text{ is } C_k,\ k = 1, 2, \cdots, p, \tag{6.5.7}$$

where $D_k \in \mathcal{F}(X \times Y)$ and $C_k \in \mathcal{F}(Z)$, such that the fuzzy system $\overline{s}$ constructed by the group of fuzzy inference rules can approximate the discrete stochastic system $\underline{s}$ to some precision $\varepsilon > 0$, i.e.,

$$(\forall (i, j) \in \{1, \cdots, n\} \times \{1, \cdots, m\})\left(\left|\overline{s}\left(x_i, y_j\right) - \underline{s}\left(x_i, y_j\right)\right| \le \varepsilon\right).$$

And the smaller is $\lambda = \max_{1 \le k \le p} \{\Delta z_k\}$, the higher is precision, where

$$\Delta z_k = z_k - z_{k-1}\ (k = 1, 2, \cdots, p).$$

The proof is the same as one of Theorem 6.5.1, and we omit it. □

6.6 Reducibility in the Transformations between Fuzzy Systems and Stochastic Systems

Take single-input single-output open-loop system $s = S(X, Y)$ as an example to discuss the problem on reducibility in the transformations between fuzzy systems and stochastic systems. We only consider continuous systems as discrete systems are special cases of continuous systems and can be treated with no difficulty. Here $X=[a_1,b_1]$ and $Y=[a_2,b_2]$ are finite real number intervals.

First, suppose that we have known a fuzzy system as the following:

$$\overline{s}=S(X,Y,\mathcal{A},\mathcal{B}),$$

where $\mathcal{A}=\{A_i|1\le i\le n\}$ and $\mathcal{B}=\{B_i|1\le i\le n\}$ are fuzzy partitions of X and Y respectively. $\mathcal{A}$ and $\mathcal{B}$ are regarded as linguistic variables, and we can get a group of fuzzy inference rules:

$$\text{If } x \text{ is } A_i \text{ then } y \text{ is } B_i,\ \ i=1,2,\cdots,n.$$

For convenience, the group of fuzzy inference rules is simply denoted by the following:

$$\mathcal{A}\to\mathcal{B}. \tag{6.6.1}$$

By (6.6.1) we have the input output function of fuzzy system $\overline{s}$:

$$\overline{s}(x)=\frac{\int_{a_2}^{b_2}\left[\bigvee_{i=1}^{n}\theta\left(\mu_{A_i}(x),\mu_{B_i}(y)\right)\right]y\mathrm{d}y}{\int_{a_2}^{b_2}\left[\bigvee_{i=1}^{n}\theta\left(\mu_{A_i}(x),\mu_{B_i}(y)\right)\right]\mathrm{d}y}, \tag{6.6.2}$$

where θ is a fuzzy implication operator with the condition:

$$\left(\forall(a,b)\in[0,1]\right)\left(\theta(a,1)=a,\,\theta(a,0)=0\right) \tag{6.6.3}$$

From above discuss, there exists a joint probability space $(\Omega,\mathcal{F},P)$, where $\Omega=X\times Y$, $\mathcal{F}=\mathcal{F}_1\times\mathcal{F}_2$ and $P=P_1\times P_2$, and random variables ξ and η are defined in probability spaces $(X,\mathcal{F}_1,P_1)$ and $(Y,\mathcal{F}_2,P_2)$. After redefining ξ and η in $(\Omega,\mathcal{F},P)$, a random vector (ξ,η) is obtained, which obeys the probability distribution based on the following probability density:

$$f(x,y)=\frac{\overset{n}{\underset{i=1}{\vee}}\theta\left(\mu_{A_i}(x),\mu_{B_i}(y)\right)}{H(2,n,\theta,\vee)},$$

$$H(2,n,\theta,\vee)=\int_{a_1}^{b_1}\int_{a_2}^{b_2}\left[\overset{n}{\underset{i=1}{\vee}}\theta\left(\mu_{A_i}(x),\mu_{B_i}(y)\right)\right]\mathrm{d}x\mathrm{d}y \tag{6.6.4}$$

By (6.2.5), we can get a stochastic system $\underline{s}=S\left(X,Y,f(x,y)\right)$ which input output function is as follows:

$$\underline{s}(x)=\frac{\int_{a_2}^{b_2}f(x,y)y\mathrm{d}y}{\int_{a_2}^{b_2}f(x,y)\mathrm{d}y}.$$

It is easy to know that above equation is the same as equation (6.6.2), i.e., $\overline{s}(x)\equiv\underline{s}(x)$. Now we show that $f(x,y)$ defined by (6.6.4) can be returned into the original fuzzy inference rule group $\mathcal{A}\to\mathcal{B}$. In fact, by using original partition nodes $x_1<x_2<\cdots<x_n$ and $y_1<y_2<\cdots<y_n$ of X and Y, we get a fuzzy inference rule group, denoted by

$$\mathcal{A}'=\left\{A_i'\middle|1\le i\le n\right\}\to\mathcal{B}'=\left\{B_i'\middle|1\le i\le n\right\}.$$

First we put $\mu_{A_i'}(x)\triangleq f\left(x,y_i\right)/M$, where

$$M\triangleq\max\left\{f(x,y)\mid(x,y)\in X\times Y\right\}.$$

It is easy to learn the following equation:

$$M=\frac{\max\limits_{(x,y)\in X\times Y}\left\{\overset{n}{\underset{i=1}{\vee}}\theta\left(\mu_{A_i}(x),\mu_{B_i}(y)\right)\right\}}{H(2,n,\theta,\vee)}=\frac{1}{H(2,n,\theta,\vee)}$$

So we have fact that $M\cdot H(2,n,\theta,\vee)=1$. It is easy to verify that, for any a natural number $i\in\{1,2,\cdots,n\}$, we have the following expression:

$$\mu_{A_i'}(x) = \frac{f(x, y_i)}{M} = \frac{\bigvee_{j=1}^{n} \theta\left(\mu_{A_j}(x), \mu_{B_j}(y)\right)}{MH(2, n, \theta, \vee)} = \mu_{A_i}(x).$$

This means that $\mathcal{A}' = \mathcal{A}$. Constructing $\mathcal{B}' = \left\{B_i' \middle| 1 \le i \le n\right\}$ is simple and of some freedom since we only demand that they are a kind of fuzzification of the peak points y_i $(i = 1, 2, \cdots, n)$ and a partition of Y. Thus, we can directly take that $B_i' = B_i$, $i = 1, 2, \cdots, n$. Then we have $\mathcal{B}' = \mathcal{B}$. Thus we have reverted $f(x, y)$ into the original fuzzy inference rule group $\mathcal{A} \to \mathcal{B}$. This is one side reducibility.

Now we consider another side reducibility. Given a stochastic system as the following:

$$\underline{s} = S\left(X, Y, f(x, y)\right).$$

We know that its input output function is as the following:

$$\underline{s}(x) = \int_{a_2}^{b_2} f(x, y)\, y\mathrm{d}y \Big/ \int_{a_2}^{b_2} f(x, y)\mathrm{d}y.$$

By Theorem 6.3.1, there exists a group of fuzzy inference rules $\mathcal{A} \to \mathcal{B}$ such that the fuzzy system $\overline{s} = S\left(X, Y, \mathcal{A}, \mathcal{B}\right)$ constructed by $\mathcal{A} \to \mathcal{B}$ can approximate the stochastic system $\underline{s} = S\left(X, Y, f(x, y)\right)$ to a given precision, i.e., $\overline{s}(x) \approx \underline{s}(x)$ (Notice that is not $\overline{s}(x) \equiv \underline{s}(x)$), in other words,

$$(\forall x \in X)\left(\lim_{\lambda \to 0} \overline{s}(x) = \underline{s}(x)\right), \tag{6.6.5}$$

where $\lambda = \max\left\{\Delta y_j \middle| j = 1, 2, \cdots, n\right\}$. These A_i can be made by using (6.3.4) or (6.3.9) and B_i can be taken as triangle waves membership functions referring to Figure 6.3.1. Then the input output function of the fuzzy system $\overline{s} = S(X, Y, \mathcal{A}, \mathcal{B})$, which is more general than one in (6.3.7), is as follows:

$$\overline{s}(x)=\frac{\int_{a_2}^{b_2}\left[\mathop{\vee}\limits_{i=1}^{n}\theta\left(\mu_{A_i}(x),\mu_{B_i}(y)\right)\right]y\mathrm{d}y}{\int_{a_2}^{b_2}\left[\mathop{\vee}\limits_{i=1}^{n}\theta\left(\mu_{A_i}(x),\mu_{B_i}(y)\right)\right]\mathrm{d}y},$$

where the fuzzy implication operator θ still needs to meet the condition (6.6.3). So we get a stochastic system $\underline{s}=S\left(X,Y,f'(x,y)\right)$, where

$$f'(x,y)=\frac{\mathop{\vee}\limits_{i=1}^{n}\theta\left(\mu_{A_i}(x),\mu_{B_i}(y)\right)}{H(2,n,\theta,\vee)}.$$

The meaning of $H(2,n,\theta,\vee)$ is the same as before. We should consider two cases for the reducibility.

Case 1: By (6.3.9), stipulate $A_i(x)\triangleq f\left(x,y_i\right)/M$, then at the division points $y_j(j=1,\cdots,n)$ of Y, we have

$$\begin{aligned} f'\left(x,y_j\right)&=\frac{\mathop{\vee}\limits_{i=1}^{n}\theta\left(\mu_{A_i}(x),\mu_{B_i}\left(y_j\right)\right)}{H(2,n,\theta,\vee)}\\ &=\frac{\mu_{A_j}(x)}{H(2,n,\theta,\vee)}=\frac{f\left(x,y_j\right)}{H(2,n,\theta,\vee)M}\\ &=\alpha(n)f\left(x,y_j\right), \end{aligned} \tag{6.6.6}$$

where $\alpha(n)\triangleq\dfrac{1}{H(2,n,\theta,\vee)M}$. For given a partition on Y, n is fixed, so $\alpha(n)$ is constant. Equation (6.6.6) means that at every nodal point y_j $(j=1,2,\cdots,n)$, $f'\left(x,y_j\right)$ is reverted to $f\left(x,y_j\right)$ under ignoring a constant factor $\alpha(n)$. Because h can be decreased arbitrarily, $f'(x,y)$ should be regarded as having been reverted to $f(x,y)$ under ignoring a constant factor.

Case 2: Suppose that y_j $(j=1,2,\cdots,n)$ of Y are equidistant as the following:

$$\left(\forall j\in\{1,2,\cdots,n\}\right)\left(\Delta y_j=\lambda\right).$$

By (6.6.4), we stipulate the following symbol:

$$\mu_{A_i}(x)\triangleq\frac{f(x,y_i)}{\sum_{j=1}^{n}f(x,y_j)},$$

then at the nodal points y_j $(j=1,2,\cdots,n)$ of Y, we have the following equation:

$$\begin{aligned}f'(x,y_j)&=\frac{\bigvee_{i=1}^{n}\theta\left(\mu_{A_i}(x),\mu_{B_i}(y_j)\right)}{H(2,n,\theta,\vee)}\\&=\frac{\mu_{A_j}(x)}{H(2,n,\theta,\vee)}=\frac{f(x,y_j)}{H(2,n,\theta,\vee)\sum_{i=1}^{n}f(x,y_i)}\\&=\frac{\lambda}{H(2,n,\theta,\vee)}\cdot\frac{f(x,y_j)}{\sum_{i=1}^{n}f(x,y_i)\lambda}\\&\approx\beta(\lambda)\frac{f(x,y_j)}{\int_Y f(x,y)\mathrm{d}y}=\beta(\lambda)\frac{f(x,y_j)}{f_\xi(x)}\\&=\beta(h)f_{\eta|\xi=x}\left(y_j\middle|x\right)\end{aligned}\qquad(6.6.7)$$

where $\beta(\lambda)\triangleq\lambda/H(2,n,\theta,\vee)$, which is constant under given a partition on the universe Y, $f_\xi(x)\triangleq\int_Y f(x,y)\mathrm{d}y$ is marginal probability density, and $f_{\eta|\xi=x}(y\,|\,x)\triangleq f(x,y)/f_\xi(x)$ is conditional probability density. Based on above equation, $f'(x,y)$ should be regarded as having been reverted to the conditional probability density $f_{\eta|\xi=x}(y\,|\,x)$ under ignoring a constant factor.

Remark 6.6.1 In $\beta(\lambda)\triangleq\lambda/H(2,n,\theta,\vee)$, it is easy to learn that two parameters λ and n are correlative each other. So $\beta(\lambda)$ can also be written as $\beta(\lambda)$, but not written as $\beta(\lambda,n)$. □

Remark 6.6.2 Noticing that $f'(x,y)$ is a continuous function, from numerical analysis and based on (6.6.6), we can easily learned that $f'(x,y)$ can be regarded as a interpolation function with the node group

$$\left\{\left(y_j,\alpha(n)f\left(x,y_j\right)\right)\Big|\,j=1,2,\cdots,n\right\}.$$

At every node $y_j, j=1,2,\cdots,n$, $f'(x,y)$ is strictly equal to the nodal function value $\alpha(n)f\left(x,y_j\right)$. There is similar understanding about the Equation (6.6.7). □

6.7 Uncertainty Systems with One Dimension Random Variables and their Representations

From above sections in this article, we can find a situation that the probability density function with respective to uncertainty systems are at least two-dimensional, i.e. the random vectors we dealt with are at least two-dimensional, say (ξ,η), where ξ is in essence defined on input universe X and η on output universe Y. This is not strange because an uncertainty system is at least of one input variable $x\in X$ and one output variable $y\in Y$. However when we learn probability theory and its applications, random variables with respective to a lot of random experiments are one-dimensional, say ξ, and if it has probability density function, it is a one-dimensional function, say $f(x)$.

Naturally we should ask such a question: What kind of uncertainty systems are only with respective to one-dimensional random variables, or one-dimensional probability density functions? We can guess that such uncertainty systems may have some special characteristics or trivialities. And such uncertainty systems may have many cases. We can only discuss several typical cases.

Typical case 1: Pure certainty systems.
As a Cantor's set can be regarded as a fuzzy set, certainty systems can also be regarded as special uncertainty systems. Now we consider a special open loop system $s = S(X,Y)$, where $X = [a,b]$ and that $Y = \{y_0\}$ is a singleton. We have known that the symbol s has double meanings, i.e. it not only abstractly represents the system, but also means the relation between input and output of the system:

$$s : X \to Y, \quad x \mapsto y = s(x) \triangleq y_0 .$$

Since $(\forall x \in X)(s(x) = y_0)$, this is a special certainty system, and also a trivial system, and its output is a step function.

We will use CRI method to construct its fuzzy approximation system. First make a partition of X :

$$a = x_1 < x_2 < \cdots < x_n = b .$$

Then these nodes x_i $(i = 1, 2, \cdots, n)$ are fuzzified as Figure 6.3.1 to obtain fuzzy sets $A_i \in \mathcal{F}(X)\,(i = 1, 2, \cdots, n)$ (note that these $n+1$ subscripts $0, 1, \cdots, n$ should be changed to n subscripts $1, 2, \cdots, n$). So a fuzzy partition of X is got as $\mathcal{A} = \{A_i | i = 1, 2, \cdots, n\}$. The fuzzy sets on Y are easily formed as the following:

$$B_i \triangleq Y = \{y_0\}, \quad i = 1, 2, \cdots, n .$$

Thus a fuzzy partition of Y is also got as $\mathcal{B} = \{B_i | i = 1, 2, \cdots, n\}$. This means that we have a fuzzy inference rule group: $\mathcal{A} \to \mathcal{B}$. Therefore a fuzzy approximation system is constructed as the following:

$$\overline{s} = S\left(X = [a,b], Y = \{y_0\}, \mathcal{A}, \mathcal{B}\right).$$

For simplification, fuzzy implication operator θ is taken as $\wedge$. We have the following expression:

$$p(x,y) = p\left(x, y_0\right) = \bigvee_{i=1}^{n}\left[\mu_{A_i}(x) \wedge \mu_{B_i}\left(y_0\right)\right] = \bigvee_{i=1}^{n} \mu_{A_i}(x).$$

Then the input output relation should be the following:

$$\overline{s}(x) = \int_Y yp\left(x, y_0\right)\mathrm{d}y \Big/ \int_Y p\left(x, y_0\right)\mathrm{d}y.$$

Let $H(1,n,\wedge,\vee) \triangleq \int_X p\left(x, y_0\right)\mathrm{d}x$, and it is easy to know the fact that the integral $_X\, p\left(x, y_0\right)\mathrm{d}x > 0$. So we can put

$$f(x) \triangleq f\left(x, y_0\right) = \frac{p\left(x, y_0\right)}{H(1,n,\wedge,\vee)} = \frac{\bigvee_{i=1}^{n} \mu_{A_i}(x)}{H(1,n,\wedge,\vee)}. \tag{6.7.1}$$

So there should exist a random variable $\xi : X \to \mathbb{R}, x \mapsto \xi(x)$ defined on the probability space $(X, \mathcal{F}, P)$, to obey a probability distribution with probability density function $f(x)$, where $\mathcal{F}$ is a Borel $\sigma-$field on X. It we let $\Omega \triangleq X \times \{y_0\}$, then $\mathcal{F}$ can be regarded as a Borel $\sigma-$ field on Ω. And ξ can be regarded as a random variable defined on Ω, i.e. without changing symbol re define as follows:

$$\xi : \Omega \to \mathbb{R}, \quad \omega = \left(x, y_0\right) \mapsto \xi(\omega) = \xi\left(x, y_0\right) \triangleq \xi(x),$$

and P is also regarded as a probability on $(\Omega, \mathcal{F}, P)$. Thus we get a stochastic system $\underline{s} = S\left(X, Y, f\left(x, y_0\right)\right)$ and and its input output relation is as follows:

$$\underline{s}(x) = \int_Y yp\left(x, y_0\right)\mathrm{d}y \Big/ \int_Y p\left(x, y_0\right)\mathrm{d}y.$$

Clearly, $(\forall x \in X)(\overline{s}(x) = \underline{s}(x))$, which is consistent with the result in Section 6.

But $\overline{s}(x) = \int_Y yp(x, y_0)\mathrm{d}y \big/ \int_Y p(x, y_0)\mathrm{d}y$ is only a formal representation, because Y is a singleton and its measure is zero, and so for any a point $x \in X$, we have the following equations:

$$\int_Y yp(x, y_0)\mathrm{d}y = 0, \quad \int_Y p(x, y_0)\mathrm{d}y = 0,$$

which means that

$$\overline{s}(x) = \frac{\int_Y yp(x, y_0)\mathrm{d}y}{\int_Y p(x, y_0)\mathrm{d}y} = \frac{0}{0}.$$

Thus $\int_Y yp(x, y_0)\mathrm{d}y \big/ \int_Y p(x, y_0)\mathrm{d}y$ is meaningless.

It is not difficult to deal with. In fact, for any $\varepsilon > 0$, is it easy to know that $(\forall x \in X)(p(x, y_0) > 0)$, and so, for any $x \in X$,

$$\int_{y_0}^{y_0+\varepsilon} p(x, y_0)\mathrm{d}y = p(x, y_0)\int_{y_0}^{y_0+\varepsilon} \mathrm{d}y = p(x, y_0)\varepsilon > 0.$$

Thus, for any $x \in X$, we also have the following expression:

$$\overline{s}(x) = \frac{\int_Y yp(x, y_0)\mathrm{d}y}{\int_Y p(x, y_0)\mathrm{d}y} = \frac{\int_{\{y_0\}} yp(x, y_0)\mathrm{d}y}{\int_{\{y_0\}} p(x, y_0)\mathrm{d}y}$$

$$\triangleq \lim_{\varepsilon \to 0} \frac{\int_{y_0}^{y_0+\varepsilon} yp(x, y_0)\mathrm{d}y}{\int_{y_0}^{y_0+\varepsilon} p(x, y_0)\mathrm{d}y} = \lim_{\varepsilon \to 0} \frac{p(x, y_0)\int_{y_0}^{y_0+\varepsilon} y\mathrm{d}y}{p(x, y_0)\varepsilon}$$

$$= \lim_{\varepsilon \to 0}\left(y_0 + \frac{\varepsilon}{2}\right) = y_0.$$

Besides, clearly, $(\forall x \in X)(\overline{s}(x) = s(x))$ which means that, in this case, the fuzzy system $\overline{s}$ constructed by CRI method can accurately approximate the system s.

Example 6.7.1 Consider an illumination system. For simplification, suppose that there is only one lamp in the system. Usually, we open the lamp in evening, and suppose that the time of opening the lamp is between a and b. Let $X = [a, b]$ that is regarded as the input universe of the system. If we take $x \in X$, then it means that the lamp is opened at time x, and the lamp emits light, which is denoted by a symbol, say 1. Naturally we can take $Y = \{y_0\} = \{1\}$ as the output universe. Clearly, the input output relation of the system is

$$s : X \to Y, \quad x \mapsto y = s(x) \triangleq y_0 = 1.$$

This is a pure certain system, of course. We have a reason to ask: Now that this is a certain system, why does there exist a random variable ξ and a probability density function $f(x)$ that ξ obeys? In fact, if we focus our attention on "what time we should open the lamp in evening", this becomes a stochastic problem. And this is not contrary with the certain input output relation

$$s : X \to Y, \quad x \mapsto y = s(x) \triangleq y_0 = 1.$$

You know, "what time we should open the lamp in evening" depends on many factors, such as different area leads different opening lamp time due to time difference. By using random experiment, we should know that opening lamp is round about at several time, such as about 5 o'clock, about 6 o'clock, about 7 o'clock, etc. Generally suppose that the lamp is usually opened at about x_1, about $x_2, \cdots$, about x_n, and denote $a = x_1$ and $b = x_n$. If x_i $(i = 1, 2, \cdots, n)$ are fuzzified to get fuzzy sets as the following:

$$A_i \in \mathcal{F}(X), \quad i = 1, 2, \cdots, n.$$

Then we make fuzzy sets on Y as the following

$$B_i \triangleq Y = \{y_0\}, \quad \mu_{B_i}(y) = \chi_Y(y) = \chi_{\{y_0\}}(y)$$
$$i = 1, 2, \cdots, n,$$

and $\mathcal{B} = \{B_i | i = 1, 2, \cdots, n\}$ is formed. Thus we have a fuzzy inference rule group: $\mathcal{A} \to \mathcal{B}$, which means that we get a fuzzy system as follows:

$$\overline{s} = S(X, Y, \mathcal{A}, \mathcal{B}).$$

This come back to the way obtaining (6.7.1), and the rest is clear. □

Typical case 2: Pure stochastic systems.
We consider another special open loop system $s = S(X, Y)$, where the set $X \triangleq \{x_0\}$ is a singleton and $Y = [a, b]$, and its input output relation should be as follows

$$s : X \to Y, \quad x_0 \mapsto y_0 = s(x_0).$$

Due to the uncertainty of the system, for the input x_0, we do not in advance know which y_0 in Y should correspond to x_0. So $s = S(X, Y)$ is a pure stochastic system. After x_0 is input, by using statistic method there are several output to correspond to it: about y_1, about $y_2, \ldots$, about y_n. After $y_0, y_1, \cdots, y_n$ are fuzzified, we get fuzzy sets as the following:

$$B_i \in \mathcal{F}(Y), \quad i = 0, 1, \cdots, n,$$

which are demanded to form a fuzzy partition of Y. Let

$$A_i \triangleq X = \{x_0\}, \quad \mu_{A_i}(y) = \chi_X(x) = \chi_{\{x_0\}}(x),$$
$$i = 1, 2, \cdots, n,$$

and denote $\mathcal{A} = \{A_i | i = 1, 2, \cdots, n\}$ and $\mathcal{B} = \{B_i | i = 1, 2, \cdots, n\}$ (not use B_0). Then a fuzzy inference rule group is got as $\mathcal{A} \to \mathcal{B}$. So we obtain a fuzzy system $\overline{s} = S(X, Y, \mathcal{A}, \mathcal{B})$. By CRI method, we have the fact as the following:

$$p(x, y) = p(x_0, y) = \bigvee_{i=1}^{n} \left[\mu_{A_i}(x_0) \wedge \mu_{B_i}(y) \right] = \bigvee_{i=1}^{n} \mu_{B_i}(y).$$

Because of the following facts:

$$(\forall y \in Y)\left(p(x_0, y) > 0\right), \quad H(1, n, \wedge, \vee) \triangleq \int_Y p(x_0, y) \mathrm{d}y > 0,$$

we can let

$$g(y) \triangleq g(x_0, y) = \frac{p(x_0, y)}{H(1, n, \wedge, \vee)} = \frac{\bigvee_{i=1}^{n} \mu_{B_i}(y)}{H(1, n, \wedge, \vee)} \tag{6.7.2}$$

Noticing that $\int_Y g(x_0, y) \mathrm{d}y = 1$, the input output relation should be as the following:

$$\overline{s}(x) = \frac{\int_Y y g(x_0, y) \mathrm{d}y}{\int_Y g(x_0, y) \mathrm{d}y} = \int_Y y g(x_0, y) \mathrm{d}y = \frac{\int_a^b y \left[\bigvee_{i=1}^{n} \mu_{B_i}(y) \right] \mathrm{d}y}{H(1, n, \wedge, \vee)}$$

Therefore there should be a probability space $(Y, \mathcal{F}, P)$ and a random variable η defined on $(Y, \mathcal{F}, P)$, which obeys the probability density function $g(y)$, where $\mathcal{F}$ is a Borel $\sigma-$field on Y.

If we put $\Omega \triangleq \{x_0\} \times Y$, then $\mathcal{F}$ can regarded as a Borel $\sigma-$field on, η as a random variable defined on Ω, and P as a probability on $(\Omega, \mathcal{F}, P)$. Thus we get a stochastic system as follows:

$$\underline{s} = S(X, Y, g(x_0, y)),$$

which its input output relation is also as the following:

$$\underline{s}(x) = \frac{\int_Y yp(x_0, y)dy}{\int_Y p(x_0, y)dy}.$$

Now let $\Delta y_j \triangleq y_j - y_{j-1}$ $(j = 1, 2, \cdots, n)$. We have the following result:

$$\underline{s}(x_0) = \frac{\int_Y p(x_0, y)\, y\mathrm{d}y}{\int_Y p(x_0, y)\mathrm{d}y} = \frac{\int_a^b y\left[\bigvee_{i=1}^{n} \mu_{B_i}(y)\right]\mathrm{d}y}{\int_a^b \left[\bigvee_{i=1}^{n} \mu_{B_i}(y)\right]\mathrm{d}y}$$

$$\approx \frac{\sum_{j=1}^{n}\left[\bigvee_{i=1}^{n} \mu_{B_i}(y_j)\right] y_j \Delta y_j}{\sum_{j=1}^{n}\left[\bigvee_{i=1}^{n} \mu_{B_i}(y_j)\right] \Delta y_j} = \frac{\sum_{j=1}^{n} y_j \Delta y_j}{b-a} = \sum_{j=1}^{n} a_j y_j, \tag{6.7.3}$$

$$a_j \triangleq \Delta y_j / (b-a), \quad j = 1, 2, \cdots, n$$

So $\underline{s}(x_0)$ corresponding to x_0 is approximately equal to the weighted average of $y_1, y_2, \cdots, y_n$.

Especially, when the partition $a = y_0 < y_1 < \cdots < y_n = b$ is equidistant, i.e. $\Delta y_j = h\,(j = 1, \cdots, n)$, we as well as have the following result:

$$\underline{s}(x_0) = \frac{\int_Y p(x_0, y)\, y\mathrm{d}y}{\int_Y p(x_0, y)\mathrm{d}y}$$

$$\approx \frac{\sum_{j=1}^{n}\left[\bigvee_{i=1}^{n} \mu_{B_i}(y_j)\right] y_j \Delta y_j}{\sum_{j=1}^{n}\left[\bigvee_{i=1}^{n} \mu_{B_i}(y_j)\right] \Delta y_j} = \frac{\sum_{j=1}^{n} y_j}{n} \tag{6.7.4}$$

i.e. $\underline{s}(x_0)$ corresponding to x_0 is approximately equal to the arithmetic average of $y_1, y_2, \cdots, y_n$.

Example 6.7.2 Consider a shooting practice system. For simplification, suppose that there is only one gun in the system. Every experiment, i.e. every shooting, only one bullet is shot to a target and the bullet is denoted by x_0. Because the same kind of guns shoot the same kind of bullets and the bullets in the same kind of bullets are all regarded as x_0, we get the input universe of the system as $X \triangleq \{x_0\}$. Every shooting, that the bullet x_0 is shot to the target is regarded as putting an input to the system, and the point of impact in the target is thought as the response of the system to the input x_0. How to measure the system response? There are many methods. Here we take the distance between the point of impact y and the center of the target as the output of the system. If we ignore missing the target of shooting, the distance between the point of impact and the center of the target is surely bounded. A felicitous upper bound is denoted by b, for example, b may be the distance between the center of the target and the edge of the target. The lower bound of the distance between the point of impact and the center of the target is clearly zero, denoted by $a=0$. And we get a output universe $Y=[a,b]$. Since we do not in advance know which y_0 in Y should correspond to x_0 when x_0 is put into the system as an input, this is a pure stochastic system. Suppose we test the shooting level of a shooting team with n shooters. By some shooting practices, we can find the distances between the point of impact and the center of the target, of the n shooters, are respectively as about y_1, about $y_2, \cdots$, about y_n. We can assume that

$$a=y_0<y_1<\cdots<y_n=b.$$

After $y_0, y_1, \cdots, y_n$ are fuzzified to get fuzzy sets as the following:

$$B_i \in \mathcal{F}(Y), \quad i=0,1,\cdots,n,$$

which are demanded to be a fuzzy partition of Y , thus a class of fuzzy set as being $\mathcal{B} \triangleq \{B_i | i=1,2,\cdots,n\}$ is formed. Then let

$$A_i \triangleq X = \{x_0\}, \quad \mu_{A_i}(x) = \chi_X(x) = \chi_{\{x_0\}}(x),$$
$$i = 1,2,\cdots,n,$$

and $\mathcal{A} \triangleq \{A_i | i=1,2,\cdots,n\}$. So a fuzzy inference rule group $\mathcal{A} \to \mathcal{B}$ is got. And we obtain a fuzzy system $\overline{s} = S(X,Y,\mathcal{A},\mathcal{B})$. This come back to the way obtaining (6.7.2), and the rest is clear. □

We turn to discuss problems of fuzzy reasoning representations with one dimensional random variables and their approximations to the stochastic systems. Also two typical cases are considered.

Typical case 1*: This case is the contraposition of above typical case 1. Given a stochastic system

$$\underline{s} = \left(X, Y \triangleq \{y_0\}, f(x) \triangleq f(x, y_0)\right),$$

this means there are a probability space $(\Omega, \mathcal{F}, P)$ and a random variable ξ defined on $(\Omega, \mathcal{F}, P)$ obeys probability density function as the following:

$$f(x) \triangleq f(x, y_0),$$

where $\Omega \triangleq X \times \{y_0\}$. From above discussion, we know that the input output relation of the system is as the following:

$$\underline{s}(x) = \frac{\int_Y f(x, y_0)\, y_0 \mathrm{d}y}{\int_Y f(x, y_0)\mathrm{d}y} = \lim_{\varepsilon \to 0} \frac{\int_{y_0}^{y_0+\varepsilon} f(x, y_0)\, y\mathrm{d}y}{\int_{y_0}^{y_0+\varepsilon} f(x, y_0)\mathrm{d}y} = y_0,$$

where $(\forall x \in X)(f(x, y_0) > 0)$ is supposed, and so

$$(\forall x \in X)\left(\int_{y_0}^{y_0+\varepsilon} f(x, y_0)\,\mathrm{d}y > 0\right).$$

Make a partition of X: $a = x_1 < x_2 < \cdots < x_n = b$ and the nodes x_i are fuzzified to get fuzzy sets $A_i \in \mathcal{F}(X)$, which are demanded to be a fuzzy partition of X. And we let

$$B_i \triangleq Y = \{y_0\}, \quad \mu_{B_i}(y) = \chi_Y(y) = \chi_{\{y_0\}}(y),$$
$$i = 1, 2, \cdots, n.$$

We can get two classes of fuzzy sets as the following:

$$\mathcal{A} \triangleq \{A_i \mid i = 1, 2, \cdots, n\}, \quad \mathcal{B} \triangleq \{B_i \mid i = 1, 2, \cdots, n\}.$$

So we obtain a fuzzy inference rule group: $\mathcal{A} \to \mathcal{B}$. Thus a fuzzy system as the follows is got

$$\overline{s} = \left(X, Y = \{y_0\}, \mathcal{A}, \mathcal{B}\right).$$

Because $\mathcal{A} = \{A_i \mid i = 1, 2, \cdots, n\}$ is a fuzzy partition of X, and we have

$$(\forall x \in X)\left(p(x, y_0) = \bigvee_{i=1}^{n} \mu_{A_i}(x) > 0\right)$$

We can understand the following fact:

$$(\forall x \in X)\left(\int_{y_0}^{y_0+\varepsilon} p(x, y_0)\,\mathrm{d}y > 0\right).$$

So the input output relation of the fuzzy system is as follows:

$$\overline{s}(x) = \frac{\int_Y p(x, y_0)\, y_0 \mathrm{d}y}{\int_Y p(x, y_0)\,\mathrm{d}y} = \lim_{\varepsilon \to 0} \frac{\int_{y_0}^{y_0+\varepsilon} p(x, y_0)\, y\mathrm{d}y}{\int_{y_0}^{y_0+\varepsilon} p(x, y_0)\,\mathrm{d}y} = y_0.$$

Clearly $(\forall x \in X)(\overline{s}(x) = \underline{s}(x))$, which means that the fuzzy system $\overline{s}$ can accurately approximate the stochastic system $\underline{s}$.

Typical case 2*: This case is the contraposition of above typical case 2. Given a stochastic system:

$$\underline{s} = \left(X \triangleq \{x_0\}, Y \triangleq [a,b], g(y) \triangleq g(x_0, y)\right),$$

this means that there are a probability space $(\Omega, \mathcal{F}, P)$ and a random variable η defined on $(\Omega, \mathcal{F}, P)$ obeys the probability density function $g(y) = g(x_0, y)$, where $\Omega \triangleq \{x_0\} \times Y$. Noticing that

$$\int_Y g(x_0, y)\mathrm{d}y = \int_Y g(y)\mathrm{d}y = 1,$$

from above discussion, we know that the input output relation of the system is as the following:

$$\begin{aligned}\underline{s}(x_0) &= \frac{\int_Y g(x_0, y)\, y\mathrm{d}y}{\int_Y g(x_0, y)\mathrm{d}y} = \int_a^b g(x_0, y)\, y\mathrm{d}y \\ &= \int_a^b g(y)\, y\mathrm{d}y = E(\eta),\end{aligned}$$

where the output of the system $\underline{s}(x_0)$ is just the mathematical expectation of random variable η: $E(\eta)$.

Theorem 6.7.1 Given a continuous stochastic system as the following:

$$\underline{s} = \left(X = \{x_0\}, Y = [a,b], g(y) = g(x_0, y)\right),$$

there must exist a group of fuzzy inference rules $\mathcal{A} \to \mathcal{B}$, where

$$\mathcal{A} = \{A_i \mid i = 1, 2, \cdots, n\}, \quad \mathcal{B} = \{B_i \mid i = 1, 2, \cdots, n\},$$
$$A_i \in \mathcal{F}(X), \quad B_i \in \mathcal{F}(Y), \quad i = 1, 2, \cdots, n,$$

such that the fuzzy system $\overline{s}$ constructed by the group of fuzzy inference rules can approximate the continuous stochastic system $\underline{S}$ to arbitrarily given precision.

Proof. First we make a partition of Y as the following:

$$a=y_0<y_1<\cdots<y_n=b$$

and triangle fuzzy sets as being $B_i^* \in \mathcal{F}(Y), i=0,1,\cdots,n$. Let

$$M \triangleq \max\{g(y) \mid y \in Y\}.$$

Then y_i $(i=0,1,\cdots,n)$ are fuzzified to become fuzzy sets:

$$\mu_{B_i}(y) \triangleq \frac{\mu_{B_i^*}(y)g(y)}{M}, \quad i=0,1,\cdots,n.$$

Clearly $B_i \in \mathcal{F}(Y)\,(i=0,1,\cdots,n)$. Put $A_i \triangleq \{x_0\}\,(i=1,2,\cdots,n)$, and we should take the two classes of fuzzy sets as follows:

$$\mathcal{A} \triangleq \{A_i | i=1,2,\cdots,n\}, \quad \mathcal{B} \triangleq \{B_i | i=1,2,\cdots,n\}$$

We have a group of fuzzy inference rules as follows:

$$\mathcal{A} \to \mathcal{B}.$$

Then a fuzzy system as the following:

$$\overline{s} = \left(X=\{x_0\}, Y=[a,b], \mathcal{A}, \mathcal{B}\right)$$

is got, which input output relation is as the following:

$$\overline{s}(x_0)=\frac{\int_a^b p(x_0,y)y\mathrm{d}y}{\int_a^b p(x_0,y)\mathrm{d}y}=\frac{\int_a^b\left(\bigvee_{i=1}^{n}\left(\mu_{A_i}(x_0)\wedge\mu_{B_i}(y)\right)\right)y\mathrm{d}y}{\int_a^b\left(\bigvee_{i=1}^{n}\left(\mu_{A_i}(x_0)\wedge\mu_{B_i}(y)\right)\right)\mathrm{d}y}$$

$$=\frac{\int_a^b\left(\bigvee_{i=1}^{n}\mu_{B_i}(y)\right)y\mathrm{d}y}{\int_a^b\left(\bigvee_{i=1}^{n}\mu_{B_i}(y)\right)\mathrm{d}y}=\frac{\int_a^b\left(\bigvee_{i=1}^{n}\frac{\mu_{B_i^*}(y)g(y)}{M}\right)y\mathrm{d}y}{\int_a^b\left(\bigvee_{i=1}^{n}\frac{\mu_{B_i^*}(y)g(y)}{M}\right)\mathrm{d}y}$$

$$\approx\frac{\sum_{j=1}^{n}\left(\bigvee_{i=1}^{n}\frac{\mu_{B_i^*}(y_j)g(y_j)}{M}\right)y_j\Delta y_j}{\sum_{j=1}^{n}\left(\bigvee_{i=1}^{n}\frac{\mu_{B_i^*}(y_j)g(y_j)}{M}\right)\Delta y_j}=\frac{\sum_{j=1}^{n}\mu_{B_i^*}(y_j)g(y_j)y_j\Delta y_j}{\sum_{j=1}^{n}\mu_{B_i^*}(y_j)g(y_j)\Delta y_j}$$

$$=\frac{\sum_{j=1}^{n}g(y_j)y_j\Delta y_j}{\sum_{j=1}^{n}g(y_j)\Delta y_j}\approx\frac{\int_a^b g(y)y\mathrm{d}y}{\int_a^b g(y)\mathrm{d}y}=E(\eta)=\underline{s}(x_0).$$

Because the Riemann sums of $\int_a^b p(x_0,y)y\mathrm{d}y$ and $\int_a^b p(x_0,y)\mathrm{d}y$ are respectively as the following:

$$\sum_{j=1}^{n}\left(\bigvee_{i=1}^{n}\frac{\mu_{B_i^*}(y_j)g(y_j)}{M}\right)y_j\Delta y_j,\quad \sum_{j=1}^{n}\left(\bigvee_{i=1}^{n}\frac{\mu_{B_i^*}(y_j)g(y_j)}{M}\right)\Delta y_j,$$

and $\sum_{j=1}^{n}g(y_j)y_j\Delta y_j$ and $\sum_{j=1}^{n}g(y_j)\Delta y_j$ are respectively the Riemann sums of the integrals $\int_a^b g(y)y\mathrm{d}y$ and $\int_a^b g(y)\mathrm{d}y$, based on Lemma 6.3.3, for any given an approximation precision $\varepsilon>0$, there must exist

$\delta > 0$, when $\lambda = \max\{\Delta y_i = y_i - y_{i-1} | i = 1, 2, \cdots, n\} < \delta$, we simultaneously have the following inequalities:

$$\left| \frac{\int_a^b p(x_0, y)\, y\mathrm{d}y}{\int_a^b p(x_0, y)\mathrm{d}y} - \frac{\sum_{j=1}^{n} \left(\bigvee_{i=1}^{n} \frac{\mu_{B_i^*}(y_j) g(y_j)}{M} \right) y_j \Delta y_j}{\sum_{j=1}^{n} \left(\bigvee_{i=1}^{n} \frac{\mu_{B_i^*}(y_j) g(y_j)}{M} \right) \Delta y_j} \right| < \frac{\varepsilon}{2},$$

$$\left| \frac{\int_a^b g(y)\, y\mathrm{d}y}{\int_a^b g(y)\mathrm{d}y} - \frac{\sum_{j=1}^{n} g(y_j)\, y_j \Delta y_j}{\sum_{j=1}^{n} g(y_j) \Delta y_j} \right| < \frac{\varepsilon}{2}$$

From these, it is easy to know that $|\overline{s}(x_0) - \underline{s}(x_0)| < \varepsilon$. □

6.8 Unification on Uncertainty Systems

In the chapter, an important fact is revealed that for arbitrarily given a fuzzy system $\overline{s} = S(X, Y, \mathcal{A}, \mathcal{B})$ there is a probability space $(\Omega, \mathcal{F}, P)$ and a random vector (ξ, η) defined on $(\Omega, \mathcal{F}, P)$ such that (ξ, η) obeys the probability density $f(x, y)$. Thus we can get a stochastic system as the following:

$$\underline{s} = S(X, Y, f(x, y)).$$

Then based on the conclusions of this paper, for arbitrarily given a stochastic system as follows:

$$\underline{s} = S(X, Y, f(x, y)),$$

we can always obtain a group of fuzzy inference rules $\mathcal{A} \to \mathcal{B}$ such that a fuzzy system as the expression:

$$\overline{s} = S(X, Y, \mathcal{A}, \mathcal{B})$$

can be formed by using $\mathcal{A} \to \mathcal{B}$. And above section tells us that there is reducibility in the transformations between fuzzy systems and stochastic systems. This means that fuzzy systems and stochastic systems are unified under system viewpoint. They look like two weights with same weight in the trays of a balance, one on a tray looking older and another one on other tray looking newer. Here older one means probability theory, and newer one is just fuzzy system theory. They have their special merits and support each other but no exclude.

It is worthy of indicating that, for an uncertainty system, if you want to use probability theory to solve the problem, it is very difficult to get a kind of probability distribution, but you can try to use fuzzy system method to overcome it because obtaining a group of fuzzy inference rules is not so difficult, and sometimes it is easy. When you get a group of fuzzy inference rules, you can immediately transform the group of fuzzy inference rules into a probability density. So this is a very interesting thing.

6.9 Conclusions

The present chapter has discussed a kind of united theory of uncertainty systems. As we know, the theories or methods dealing with uncertainty systems are usually of using probability theory and fuzzy set theory. It is interesting to communicate the relationship between probability theory and fuzzy set theory with respect to uncertainty systems. Firstly, we studied the probability representation problem of fuzzy systems in detail and indicated that there exists close relation between fuzzy systems and probability theory. Secondly, the fuzzy reasoning significance of stochastic systems is revealed. The main results are as follows:

1) For arbitrarily given a stochastic system $\underline{s} = S(X, Y, f(x, y))$, we can always obtain a group of fuzzy inference rules $\mathcal{A} \to \mathcal{B}$ such that a fuzzy system $\overline{s} = S(X, Y, \mathcal{A}, \mathcal{B})$ can be formed by using the fuzzy inference $\mathcal{A} \to \mathcal{B}$ and $\overline{s}$ can approximate $\underline{s}$ to arbitrarily given precision.

2) It is pointed out that there is reducibility in the transformations between fuzzy systems and stochastic systems. One side, under knowing a fuzzy system $\overline{S} = S(X, Y, \mathcal{A}, \mathcal{B})$, the reducibility is complete. On the other side, under knowing a stochastic system $\underline{S} = S(X, Y, f(x, y))$, the reducibility is approximate.

3) One side, we have shown that for arbitrarily given a fuzzy system $\overline{S}$, its fuzzy inference rule group $\mathcal{A} \to \mathcal{B}$ can be transformed into a probability density f of a stochastic system $\underline{S}$. On the other side, the case is just opposite, i.e., for arbitrarily given a stochastic system $\underline{S}$, its probability density f can must be transformed into a fuzzy inference rule group $\mathcal{A} \to \mathcal{B}$ of a fuzzy system $\overline{S}$. Therefore, with respect to an uncertainty system, the probability density of the stochastic system and fuzzy inference rule group of the fuzzy system can be transformed each other. In other words, with respect to an uncertainty system, fuzziness and randomness are two different sides and regarded as two different description approaches, and they are in essence belonging to same thing: uncertainty. We may regard fuzziness and randomness as interlacing together, and it is hard to separate them into two self-governed parts. They look like two weights with same weight in the trays of a balance, one on a tray looking older and another one on other tray looking newer. Here older one means probability theory, and newer one is just fuzzy system theory. They have their special merits and support each other but no exclude.

4) For an uncertainty system, if you want to use probability theory to solve the problem, it is very difficult to get a kind of probability distribution, but you can try to use fuzzy system method to overcome it because obtaining a group of fuzzy inference rules is not so difficult, and sometimes it is easy. When you get a group of fuzzy inference rules, you can immediately transform the group of fuzzy inference rules into a probability density. In this way, a lot of good tools in probability theory can be used to treat with the uncertainty system. So this is a very interesting thing.

5) Just with COG method, the relation between fuzzy systems and probability theory has been established. From the viewpoint of methodology, in a certain bound, one may use the method of probability theory to investigate fuzzy systems. From the viewpoint of philosophy,

uncertainty originally contains randomness as well as fuzziness. Randomness and fuzziness are often interwoven, so it is very difficult to divide up them.

Reference

1. Zadeh, L.A. (1973). Outline of a new approach to the analysis of complex systems and decision processes, IEEE Trans. SMC, 3, pp. 28-44.
2. Zadeh, L. A. (1974). The concept of a linguistic variable and its applications to approximate reasoning (I), Information Sciences, 8(2), pp. 199-249.
3. Zadeh, L. A. (1974). The concept of a linguistic variable and its applications to approximate reasoning (II), Information Sciences, 8(3), pp. 301-357.
4. Zadeh, L. A. (1975). The concept of a linguistic variable and its applications to approximate reasoning (III), Information Sciences, 9(1), pp. 43-80.
5. Wu, W. M. (1994). *Principle and Methods of Fuzzy Reasoning.* (Guizhou Science and Technology Press, Guiyang). (in Chinese)
6. Li, H. X. (1998). Interpolation mechanism of fuzzy control, Science in China (Series E), 41(3), pp. 312-320.
7. Li, H. X. (1995). To see the success of fuzzy logic from mathematical essence of fuzzy control, Fuzzy Systems and Mathematics, 9(4), pp. 1-14 (in Chinese).
8. Hou, J., You, F. and Li, H. X. (2005). Some fuzzy controllers constructed by triple I method and their response capability, Progress in Natural Science, 15(1), pp. 29-37 (in Chinese).
9. Li, H. X., You, F. and Peng, J. Y. (2004). Fuzzy controllers based on some fuzzy implication operators and their response functions, Progress in Natural Science, 14(1), pp. 15-20.
10. Wang, P. Z. and Li, H. X. (1995). *Fuzzy Systems Theory and Fuzzy Computers.* (Science Press, Beijing). (in Chinese).
11. Zhang, W. X. and Liang, G. X. (1998). *Fuzzy Control and Systems.* (Xi'an Jiaotong University Press, Xi'an). (in Chinese).
12. Wang, G. J. (1999). A new method for fuzzy reasoning, Fuzzy Systems and Mathematics, 1999, 13(3), pp. 1-10 (in Chinese).
13. Wang, G. J. (1997). A formal deductive system of fuzzy propositional calculus, Chinese Science Bulletin, 42(10), pp. 1041-1045 (in Chinese).
14. You, F., Feng, Y. B. and Li, H. X. (2003). Fuzzy implication operators and their construction (I), Journal of Beijing Normal University, 39(5), pp. 606-611 (in Chinese).
15. You, F., Feng, Y. B., Wang, J. Y. and Li, H. X. (2004). Fuzzy implication operators and their construction (II), Journal of Beijing Normal University, 40(2), pp. 168-176 (in Chinese).

16. You, F., Yang, X. Y. and Li, H. X. (2004). Fuzzy implication operators and their construction (III), Journal of Beijing Normal University, 40(4), pp. 427-432 (in Chinese).
17. You, F. and Li, H. X. (2004). Fuzzy implication operators and their construction (IV), Journal of Beijing Normal University, 40(5), pp. 588-599 (in Chinese).
18. Dubois, D. and Prade, H. (1991). Fuzzy sets in approximate reasoning, Part 1: Inference with possibility distributions, Fuzzy Sets and Systems, 40(1), pp. 143-202.
19. Dubois, D. and Prade, H. (1991). Fuzzy sets in approximate reasoning, Part 2: Logical approaches, Fuzzy Sets and Systems, 40(1), pp. 203-244.
20. Wang, G. J. (2000). *Non-classical Mathematical Logic and Approximate Reasoning.* (Science Press, Beijing). (in Chinese).
21. Wang, G. J. (1999). Full implication triple I method for fuzzy reasoning, Science in China (Series E), 29(1), pp. 43-53 (in Chinese).
22. Pei, D. W. (2001). Two triple I methods for FMT problem and their reductivity, Fuzzy Systems and Mathematics, 15(4), pp. 1-7 (in Chinese).
23. Wang, G. J. and Song, Q. Y. (2003). A new kind of triple I method and its logical foundation, Progress in Natural Science, 13(6), pp. 575-581 (in Chinese).
24. Guo, F. F., Chen, T. Y. and Xia, Z. Q. (2003). Triple I methods for fuzzy reasoning based on maximum fuzzy entropy principle, Fuzzy Systems and Mathematics, 17(4), pp. 55-59 (in Chinese).
25. Song, S. J. and Wu, C. (2002). Reverse triple I method of fuzzy reasoning, Science in China (Series F), 45(5), pp. 344-364.
26. Song, S. J. and Wu, C. (2002). Reverse triple I method with restrictions of fuzzy reasoning, Progress in Natural Science, 12(1), pp. 95-100 (in Chinese).
27. Song, S. J., Feng, C. B. and Wu, C. X. (2001). Theory of restriction degree of triple I method with total inference rules of fuzzy reasoning, Progress in Natural Science, 11(1), pp. 58-66.
28. Li, H. X. (2006). Probability representations of fuzzy systems, Science in China (Series F), 49(3), pp. 339-363.

Chapter 7

The Normal Numbers of Fuzzy Systems and Their Classes

7.1 Introduction

$\overline{\mathbb{R}}$ – fuzzy sets are defined firstly in this chapter, which are regarded as the generalization of the Zadeh fuzzy sets. Then bounded fuzzy sets are defined, which are also regarded as the generalization of the Zadeh fuzzy sets and particular examples of $\overline{\mathbb{R}}$ – fuzzy sets. Based on a class of $\overline{\mathbb{R}}$ – fuzzy sets, a fuzzy system is constructed by means of CRI method such that the connection between the input and the output of the system is just a quasi-interpolation function. And then, by suitably using several kinds of $\overline{\mathbb{R}}$ – fuzzy sets as fuzzy inference antecedents, several fuzzy systems are respectively obtained, such as the piecewise linear fuzzy system and Lagrange fuzzy system. Afterward, based on a particular class of $\overline{\mathbb{R}}$ – fuzzy sets, a fuzzy system is constructed by also means of CRI method such that the connection between the input and the output of the system is just a generalized Bernstein polynomial. On generalized Bernstein polynomials, it is proved that generalized Bernstein polynomials are uniformly convergent in $C[a,b]$ under a weaker condition, and it is pointed out that there exist generalized Bernstein polynomials to be not convergent in $C[a,b]$ by use of constructing a counterexample. A notion of normal numbers of fuzzy systems is defined here, which is regarded as an invariant on a fuzzy system; in other words, the normal numbers of fuzzy systems are able quantitatively holistically to describe fuzzy systems. Under the significance of the normal numbers of fuzzy systems, all fuzzy systems are able to be classified as three classes such as the normal fuzzy systems, the regular fuzzy systems and the singular fuzzy systems. Based on another class of $\overline{\mathbb{R}}$ – fuzzy sets as fuzzy inference consequents, a kind of fuzzy system is constructed by still using CRI method such that the connection between the input and the output of the system is just a fitted function, although it is not suitable for the interpolation condition, it does have more approximate performance to actual uncertain systems. At last, on the assumption of the input universe partitions on the fuzzy systems being compatible, based on a class of $\overline{\mathbb{R}}$ – fuzzy sets, Hermite fuzzy systems are formed by CRI method too, and the collocation factor fuzzy systems are defined from Hermite fuzzy system, so that ability of modeling on uncertain systems is improved and application area of fuzzy systems is expanded.

It is not difficult to understand that fuzzy systems are a sort of representations to uncertain systems, especially to ones with fuzziness. What is a representation to an uncertain system? Generally speaking, so called a representation to a system is just to establish a mathematical model for the system. It is well-known that a differential equation is usually regarded as a model for a given certain system, and under given conditions for determining solutions we are able to obtain a unique solution $y = s(x)$. In many situations, a solution $y = s(x)$ usually represents the connection between the input and the output of the system. If the system is denoted by S, then S can be simply shown as Figure 7.1.1, where the input variable x takes values in an input universe X and the output variable y takes values in an output universe Y.

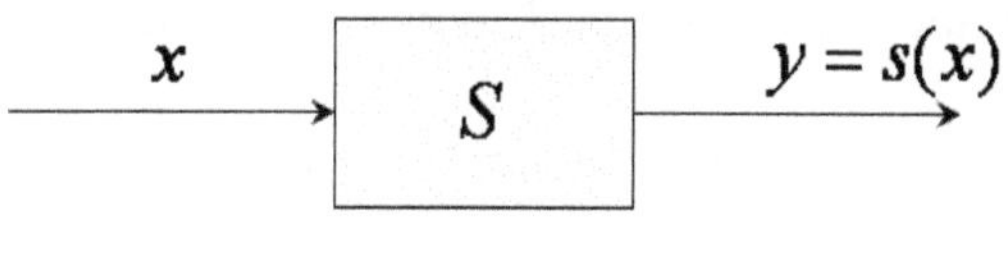

Fig. 7.1.1. A single-input single-output open-loop system

It is considering of how to model on the systems with fuzziness that Zadeh defined fuzzy sets and designed modeling method by means of fuzzy inference so that it is possible to make good models to such uncertain systems (for example, see [10–14,16–21]). Under the fuzzy inference significance, CRI method (consult [10]) was designed by Zadeh which can be used for a system with fuzziness such that we are able to get a model to represent the connection between the input and the output of the system, in which connection is denoted by $\underline{s}(x)$ regarded as an approximate function to $\underline{s}(x)$ in Figure 7.7.1. Usually $\underline{s}$ is called a fuzzy system in the narrow sense. In [11], $\underline{s}(x)$ is proved to be a certain interpolation function; especially under some conditions it is a piecewise interpolation function, that is

$$s(x) \approx \underline{s}(x) = \sum_{i=0}^{n} \mu_{A_i}(x) y_i , \tag{7.1.1}$$

where A_i $(i = 0, 1, \cdots, n)$ are a group of antecedents of the fuzzy inference rules as follows:

$$\left.\begin{array}{c} \text{If } x \text{ is } A_0 \text{ then } y \text{ is } B_0 \\ \text{or} \\ \text{If } x \text{ is } A_1 \text{ then } y \text{ is } B_1 \\ \text{or} \\ \cdots\cdots \\ \text{or} \\ \text{If } x \text{ is } A_n \text{ then } y \text{ is } B_n \end{array}\right\} \tag{7.1.2}$$

and y_i are the peak-points of the fuzzy sets B_i as the consequents of the fuzzy inference rules, which the peak-points mean the following equation:

$$\left(\forall i \in \{0, 1, \cdots, n\}\right)\left(\mu_{B_i}(y_i) = 1\right).$$

The input variable x takes values in an input universe X and the output variable y takes values in an output universe Y.

The statement mentioned above means a fuzzy system usually is an interpolation function. Whereas, from another point of view, we may find such meaning: given a piecewise interpolation function suiting with some conditions as the following:

$$F_{n+1}: X \to Y, \quad x \mapsto F_{n+1}(x) = \sum_{i=0}^{n} \psi_i(x) y_i$$

there exists a group of fuzzy inference rules as (7.1.2) such that, based on the group of fuzzy inference rules, we are able to form a fuzzy system $\underline{s}$ by means of the CRI method, in which the connection $\underline{s}(x)$ between the input and the output of the system equates approximately or even accurately to $F_{n+1}(x)$ and the base functions $\psi_i(x)$ $(i = 0, 1, \cdots, n)$ in the interpolation meet the following condition:

$$\left(\forall i \in \{0, 1, \cdots, n\}\right)\left(\psi_i(x) \equiv \mu_{A_i}(x)\right).$$

This suggests us concern with such a problem that, in numerical approximation theory, there exist many interpolation methods (for example, see [3]) that all are able to form an interpolation function, denoted by $F_{n+1}(x)$, and for such every method, whether can we make a group of fuzzy inference rules as the Expression (7.1.2) such that, based on the group of fuzzy inference rules, a fuzzy system s may be constructed in which the connection $\underline{s}(x)$ between the input and the output of the system holds the equation as being $\underline{s}(x) \approx F_{n+1}(x)$ or the equation $\underline{s}(x) = F_{n+1}(x)$? This is one of motivations of this chapter.

It is well known that the fuzzy system is a kind of approximation to certain or uncertain system. So, it is very interesting to analysis holistically and to describe quantitatively fuzzy systems from the view point of functional analysis, which is another motivation of this chapter.

In order to solve the above problem, CRI method designed by Zadeh should be generalized to general case in which the antecedents and consequents are a special class of *L*-fuzzy sets. So, fuzzy reference based on *L*-fuzzy sets can be regarded as a generalization of one based on Zadeh fuzzy sets. In fact, *L*-fuzzy set was introduced by Gougen in [7] which is a generalization of Zadeh fuzzy set. Since then, different kinds of *L*-fuzzy sets are studied such as interval valued fuzzy sets [29], intuitionistic fuzzy sets [2], type-2 fuzzy sets [22] and so on. The toll set [5] over domain of discourse *X* which was studied by Dubois and Prade is a mapping $A: X \to [0,+\infty) \bigcup \{+\infty\}$. Since the set $L = [0,+\infty) \bigcup \{+\infty\}$ with the order "$\leq$" (the order of real numbers set $\mathbb{R}$) is a complete lattice, toll set is a special class of *L*-fuzzy sets.

In this chapter, we first introduce a class of *L*-fuzzy sets called $\overline{\mathbb{R}}-$fuzzy set as a kind of generalization of toll sets where we use the symbol $\overline{\mathbb{R}} = \mathbb{R} \bigcup \{-\infty,+\infty\}$. Based on a class of $\overline{\mathbb{R}}-$ sets, a fuzzy system is constructed by means of CRI method such that the connection between the input and the output of the system is just a quasi-interpolation function. And then, by suitably using several kinds of $\overline{\mathbb{R}}-$ sets as fuzzy inference antecedents, several fuzzy systems are respectively obtained, such as the piecewise linear fuzzy system and Lagrange fuzzy system. Afterward, based on a particular class of $\overline{\mathbb{R}}-$ sets, a fuzzy system is constructed by also means of CRI method such that the connection between the input and the output of the system is just a generalized Bernstein polynomial. On generalized Bernstein polynomials, it is proved that generalized Bernstein polynomials are uniformly convergent in $C[a,b]$ under a weaker condition, and it is pointed out that there exist generalized Bernstein polynomials to be not convergent in $C[a,b]$ by use of constructing a counterexample. A notion of normal numbers of fuzzy systems is defined here, which is regarded as an invariant on a fuzzy system; in other words, the normal numbers of fuzzy systems are able quantitatively holistically to describe fuzzy systems. Under the significance of the normal numbers of fuzzy systems, all fuzzy systems are able to be classified as three classes such as the normal fuzzy systems, the regular fuzzy systems and the singular fuzzy systems. Based on another class of $\overline{\mathbb{R}}-$ sets as fuzzy inference consequents, a kind of fuzzy system is constructed by still using CRI method such that the connection between the input and the output of the system is just a fitted function, although it is not suitable for the interpolation condition, it does have more approximate performance to actual uncertain systems. At last, on the assumption of the input universe partitions on the fuzzy systems being compatible, based on a class of $\overline{\mathbb{R}}-$ sets, Hermite fuzzy systems are formed by CRI method too, and the collocation factor fuzzy systems are defined from

Hermite fuzzy system, so that ability of modeling on uncertain systems is improved and application area of fuzzy systems is expanded.

This chapter is organized as follows. In section 7.2, $\overline{\mathbb{R}}-$ set is introduced. In section 7.3, $\overline{\mathbb{R}}-$ implication operations are defined. In section 7.4, the fuzzy systems based on $\overline{\mathbb{R}}-$ sets are discussed. In section 7.5, Normal numbers of fuzzy systems are introduced in order to discuss some analysis properties of fuzzy systems from functional analysis point of view. In section 7.6, Bernstein fuzzy systems are introduced, and the approximation properties of such fuzzy systems are discussed. In section 7.7, fitted type fuzzy systems and Hermite fuzzy systems are discussed in section 7.7 and section 7.8, respectively. In section 7.9, the normal numbers of Hermite fuzzy systems is discussed. In section 7.10, weighed fuzzy sets are introduced. The conclusions are presented in section 7.11.

7.2 $\overline{\mathbb{R}}-$ Fuzzy Sets

Given a nonempty universe X, a Zadeh fuzzy set A on a set X is a mapping $\mu_A : X \to [0,1]$, where μ_A is called the membership function of A and also denoted by the following symbol:

$$(\forall x \in X)\left(A(x) \triangleq \mu_A(x)\right),$$

for us being more convenient. We know very well that $[0,1]$ for the operations as the following:

$$\vee \triangleq \sup, \quad \wedge \triangleq \inf, \quad x^c \triangleq 1-x$$

should form an F-lattice (see [29]). It is taking notice of that the generalized real number set as the following:

$$\overline{\mathbb{R}} = \mathbb{R} \cup \{-\infty, +\infty\},$$

where $\mathbb{R}$ is well-known the field of real numbers, for the operations $\vee \triangleq \sup$, $\wedge \triangleq \inf$ and $x^c \triangleq 1-x$, forms an F-lattice, too. $\left([0,1], \vee, \wedge\right)$ is obviously isomorphic with $\left(\overline{\mathbb{R}}, \vee, \wedge\right)$. In fact, we make a mapping as the following:

$$f:([0,1],\vee,\wedge)\to(\overline{\mathbb{R}},\vee,\wedge)$$

$$x\mapsto f(x)\triangleq\begin{cases}-\infty, & x=0;\\ \tan[\pi(x-0.5)], & x\in(0,1);\\ +\infty, & x=1\end{cases}$$

It is easy to verify that the mapping is a bijection and keeping operations. So it is an isomorphic mapping. Now we define a complement operation in $\overline{\mathbb{R}}$ as follows:

$$c:\overline{\mathbb{R}}\to\overline{\mathbb{R}},\quad x\mapsto c(x)\triangleq x^c\triangleq -x.$$

For any a point $x\in[0,1]$, we have the following facts:

$$\begin{aligned}x=0\Rightarrow f\left(x^c\right)&=f(1-x)=f(1)=+\infty=-(-\infty)\\&=-f(0)=[f(0)]^c=[f(x)]^c,\\x=1\Rightarrow f\left(x^c\right)&=f(1-x)=f(0)=-\infty=-(+\infty)\\&=-f(1)=[f(1)]^c=[f(x)]^c,\\0<x<1\Rightarrow f\left(x^c\right)&=f(1-x)=\tan[\pi(1-x-0.5)]\\&=-\tan[\pi(1-x-0.5)]=-f(x)=[f(x)]^c\end{aligned}$$

These mean that the mapping $f:([0,1],\vee,\wedge,c)\to(\overline{\mathbb{R}},\vee,\wedge,c)$ is also an isomorphic mapping. So we can learn that $(\overline{\mathbb{R}},\vee,\wedge,c)$ is a fuzzy lattice which is a kind of algebraic structure.

Especially, for any $c,d\in\mathbb{R},\ c<d,\ [c,d]$ can also be a fuzzy lattice with respect to the operations $\vee,\ \wedge,\ c$. And we can prove the fact that the algebraic structure $([0,1],\vee,\wedge,c)$ is isomorphic with the algebraic structure $([0,1],\vee,\wedge,c)$.

In fact, if we make a mapping as the following:

$$f:([0,1],\vee,\wedge,c)\to([c,d],\vee,\wedge,c)$$
$$x\mapsto f(x)\triangleq(d-c)x+c,$$

then it is easy to know that f is an isomorphic mapping, where the complement operation in $([c,d],\vee,\wedge,c)$ as follows:

$$c:[c,d]\to[c,d],\quad x\mapsto c(x)\triangleq x^c\triangleq d+c-x$$

Of course we can verify the fact as the following: $\forall x\in[0,1]$,

$$f\left(x^c\right)=f(1-x)=(d-c)(1-x)+c$$
$$=d+c-[(d-c)x+c]=d+c-f(x)=[f(x)]^c.$$

Generally speaking, if we let $(L,\vee,\wedge)$ be a complete lattice, then every mapping $A:X\to L$ is called an L-fuzzy set (see [7]), and the set of all such L-fuzzy sets is denoted by L^X.

When $L=\overline{\mathbb{R}}$, the elements in the set: $\overline{\mathbb{R}}^X=\left\{A\middle|A:X\to\overline{\mathbb{R}}\right\}$ are naturally called $\overline{\mathbb{R}}-$ fuzzy sets. In [28], the category of such generalized fuzzy sets with the degree set $L=\hat{\mathbb{R}}\triangleq\mathbb{R}\bigcup\{+\infty\}$ was researched, and the category is with good properties. For that reason mentioned above, we can and should generalize Zadeh's fuzzy sets as follows.

Definition 7.2.1 Given a nonempty universe X, a generalized real-valued function $A:X\to\overline{\mathbb{R}}$ is called an $\overline{\mathbb{R}}-$ fuzzy set. The set of all the $\overline{\mathbb{R}}-$ fuzzy sets on X is denoted by $\overline{\mathbb{R}}^X$. Particularly, when A is a bounded function, A is named a bounded fuzzy set, and the set of all the bounded fuzzy sets on X is denoted by $BF(X)$. □

Apparently, $BF(X)\subset\overline{\mathbb{R}}^X$. Let A be a bounded fuzzy set on X. Then there exist $c,d\in\mathbb{R}$ with $c\le d$, such that $A:X\to\overline{\mathbb{R}}$ can be shown as $A:X\to[c,d]$. When $c\ge0$ and $d\le1$, such bounded fuzzy sets will degenerate Zadeh fuzzy sets.

Example 7.2.1 Given a nonempty universe X, let $c=-1$ and $d=1$. Then the mapping $A: X \to [-1,1]$ is a bounded fuzzy set. □

Remark 7.2.1 In [25], a notion of the double branch fuzzy sets was defined as the statement: given a nonempty universe X, making a partition for X as $\{X^+, X^-, X^0\}$, i.e., the sets X^+, X^-, X^0 are not disjoint each other and $X = X^+ \cup X^- \cup X^0$, so-called a double branch fuzzy set A means, when $x \in X^+$, $A(x) \in (0,1]$, when $x \in X^-$, $A(x) \in [-1,0)$ and when $x \in X^0$, $A(x) = 0$. Clearly, a double branch fuzzy set is a particular bounded fuzzy set as shown as in Example 7.2.1. As a matter of fact, for a bounded fuzzy set A as mentioned in Example 7.2.1, let

$$X^+ \triangleq \{x \in X \mid A(x) \in (0,1]\},$$
$$X^- \triangleq \{x \in X \mid A(x) \in [-1,0)\},$$
$$X^0 \triangleq \{x \in X \mid A(x) = 0\}$$

Then $\{X^+, X^-, X^0\}$ forms a partition on X and the A is indeed a double branch fuzzy set. □

Remark 7.2.2 For a bounded fuzzy set $A: X \to [c,d]$, if we have the inclusion $A(X) \subset [0,1]$, then A degenerates a Zadeh fuzzy set. □

Example 7.2.2 Let $X = [a,b] \subset \mathbb{R}$. Making a partition on X as the following:

$$a = x_0 < x_1 < \cdots < x_n = b,$$

we form the bounded fuzzy sets $A_{ij}: X \to [c,d]$ as the following (their shapes are shown as Figure 7.2.1):

$$\begin{aligned} &A_{ij}(x) = (x - x_j)/(x_i - x_j), \\ &i \neq j; \quad i, j = 0,1,\cdots,n. \end{aligned} \tag{7.2.1}$$

Clearly, we have $A_{ij}(X)=\left[c_{ij},d_{ij}\right]$, where we have put:

$$c_{ij}\triangleq\min\left\{A_{ij}(x)\middle|x\in X\right\},\quad d_{ij}\triangleq\max\left\{A_{ij}(x)\middle|x\in X\right\},$$

then the mappings $A_{ij}:X\to[c,d]$ are significant. □

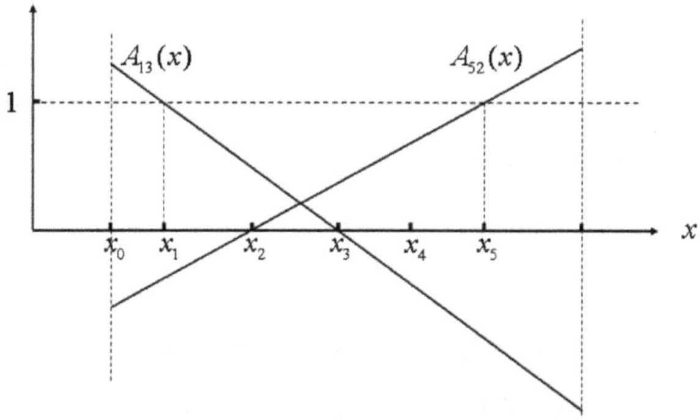

Fig. 7.2.1. A class of bounded fuzzy sets

Now we reconsider the bounded fuzzy set $A:X\to[c,d]$. We are able to understand that the interval $[c,d]$ is a kind of description of membership degree for an element $x\in X$ belonging to a bounded fuzzy set A, only in which the scale by use of $[c,d]$ is different to the one by using $[0,1]$. For example, when $A(x)=d$, it is regarded as that x fully belongs to A, when $A(x)=c$, as that x does fully not belong to A and when the situation: $c<A(x)<d$, as the membership degree is a number between c and d. Especially, when $c<0$ and $d\geq 0$, that the value $A(x)\in[0,d]$ means a degree that x does belong to A, and that the value $A(x)\in[c,0)$ means a degree that x do does not belong to A. Of course, this is only one kind of interpretation, and there may be other ones. Actually membership meanings of $A(x)$ should be defined in accordance with practical situations, so that the abilities for applications can greatly be improved. For the situation of $\overline{\mathbb{R}}$ – fuzzy set $A:X\to\overline{\mathbb{R}}$, there is a similar interpretation.

7.3 $\overline{\mathbb{R}}$ – Fuzzy Implication Operations

Definition 7.3.1 A generalized binary real-valued function as follows

$$\theta : \overline{\mathbb{R}} \times \overline{\mathbb{R}} \to \overline{\mathbb{R}}, \quad (a,b) \mapsto \theta(a,b)$$

is called an $\overline{\mathbb{R}}$ – fuzzy implication operations, if $\theta\big|_{[0,1]^2}$ is a fuzzy implication operator. □

Because the generalized real-valued functions are able to take their values in $\{\pm\infty\}$, in order to avoid making mistakes, we emphasize some common stipulations as follows:

$$\begin{aligned}
&-\infty < +\infty; \quad x \in \mathbb{R} \Rightarrow -\infty < x < +\infty; \\
&\pm\infty + (\pm\infty) = \pm\infty - (\mp\infty); \\
&(\forall x \in \mathbb{R})\big(\pm\infty + x = \pm\infty = x - (\mp\infty)\big); \\
&(\forall x \in (0,+\infty))\big(\pm\infty \cdot x = \pm\infty\big); \\
&(\forall x \in [-\infty,0))\big(\pm\infty \cdot x = \mp\infty\big); \\
&(\forall x \in \mathbb{R})\left(\pm\infty \cdot 0 = 0 = \frac{x}{\pm\infty}\right); \\
&|\pm\infty| = +\infty; \quad (\pm\infty)\cdot(\pm\infty) = +\infty; \\
&(\pm\infty)\cdot(\mp\infty) = -\infty.
\end{aligned}$$

Sometimes, $+\infty$ is simply denoted by ∞. Be carefully, such as the situations: $\pm\infty - (\pm\infty)$, $(\pm\infty) + (\mp\infty)$, and so on are insignificant.

Example 7.3.1 Suppose we take a binary function as the following form:

$$\theta \triangleq \cdot : \overline{\mathbb{R}} \times \overline{\mathbb{R}} \to \overline{\mathbb{R}}, \quad (x,y) \mapsto \theta(x,y) = x \cdot y$$

Then θ is an $\overline{\mathbb{R}}$ – fuzzy implication operation. And let

$$\theta \triangleq \wedge : \overline{\mathbb{R}} \times \overline{\mathbb{R}} \to \overline{\mathbb{R}}, \quad (x,y) \mapsto \theta(x,y) = x \wedge y$$

Then θ is also an $\overline{\mathbb{R}}-$ fuzzy implication operation. □

Remark 7.3.1 In the chapter, we often use $\overline{\mathbb{R}}-$ relations and the bounded fuzzy relations which are regarded respectively as particular ones of $\overline{\mathbb{R}}-$ sets and the bounded fuzzy sets. Besides, very like Definition 7.3.1, we are able to generalize T-norm and co-T-norm as $\overline{\mathbb{R}}-$ T-norm, $\overline{\mathbb{R}}-$ co-T-norm, the bounded T-norm and the bounded co-T-norm. □

7.4 Fuzzy Systems Based on $\overline{\mathbb{R}}-$ sets

Now we again review the single input and single output fuzzy system with the input universe $X=[a,b]$ and the output universe $Y=[c,d]$. Suppose we have known a group of the input-output data as the following:

$$\mathrm{IOD}=\{(x_i,y_i)\mid i=0,1,\cdots,n\}$$

with the partitions on the universes X and Y, as the following:

$$a=x_0<x_1<\ldots<x_n=b,$$
$$c=y_{k_0}<y_{k_1}<\ldots<y_{k_n}=d,$$

respectively, where $k_i=\sigma(i)$ and the mapping σ is an $(n+1)-$ elements permutation:

$$\sigma=\begin{pmatrix}0 & 1 & \cdots & n\\ k_0 & k_1 & \cdots & k_n\end{pmatrix}.$$

Let

$$\Delta y_{k_i}=y_{k_{i+1}}-y_{k_i},\ i=0,1,\cdots,n-1,\ \Delta y_{k_n}=\frac{1}{n}\sum_{i=0}^{n-1}\Delta y_{k_i}$$

Then we construct the bounded fuzzy sets $A_i\in BF(X)\ (i=0,1,\cdots,n)$ as fuzzy inference antecedents and the $\overline{\mathbb{R}}-$fuzzy sets as follows:

$$B_i \in \overline{\mathbb{R}}^Y, \quad i = 0, 1, \cdots, n$$

as fuzzy inference consequents, where the antecedent bounded fuzzy sets hold the normalizing condition:

$$(\forall x \in X)\left(\sum_{i=0}^{n} \mu_{A_i}(x) = 1\right)$$

And in order to make the fuzzy inference consequent $\overline{\mathbb{R}}-$fuzzy sets as being $B_i \in \overline{\mathbb{R}}^Y$, we firstly form a group of the triangle wave fuzzy sets as being $\overline{B}_{k_i} \in \mathcal{F}(Y)$ as the following (see Figure 7.4.1):

$$\overline{B}_{k_0}(y) = \begin{cases} \left(y - y_{k_1}\right)/\left(y_{k_0} - y_{k_1}\right), & y \in \left[y_{k_0}, y_{k_1}\right]; \\ 0, & \text{otherwise}, \end{cases}$$

$$\overline{B}_{k_i}(y) = \begin{cases} \left(y - y_{k_{i-1}}\right)/\left(y_{k_i} - y_{k_{i-1}}\right), & y \in \left[y_{k_{i-1}}, y_{k_i}\right]; \\ \left(y - y_{k_{i+1}}\right)/\left(y_{k_i} - y_{k_{i+1}}\right), & y \in \left[y_{k_i}, y_{k_{i+1}}\right]; \\ 0, & \text{otherwise}; \end{cases}$$

$$i = 1, 2, \cdots, n-1,$$

$$\overline{B}_{k_n}(y) = \begin{cases} \left(y - y_{k_{n-1}}\right)/\left(y_{k_n} - y_{k_{n-1}}\right), & y \in \left[y_{k_{n-1}}, y_{k_n}\right]; \\ 0, & \text{otherwise}. \end{cases}$$

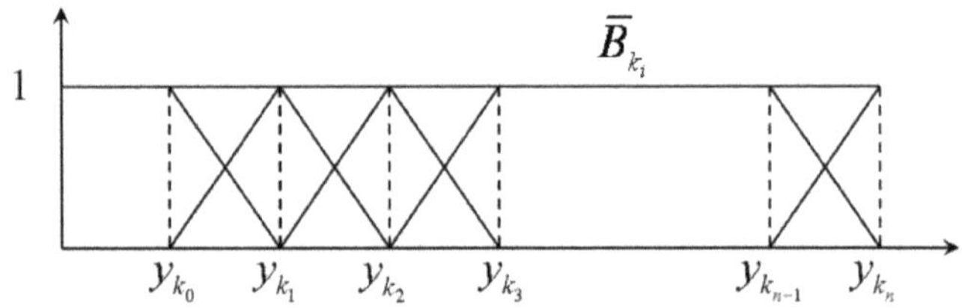

Fig. 7.4.1. Triangle wave fuzzy sets

Then these $\overline{B}_i$ are expanded to be as the $\overline{\mathbb{R}}-$fuzzy sets $B_i \in \overline{\mathbb{R}}^Y$ as the following:

$$\mu_{B_i}(y) = \mu_{\overline{B}_i}(x) \Big/ (\Delta y_i)^2, \quad i = 0, 1, \cdots, n. \tag{7.4.1}$$

It is not difficult to understand that every $1\big/(\Delta y_i)^2$ in Equation (7.4.1) plays such a role that every $\overline{B}_i$ is weighted by $1\big/(\Delta y_i)^2$ to become a B_i.

For the fuzzy inference consequents, the smaller is Δy_i, the bigger is the number $\gamma_i = 1\big/(\Delta y_i)^2$. So under the condition as the following:

$$\lim_{n\to\infty} \max_i \Delta y_i = 0,$$

we have the following result:

$$\lim_{n\to\infty} B_i = \lim_{\Delta y_i \to 0} B_i = \lim_{\Delta y_i \to 0} \left(\overline{B}_i \big/ (\Delta y_i)^2 \right) = \{y_i\}_{\overline{\mathbb{R}}},$$

where $\{y_i\}_{\overline{\mathbb{R}}}$ is called a $\overline{\mathbb{R}}$-singleton, which means the truth value set of singletons is generalized from $\{0,1\}$ to $\{-\infty, +\infty\}$, i.e.,

$$(\forall y \in Y)\left(\mu_{\{y_i\}_{\overline{\mathbb{R}}}}(y) = \begin{cases} +\infty, & y = y_i \\ -\infty, & y \neq y_i \end{cases} \right).$$

Absolutely we are able to regard it as reasonable. It is the time to give our fuzzy inference rules and they are as follows:

$$\text{If } x \text{ is } A_i \text{ then } y \text{ is } B_i, \quad i = 0, 1, \cdots, n. \tag{7.4.2}$$

From every rule in Expression (7.4.2), the $\overline{\mathbb{R}}$ – fuzzy inference relations as the following:

$$R_i = \theta(A_i, B_i), \quad i = 0, 1, \cdots, n$$

are able to be determined, where θ is an $\overline{\mathbb{R}}$ – implication operator selected by us, that is

$$\mu_{R_i}(x,y) = \theta\left(\mu_{A_i}(x), \mu_{B_i}(y)\right), \quad i = 0,1,\cdots,n. \tag{7.4.3}$$

In the chapter, we often choose the $\overline{\mathbb{R}}$ – fuzzy implication operator as the form of $\theta \triangleq \cdot$, and thus

$$\mu_{R_i}(x,y) = \mu_{A_i}(x) \cdot \mu_{B_i}(y), \quad i = 0,1,\cdots,n. \tag{7.4.4}$$

In [31], an idea of weighted fuzzy inference was discussed, and then some applications were researched in [27]. Here we will use such weighted fuzzy inferences to deal with our problem. As a matter of fact, there $\overline{\mathbb{R}}$ – fuzzy relations obtained in Equation (7.4.4) are aggregated by the weighted from to become a whole $\overline{\mathbb{R}}$ – fuzzy relations on all rules as Expression (7.4.2) as $R \triangleq \sum_{i=0}^{n} w_i R_i$ that is

$$\mu_R(x,y) = \sum_{k=0}^{n} w_i \mu_{R_i}(x,y) = \sum_{k=0}^{n} w_i \mu_{A_i}(x) \mu_{B_i}(y) \tag{7.4.5}$$

These w_i represent for the portions of the $\overline{\mathbb{R}}$ – fuzzy inference relations R_i to occupy in the whole $\overline{\mathbb{R}}$ – fuzzy inference relation R, respectively. Here we take the weights as follows:

$$w_i = \frac{\Delta y_i}{\sum_{i=0}^{n} \Delta y_k}, \quad i = 0,1,\cdots,n. \tag{7.4.6}$$

We take notice of these w_i are just Δy_i essentially respectively, and that $\sum_{k=0}^{n} \Delta y_k$ plays only a normalizing role for the weights. Clearly Δy_k shows a subinterval of the universe $Y = [c,d]$ taken up by i-th inference rule. It is easy to learn that, the bigger the subinterval is taken up, the more important the fuzzy inference rule possesses in the whole. So we think of such a selection for the weights is indeed reasonable.

We should notice the difference between these weights w_i and those weights $\gamma_i = 1/(\Delta y_i)^2$, mentioned above. The former is on the i-th inference rule, and the latter is only on the consequent $\overline{B}_i$ of the i-th inference rule, which is with different meanings. Moreover, the $\overline{\mathbb{R}}$ – fuzzy relation R is a $\overline{\mathbb{R}}$ – fuzzy set on $\overline{\mathbb{R}} \times \overline{\mathbb{R}}$, i.e., $R \in \overline{\mathbb{R}}^{[a,b]\times[c,d]}$. For the use of the $\overline{\mathbb{R}}$ – fuzzy inference relation, we denote two symbols as the following:

$$
\begin{aligned}
M &\triangleq \sup\{\mu_R(x,y) \mid (x,y) \in [a,b]\times[c,d]\} \\
&= \sup\left\{\sum_{k=0}^{n} w_i \mu_{A_i}(x)\mu_{B_i}(y) \,\middle|\, (x,y) \in [a,b]\times[c,d]\right\}, \\
m &\triangleq \inf\{\mu_R(x,y) \mid (x,y) \in [a,b]\times[c,d]\} \\
&= \inf\left\{\sum_{k=0}^{n} w_i \mu_{A_i}(x)\mu_{B_i}(y) \,\middle|\, (x,y) \in [a,b]\times[c,d]\right\}.
\end{aligned}
$$

For the requirements in what follows, we introduce a new concept, quasi-interpolation functions. So-called a quasi-interpolation function $F_{n+1}(x)$ means it holding the conditions as the following:

1) $F_{n+1}(x)$ is a linear combination of the group of base functions as the following:

$$\left\{\mu_{A_i}(x) \mid i = 0,1,\cdots,n\right\},$$

i.e., there exists a group of real numbers $\{c_i \in \mathbb{R} \mid i = 0,1,\cdots,n\}$ such that

$$F_{n+1}(x) = \sum_{i=0}^{n} \mu_{A_i}(x) c_i\,;$$

2) $\left(\forall i\in\{0,1,\cdots,n\}\right)\left(c_i=y_i\right)$.

Clearly we know that, only with above two conditions, well-known interpolation condition:

$$\left(\forall i\in\{0,1,\cdots,n\}\right)\left(F_{n+1}\left(x_i\right)=y_i\right),$$

cannot be met yet. It is easy to see the fact that, if the group of base functions $\left\{\mu_{A_i}(x)\middle|\,i=0,1,\cdots,n\right\}$ satisfies Kronecker condition:

$$A_i\left(x_j\right)=\begin{cases}1, & i=j;\\ 0, & i\neq j,\end{cases}$$
$$i,j=0,1,\cdots,n$$

then that $F_{n+1}(x)=\sum_{i=0}^{n}\mu_{A_i}(x)y_i$ holds the interpolation condition.

Theorem 7.4.1 By still using notations and notions mentioned above, based on the group of fuzzy inference rules as Expression (7.4.2), a fuzzy system $\underline{s}$ is obtained by means of CRI method is approximately equal to a quasi-interpolation function in which its basis functions are just the bounded fuzzy sets $\left\{\mu_{A_i}(x)\middle|\,i=0,1,\cdots,n\right\}$, as the following

$$\underline{s}(x)\approx F_{n+1}(x)\triangleq\sum_{i=0}^{n}\mu_{A_i}(x)y_i\,. \tag{7.4.7}$$

Proof. By CRI method, from the $\overline{\mathbb{R}}$ – fuzzy inference relation R (see Equation (7.4.5)), a $\overline{\mathbb{R}}$ – fuzzy transformation "$\circ$" is induced as follows

$$\begin{aligned}&\circ:\ \overline{\mathbb{R}}^X\rightarrow\overline{\mathbb{R}}^Y,\quad A\mapsto B\triangleq A\circ R,\\ &\left(\forall y\in Y\right)\left(\mu_B(y)=\bigvee_{x\in X}\left[\mu_A(x)\wedge\mu_R(x,y)\right]\right)\end{aligned} \tag{7.4.8}$$

For any a point $x^* \in X$, denoting the following $\overline{\mathbb{R}}$ – fuzzy set:

$$\mu_{A^*}(x) \triangleq \begin{cases} M, & x = x^*, \\ m, & x \neq x^*, \end{cases}$$

and being substituted in Equation (7.4.8), we get a fuzzy inference consequent $B^* \in \overline{\mathbb{R}}^Y$ as the following

$$\begin{aligned} \mu_{B^*}(y) &= \bigvee_{x\in X}\left(\mu_{A^*}(x) \wedge \mu_R(x,y)\right) \\ &= \sum_{i=0}^{n} w_i \mu_{A_i}\left(x^*\right) \mu_{B_i}(y) \end{aligned} \tag{7.4.9}$$

If the following conditions are satisfied

$$\int_Y \left|y\mu_{B^*}(y)\right| \mathrm{d}y < \infty, \quad 0 < \int_Y \left|\mu_{B^*}(y)\right| \mathrm{d}y < \infty,$$

then we are able to obtain a corresponding point $y^* \in Y$ with respect to the given point x^*, i.e.,

$$y^* = \frac{\int_Y y\mu_{B^*}(y)\mathrm{d}y}{\int_Y \mu_{B^*}(y)\mathrm{d}y},$$

by using the barycenter method. Because x^* is arbitrary, above expression should be generalized as the following

$$\begin{aligned} & y = \frac{\int_Y \mu_B(y) y \mathrm{d}y}{\int_Y \mu_B(y)\mathrm{d}y}, \\ & (\forall y \in Y)\left(\mu_B(y) = \sum_{i=0}^{n} w_i \mu_{A_i}(x) \mu_{B_i}(y)\right). \end{aligned} \tag{7.4.10}$$

In accordance with the significance of Riemannian Sum in the definition of definite integral, we have the following equation:

$$y = \frac{\int_Y \mu_B(y) y \mathrm{d}y}{\int_Y \mu_B(y) \mathrm{d}y} \approx \frac{\sum_{i=0}^{n} \mu_B\left(y_{k_i}\right) y_{k_i} \Delta y_{k_i}}{\sum_{i=0}^{n} \mu_B\left(y_{k_i}\right) \Delta y_{k_i}}$$
$$= \frac{\sum_{i=0}^{n} y_i \mu_B\left(y_i\right) \Delta y_i}{\sum_{i=0}^{n} \mu_B\left(y_i\right) \Delta y_i} \tag{7.4.11}$$

Since the bounded fuzzy sets $\left\{\mu_{A_i}(x) \middle| i = 0, 1, \cdots, n\right\}$ hold the normalizing condition: $\sum_{i=0}^{n} \mu_{A_i}(x) \equiv 1$, by Equations (7.4.1) and (7.4.6), we know the fact that

$$\mu_B\left(y_i\right) \Delta y_i = \Delta y_i \sum_{k=0}^{n} w_k \mu_{A_k}(x) \mu_{B_k}\left(y_i\right)$$
$$= \Delta y_i w_i \mu_{A_i}(x) \frac{1}{\left(\Delta y_i\right)^2} = \frac{1}{\sum_{i=0}^{n} \Delta y_k} \mu_{A_i}(x).$$

Thus Expression (7.4.11) can be shown as follows

$$y \approx \frac{\sum_{i=0}^{n} y_i \mu_B\left(y_i\right) \Delta y_i}{\sum_{i=0}^{n} \mu_B\left(y_i\right) \Delta y_i} = \frac{\sum_{i=0}^{n} \frac{1}{\sum_{k=0}^{n} \Delta y_k} \mu_{A_i}(x) y_i}{\sum_{i=0}^{n} \frac{1}{\sum_{k=0}^{n} \Delta y_k} \mu_{A_i}(x)}$$
$$= \frac{\sum_{i=0}^{n} \mu_{A_i}(x) y_i}{\sum_{i=0}^{n} \mu_{A_i}(x)} = \sum_{i=0}^{n} \mu_{A_i}(x) y_i \tag{7.4.12}$$

Substituting $\underline{s}(x)$ for y and taking the function as the following:

$$F_{n+1}(x) \triangleq \sum_{i=0}^{n} \mu_{A_i}(x) y_i ,$$

we have the following result:

$$\underline{s}(x) \approx F_{n+1}(x) = \sum_{i=0}^{n} \mu_{A_i}(x) y_i , \tag{7.4.13}$$

This is the end of our proof. □

Example 7.4.1 From the partition of the universe X as the following:

$$a = x_0 < x_1 < \ldots < x_n = b ,$$

the bounded fuzzy sets as the antecedents of fuzzy inference rules are formed as the following:

$$\begin{aligned} \mu_{A_i}(x) &= \prod_{\substack{j=0 \\ j \neq i}}^{n} \frac{x - x_j}{x_i - x_j} \\ &= \frac{(x - x_0)\cdots(x - x_{i-1})(x - x_{i+1})\cdots(x - x_n)}{(x_i - x_0)\cdots(x_i - x_{i-1})(x_i - x_{i+1})\cdots(x_i - x_n)}, \\ i &= 0, 1, \cdots, n. \end{aligned} \tag{7.4.14}$$

From Fundamental Theorem of Algebra, it is easy to know the fact that

$$\sum_{i=0}^{n} \mu_{A_i}(x) = \sum_{i=0}^{n} \prod_{\substack{j=0 \\ j \neq i}}^{n} \frac{x - x_j}{x_i - x_j} \equiv 1 .$$

So the connection between the input and the output of the fuzzy system $\underline{s}$ constructed just above is approximately equal to a quasi-interpolation function in which its base functions are just the group of functions as being $\left\{\mu_{A_i}(x)\right\}_{i=0}^{n}$, i.e.,

$$\underline{s}(x) \approx F_{n+1}(x) = \sum_{i=0}^{n} \mu_{A_i}(x) y_i = \sum_{i=0}^{n} \prod_{\substack{j=0 \\ j \neq i}}^{n} \frac{x - x_j}{x_i - x_j} y_i \tag{7.4.15}$$

Because the bounded fuzzy sets $\{A_i\}_{i=0}^{n}$ here are typical Lagrange interpolation basis functions, that hold Kronecker condition, the following function:

$$F_{n+1}(x) = \sum_{i=0}^{n} \prod_{\substack{j=0 \\ j \neq i}}^{n} \frac{x - x_j}{x_i - x_j} y_i$$

is just an interpolation function. Such fuzzy systems are called by us Lagrange Fuzzy Systems. □

Example 7.4.2 From the partition of the universe as the following:

$$a = x_0 < x_1 < \ldots < x_n = b \text{ ,}$$

the bounded fuzzy sets as the antecedents of fuzzy inference rules are formed as the triangle wave Zadeh fuzzy sets very like Figure 7.4.1 as the following:

$$\mu_{A_0}(x) = \begin{cases} (x - x_1)/(x_0 - x_1), & x \in [x_0, x_1]; \\ 0, & \text{otherwise}; \end{cases}$$

$$\mu_{A_i}(x) = \begin{cases} (x - x_{i-1})/(x_i - x_{i-1}), & x \in [x_{i-1}, x_i]; \\ (x - x_{i+1})/(x_i - x_{i+1}), & x \in [x_i, x_{i+1}]; \\ 0, & \text{otherwise}; \end{cases}$$

$$i = 1, \cdots, n-1,$$

$$\mu_{A_n}(x) = \begin{cases} (x - x_{n-1})/(x_n - x_{n-1}), & x \in [x_{n-1}, x_n]; \\ 0, & \text{otherwise}; \end{cases}$$

Clearly $\sum_{i=0}^{n} \mu_{A_i}(x) \equiv 1$. So the connection between the input and the output of the fuzzy system $\underline{s}$ constructed just above is approximately equal to a quasi-interpolation function in which its base functions are just those membership functions as being $\{\mu_{A_i}(x)\}_{i=0}^{n}$, i.e.,

$$\underline{s}(x) \approx F_{n+1}(x) = \sum_{i=0}^{n} \mu_{A_i}(x) y_i . \tag{7.4.16}$$

Apparently the group of base functions, $\{\mu_{A_i}(x)\}_{i=0}^{n}$, hold Kronecker condition. Thus that $F_{n+1}(x) = \sum_{i=0}^{n} \mu_{A_i}(x) y_i$ is just an interpolation function. So such fuzzy systems are called by us Piecewise Linear Fuzzy Systems. □

Example 7.4.3 On the input universe X, the bounded fuzzy sets as the antecedents of fuzzy inference rules are formed as the following:

$$\mu_{A_i}(x) = C_n^i \left(\frac{x-a}{b-a}\right)^i \left(\frac{b-x}{b-a}\right)^{n-i}, \quad i = 0, 1, \cdots, n \tag{7.4.17}$$

Clearly we know the fact : $\sum_{i=0}^{n} \mu_{A_i}(x) \equiv 1$.

So the connection between the input and the output of the fuzzy system $\underline{s}$ constructed just above is approximately equal to a quasi-interpolation function in which its basis functions are just those membership functions as being $\{\mu_{A_i}(x)\}_{i=0}^{n}$, i.e.,

$$\begin{aligned} \underline{s}(x) &\approx F_{n+1}(x) = \sum_{i=0}^{n} \mu_{A_i}(x) y_i \\ &= \sum_{i=0}^{n} C_n^i \left(\frac{x-a}{b-a}\right)^i \left(\frac{b-x}{b-a}\right)^{n-i} y_i \end{aligned} \tag{7.4.18}$$

□

Remark 7.4.1 The fuzzy system $\underline{s}$ as Equation (7.4.18) is called by us a Bernstein Fuzzy System. Particularly, when $a=0$ and $b=1$, we have

$$\mu_{A_i}(x)=C_n^i(x)^i(1-x)^{n-i},\quad i=0,1\cdots,n,$$

which are typical base functions from Bernstein polynomials.

However here the base function group as being $\left\{\mu_{A_i}(x)\right\}_{i=0}^{n}$ does not hold Kronecker condition. It is not difficult to learn that the following function:

$$F_{n+1}(x)=\sum_{i=0}^{n}\mu_{A_i}(x)y_i$$

is not an interpolation function but a quasi-interpolation function. □

7.5 Normal Numbers of Fuzzy Systems

In this section, we will discuss some analysis properties of fuzzy systems from functional analysis point of view.

We still take account of the single input and single output open loop uncertain system as shown as Figure 7.1.1, i.e.,

$$s:X\to Y,\quad x\mapsto y=s(x).$$

The group of $\overline{\mathbb{R}}-$ fuzzy inference rules describing the uncertain system is as Expression (7.4.2), that is,

$$A_i\to B_i,\quad i=0,1,\cdots,n,$$

where $A_i\in\overline{\mathbb{R}}^X$ and $B_i\in\overline{\mathbb{R}}^Y$, $i=0,1,\cdots,n$.

In this chapter or even in this book, we often regard $\mu_A(x)$ as the same as $A(x)$, because $A(x)$ is more convenient than $\mu_A(x)$.

By noticing that $A_i:X\to\overline{\mathbb{R}}$ and $B_i:Y\to\overline{\mathbb{R}}, i=0,1,\cdots,n$, we can know the fact as following:

$$\mathcal{A} \triangleq \{A_0, \cdots, A_n\} \subset \overline{\mathbb{R}}^X \triangleq \{f \mid f : X \to \overline{\mathbb{R}}\}$$

$$\mathcal{B} \triangleq \{B_0, \cdots, B_n\} \subset \overline{\mathbb{R}}^Y \triangleq \{g \mid g : Y \to \overline{\mathbb{R}}\}.$$

In $\overline{\mathbb{R}}^X$, we define the addition and the scalar multiplication operations respectively as follows:

$$(\forall f, g \in \mathbb{R}^X)\big((\forall x \in X)((f+g)(x) \triangleq f(x) + g(x))\big);$$
$$(\forall f \in \mathbb{R}^X)(\forall a \in \mathbb{R})\big((\forall x \in X)((a \cdot f)(x) = a \cdot f(x))\big).$$

It is easy to know that $(\overline{\mathbb{R}}^X, +, \cdot)$ is a linear space over the real number field $\mathbb{R}$, and so $(\overline{\mathbb{R}}^Y, +, \cdot)$ is. In the function spaces $\overline{\mathbb{R}}^X$ and $\overline{\mathbb{R}}^Y$, the norm $\|\cdot\|_X$ and $\|\cdot\|_Y$ are defined respectively such that $(\overline{\mathbb{R}}^X, \|\cdot\|_X)$ and $(\overline{\mathbb{R}}^Y, \|\cdot\|_Y)$ all become the normed linear spaces. Thus $\mathcal{A}$ and $\mathcal{B}$ are able to be regarded as the subsets of the normed linear spaces $\overline{\mathbb{R}}^X$ and $\overline{\mathbb{R}}^Y$, respectively. So-called a group of fuzzy inference rules,

$$A_i \to B_i, \quad i = 0, 1, \cdots, n,$$

is actually a transformation from a subset $\mathcal{A}$ of the normed linear space $\overline{\mathbb{R}}^X$ to a subset $\mathcal{B}$ of the normed linear space $\overline{\mathbb{R}}^Y$, denoted by T_{n+1}, i.e.

$$T_{n+1} : \mathcal{A} \to \mathcal{B}, \quad A_i \mapsto T_{n+1}(A_i) \triangleq B_i, \qquad (7.5.1)$$
$$i = 0, 1, \cdots, n$$

Whether can this transformation be expanded as a kind of transformation from the normed linear space $\overline{\mathbb{R}}^X$ to the normed linear space $\overline{\mathbb{R}}^Y$? If it can, then the transformation is denoted by the following mapping:

$$T:\overline{\mathbb{R}}^X \to \overline{\mathbb{R}}^Y, \quad A \mapsto B \triangleq T(A).$$

In fact this thing has already almost been done (see Equation (7.4.8)), i.e., $T = \circ$. However T is not a linear transformation but a nonlinear transformation. In other words, T is not a bounded linear operator from the normed linear space $\left(\overline{\mathbb{R}}^X, \|\cdot\|_X\right)$ to the normed linear space $\left(\overline{\mathbb{R}}^Y, \|\cdot\|_Y\right)$. Moreover, the transformation as Equation (7.4.8) has a bad property, that is, $T\big|_{\mathcal{A}} \neq T_{n+1}$, or T does not hold the following condition:

$$(\forall i \in \{0,1,\cdots,n\})\left(T\left(A_i\right) = B_i\right).$$

But this does not retard us to use the norms. As a matter of fact, although $T\left(A_i\right) \neq B_i$, the difference $\left\|T\left(A_i\right) - B_i\right\|_Y$ does describe the degree for $T\left(A_i\right)$ approximating B_i, which means the transformation as Equation (7.4.8) is not an interpolation operator but is a fitted operator in accordance with Equation (7.5.1).

In section 7.5, we have denoted $X = [a,b]$ and $Y = [c,d]$. that represent the input-output connection of the uncertain system shown as Figure 7.1.1 to be a function, as the following:

$$s:[a,b] \to [c,d], \ x \mapsto s(x).$$

In fact, $s(x)$ is usually a continuous function, i.e., $s \in C[a,b]$. So we take account of our problems in the space $C[a,b]$. Firstly, $\forall s \in C[a,b]$, a norm in $C[a,b]$ is defined as follows:

$$\|s\|_\infty \triangleq \max\left\{s(x) \mid x \in [a,b]\right\}.$$

Reviewing the group of fuzzy inference rules as Expression (7.1.2), when A_i and B_i are all normal fuzzy sets which mean, $\exists x_i \in X$ and $\exists y_i \in Y$, such that $A\left(x_i\right) = 1$ and $B\left(y_i\right) = 1$, this shows us to know that, designing a group of fuzzy inference rules as Equation (7.1.2) and obtaining a group of input-output data as being the following set:

$$\mathrm{IOD} = \{(x_i, y_i) | i = 0, 1, \cdots, n\}$$

is almost a same thing, where this group of data should satisfy the following interpolation condition:

$$(\forall i \in \{0, 1, \cdots, n\})(y_i = s(x_i)). \tag{7.5.2}$$

So we can know that theorem 7.4.1 means the following equation:

$$s(x) \approx \underline{s}(x) \approx F_{n+1}(x) = \sum_{i=0}^{n} A_i(x) y_i = \sum_{i=0}^{n} A_i(x) s(x_i)$$

and we are able to get a bounded linear operator from $(C[a,b], \|\cdot\|_\infty)$ to $(C[a,b], \|\cdot\|_\infty)$ as the following:

$$\begin{aligned} &L_{n+1} : C[a,b] \to C[a,b],\, s \mapsto L_{n+1}(s), \\ &L_{n+1}(s)(x) \triangleq F_{n+1}(x) = \sum_{i=0}^{n} A_i(x) s(x_i). \end{aligned} \tag{7.5.3}$$

Based on this operator, a sort of numerical characters of the fuzzy systems shown in Theorem 1 can be described by the normal number of the operator as $\|L_{n+1}\|$, called by us Normal Numbers of fuzzy systems.

Proposition 7.5.1 If the bounded fuzzy sets as the antecedents of fuzzy inference rules are $A_i \in C[a,b], i = 0, 1, \cdots, n$, then the normal number of the fuzzy system is the following:

$$\|L_{n+1}\| = \max_{x \in [a,b]} \sum_{i=0}^{n} |A_i(x)|. \tag{7.5.4}$$

Proof. Let $M = \max_{x \in [a,b]} \sum_{i=0}^{n} |A_i(x)|$. One side we have the following inequality:

$$\|L_{n+1}(s)\|_\infty \le \max_{x\in[a,b]}\sum_{i=0}^{n}\left|A_i(x)s(x_i)\right| \le \|s\|_\infty \max_{x\in[a,b]}\sum_{i=0}^{n}|A_i(x)| = M\|s\|_\infty .$$

So we get the following inequality:

$$\|L_{n+1}\| = \sup_{\|s\|_\infty\le 1}\|L_{n+1}(s)\|_\infty \le M .$$

On the other side, as $\sum_{i=0}^{n}|A_i(x)| \in C[a,b]$, there must exist a $x_0 \in [a,b]$ such that

$$\sum_{i=0}^{n}\left|A_i(x_0)\right| = M .$$

Choosing a $s_0 \in C[a,b]$ such that $\|s_0\|_\infty = 1$ and

$$(\forall i \in \{0,1,\cdots,n\})\left(s_0(x_i) = \operatorname{sgn} A_i(x_i)\right),$$

i.e., $|s_0(x)| \le 1$, we have the following expression:

$$\begin{aligned}\|L_{n+1}\| &= \sup_{\|s\|_\infty=1}\|L_{n+1}(s)\|_\infty \ge \|L_{n+1}(s_0)\|_\infty \\ &= \sup_{x\in[a,b]}\left|L_{n+1}(s_0)(x)\right| \ge \left|L_{n+1}(s_0)(x_0)\right| \\ &= \left|\sum_{i=0}^{n}A_i(x_0)\operatorname{sgn} A_i(x_i)\right| = \sum_{i=0}^{n}\left|A_i(x_0)\right| = M,\end{aligned}$$

Therefore, we get $\|L_{n+1}\| = \max_{x\in[a,b]}\sum_{i=0}^{n}|A_i(x)|$. □

Remark 7.5.1 This means $\|L_{n+1}\| = \max_{x\in[a,b]}\sum_{i=0}^{n}|A_i(x)|$ is a center invariant, which its quantity is sometimes only depending on the partitions on the input universe X . □

Example 7.5.1 When the bounded fuzzy sets $A_i (i = 0,1,\cdots,n)$ as the antecedents of fuzzy inference rules are taken as the triangle wave fuzzy sets (see Example 7.4.2), the normal number of the fuzzy system has a unit quantity:

$$\|L_{n+1}\| = \max_{x\in[a,b]} \sum_{i=0}^{n} |A_i(x)| = \max_{x\in[a,b]} \sum_{i=0}^{n} A_i(x) = 1. \qquad (7.5.5)$$

In what follows, a fuzzy system having the normal number with a unit quantity is called a Normal Fuzzy System. □

Example 7.5.2 When the bounded fuzzy sets $A_i (i = 0,1,\cdots,n)$ as the antecedents of fuzzy inference rules are taken as Lagrange basis functions as the following (see Example 7.4.1):

$$A_i(x) = \prod_{\substack{j=0 \\ j\neq i}}^{n} \frac{x - x_j}{x_i - x_j}, \quad i = 0,1,\cdots,n,$$

the normal number of the fuzzy system has the following inequality (see [3]):

$$\|L_{n+1}\| = \max_{x\in[a,b]} \sum_{i=0}^{n} |A_i(x)| > \frac{2}{\pi}\ln(n+1) + 0.5212$$

Clearly $\lim_{n\to\infty} \|L_{n+1}\| = +\infty$. This means Lagrange fuzzy systems are not the normal fuzzy systems.

For general cases, we define that, when the bounded linear operator L_{n+1} in Equation (7.5.4) is uniformly bounded, i.e.,

$$(\exists M > 0)\left(\sup\{\|L_{n+1}\| \mid n = 0,1,\cdots\} < M\right)$$

the corresponding fuzzy systems are called Regular Fuzzy Systems, or else called Singular Fuzzy Systems. Apparently, the normal fuzzy systems must be the regular fuzzy systems. Therefore, Lagrange fuzzy systems are not the regular fuzzy systems but the singular fuzzy systems. □

Remark 7.5.2 For the bounded linear operator as the follows:

$$L_{n+1} \in C[a,b]^{C[a,b]}$$

i.e., $L_{n+1} \in B(C[a,b], C[a,b])$ as Equation (7.5.4), if it holds the following condition: for any a function $s \in C[a,b]$,

$$(\exists M_s > 0)\left(\sup\left\{\|L_{n+1}(s)\|_\infty \middle| n = 0,1,\cdots\right\} < M_s\right),$$

then the linear operator L_{n+1} is called pointwise bounded. Because the function space $C[a,b]$ is a Banach space, by utilizing Resonance Theorem in functional analysis (see [6]): if a bounded linear operator L_{n+1} is pointwise bounded, then L_{n+1} must be uniformly bounded. Thus, the bounded linear operator L_{n+1} in Lagrange fuzzy systems is not point-wise bounded, which means the following expression:

$$(\exists s \in C[a,b])\left(\sup\left\{\|L_{n+1}(s)\|_\infty \middle| n = 0,1,\cdots\right\} = +\infty\right).$$

In other words, there must exit a function $s(x)$ in $C[a,b]$ such that the sequence of functions $L_{n+1}(s)(x)$ does not converge to $s(x)$. So when using Lagrange fuzzy systems, we should firstly verify their convergence.

Actually, Runge had found the flaw as "singular" on Lagrange fuzzy systems (see [23]) and he gave a counterexample: considering a continuous function in $C[-1,1]$ as the following:

$$s(x) = \frac{1}{1+25x^2}$$

making an equidistant partition on $[-1,1]$ as follows:

$$x_i = -1 + \frac{2i}{n}, \quad i = 0,1,\cdots,n$$

straightaway from numerical values we are able to learn that v does not converge to $s(x)$. For example, when $n=10$, it is not difficult to calculate the following values:

$$L_{n+1}(s)(-0.96)=L_{11}(s)(-0.96)\approx 1.80438,$$
$$s(-0.96)\approx 0.04160$$

We are able to see how big the difference between them in a neighborhood at an endpoint.

Similarly, the difference between $L_{11}(s)(0.96)$ and $s(0.96)$ is also big, in a neighborhood at another endpoint. If the counterexample given by Runge showed us a kind of no convergence of the interpolation function only at endpoints, then ones must ask such a question: whether can we really find a continuous function $s\in C[a,b]$ such that $L_{n+1}(s)(x)$ does not converge to $s(x)$ a. e. in $[a,b]$?

In fact, in [23], Bernstein for this thing had given a theorem: for the continuous function $s(x)=|x|\in C[-1,1]$, by making an equidistant partition on $[-1,1]$ as follows:

$$x_i=-1+\frac{2i}{n},\quad i=0,1,\cdots,n,$$

$L_{n+1}(s)(x)$ does not converge to $s(x)=|x|$ at any point in $[-1,1]$ except the three points: $x=-1,0,1$, with $n\to\infty$. □

Example 7.5.3 When the bounded fuzzy sets $A_i(i=0,1,\cdots,n)$ as the antecedents of fuzzy inference rules are taken as Bernstein polynomial basis functions as follows:

$$A_i(x)=C_n^i\left(\frac{x-a}{b-a}\right)^i\left(\frac{b-x}{b-a}\right)^{n-i},\quad i=0,1,\cdots,n,$$

or $A_i(x)=C_n^i(x)^i(1-x)^{n-i}, i=0,1,\cdots,n$ (see Example 7.4.1), the normal number of the fuzzy system has a unit quantity:

$$\|L_{n+1}\| = \max_{x\in[a,b]} \sum_{i=0}^{n} |A_i(x)| = \max_{x\in[a,b]} \sum_{i=0}^{n} A_i(x) = 1$$

So Bernstein fuzzy systems are the normal fuzzy systems. □

Remark 7.5.3 It is easy to know that $\{A_0, A_1, \cdots, A_n\}$ from Example 7.4.1 to Example 7.4.3, is a group of $n+1$ linearly independent functions in $C[a,b]$, and then a $n+1$ dimensional linear subspace of $C[a,b]$ as the following:

$$\text{span}\{A_0, A_1, \cdots, A_n\} \subset C[a,b],$$

can be generated by $\{A_0, A_1, \cdots, A_n\}$ as base functions of the linear subspace. This means, for an uncertain system, $s: X \to Y$, where the universes $X = [a,b] \subset \mathbb{R}$ and $Y = [c,d] \subset \mathbb{R}$, $s(x)$ is an undetermined input-output connection in which $s(x)$ is requested to be a continuous function, i.e., $s \in C[a,b]$.

However, we only know a group of the input-output experiment data as $\text{IOD} = \{(x_i, y_i) | i = 0, 1, \cdots, n\}$ holding the interpolation condition as Equation (7.5.2) as follows:

$$(\forall i \in \{0,1,\cdots,n\})(y_i = s(x_i)).$$

From this group of basic data we can generate a group of fuzzy inference rules (also can see Equations (7.1.2) or (7.4.2)):

$$A_i \to B_i,\ i = 0,1,\cdots,n, \tag{7.5.6}$$

where $A_i (i = 0,1,\cdots,n)$ are able to be the triangle wave fuzzy sets required of holding the double-phase property as the following:

$$(\forall x \in X)(\exists i \in \{0,1,\cdots,n-1\})(A_i(x) + A_{i+1}(x) = 1)$$

or Lagrange base functions or Bernstein base functions, which are the bounded fuzzy sets and just forming the base functions of the function space: $\text{span}\{A_0, A_1, \cdots, A_n\}$, and the fuzzy sets B_i $(i = 0,1,\cdots,n)$ are shown as Figure 7.4.1. By function approximation theory (for example, see [3,23]), we know that, arbitrarily given $s \in C[a,b]$, for any $\varepsilon > 0$, there exists a group of fuzzy inference rules as Equation (7.5.6), that is equivalent to a group of input-output data as follows:

$$\text{IOD} = \{(x_i, y_i) | i = 0,1,\cdots,n\},$$

required of holding Equation (7.5.3), such that $\|L_{n+1}(s) - s\|_\infty < \varepsilon$. By noticing the fact that

$$L_{n+1}(s) \in \text{span}\{A_0, A_1, \cdots, A_n\},$$

we know that, for any function $f(x)$ in the infinite dimensional function space $C[a,b]$, we are able to use a function in the finite dimensional function space as the following:

$$\text{span}\{A_0, A_1, \cdots, A_n\}$$

to approximate it. This makes a part of fuzzy system analysis are able to be framed into the approximation theory of functions. □

7.6 Bernstein Fuzzy Systems

We have introduced Bernstein fuzzy systems in Example 7.4.3, and now we begin to discuss universal approximation of such fuzzy systems. The single input and single output open loop uncertain system shown as Figure 7.1.1 is still considered, here supposing that $X = [a,b] \subset \mathbb{R}$ and $Y = [c,d] \subset \mathbb{R}$, in which we are able to assume that $a = 0$ and $b = 1$, or else, we are able to make a kind of change of variable as $u = \dfrac{x-a}{b-a}$, then $u \in [0,1]$. Therefore, we regarded the input-output connection of the system $s: X \to Y$ as $s \in C[0,1]$. Assume that, for the information of $s(x)$, we only learn a group of the input-output data as the following:

$$\text{IOD} = \{(x_i, y_i) | i = 0, 1, \cdots, n\}$$

holding the condition:

$$0 = x_0 < x_1 < \cdots < x_n = 1,$$
$$(\forall\, i \in \{0, 1, \cdots, n\})(y_i = s(x_i)).$$

The bounded fuzzy sets $A_i \in BF(X)\ (i = 0, 1, \cdots n)$ as the antecedents of fuzzy inference are taken as the following:

$$A_i(x) = C_n^i x^i (1-x)^{n-i}, \quad i = 0, 1, \cdots, n\ . \tag{7.6.1}$$

Clearly $\{A_0, A_1, \cdots, A_n\}$ is a group of linearly independent functions in the function space $C[0,1]$ and easy to know it holding the normalizing condition: $\sum_{i=0}^{n} A_i(x) \equiv 1$. The bounded fuzzy sets $B_i\ (i = 0, 1, \cdots, n)$ as the consequents of fuzzy inference rules are still taken as equation (7.6.1). Thus we get a group of fuzzy inference rules:

$$A_i \to B_i, \ i = 0, 1, \cdots, n.$$

From the group of fuzzy inference rules, by means of CRI method, a fuzzy system $\underline{s}$ can be constructed to approximately be a Generalized Bernstein Polynomial as the following

$$\begin{aligned} s(x) &\approx \underline{s}(x) \approx \overline{B}_n(s; x) \\ &\triangleq \sum_{i=0}^{n} A_i(x) y_i = \sum_{i=0}^{n} s(x_i) C_n^i x^i (1-x)^{n-i} \end{aligned} \tag{7.6.2}$$

This is a particular example of Example 7.4.2. It is well-known that a Bernstein polynomial is a polynomial as follows:

$$B_n(s;x) \triangleq \sum_{i=0}^{n} s\left(\frac{i}{n}\right) C_n^i x^i (1-x)^{n-i} . \qquad (7.6.3)$$

Be careful, in a Bernstein polynomial, the partition on $X=[0,1]$ is equidistant as

$$x_i = \frac{i}{n}, \quad i = 0,1,\cdots,n;$$

but in a generalized Bernstein polynomial $\overline{B}_n(s;x)$, the partition on the interval $X=[0,1]$ is unnecessarily equidistant (see x_i in $s(x_i)$ in equation (7.6.2)). Bernstein polynomial $B_n(s;x)$ had been ever used to prove Weierstrass First Approximation Theorem, which means $B_n(s;x)$ can uniformly converge to $s(x)$ on $[0,1]$, i.e.,

$$\lim_{n\to\infty} \left\| s - B_n(s) \right\|_\infty = 0 .$$

However we have such a question: whether can a generalized Bernstein polynomial $\overline{B}_n(s;x)$ uniformly converge to $s(x)$ on $[0,1]$, too?

The answer should be not. Now we concern with under some condition to prove the proposition: $\lim\limits_{n\to\infty} \left\| s - \overline{B}_n(s) \right\|_\infty = 0$.

How to give a right condition to make $\lim\limits_{n\to\infty} \left\| s - \overline{B}_n(s) \right\|_\infty = 0$ to be true?

We think that, when we make a non-equidistant partition, the making cannot be too arbitrary and it should comply with some rule. What kind of rule? The rule should be that a non-equidistant partition must have some relationship with an equidistant partition. We deem that, considering the relationship between the non-equidistant partition points as being x_i $(i=0,1,\cdots,n)$ and the equidistant partition points $\frac{i}{n}(i=0,1,\cdots,n)$, $\max\limits_i \left| x_i - \frac{i}{n} \right|$ should not be over some proportion of $\frac{1}{n}$ that is the measure of every subinterval for an equidistant partition; so the expression is the following:

$$\max_i \left| x_i - \frac{i}{n} \right| \le \rho \cdot \frac{1}{n}, \quad 0 < \rho \in \mathbb{R}.$$

Let $B[0,1]$ be the set of all bounded functions defined on $[0,1]$. We firstly in $B[0,1]$ take account of the convergence of generalized Bernstein polynomials $\overline{B}_n(s;x)$.

Theorem 7.6.1 Let $s \in B[0,1]$ and that $x \in [0,1]$ be any continuous point of $s(x)$. For any given real number $\rho > 0$, if a partition on $[0,1]$, as being $0 = x_0 < x_1 < \cdots < x_n = 1$, satisfies the condition:

$$\max_i \left| x_i - \frac{i}{n} \right| \le \frac{\rho}{n},$$

then $n-$th $(n \ge 1)$ generalized Bernstein polynomial $\overline{B}_n(s;x)$ converges to $s(x)$, i.e.,

$$\lim_{n\to\infty} \overline{B}_n(s;x) = s(x). \tag{7.6.4}$$

Proof. **Step 1**. We firstly prove a useful inequality: for any $\delta > 0$, and for any a point $x \in [0,1]$, we have the following inequality:

$$\sum_{|x_i - x| \ge \delta} C_n^i x^i (1-x)^i \le \frac{4\rho^2 + n}{2n^2\delta}, \tag{7.6.5}$$

where $\sum\limits_{|x_i - x| \ge \delta}$ means to do sum for all i that hold $|x_i - x| \ge \delta$. In fact, as $|x_i - x| \ge \delta$, we know that $\frac{1}{\delta^2}(x_i - x)^2 \ge 1$. Thus

$$\sum_{|x_i-x|\ge\delta} C_n^i x^i (1-x)^{n-i} \le \sum_{|x_i-x|\ge\delta} \frac{1}{\delta^2}(x_i-x)^2 C_n^i x^i (1-x)^{n-i}$$

$$=\frac{1}{n^2\delta^2}\sum_{|x_i-x|\ge\delta}(nx_i-nx)^2 C_n^i x^i (1-x)^{n-i}$$

$$\le\frac{1}{n^2\delta^2}\sum_{|x_i-x|\ge\delta}\left(|nx_i-i|+|i-nx|\right)^2 C_n^i x^i (1-x)^{n-i}$$

$$\le\frac{2}{n^2\delta^2}\sum_{|x_i-x|\ge\delta}\left[(nx_i-i)^2+(i-nx)^2\right] C_n^i x^i (1-x)^{n-i}$$

$$=\frac{2}{n^2\delta^2}\sum_{|x_i-x|\ge\delta}(nx_i-i)^2 C_n^i x^i (1-x)^{n-i}$$

$$+\frac{2}{n^2\delta^2}\sum_{|x_i-x|\ge\delta}(i-nx)^2 C_n^i x^i (1-x)^{n-i}$$

For convenience, we use the following two symbols:

$$\mathrm{I} \triangleq \frac{2}{n^2\delta^2}\sum_{|x_i-x|\ge\delta}(nx_i-i)^2 C_n^i x^i (1-x)^{n-i},$$

$$\mathrm{II} \triangleq \frac{2}{n^2\delta^2}\sum_{|x_i-x|\ge\delta}(i-nx)^2 C_n^i x^i (1-x)^{n-i}$$

And it is not difficult to prove the identity:

$$\sum_{i=0}^{n}(i-nx)^2 C_n^i x^i (1-x)^{n-i} \equiv nx(1-x).$$

Now by using our condition: $\max_i \left|x_i - \frac{i}{n}\right| \le \frac{\rho}{n}$, we can know the fact that $(nx_i-i)^2 \le \rho^2$, and then we have the following results:

$$\mathrm{I} \leq \frac{2\rho^2}{n^2\delta^2} \sum_{|x_i - x| \geq \delta} C_n^i x^i (1-x)^{n-i} \leq \frac{2\rho^2}{n^2\delta^2} \sum_{i=0}^{n} C_n^i x^i (1-x)^{n-i} = \frac{2\rho^2}{n^2\delta^2},$$

$$\mathrm{II} \leq \frac{2}{n^2\delta^2} \sum_{i=0}^{n} (i - nx)^2 C_n^i x^i (1-x)^{n-i} \leq \frac{2}{n^2\delta^2} nx(1-x) \leq \frac{n}{2n^2\delta^2},$$

$$\mathrm{I} + \mathrm{II} \leq \frac{2\rho^2}{n^2\delta^2} + \frac{n}{2n^2\delta^2} = \frac{4\rho^2 + n}{2n^2\delta^2}.$$

From these we know that Equation (7.6.5) is true.

Step 2. We prove that Equation (7.6.4) is also true. Actually, as that $s \in B[0,1]$ means s being bounded on $[0,1]$, we have the fact that

$$(\exists M > 0)(\forall x \in [0,1])(|s(x)| \leq M);$$

and since x is a continuous point of $s(x)$, we must have the result: for any $\varepsilon > 0$, $\exists \delta > 0$, such that

$$(\forall x' \in [0,1])\left(|x - x'| \leq \delta \Rightarrow |s(x) - s(x')| < \varepsilon/2\right).$$

Besides by the limitation $\lim\limits_{n\to\infty} \frac{4\rho^2 + n}{2n^2\delta^2} = 0$, for above ε, there exists a number $N \in \mathbb{N}_+$ ($\mathbb{N}_+$ is the set of all natural numbers), such that

$$(\forall n \in \mathbb{N}_+)\left(n \geq N \Rightarrow \frac{4\rho^2 + n}{2n^2\delta^2} < \frac{\varepsilon}{4M}\right)$$

Thus, $\forall n \geq N$, we have the following result:

$$\left|s(x)-\overline{B}_n(s;x)\right| = \left|s(x)\sum_{i=0}^{n} C_n^i x^i (1-x)^{n-i} - \sum_{i=0}^{n} s(x_i) C_n^i x^i (1-x)^{n-i}\right|$$
$$\leq \sum_{i=0}^{n} \left|s(x)-s(x_i)\right| C_n^i x^i (1-x)^{n-i}$$
$$= \sum_{|x_i-x|\geq\delta} \left|s(x)-s(x_i)\right| C_n^i x^i (1-x)^{n-i} + \sum_{|x_i-x|<\delta} \left|s(x)-s(x_i)\right| C_n^i x^i (1-x)^{n-i}$$
$$\leq 2M \sum_{|x_i-x|\geq\delta} C_n^i x^i (1-x)^{n-i} + \frac{\varepsilon}{2} \sum_{|x_i-x|<\delta} C_n^i x^i (1-x)^{n-i} < 2M \frac{\varepsilon}{4M} + \frac{\varepsilon}{2} = \varepsilon$$

This means that $\lim_{n\to\infty} \overline{B}_n(s;x) = s(x)$. □

Theorem 7.6.2 Let $s \in C[0,1]$. For any real number $\rho > 0$, if a partition on $X = [0,1]$, $0 = x_0 < x_1 < \cdots < x_n = 1$, holds the following condition:

$$\max_i \left| x_i - \frac{i}{n} \right| \leq \frac{\rho}{n},$$

then n-th $(n > 1)$ generalized Bernstein polynomial $\overline{B}_n(s;x)$ converges uniformly to $s(x)$, i.e.,

$$\lim_{n\to\infty} \left\|\overline{B}_n(s) - s\right\|_\infty = \lim_{n\to\infty} \max_{x\in[0,1]} \left|\overline{B}_n(s;x) - s(x)\right| = 0. \tag{7.6.6}$$

Proof. For any $\varepsilon > 0$, by knowing that the typical Bernstein polynomial $B_n(s;x)$ can converges uniformly to $s(x)$, there must exist a natural number $N_1 \in \mathbb{N}_+$, such that

$$(\forall n \in \mathbb{N}_+)\left(n \geq N_1 \Rightarrow \left|B_n(s;x) - s(x)\right| < \frac{\varepsilon}{2} \right).$$

Since $s(x) \in C[0,1]$, $s(x)$ must be uniformly continuous on $[0,1]$. So $\exists \delta > 0$, such that, $\forall x_1, x_2 \in [0,1]$, we have the following implication:

$$|x_1 - x_2| < \delta \Rightarrow |s(x_1) - s(x_2)| < \frac{\varepsilon}{2}.$$

By using our condition: $\max_i \left| x_i - \frac{i}{n} \right| \le \frac{\rho}{n}$, there must exist a $N_2 \ge N_1$, such that

$$(\forall n \in \mathbb{N}_+)\left(n \ge N_2 \Rightarrow \max_i \left| x_i - \frac{i}{n} \right| \le \frac{\rho}{n} < \delta \right),$$

and then

$$(\forall i \in \{0,1,\cdots,n\})\left(\left| s(x_i) - s\left(\frac{i}{n}\right) \right| < \frac{\varepsilon}{2} \right).$$

Thus

$$\begin{aligned} |\overline{B}_n(s;x) - s(x)| &\le |\overline{B}_n(s;x) - B_n(s;x)| + |B_n(s;x) - s(x)| \\ &< \sum_{i=0}^{n} \left| s(x_i) - s\left(\frac{i}{n}\right) \right| C_n^i x^i (1-x)^{n-i} + \frac{\varepsilon}{2} < \frac{\varepsilon}{2} + \frac{\varepsilon}{2} = \varepsilon, \end{aligned}$$

This finishes the proof of $\lim_{n\to\infty} \|\overline{B}_n(s) - s\|_\infty = 0$. □

Remark 7.6.1 We are able to give a counterexample to show that there at least exists a generalized Bernstein polynomial $\overline{B}_n(s;x)$ such that it does not converge to $s(x)$; in other words, for a generalized Bernstein polynomial $\overline{B}_n(s;x)$, there at least exists a continuous function $s \in C[0,1]$, by making a particular partition on $[0,1]$ as the following:

$$0 = x_0 < x_1 < \cdots < x_n = 1,$$

such that $\overline{B}_n(s;x)$ does not converge to $s(x)$ in $[0,1]$.

As a matter of fact, that we concern with how to choose a particular partition on $[0,1]$, as being $0 = x_0 < x_1 < \cdots < x_n = 1$, is based on such an idea: along with n increasing, breakpoints x_i $(i=0,1,\cdots,n)$ are gradually increasing and adequately moving to right end-point 1, such that $\overline{B}_n(s;x)$ holds that

$$\left(\forall x\in[0,1]\right)\left(\lim_{n\to\infty}\overline{B}_n(s;x)\to s(1)\right).$$

Please see the following example. □

Remark 7.6.2 We now give the proof of the following identity:

$$\sum_{i=0}^{n}(i-nx)^2 C_n^i x^i (1-x)^{n-i} \equiv nx(1-x)$$

We can use probability method to do it. In fact, let random variable ξ obey binomial distribution $b(n, x)$ which its distribution sequence is as the follows:

$$P(\xi=i)=C_n^i x^i(1-x)^{n-i},\quad i=0,1,\cdots,n.$$

Thus we get the equation $\sum_{i=0}^{n}P(\xi=i)=1$ which means the following equation:

$$\sum_{i=0}^{n}C_n^i x^i(1-x)^{n-i}=1.$$

It is well-known that the mathematical expectation of the distribution sequence is the form as the following:

$$E(\xi)=\sum_{i=0}^{n}iP(\xi=i)=nx,$$

i.e., being as the following equation:

$$\sum_{i=0}^{n}iC_n^i x^i(1-x)^{n-i}=nx.$$

And then by use of the variance expression of the binomial distribution as the following expression:

$$D(\xi) = E\left(\xi^2\right) - E(\xi)^2 = nx(1-x),$$

we can get the fact that $E\left(\xi^2\right) = nx(1-x) + E(\xi)^2$. In other words, this means the following equation:

$$\sum_{i=0}^{n} i^2 C_n^i x^i (1-x)^{n-i} = nx(1-x) + n^2x^2.$$

Finally, we have result as the following:

$$\begin{aligned}
&\sum_{i=0}^{n} (i-nx)^2 C_n^i x^i (1-x)^{n-i} \\
&= \sum_{i=0}^{n} i^2 C_n^i x^i (1-x)^{n-i} - \sum_{i=0}^{n} 2nixC_n^i x^i (1-x)^{n-i} \\
&\quad + \sum_{i=0}^{n} n^2x^2 C_n^i x^i (1-x)^{n-i} \\
&= nx(1-x) + n^2x^2 - 2nx \cdot nx + n^2x^2 = nx(1-x)
\end{aligned}$$

This is the end of the proof. □

Example 7.6.1 For $n \geq 2$, we should choose a partition on $[0,1]$ as the form: $0 = x_0 < x_1 < \cdots < x_n = 1$, where x_i $(i = 0,1,\cdots,n)$ are defined as the following:

$$x_i = \begin{cases} \dfrac{i}{\ln n}, & 0 \leq i \leq [\ln n]; \\ \dfrac{[\ln n]}{\ln n} + \dfrac{\ln n - [\ln n]}{\ln n} \cdot \dfrac{i - [\ln n]}{n - [\ln n]}, & [\ln n] + 1 \leq i \leq n. \end{cases}$$

Figure 7.6.1 shows the distributing cases of the two partitions on the closed interval $[0,1]$ of x_i $(i = 0,1,\cdots,n)$, when $n = 10$ and $n = 30$.

It is easy to learn such the partitions holding our idea mentioned above. Clearly, we have the following limit expression:

$$\lim_{n\to\infty}\max_{1\le i\le n}\left(x_i - x_{i-1}\right) = \lim_{n\to\infty}\frac{1}{\ln n} = 0 .$$

For any a given bounded function $s(x)$ on $[0,1]$, it is supposed that $s(x)$ holds the weak Lipschitz condition:

$$(\exists L > 0)(\forall x \in [0,1])\left(|s(1) - s(x)| \le L(1-x)\right). \tag{7.6.7}$$

By noticing fact that $\lim_{x\to 0} x^x = 1$, we should stipulate that $0^0 = 1$. Then the generalized Bernstein polynomial as follows:

$$\overline{B}_n(s;x) = \sum_{i=0}^{n} s\left(x_i\right) C_n^i x^i (1-x)^{n-i}$$

must satisfy the bounded condition: $\overline{B}_n(s;0) = s(0), \overline{B}_n(s;1) = s(1)$.

When $x \in (0,1)$, by denoting that $\hat{x} \triangleq \max\{x, 1-x\}$, we have the following inequality:

$$\left|s(1)-\overline{B}_n(s;x)\right| = \left|s(1)\sum_{i=0}^{n} C_n^i x^i (1-x)^{n-i} - \sum_{i=0}^{n} s(x_i) C_n^i x^i (1-x)^{n-i}\right|$$

$$\leq \sum_{i=0}^{n} \left|s(1)-s(x_i)\right| C_n^i x^i (1-x)^{n-i} \leq L\sum_{i=0}^{n} (1-x_i) C_n^i x^i (1-x)^{n-i}$$

$$= L\sum_{i=0}^{[\ln n]} \left(1-\frac{i}{\ln n}\right) C_n^i x^i (1-x)^{n-i} +$$

$$L\sum_{i=[\ln n]+1}^{n} \left(1-\frac{[\ln n]}{\ln n} - \frac{\ln n-[\ln n]}{\ln n}\cdot\frac{i-[\ln n]}{n-[\ln n]}\right) C_n^i x^i (1-x)^{n-i}$$

$$\leq L\sum_{i=0}^{[\ln n]} C_n^i \hat{x}^i \hat{x}^{n-i} + L\frac{\ln n-[\ln n]}{\ln n} \sum_{i=[\ln n]+1}^{n} C_n^i x^i (1-x)^{n-i}$$

$$\leq L\hat{x}^n \sum_{i=0}^{[\ln n]} C_n^i + \frac{L}{\ln n}\sum_{i=0}^{n} C_n^i x^i (1-x)^{n-i} \leq L\hat{x}^n n^{\ln n+1} + \frac{L}{\ln n},$$

$$\leq L\sum_{i=0}^{[\ln n]} C_n^i \hat{x}^i \hat{x}^{n-i} + L\frac{\ln n-[\ln n]}{\ln n} \sum_{i=[\ln n]+1}^{n} C_n^i x^i (1-x)^{n-i}$$

$$\leq L\hat{x}^n \sum_{i=0}^{[\ln n]} C_n^i + \frac{L}{\ln n}\sum_{i=0}^{n} C_n^i x^i (1-x)^{n-i} \leq L\hat{x}^n n^{\ln n+1} + \frac{L}{\ln n}$$

In above expression, we use two zooming inequalities as follows:

$$\sum_{i=0}^{[\ln n]} \left(1-\frac{i}{\ln n}\right) C_n^i x^i (1-x)^{n-i} \leq \sum_{i=0}^{[\ln n]} C_n^i x^i (1-x)^{n-i} \leq \sum_{i=0}^{[\ln n]} C_n^i \hat{x}^n,$$

$$C_n^i = \frac{n(n-1)\cdots(n-i+1)}{1\cdot 2\cdot\cdots\cdot i} \leq n(n-1)\cdots(n-i+1) \leq n^i < n^{\ln n}.$$

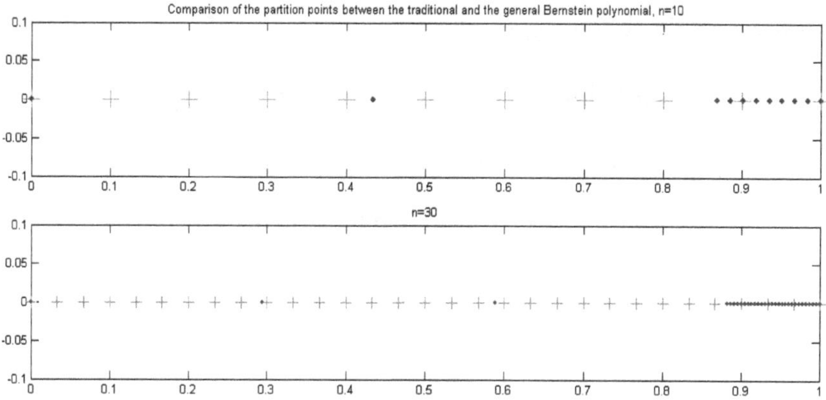

Fig. 7.6.1. The non-equidistant partitions on $[0,1]$ when $n = 10, 30$

Moreover, we need to verify a limit equation:

$$\lim_{n\to\infty} \hat{x}^n n^{\ln n+1} = 0.$$

In fact, by using in L'Hospital rule, we have the fact as the following:

$$\lim_{x\to+\infty} \frac{(\ln x+1)\ln x}{x} = 0.$$

So we have the limit expression $\lim_{n\to\infty} \frac{(\ln n+1)\ln n}{n} = 0$. Thus, there must exist a natural number $N \in \mathbb{N}_+$, such that, $\forall n > N$, the following inequality holds

$$\ln \hat{x} < \ln \hat{x} + \frac{(\ln n+1)\ln n}{n} < \frac{\ln \hat{x}}{2}.$$

Then we must have the following inequality: $\forall n > N$,

$$\exp\left(n\left(\ln \hat{x} + \frac{(\ln n+1)\ln n}{n} \right)\right) < \exp\left(\frac{n \ln \hat{x}}{2} \right).$$

Thus we get the following result:

$$\begin{aligned} 0 &\le \lim_{n\to\infty} \hat{x}^n n^{\ln n+1} = \lim_{n\to\infty} \exp\left(\ln\left(\hat{x}^n n^{\ln n+1}\right)\right) \\ &= \lim_{n\to\infty} \exp\left(n \ln \hat{x} + (\ln n+1)\ln n\right) \\ &= \lim_{n\to\infty} \exp\left(n\left(\ln \hat{x} + \frac{(\ln n+1)\ln n}{n}\right)\right) \\ &\le \lim_{n\to\infty} \exp\left(\frac{n \ln \hat{x}}{2}\right) = 0. \end{aligned}$$

So $\lim_{n\to\infty} \hat{x}^n n^{\ln n+1} = 0$, and then we have $\lim_{n\to\infty} \overline{B}_n(s;x) = s(1)$. Therefore, this kind of generalized Bernstein polynomial $\overline{B}_n(s;x)$ converges to $s(1)$ for any $x \in (0,1]$, but not $s(x)$.

By the way, we should point out that there are many bounded functions to hold the weak Lipschitz condition (7.6.7); for example, all the functions $s \in C^1[a,b]$ do hold it, for example, the well-known functions $s(x) = x$ and $s(x) = \sin x$. □

7.7 Fitted Type Fuzzy Systems

A group of fuzzy inference rules (see Equation (7.1.2) or (7.4.2) or (7.5.6)) plays a very important and basic role in modeling on uncertain systems. However, we should use flexibly the group of fuzzy inference rules. In this section, we concern with how to design the bounded fuzzy sets as the consequents of fuzzy inference rules and how to choose the weights for aggregating R_i with respect to every fuzzy inference rule to become the whole fuzzy inference relation R, such that the fuzzy system $\underline{s}$ and the approximate function $F_{n+1}(x) = \sum_{i=0}^{n} A_i(x) y_i$ for $\underline{s}(x)$ have the identical equation as follows:

$$\underline{s}(x) = F_{n+1}(x) = \sum_{i=0}^{n} A_i(x) y_i \,, \tag{7.7.1}$$

but not an approximate equation as being $\underline{s}(x) \approx F_{n+1}(x)$ (see Equation (7.4.7)). We are able to finish this intention under dealing little with the group of the breakpoints $\{y_i \,|\, i = 0,1,\cdots,n\}$ in the output universe Y.

In fact, by noticing that x^* is arbitrary in Equation (7.4.9), Equation (7.4.9) can be written as more general form as follows:

$$B(y) = \sum_{i=0}^{n} w_i A_i(x) B_i(y) \,. \tag{7.7.2}$$

For replacing Equation (7.4.1), we should expand the Zadeh fuzzy sets $\overline{B}_i (i = 0,1,\cdots,n)$ to be the bounded fuzzy sets as $B_i \ (i = 0,1,\cdots,n)$ as the following:

$$B_i(y) = \frac{\overline{B}_i(y)}{\left(\int_c^d \overline{B}_i(y)\,\mathrm{d}y\right)^2}, \quad y \in Y, \qquad i = 0,1,\cdots,n. \tag{7.7.3}$$

And the weights in Equation (7.4.1) are replaced by the following form with the integrals:

$$w_i = \frac{\int_c^d \overline{B}_i(y)\,\mathrm{d}y}{\sum_{i=0}^{n} \int_c^d \overline{B}_i(y)\,\mathrm{d}y}, \quad i = 0,1,\cdots,n. \tag{7.7.4}$$

Here the weights $w_i \ (i = 0,1,\cdots,n)$ mean that, for the consequent fuzzy sets $\overline{B}_i (i = 0,1,\cdots,n)$ of the fuzzy inference rules, the bigger is the area of $\overline{B}_i$, the bigger portion in the whole $\overline{B}_i$ occupies. Clearly this is reasonable.

By Equation (7.4.10) and the normalizing condition: $\sum_{i=0}^{n} A_i(x) \equiv 1$, we surely have the following equation:

$$y = \frac{\int_Y B(y) y \mathrm{d}y}{\int_Y B(y) \mathrm{d}y} = \frac{\int_c^d y \sum_{i=0}^{n} w_i A_i(x) B_i(y) \mathrm{d}y}{\int_c^d \sum_{i=0}^{n} w_i A_i(x) B_i(y) \mathrm{d}y}$$

$$= \frac{\sum_{i=0}^{n} A_i(x) \int_c^d \frac{1}{\int_c^d \overline{B}_i(y)\, \mathrm{d}y} \cdot \overline{B}_i(y) y \mathrm{d}y}{\sum_{i=0}^{n} A_i(x) \int_c^d \frac{1}{\int_c^d \overline{B}_i(y) \mathrm{d}y} \cdot \overline{B}_i(y)\, \mathrm{d}y}$$

$$= \sum_{i=0}^{n} A_i(x) \frac{\int_c^d \overline{B}_i(y) y \mathrm{d}y}{\int_c^d \overline{B}_i(y) \mathrm{d}y}.$$

By stipulating that $y_{-1} \triangleq y_0$, $y_{n+1} \triangleq y_n$, and calculating above definite integrals, we have the following result:

$$\overline{y}_i \triangleq \frac{\int_c^d \overline{B}_i(y) y \mathrm{d}y}{\int_c^d \overline{B}_i(y) \mathrm{d}y} = \frac{1}{3}\left(y_{i-1} + y_i + y_{i+1}\right), \tag{7.7.5}$$

$$i = 0, 1, \cdots, n$$

By denoting $F_{n+1}(x) \triangleq \sum_{i=0}^{n} A_i(x) \overline{y}_i$, we sum above result up to get a theorem as follows.

Theorem 7.7.1 Following the notations and notions mentioned above, based on the group of fuzzy inference rules as Equation (7.4.2) (or (7.1.2) or (7.5.6)), the fuzzy system obtained by using CRI method is a fitted function that its basis functions are just the bounded fuzzy sets $A_i(x)$, i.e., as the following expression:

$$\left.\begin{aligned} &\underline{s}(x) = F_{n+1}(x) \triangleq \sum_{i=0}^{n} A_i(x)\overline{y}_i, \\ &\overline{y}_i \triangleq \frac{\int_c^d \overline{B}_i(y)y\mathrm{d}y}{\int_c^d \overline{B}_i(y)\mathrm{d}y} = \frac{y_{i-1}+y_i+y_{i+1}}{3}, \\ &i = 0,1,\cdots,n, \\ &y_{-1} \triangleq y_0, \quad y_{n+1} \triangleq y_n. \end{aligned}\right\} \tag{7.7.6}$$

This sort of fuzzy systems are called Fitted Type Fuzzy System. □

Remark 7.7.1 In Equation (7.7.6), we have known the fact:

$$\overline{y}_i = \frac{y_{i-1}+y_i+y_{i+1}}{3}, \quad i = 0,1,\cdots,n,$$

which mean that y_i is the mean valve with y_{i-1} and y_{i+1}; clearly this is reasonable and of more accurate value. □

Remark 7.7.2 Under supposing the interpolation condition (7.5.3) be satisfied, by Equation (7.7.6), we are able to make a bounded linear operator $\overline{L}_{n+1}$ as follows:

$$\left.\begin{aligned} &\overline{L}_{n+1} : C[a,b] \to C[a,b],\ s \mapsto \overline{L}_{n+1}(s), \\ &\overline{L}_{n+1}(s)(x) \triangleq F_{n+1}(x) = \sum_{i=0}^{n} A_i(x)\overline{y}_i \end{aligned}\right\} \tag{7.7.7}$$

Very similar to the proof of Proposition 7.5.1, we are able to get a result on the normal numbers of the fitted type fuzzy systems as the following:

$$\left\|\overline{L}_{n+1}\right\| = \max_{x\in[a,b]} \sum_{i=0}^{n} \left|A_i(x)\right|. \qquad \square$$

7.8 Hermite Fuzzy Systems and Collocation Factor Fuzzy Systems

For improving differentiability of the fuzzy systems obtained by us, in this section, we take account of a new kind of fuzzy inference structure and the fuzzy systems generated by them. Now we turn to concern with a sort of single input double outputs open loop uncertain systems shown as Figure 7.8.1, where the input universe and the output universe are respectively as the following:

$$X=[a,b]\subset\mathbb{R},\quad Y\times Y'=[c,d]\times[c',d']\subset\mathbb{R}\times\mathbb{R}$$

From Figure 7.8.1, we are able to learn that the double outputs variables y and y' are not independent, in which first output is that $y=s(x)$ and second output is that $y'=s'(x)$ generated in essence by first output.

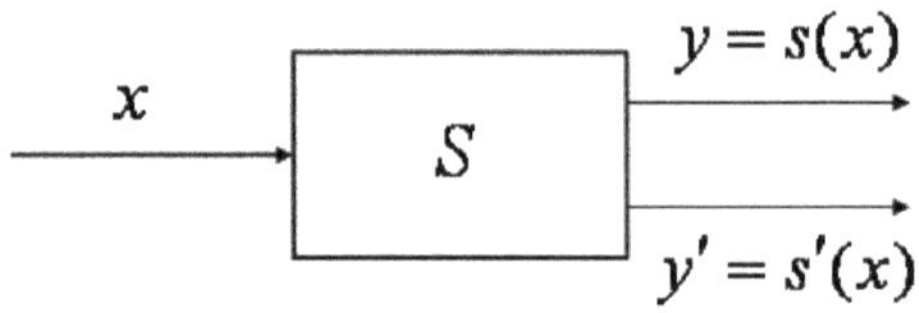

Fig. 7.8.1. Single input double outputs open loop uncertain systems

Suppose a group of the input-output data have been got by us by use of experiments as being $\{(x_i,(y_i,y'_i))\,|\,i=0,1,\cdots,n\}$, where the input data set $\{x_i\,|\,i=0,1,\cdots,n\}$ can form a partition on the input universe $X=[a,b]\subset\mathbb{R}$ as being $a=x_0<x_1<\cdots<x_n=b$, and the output data set: $\{(y_i,y'_i)\,|\,i=0,1,\cdots,n\}$ is a group of 2 dimensional vectors holding the following conditions:

1) The interpolation condition:

$$s(x_i)=y_i,\quad s'(x_i)=\left.\frac{\mathrm{d}s}{\mathrm{d}x}\right|_{x=x_i}=y'_i,\quad i=0,1,\cdots,n;$$

2) The partition condition:

$$c = y_{k_0} < y_{k_1} < \cdots < y_{k_n} = d, \quad c' = y'_{p_0} < y'_{p_1} < \cdots < y'_{p_n} = d',$$

where $k_i = \sigma(i), p_i = \tau(i), i = 0,1,\cdots,n$, and σ and τ are two permutations as the following:

$$\sigma = \begin{pmatrix} 0 & 1 & \cdots & n \\ k_0 & k_1 & \cdots & k_n \end{pmatrix}, \quad \tau = \begin{pmatrix} 0 & 1 & \cdots & n \\ p_0 & p_1 & \cdots & p_n \end{pmatrix}$$

We take account of how to construct the fuzzy inference rules for the uncertain system. Let

$$\Delta y_{k_i} = y_{k_{i+1}} - y_{k_i}, \; i = 0,1,\cdots,n-1,$$
$$\Delta y'_{p_i} = y'_{p_{i+1}} - y'_{p_i}, \; i = 0,1,\cdots,n-1,$$
$$\Delta y_{k_n} = \frac{\sum_{i=0}^{n-1} \Delta y_{k_i}}{n}, \quad \Delta y'_{p_n} = \frac{\sum_{i=0}^{n-1} \Delta y'_{p_i}}{n},$$

Firstly, the two groups of $\overline{\mathbb{R}}-$fuzzy sets as the following:

$$B_i \in \overline{\mathbb{R}}^Y, \quad \hat{B}_i \in \overline{\mathbb{R}}^Y, \quad i = 0,1,\cdots,n,$$

as the consequents of the fuzzy inference rules as follows:

$$\left.\begin{aligned} B_i(y) &= \frac{\overline{B}_i(y)}{(\Delta y_i)^2 \sum_{j=0}^{n} \Delta y'_j}, \quad i = 0,1,\cdots,n, \; y \in Y \\ \hat{B}_i(y') &= \frac{B'_i(y')}{(\Delta y'_i)^2 \sum_{j=0}^{n} \Delta y_j}, \quad i = 0,1,\cdots,n, \; y' \in Y' \end{aligned}\right\} \tag{7.8.1}$$

where the shapes of the Zadeh's fuzzy sets as being $\overline{B}_{k_i} \in \mathcal{F}(Y)$ are shown similarly in Figure 7.4.1, and the structures of the Zadeh's fuzzy sets as being $B'_{p_i} \in \mathcal{F}(Y')$ fully resemble the ones of $\overline{B}_{k_i} \in \mathcal{F}(Y)$ (still see Figure 7.4.1).

And then, we can easily make the two groups of the bounded fuzzy sets as $A_i \in BF(X)$ and $\hat{A}_i \in BF(X)$ as the antecedents of the fuzzy inference rules as the following:

$$A_0(x) = \begin{cases} \left(1 + 2\dfrac{x - x_0}{x_1 - x_0}\right)\left(\dfrac{x - x_1}{x_0 - x_1}\right)^2, & x \in [x_0, x_1]; \\ 0, & \text{otherwise}, \end{cases}$$

$$A_i(x) = \begin{cases} \left(1 + 2\dfrac{x - x_i}{x_{i-1} - x_i}\right)\left(\dfrac{x - x_{i-1}}{x_i - x_{i-1}}\right)^2, & x \in [x_{i-1}, x_i]; \\ \left(1 + 2\dfrac{x - x_i}{x_{i+1} - x_i}\right)\left(\dfrac{x_{i+1} - x}{x_{i+1} - x_i}\right)^2, & x \in [x_i, x_{i+1}]; \\ 0, & \text{otherwise}; \end{cases}$$

$$i = 1, 2, \cdots, n-1,$$

$$A_n(x) = \begin{cases} \left(1 + 2\dfrac{x_n - x}{x_n - x_{n-1}}\right)\left(\dfrac{x - x_{n-1}}{x_n - x_{n-1}}\right)^2, & x \in [x_{n-1}, x_n]; \\ 0, & \text{otherwise}. \end{cases}$$

$$\hat{A}_0(x) = \begin{cases} (x - x_0)\left(\dfrac{x - x_1}{x_0 - x_1}\right)^2, & x \in [x_0, x_1]; \\ 0, & \text{otherwise}, \end{cases}$$

$$\hat{A}_i(x) = \begin{cases} (x - x_i)\left(\dfrac{x - x_{i-1}}{x_i - x_{i-1}}\right)^2, & x \in [x_{i-1}, x_i]; \\ (x - x_i)\left(\dfrac{x_{i+1} - x}{x_{i+1} - x_i}\right)^2, & x \in [x_i, x_{i+1}]; \\ 0, & \text{otherwise}; \end{cases}$$

$$i = 1, 2, \cdots, n-1,$$

$$\hat{A}_n(x) = \begin{cases} (x - x_n)\left(\dfrac{x - x_{n-1}}{x_n - x_{n-1}}\right)^2, & x \in [x_{n-1}, x_n]; \\ 0, & \text{otherwise.} \end{cases}$$

And we write the following four $\overline{\mathbb{R}}$ – fuzzy set classes:

$$\mathcal{A} \triangleq \{A_i \mid i = 0, 1, \cdots, n\}, \quad \hat{\mathcal{A}} \triangleq \left\{\hat{A}_i \middle| i = 0, 1, \cdots, n\right\},$$

$$\mathcal{B} \triangleq \{B_i \mid i = 0, 1, \cdots, n\}, \quad \hat{\mathcal{B}} \triangleq \left\{\hat{B}_i \middle| i = 0, 1, \cdots, n\right\}.$$

It is easy to verify that the elements in $\mathcal{A}, \hat{\mathcal{A}}, \mathcal{B}, \hat{\mathcal{B}}$ satisfy the following conditions:

1) A_i and $\hat{A}_i$ hold Hermite interpolation condition:

$$A_i(x_j) = \delta_{ij}, \quad \left.\frac{\mathrm{d}A_i(x)}{\mathrm{d}x}\right|_{x=x_j} = 0;$$

$$\hat{A}_i(x_j) = 0, \quad \left.\frac{\mathrm{d}\hat{A}_i(x)}{\mathrm{d}x}\right|_{x=x_j} = \delta_{ij};$$

$$i, j = 0, 1, \cdots, n.$$

2) A_i meet the normalizing condition: $\sum_{i=0}^{n} A_i(x) \equiv 1$ and

$$A_i(x)A_j(x) \neq 0, \ \text{for } |j - i| \leq 1,$$
$$A_i(x)A_j(x) = 0, \ \text{for } |j - i| \geq 2,$$
$$i, j = 0, 1, \cdots, n$$

By use of $\mathcal{A}, \hat{\mathcal{A}}, \mathcal{B}, \hat{\mathcal{B}}$, a group of 2 dimensional vector fuzzy inference rules is able to be formed as the following:

$$\left.\begin{array}{l}\left(\mathcal{A},\hat{\mathcal{A}}\right)\to\left(\mathcal{B},\hat{\mathcal{B}}\right)\\ \left(\forall i\in\{0,1,\cdots,n\}\right)\left[\left(A_i,\hat{A}_i\right)\to\left(B_i,\hat{B}_i\right)\right]\end{array}\right\}\tag{7.8.2}$$

We feel that the vector fuzzy inference may be very interesting. Now we first give a brief out-line, and then turn to concern with the problem for 2 dimensional vector fuzzy inferences as Equation (7.8.2).

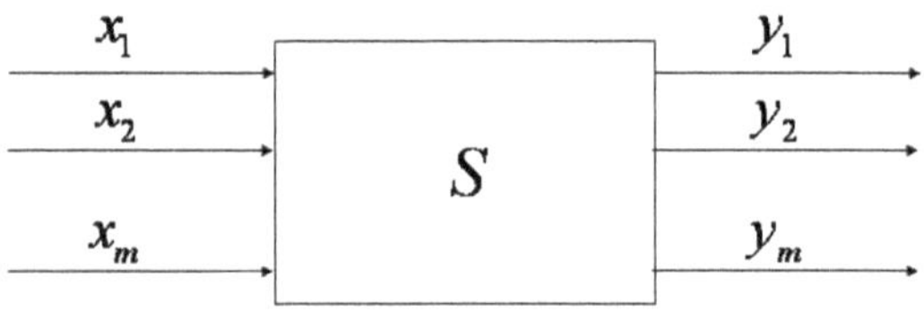

Fig. 7.8.2. Uncertain systems with m inputs and m outputs

We take account of the m dimensional vector fuzzy inference with the application back-ground shown as Figure 7.8.2 in which the input is with m variables and the output is with m variables too (More general case with p inputs and q outputs has been discussed in [10]).

Let $X_k, Y_k, k=1,2,\cdots,m$ be all nonempty universes in which the input variables $x_k (k=1,2,\cdots m)$ and $y_k (k=1,2,\cdots m)$ take their values, respectively. Given $\overline{\mathbb{R}}-$fuzzy sets as the following:

$$A_{ki}\in\overline{\mathbb{R}}^{X_k},\quad B_{ki}\in\overline{\mathbb{R}}^{Y_k},$$
$$i=0,1,\cdots,n,\ k=1,2,\cdots,m$$

they are able to form a group of m dimensional vector fuzzy inference rules as follows:

$$\left(A_{1i},A_{2i},\cdots,A_{mi}\right)\to\left(B_{1i},B_{2i},\cdots,B_{mi}\right),\quad i=0,1,\cdots,n\tag{7.8.3}$$

More essential form of Equation (7.8.3) is as follows:

$$\left.\begin{array}{l}\begin{cases}\text{If } x_1 \text{ is } A_{11} \text{ and } \cdots \text{ and } x_m \text{ is } A_{m1} \\ \text{then } y_1 \text{ is } B_{11} \text{ and } \cdots \text{ and } y_m \text{ is } B_{m1}\end{cases} \\ \begin{cases}\text{If } x_1 \text{ is } A_{12} \text{ and } \cdots \text{ and } x_m \text{ is } A_{m2} \\ \text{then } y_1 \text{ is } B_{12} \text{ and } \cdots \text{ and } y_m \text{ is } B_{m2}\end{cases} \\ \cdots\cdots \\ \begin{cases}\text{If } x_1 \text{ is } A_{1n} \text{ and } \cdots \text{ and } x_m \text{ is } A_{mn} \\ \text{then } y_1 \text{ is } B_{1n} \text{ and } \cdots \text{ and } y_m \text{ is } B_{mn}\end{cases}\end{array}\right\} \tag{7.8.4}$$

It is well-known that, after the group of fuzzy inference rules as Equation (7.8.4) is got, every $\overline{\mathbb{R}}-$fuzzy inference relations R_i, on every fuzzy inference rule, should be generated by using some $\overline{\mathbb{R}}-$fuzzy implication operator θ, that is

$$\left.\begin{array}{l} R_i = \theta\left(\left(A_{1i}, A_{2i}, \cdots, A_{mi}\right), \left(B_{1i}, B_{2i}, \cdots, B_{mi}\right)\right), \\ R_i\left(\left(x_1, x_2, \cdots, x_m\right), \left(y_1, y_2, \cdots, y_m\right)\right) \\ = \theta\left(\left(A_{1i}\left(x_1\right), \cdots, A_{mi}\left(x_m\right)\right), \left(B_{1i}\left(y_1\right), \cdots, B_{mi}\left(y_m\right)\right)\right), \\ i = 0, 1, \cdots, n. \end{array}\right\} \tag{7.8.5}$$

First Scheme: Suppose $\vec{\theta}$ be a mapping from $\overline{\mathbb{R}}^m \times \overline{\mathbb{R}}^m \to \overline{\mathbb{R}}^m$. We denote the following vector symbol:

$$\left(c_1, c_2, \cdots, c_m\right) \triangleq \vec{\theta}\left(\left(a_1, a_2, \cdots, a_m\right), \left(b_1, b_2, \cdots, b_m\right)\right)$$

Then we should concern with how to evaluate c_k $(k = 0, 1, \cdots, m)$. At first, it is easy to bethink of using some well-known $\overline{\mathbb{R}}-$fuzzy implication operator $\vec{\theta}$ to generate a vector $\overline{\mathbb{R}}-$fuzzy implication operator $\vec{\theta}$ like Hadamard product, i.e.,

$$\vec{\theta}\left(\left(a_1, \cdots, a_m\right), \left(b_1, \cdots, b_m\right)\right) \triangleq \left(\theta\left(a_1, b_1\right), \cdots, \theta\left(a_m, b_m\right)\right), \tag{7.8.6}$$

where θ is some chosen $\overline{\mathbb{R}}-$fuzzy implication operator, i.e., $\theta \in \overline{\mathbb{R}}^{\overline{\mathbb{R}} \times \overline{\mathbb{R}}}$.

When $\theta \triangleq \cdot$, that is, θ is taken as Larsen implication, Equation (7.8.6) becomes the following:

$$\vec{\theta}\left(\left(a_1,\cdots,a_m\right),\left(b_1,\cdots,b_m\right)\right)=\left(a_1\cdot b_1,\cdots,a_m\cdot b_m\right) \tag{7.8.7}$$

Here $\vec{\theta}$ is called Larsen-Hadamard Vector $\overline{\mathbb{R}}$ – fuzzy Implication Operator. When $\theta \triangleq \wedge$, that is, θ is taken as Mamdani implication, Equation (7.8.6) becomes the following:

$$\vec{\theta}\left(\left(a_1,\cdots,a_m\right),\left(b_1,\cdots,b_m\right)\right)=\left(a_1\wedge b_1,\cdots,a_m\wedge b_m\right) \tag{7.8.8}$$

Here $\vec{\theta}$ is also called Mamdani-Hadamard Vector $\overline{\mathbb{R}}$ – fuzzy Implication Operator.

Second Scheme: Suppose $\vec{\theta}$ be a mapping as the following:

$$\vec{\theta}:\overline{\mathbb{R}}^m\times\overline{\mathbb{R}}^m\to\overline{\mathbb{R}}$$
$$\left(\left(a_1,\cdots,a_m\right),\left(b_1,\cdots,b_m\right)\right)\mapsto\beta\triangleq\vec{\theta}\left(\left(a_1,\cdots,a_m\right),\left(b_1,\cdots,b_m\right)\right)$$

And then we also concern with how to evaluate. For infecting us by Larsen implication operator, we imagine that the product operation in Larsen implication operator should be expanded to be some kind of inner product operation which is not common inner product operation but a kind of Weighted Inner Product Operation as the following:

$$\begin{aligned}&\vec{\theta}\left(\left(a_1,\cdots,a_m\right),\left(b_1,\cdots,b_m\right)\right)\\&\triangleq\left(a_1,\cdots,a_m\right)*\left(b_1,\cdots,b_m\right)\triangleq\sum_{k=1}^{m}\omega_k a_k b_k,\end{aligned} \tag{7.8.9}$$

where $\omega_k\,(k=1,2,\cdots,m)$ are a group of the weights chosen by us that should meet the well-known weight condition:

$$\left.\begin{aligned}&\left(\forall k\in\{1,2,\cdots,m\}\right)\left(\omega_k>0\right),\\&\sum_{k=1}^{m}\omega_k=1\end{aligned}\right\}$$

Under first scheme, when $\theta \triangleq \cdot$, i.e., θ is taken as Larsen implication operator, Equation (7.8.4) can be implemented by the following form:

$$\begin{aligned}
&R_i\left((x_1,x_2,\cdots,x_m),(y_1,y_2,\cdots,y_m)\right)\\
&=\vec{\theta}\left(\left(A_{1i}(x_1),\cdots,A_{mi}(x_m)\right),\left(B_{1i}(y_1),\cdots,B_{mi}(y_m)\right)\right)\\
&=\left(R_{1i}(x_1,y_1),\cdots,R_{mi}(x_m,y_m)\right)\\
&=\left(A_{1i}(x_1)B_{1i}(y_1),\cdots,A_{mi}(x_m)B_{mi}(y_m)\right),\\
&i=0,1,\cdots,n;\\
&R_{ki}(x_k,y_k)\triangleq A_{ki}(x_k)B_{ki}(y_k),\quad k=1,2,\cdots,m.
\end{aligned}$$

Distinctly, $\overline{\mathbb{R}}-$fuzzy inference relations R_i $(i=0,1,\cdots,n)$ obtained by us above are all the vector forms, and in order to be simple, they are still denoted by R_i $(i=0,1,\cdots,n)$ but not by $\vec{R}_i$ $(i=0,1,\cdots,n)$. When $\theta \triangleq \wedge$, i.e., θ is taken as Mamdani implication operator, Equation (7.8.5) can be implemented by the following form:

$$\begin{aligned}
&R_i\left((x_1,x_2,\cdots,x_m),(y_1,y_2,\cdots,y_m)\right)\\
&=\vec{\theta}\left(\left(A_{1i}(x_1),\cdots,A_{mi}(x_m)\right),\left(B_{1i}(y_1),\cdots,B_{mi}(y_m)\right)\right)\\
&=\left(R_{1i}(x_1,y_1),R_{2i}(x_2,y_2),\cdots,R_{mi}(x_m,y_m)\right)\\
&=\left(A_{1i}(x_1)\wedge B_{1i}(y_1),\cdots,A_{mi}(x_m)\wedge B_{mi}(y_m)\right),
\end{aligned}$$

where

$$\begin{aligned}
&R_{ki}(x_k,y_k)\triangleq A_{ki}(x_k)\wedge B_{ki}(y_k),\\
&i=0,1,\cdots,n;\quad k=1,2,\cdots,m.
\end{aligned}$$

And then, such $\overline{\mathbb{R}}-$ fuzzy inference relations R_i $(i=0,1,\cdots,n)$ should be aggregate a whole $\overline{\mathbb{R}}-$fuzzy inference relation R. However, how to aggregate R from R_i $(i=0,1,\cdots,n)$ is a very interesting problem. Here we are using the weighted sum to implement the aggregation. For doing this, we choose a group of weight vectors as the follows:

$$W_i = (w_{1i}, w_{2i}, \cdots, w_{mi}), \quad i = 0, 1, \cdots, n,$$

that meet the following condition:

$$(\forall (k,i) \in \{1,\cdots,m\} \times \{0,\cdots,n\})(w_{ki} > 0),$$
$$(\forall k \in \{1,\cdots,m\})\left(\sum_{i=1}^{n} w_{ki} = 1\right).$$

By using this group of weight vectors W_i, and using Larsen implication operator (or Mamdani implication operator, but we usually use Larsen implication operator), and after noticing the weight vectors W_i and R_i representing inner product of vectors, we have the following result:

$$R = \sum_{i=0}^{n} W_i \cdot R_i = \sum_{i=0}^{n} (w_{1i}, \cdots, w_{mi}) \cdot (R_{1i}, \cdots, R_{mi})$$
$$= \sum_{i=0}^{n} \sum_{k=1}^{m} w_{ki} R_{ki} = \sum_{i=0}^{n} \sum_{k=1}^{m} w_{ki} A_{ki} B_{ki},$$
$$R_i = (R_{1i}, R_{2i}, \cdots, R_{mi}), \quad R_{ki} = A_{ki} B_{ki},$$
$$k = 1, 2, \cdots, m, \quad i = 0, 1, \cdots, n.$$

So we have got the following form:

$$\begin{aligned} &R((x_1, x_2, \cdots, x_m), (y_1, y_2, \cdots, y_m)) \\ &= \sum_{i=0}^{n} W_i \cdot R_i((x_1, x_2, \cdots, x_m), (y_1, y_2, \cdots, y_m)) \\ &= \sum_{i=0}^{n} (w_{1i}, \cdots, w_{mi}) \cdot (R_{1i}(x_1, y_1), \cdots, R_{mi}(x_m, y_m)) \\ &= \sum_{i=0}^{n} \sum_{k=1}^{m} w_{ki} R_{ki}(x_k, y_k) = \sum_{i=0}^{n} \sum_{k=1}^{m} w_{ki} A_{ki}(x_k) B_{ki}(y_k). \end{aligned} \tag{7.8.10}$$

Now we turn to deal with the 2 dimensional vector fuzzy inference rules as Equation (7.8.3) by use of the first scheme. At first, from Equation (7.8.10), it is easy to know the fact that

$$R_i = \left(A_i B_i, \hat{A}_i \hat{B}_i \right), \quad i = 0, 1, \cdots, n.$$

And from Equation (7.8.10), the whole $\overline{\mathbb{R}}-$ fuzzy inference relation should formally have the following form:

$$R\left(\left(x_1, x_2\right), \left(y_1, y_2\right)\right) = \sum_{i=0}^{n} W_i R_i \left(\left(x_1, x_2\right), \left(y_1, y_2\right)\right)$$
$$= \sum_{i=0}^{n} \left(w_{1i} R_{1i}\left(x_1, y_1\right) + w_{2i} R_{2i}\left(x_2, y_2\right)\right)$$
$$= \sum_{i=0}^{n} \left(w_{1i} A_{1i}\left(x_1\right) B_{2i}\left(y_1\right) + w_{2i} A_{2i}\left(x_2\right) B_{2i}\left(y_2\right)\right).$$

By noticing the following fact that

$$A_{1i}\left(x_1\right) = A_i(x), \quad A_{2i}\left(x_2\right) = \hat{A}_i(x),$$
$$B_{1i}\left(y_1\right) = B_i(y), \quad B_{2i}\left(y_2\right) = \hat{B}_i\left(y'\right),$$
$$i = 0, 1, \cdots, n,$$

especially learning that the input variables $\left(x_1, x_2\right)$ take values only in the diagonal of $\overline{\mathbb{R}} \times \overline{\mathbb{R}}$, i.e.,

$$\left(x_1, x_2\right) \in \left\{ \overline{\mathbb{R}} \times \overline{\mathbb{R}} \middle| x_1 = x_2 \right\} \subset \overline{\mathbb{R}} \times \overline{\mathbb{R}},$$

in other words, x_1 and x_2 being not independent, the whole $\overline{\mathbb{R}}-$fuzzy inference relation R should be with the following form:

$$\begin{aligned} R\left(x, \left(y, y'\right)\right) &= \sum_{i=0}^{n} W_i R_i\left(x, \left(y, y'\right)\right) \\ &= \sum_{i=0}^{n} \left(w_{1i} A_i(x) B_i(y) + w_{2i} \hat{A}_i(x) \hat{B}_i\left(y'\right)\right) \end{aligned} \tag{7.8.11}$$

At present, these weight vectors $W_i = (w_{1i}, w_{2i})$ have not been practically defined, and then we take them as the following forms:

$$w_{1i} \triangleq \frac{\Delta y_i}{\sum_{j=0}^{n} \Delta y_i}, \quad w_{2i} \triangleq \frac{\Delta y_i'}{\sum_{j=0}^{n} \Delta y_i'}, \quad i = 0, 1, \cdots, n. \tag{7.8.12}$$

Clearly they meet the condition:

$$(\forall i \in \{0,1,\cdots,n\})(\forall k \in \{1,2\})(w_{ki} > 0),$$

$$(\forall k \in \{1,2\})\left(\sum_{j=0}^{n} w_{ki} = 1\right)$$

Theorem 7.8.1 Reserving the notations and the notions defined above, based on the 2 dimensional vector fuzzy inference rules as Equation (7.8.2), by means of CRI method, a fuzzy system $\underline{s}$ obtained by us is approximately equal to a Hermite interpolation function which basis functions of it are just the bounded fuzzy sets $A_i(x)$ and $\hat{A}_i(x)$, i.e.,

$$\underline{s}(x) \approx F_{n+1}(x) \triangleq \sum_{i=0}^{n} \left(A_i(x) y_i + \hat{A}_i(x) y_i' \right). \tag{7.8.13}$$

Proof. By CRI method, from the $\overline{\mathbb{R}}-$ fuzzy inference relation (see Equation (7.8.11)), a $\overline{\mathbb{R}}-$fuzzy transformation "$\circ$" is induced as follows

$$\begin{aligned} &\circ: \overline{\mathbb{R}}^X \to \overline{\mathbb{R}}^Y \times \overline{\mathbb{R}}, \quad A \mapsto B \triangleq \circ(A) \triangleq A \circ R, \\ &B(y, y') = \bigvee_{x \in X} \left(A(x) \wedge R(x, (y, y')) \right), (y, y') \in Y \times Y' \end{aligned} \tag{7.8.14}$$

For any a point $x^* \in X$, we make a $\overline{\mathbb{R}}-$fuzzy set as the following:

$$A^*(x) \triangleq \begin{cases} M, & x = x^*; \\ m, & x \neq x^*, \end{cases}$$

where the two number M and m are defined as the following:

$$M \triangleq \sup\left\{R\left(x,\left(y,y'\right)\right)\middle|\left(x,\left(y,y'\right)\right)\in[a,b]\times\left([c,d]\times\left[c',d'\right]\right)\right\},$$

$$m \triangleq \inf\left\{R\left(x,\left(y,y'\right)\right)\middle|\left(x,\left(y,y'\right)\right)\in[a,b]\times\left([c,d]\times\left[c',d'\right]\right)\right\}.$$

And after x^* is substituted into Equation (7.8.14), a fuzzy inference result $B^* \in \overline{\mathbb{R}}^{Y}\times\overline{\mathbb{R}}^{Y'}$ is got as the following:

$$\left.\begin{aligned}
&B^*\left(y,y'\right)=\bigvee_{x\in X}\left(A^*(x)\wedge R\left(x,\left(y,y'\right)\right)\right)\\
&=R\left(x^*,\left(y,y'\right)\right)=B_1^*(y)+B_2^*\left(y'\right),\\
&B_1^*(y)\triangleq\sum_{i=0}^{n}w_{1i}A_i\left(x^*\right)B_i(y),\\
&B_2^*\left(y'\right)\triangleq\sum_{i=0}^{n}w_{2i}\hat{A}_i\left(x^*\right)\hat{B}_i\left(y'\right).
\end{aligned}\right\}\tag{7.8.16}$$

Now we take account of the method how to change the binary $\overline{\mathbb{R}}-$ fuzzy set $B^*\left(y,y'\right)$ into a corresponding point $y^*\in Y$ for $x^*\in \mathrm{X}$. If the following conditions are satisfied

$$\begin{aligned}
&\int_Y\left|yB_1^*(y)\right|\mathrm{d}y<\infty,\quad \int_{Y'}\left|y'B_2^*\left(y'\right)\right|\mathrm{d}y'<\infty,\\
&\int_Y\left|B_1^*(y)\right|\mathrm{d}y<\infty,\quad \int_{Y'}\left|B_2^*\left(y'\right)\right|\mathrm{d}y'<\infty,\\
&\int_Y B_1^*(y)\mathrm{d}y\neq 0,\quad \int_{Y'} B_2^*\left(y'\right)\mathrm{d}y'\neq 0,
\end{aligned}$$

then we write the following symbols:

$$y_1^*\triangleq\frac{\int_Y yB_1^*(y)\mathrm{d}y}{\int_Y B_1^*(y)\mathrm{d}y},\quad y_2^*\triangleq\frac{\int_{Y'} y'B_2^*\left(y'\right)\mathrm{d}y'}{\int_{Y'} B_2^*\left(y'\right)\mathrm{d}y'}$$

And now we are going to use the weighted sum to determine the following equations:

$$y^* = \lambda_1 y_1^* + \lambda_2 y_2^*,$$

$$\lambda_1 \triangleq \frac{\int_Y B_1^*(y)\mathrm{d}y}{\int_Y B_1^*(y)\mathrm{d}y + \int_{Y'} B_2^*(y')\,\mathrm{d}y'},$$

$$\lambda_2 \triangleq \frac{\int_{Y'} B_2^*(y')\,\mathrm{d}y'}{\int_Y B_1^*(y)\mathrm{d}y + \int_{Y'} B_2^*(y')\,\mathrm{d}y'}.$$

Then, it is easy to know that $\lambda_1 \geq 0, \lambda_2 \geq 0$ and $\lambda_1 + \lambda_2 = 1$.

Let $y^* = \lambda_1 y_1^* + \lambda_2 y_2^*$, (which is called Linearly Amalgamated Barycenter Method). Thus we have the following result:

$$y^* = \lambda_1 y_1^* + \lambda_2 y_2^* =$$

$$\frac{\int_Y y \sum_{i=0}^{n} w_{1i} A_i\left(x^*\right) B_i(y)\mathrm{d}y + \int_{Y'} y' \sum_{i=0}^{n} w_{2i} \hat{A}_i\left(x^*\right) \hat{B}_i(y')\mathrm{d}y'}{\int_Y \sum_{i=0}^{n} w_{1i} A_i\left(x^*\right) B_i(y)\mathrm{d}y + \int_{Y'} \sum_{i=0}^{n} w_{2i} \hat{A}_i\left(x^*\right) \hat{B}_i(y')\mathrm{d}y'}. \tag{7.8.16}$$

Since x^* is arbitrarily chosen in the universe X, $\left(x^*, y^*\right)$ can be generalized to be rewritten as (x, y), and $\underline{s}(x)$ is replaced by y. By noticing the fact as the following:

$$(\forall x \in X)\left(\sum_{i=0}^{n} A_i(x) = 1\right)$$

and that the define integrals in Equation (7.8.16) are replaced by Riemann sums, we have the following form:

$$\underline{s}(x) = \frac{\int_Y y \sum_{i=0}^{n} w_{1i} A_i(x) B_i(y)\mathrm{d}y + \int_{Y'} y' \sum_{i=0}^{n} w_{2i} \hat{A}_i(x) \hat{B}_i(y')\mathrm{d}y'}{\int_Y \sum_{i=0}^{n} w_{1i} A_i(x) B_i(y)\mathrm{d}y + \int_{Y'} \sum_{i=0}^{n} w_{2i} \hat{A}_i(x) \hat{B}_i(y')\mathrm{d}y'}$$

$$
= \frac{\sum_{i=0}^{n} w_{1i} A_i(x) \int_Y y B_i(y) \mathrm{d}y + \sum_{i=0}^{n} w_{2i} \hat{A}_i(x) \int_{Y'} y' \hat{B}_i(y') \mathrm{d}y'}{\sum_{i=0}^{n} w_{1i} A_i(x) \int_Y B_i(y) \mathrm{d}y + \sum_{i=0}^{n} w_{2i} \hat{A}_i(x) \int_{Y'} \hat{B}_i(y') \mathrm{d}y'}
$$

$$
= \frac{\sum_{i=0}^{n} \frac{\Delta y_i A_i(x)}{\sum_{j=0}^{n} \Delta y_j} \int_c^d \frac{y \overline{B}_i(y)}{(\Delta y_i)^2 \sum_{j=0}^{n} \Delta y'_j} \mathrm{d}y + \sum_{i=0}^{n} \frac{\Delta y'_i \hat{A}_i(x)}{\sum_{j=0}^{n} \Delta y'_j} \int_{c'}^{d'} \frac{y' B'_i(y')}{(\Delta y'_i)^2 \sum_{j=0}^{n} \Delta y_j} \mathrm{d}y'}{\sum_{i=0}^{n} \frac{\Delta y_i A_i(x)}{\sum_{j=0}^{n} \Delta y_j} \int_c^d \frac{\overline{B}_i(y)}{(\Delta y_i)^2 \sum_{j=0}^{n} \Delta y'_j} \mathrm{d}y + \sum_{i=0}^{n} \frac{\Delta y'_i \hat{A}_i(x)}{\sum_{j=0}^{n} \Delta y'_j} \int_{c'}^{d'} \frac{B'_i(y')}{(\Delta y'_i)^2 \sum_{j=0}^{n} \Delta y_j} \mathrm{d}y'}
$$

$$
\approx \frac{\sum_{i=0}^{n} \frac{\Delta y_i A_i(x)}{\sum_{j=0}^{n} \Delta y_j} \cdot \frac{y_i \overline{B}_i(y_i)}{(\Delta y_i)^2 \sum_{j=0}^{n} \Delta y'_j} \Delta y_i + \sum_{i=0}^{n} \frac{\Delta y'_i \hat{A}_i(x)}{\sum_{j=0}^{n} \Delta y'_j} \cdot \frac{y'_i B'_i(y'_i)}{(\Delta y'_i)^2 \sum_{j=0}^{n} \Delta y_j} \Delta y'}{\sum_{i=0}^{n} \frac{\Delta y_i A_i(x)}{\sum_{j=0}^{n} \Delta y_j} \cdot \frac{\overline{B}_i(y_i)}{(\Delta y_i)^2 \sum_{j=0}^{n} \Delta y'_j} \Delta y_i + \sum_{i=0}^{n} \frac{\Delta y'_i \hat{A}_i(x)}{\sum_{j=0}^{n} \Delta y'_j} \cdot \frac{B'_i(y'_i)}{(\Delta y'_i)^2 \sum_{j=0}^{n} \Delta y_j} \Delta y'}
$$

$$
= \frac{\sum_{i=0}^{n} A_i(x) y_i + \sum_{i=0}^{n} \hat{A}_i(x) y'}{\sum_{i=0}^{n} A_i(x) + \sum_{i=0}^{n} \hat{A}_i(x)} = \frac{\sum_{i=0}^{n} A_i(x) y_i + \sum_{i=0}^{n} \hat{A}_i(x) y'}{1 + \sum_{i=0}^{n} \hat{A}_i(x)}
$$

$$
= \frac{\sum_{i=0}^{n} A_i(x) y_i + \sum_{i=0}^{n} \hat{A}_i(x) y'}{1 + \alpha_{n+1}(x)} = \frac{\sum_{i=0}^{n} A_i(x) y_i + \sum_{i=0}^{n} \hat{A}_i(x) y'}{\lambda_{n+1}(x)} = \frac{F_{n+1}(x)}{\lambda_{n+1}(x)},
$$

where we have put

$$
\alpha_{n+1}(x) \triangleq \sum_{i=0}^{n} \hat{A}_i(x), \quad \lambda_{n+1}(x) \triangleq 1 + \alpha_{n+1}(x),
$$

$$
F_{n+1}(x) \triangleq \sum_{i=0}^{n} A_i(x) y_i + \sum_{i=0}^{n} \hat{A}_i(x) y'
$$

Or we have the following form:

$$\lambda_{n+1}(x)\underline{s}(x) \approx F_{n+1}(x) = \sum_{i=0}^{n} A_i(x)y_i + \sum_{i=0}^{n} \hat{A}_i(x)y' \qquad (7.8.17)$$

Now we prove that $\lim_{n\to\infty} \lambda_{n+1}(x) = 1$, and this only needs to prove the following limit expression:

$$\lim_{n\to\infty} \alpha_{n+1}(x) = 0 .$$

For doing this thing, we introduce a new notion for the universe partitions. In fact, we let

$$\begin{aligned} &h_i \triangleq x_{i+1} - x_i,\ i = 0,1,\cdots,n-1; \\ &h_n \triangleq x_{n+1} - x_n = x_n - x_n = 0; \\ &h_{-1} \triangleq x_0 - x_{-1} = x_0 - x_0 = 0; \\ &d_n \triangleq \max\{h_i \mid i = 0,1,\cdots,n\}, \end{aligned}$$

A partition as $a = x_0 < x_2 < \cdots < x_n = b$ on the universe $X = [a,b]$ is called Conforming, if it meets the condition: $\lim_{n\to\infty} d_n = 0$.

Actually, the conforming for the partitions on universes is really reasonable, so that we assume that the partitions doing by us on the input universe X are always conforming. Now we define the following symbol:

$$x_{i+\frac{1}{2}} \triangleq \frac{x_i + x_{i+1}}{2}$$

and now we take an $x \in X$ arbitrarily. Clearly, $\exists i \in \{0,1,\cdots,n-1\}$ such that $x \in [x_i, x_{i+1}]$, and it is easy to know the fact that

$$\alpha_{n+1}(x) = \sum_{i=0}^{n} \hat{A}_i(x) = -2\frac{(x-x_i)(x_{i+1}-x)\left(x-x_{i+\frac{1}{2}}\right)}{(x_{i+1}-x_i)^2}$$

By using the elementary inequality as follows:

$$\prod_{k=1}^{p} a_k \le \left(\left(\sum_{k=1}^{p} a_k\right)/p\right)^p, \quad a_k \ge 0,\ p \ge 1,\ k = 1, 2, \cdots, p$$

when the variable $x \in \left[x_i,\ x_{i+\frac{1}{2}}\right]$, the function $\alpha_{n+1}(x)$ has the following estimating expression:

$$\alpha_{n+1}(x) < \frac{1}{(x_{i+1} - x_i)^2} \cdot \left(\frac{1}{3}\left(2x - 2x_i + x_{i+1} - x + x_{i+\frac{1}{2}} - x\right)\right)^3 = \frac{h_i}{8},$$

And when $x \in \left[x_{i+\frac{1}{2}}, x_{i+1}\right]$, $-\alpha_{n+1}(x)$ is of the following estimating expression:

$$-\alpha_{n+1}(x) < \frac{1}{(x_{i+1} - x_i)^2} \cdot \left(\frac{1}{3}\left(x - x_i + 2x_{i+1} - 2x + x - x_{i+\frac{1}{2}}\right)\right)^3 = \frac{h_i}{8},$$

From above reasoning and the partition on X being conforming, we have the following result:

$$(\forall x \in X)\left(|\alpha_{n+1}(x)| \le \frac{h_i}{8} \le \frac{d_n}{8} \xrightarrow{n\to\infty} 0\right)$$

This means that $\alpha_{n+1}(x) \xrightarrow{n\to\infty} 0$ or $\lambda_{n+1}(x) \xrightarrow{n\to\infty} 1$. Therefore, Equation (7.8.17) should become the following equation:

$$\underline{s}(x) \approx F_{n+1}(x) = \sum_{i=0}^{n} A_i(x) y_i + \sum_{i=0}^{n} \hat{A}_i(x) y'. \tag{7.8.18}$$

It is well-known that $F_{n+1}(x) = \sum_{i=0}^{n} A_i(x) y_i + \sum_{i=0}^{n} \hat{A}_i(x) y'$ is just a Hermite interpolation function, where not only $F_{n+1}(x)$ converges uniformly to $\underline{s}(x)$ but also $\frac{\mathrm{d}F_{n+1}(x)}{\mathrm{d}x}$ converges uniformly to $\frac{\mathrm{d}\underline{s}(x)}{\mathrm{d}x}$. Here such $\underline{s}$ is called a Hermite Fuzzy System. □

Remark 7.8.1 Reviewing Equation (7.8.17) as the follows:

$$\lambda_{n+1}(x)\underline{s}(x) \approx F_{n+1}(x) = \sum_{i=0}^{n} A_i(x)y_i + \sum_{i=0}^{n} \hat{A}_i(x)y',$$

which makes us to discover a phenomenon: for a fuzzy system $\underline{s}$, although its input-output function $\underline{s}(x)$ is often not approximately equal to a typical interpolation function, as if the integrating factor method in differential equations, there may exists a non-zero function $\lambda_{n+1}(x)$ such that $\lambda_{n+1}(x)\underline{s}(x)$ is just approximately equal to a typical interpolation function. The fuzzy system $\underline{s}$ is called a Collocation Factor Fuzzy System. Under this significance, Hermite fuzzy systems are a kind of particular collocation factor fuzzy systems. □

Remark 7.8.2 Now we rewrite the typical triangle wave Zadeh fuzzy sets (Their shapes are very like the ones in Figure 7.4.1) in Example 7.4.2 to be $\overline{A}_i\ (i = 0, 1, \cdots, n)$ as the following:

$$\overline{A}_0(x) = \begin{cases} (x - x_i)/(x_0 - x_1), & x \in [x_0, x_1]; \\ 0, & \text{otherwise}; \end{cases}$$

$$\overline{A}_i(x) = \begin{cases} (x - x_{i-1})/(x_i - x_{i-1}), & x \in [x_{i-1}, x_i]; \\ (x - x_{i+1})/(x_i - x_{i+1}), & x \in [x_i, x_{i+1}]; \\ 0, & \text{otherwise}; \end{cases}$$

$$i = 1, 2, \cdots, n-1,$$

$$\overline{A}_n(x) = \begin{cases} (x - x_{n-1})/(x_n - x_{n-1}), & x \in [x_{n-1}, x_n]; \\ 0, & \text{otherwise} \end{cases}$$

Then the bounded fuzzy sets as the antecedents of fuzzy inference rules, $A_i(x)\ (i = 0, 1, \cdots, n)$ and $\overline{A}_i(x)\ (i = 0, 1, \cdots, n)$, are all assembled by using as the following:

$$\begin{cases} A_i(x) = 3\left(\overline{A}_i(x)\right)^2 - 2\left(\overline{A}_i(x)\right)^3, \ x \in [a,b], \\ i = 0,1,\cdots,n; \end{cases}$$

$$\begin{cases} \hat{A}_0(x) = h_0\overline{A}_1(x)\left(\overline{A}_0(x)\right)^2 \\ \qquad = h_0\left(1-\overline{A}_0(x)\right)\left(\overline{A}_0(x)\right)^2, \quad x \in [a,b] \\ \hat{A}_i(x) = \begin{cases} -h_{i-1}\overline{A}_{i-1}(x)\left(\overline{A}_i(x)\right)^2 = h_{i-1}\left(\overline{A}_i(x)-1\right)\left(\overline{A}_i(x)\right)^2, x \in [a, x_i); \\ h_i\overline{A}_{i+1}(x)\left(\overline{A}_i(x)\right)^2 = h_i\left(1-\overline{A}_i(x)\right)\left(\overline{A}_i(x)\right)^2, \quad x \in [x_i, b]; \end{cases} \\ i = 1,2\cdots,n-1; \\ \hat{A}_n(x) = -h_{n-1}\overline{A}_{n-1}(x)\left(\overline{A}_n(x)\right)^2 \\ \qquad = h_{n-1}\left(\overline{A}_n(x)-1\right)\left(\overline{A}_n(x)\right)^2, \quad x \in [a,b] \end{cases}$$

This means, in many cases, the triangle wave Zadeh's fuzzy sets are the kernels of bounded fuzzy sets, in which the kernels play roles in generating these bounded fuzzy sets. □

7.9 Normal Numbers of Hermite Fuzzy Systems

It is the time to calculate the normal numbers of Hermite fuzzy systems. At first, the norm in $\left(C^1[a,b], \ \|\cdot\|_{C^1}\right)$ is defined as the following:

$$\|s\|_{C^1} \triangleq \max\left\{|s(x)|, |s'(x)| \mid x \in [a,b]\right\}$$

Secondly, we define a bounded linear operator from $\left(C^1[a,b], \ \|\cdot\|_{C^1}\right)$ to the function space $\left(C^1[a,b], \ \|\cdot\|_{\infty}\right)$ as follows:

$$\left.\begin{aligned} &L_{n+1} : C^1[a,b] \to C^1[a,b], s \mapsto L_{n+1}(s), \\ &L_{n+1}(s)(x) \triangleq \sum_{i=0}^{n}\left(A_i(x)s\left(x_i\right) + \hat{A}_i(x)s'\left(x_i\right)\right) \end{aligned}\right\} \tag{7.9.1}$$

where

$$s(x_i) = y_i, \quad s'(x_i) = \left.\frac{\mathrm{d}s(x)}{\mathrm{d}x}\right|_{x=x_i} = y_i', \quad i = 0,1,\cdots,n.$$

Theorem 7.9.1 We still denote $d_n \triangleq \max\{h_i \mid i = 0,1,\cdots,n\}$, then the normal numbers of Hermite fuzzy systems are as the following:

$$\|L_{n+1}\| = 1 + \frac{d_n}{4}. \tag{7.9.2}$$

Proof. Firstly from the following condition which we always use:

$$(\forall x \in X)\left(A_i(x) \geq 0, \sum_{i=0}^{n} A_i(x) = 1\right),$$

we have the following inequalities:

$$\|L_{n+1}(s)\|_\infty = \max_{x\in[a,b]} |L_{n+1}(s)(x)| \leq \max_{x\in[a,b]} \sum_{i=0}^{n} \left|A_i(x)s(x_i) + \hat{A}_i(x)s'(x_i)\right|$$

$$\leq \|s\|_{C^1} \max_{x\in[a,b]} \sum_{i=0}^{n}\left(A_i(x) + \left|\hat{A}_i(x)\right|\right) = \|s\|_{C^1}\left(1 + \max_{x\in[a,b]}\sum_{i=0}^{n}\left|\hat{A}_i(x)\right|\right).$$

By the structures of the bounded fuzzy set $\hat{A}_i$ $(i = 0,1,\cdots,n)$, for arbitrarily given a point $x \in X$, there must exist a $i \in \{0,1,\cdots,n-1\}$, such that $x \in [x_i, x_{i+1}]$. Thus we have the following inequality:

$$\sum_{k=0}^{n}\left|\hat{A}_k(x)\right| = \left|\hat{A}_i(x)\right| + \left|\hat{A}_{i+1}(x)\right| = \frac{(x_{i+1} - x)(x - x_i)}{x_{i+1} - x_i}$$

$$\leq \frac{\left(\dfrac{x_{i+1} - x + x - x_i}{2}\right)^2}{x_{i+1} - x_i} = \frac{h_i}{4} \leq \frac{d_n}{4},$$

So we get that the following one side inequality:

$$\|L_{n+1}\| = \sup_{\|s\|_{C^1} \le 1} \|L_{n+1}(s)\|_\infty \le 1 + \frac{d_n}{4}.$$

On the other hand, for arbitrarily given $\varepsilon \in (0, 0.1]$, we construct a function $\tilde{s}(x)$ as follows

$$\tilde{s}(x) = \begin{cases} \exp\left[(1-\varepsilon)\left(x - x_{i_0}\right)\right] - \varepsilon, & x \in \left[a, x_{i_0}\right]; \\ \left\{ \begin{array}{l} 1 + (1-9\varepsilon)\left(\dfrac{x - x_{i_0+\frac{1}{2}}}{d_n}\right)^2 \\ -(4-20\varepsilon)\left(\dfrac{x - x_{i_0+\frac{1}{2}}}{d_n}\right)^4 \end{array} \right\}, & x \in \left(x_{i_0}, x_{i_0+1}\right); \\ \exp\left[-(1-\varepsilon)\left(x - x_{i_0+1}\right)\right] - \varepsilon, & x \in \left[x_{i_0+1}, b\right]; \end{cases}$$

where we have put the following two symbols:

$$i_0 \triangleq \min\left\{ i \in \{0, 1, \cdots, n-1\} \,\middle|\, h_i = d_n \right\},$$

$$x_{i_0+\frac{1}{2}} = \frac{x_{i_0} + x_{i_0+1}}{2}.$$

We now prove that $\tilde{s} \in C^1[a,b]$. In fact, we firstly calculate the following two one-sided limits:

$$\begin{aligned} \lim_{x \to x_{i_0}+0} \tilde{s}(x) &= 1 + (1-9\varepsilon)\left(\frac{x_{i_0} - x_{i_0+\frac{1}{2}}}{d_n}\right)^2 \\ &\quad - (4-20\varepsilon)\left(\frac{x_{i_0} - x_{i_0+\frac{1}{2}}}{d_n}\right)^4 \\ &= 1 + \frac{1-9\varepsilon}{4} - \frac{4-20\varepsilon}{16} = 1 - \varepsilon = \tilde{s}\left(x_{i_0}\right), \end{aligned}$$

$$\lim_{x\to x_{i_0+1}-0}\tilde{s}(x)=1+(1-9\varepsilon)\left(\frac{x_{i_0+1}-x_{i_0+\frac{1}{2}}}{d_n}\right)^2$$
$$-(4-20\varepsilon)\left(\frac{x_{i_0+1}-x_{i_0+\frac{1}{2}}}{d_n}\right)^4$$
$$=1+\frac{1-9\varepsilon}{4}-\frac{4-20\varepsilon}{16}=1-\varepsilon=\tilde{s}\left(x_{i_0+1}\right),$$

So we know that $\tilde{s}(x)$ is continuous in $[a,b]$. And then, by noticing the following expressions:

$$\tilde{s}'(x)=\begin{cases}(1-\varepsilon)\exp\left[(1-\varepsilon)\left(x-x_{i_0}\right)\right], & x\in\left[a,x_{i_0}\right);\\ \left.\begin{array}{l}(2-18\varepsilon)\dfrac{x-x_{i_0+\frac{1}{2}}}{d_n}\\ -(16-80\varepsilon)\left(\dfrac{x-x_{i_0+\frac{1}{2}}}{d_n}\right)^3\end{array}\right\}, & x\in\left(x_{i_0},x_{i_0+1}\right);\\ -(1-\varepsilon)\exp\left[-(1-\varepsilon)\left(x-x_{i_0+1}\right)\right], & x\in\left(x_{i_0+1},b\right];\end{cases}$$

And the calculating the following two one-sided limits:

$$\lim_{x\to x_{i_0}+0}\tilde{s}'(x)=(2-18\varepsilon)\frac{x_{i_0}-x_{i_0+\frac{1}{2}}}{d_n}-(16-80\varepsilon)\left(\frac{x_{i_0}-x_{i_0+\frac{1}{2}}}{d_n}\right)^3$$
$$=(2-18\varepsilon)\left(-\frac{1}{2}\right)-(16-80\varepsilon)\left(-\frac{1}{8}\right)=1-\varepsilon=\lim_{x\to x_{i_0}-0}\tilde{s}'(x),$$

$$\lim_{x\to x_{i_0+1}-0}\tilde{s}'(x)=(2-18\varepsilon)\frac{x_{i_0+1}-x_{i_0+\frac{1}{2}}}{d_n}-(16-80\varepsilon)\left(\frac{x_{i_0+1}-x_{i_0+\frac{1}{2}}}{d_n}\right)^3$$
$$=(2-18\varepsilon)\frac{1}{2}-(16-80\varepsilon)\frac{1}{8}=\varepsilon-1=\lim_{x\to x_{i_0+1}+0}\tilde{s}'(x),$$

we also know that $\tilde{s}(x)$ is continuous in $[a,b]$; so $\tilde{s} \in C^1[a,b]$. At last, from the expressions of $\tilde{s}(x)$ and $\tilde{s}'(x)$ in $[a,b]$, it is easy to know the following results:

$$\begin{aligned}
&\max\left\{|s(x)|,|s'(x)| \,\middle|\, x\in\left[a,x_{i_0}\right]\right\} \\
&= \max\left\{e^{(1-\varepsilon)\left(x-x_{i_0}\right)}-\varepsilon,\,(1-\varepsilon)e^{(1-\varepsilon)\left(x-x_{i_0}\right)} \,\middle|\, x\in\left[a,x_{i_0}\right]\right\} \\
&= 1-\varepsilon, \\
&\max\left\{|s(x)|,|s'(x)| \,\middle|\, x\in\left[x_{i_0+1},b\right]\right\} \\
&= \max\left\{e^{-(1-\varepsilon)\left(x-x_{i_0+1}\right)}-\varepsilon,\,(1-\varepsilon)e^{-(1-\varepsilon)\left(x-x_{i_0+1}\right)} \,\middle|\, x\in\left[x_{i_0+1},b\right]\right\} \\
&= 1-\varepsilon,
\end{aligned}$$

And when $x\in\left(x_{i_0},x_{i_0+1}\right)$, it is also easy to know the following equations:

$$|s(x)| = 1+(1-9\varepsilon)\left(\frac{x-x_{i_0+\frac{1}{2}}}{d_n}\right)^2-(4-20\varepsilon)\left(\frac{x-x_{i_0+\frac{1}{2}}}{d_n}\right)^4,$$

$$|s'(x)| = \left|(2-18\varepsilon)\frac{x-x_{i_0+\frac{1}{2}}}{d_n}-(16-80\varepsilon)\left(\frac{x-x_{i_0+\frac{1}{2}}}{d_n}\right)^3\right|,$$

Thus $\max\left\{|s(x)|,|s'(x)| \,\middle|\, x\in\left(x_{i_0},x_{i_0+1}\right)\right\}=1$. Based on above three cases, we have that $\|\tilde{s}\|_{C^1}=1$.

And then by noticing the following fact that

$$\begin{cases}
\tilde{s}\left(x_{i_0}\right)=\tilde{s}\left(x_{i_0+1}\right)=\tilde{s}'\left(x_{i_0}\right)=1-\varepsilon, \\
\tilde{s}'\left(x_{i_0+1}\right)=\varepsilon-1
\end{cases}$$

we have get the following inequality:

$$\begin{aligned}
\|L_{n+1}\| &= \sup_{\|s\|_{C^1}=1} \|L_{n+1}(s)\|_\infty \geq \|L_{n+1}(\tilde{s})\|_\infty \\
&= \max_{x\in[a,b]} |L_{n+1}(\tilde{s})(x)| \geq |L_{n+1}(\tilde{s})(x_0)| \\
&= A_{i_0}(x_0)\tilde{s}(x_{i_0}) + \hat{A}_{i_0}(x_0)\tilde{s}'(x_{i_0}) \\
&\quad + A_{i_0+1}(x_0)\tilde{s}(x_{i_0+1}) + \hat{A}_{i_0+1}(x_0)\tilde{s}'(x_{i_0+1}) \\
&= (1-\varepsilon)\left(A_{i_0}(x_0) + \hat{A}_{i_0}(x_0) + A_{i_0+1}(x_0) - \hat{A}_{i_0+1}(x_0)\right) \\
&= (1-\varepsilon)\left(1+\frac{d_n}{4}\right),
\end{aligned}$$

Because ε is arbitrary, it must be true that $\|L_{n+1}\| \geq 1+\frac{d_n}{4}$. Therefore, we have got our result:

$$\|L_{n+1}\| = 1+\frac{d_n}{4}. \qquad \square$$

We easily know that, when the partition on the universe X is conforming, the sequence of numbers $d_n \xrightarrow{n\to\infty} 0$; so d_n is bounded. Thus Hermite fuzzy systems are not the singular fuzzy systems, but the regular fuzzy systems. Although Hermite fuzzy systems are not the normal fuzzy systems, their limit systems are just the normal fuzzy systems, which is very like the effect for central limit theorem in probability theory; that is very interesting.

7.10 Weighted Fuzzy Sets

In this section, we further take account of the significance of $\overline{\mathbb{R}}-$ fuzzy sets and bounded fuzzy sets. This needs a more extensive formwork to deal with them. So we introduce a new concept of weighed fuzzy sets.

Definition 7.10.1 Given a nonempty universe X, a quaternary form as the following:

$$\left(X, A, W, W \rhd A\right)$$

is called a weighed fuzzy set, where $A \in \mathcal{F}(X)$, $W, W \rhd A \in \overline{\mathbb{R}}^X$; and $W \rhd A$ means an action of W to A, and W is called the weight function of the weighed fuzzy set. □

In order to understand weighed fuzzy sets, we first review intuitionistic fuzzy sets (see [2]). Given a nonempty universe X, an intuitionistic fuzzy set A defined on X is denoted by a ternary form as follows:

$$A = \left(X, \mu_A, \nu_A\right),$$

where $\mu_A : X \to [0,1]$, and $\nu_A : X \to [0,1]$, which satisfy the following condition:

$$\left(\forall x \in X\right)\left(\mu_A(x) + \nu_A(x) \le 1\right),$$

and where $\mu_A(x)$ means the degree of x belonging to A and $\nu_A(x)$ means the degree of x not belonging to A.

Example 7.10.1 Given an intuitionistic fuzzy set $A = \left(X, \mu_A, \nu_A\right)$ on X, take fuzzy sets $\overline{A}, W \in \mathcal{F}(X)$, which their membership functions are respectively defined as the following:

$$\overline{A}(x) \triangleq \mu_A(x), \quad W(x) \triangleq \nu_A(x).$$

The action of W to $\overline{A}$, $W \rhd \overline{A}$, is defined by the following mapping:

$$W \rhd \overline{A} : X \to \mathbb{R}$$
$$x \mapsto \left(W \rhd \overline{A}\right)(x) \triangleq 1 - \overline{A}(x) - W(x)$$

Thus it is easy to know that the quaternary $\left(X, \overline{A}, W, W \rhd \overline{A}\right)$ is just a weighed fuzzy set. □

On the contrary, we can chose two fuzzy set $B, W \in \mathcal{F}(X)$, such that W and B, and the action of W to B, $W \triangleright B$, should satisfy the following condition:

$$W \triangleright B : X \to \overline{\mathbb{R}}$$
$$x \mapsto (W \triangleright B)(x) \triangleq 1 - B(x) - W(x)$$

Such quaternary $(X, B, W, W \triangleright B)$ is of course a weighed fuzzy set. However, if $\left(\forall x \in X\right)\left((W \triangleright B)(x) \geq 0\right)$, then we should take

$$\mu_A(x) \triangleq B(x), \quad \nu_A(x) \triangleq W(x).$$

So the ternary form $A = \left(X, \mu_A, \nu_A\right)$ is just an intuitionistic fuzzy set.

Example 7.10.2 Suppose $X = [a,b] \subset \mathbb{R}$, where $a < b$ and

$$x_1, x_2 \in (a,b), \quad x_1 < x_2 .$$

We take a fuzzy $A \in \mathcal{F}(X)$ to be the following saw tooth wave fuzzy set (see Figure 7.10.1):

$$A(x) = \begin{cases} (x - x_1)/(x_2 - x_1), & x \in [x_1, x_2]; \\ 0, & x \notin [x_1, x_2], \end{cases}$$

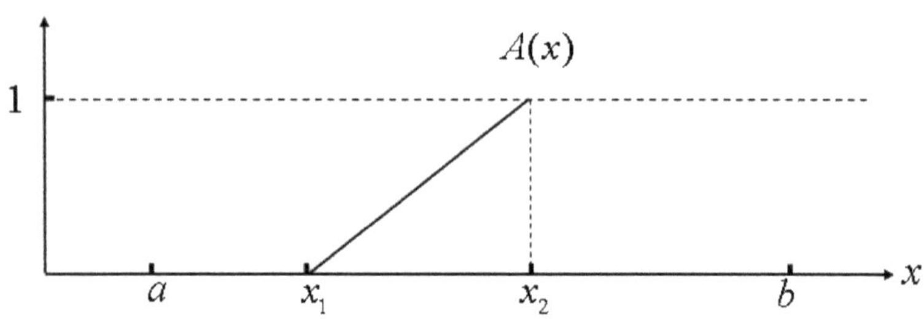

Fig. 7.10.1 Saw tooth wave fuzzy set

And we define a weight function as the following:

$$W(x) \triangleq (x - x_1)/(x_2 - x_1), \quad x \in X;$$

The action of W to A is de fined as the following:

$$(W \rhd A)(x) = \begin{cases} A(x) \vee W(x), & x \geq x_2; \\ A(x) \wedge W(x), & x < x_2. \end{cases}$$

Clearly $(X, A, W, W \rhd A)$ is a weighed fuzzy set. It is easy to learn that $W \rhd A$ is a bounded fuzzy set (see Figure 7.10.2). □

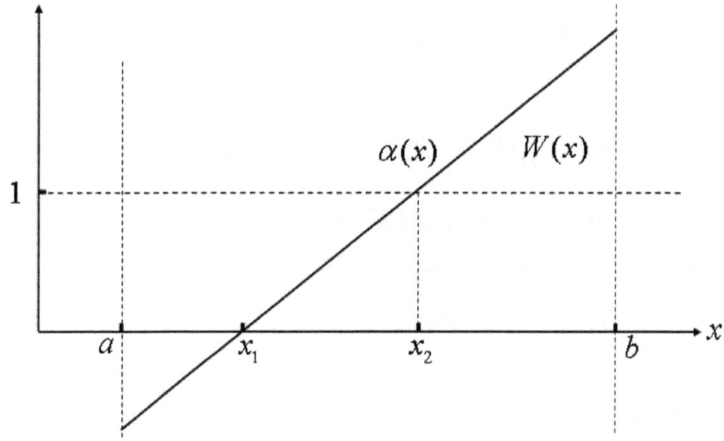

Fig. 7.10.2. A kind of weighed fuzzy sets

Example 7.10.3 Given a fuzzy set $A \in \mathcal{F}(X)$, we define a weight function as the following:

$$W : X \to \overline{\mathbb{R}}, \quad x \mapsto W(x) \triangleq c$$

where $c \in \mathbb{R}$ is a constant. And an action of W to A, $W \rhd A$, is defined as the following:

$$\left(\forall x \in X\right)\left[(W \rhd A)(x) = c \cdot A(x)\right]$$

Clearly $W \rhd A$ is a bounded fuzzy set on X, i.e., $W \rhd A \in BF(X)$. This kind of bounded fuzzy sets are of commonly use. Besides, we will learn that they can reveal the practical meanings between $\overline{\mathbb{R}}-$fuzzy sets and bounded fuzzy sets. □

Proposition 7.10.1 Given a nonempty universe X, any a bounded fuzzy set on X is always becoming a weight function of a weighed fuzzy set on X.

Proof. For any a bounded fuzzy set $B: X \to [c,d]$, we can prove our result by the following three cases.

Case 1. $d<0$. We arbitrarily take a fuzzy set $A \in \mathcal{F}(X)$, and let $W(x) = B(x)$, and an action of W to A, $W \rhd A$, is defined as the following:

$$\left(\forall x \in X\right)\left[(W \rhd A)(x) = A(x) \wedge B(x) = B(x)\right].$$

It is not difficult to verify that $(X, A, W, W \rhd A)$ is surely a weighed fuzzy set, where B is just the weight function of the bounded fuzzy set.

Case 2. $c>1$. We also arbitrarily take a fuzzy set $A \in \mathcal{F}(X)$, and we still let $W(x) = B(x)$, and an action of W to A, $W \rhd A$, is defined as the following:

$$\left(\forall x \in X\right)\left[(W \rhd A)(x) = A(x) \vee B(x) = B(x)\right],$$

Thus $(X, A, W, W \rhd A)$ is surely a weighed fuzzy set, where B is also just the weight function of the bounded fuzzy set.

Case 3. We should the situation of $[c,d] \bigcap [0,1] \neq \varnothing$. Now we write the following symbols:

$$X_1 \triangleq B^{-1}([0,1]),\ X_2 \triangleq B^{-1}\left([c,d] \bigcap (-\infty, 0)\right),$$
$$X_3 \triangleq B^{-1}\left([c,d] \bigcap (1, +\infty)\right)$$

Then we define a fuzzy set $A \in \mathcal{F}(X)$ as the form:

$$(\forall x \in X)\left(A(x) \triangleq \chi_{X_1}(x)\right).$$

And take $W(x) = B(x)$, and an action of W to A, $W \rhd A$, is defined as the following:

$$(W \rhd A)(x) = \begin{cases} A(x) \wedge B(x), & x \in X_1; \\ A(x) \wedge B(x), & x \in X_2; \\ A(x) \vee B(x), & x \in X_3. \end{cases}$$

It is clear to know that $(W \rhd A)(x) = B(x)$.

So we can know that $(X, A, W, W \rhd A)$ is also a weighed fuzzy set, where B is surely a the weight function of the weighed fuzzy set. □

Remark 7.10.1 For any a bounded fuzzy set $A \in \mathcal{F}(X)$, we also make a weighed fuzzy set $(X, A, W, W \rhd A)$ by this A, such that the A cannot weight be a function in the $(X, A, W, W \rhd A)$. Please see the following example. □

Example 7.10.4 Zadeh's fuzzy set is a bounded fuzzy set, and then it is also a weight function of some weighed fuzzy set; but the action of weight function to fuzzy set A is not unique.

As a matter of fact, given a nonempty universe X, we arbitrarily take a Zadeh's fuzzy set $A \in \mathcal{F}(X)$ and let $W(x) \equiv 1$; now we define an action of W to A, $W \rhd A$, as the following:

$$(\forall x \in X)\left[(W \rhd A)(x) \triangleq W(x) - A(x) = 1 - A(x)\right].$$

Thus $(X, A, W, W \rhd A)$ degrades into a Zadeh's fuzzy set. Here we should notice that the bounded fuzzy set A is not the weight function of the weighed fuzzy set $(X, A, W, W \rhd A)$. □

Now we want to discuss the effect of weight function $W(x)$ in weighed fuzzy set $(X, A, W, W \triangleright A)$ by means of Example 7.10.4. In fact, when $x \in [x_1, x_2]$, $A(x) = (x - x_1)/(x_2 - x_1)$; as long as x moves from x_1 to x_2, $A(x)$ goes up along the segment: $(x - x_1)/(x_2 - x_1)$. Under some cases, this kind of ascending situation will continue after $x > x_2$. So there should be a kind of weight to realize the mechanism. When x reversely moves from x_2 to x_1, $A(x)$ will appear declining situation; then after $x < x_1$, it is the same way that $A(x)$ will decline.

Generally, given a function $f : X \to \mathbb{R}$, so-called a weight action to the function f means that there exists a weight function $W : X \to \mathbb{R}$, such that we can get a weighed function $F : X \to \mathbb{R}$, by means of W, as the following:

$$F : X \to \mathbb{R}, \quad x \mapsto F(x) \triangleq W(x) \cdot f(x)$$

where the action of W to f is actually multiplication operation, i.e., $W \triangleright f \triangleq W \cdot f$. Clearly, this multiplication action can be generalized.

For example, we can use $\wedge$ operation or $\vee$ operation, and even we can partly use $\wedge, \vee$, or multiplication, etc. In fact, in example 7.10.4, we actually partly use $\wedge, \vee$, to realize the weight action of W to A.

7.11 Conclusions

Under the significance of $\overline{\mathbb{R}}-$fuzzy sets the constructions of fuzzy systems are researched and their approximation properties are discussed, in details. Our main results are as follows.

1) Based on a very extensive class of $\overline{\mathbb{R}}-$fuzzy sets, by means of CRI method, such fuzzy systems are constructed that the connection between the input and the output are just the quasi-interpolations.

2) By becomingly choosing $\overline{\mathbb{R}}-$fuzzy sets as the fuzzy inference antecedents, the piecewise linear fuzzy systems and Lagrange fuzzy systems are formed respectively.

3) Based on a very particular class of $\overline{\mathbb{R}}-$fuzzy sets, by means of CRI method, such fuzzy systems are constructed that the connection between the input and the output are just the generalized Bernstein polynomials.

4) Under a weaker condition, it is proved that the generalized Bernstein polynomials are uniformly convergent in $C[a,b]$, and a counterexample is given to show that there exist the generalized Bernstein polynomials with being not convergent in $C[a,b]$.

5) The normal numbers of fuzzy systems are defined so that they are regarded as the center invariants of fuzzy systems which can quantitatively describe fuzzy systems. Based on them, three classes of fuzzy systems are defined such as the normal fuzzy systems, the regular fuzzy systems and the singular fuzzy systems. On such significance, Lagrange fuzzy systems are the singular fuzzy systems, and Bernstein fuzzy systems are the normal fuzzy systems.

6) By becomingly choosing $\overline{\mathbb{R}}-$fuzzy sets as the fuzzy inference consequents, a class of fitted type fuzzy systems are constructed, and although they do not meet the interpolation condition, they are able to accurately approximate fuzzy systems.

7) Under supposing universe partitions be compatible, based on a class of $\overline{\mathbb{R}}-$fuzzy sets, by using CRI method, such fuzzy systems are constructed that the connection between the input and the output are just Hermite fuzzy systems and it is shown that Hermite fuzzy systems are the regular fuzzy systems.

8) Based on the process of forming Hermite fuzzy systems, the collocation factor fuzzy systems are defined, which not only improve flexibility of modeling on uncertain systems, but also expand application area for fuzzy systems.

9) When researching Hermite fuzzy systems, we find that, although they are not the normal fuzzy systems, their limit systems are just the normal fuzzy systems, which is very like the effect for the central limit theorem in probability theory.

10) It should be to say it is us who use functional analysis to describe fuzzy systems quantitatively, so that we are more profoundly able to reveal the inner mechanism of fuzzy systems. In fact, in

substance, a class of fuzzy systems is just a bounded linear operator from a Banach space to a normed linear space; it is based on such bounded linear operators that almost all fuzzy systems are classed as three classes of types such as the normal fuzzy systems, the regular fuzzy systems and the singular fuzzy systems. It is more important that, based on well-know the Resonance Theorem (or the Uniform Boundedness Principle), we are able to expediently verify the convergence of the universal approximation for fuzzy systems. We should know that, a fuzzy system with bad universal approximation is hardly useful. Thus, whether a bounded linear operator regarded as a fuzzy system is uniformly bounded looks very important.

Reference

1. Ahmed, F., Capretz, L. F. and Samarabandu, J. (2008). Fuzzy inference systems for software product family process evaluation, Information Sciences, 178, pp. 2780-2793.
2. Atanassov, K. (1986). Intuitionistic fuzzy sets, Fuzzy Sets and Systems, 20, pp. 87-96.
3. Cheney, W. and Light, W. (2000) *A Course in Approximation Theory*. (Brook/Cole Publishing Company, a division of Thomson Learning).
4. Dong, J. X. and Yang, G. H. (2008). State feedback control of continuous-time T-S fuzzy systems via switched fuzzy controls, Information Sciences, 178, pp. 1680-1695.
5. Dubois, D and Prade, H. (1991). Toll Sets, *Proceedings of IFSA'91*, Brussels, pp. 21- 24.
6. Edwards, R. E. (1995) *Functional Analysis (Theory and Applications)*. (Dover Publications, Inc., New York).
7. Goguen, J. A. (1967). L-fuzzy sets, Journal of Mathematics Analysis and Applications, 18, pp. 145-174.
8. Juang, Y. T., Chang, Y. T. and Huang, C. P. (2008). Design of fuzzy PID controllers using modified triangular membership functions, Information Sciences, 178, pp. 1325-1333.
9. Li, D. C., Shi, Z. K. and Li, Y. M. (2008). Sufficient and necessary conditions for Boolean fuzzy systems as universal approximators, Information Sciences, 178, pp. 414-424.
10. Li, H. X. (2006). Probability representations of fuzzy systems, Science in China (Series F), 49, pp. 339-363.
11. Li, H. X. (1998). Interpolation mechanism of fuzzy control, Science in China (Series E), 41, pp. 312-320.

12. Li, H. X., Wang, J. Y. and Miao, Z. H. (2002). Modeling on fuzzy control systems, Science in China (Series A), 45, pp. 1506-517.
13. Li, H. X., Wang, J. Y. and Miao, Z. H. (2003). Marginal linearization method in modeling on fuzzy control systems, Progress in Natural Science, 13, pp. 489-496.
14. Li, H. X., Li, Y. D., Miao, Z. H. and Lee, E. S. (2003). Control functions of fuzzy controllers, Computers & Mathematics with Applications, 46, pp. 875-890.
15. Liu, F. (2008). An efficient centroid type-reduction strategy for general type-2 fuzzy logic system, Information Sciences, 178, pp. 2224-2236.
16. Liu, P. Y. and Li, H. X. (2000). Equivalence of generalized Takagi-Sugeno fuzzy system and its hierarchical systems, Journal of Beijing Normal University (Natural Science), 36, pp. 613-618.
17. Liu, P. Y. and Li, H. X. (2001). Analyses for Lp(μ)-norm approximation capability of generalized Mamdani fuzzy systems, Information Sciences, 138, pp. 195-210.
18. Liu, P. Y. and Li, H. X. (2000). Approximation of generalized fuzzy systems to integrable functions, Science in China (Series E), 43, pp. 613-624.
19. Liu, P. Y. and Li, H. X. (2005). Hierarchical TS fuzzy system and its universal approximation, Information Sciences, 169, pp. 279-303.
20. Liu, P. Y. and Li, H. X. (2005). Approximation of stochastic processes by T-S fuzzy systems, Fuzzy Sets and Systems, 155, pp. 215-235.
21. Luo, Q., Yang, W. Q. and Yi, D. Y. (2008). Kernel shapes of fuzzy sets in fuzzy systems for function approximation, Information Sciences, 178, pp. 836-857.
22. Mendel, J. M. (2007). Advances in type-2 fuzzy sets and systems, Information Sciences, 177, pp. 84-110.
23. Natanson, I. P. (1961) *Constructive Theory of Functions*. (U.S. Atomic Energy Commission, Office of Technical Information, ACE-tr-4503, 1961. Original Russian Text, Moscow, 1949).
24. Daowu Pei, D. W. (2008). Unified full implication algorithms of fuzzy reasoning, Information Sciences, 178, pp. 520-530.
25. Shi, K. Q. (1998). Double branch fuzzy sets (I), Journal of Shan Dong Industrial University, 28 , pp. 127-134.
26. Wang, G. J. (1988) *Fuzzy topology space theory*. (Shanxi Normal University Press, Shanxi).
27. Yeung, D. S. and Tsang, E. C. C. (1997). Weighted fuzzy production rules, Fuzzy Sets and Systems, 88, pp. 299-313.
28. Yuan, X. H. and Xia, Z. Q. (2006). Properties of weak Topos on the category of real valued functions, The Journal of Fuzzy Mathematics, 14, pp. 431-440.
29. Zadeh, L.A. (1973). Outline of a new approach to the analysis of complex systems and decision processes, interval-valued fuzzy sets, IEEE Transactions on Systems, Man, Cybernetics, 3, pp. 28-44.
30. Zeng, W. Y. and Li, H. X. (2005). Inner product truth-valued flow inference, Uncertainly, Fuzziness and Knowledge-Based Systems, 13, 601-612.

31. Zhang, Y. Z. and Li, H. X. (2006). Variable weighted synthesis inference method for fuzzy reasoning and fuzzy systems, Computers & Mathematics with Applications, 52, pp. 305-322.

Chapter 8

Unified Theory of Classic Mechanics and Quantum Mechanics

8.1 Introduction

As we all know, classic mechanics is the scope of macroscopical physics in which Newtonian mechanics is its main part. Classic mechanics is very different with microphysics, especially with quantum mechanics. For example, the motions of microscopic particles have wave-particle duality; but the motion of mass points in macroscopical physics only has mass point characters and no wave natures; in other words, there is no wave-mass-point duality in macroscopical physics. However, there exists a **correspondence principle**: considering a kind of motion state in quantum physics, when quantum number $n \to \infty$, the limit situation of the motion state in quantum physics must become a kind of motion state in macroscopical physics. In other words, the limit situation of the motion low in quantum physics is just some motion low in macroscopical physics.

Generally, Bohr suggested a **generalized correspondence principle**: the limit situation of any new theory must be in line with some old theory.

It is worth noting that above correspondence principle or generalized correspondence principle is all of unipolarity: the limit situation of the motion low in quantum physics is just some motion low in macroscopical physics, but the converse principle is clearly meaningless.

However, we can consider an important problem: must any one of motion states in macroscopical physics be the limit situation of some the motion states in quantum physics?

Apparently, this problem has not been observed, and of course there is no any answer. For example, we consider the well-known projectile motion. As we all know, a projectile motion can be used by the equation of locus of the projectile motion as following:

$$y(x) = x\tan\alpha - \frac{g}{2v_0^2\cos^2\alpha}x^2,$$

$$x \in [0, d_0], \quad d_0 = \frac{2v_0^2}{g}\sin 2\alpha$$

where $\alpha \in \left(0, \frac{\pi}{2}\right)$ is a mass ejection angle, $d_0 \in (0, +\infty)$ is the maximum range of fire, and $v_0 \in (0, +\infty)$ is the initial velocity; here the air friction is omitted.

Clearly $y(x) \in C[0, d_0]$, i.e., a projectile motion can be described by an unary continuous function. For this continuous function, can we find some microscopic particles such that the limit of the group behavior of these microscopic particles is just this continuous function $y(x)$ when quantum number $n \to \infty$?

In this chapter, we will give a positive answer for this problem. It is easy to understand that almost all laws of classic mechanics are described by continuous functions. So we can generalize above problem as such problem: for any a continuous function f, unary continuous function or multivariate continuous function, which should describe some motion law of some mass point in microscopically physics, can we find some microscopic particles such that the limit of the group behavior of these microscopic particles is just this continuous function f when quantum number $n \to \infty$?

From the following section, we start to try to solve out the problem.

8.2 Quantum Mechanics Representation of Classic Mechanics

Firstly, we consider the case of unary continuous functions. For any an unary continuous function $f(x) \in C[a, b]$, we can use a linear transformation as the following:

$$u:[a,b]\to[0,1],$$
$$x\mapsto u=u(x)=\frac{x-a}{b-a}$$

to redefine the continuous function $f(x)$ on the closed interval $[0,1]$, denoted by $g(u)$, i.e.,

$$g(u)=f\left((b-a)u+a\right)\in C[0,1].$$

Therefore, without loss of generality, we can only consider such continuous functions as being $f(x)\in C[0,1]$. However, we do not consider constant functions because constant functions are almost meaningless in physics.

In order to prover the following main theorem, we have to a lemma as the following.

Lemma 8.2.1 Arbitrarily taken $m+1$ real numbers $a_0,a_1,\cdots,a_m\in\mathbb{R}$, we denote the following symbol:

$$e_m=\max\left\{|a_i-a_{i-1}|\,\middle|\,i=1,2,\cdots,m\right\}.$$

And we take a permutation as the following:

$$\sigma=\begin{pmatrix}0 & 1 & \cdots & m\\ k_0 & k_1 & \cdots & k_m\end{pmatrix},$$

such that $a_{k_0}\le a_{k_1}\le\cdots\le a_{k_m}$. If we write

$$d_m=\max\left\{a_{k_i}-a_{k_{i-1}}\,\middle|\,i=1,2,\cdots,m\right\},$$

then $d_n\le e_n$.

Proof. By the definition of d_n, we can know the following fact:

$$\left(\exists i\in\{1,2,\cdots,m\}\right)\left(d_m=a_{k_i}-a_{k_{i-1}}\right).$$

If $d_m=0$, then the conclusion of the lemma is clearly true. Now we assume $d_m>0$. We know that σ is a bijection, and then $k_i\ne k_{i-1}$.

Let $s = k_i, t = k_{i-1}$. So $a_s - a_t = d_m$. We consider two cases: (i) and (ii) as follows.

(i) $s < t$. If we pay attention to the total order relation:

$$a_{k_0} \le a_{k_1} \le a_{k_{i-1}} < a_{k_i} \le \cdots \le \cdots \le a_{k_m},$$

then we can learn the fact:

$$a_s, a_{s+1}, a_{s+2}, \cdots, a_{t-1}, a_t \notin (a_t, a_s) = \left(a_{k_{i-1}}, a_{k_i}\right),$$

which means $a_s, a_{s+1}, a_{s+2}, \cdots, a_{t-1}, a_t \in (-\infty, a_t] \cup [a_s, +\infty)$. Let

$$l = \min\left\{i \in \{s, s+1, \cdots, t\} \middle| a_i \in (-\infty, a_t]\right\}.$$

Clearly $l \ne s$; or else $a_l = a_s \in [a_s, +\infty)$; this will be contradictory with the fact that $a_l \in (-\infty, a_t]$. By the meaning of the subscript l, it is easy understand that $a_{l-1} \in [a_s, +\infty)$. Thus we have the result:

$$e_m \ge |a_l - a_{l-1}| \ge a_s - a_t = d_m.$$

(ii) $t < s$. This time we have the following result:

$$a_t, a_{t+1}, a_{t+2}, \cdots, a_{s-1}, a_s \notin (a_t, a_s) = \left(a_{k_{i-1}}, a_{k_i}\right),$$

which means the following expression is true:

$$a_t, a_{t+1}, a_{t+2}, \cdots, a_{s-1}, a_s \in (-\infty, a_t] \cup [a_s, +\infty).$$

Let $l = \max\left\{i \in \{t, t+1, \cdots, s\} \middle| a_i \in (-\infty, a_t]\right\}$. Clearly $l \ne s$, or else we have $a_l = a_s \in [a_s, +\infty)$; this will also be contradictory with this expression $a_l \in (-\infty, a_t]$. So $a_{l+1} \in [a_s, +\infty)$. Thus we have the result:

$$e_m \ge |a_{l+1} - a_l| \ge a_s - a_t = d_m.$$

We complete the proof of the proposition. □

Theorem 8.2.1 Given arbitrarily a non-constant function $f(x) \in C[0,1]$, there must exist some microscopic particles such that the limit of the group behavior of these microscopic particles is just this continuous function $f(x)$ when the quantum number $n \to \infty$.

Proof. **Step 1**. We consider the wave function of a microscopic particle in infinite deep square potential well.

As a matter of fact, we take a particle M with quality m, and M moves along Ox axis and is of determined momentum $p = mv_x$ and determined energy $E = \frac{1}{2}mv_x^2 = \frac{p^2}{2m}$ where v_x is the velocity of M moving along Ox. We take a special infinite deep square potential well as follows (see Figure 8.2.1):

$$V(x) = \begin{cases} 0, & x \in [0,1], \\ +\infty, & x \in (-\infty, 0) \cup (1, +\infty) \end{cases}$$

The particle M is complete free inside the potential well; only at two endpoints $x = 0, x = 1$, there are infinite forces to impose restrictions on M not to escape.

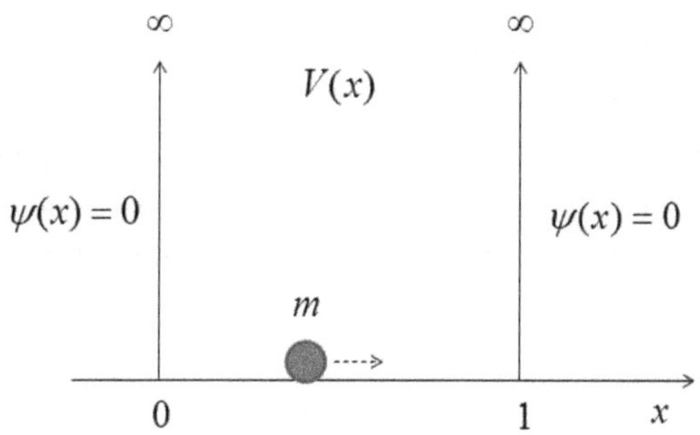

Fig. 8.2.1. Particle movement in the infinite deep square potential well

At outside of the potential well, i.e. $x \in (-\infty, 0) \cup (1, +\infty)$, we now notice the steady state Schrodinger Equation as the following:

$$\left[-\frac{\hbar^2}{2m}\frac{\partial^2}{\partial x^2}+V(x)\right]\psi(x)=E\psi(x)$$

It is easy to know that $\psi(x)=0$; so the probability of finding the particle in the interval $(-\infty,0)\cup(1,+\infty)$ is zero. However inside the potential well, i.e. $x\in[0,1]$, we have $V(x)=0$; then the Schrodinger Equation turn into the following form:

$$\frac{d^2\psi(x)}{dx^2}=-\left(\frac{\sqrt{2mE}}{\hbar}\right)^2\psi(x).$$

Let $k=\frac{\sqrt{2mE}}{\hbar}$; then we have the following form:

$$\frac{d^2\psi(x)}{dx^2}+k^2\psi(x)=0,$$

which is the equation of motion of a simple harmonic oscillation, and its general solution is as following:

$$\psi(x)=A\sin kx+B\cos kx,$$

where A,B are two arbitrary constants that can be determined by some boundary conditions.

Then, what are the boundary conditions? In fact, in quantum mechanics, the solution of a Schrodinger Equation in three-dimension space, i.e. the wave function $\Psi(x,y,z,t)$ should satisfy the following established standard conditions:

i) $\int_{\mathbb{R}^3}|\Psi|^2dxdydz=1$;

ii) Ψ and its three partial derivatives $\frac{\partial\Psi}{\partial x},\frac{\partial\Psi}{\partial y},\frac{\partial\Psi}{\partial z}$ are continuous everywhere;

iii) Ψ is a single-valued function about coordinates.

By means of above conditions, when the potential function approaches infinite, based on the continuity of $\psi(x)$, we can get the result as being $\psi(0)=\psi(1)=0$, which can make the solution be continuous at both inside and outside of the potential well. Because of the following expression:

$$0=\psi(0)=A\sin k0+B\cos k0=B,$$

we get $B=0$; thus we have the following equation:

$$\psi(x)=A\sin kx$$

And then we take notice of the equation: $0=\psi(1)=A\sin k$, if $A=0$, then $\psi(x)\equiv 0$ which is a trivial solution and cannot be normalized. Thus we only get the result: $\sin k=0$, and we know the following fact:

$$k=0,\pm\pi,\pm 2\pi,\pm 3\pi,\cdots$$

Clearly that $k=0$ is meaningless, for this can also make that $\psi(x)\equiv 0$. Besides, k with negative values cannot generate any new solutions because of the fact that $\sin(-\theta)=-\sin\theta$ and we can make the minus signs enter into the coefficient A. Therefore, we have the result:

$$k=k_n=n\pi,\quad n=1,2,3,\cdots$$

We should notice a fact that, the boundary condition at $x=1$ is not used to determine the coefficient A, but to determine the energy E because of the expression: $k=\dfrac{\sqrt{2mE}}{\hbar}$, i.e.,

$$E=E_n=\frac{\hbar^2k_n^2}{2m}=\frac{n^2\pi^2\hbar^2}{2m},\quad n=1,2,3,\cdots \tag{8.2.1}$$

It is well-known that $E_1=\dfrac{\pi^2\hbar^2}{2m}$ is ground state, and others are follows:

$$E_2 = 4E_1,\ E_3 = 9E_1,\ E_4 = 16E_1, \cdots$$

which means that the energy of a particle can only take discrete values; in other words, the energy of a particle is quantized. And positive integer n is called the quantum number of the energy of a particle. So we can learn that the quantization of the energy of a particle is very natural in quantum mechanics.

Thus the solution of the Schrodinger Equation can be expressed by the quantum number as the following:

$$\psi_n(x) = A\sin(n\pi x), \quad n = 1,2,3,\cdots \tag{8.2.2}$$

In order to determine the coefficient A, we can use the normalization condition $\int_0^1 |\psi_n(x)|^2 dx = 1$ to get $A = \sqrt{2}$. Then we get the solution of the Schrodinger Equation inside the potential well as the following:

$$\psi_n(x) = \sqrt{2}\sin(n\pi x), \quad x \in [0,1], \quad n = 1,2,3,\cdots \tag{8.2.3}$$

Let

$$\alpha_n(x) = \sin(n\pi x), \quad x \in [0,1], \quad n = 1,2,3,\cdots,$$

and we have the following form:

$$\psi_n(x) = \sqrt{2}\alpha_n(x), \quad x \in [0,1], \quad n = 1,2,3,\cdots \tag{8.2.4}$$

The function $\alpha_n(x)$ is called **essence wave function** of the wave function $\psi_n(x)$.

Step 2. Based on an important fact that will be described as follows, we should consider to weaken three standard conditions about the wave function $\Psi(x,y,z,t)$ mentioned above.

As a matter of fact, we can see that the derived function $\dfrac{\partial \psi_n(x)}{\partial x}$ of the wave function $\psi_n(x) = \sqrt{2}\sin(n\pi x)$ is not continuous at $x = 0,1$.

For this we only notice the following implication is true:

$$\frac{\partial \psi_n(x)}{\partial x} = \frac{\sqrt{2}}{n\pi}\cos(n\pi x) \Rightarrow$$
$$\left(\frac{\partial \psi_n(0)}{\partial x} = \frac{\sqrt{2}}{n\pi} \neq 0, \quad \frac{\partial \psi_n(1)}{\partial x} = \frac{\sqrt{2}}{n\pi}\cos(n\pi) \neq 0\right).$$

It is well known that the movement of a particle in the infinite potential well is a typical example in quantum mechanics. However, as we have learned above, its wave function Ψ and its three partial derivatives $\frac{\partial \Psi}{\partial x}, \frac{\partial \Psi}{\partial y}, \frac{\partial \Psi}{\partial z}$ are not continuous as everywhere (of course, in above case, there is only one partial derivative $\frac{\partial \Psi}{\partial x}$, in fact $\frac{\partial \Psi}{\partial x} = \frac{\mathrm{d}\Psi}{\mathrm{d}x}$ here).

We should forget a fact that wave function Ψ does not represent a physical wave but only a mathematical wave; in other words, $|\Psi|^2$ is a probability density function where it should be normalized.

We also know such a fact that, in probability theory, any probability density function is not required to be continuous at everywhere but only required to be almost everywhere continuous. Thus, we have enough reason to revise the three standard conditions which the wave function $\Psi(x, y, z, t)$ should satisfy mentioned above to be as the following:

(i) $\int_{\mathbb{R}^3} |\Psi|^2 dxdydz = 1$;

(ii) Ψ and its three partial derivatives $\frac{\partial \Psi}{\partial x}, \frac{\partial \Psi}{\partial y}, \frac{\partial \Psi}{\partial z}$ cannot be not continuous only at finite points (clearly the requirement is a little stronger than almost everywhere continuous);

(iii) Ψ is a single-valued function about coordinates.

Moreover, by the viewpoint of Von Neumann, wave function Ψ is defined in a Hilbert space $\mathcal{L}^2\left(\mathbb{R}^3\right)$, where the operations in quantum mechanics (momentum, work, and so on) are inner product operations, which may be enlightened by $\int_{\mathbb{R}^3} |\Psi|^2 dxdydz = 1$ and form a mathematical formalization structure. We all know the fact that, in a Hilbert space $\mathcal{L}^2(\mathbb{R}^3)$, we have no need to require wave function Ψ to be continuous at everywhere but almost everywhere continuous to be enough.

Step 3. We continue to consider the wave function of the particle in the one dimension infinite deep potential well. We have known its general solution being as

$$\psi(x) = A\sin kx + B\cos kx,$$

where A, B are arbitrary constants which can be determined by the boundary conditions. This time, we suppose $\frac{\partial\psi(x)}{\partial x}$ be continuous at the boundary points $x = 0,1$. We take notice of the following implication:

$$\frac{\partial\psi(x)}{\partial x} = \frac{A}{k}\cos kx - \frac{B}{k}\sin kx \Rightarrow 0 = \frac{\partial\psi(0)}{\partial x} = \frac{A}{k} \Rightarrow A = 0$$

Then we get the following result:

$$\psi(x) = B\cos kx.$$

And then we pay attention to the equation $\frac{\partial\psi(x)}{\partial x} = -\frac{B}{k}\sin kx$, so that

$$0 = \frac{\partial\psi(1)}{\partial x} = -\frac{B}{k}\sin k.$$

Because $\frac{B}{k} \neq 0$, we solve out the values of k as follows:

$$k = k_n = n\pi, \quad n = 1, 2, 3, \cdots$$

Very similar to the method in Step 1, we have the expression of E again as follows:

$$E = E_n = \frac{\hbar^2 k_n^2}{2m} = \frac{n^2\pi^2\hbar^2}{2m}, \quad n = 1,2,3,\cdots$$

So the solution of the Schrodinger Equation can be expressed by means of quantum numbers as the following:

$$\varphi_n(x) = B\cos(n\pi x), \quad n = 1,2,3,\cdots \tag{8.2.5}$$

Again by using the normalization condition, we can get that $B = \sqrt{2}$. Thus another solution of the Schrodinger Equation in the potential well is as the following:

$$\varphi_n(x) = \sqrt{2}\cos(n\pi x), \quad x \in [0,1], \quad n = 1,2,3,\cdots \tag{8.2.6}$$

Let $\beta_n(x) = \cos(n\pi x), x \in [0,1], n = 1,2,3,\cdots$, and we have

$$\varphi_n(x) = \sqrt{2}\beta_n(x), \quad x \in [0,1], \quad n = 1,2,3,\cdots \tag{8.2.7}$$

The function $\beta_n(x)$ is also called **essence wave function** of the wave function $\varphi_n(x)$.

It is interesting to note that the wave function $\varphi_n(x) = \sqrt{2}\cos(n\pi x)$ is not continuous at boundary points $x = 0,1$ this time. Besides, since

$$\begin{aligned}\psi_n\left(x + \frac{1}{2n}\right) &= \sqrt{2}\sin\left[n\pi\left(x + \frac{1}{2n}\right)\right] \\ &= \sqrt{2}\sin\left(n\pi x + \frac{\pi}{2}\right) = \sqrt{2}\cos(n\pi x) = \varphi_n(x)\end{aligned}$$

when the quantum number n is very large, the two wave functions $\psi_n(x)$ and $\varphi_n(x)$ are almost no different; in other words, $\varphi_n(x)$ is just the situation that $\psi_n(x)$ translates a $\frac{\pi}{2}$ phase position to the right side.

For visualization, the function $\psi_n(x)$ can be vividly called Adam wave function and $\varphi_n(x)$ be called Eve wave function. In fact, we care more about the function family of essence wave functions of Adam and Eve wave functions, denoted by $\{\alpha_n(x), \beta_n(x)\}_{n=1}^{\infty}$, and we can call $\alpha_n(x)$ to be Adam essence wave function and $\beta_n(x)$ to be Eve essence wave function. Clearly $\alpha_n(x)$ and $\beta_n(x)$ are defined on the unit interval $X = [0,1]$.

Step 4. Supplementary instruction for the revision of the three standard requirements on the wave function Ψ

It is well known that, in physics, harmonic oscillation is often described by complex exponential form; for example, the two wave functions that we just get can be described as the following:

$$\begin{aligned}\Psi(x) &= \sqrt{2}e^{i(n\pi x)} \\ &= \sqrt{2}\cos(n\pi x) + i\sqrt{2}\sin(n\pi x) \\ &= \varphi_n(x) + i\psi_n(x)\end{aligned} \tag{8.2.8}$$

In classic physics, this kind of expression is said to be more convenient for operation but with no more physical significance. However, here we can find its physical significance of the complex variables function $\Psi(x) = \sqrt{2}e^{in\pi x}$ coming from quantum mechanics. As its real part of the $\Psi(x) = \sqrt{2}e^{in\pi x}$, Eve wave function as being $\varphi_n(x) = \sqrt{2}\cos(n\pi x)$ is determined by the second boundary condition; and its imaginary part, Adam wave function as being $\psi_n(x) = \sqrt{2}\sin(n\pi x)$ is determined by the first boundary condition. These mean that the two boundary conditions are all useful and we cannot give up any one of them. Therefore, the revision of the three standard requirements is quite reasonable.

Step 5. The extension of the domain of definition of the wave functions

For any a finite closed interval $[a,b]$, by means of the linear transformation as follows:

$$t = (b-a)x + a,$$

the essence wave function family $\{\sin(n\pi x), \cos(n\pi x)\}_{n=1}^{\infty}$ defined on the interval $[0,1]$ can be extended to the closed interval $[a,b]$; we rewrite the variable t to be x, and we have the following form:

$$\left\{\sin\frac{n\pi(x-a)}{b-a}, \cos\frac{n\pi(x-a)}{b-a}\right\}_{n=1}^{\infty}, \quad x \in [a,b].$$

We can easily know that the mapping as follows

$$u:[a,b] \to [0,1], \quad x \mapsto u(x) = \frac{x-a}{b-a}$$

is a topological homeomorphism from $[a,b]$ to $[0,1]$. This means that the essence wave function family $\{\sin(n\pi x), \cos(n\pi x)\}_{n=1}^{\infty}$ and the family of essence wave functions

$$\left\{\sin\frac{n\pi(x-a)}{b-a}, \cos\frac{n\pi(x-a)}{b-a}\right\}_{n=1}^{\infty}$$

are not essentially different; so they are can be regarded the same.

It is worth noting that, for Adam wave function, in the infinite deep square potential well, it should be written as the following complete form:

$$\Psi(x,t) = \psi_n(x)e^{-\frac{i}{\hbar}E_n t} = \sqrt{2}\sin(n\pi x)e^{-\frac{i}{\hbar}E_n t}, \quad x \in [0,1], \quad (8.2.9)$$

where we only write out the expression just as being $x \in [0,1]$. And for Eve wave function, in the infinite deep square potential well, it should be written as the following complete form:

$$\Psi(x,t) = \varphi_n(x)e^{-\frac{i}{\hbar}E_n t} = \sqrt{2}\cos(n\pi x)e^{-\frac{i}{\hbar}E_n t}, \quad x \in [0,1], \quad (8.2.10)$$

where we also only write out the expression just as being $x \in [0,1]$.

Based on the statistical interpretation of wave functions, $|\Psi(x,t)|^2$ should be a kind of probability density function. Then from Equations (8.3.9) and (8.2.10), we can learn that $2\sin^2(n\pi x)$ is a probability density function and $2\cos^2(n\pi x)$ is a probability density function too. We have enough reason to call $\sin^2(n\pi x)$ and $\cos^2(n\pi x)$ essence probability density function of the probability density functions. So we get the essence probability density function family of Adam wave functions and Eve functions as the following:

$$\left\{\sin^2(n\pi x), \cos^2(n\pi x)\right\}_{n=1}^{\infty}. \tag{8.2.11}$$

It is easy to see that $\left\{\sin^2(n\pi x), \cos^2(n\pi x)\right\}_{n=1}^{\infty}$ is of two-phase normalization property:

$$\sin^2(n\pi x) + \cos^2(n\pi x) = 1.$$

Step 6. The construction of the sequence of two-dimension probability density functions

Given arbitrarily a continuous function $f \in C[0,1]$, clearly $f([0,1])$ is a closed interval, denoted by $Y = [c,d] = f([0,1])$. Let

$$X(n) = \left\{x \in [0,1] \middle| \sin(n\pi x) = 0, \cos(n\pi x) = 0\right\}.$$

And we can easily know that $\text{card}(X(n)) = 2n+1$. Hence we have the following expression:

$$X(n) = \left\{x_i^{(n)} \middle| i = 0,1,2,\cdots,2n\right\},$$

where $x_i^{(n)} = \dfrac{i}{2n}, i = 0,1,2,\cdots,2n$. This expression means that the closed interval $X = [0,1]$ are equidistantly partitioned as the following:

$$\Delta x_i^{(n)} = x_i^{(n)} - x_{i-1}^{(n)} = \frac{1}{2n}, \quad i = 1,2,\cdots,2n.$$

And we let

$$Y(n)=\left\{y_i^{(n)}=f\left(x_i^{(n)}\right)\middle|i=0,1,2,\cdots,2n\right\}.$$

For convenience, let $m=2n$; but be careful, here m means subscript but not the quality of some particle. We are going to discuss our problem from the following two cases.

Case 1. Suppose $f(x)$ is a strict monotonous function. It assumes that $f(x)$ be a strict monotonous rising function because its proof is not of essence difference when $f(x)$ is a strict monotonous declining function. Therefore, we have the following partition:

$$c=y_0^{(n)}<y_1^{(n)}<\cdots<y_{m-1}^{(n)}<y_m^{(n)}=d.$$

Then we consider the particle wave functions defined in the following subintervals one by one:

$$\left[y_0^{(n)},y_1^{(n)}\right],\left[y_1^{(n)},y_2^{(n)}\right],\cdots,\left[y_{m-2}^{(n)},y_{m-1}^{(n)}\right],\left[y_{m-1}^{(n)},y_m^{(n)}\right].$$

Firstly we treat with it in the closed interval $\left[y_0^{(n)},y_1^{(n)}\right]$. And we consider the movement of a particle in the infinite deep square potential well that the closed interval $\left[0,2\left(y_1^{(n)}-y_0^{(n)}\right)\right]$ is just the bottom margin of the potential well. The particle is denoted by $M_1^{(n)}$ which can be regarded as a descendant particle generated by the Adam wave function and Eve wave function of the original particle M in the case of energy level being n. The descendant particle $M_1^{(n)}$ moves along Oy axis with determined quality $m_1^{(n)}$ and determined momentum $p_1^{(n)}=m_1^{(n)}v_y^{(n,1)}$ and determined energy

$$E_1^{(n)}=\frac{1}{2}m_1^{(n)}\left(v_y^{(n,1)}\right)^2=\frac{\left(p_1^{(n)}\right)^2}{2m_1^{(n)}},$$

where $v_y^{(n,1)}$ is the velocity of movement of $M_1^{(n)}$ along Oy axis. By means of the continuity of the wave function, it is easy to get the solution of the wave function in $\left[0,2\left(y_1^{(n)}-y_0^{(n)}\right)\right]$ as following:

$$\psi_p^{(n,1)}(y)=\sqrt{\frac{2}{2\left(y_1^{(n)}-y_0^{(n)}\right)}}\sin\frac{p\pi}{2\left(y_1^{(n)}-y_0^{(n)}\right)}y, \quad p=1,2,3,\cdots \tag{8.2.12}$$

Then again, by means of the continuity of the derived function of the wave function, we can get another solution of the wave function in the closed interval $\left[0,2\left(y_1^{(n)}-y_0^{(n)}\right)\right]$ as following:

$$\varphi_p^{(n,1)}(y)=\sqrt{\frac{2}{2\left(y_1^{(n)}-y_0^{(n)}\right)}}\cos\frac{p\pi}{2\left(y_1^{(n)}-y_0^{(n)}\right)}y, \quad p=1,2,3,\cdots \tag{8.2.13}$$

Now we care more for the ground state of $\psi_p^{(n,1)}(y)$ and $\varphi_p^{(n,1)}(y)$, i.e., the wave functions when $p=1$ as follows:

$$\psi_1^{(n,1)}(y)=\sqrt{\frac{2}{2\left(y_1^{(n)}-y_0^{(n)}\right)}}\sin\frac{\pi}{2\left(y_1^{(n)}-y_0^{(n)}\right)}y, \tag{8.2.14}$$

$$\varphi_1^{(n,1)}(y)=\sqrt{\frac{2}{2\left(y_1^{(n)}-y_0^{(n)}\right)}}\cos\frac{\pi}{2\left(y_1^{(n)}-y_0^{(n)}\right)}y, \tag{8.2.15}$$

We can omit the amplitudes of the wave and keep the essence wave function and do squaring operation on the essence wave functions, and get the probability essence wave functions as the following:

$$\sin^2\frac{\pi}{2\left(y_1^{(n)}-y_0^{(n)}\right)}y, \quad \cos^2\frac{\pi}{2\left(y_1^{(n)}-y_0^{(n)}\right)}y. \tag{8.2.16}$$

The graphs of the probability essence wave functions in $\left[0, y_1^{(n)} - y_0^{(n)}\right]$ are shown in Figure 8.2.2.

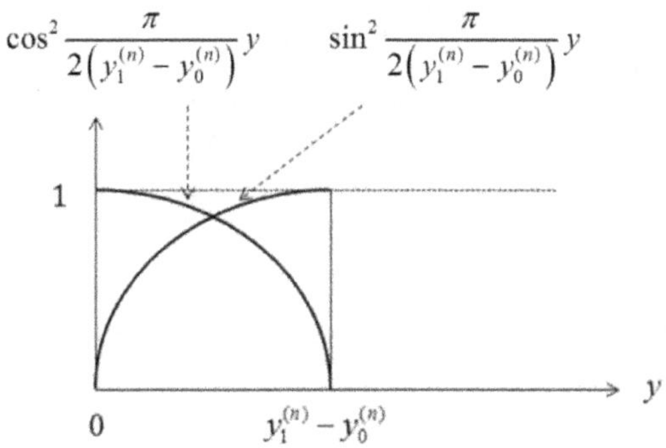

Fig. 8.2.2. The probability essence wave functions in $\left[0, y_1^{(n)} - y_0^{(n)}\right]$

The next, we make a coordinate translation: $t = y + y_0^{(n)}$, and then we have the following expressions:

$$\sin^2 \frac{\pi}{2\left(y_1^{(n)} - y_0^{(n)}\right)} y = \sin^2 \frac{\pi}{2\left(y_1^{(n)} - y_0^{(n)}\right)} \left(t - y_0^{(n)}\right),$$

$$\cos^2 \frac{\pi}{2\left(y_1^{(n)} - y_0^{(n)}\right)} y = \cos^2 \frac{\pi}{2\left(y_1^{(n)} - y_0^{(n)}\right)} \left(t - y_0^{(n)}\right)$$

Thus we transfer the probability essence wave functions defined in the closed interval $\left[0, y_1^{(n)} - y_0^{(n)}\right]$ into the probability essence wave functions in in closed interval $\left[y_0^{(n)}, y_1^{(n)}\right]$. And we rewrite the variable t back to y, and then we get the following expressions:

$$\sin^2 \frac{\pi}{2\left(y_1^{(n)} - y_0^{(n)}\right)} \left(y - y_0^{(n)}\right), \cos^2 \frac{\pi}{2\left(y_1^{(n)} - y_0^{(n)}\right)} \left(y - y_0^{(n)}\right) \quad (8.2.17)$$

The graphs of the probability essence wave functions in $\left[y_0^{(n)}, y_1^{(n)}\right]$ are shown in Figure 8.2.3.

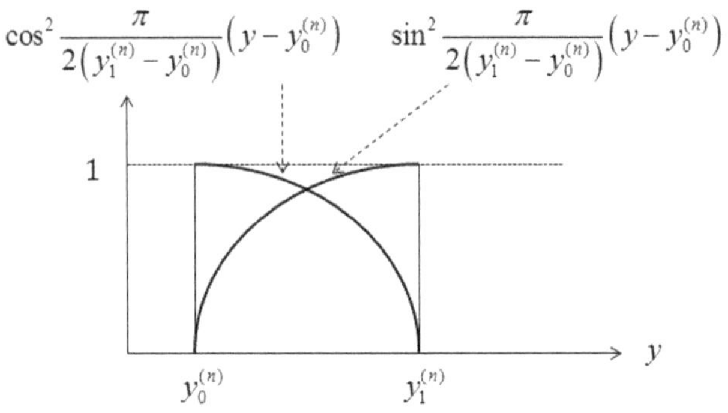

Fig. 8.2.3. The probability essence wave functions in $\left[y_0^{(n)}, y_1^{(n)}\right]$

In that way, we can regard $\sin^2 \frac{\pi}{2\left(y_1^{(n)}-y_0^{(n)}\right)}\left(y-y_0^{(n)}\right)$ as Adam probability essence wave function of the movement of the descendant particle $M_1^{(n)}$ in $\left[y_0^{(n)}, y_1^{(n)}\right]$, and regard $\cos^2 \frac{\pi}{2\left(y_1^{(n)}-y_0^{(n)}\right)}\left(y-y_0^{(n)}\right)$ as Eve probability essence wave function of the movement of the descendant particle $M_1^{(n)}$ in $\left[y_0^{(n)}, y_1^{(n)}\right]$.

In the same way, we can get Adam and Eve probability essence wave functions of the movement of the descendant particles $M_2^{(n)}, \cdots, M_m^{(n)}$ in the closed intervals $\left[y_1^{(n)}, y_2^{(n)}\right], \cdots, \left[y_{m-1}^{(n)}, y_m^{(n)}\right]$ respectively as the following:

$$\sin^2 \frac{\pi}{2\left(y_2^{(n)}-y_1^{(n)}\right)}\left(y-y_1^{(n)}\right), \quad \cos^2 \frac{\pi}{2\left(y_2^{(n)}-y_1^{(n)}\right)}\left(y-y_1^{(n)}\right),$$

......

$$\sin^2 \frac{\pi}{2\left(y_m^{(n)}-y_{m-1}^{(n)}\right)}\left(y-y_{m-1}^{(n)}\right), \quad \cos^2 \frac{\pi}{2\left(y_m^{(n)}-y_{m-1}^{(n)}\right)}\left(y-y_{m-1}^{(n)}\right)$$

We get all these graphs of the probability essence wave functions together in the following closed intervals:

$$\left[y_0^{(n)},y_1^{(n)}\right],\left[y_1^{(n)},y_2^{(n)}\right],\cdots,\left[y_{m-1}^{(n)},y_m^{(n)}\right]$$

and they are shown in Figure 8.2.4.

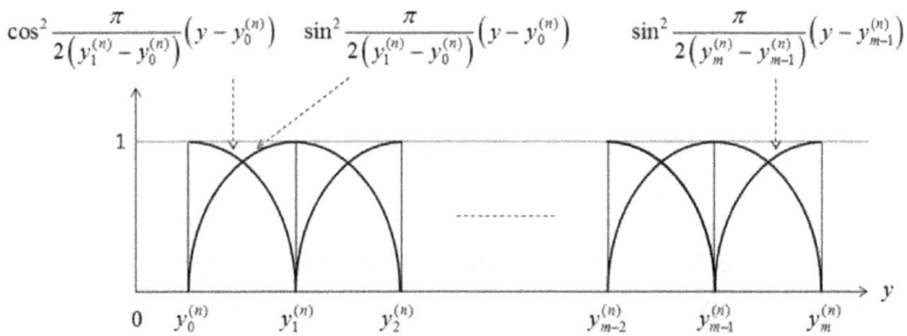

Fig. 8.2.4. All the probability essence wave functions in $\left[y_0^{(n)},y_1^{(n)}\right],\cdots,\left[y_{m-1}^{(n)},y_m^{(n)}\right]$

Now we need to summarize the work that we have done as follows.

When $x\in\left[x_0^{(n)},x_1^{(n)}\right]$, from the information of Adam and Eve probability essence wave functions $\sin^2(n\pi x)$ and $\cos^2(n\pi x)$ at the nodes as the following:

$$y_0^{(n)}=f\left(x_0^{(n)}\right),\quad y_1^{(n)}=f\left(x_1^{(n)}\right),$$

we get Adam and Eve probability essence wave functions in $\left[y_0^{(n)},y_1^{(n)}\right]$ as follows:

$$\sin^2\frac{\pi}{2\left(y_1^{(n)}-y_0^{(n)}\right)}\left(y-y_0^{(n)}\right),\quad \cos^2\frac{\pi}{2\left(y_1^{(n)}-y_0^{(n)}\right)}\left(y-y_0^{(n)}\right)$$

They have some interesting properties: one is that they can have the form of Adam probability essence wave functions; another is that they can also have the form of Eve probability essence wave functions; they are all at ground state, and they are all regarded as the probability essence wave functions of the descendant particles of M when the quantum number is the natural number n.

When $x \in \left[x_1^{(n)}, x_2^{(n)}\right]$, from the information of Adam and Eve probability essence wave functions $\sin^2(n\pi x)$ and $\cos^2(n\pi x)$ at the nodes as the following: $y_1^{(n)} = f\left(x_1^{(n)}\right), y_2^{(n)} = f\left(x_2^{(n)}\right)$, we can get Adam and Eve probability essence wave functions in $\left[y_1^{(n)}, y_2^{(n)}\right]$ as follows:

$$\sin^2 \frac{\pi}{2\left(y_2^{(n)} - y_1^{(n)}\right)}\left(y - y_1^{(n)}\right), \quad \cos^2 \frac{\pi}{2\left(y_2^{(n)} - y_1^{(n)}\right)}\left(y - y_1^{(n)}\right)$$

They also have the properties: one is that they can have the form of Adam probability essence wave functions; another is that they can also have the form of Eve probability essence wave functions; they are all at ground state, and they are all regarded as the probability essence wave functions of the descendant particles of M when the quantum number is also the natural number n.

At last, when $x \in \left[x_{m-1}^{(n)}, x_m^{(n)}\right]$, from the information of Adam and Eve probability essence wave functions $\sin^2(n\pi x)$ and $\cos^2(n\pi x)$ at the nodes: $y_{m-1}^{(n)} = f\left(x_{m-1}^{(n)}\right), y_m^{(n)} = f\left(x_m^{(n)}\right)$, we get Adam and Eve probability essence wave functions in $\left[y_{m-1}^{(n)}, y_m^{(n)}\right]$ as follows:

$$\sin^2 \frac{\pi}{2\left(y_m^{(n)} - y_{m-1}^{(n)}\right)}\left(y - y_{m-1}^{(n)}\right), \quad \cos^2 \frac{\pi}{2\left(y_m^{(n)} - y_{m-1}^{(n)}\right)}\left(y - y_{m-1}^{(n)}\right)$$

They have the same properties: one is that they can have the form of Adam probability essence wave functions; another is that they can also have the form of Eve probability essence wave functions; they are all at ground state, and they are all regarded as the probability essence wave functions of the descendant particles of M when quantum number is n.

Based on these probability essence wave functions, we try to make some useful base functions defined respectively on the intervals $[0,1]$ and $[c,d] = \left[y_0^{(n)}, y_m^{(n)}\right]$: $A_0^{(n)}, A_1^{(n)}, \cdots, A_m^{(n)}, B_0^{(n)}, B_1^{(n)}, \cdots, B_m^{(n)}$ as the following expressions:

$$A_0^{(n)}(x) = \chi_{\left[0,\frac{1}{m}\right]}(x)\cos^2(n\pi x),$$

$$A_1^{(n)}(x) = \chi_{\left[0,\frac{2}{m}\right]}(x)\sin^2(n\pi x),$$

$$A_2^{(n)}(x) = \chi_{\left[\frac{1}{m},\frac{3}{m}\right]}(x)\cos^2(n\pi x)$$

……

$$A_{m-2}^{(n)}(x) = \chi_{\left[\frac{m-3}{m},\frac{1}{m}\right]}(x)\cos^2(n\pi x),$$

$$A_{m-1}^{(n)}(x) = \chi_{\left[\frac{m-2}{m},1\right]}(x)\sin^2(n\pi x),$$

$$A_m^{(n)}(x) = \chi_{\left[\frac{m-1}{m},1\right]}(x)\cos^2(n\pi x);$$

$$B_0^{(n)}(y) = \chi_{\left[y_0^{(n)},y_1^{(n)}\right]}(y)\cos^2\frac{\pi}{2\left(y_1^{(n)}-y_0^{(n)}\right)}\left(y-y_0^{(n)}\right),$$

$$B_1^{(n)}(y) = \chi_{\left[y_0^{(n)},y_1^{(n)}\right]}(y)\sin^2\frac{\pi}{2\left(y_1^{(n)}-y_0^{(n)}\right)}\left(y-y_0^{(n)}\right)$$

$$+\chi_{\left[y_1^{(n)},y_2^{(n)}\right]}(y)\cos^2\frac{\pi}{2\left(y_2^{(n)}-y_1^{(n)}\right)}\left(y-y_1^{(n)}\right),$$

……

$$B_{m-1}^{(n)}(y) = \chi_{\left[y_{m-2}^{(n)},y_{m-1}^{(n)}\right]}(y)\sin^2\frac{\pi}{2\left(y_{m-1}^{(n)}-y_{m-2}^{(n)}\right)}\left(y-y_{m-2}^{(n)}\right)$$

$$+\chi_{\left[y_{m-1}^{(n)},y_m^{(n)}\right]}(y)\cos^2\frac{\pi}{2\left(y_m^{(n)}-y_{m-1}^{(n)}\right)}\left(y-y_{m-1}^{(n)}\right),$$

$$B_m^{(n)}(y) = \chi_{\left[y_{m-1}^{(n)},y_m^{(n)}\right]}(y)\sin^2\frac{\pi}{2\left(y_m^{(n)}-y_{m-1}^{(n)}\right)}\left(y-y_{m-1}^{(n)}\right)$$

where χ_A is the characteristic function of the set A; for example,

$$\chi_{\left[0,\frac{1}{m}\right]}(x)=\begin{cases}1, & x\in\left[0,\dfrac{1}{m}\right],\\ 0, & x\in[0,1]-\left[0,\dfrac{1}{m}\right],\end{cases}$$

$$\chi_{\left[y_0^{(n)},y_1^{(n)}\right]}(y)=\begin{cases}1, & y\in\left[y_0^{(n)},y_1^{(n)}\right],\\ 0, & y\in[c,d]-\left[y_0^{(n)},y_1^{(n)}\right]\end{cases}$$

Let us denote two classes of sets as the following:

$$\mathcal{A}(n)=\left\{A_0^{(n)},A_1^{(n)},\cdots,A_m^{(n)}\right\},\quad \mathcal{B}(n)=\left\{B_0^{(n)},B_1^{(n)},\cdots,B_m^{(n)}\right\}$$

Clearly they are just the groups of base functions defined respectively on the closed intervals $X=[0,1]$ and $Y=[c,d]$. Clearly $\mathcal{A}(n)$ is a linearly independent group in the continuous function space $C[0,1]$ and $\mathcal{B}(n)$ is a linearly independent group in the continuous function space $C[c,d]$. Put

$$\mathcal{A}(n)\cdot\mathcal{B}(n)=\left\{A_i^{(n)}\cdot B_j^{(n)}\,\middle|\, i,j=0,1,\cdots,m\right\},$$
$$A_i^{(n)}\cdot B_j^{(n)}:[0,1]\times[c,d]\to[0,1]$$
$$(x,y)\mapsto\left(A_i^{(n)}\cdot B_j^{(n)}\right)(x,y)=A_i^{(n)}(x)\cdot B_j^{(n)}(y)$$

It is easy to know that $\mathcal{A}(n)\cdot\mathcal{B}(n)$ a linearly independent group in the continuous function space $C\left([0,1]\times[c,d]\right)$. Now we take the diagonal elements of $\mathcal{A}(n)\cdot\mathcal{B}(n)$ to make a set as follows:

$$\mathcal{C}(n)=\left\{A_i^{(n)}\cdot B_i^{(n)}\,\middle|\, i=0,1,\cdots,m\right\},$$

which is clearly a linearly independent group with $m+1=2n+1$ dimension in the continuous function space $C\left([0,1]\times[c,d]\right)$. By using $\mathcal{C}(n)$, we can get a sequence of binary nonnegative continuous functions as the following:

$$\mu_n : [0,1]\times[c,d]\to[0,1]$$
$$(x,y)\mapsto \mu_n(x,y)=\bigvee_{i=1}^{m}\left[A_i^{(n)}(x)\cdot B_i^{(n)}(y)\right],$$
$$n=1,2,3,\cdots$$

where

$$\bigvee_{i=0}^{m}\left[A_i^{(n)}(x)\cdot B_i^{(n)}(y)\right]=\max_{0\le i\le m}\left\{A_i^{(n)}(x)\cdot B_i^{(n)}(y)\right\}.$$

Then this sequence of binary nonnegative continuous functions as being $\{\mu_n(x,y)\}_{n=1}^{\infty}$ are normalized as the following:

$$p_n(x,y)=\chi_{[0,1]\times[c,d]}(x,y)\frac{\mu_n(x,y)}{\int_c^d\int_0^1\mu_n(x,y)dxdy},$$
$$n=1,2,3,\cdots,$$

where

$$\chi_{[0,1]\times[c,d]}(x,y)=\begin{cases}1, & (x,y)\in[0,1]\times[c,d],\\ 0, & (x,y)\in\mathbb{R}^2-[0,1]\times[c,d]\end{cases}$$

Therefore $\{p_n(x,y)\}_{n=1}^{\infty}$ becomes a sequence of probability density functions defined on $\mathbb{R}^2$, and $p_n(x,y)$ is called the probability density function when the quantum number is just n.

And now by means of the sequence $\{p_n(x,y)\}_{n=1}^{\infty}$, we can construct a sequence of functions of one variable as follows:

$$f_n(x)=\frac{\int_{-\infty}^{+\infty}yp_n(x,y)dy}{\int_{-\infty}^{+\infty}p_n(x,y)dy},\quad n=1,2,3,\ldots \tag{8.2.18}$$

Apparently, $\{f_n(x)\}_{n=1}^{\infty}$ is just the sequence of conditional mathematical expectations formed by $\{p_n(x,y)\}_{n=1}^{\infty}$.

Case 2. Suppose $f: X \to Y$ be not strict monotonous function and not constant function.

Because the elements of the set $Y(n)$ may not always satisfy the monotonicity about the subscript i as $y_0 \le y_1 \le \cdots \le y_m$, it is of a little difficulty to make the continuous base functions as follows:

$$B_i^{(n)}(y), \quad i = 0,1,\cdots,m.$$

So we have to make a permutation on the subscript set $\{0,1,\cdots,m\}$ as the following:

$$\sigma = \begin{pmatrix} 0 & 1 & \cdots & m \\ k_0 & k_1 & \cdots & k_m \end{pmatrix},$$
$$\big(\forall i \in \{0,1,\cdots,m\}\big)\big(k_i = \sigma(i)\big)$$

such that the subscript set after the permutation is denoted by the following symbol:

$$K(n) = \{k_0, k_1, \cdots, k_m\}$$

and satisfies the following condition:

$$c(n) = y_{k_0}^{(n)} \le y_{k_1}^{(n)} \le \cdots \le y_{k_m}^{(n)} = d(n). \qquad (8.2.19)$$

Since (8.2.19) shows that the inequalities may not be strict, we have to consider the following two situations.

1) Assume that $c(n) = y_{k_0}^{(n)} < y_{k_1}^{(n)} < \cdots < y_{k_m}^{(n)} = d(n)$. Based on these nodes $y_{k_0}^{(n)}, y_{k_1}^{(n)}, \cdots, y_{k_m}^{(n)}$ in $[c,d]$ and doing in imitation of Case 1, we can get the continuous base functions $B_{k_j}^{(n)}$ $(j = 0,1,\cdots,m)$ as following:

$$B_{k_0}^{(n)}(y) = \chi_{\left[y_{k_0}^{(n)}, y_{k_1}^{(n)}\right]}(y)\cos^2 \frac{\pi}{2\left(y_{k_1}^{(n)} - y_{k_0}^{(n)}\right)}\left(y - y_{k_0}^{(n)}\right),$$

$$B_{k_1}^{(n)}(y) = \chi_{\left[y_{k_0}^{(n)}, y_{k_1}^{(n)}\right]}(y)\sin^2\frac{\pi}{2\left(y_{k_1}^{(n)} - y_{k_0}^{(n)}\right)}\left(y - y_{k_0}^{(n)}\right)$$

$$+\chi_{\left[y_{k_1}^{(n)}, y_{k_2}^{(n)}\right]}(y)\cos^2\frac{\pi}{2\left(y_{k_2}^{(n)} - y_{k_1}^{(n)}\right)}\left(y - y_{k_1}^{(n)}\right),$$

……

$$B_{k_{m-1}}^{(n)}(y) = \chi_{\left[y_{k_{m-2}}^{(n)}, y_{k_{m-1}}^{(n)}\right]}(y)\sin^2\frac{\pi}{2\left(y_{k_{m-1}}^{(n)} - y_{k_{m-2}}^{(n)}\right)}\left(y - y_{k_{m-2}}^{(n)}\right)$$

$$+\chi_{\left[y_{k_{m-1}}^{(n)}, y_{k_m}^{(n)}\right]}(y)\cos^2\frac{\pi}{2\left(y_{k_m}^{(n)} - y_{k_{m-1}}^{(n)}\right)}\left(y - y_{k_{m-1}}^{(n)}\right),$$

$$B_{k_m}^{(n)}(y) = \chi_{\left[y_{k_{m-1}}^{(n)}, y_{k_m}^{(n)}\right]}(y)\sin^2\frac{\pi}{2\left(y_{k_m}^{(n)} - y_{k_{m-1}}^{(n)}\right)}\left(y - y_{k_{m-1}}^{(n)}\right)$$

Then we easily make a sequence of binary nonnegative continuous functions defined on $X \times Y = [0,1]\times[c,d]$ as follows:

$$\mu_n(x,y) = \bigvee_{j=1}^{m}\left[A_{k_j}^{(n)}(x)\cdot B_{k_j}^{(n)}(y)\right], \quad n = 1,2,3,\cdots \tag{8.2.20}$$

2) Assume $c(n) = y_{k_0}^{(n)} \le y_{k_1}^{(n)} \le \cdots \le y_{k_m}^{(n)} = d(n)$. Firstly we do a kind of screen work on the elements in the following node set:

$$Y(n) = \left\{y_{k_0}^{(n)}, y_{k_1}^{(n)}, \cdots, y_{k_m}^{(n)}\right\}.$$

In fact, let $K(n) = \{k_0, k_1, \cdots, k_m\}$. We define a equivalence relation on the set $K(n)$ as being "$\sim$" as follows:

$$\left(\forall s,t \in \{0,1,\cdots,m\}\right)\left(k_s \sim k_t \Leftrightarrow y_{k_s}^{(n)} = y_{k_t}^{(n)}\right).$$

Then we get the quotient set of $K(n)$ as the following:

$$K(n)/\sim = \left\{\left[k_j\right] \middle| j = 0,1,\cdots,m\right\},$$

where $\left[k_j\right]$ is the equivalence class in which k_j belongs.

Let all the elements of the quotient set $K(n)/\sim$ be the following:

$$\left[k_{j_0}\right],\left[k_{j_1}\right],\cdots,\left[k_{j_{q(m)}}\right],$$

where $0 \le q(m) \le m$, and stipulate the representative element k_{j_s} be the smallest element in $\left[k_{j_s}\right]$. Thus we have the following inequalities:

$$y_{k_{j_0}}^{(n)} < y_{k_{j_1}}^{(n)} < \cdots < y_{k_{j_{q(m)}}}^{(n)}.$$

Based on the nodes $y_{k_{j_0}}^{(n)}, y_{k_{j_1}}^{(n)}, \cdots, y_{k_{j_{q(m)}}}^{(n)}$ in $[c,d]$, we make the continuous base functions $B_{k_{j_s}}^{(n)}\ (s = 0,1,\cdots,q(m))$ as follows:

$$B_{k_{j_0}}^{(n)}(y) = \chi_{\left[y_{k_{j_0}}^{(n)},\, y_{k_{j_1}}^{(n)}\right]}(y)\cos^2 \frac{\pi}{2\left(y_{k_{j_1}}^{(n)} - y_{k_{j_0}}^{(n)}\right)}\left(y - y_{k_{j_0}}^{(n)}\right),$$

$$B_{k_{j_1}}^{(n)}(y) = \chi_{\left[y_{k_{j_0}}^{(n)},\, y_{k_{j_1}}^{(n)}\right]}(y)\sin^2 \frac{\pi}{2\left(y_{k_1}^{(n)} - y_{k_0}^{(n)}\right)}\left(y - y_{k_{j_0}}^{(n)}\right)$$

$$+ \chi_{\left[y_{k_{j_1}}^{(n)},\, y_{k_{j_2}}^{(n)}\right]}(y)\cos^2 \frac{\pi}{2\left(y_{k_{j_2}}^{(n)} - y_{k_{j_1}}^{(n)}\right)}\left(y - y_{k_{j_1}}^{(n)}\right),$$

……

$$B_{k_{j_{q(m)-1}}}^{(n)}(y) = \chi_{\left[y_{k_{j_{q(m)-2}}}^{(n)},\, y_{k_{j_{q(m)-1}}}^{(n)}\right]}(y)\sin^2 \frac{\pi}{2\left(y_{k_{j_{q(m)-1}}}^{(n)} - y_{k_{j_{q(m)-2}}}^{(n)}\right)}\left(y - y_{k_{j_{q(m)-2}}}^{(n)}\right)$$

$$+ \chi_{\left[y_{k_{j_{q(m)-1}}}^{(n)},\, y_{k_{j_{q(m)}}}^{(n)}\right]}(y)\cos^2 \frac{\pi}{2\left(y_{k_{j_{q(m)}}}^{(n)} - y_{k_{j_{q(m)-1}}}^{(n)}\right)}\left(y - y_{k_{j_{q(m)-1}}}^{(n)}\right),$$

$$B_{k_{j_{q(m)}}}^{(n)}(y) = \chi_{\left[y_{k_{j_{q(m)-1}}}^{(n)},\, y_{k_{j_{q(m)}}}^{(n)}\right]}(y)\sin^2 \frac{\pi}{2\left(y_{k_{j_{q(m)}}}^{(n)} - y_{k_{j_{q(m)-1}}}^{(n)}\right)}\left(y - y_{k_{j_{q(m)-1}}}^{(n)}\right)$$

Hence for the nodes $y_{k_{j0}}^{(n)}, y_{k_{j1}}^{(n)}, \cdots, y_{k_{jq(m)}}^{(n)}$ which corresponds to the representative elements $k_{j_0}, k_{j_1}, \cdots, k_{j_{q(m)}}$ coming from these equivalence classes as being $\left[k_{j_0}\right], \left[k_{j_1}\right], \cdots, \left[k_{j_{q(m)}}\right]$, we have made the continuous base functions as follows:

$$B_{k_{j0}}^{(n)}(y), B_{k_{j1}}^{(n)}(y), \cdots, B_{k_{jq(m)}}^{(n)}(y).$$

For any $s \in \{0,1,\cdots,q(m)\}$ and we can define the continuous base functions corresponding to the elements in $\left[k_{j_s}\right]-\left\{k_{j_s}\right\}$ as following:

$$\left(\forall \tau \in \left[k_{j_s}\right]-\left\{k_{j_s}\right\}\right)\left(B_{\tau}^{(n)}(y) \equiv B_{k_{j_s}}^{(n)}(y)\right)$$

So for all the nodes $y_{k_0}^{(n)} \leq y_{k_1}^{(n)} \leq \cdots \leq y_{k_m}^{(n)}$ in $[c,d]$, we have got the corresponding continuous base functions as follows:

$$B_{k_0}^{(n)}(y), B_{k_1}^{(n)}(y), \cdots, B_{k_m}^{(n)}(y).$$

By using these continuous base functions, we get a sequence of binary nonnegative continuous functions defined on $X \times Y = [0,1] \times [c,d]$ as the following:

$$\mu_n(x,y) = \bigvee_{j=1}^{m}\left[A_{k_j}^{(n)}(x) \cdot B_{k_j}^{(n)}(y)\right], \quad n = 1,2,3,\cdots \tag{8.2.21}$$

Based on above two cases, we have got the sequence of binary nonnegative continuous functions defined on $X \times Y = [0,1] \times [c,d]$ as being $\{\mu_n(x,y)\}_{n=1}^{\infty}$. Now we normalize $\{\mu_n(x,y)\}_{n=1}^{\infty}$ as follows:

$$p_n(x,y) = \chi_{[0,1]\times[c,d]}(x,y)\frac{\mu_n(x,y)}{\int_c^d \int_0^1 \mu_n(x,y)dxdy},$$

$$n = 1,2,3,\cdots$$

where

$$\chi_{[0,1]\times[c,d]}(x,y)=\begin{cases}1, & (x,y)\in[0,1]\times[c,d],\\ 0, & (x,y)\in\mathbb{R}^2-[0,1]\times[c,d]\end{cases}$$

Therefore $\{p_n(x,y)\}_{n=1}^{\infty}$ becomes a sequence of probability density functions defined on $\mathbb{R}^2$, and $p_n(x,y)$ is also called the probability density function when the quantum number is just n. And by means of $\{p_n(x,y)\}_{n=1}^{\infty}$, we can construct a sequence of functions of one variable defined on $[0,1]$ as follows:

$$f_n(x)=\frac{\int_{-\infty}^{+\infty} y p_n(x,y)dy}{\int_{-\infty}^{+\infty} p_n(x,y)dy}, \quad x\in[0,1], \qquad (8.2.18)$$
$$n=1,2,3,\cdots$$

Apparently, $\{f_n(x)\}_{n=1}^{\infty}$ is just the sequence of conditional mathematical expectations formed by $\{p_n(x,y)\}_{n=1}^{\infty}$. Besides, it is not under the following expression:

$$f_n(x)=\frac{\int_{-\infty}^{+\infty} y \mu_n(x,y)dy}{\int_{-\infty}^{+\infty} \mu_n(x,y)dy}, \quad x\in[0,1], \quad n=1,2,3,\cdots$$

Step 7. Proof of the conclusion: the sequence of conditional mathematical expectations $\{f_n(x)\}_{n=1}^{\infty}$ can uniformly converge to $f(x)$ on the closed interval $[0,1]$.

Situation 1. Suppose $f:X\to Y$ be strict monotonous. We only consider the case that $f(x)$ is a strict monotone increasing function because we can treat it in the same way when $f(x)$ is strict monotone decreasing function.

First of all, for the sequence of binary nonnegative continuous functions $\{\mu_n(x,y)\}_{n=1}^{\infty}$, we prove the following fact:

$$(\forall n \in \mathbb{N}_+)(\forall x \in [0,1])\left(\int_c^d \mu_n(x,y)dy > 0\right).$$

In fact, for any a point $x \in [0,1]$, we can easily know the fact that

$$(\exists i \in \{1,2,\cdots,m\})\left(x \in \left[x_{i-1}^{(n)}, x_i^{(n)}\right]\right).$$

Then for any a point $y \in [c,d]$, we can learn the following fact:

$$\mu_n(x,y) = \mathop{\vee}_{k=0}^{m}\left(A_k^{(n)}(x)\cdot B_k^{(n)}(y)\right)$$
$$= \begin{cases} \left(A_{i-1}^{(n)}(x)\cdot B_{i-1}^{(n)}(y)\right)\vee\left(A_i^{(n)}(x)\cdot B_i^{(n)}(y)\right), & y \in \left[y_{i-2}^{(n)}, y_{i+1}^{(n)}\right], \\ 0, & y \in [c,d] - \left[y_{i-2}^{(n)}, y_{i+1}^{(n)}\right] \end{cases}$$

It is easy to know the fact as the following:

$$\left(\exists y' \in \left(y_{i-2}^{(n)}, y_{i+1}^{(n)}\right)\right)\left(\mu_n(x,y') > 0\right).$$

Since for this fixed point $x \in [a,b]$, $\mu_n(x,y)$ is continuous with respect to y, we have the following results:

$$(\exists \delta > 0)\left((y'-\delta, y'+\delta) \subset \left(y_{i-2}^{(n)}, y_{i+1}^{(n)}\right)\right),$$
$$\left(\forall y \in (y'-\delta, y'+\delta)\right)\left(\mu_n(x,y) > 0\right)$$

By using mean value theorem of integrals, there exists a point as follows:

$$\xi \in \left[y' - \frac{\delta}{2}, y' + \frac{\delta}{2}\right],$$

such that

$$\int_c^d \mu_n(x,y)dy \geq \int_{(y'-\delta,y'+\delta)} \mu_n(x,y)dy$$
$$\geq \int_{\left[y'-\frac{\delta}{2},y'+\frac{\delta}{2}\right]} \mu_n(x,y)dy = \mu_n(x,\xi)\cdot\delta > 0$$

So the fact we want to prove is true. Thus for every $n \in \mathbb{N}_+$, the following function

$$f_n(x) = \frac{\int_c^d y\mu_n(x,y)dy}{\int_c^d \mu_n(x,y)dy}$$

must be meaningful.

Then we prove that the sequence of single variable functions $\{f_n(x)\}_{n=1}^{\infty}$ can converge to $f(x)$ at everywhere in $[0,1]$.

As a matter of fact, for any a point $x \in [0,1]$, we must have the following fact:

$$(\exists i \in \{1,2,\cdots,n\})\left(x \in \left[x_{i-1}^{(n)}, x_i^{(n)}\right]\right).$$

So we have the following expression:

$$\mu_n(x,y) = \bigvee_{k=0}^{n}\left(A_k^{(n)}(x)\cdot B_k^{(n)}(y)\right)$$
$$= \begin{cases} \left(A_{i-1}^{(n)}(x)\cdot B_{i-1}^{(n)}(y)\right)\vee\left(A_i^{(n)}(x)\cdot B_i^{(n)}(y)\right), & y \in \left[y_{i-2}^{(n)}, y_{i+1}^{(n)}\right], \\ 0, & y \in [c,d]-\left[y_{i-2}^{(n)}, y_{i+1}^{(n)}\right] \end{cases}$$

By means of the first mean value theorem of integrals, we know the fact that, there exists $\eta_n(x) \in \left[y_{i-2}^{(n)}, y_{i+1}^{(n)}\right]$, such that

$$f_n(x) = \frac{\int_c^d y\mu_n(x,y)dy}{\int_c^d \mu_n(x,y)dy} = \frac{\eta_n(x)\int_{y_{i-2}^{(n)}}^{y_{i+1}^{(n)}} R_n(x,y)dy}{\int_{y_{i-2}^{(n)}}^{y_{i+1}^{(n)}} R_n(x,y)dy} = \eta_n(x)$$

Because $f(x)$ is continuous and taking notice of $\eta_n(x) \in \left[y_{i-2}^{(n)}, y_{i+1}^{(n)} \right]$, based on intermediate value theorem on continuous functions, we can know the following result:

$$\left(\exists \overline{x} \in \left[x_{i-2}^{(n)}, x_{i+1}^{(n)} \right] \right) \left(f\left(\overline{x} \right) = \eta_n(x) \right).$$

And taking notice of the fact that $f(x) \in \left[y_{i-1}^{(n)}, y_{i+1}^{(n)} \right] \subset \left[y_{i-2}^{(n)}, y_{i+1}^{(n)} \right]$, we have the following implication:

$$\begin{aligned} & n \to \infty \Rightarrow \left| y_{i+1}^{(n)} - y_{i-2}^{(n)} \right| \to 0 \\ & \Rightarrow \eta_n(x) = f\left(\overline{x} \right) \to f(x) \end{aligned} \tag{8.2.22}$$

By means of the fact that x is arbitrarily taken in $[0,1]$, we get the following result:

$$(\forall x \in [0,1]) \left(\lim_{n\to\infty} f_n(x) = f(x) \right).$$

And then we prove the fact that the sequence of single variable functions $\{f_n(x)\}_{n=1}^{\infty}$ can uniformly converge to $f(x)$ in $[0,1]$.

As a matter of fact, since $f(x)$ is continuous in the closed interval $[0,1]$, $f(x)$ must be uniformly continuous in $[0,1]$. So for any $\varepsilon > 0$, there exists $N \in \mathbb{N}_+$, such that

$$(\forall n \in \mathbb{N}_+) \left(n > N \Rightarrow \max \left\{ \left| \Delta y_i^{(n)} \right| \middle| i = 1, 2, \cdots, m \right\} < \frac{\varepsilon}{3} \right)$$

By use of (8.2.22), for any a point $x \in [0,1]$, for any a number $n \in \mathbb{N}_+$, when $n > N$, we have the following expression:

$$\begin{aligned} & \left| f_n(x) - f(x) \right| = \left| \eta_n(x) - f(x) \right| \le \left| y_{i+1}^{(n)} - y_{i-2}^{(n)} \right| \\ & \le 3 \max \left\{ \left| \Delta y_i^{(n)} \right| \middle| i = 1, 2, \cdots, n \right\} < 3 \cdot \frac{\varepsilon}{3} = \varepsilon \end{aligned}$$

All in all, we draw a conclusion: for any $\varepsilon > 0$ and for any $n \in \mathbb{N}_+$, there must exist $N \in \mathbb{N}_+$, such that

$$(\forall n \in \mathbb{N}_+)\Big(n > N \Rightarrow (\forall x \in [0,1])\big(|f_n(x) - f(x)| < \varepsilon\big)\Big)$$

This means that $\{f_n(x)\}_{n=1}^{\infty}$ can uniformly converge to $f(x)$ in $[0,1]$.

Situation 2. Assume $f(x)$ be not strict monotonous and not a constant function. We also consider two situations.

1) Suppose $c(n) = y_{k_0}^{(n)} < y_{k_1}^{(n)} < \cdots < y_{k_m}^{(n)} = d(n)$. From (8.2.19), we have the following expression:

$$\mu_n(x, y) = \bigvee_{j=1}^{m}\Big[A_{k_j}^{(n)}(x) \cdot B_{k_j}^{(n)}(y)\Big], \quad n = 1, 2, 3, \cdots$$

First it is not difficult to know the fact that

$$(\forall n \in \mathbb{N}_+)(\forall x \in [0,1])\left(\int_c^d \mu_n(x, y)dy > 0\right).$$

We have necessity to define that $k_{-1} = k_0, k_{n+1} = k_n$. Arbitrarily taken a point $x \in [0,1]$, clearly we have the fact as the following:

$$(\exists s, t \in \{0, 1, \cdots, n\})\Big(x \in \big[x_{k_s}, x_{k_t}\big]\Big),$$

and so we have the following expression:

$$\mu_n(x, y) = \bigvee_{j=0}^{n}\Big(A_{k_j}^{(n)}(x) \cdot B_{k_j}^{(n)}(y)\Big)$$
$$= \begin{cases} \Big(A_{k_s}^{(n)}(x) \cdot B_{k_s}^{(n)}(y)\Big) \vee \Big(A_{k_t}^{(n)}(x) \cdot B_{k_t}^{(n)}(y)\Big), & y \in E_n, \\ 0, & y \in [c, d] - E_n \end{cases}$$
$$E_n \triangleq \Big[y_{k_{s-1}}^{(n)}, y_{k_{s+1}}^{(n)}\Big] \cup \Big[y_{k_{t-1}}^{(n)}, y_{k_{t+1}}^{(n)}\Big]$$

Let $y_* = \min\left\{y_{k_{s-1}}^{(n)}, y_{k_{t-1}}^{(n)}, y_{k_{s+1}}^{(n)}, y_{k_{t+1}}^{(n)}\right\}$ and $y^* = \max\left\{y_{k_{s-1}}^{(n)}, y_{k_{t-1}}^{(n)}, y_{k_{s+1}}^{(n)}, y_{k_{t+1}}^{(n)}\right\}$. For clarity, we can assume that $y_* = y_{k_{s-1}}^{(n)}, y^* = y_{k_{t+1}}^{(n)}$, this makes the following inclusion:

$$\left[y_*, y^*\right] = \left[y_{k_{s-1}}^{(n)}, y_{k_{t+1}}^{(n)}\right] \supset \left[y_{k_{s-1}}^{(n)}, y_{k_{s+1}}^{(n)}\right] \cup \left[y_{k_{t-1}}^{(n)}, y_{k_{t+1}}^{(n)}\right].$$

So above expression can be written as the following:

$$\mu_n(x,y) = \overset{n}{\underset{j=0}{\vee}} \left(A_{k_j}^{(n)}(x) \cdot B_{k_j}^{(n)}(y)\right)$$
$$= \begin{cases} \left(A_{k_s}^{(n)}(x) \cdot B_{k_s}^{(n)}(y)\right) \vee \left(A_{k_t}^{(n)}(x) \cdot B_{k_t}^{(n)}(y)\right), & y \in \left[y_{k_{s-1}}^{(n)}, y_{k_{t+1}}^{(n)}\right], \\ 0, & y \in [c,d] - \left[y_{k_{s-1}}^{(n)}, y_{k_{t+1}}^{(n)}\right] \end{cases}$$

By means of the first mean value theorem of integrals, there must be $\eta_n(x) \in \left[y_{k_{s-1}}^{(n)}, y_{k_{t+1}}^{(n)}\right]$, such that

$$f_n(x) = \frac{\int_c^d y\mu_n(x,y)dy}{\int_c^d \mu_n(x,y)dy} = \frac{\eta_n(x)\int_{y_{k_{s-1}}^{(n)}}^{y_{k_{t+1}}^{(n)}} \mu_n(x,y)dy}{\int_{y_{k_{s-1}}^{(n)}}^{y_{k_{t+1}}^{(n)}} \mu_n(x,y)dy} = \eta_n(x)$$

Let $d_n = \max\left\{\Delta y_{k_j}^{(n)} \middle| j = 1,2,\cdots,m\right\}$, where we have put

$$\Delta y_{k_j}^{(n)} = y_{k_j}^{(n)} - y_{k_{j-1}}^{(n)}, \quad j = 1,2,\cdots,m.$$

We can prove the fact that $\lim_{n\to\infty} d_n = 0$. In fact, let

$$e_n = \max\left\{\left|y_i^{(n)} - y_{i-1}^{(n)}\right| \middle| i = 1,2,\cdots,m\right\}.$$

Based on Lemma 8.2.1, we must have the following result:

$$(\forall n \in \mathbb{N}_+)(d_n \le e_n).$$

By using this result and by means of the fact that $f(x)$ uniformly continuous in the closed interval $[0,1]$, we can get $\lim_{n\to\infty} e_n = 0$, and then that the limit $\lim_{n\to\infty} d_n = 0$ must be true.

Then we return to the proof of the theorem. By means of above conclusion, we have the result: for any $\varepsilon > 0$,

$$(\exists N_1 \in \mathbb{N}_+)(\forall n \in \mathbb{N}_+)\left(n > N_1 \Rightarrow d_n < \frac{\varepsilon}{3}\right).$$

By notice of the following implications:

$$\begin{aligned} & n \to \infty \Rightarrow x_{k_s}^{(n)} - x_{k_t}^{(n)} \to 0 \\ & \Rightarrow \left|y_{k_s}^{(n)} - y_{k_t}^{(n)}\right| = \left|f\left(x_{k_s}^{(n)}\right) - f\left(x_{k_t}^{(n)}\right)\right| \to 0 \end{aligned}$$

We get the result: there must exist a number $N_2 \in \mathbb{N}_+$, such that

$$(\forall n \in \mathbb{N}_+)\left(n > N_2 \Rightarrow \left|y_{k_s}^{(n)} - y_{k_t}^{(n)}\right| < \frac{\varepsilon}{3}\right). \tag{8.2.23}$$

And we take $N = \max\{N_1, N_2\}$; for any $n \in \mathbb{N}_+$, when $n > N$, we get the following inequalities:

$$\begin{aligned} & \left|y_{k_{t+1}}^{(n)} - y_{k_{s-1}}^{(n)}\right| \le \left|y_{k_{t+1}}^{(n)} - y_{k_t}^{(n)}\right| + \left|y_{k_t}^{(n)} - y_{k_s}^{(n)}\right| + \left|y_{k_s}^{(n)} - y_{k_{s-1}}^{(n)}\right| \\ & < d_n + \frac{\varepsilon}{3} + d_n < \frac{\varepsilon}{3} + \frac{\varepsilon}{3} + \frac{\varepsilon}{3} = \varepsilon \end{aligned}$$

By this expression we get $\left|y_{k_{t+1}}^{(n)} - y_{k_{s-1}}^{(n)}\right| \xrightarrow{n\to\infty} 0$, and then we have

$$\left|y_{k_s}^{(n)} - \eta_n(x)\right| \xrightarrow{n\to\infty} 0.$$

By (8.2.22) we can easily know the following limit:

$$\left|f(x) - y_{k_s}^{(n)}\right| \xrightarrow{n\to\infty} 0.$$

At last, we have the result:

$$\left|f(x)-\eta_n(x)\right| \le \left|f(x)-y_{k_s}^{(n)}\right| + \left|y_{k_s}^{(n)}-\eta_n(x)\right| \xrightarrow{n\to\infty} 0 .$$

This means that $\eta_n(x) \xrightarrow{n\to\infty} f(x)$. So we have the following expression:

$$\left(\forall x \in [0,1]\right)\left(\lim_{n\to\infty} f_n(x) = f(x)\right).$$

Furthermore, very similar to the process we just did in Situation 1, we can prove that $\{f_n(x)\}_{n=1}^{\infty}$ can uniformly converge to $f(x)$ in $[0,1]$.

2) Let $c(n) = y_{k_0}^{(n)} \le y_{k_1}^{(n)} \le \cdots \le y_{k_m}^{(n)} = d(n)$. By (8.2.21), we have

$$\mu_n(x,y) = \bigvee_{j=1}^{m}\left[A_{k_j}^{(n)}(x)\cdot B_{k_j}^{(n)}(y)\right], \quad n = 1,2,3,\cdots$$

It is easy to know the fact that

$$\left(\forall n \in \mathbb{N}_+\right)\left(\forall x \in [0,1]\right)\left(\int_c^d \mu_n(x,y)dy > 0\right).$$

Now arbitrarily taken a point $x \in [0,1]$, we must have the following expression:

$$\left(\exists s,t \in \{0,1,\cdots,m\}\right)\left(x \in \left[x_{k_s}^{(n)}, x_{k_t}^{(n)}\right]\right).$$

Then we again consider two cases the following:

i) When $B_{k_s}^{(n)}(y) \equiv B_{k_t}^{(n)}(y)$, we have the expression:

$$\mu_n(x,y) = \bigvee_{j=0}^{m}\left(A_{k_j}^{(n)}(x)\cdot B_{k_j}^{(n)}(y)\right)$$
$$= \begin{cases} \left(A_{k_s}^{(n)}(x)\cdot B_{k_s}^{(n)}(y)\right) \vee \left(A_{k_t}^{(n)}(x)\cdot B_{k_t}^{(n)}(y)\right), & y \in \left[y_{k_{s-1}}^{(n)}, y_{k_{s+1}}^{(n)}\right], \\ 0, & y \in [c,d] - \left[y_{k_{s-1}}^{(n)}, y_{k_{s+1}}^{(n)}\right] \end{cases}$$

ii) When $B_{k_s}^{(n)}(y) \lesseqgtr B_{k_t}^{(n)}(y)$, we have the following:

$$\mu_n(x,y) = \mathop{\vee}_{j=0}^{m} \left(A_{k_j}^{(n)}(x) \cdot B_{k_j}^{(n)}(y) \right)$$

$$= \begin{cases} \left(A_{k_s}^{(n)}(x) \cdot B_{k_s}^{(n)}(y) \right) \vee \left(A_{k_t}^{(n)}(x) \cdot B_{k_t}^{(n)}(y) \right), & y \in G_n, \\ 0, & y \in [c,d] - G_n \end{cases}$$

$$G_n \triangleq \left[y_{k_{s-1}}^{(n)}, y_{k_{s+1}}^{(n)} \right] \cup \left[y_{k_{t-1}}^{(n)}, y_{k_{t+1}}^{(n)} \right]$$

Nevertheless, in either case, similar to the method we have used in 1), we have proved the following conclusion:

$$\left(\forall x \in [0,1] \right) \left(\lim_{n \to \infty} f_n(x) = f(x) \right),$$

and $\{f_n(x)\}_{n=1}^{\infty}$ must uniformly converge to $f(x)$ in $[0,1]$.

Paying attention to the process of the theorem, when the quantum number is n, the set of the descendant particles generated by the particle M is the following:

$$\mathcal{M}_n = \left\{ M_1^{(n)}, M_2^{(n)}, \cdots, M_{2n}^{(n)} \right\},$$

When $n \to \infty$, the set of all descendant particles generated by the particle M is $\mathcal{M} = \bigcup_{n=1}^{\infty} \mathcal{M}_n$. Clearly the cardinal number of the set is as being: $\text{card}(\mathcal{M}) = \aleph_0$; i.e., we all use countable infinite particles. These particles can be expressed as the following expression:

$$M \overset{n=1,2,3,\cdots}{\Rightarrow} \begin{cases} M_1^{(1)}, M_2^{(1)}; \\ M_1^{(2)}, M_2^{(2)}, M_3^{(2)}, M_4^{(2)}; \\ M_1^{(3)}, M_2^{(3)}, M_3^{(3)}, M_4^{(3)}, M_5^{(3)}, M_6^{(3)}; \\ \cdots\cdots \\ M_1^{(n)}, M_2^{(n)}, \cdots, M_{2n-1}^{(n)}, M_{2n}^{(n)}; \\ \cdots\cdots \end{cases}$$

where only the particle M moves along Ox axis, but all the descendant particles $M_1^{(1)}, M_2^{(1)}, \cdots M_1^{(n)}, \cdots M_{2n}^{(n)}, \cdots$ move along Oy axis.

This means that the motion curve of a mass point in classic physics $y = f(x)$ can be constructed by an infinite sequence of microscopic particles wave functions. In other words, this motion curve of a mass point $y = f(x)$ have been quantization, which is the limit state of these microscopic particles wave functions when $n \to \infty$. Clearly this fact meets the Bohr's correspondence principle.

We finally end the proof of the theorem. □

Example 8.2.1 Suppose we cast an object B with quality m_0, which is regarded as a mass point. So the movement of B can be described by its equation of locus as follows:

$$y = f(x) = x \tan \alpha - \frac{g}{2v_0^2 \cos^2 \alpha} x^2,$$

$$x \in [0, d_0], \quad d_0 = \frac{v_0^2}{g} \sin 2\alpha$$

where $\alpha \in \left(0, \frac{\pi}{2}\right)$ is a mass ejection angle, $d_0 \in (0, +\infty)$ is the maximum range of fire, and $v_0 \in (0, +\infty)$ is the initial velocity; here the air friction is omitted. Clearly $y(x) \in C[0, d_0]$, which means that the projectile motion is expressed by an unary continuous function.

Now if we take $\alpha = \frac{\pi}{4}, v_0 = \sqrt{g}$, then $d_0 = 1$; then we have the following equation:

$$y = f(x) = x - x^2 = x(1 - x).$$

When the quantum number $n = 5, 10, 20$, the approximation situations of the sequence of conditional mathematical expectations $f_n(x)$ to $f(x)$ are respectively shown in Figure 8.2.5, 8.2.6 and 7.2.7., where red curve means $f_n(x)$, and blue curve indicates $f(x)$. □

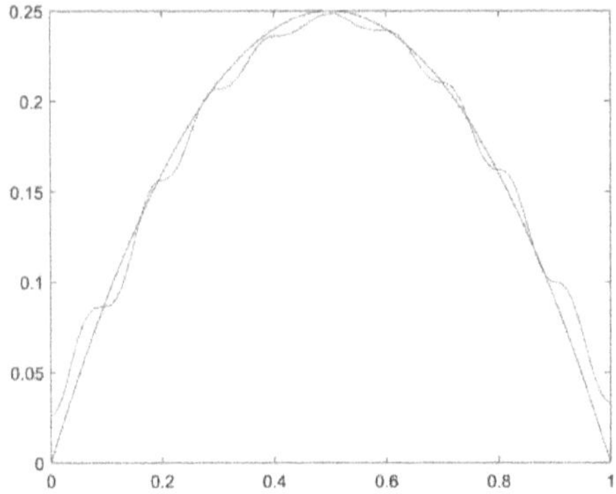

Fig. 8.2.5. Approximation of $f_5(x)$ to $f(x)$

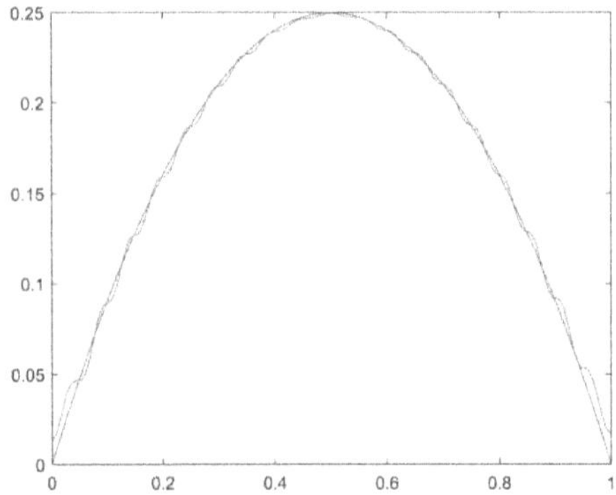

Fig. 8.2.6. Approximation of $f_{10}(x)$ to $f(x)$

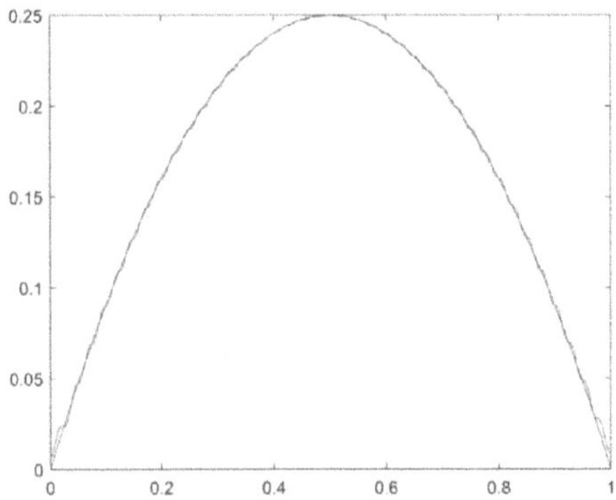

Fig. 8.2.7. Approximation of $f_{20}(x)$ to $f(x)$

8.3 Duality of Mass Point Motion

We firstly review the projectile motion in Example 8.2.1. The property of mass point motion is shown as its momentum $p = m_0 v_0$ and its energy as the following:

$$E = E_k = \frac{1}{2} m_0 v_0^2 .$$

Actually, more straightway, its property of mass point should be described by its equation of locus as the following:

$$y = f(x) = x \tan\alpha - \frac{g}{2v_0^2 \cos^2\alpha} x^2$$

In other words, either the property of mass point can be described by its momentum and energy or by its equation of locus; these two methods are equivalent.

Then we raise an interesting and important problem: is there wave nature on mass point motion in classic physics? Alternatively, we can ask the question: is there wave mass point duality in classic physics?

For answering this problem, we firstly review the particle nature and wave nature in quantum mechanics. As we all know, a microscopic particle has no determinate movement locus so that it has no an equation describing its movement locus. Thus, its nature of particle can only be described by its momentum $p = mv$ and its energy $E = \frac{1}{2} mv^2$. Based on the viewpoint of de Broglie, an object particle is of wave-particle duality, which means the particle also has its nature of wave. The nature of wave should be shown by its wave function Ψ, and the wave function Ψ should be the solution of. The wave as being the solution of Schrodinger Equation is called de Broglie wave. Then Born gave Schrodinger Equation the statistical interpretation of de Broglie wave, which means that $|\Psi|^2$ should be a kind of probability density function. So $|\Psi|^2$ is often called probability wave. In fact, in quantum mechanics, the probability wave $|\Psi|^2$ is much more important than the wave function Ψ itself.

Again, we consider the movement of the particle in the infinite deep square potential well as we have discussed in Step 1 in Theorem 8.2.1, where the wave function is as following:

$$\psi_n(x) = \sqrt{2}\sin(n\pi x), \quad x \in [0,1], \quad n = 1,2,3,\cdots$$

Then, its probability wave is $|\psi_n(x)|^2 = 2\sin^2(n\pi x)$, which figure is shown in Figure 8.3.1.

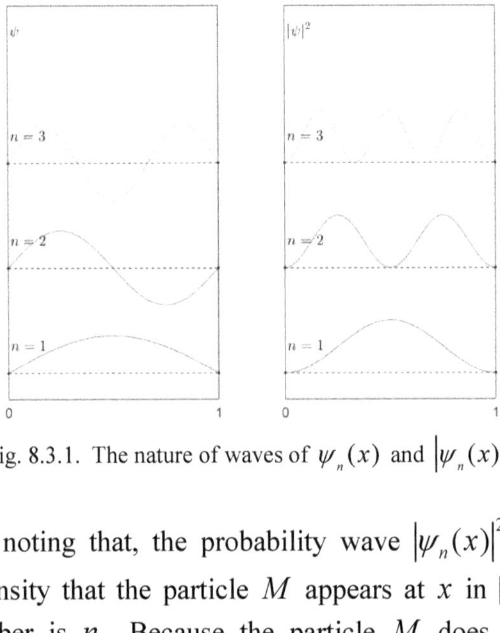

Fig. 8.3.1. The nature of waves of $\psi_n(x)$ and $|\psi_n(x)|^2$

It is worth noting that, the probability wave $|\psi_n(x)|^2$ describes the probability density that the particle M appears at x in $[0,1]$ when the quantum number is n. Because the particle M does one-dimension motion along Ox axis, $|\psi_n(x)|^2$ is a curve on two-dimension plane.

It is well-known that the wave nature of simple harmonic wave is constructed by its frequency ν and its wave length λ. When the quantum number is n, its energy expression is $E_n = \dfrac{n^2\pi^2\hbar^2}{2m}$, and the wave frequency is as following:

$$\nu_n = \frac{1}{T_n} = \frac{k_n}{2\pi} = \frac{n\pi}{2\pi} = \frac{n}{2} = \frac{\sqrt{mE_n}}{\sqrt{2}\pi\hbar}.$$

Based on the definition of wave length, we know the wave length is $\lambda_n = \frac{2}{n}$ so that

$$\lambda_n = \frac{2}{n} = \frac{\sqrt{2}\pi\hbar}{\sqrt{mE_n}}.$$

This just gives the result that $\nu_n \cdot \lambda_n = 1$, which means that the relation between the wave nature and the particle nature can be established by using Planck number $\hbar$.

Now we return to continue to discuss the motion of projectile. Its mass point nature reflected in its equation of locus.

Especially, when $\alpha = \frac{\pi}{4}, v_0 = \sqrt{g}$, the equation of locus is as follows:

$$y = f(x) = x - x^2 = x(1-x), \quad x \in [0,1].$$

Because this sequence of conditional mathematical expectations as being $\{f_n(x)\}_{n=1}^{\infty}$ uniformly converges to $y = f(x)$ in $[0,1]$, for arbitrarily given a $\varepsilon > 0$, there must exist a natural number $N \in \mathbb{N}_+$, such that

$$(\forall n \in \mathbb{N}_+)(n > N \Rightarrow \|f_n - f\| < \varepsilon),$$

where $\|\cdot\|$ is a kind of norm in the linear normed space $(C[0,1], \|\cdot\|)$ and defined as the following:

$$(\forall f \in C[0,1])\left(\|f\| = \max_{x\in[0,1]} |f(x)|\right).$$

For $\varepsilon > 0$ is small enough, that $\|f_n - f\| < \varepsilon$ means that the difference between f_n and f is very small so that f_n can be replaced by f approximately.

We now take notice of the following important expression:

$$f(x) \approx f_n(x) = \frac{\int_c^d y p_n(x,y)dy}{\int_c^d p_n(x,y)dy} = \frac{\int_0^1 y p_n(x,y)dy}{\int_0^1 p_n(x,y)dy},$$

for above the motion of projectile where $c = 0, d = 1$, where $p_n(x, y)$ is a binary probability density function.

When the quantum number $n = 5, 10, 15$, the graphed of the probability density function $p_n(x, y)$ are respectively shown in Figure 8.3.2, 8.3.3 and 8.3.4.

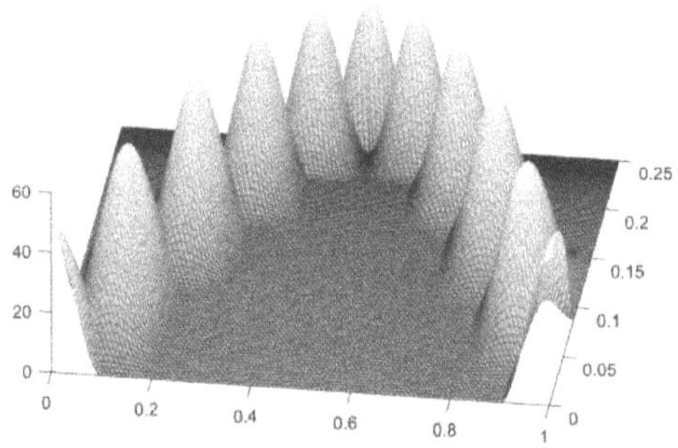

Fig. 8.3.2. Graph of $p_5(x, y)$

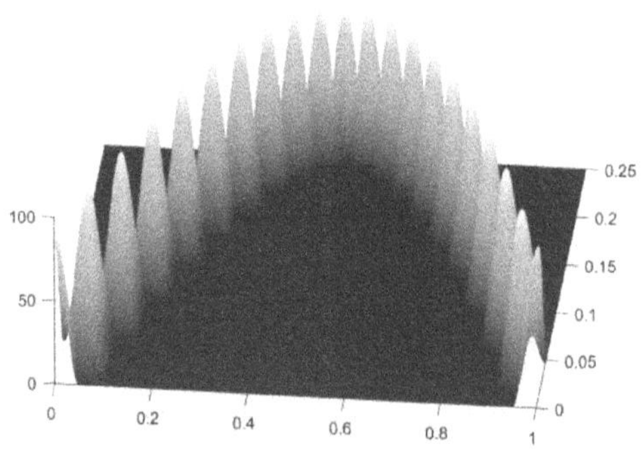

Fig. 8.3.3. Graph of $p_{10}(x, y)$

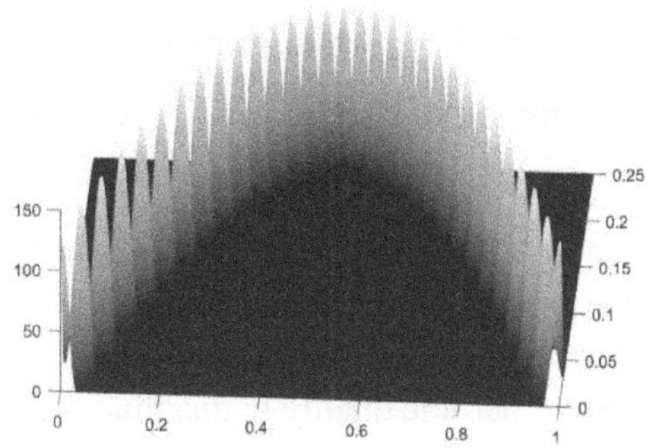

Fig. 8.3.4. Graph of $p_{15}(x, y)$

Apparently, the probability density function $p_n(x, y)$ shows up waviness. We observe the motion curve of the projectile, and suppose some mass point B moves in the rectangle as in Fig 8.3.5, and the probability density function that B falls into the set of graph of $f(x)$ as follows

$$G_f = \{(x, y) \in [0,1] \times [0, 0.25] \,|\, y = f(x)\} \tag{8.3.1}$$

is just $p_n(x, y)$.

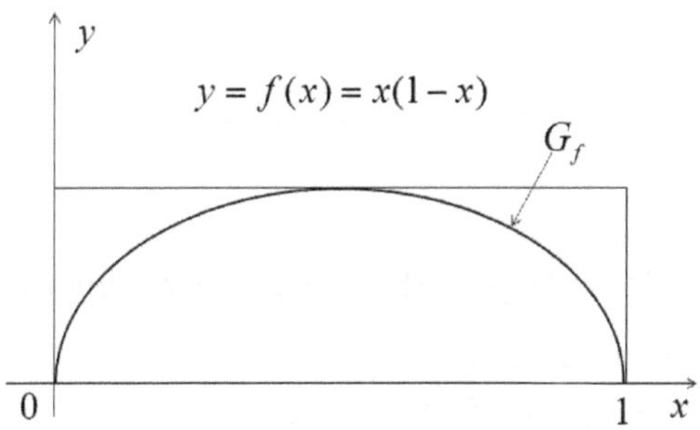

Fig. 8.3.5. Graph of the motion of projectile

It is worth noting that, since the mass point B moves in a two-dimension region, the probability density function $p_n(x, y)$ is a wave surface in three-dimension space. From Figure 8.3.1, we can learn that, since the particle M moves in $[0,1]$ on Ox axis, the probability wave

$|\psi_n(x)|^2$ mainly roots in $[0,1]$; while from Figure 8.3.4, we also can learn that, since the mass point B moves in G_f on $x-y$ plane, the probability wave $p_n(x,y)$ roots in G_f.

Above discussion reveals an important conclusion: the motion of mass point in classic mechanics is surely of waviness so that the motion of mass point in classic mechanics also has wave mass point duality, which is very same with wave-particle duality in quantum mechanics.

Furthermore, the relationship between the wave nature and particle nature is established by means of Schrodinger Equation and the energy of the particle E and the momentum of the particle p can be respectively expressed by the frequency ν and the wavelength λ of the particle as the following:

$$E = 2\pi\hbar\nu, \quad p = \frac{2\pi\hbar}{\lambda}.$$

While in classic mechanics, the relation between the mass point nature and waviness of motion of mass point is related by means of the following integral equation:

$$\frac{\int_c^d yp(x,y)dy}{\int_c^d p(x,y)dy} = f(x), \quad (x,y)\in[a,b]\times[c,d] \tag{8.3.2}$$

where $p(x,y)\in C\left([a,b]\times[c,d]\right)$ is an unknown binary function satisfying the following conditions:

(1) $\left(\forall(x,y)\in[a,b]\times[c,d]\right)\left(p(x,y)\geq 0\right)$;

(2) $\left(\forall x\in[a,b]\right)\left(\int_c^d p(x,y)\mathrm{d}y > 0\right)$.

(3) $\int_c^d\int_a^b p(x,y)\mathrm{d}x\mathrm{d}y = 1$.

Because $y = f(x)$ is the equation of locus of motion of the mass point, it completely represents the mass point nature of motion of the mass point; while $p(x,y)$ is the probability density function which is the probability wave of itself so that $p(x,y)$ itself represents the waviness of motion of the mass point. And the relation between the mass point nature and the wave nature is related by means of the integral equation (8.3.2). This adequately explains that the motion of mass point in classic mechanics has the duality of wave mass point, or written by **wave-mass-point duality**.

Here we need to explain that to solve the integral equation (8.3.2) is not an easy thing; however, we have given a kind of approximate method to do it; actually, $\{p_n(x,y)\}_{n=1}^{\infty}$ is a sequence of approximate solutions of the integral equation because if we write

$$f_n(x)=\frac{\int_c^d yp_n(x,y)dy}{\int_c^d p_n(x,y)dy},$$

then we have $\lim_{n\to\infty}\|f_n-f\|=0$ based on Theorem 8.2.1.

How about the properties of convergence of the sequence $\{p_n(x,y)\}_{n=1}^{\infty}$? We see the following theorem.

Theorem 8.3.1 1) $p_n(x,y)\overset{n\to\infty}{\Rightarrow}0$, i.e. $\{p_n(x,y)\}_{n=1}^{\infty}$ converges in measure to zero function 0 as follows:

$$0:[a,b]\times[c,d]\to\mathbb{R},\quad (x,y)\mapsto 0(x,y)=0.$$

2) The sequence of binary functions $\{p_n(x,y)\}_{n=1}^{\infty}$ does not converge in the set $G_f-\{(a,f(a)),(b,f(b))\}$.

We omit the proof. □

Because the sequence $\{p_n(x,y)\}_{n=1}^{\infty}$ converges in measure and the two functions $p_n(x,y)$ and $yp_n(x,y)$ are bounded in $\mathbb{R}^2$ with respect with every n, based on Lebesque dominated convergence theorem, the limit operation and integral operation can exchange order, i.e.,

$$\lim_{n\to\infty}\int_{-\infty}^{+\infty} yp_n(x,y)dy = \int_{-\infty}^{+\infty} y\lim_{n\to\infty} p_n(x,y)dy = 0,$$

$$\lim_{n\to\infty}\int_{-\infty}^{+\infty} p_n(x,y)dy = \int_{-\infty}^{+\infty} \lim_{n\to\infty} p_n(x,y)dy = 0$$

so that

$$\frac{\lim_{n\to\infty}\int_{-\infty}^{+\infty} yp_n(x,y)dy}{\lim_{n\to\infty}\int_{-\infty}^{+\infty} p_n(x,y)dy} = \frac{0}{0} \neq f(x) = \lim_{n\to\infty} f_n(x) = \lim_{n\to\infty}\frac{\int_{-\infty}^{+\infty} yp_n(x,y)dy}{\int_{-\infty}^{+\infty} p_n(x,y)dy}$$

This means that the limit function of convergence in measure as follows:

$$\lim_{n\to\infty} p_n(x,y) = 0$$

is not a solution of the integral Equation (8.3.2). But for every quantum number $n \in \mathbb{N}_+$, the probability wave function $p_n(x,y)$ must be a solution of the following integral equation:

$$\frac{\int_c^d yp(x,y)dy}{\int_c^d p(x,y)dy} = f_n(x), \tag{8.3.3}$$

And the sequence of functions $f_n(x)$ can uniformly converge to $f(x)$. In other words, the sequence of binary functions $\{p_n(x,y)\}_{n=1}^{\infty}$ must be approximate solutions of the integral Equation (8.3.2).

Another thing we should point out is that, about the probability wave function $p_n(x,y)$, there should be a binary function $\Phi_n(x,y)$, such that

$$|\Phi_n(x,y)|^2 = p_n(x,y);$$

while $\Phi_n(x,y)$ should be a solution of a kind of 2 order partial differential equation. From the structure of $p_n(x,y)$, we can learn that $\Phi_n(x,y)$ has not determined frequency and determined wave length but has frequency conversion and length conversion. Thus we can think that the 2 order partial differential equation should be a kind of 2 order partial differential equation with variable coefficients.

8.4 An Important Mathematical Conclusion Generated By Theorem 8.2.1

Based on Theorem 8.2.1, we can get an important and interesting mathematical conclusion.

Theorem 8.4.1 For arbitrarily given a continuous function $f \in C[a,b]$, there must exist a sequence of probability spaces $\{(\Omega, \mathcal{F}, P_n)\}_{n=1}^{\infty}$ and a sequence of random vectors $\{(\xi_n, \eta_n)\}_{n=1}^{\infty}$, where every random vectors (ξ_n, η_n) is defined on the probability space $(\Omega, \mathcal{F}, P_n)$, such that the sequence of conditional mathematical expectations $\{E(\eta_n | \xi_n = x)\}_{n=1}^{\infty}$ converges uniformly to $f(x)$ in $[a,b]$, i.e., for any $\varepsilon > 0$, there must exist a natural number $N \in \mathbb{N}_+$, such that, for any $n \in \mathbb{N}_+$, if $n > N$, then we have the following result:

$$(\forall x \in [a,b])\left(\left|E(\eta_n | \xi_n = x) - f(x)\right| < \varepsilon\right),$$

where $\mathbb{N}_+ = \{1,2,3,\cdots\}$ and $\mathbb{N} = \{0,1,2,\cdots\}$.

Proof. **Case 1**. Suppose $f(x)$ be not constant function. By means of the method in the proof of Theorem 8.2.1, we can get the sequence of probability density functions $\{p_n(x,y)\}_{n=1}^{\infty}$. If we let

$$F_n(x,y) = \int_{-\infty}^{x} \int_{-\infty}^{y} p_n(u,v)\,du\,dv.$$

Then $\{F_n(x,y)\}_{n=1}^{\infty}$ must be a sequence of distribution functions. Now we can take $\Omega = \mathbb{R}^2, \mathcal{F} = \mathcal{B}_2$, where $\mathcal{B}_2$ is a Borel σ algebra on $\mathbb{R}^2$, and P_n is taken as the probability measure corresponding to $F_n(x,y)$, which we know that P_n is existing and unique. Thus, we get a sequence of probability spaces as follows:

$$\left\{\left(\Omega,\mathcal{F},P_n\right)\right\}_{n=1}^{\infty}=\left\{\left(\mathbb{R}^2,\mathcal{B}_2,P_n\right)\right\}_{n=1}^{\infty}.$$

Then, on every probability space $\left(\Omega,\mathcal{F},P_n\right)$, we define a random vector as following:

$$\begin{aligned}&\zeta_n=\left(\xi_n,\eta_n\right):\Omega\to\mathbb{R}^2\\&\omega=\left(\omega_1,\omega_2\right)\mapsto\zeta_n(\omega)=\left(\xi_n(\omega),\eta_n(\omega)\right)=\left(\omega_1,\omega_2\right)\end{aligned}$$

For any $(x,y)\in\mathbb{R}^2$, we take notice of the following fact:

$$\begin{aligned}&\left\{\omega\in\Omega\middle|\xi_n(\omega)\le x\right\}=\left\{\omega\in\Omega\middle|\omega_1\le x\right\}\\&=\left\{\omega\in\Omega\middle|\omega_1\in(-\infty,x],\omega_2\in(-\infty,+\infty)\right\}\\&=(-\infty,x]\times(-\infty,+\infty)\in\mathcal{B}_2=\mathcal{F}\end{aligned}$$

This means that $\xi_n(\omega)$ is surely a random variable defined on $\left(\Omega,\mathcal{F},P_n\right)$; in the same way, $\eta_n(\omega)$ is also a random variable defined on $\left(\Omega,\mathcal{F},P_n\right)$. So $\zeta_n(\omega)=\left(\xi_n(\omega),\eta_n(\omega)\right)=\left(\omega_1,\omega_2\right)=\omega$ is just a random vector defined on $\left(\Omega,\mathcal{F},P_n\right)$.

Let the distribution function of $\zeta_n(\omega)$ be $F_{\zeta_n}(x,y)$. For any a binary point $(x,y)\in\mathbb{R}^2$, since P_n is the probability measure corresponding to the distribution function $F_n(x,y)$, we have the following expression:

$$\begin{aligned}&F_{\zeta_n}(x,y)=P_n\left(\left\{\omega\in\Omega\middle|\xi_n(\omega)\le x,\eta_n(\omega)\le y\right\}\right)\\&=P_n\left(\left\{\omega\in\Omega\middle|\omega_1\le x,\omega_2\le y\right\}\right)\\&=P_n\left((-\infty,x]\times(-\infty,y]\right)=F_n(x,y)\end{aligned}$$

This means that the distribution function $F_{\zeta_n}(x,y)$ of $\zeta_n(\omega)$ is just the distribution function $F_n(x,y)$, i.e.,

$$F_{\zeta_n}(x,y) \equiv F_n(x,y).$$

Therefore, we can get the sequence of conditional mathematical expectations as follows:

$$\left\{E\left(\eta_n \middle| \xi_n = x\right)\right\}_{n=1}^{\infty}$$

of the random vectors $\{\zeta_n\}_{n=1}^{\infty} = \{(\xi_n, \eta_n)\}_{n=1}^{\infty}$, where

$$E\left(\eta_n \middle| \xi_n = x\right) = \frac{\int_{-\infty}^{+\infty} y p_n(x,y)dy}{\int_{-\infty}^{+\infty} p_n(x,y)dy}, \quad n = 1,2,3,\cdots$$

By noticing the significance of $\{f_n(x)\}_{n=1}^{\infty}$ in Theorem 8.2.1, we have

$$(\forall n \in \mathbb{N}_+)\left(E\left(\eta_n \middle| \xi_n = x\right) = f_n(x)\right).$$

Because $\lim_{n\to\infty}\|f_n - f\| = 0$, the sequence of conditional mathematical expectations $\left\{E\left(\eta_n \middle| \xi_n = x\right)\right\}_{n=1}^{\infty}$ uniformly converges to $f(x)$ in $[a,b]$.

Case 2. Suppose $f(x)$ be a constant function, i.e.,

$$(\exists \beta \in \mathbb{R})(\forall x \in [a,b])(f(x) = \beta).$$

This is a kind of degenerate situation so that we take the following degenerate distribution function:

$$F_\eta(y) = \begin{cases} 0, & y \in (-\infty, \beta), \\ 1, & y \in [\beta, +\infty) \end{cases}$$

We can make a probability space $(\Omega,\mathcal{F},P)$ such that P is just a the probability measure corresponding to $F_\eta(y)$ and $\Omega=\mathbb{R}^1,\mathcal{F}=\mathcal{B}_1$. We define a random variable as the following:

$$\eta:\Omega\to\mathbb{R}^1,\quad \omega\mapsto\eta(\omega)=\omega\,.$$

It is easy to know that the distribution function of η is just $F_\eta(y)$. Take the notice of the following fact:

$$\begin{aligned}&P\left(\{\omega\in\Omega|\eta(\omega)=\beta\}\right)=P\left(\{\omega\in\Omega|\omega=\beta\}\right)\\&=F_\eta(\beta)-F_\eta(\beta-0)=1-0=1\end{aligned}$$

And we know that $E(\eta)=\beta$ which means that $f(x)\equiv E(\eta)$. Then we take another random variable ξ defined on $(\Omega,\mathcal{F},P)$ with requirement that ξ is independent with η; hence, (ξ,η) can be regarded as a random vector defined on $(\Omega,\mathcal{F},P)$. Thus, we have the following expression:

$$E\left(\eta|\xi=x\right)\equiv E(\eta)=\beta\,.$$

Furthermore, we can define a sequence of random vectors $\{(\xi_n,\eta_n)\}_{n=1}^{\infty}$ as the following

$$(\forall n\in\mathbb{N}_+)\left((\xi_n,\eta_n)=(\xi,\eta)\right).$$

Clearly $\{E\left(\eta_n|\xi_n=x\right)\}_{n=1}^{\infty}$ can uniformly converges to $f(x)$ in the closed interval $[a,b]$. □

8.5 Approximation Theory Significance of Theorem 8.2.1

In above section, we prove an important conclusion: the sequence of conditional mathematical expectations $\left\{E\left(\eta_n \middle| \xi_n = x\right)\right\}_{n=1}^{\infty}$ uniformly converges to the continuous function $f(x) \in C[a,b]$ in $[a,b]$. Now we consider the signification of approximation theory of $\left\{E\left(\eta_n \middle| \xi_n = x\right)\right\}_{n=1}^{\infty}$ with respect to the continuous function $f(x)$.

Our discussion is under the form on the continuous function space $C[a,b]$. For doing this work, we define two algebraic operations in the space $C[a,b]$, additive operation "$+$" and scalar multiplication "$\cdot$" as the following:

$$\begin{aligned}
&+ : C[a,b] \times C[a,b] \to C[a,b] \\
&\qquad (f,g) \mapsto +(f,g) = f+g, \\
&\left(\forall x \in [a,b]\right)\left[(f+g)(x) = f(x)+g(x)\right]; \\
&\cdot : \mathbb{R} \times C[a,b] \to C[a,b] \\
&\qquad (a,f) \mapsto \cdot(a,f) = a \cdot f, \\
&\left(\forall x \in [a,b]\right)\left[(a \cdot f)(x) = a \cdot f(x)\right]
\end{aligned}$$

Clear $\left(C[a,b], +, \mathbb{R}, \cdot\right)$ is a linear space, simply denoted by $C[a,b]$. In the space $C[a,b]$, we define a norm as follows:

$$\begin{aligned}
&\|\cdot\| : C[a,b] \to [0,+\infty) \\
&f \mapsto \|\cdot\|(f) = \|f\| = \max_{x \in [a,b]} |f(x)|
\end{aligned}$$

Then $\left(C[a,b], \|\cdot\|\right)$ is a linear normed space, also simply denoted by $C[a,b]$. In fact, we all know that $C[a,b]$ is a Banach space with infinite dimension.

Suppose $f(x) \in C[a,b]$ be a "complicated" function. For every natural number $m \in \mathbb{N}_+$, we try to find $m+1$ a group of simple functions:

$$\Phi(m) = \left\{\varphi_0^{(m)}(x), \varphi_1^{(m)}(x), \cdots, \varphi_m^{(m)}(x)\right\} \subset C[a,b],$$

and $m+1$ constants $a_0^{(m)}, a_1^{(m)}, \cdots, a_m^{(m)} \in \mathbb{R}$, which there at least be one number not being zero, such that the function $f(x)$ can be linearly expressed by $\Phi(m)$ approximately as the following:

$$(\forall x \in [a,b])\left(\left|f(x) - \sum_{i=0}^{m} a_i^{(m)} \varphi_i^{(m)}(x)\right| < \varepsilon\right).$$

where $\varepsilon > 0$ is a kind of approximation accuracy beforehand given by us. Let

$$F_m(x) = \sum_{i=0}^{m} a_i^{(m)} \varphi_i^{(m)}(x),$$

and we get a sequence of continuous functions $\{F_m(x)\}_{m=1}^{\infty}$ coming from $C[a,b]$. Above expression means that the sequence of continuous functions $\{F_m(x)\}_{m=1}^{\infty}$ uniformly converges to $f(x)$ in $[a,b]$, which tells us the fact as follows:

$$(\forall \varepsilon > 0)(\exists N \in \mathbb{N}_+)(\forall m \in \mathbb{N}_+)(m > N \Rightarrow \|F_m - f\| < \varepsilon).$$

For this ε, when $m > N$, $(\text{span}\Phi(n), \|\cdot\|)$ is regarded as a $m+1$ dimension linear subspace of $(C[a,b], \|\cdot\|)$, such that

$$\left(\exists a_0^{(m)}, a_1^{(m)}, \cdots, a_m^{(m)} \in \mathbb{R}\right)\left(\|f_m - f\| < \varepsilon\right)$$

Where $\text{span}\Phi(m)$ is the linear subspace of $C[a,b]$ generated by the group of linearly independent elements as the following:

$$\Phi(m) = \{\varphi_0^{(m)}(x), \varphi_1^{(m)}(x), \cdots, \varphi_m^{(m)}(x)\}.$$

In other words, under the condition that ε is given in advance, we can use a kind of linear combination of the base elements of the linear normed subspace $\text{span}\Phi(m)$, as follows:

$$F_m(x) = \sum_{i=1}^{m} a_i^{(m)} \varphi_i^{(m)}(x)$$

to approximately replace $f(x)$, or we can say that, $f_n(x)$ can approximates to $f(x)$ reaching the precision ε given by us in advance. This is the base idea of function approximation theory.

We have known the fact that the sequence of functions $F_m(x)$ uniformly converges to $f(x)$ in $[a,b]$; however, we need more requirements for the sequence of functions $\{F_m(x)\}_{m=1}^{\infty}$, which is stated as being: for any a point $x \in [a,b]$ and for any $\delta > 0$, there must exist $N \in \mathbb{N}_+$, such that, for any a natural number $m \in \mathbb{N}_+$, if $m > N$, then

$$\left(\exists x_\delta \in (x-\delta, x+\delta) \cap [a,b]\right)\left(F_m(x_\delta) = f(x_\delta)\right).$$

This means that there are many points x_δ in $[a,b]$, such that

$$F_m(x_\delta) = f(x_\delta),$$

and these points spread all over $[a,b]$. This just leads to the interpolation approximation problem.

First, we make a partition on $[a,b]$ as the following:

$$a = x_0^{(m)} < x_1^{(m)} < \cdots < x_m^{(m)} = b,$$

where the partition does not need to be equidistant. Let

$$X(m) = \left\{x_i^{(m)} \middle| i = 0,1,\cdots,m\right\},$$
$$y_i^{(m)} = f\left(x_i^{(m)}\right), i = 0,1,\cdots,m,$$
$$Y(m) = \left\{y_i^{(m)} \middle| i = 0,1,\cdots,m\right\}$$

By using the set of nodes $X(n)$, we make the group of base functions as follows:

$$\Phi(m) = \left\{\varphi_0^{(m)}(x), \varphi_1^{(m)}(x), \cdots, \varphi_m^{(m)}(x)\right\},$$
$$\left(\forall i \in \{0,1,\cdots,m\}\right)\left(\varphi_i^{(m)}(x) \in C[a,b]\right),$$

and $\varphi_0^{(m)}(x), \varphi_1^{(m)}(x), \cdots, \varphi_m^{(m)}(x)$ are linearly independent and with Kronecker condition:

$$\varphi_i^{(m)}\left(x_j^{(m)}\right) = \delta_{ij}, \quad i, j = 0, 1, \cdots, m.$$

In $F_m(x) = \sum_{i=0}^{m} a_i^{(m)} \varphi_i^{(m)}(x)$, we take $a_i^{(m)} = y_i^{(m)}$, and we have following expression:

$$F_m(x) = \sum_{i=0}^{m} y_i^{(m)} \varphi_i^{(m)}(x) = \sum_{i=0}^{n} f\left(x_i^{(m)}\right) \varphi_i^{(m)}(x)$$

This is just an interpolation function, which satisfies the interpolation condition:

$$\left(\forall i \in \{0, 1, \cdots, m\}\right)\left(F_m\left(x_i^{(m)}\right) = f\left(x_i^{(m)}\right)\right).$$

All in all, because $F_m(x) \in \text{span}\Phi(m)$ and $f(x) \in C[a,b]$, and by noticing that $\text{span}\Phi(m)$ is a linear subspace with finite dimension of $C[a,b]$, for any $\varepsilon > 0$, there must exist $m \in \mathbb{N}_+$, such that the element in $C[a,b]$, $f(x)$, can be approximate by the element in $\text{span}\Phi(m)$, $F_m(x)$, which means $\|F_m - f\| < \varepsilon$.

Definition 8.5.1 The sequence of conditional mathematical expectations as the following:

$$\left\{E\left(\eta_n \middle| \xi_n = x\right)\right\}_{n=1}^{\infty}$$

in Theorem 8.4.1 is called the sequence of conditional mathematical expectations generated by the continuous function $f(x)$. □

Theorem 8.5.1 Arbitrarily given a continuous function $f(x) \in C[a,b]$, but $f(x)$ not being a constant function, $\left\{E\left(\eta_n \middle| \xi_n = x\right)\right\}_{n=1}^{\infty}$ is the sequence of conditional mathematical expectations generated by the continuous function $f(x)$, then by means of $\left\{E\left(\eta_n \middle| \xi_n = x\right)\right\}_{n=1}^{\infty}$ we can make a group of continuous base functions as follows:

$$\Phi(m) = \left\{\varphi_0^{(m)}(x), \varphi_1^{(m)}(x), \cdots, \varphi_m^{(m)}(x)\right\},$$

where $m = 2n, \varphi_l^{(m)}(x) \in C[a,b], l = 0,1,\cdots,m$, such that the sequence of interpolation functions formed by using $\{\Phi(m)\}$ as the following:

$$F_m(x) = \sum_{l=0}^{m} \varphi_l^{(m)}(x) y_l^{(m)}, \quad m = 2n, \quad n = 1,2,3,\cdots$$

can uniformly converges to $f(x)$ in $[a,b]$.

Proof. For convenience, we only consider the situation as $[a,b] = [0,1]$, since for the general situation $[a,b]$, we can use a kind of linear transformation to transfer it into $[0,1]$.

Case 1. Suppose $f(x)$ be a strict monotonous function. We can assume $f(x)$ be a strict monotonously increasing function, because for a strict monotonously decreasing function, the proof is the same.

For any a point $x \in [0,1]$, there must exist $i \in \{1,2,\cdots,m\}, m = 2n$, such that $x \in \left[x_{i-1}^{(n)}, x_i^{(n)}\right]$. Thus

$$\mu_n(x,y) = \bigvee_{k=0}^{m} \left(A_k^{(n)}(x) \cdot B_k^{(n)}(y)\right)$$
$$= \begin{cases} \left(A_{i-1}^{(n)}(x) \cdot B_{i-1}^{(n)}(y)\right) \vee \left(A_i^{(n)}(x) \cdot B_i^{(n)}(y)\right), & y \in \left[y_{i-2}^{(n)}, y_{i+1}^{(n)}\right], \\ 0, & y \in [c,d] - \left[y_{i-2}^{(n)}, y_{i+1}^{(n)}\right] \end{cases}$$

Now we consider two integrals in the following expression:

$$E\left(\eta_n \middle| \xi_n = x\right) = \frac{\int_c^d y \mu_n(x,y) dy}{\int_c^d \mu_n(x,y) dy}$$

as being $\int_c^d y\mu_n(x,y)dy$ and $\int_c^d \mu_n(x,y)dy$. Based on the definition of definite integral, we have the following expressions:

$$\int_c^d y\mu_n(x,y)dy = \lim_{\lambda(T_k)\to 0}\sum_{l=1}^{k} y_l^{(k)}\mu_n\left(x,y_l^{(k)}\right)\Delta y_l^{(k)},$$

$$\int_c^d \mu_n(x,y)dy = \lim_{\lambda(T_k)\to 0}\sum_{l=1}^{k} \mu_n\left(x,y_l^{(k)}\right)\Delta y_l^{(k)},$$

where $\lambda\left(T_k\right)=\max\left\{\Delta y_l^{(k)}=y_l^{(k)}-y_{l-1}^{(k)}\middle| l=1,2,\cdots,k\right\}$ and T_k represents the partition of $Y=[c,d]$ as the following:

$$c=y_0^{(k)}<y_1^{(k)}<\cdots<y_k^{(k)}=d,$$
$$x_l^{(k)}=a+lh(k),\quad y_l^{(k)}=f\left(x_l^{(k)}\right),$$
$$l=0,1,\cdots,k$$

We should know that k is different with n, where n is a fixed subscript for the moment, while k is going to approach infinite.

Because $f(x)$ is continuous, $\lambda\left(T_k\right)\to 0 \Leftrightarrow k\to\infty$, and then above expressions can be written as the following:

$$\int_c^d y\mu_n(x,y)dy = \lim_{k\to\infty}\sum_{l=1}^{k} y_l^{(k)}\mu_n\left(x,y_l^{(k)}\right)\Delta y_l^{(k)},$$

$$\int_c^d \mu_n(x,y)dy = \lim_{k\to\infty}\sum_{l=1}^{k} \mu_n\left(x,y_l^{(k)}\right)\Delta y_l^{(k)}$$

Let $\Delta y_0^{(k)}=\Delta y_1^{(k)}$. Since the binary functions $\mu_n(x,y)$ are bounded, actually, $0\le\mu_n(x,y)\le 1$, and $f(x)$ is also bounded, we must have the following expression:

$$\left(\exists M(x)>0\right)\left(\forall k\in\mathbb{N}\right)\left(\left|y_0^{(k)}\mu_n\left(x,y_0^{(k)}\right)\right|<M(x)\right).$$

And then we get the following limit expression:

$$\lim_{k\to\infty}\left[y_0^{(k)}\mu_n\left(x,y_0^{(k)}\right)\Delta y_0^{(k)}\right]=0=\lim_{k\to\infty}\left[\mu_n\left(x,y_0^{(k)}\right)\Delta y_0^{(k)}\right],$$

and by this we have the following result:

$$\begin{aligned}&\lim_{k\to\infty}\sum_{l=1}^{k}y_l^{(k)}\mu_n\left(x,y_l^{(k)}\right)\Delta y_l^{(k)}\\&=\lim_{k\to\infty}\left[y_0^{(k)}\mu_n\left(x,y_0^{(k)}\right)\Delta y_0^{(k)}+\sum_{l=1}^{k}y_l^{(k)}\mu_n\left(x,y_l^{(k)}\right)\Delta y_l^{(k)}\right]\\&=\lim_{k\to\infty}\sum_{l=0}^{k}y_l^{(k)}\mu_n\left(x,y_l^{(k)}\right)\Delta y_l^{(k)},\end{aligned}$$

$$\begin{aligned}&\lim_{k\to\infty}\sum_{l=1}^{k}\mu_n\left(x,y_l^{(k)}\right)\Delta y_l^{(k)}\\&=\lim_{k\to\infty}\left[\mu_n\left(x,y_0^{(k)}\right)\Delta y_0^{(k)}+\sum_{l=1}^{k}\mu_n\left(x,y_l^{(k)}\right)\Delta y_l^{(k)}\right]\\&=\lim_{k\to\infty}\sum_{l=0}^{k}\mu_n\left(x,y_l^{(k)}\right)\Delta y_l^{(k)}\end{aligned}$$

so that

$$\int_c^d y\mu_n(x,y)dy=\lim_{k\to\infty}\sum_{l=0}^{k}y_l^{(k)}\mu_n\left(x,y_l^{(k)}\right)\Delta y_l^{(k)},$$

$$\int_c^d \mu_n(x,y)dy=\lim_{k\to\infty}\sum_{l=0}^{k}\mu_n\left(x,y_l^{(k)}\right)\Delta y_l^{(k)}$$

We easily know the two facts: $\left(\forall x\in[a,b]\right)\left(\int_c^d \mu_n(x,y)dy>0\right)$ and

$$\int_c^d \mu_n(x,y)dy=\lim_{k\to\infty}\sum_{l=0}^{k}R_n\left(x,y_l^{(k)}\right)\Delta y_l^{(k)}.$$

So, for any a point $x\in[a,b]$, there must exists a number $N(x)\in\mathbb{N}_+$, such that

$$(\forall k \in \mathbb{N}_+)\left(k > N(x) \Rightarrow \sum_{l=0}^{k} \mu_n\left(x, y_l^{(k)}\right)\Delta y_l^{(k)} > 0 \right)$$

Thus, when $k > N(x)$, we have the following result:

$$E\left(\eta_n \middle| \xi_n = x\right) = \frac{\int_c^d y\mu_n(x,y)dy}{\int_c^d \mu_n(x,y)dy} = \frac{\lim_{k\to\infty}\sum_{l=0}^{k} y_l^{(k)}\mu_n\left(x, y_l^{(k)}\right)\Delta y_l^{(k)}}{\lim_{k\to\infty}\sum_{l=0}^{k} \mu_n\left(x, y_l^{(k)}\right)\Delta y_l^{(k)}}$$

$$= \lim_{k\to\infty}\frac{\sum_{l=0}^{k} y_l^{(k)}\mu_n\left(x, y_l^{(k)}\right)\Delta y_l^{(k)}}{\sum_{l=0}^{k} \mu_n\left(x, y_l^{(k)}\right)\Delta y_l^{(k)}} = \lim_{k\to\infty}\sum_{l=0}^{k}\frac{\mu_n\left(x, y_l^{(k)}\right)\Delta y_l^{(k)}}{\sum_{j=0}^{k} \mu_n\left(x, y_j^{(k)}\right)\Delta y_j^{(k)}}\cdot y_l^{(k)}$$

$$= \lim_{k\to\infty}\frac{\sum_{l=0}^{k} y_l^{(k)}\mu_n\left(x, y_l^{(k)}\right)\Delta y_l^{(k)}}{\sum_{l=0}^{k} \mu_n\left(x, y_l^{(k)}\right)\Delta y_l^{(k)}} = \lim_{k\to\infty}\sum_{l=0}^{k}\frac{\mu_n\left(x, y_l^{(k)}\right)\Delta y_l^{(k)}}{\sum_{j=0}^{k} \mu_n\left(x, y_j^{(k)}\right)\Delta y_j^{(k)}}\cdot y_l^{(k)}$$

And we let

$$\varphi_l^{(2n)}(x) = \frac{\mu_n\left(x, y_l^{(k)}\right)\Delta y_l^{(k)}}{\sum_{j=0}^{k} \mu_n\left(x, y_j^{(k)}\right)\Delta y_j^{(k)}}, \quad l = 0,1,\cdots,k;$$

then above expression can be simply written as the following:

$$\lim_{k\to\infty}\sum_{l=0}^{k}\varphi_l^{(2n)}(x)y_l^{(k)} = E\left(\eta_n \middle| \xi_n = x\right). \tag{8.5.1}$$

If we write the following expression:

$$F_{mk}(x) = \sum_{l=0}^{k}\varphi_l^{(m)}(x)y_l^{(k)},$$

then we can get a sequence of continuous functions with the double subscripts $\{f_{nk}(x)\}_{n,k=1}^{\infty}$. Then we put

$$\Phi_m(k)=\left\{\varphi_0^{(m)}(x),\varphi_1^{(m)}(x),\cdots,\varphi_k^{(m)}(x)\right\}.$$

It is easy to know that $F_{mk}(x)=\sum_{l=0}^{k}\varphi_l^{(m)}(x)y_l^{(k)}$ is just an interpolation function where $\Phi_m(k)$ is regarded as the group of base functions.

Then we especially let $k=2n=m$, i.e., we only take a subsequence of the sequence $\{F_{mk}(x)\}_{n,k=1}^{\infty}$, so that we can gain a sequence of continuous functions with single subscript $\{F_m(x)\}_{n=1}^{\infty}$, where

$$F_m(x)=F_{m,m}(x)=\sum_{l=0}^{m}\varphi_l^{(m)}(x)y_l^{(m)},$$
$$m=2n,\quad n=1,2,3,\cdots$$

And then we let

$$\Phi(m)=\Phi_m(m)=\left\{\varphi_0^{(m)}(x),\varphi_1^{(m)}(x),\cdots,\varphi_m^{(m)}(x)\right\}.$$

Then $F_m(x)=\sum_{l=0}^{m}\varphi_l^{(m)}(x)y_l^{(m)}$ is an interpolation function whose base function group is $\Phi(m)$.

Now we can prove the conclusion: $\{F_m(x)\}_{n=1}^{\infty}$ uniformly converges to $f(x)$ in $X=[a,b]$.

We first inspect the $m+1$ unary functions with respect to variable x as being $\mu_n\left(x,y_l^{(m)}\right), l=0,1,\cdots,m$. In fact, $B_i^{(n)}\left(y_l^{(m)}\right)$ has the well-known Kronecker property:

$$(\forall i,l\in\{0,1,\cdots,m\})\left(B_i^{(n)}\left(y_l^{(m)}\right)=\delta_{il}=\begin{cases}1, & i=l,\\ 0, & i\neq l\end{cases}\right)$$

So we must have the following expression:

$$\mu_n\left(x, y_l^{(m)}\right) = \bigvee_{i=0}^{m}\left(A_i^{(n)}(x) \cdot B_i^{(n)}\left(y_l^{(m)}\right)\right) = A_l^{(n)}(x),$$

and then we have the following results:

$$\sum_{l=0}^{m} y_l \mu_n\left(x, y_l^{(m)}\right) \Delta y_l^{(m)} = \sum_{l=0}^{m} y_l^{(m)} A_l^{(n)}(x) \Delta y_l^{(m)},$$

$$\sum_{l=0}^{m} \mu_n\left(x, y_l^{(m)}\right) \Delta y_l^{(m)} = \sum_{l=0}^{n} A_l^{(n)}(x) \Delta y_l^{(m)},$$

$$\varphi_l^{(m)}(x) = \frac{\mu_n\left(x, y_l^{(m)}\right) \Delta y_l^{(m)}}{\sum_{j=0}^{m} \mu_n\left(x, y_j^{(m)}\right) \Delta y_j^{(m)}} = \frac{A_l^{(n)}(x) \Delta y_l^{(m)}}{\sum_{j=0}^{m} A_j^{(n)}(x) \Delta y_j^{(m)}},$$

$$l = 0, 1, \cdots, m,$$

so that

$$F_m(x) = \sum_{l=0}^{m} \frac{A_l^{(n)}(x) \Delta y_l^{(m)}}{\sum_{j=0}^{m} A_j^{(n)}(x) \Delta y_j^{(m)}} \cdot y_l^{(m)} = \sum_{l=0}^{m} \varphi_l^{(m)}(x) y_l^{(m)} \tag{8.5.2}$$

Because the group of functions $\left\{\varphi_l^{(m)}(x) \middle| l = 0, 1, \cdots, m\right\}$ is linearly independent, and $\sum_{l=0}^{m} \varphi_l^{(m)}(x) \equiv 1$, and span $\left\{\varphi_l^{(m)}(x) \middle| l = 0, 1, \cdots, m\right\}$ forms a $m+1$ dimension linear normed subspace of $C[a,b]$, if we regard the function group $\Phi(m) = \left\{\varphi_0^{(m)}(x), \varphi_1^{(m)}(x), \cdots, \varphi_m^{(m)}(x)\right\}$ as a group of base functions, then

$$F_m(x) = \sum_{l=0}^{m} \varphi_l^{(m)}(x) y_l^{(m)}. \tag{8.5.3}$$

is just a piecewise interpolation function based on the group of base functions $\Phi(m)$.

By above discussion, we can turn to prove the conclusion: $\{F_m(x)\}_{n=1}^{\infty}$ uniformly converges to $f(x)$ in $[a,b]$.

Actually, arbitrarily taken a point $x \in [0,1]$, then

$$(\exists i \in \{1,2,\cdots,m\})\left(x \in \left[x_{i-1}^{(n)}, x_i^{(n)}\right]\right),$$

so that

$$F_m(x) = \sum_{l=0}^{m} \varphi_l^{(m)}(x) y_l^{(m)} = \varphi_{i-1}^{(m)}(x) y_{i-1}^{(m)} + \varphi_i^{(m)}(x) y_i^{(m)}$$

Because $f(x)$ is continuous, there must exist two points as the following:

$$\xi_i^{(n)}, \eta_i^{(n)} \in \left[x_{i-1}^{(n)}, x_i^{(n)}\right],$$

such that

$$f\left(\xi_i^{(n)}\right) = \min_{x \in \left[x_{i-1}^{(n)}, x_i^{(n)}\right]} f(x), \quad f\left(\eta_i^{(n)}\right) = \max_{x \in \left[x_{i-1}^{(n)}, x_i^{(n)}\right]} f(x)$$

We can easily learn the following facts:

$$(\forall l \in \{0,1,\cdots,m\})\left(\varphi_l^{(m)}([a,b]) = [0,1]\right),$$

$$\left(\forall x \in \left[x_{i-1}^{(n)}, x_i^{(n)}\right]\right)\left(\varphi_{i-1}^{(m)}(x) + \varphi_i^{(m)}(x) = 1\right)$$

So we get the following result:

$$\left(\forall x \in \left[x_{i-1}^{(n)}, x_i^{(n)}\right]\right)\left(f\left(\xi_i^{(n)}\right) \le \varphi_{i-1}^{(m)}(x) y_{i-1}^{(m)} + \varphi_i^{(m)} y_i^{(m)} \le f\left(\eta_i^{(n)}\right)\right).$$

Since $y_{i-1}^{(n)} = f\left(x_{i-1}^{(n)}\right), y_i^{(n)} = f\left(x_i^{(n)}\right)$, for any $x \in \left[x_{i-1}^{(n)}, x_i^{(n)}\right]$, we have the following inequality:

$$\begin{aligned}|f(x)-F_m(x)| &= \left|f(x)-\left(\varphi_{i-1}^{(m)}(x)y_{i-1}^{(m)}+\varphi_i^{(m)}y_i^{(m)}\right)\right| \\ &\le \left|f\left(\eta_i^{(n)}\right)-f\left(\xi_i^{(n)}\right)\right|\end{aligned}$$

Because $f(x)$ is uniformly continuous in $[a,b]$, for any $\varepsilon>0$, there exists $\delta>0$, such that

$$\left(\forall u,v\in[a,b]\right)\left(|u-v|<\delta\Rightarrow|f(u)-f(v)|<\varepsilon\right).$$

We take $h(n)<\delta$, and we must have the following inequality:

$$\left|f\left(\eta_i^{(n)}\right)-f\left(\xi_i^{(n)}\right)\right|<\varepsilon,$$

and then we get the inequality as follows:

$$\left(\forall x\in\left[x_{i-1}^{(n)},x_i^{(n)}\right]\right)\left(|f(x)-F_m(x)|<\varepsilon\right).$$

Since $h(n)\to 0\Leftrightarrow n\to\infty$, there exists $N\in\mathbb{N}_+$, such that

$$\left(\forall n\in\mathbb{N}_+\right)\left(n>N\Rightarrow h(n)<\delta\right),$$

and we get the following expression:

$$\left(\forall m\in\mathbb{N}_+\right)\left(m>N\Rightarrow\left(\forall x\in[a,b]\right)\left(|f(x)-F_m(x)|<\varepsilon\right)\right).$$

This means that the sequence of interpolation functions $\{F_m(x)\}_{n=1}^{\infty}$ uniformly converges to the continuous function $f(x)$ in $X=[a,b]$.

Case 2. Suppose $f(x)$ not be strict monotone function. Very similar to the method in the proof of Theorem 8.2.1, we can get the following binary functions:

$$\mu_n(x,y)=\bigvee_{j=0}^{m}\left(A_{k_j}^{(n)}(x)\cdot B_{k_j}^{(n)}(y)\right)$$

By means of them we can get the following sequence of interpolation functions:

$$F_m(x)=\sum_{l=0}^{m}\frac{A_{k_l}^{(n)}(x)\Delta y_{k_l}^{(m)}}{\sum_{s=0}^{m}A_{k_s}^{(n)}(x)\Delta y_{k_s}^{(n)}}\cdot y_{k_l}^{(m)}=\sum_{l=0}^{m}\varphi_l^{(m)}(x)y_{k_l}^{(m)},$$

$$\varphi_l^{(m)}(x)=\frac{A_{k_l}^{(n)}(x)\Delta y_{k_l}^{(m)}}{\sum_{s=0}^{n}A_{k_s}^{(n)}(x)\Delta y_{k_s}^{(m)}},\quad l=0,1,\cdots,m$$

Very similar to Case 1, we can prove that the sequence of interpolation functions $\{F_m(x)\}_{n=1}^{\infty}$ uniformly converges to the continuous function $f(x)$ in the universe $X=[a,b]$.

We finally completely finish the proof of this theorem. □

Remark 8.5.1 If we let

$$w_l^{(m)}(x)=\frac{\Delta y_l^{(m)}}{\sum_{j=0}^{m}A_j^{(n)}(x)\Delta y_j^{(m)}},\quad l=0,1,\cdots,m,$$

then we have the following expression:

$$F_m(x)=\sum_{l=0}^{m}\varphi_l^{(m)}(x)y_l^{(m)}=\sum_{l=0}^{m}\frac{A_l^{(n)}(x)\Delta y_l^{(m)}}{\sum_{j=0}^{m}A_j^{(n)}(x)\Delta y_j^{(m)}}\cdot y_l^{(m)}$$

$$=\sum_{l=0}^{m}w_l^{(m)}(x)A_l^{(n)}(x)y_l^{(m)}$$

If we regard $w_0^{(n)}(x),w_1^{(n)}(x),\cdots,w_n^{(n)}(x)$ as a group of weight functions, then based on Theorem 8.5.1 we can get the following interpolation function:

$$f_n(x)=\sum_{l=0}^{n}w_l^{(n)}(x)A_l^{(n)}(x)y_l^{(n)}$$

which is clearly a kind of weighed form of the piecewise interpolation function $g_m(x)=\sum_{l=0}^{m} A_l^{(n)}(x)y_l^{(m)}$; in other words, it is a kind of amendment for the expression $g_m(x)=\sum_{l=0}^{m} A_l^{(n)}(x)y_l^{(m)}$, although the following equation:

$$F_n(x)=\sum_{l=0}^{m} w_l^{(m)}(x)A_l^{(n)}(x)y_l^{(m)}$$

is also an interpolation function. □

Remark 8.5.2 Because the piecewise interpolation function as follows

$$g_m(x)=\sum_{l=0}^{m} A_l^{(n)}(x)y_l^{(m)}$$

is based on the following group of base functions:

$$\Gamma(m)=\left\{A_0^{(n)}(x), A_1^{(n)}(x), \cdots, A_m^{(n)}(x)\right\}$$

If we let

$$W(m)=\left\{w_0^{(m)}(x), w_1^{(m)}(x), \cdots, w_m^{(m)}(x)\right\},$$

then we have the following expression:

$$\begin{aligned}
\Phi(m) &= \left\{\varphi_0^{(m)}(x), \varphi_1^{(m)}(x), \cdots, \varphi_m^{(m)}(x)\right\} \\
&= \left\{w_0^{(m)}(x)\cdot A_0^{(n)}(x), w_1^{(m)}(x)\cdot A_1^{(n)}(x), \cdots, w_m^{(m)}(x)\cdot A_m^{(n)}(x)\right\} \\
&= W(m)\cdot\Gamma(m)
\end{aligned}$$

where $W(m)\cdot\Gamma(m)$ is regarded as Hadamand product between $m+1$ vectors $W(m)$ and $\Gamma(m)$. By using the inner product action of vector $W(n)$ to $\Gamma(n)$, we can make $m+1$ dimension linear subspace as being $\operatorname{span}(\Gamma(m))$ of $C[a,b]$ turn to be another $m+1$ dimension linear subspace $\text{span}(\Phi(m))$ of $C[a,b]$. Before the transformation, we use some elements in the linear normed subspace $\text{span}(\Gamma(m))$ to approximate $f(x)$; after the transformation, we use some elements in $\text{span}(\Phi(m))$ to approximate $f(x)$. □

8.6 Conclusions

In this chapter, we an important problem: unified theory of classic mechanics and quantum mechanics. So-called unified theory here means almost every motion of a mass point in classic mechanics can be represented by the motions of an infinite sequence of particles in quantum mechanics, where limit operation plays an important role in the unified theory. Clearly this situation is just according with Bohr's Correspondence Principle.

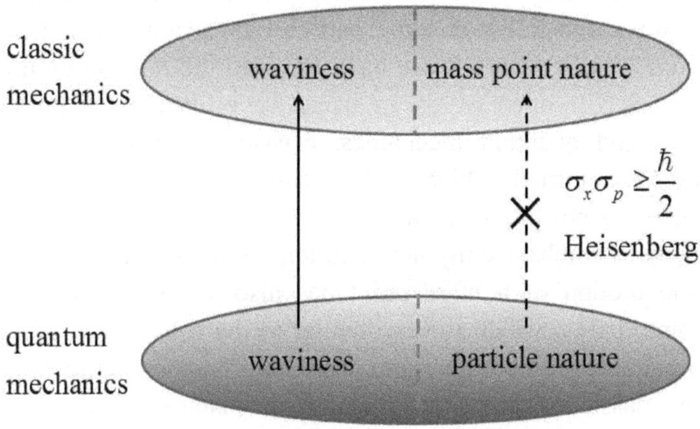

Fig. 8.6.1. Unified frame of two kinds of mechanics

It is worth noting that this kind of correspondence relation between classic mechanics and quantum mechanics cannot be expressed by the relationship between the mass point nature in classic mechanics and the particle nature in quantum mechanics because of Heisenberg's

Uncertainty Principle (see Figure 8.6.1). As we all know, in classic mechanics, the motion of a mass point has no uncertainty so that we can use continuous functions to describe the movement locus of the mass point. However, in quantum mechanics, the motion of a particle has surely uncertainty so that we cannot use continuous functions to describe the movement locus of the particle. By now, we have known that the position and momentum of a particle are all random and they are related by Planck constant $\hbar$, i.e.,

$$\sigma_x \sigma_p \geq \frac{\hbar}{2}.$$

Fortunately, we have pointed that the motion of a mass point in classic mechanics has also waviness in Section 8.3. The wave function of the motion of a mass point has surely no uncertainty. On the other hand, although the motion of a particle has surely uncertainty, the wave function of the particle must have no uncertainty. Thus, we can consider the relation between the wave function of a mass point in classic mechanics and the wave functions of some particles in quantum mechanics. As we discussed in Section 8.2, we have revealed the relation by means of Theorem 8.2.1. In other words, by using wave functions of both classic mechanics and quantum mechanics, classic mechanics and quantum mechanics are unified, which is the significance of our unified theory about the two kinds of mechanics.

We need to emphasize my new and important and interesting conclusion: The motion of a mass point has also so-called duality: wave-mass-point duality, which is very similar to the case of the motion of a particle in quantum mechanics and is an important support to our unified theory on classic mechanics and quantum mechanics. It is not difficult to understand that Theorem 8.2.1 should be the most important in physics.

Another new and important and interesting conclusion of me is coming from Theorem 8.4.1 which means that, for any a continuous function, there must be a sequence of probability spaces and a sequence of random vectors defined on the sequence of probability spaces, such that the sequence of conditional mathematical expectations of the sequence of random vectors uniformly converges to the continuous function. This conclusion can establish a new bridge between real analysis and probability theory.

Prigogine had ever pointed out his conclusion by many experiments: world is random not certain (see [20]). In fact, Theorem 8.4.1 just prove his idea, because, as we all know, a large part of physical phenomenon can be described by some kind of continuous functions, and based on Theorem 8.4.1, any one of these continuous functions must be the limit of the sequence of conditional mathematical expectations of a sequence of random vectors.

In Section 8.5, approximation theory significance of theorem 8.2.1 is discussed in detail and its main conclusion is expressed by Theorem 8.5.1. This undoubtedly gives a new kind of new method to function approximation theory.

At last, we should state the fact that, these results in this chapter can easily extended to the cases of multivariate continuous functions based the methods in Chapter 5.

References

1. Zadeh L.A. (1973). Outline of a new approach to the analysis of complex systems and decision processes, IEEE Trans. SMC, 3, pp. 28-44.
2. Zadeh, L. A. (1974). The concept of a linguistic variable and its applications to approximate reasoning (I), Information Sciences, 8(2), pp. 199-249.
3. Zadeh, L. A. (1974). The concept of a linguistic variable and its applications to approximate reasoning (II), Information Sciences, 8(3), pp. 301-357.
4. Zadeh, L. A. (1975). The concept of a linguistic variable and its applications to approximate reasoning (III), Information Sciences, 9(1), pp. 43-80.
5. Li, H. X. (1998). Interpolation mechanism of fuzzy control, Science in China (Series E), 41(3), pp. 312-320.
6. Li, H. X. (1995). To see the success of fuzzy logic from mathematical essence of fuzzy control, Fuzzy Systems and Mathematics, 9(4), pp. 1-14 (in Chinese).
7. Hou, J., You, F. and Li, H. X. (2005). Some fuzzy controllers constructed by triple I method and their response capability, Progress in Natural Science, 15(1), pp. 29-37 (in Chinese).
8. Li, H. X., You, F. and Peng, J. Y. (2004). Fuzzy controllers based on some fuzzy implication operators and their response functions, Progress in Natural Science, 14(1), pp. 15-20.
9. Wang, G. J. (1997). A formal deductive system of fuzzy propositional calculus, Chinese Science Bulletin, 42(10), pp. 1041-1045 (in Chinese).

10. You, F., Feng, Y. B. and Li, H. X. (2003). Fuzzy implication operators and their construction (I), Journal of Beijing Normal University, 39(5), pp. 606-611 (in Chinese).
11. You, F., Feng, Y. B., Wang, J. Y. and Li, H. X. (2004). Fuzzy implication operators and their construction (II), Journal of Beijing Normal University, 40(2): 168-176 (in Chinese).
12. You, F., Yang, X. Y., Li, H. X. (2004). Fuzzy implication operators and their construction (III), Journal of Beijing Normal University, 40(4), pp. 427-432 (in Chinese).
13. You, F. and Li, H. X. (2004). Fuzzy implication operators and their construction (IV), Journal of Beijing Normal University, 40(5), pp. 588-599 (in Chinese).
14. Wang, G. J. (2000) *Non-classical Mathematical Logic and Approximate Reasoning*. (Science Press, Beijing, in Chinese).
15. Wang, G. J. (1999). Full implication triple I method for fuzzy reasoning, Science in China (Series E), 29(1), pp. 43-53 (in Chinese).
16. Li, H. X. (2006). Probability representations of fuzzy systems, Science in China (Series F), 49(3), pp. 339-363.
17. David J. G. (2005) *Introduction to Quantum Mechanics*, second edition. (Prentice-Hall, Inc.).
18. Zeng J. Y. (2015) *Quantum Mechanics*, fifth edition, Vol. 1 (Science Press, Beijing, In China).
19. Loeve, M. (1977) *Probability Theory*, fourth edition, Vol.1. (Springer-Verlag, New York).
20. Prigogine, L. (1997) *The End of Certainty*. (Free Press).

Chapter 9

Unification of Riemann Integral and Lebesgue Integral

9.1 Introduction

Riemann integral and Lebasque integral are well-known and important contents in mathematical analysis and real analysis. Riemann integral is simpler than Lebasque integral considering that Lebasque integral needs measure theory. We all know that the integrable condition of Lebasque integral is much weaker than the integrable condition of Riemann integral; so Lebasque integral is major content in real analysis. And we also know that Lebasque integral is much harder to learn and teach for students and teachers. From the definitions and structures of Riemann integral and Lebasque integral, the two kinds of integrals look like quite different. In the paper, we show the fact that they are the same in essence, because their structures are the same based on function approximation theory and a kind of algebraic structure: linear normed space.

First, the structure of Riemann integral is discussed, where the integrand of a Riemann integral is regarded as the limit function of a sequence of functions; every function of the sequence of functions is just a linear combination of the base functions of a finite dimension linear space. Second, the structure of Lebesgue integral is discussed in the same way, where the integrand of a Lebesgue integral is also regarded as the limit function of a sequence of functions; every function of the sequence of functions is just a linear combination of the base functions of a finite dimension linear space. Third, the unification of Riemann integral and Lebasque integral is discussed under the meanings of function approximation theory and linear normed space, where the unification means that Riemann integral and Lebasque integral are all the limit of the integrals of a sequence of functions and every function of the sequence of functions is just a linear combination of the base functions of a finite dimension linear space. Then inspired by the wave-particle dualism from quantum mechanics, the wave-set dualism is firstly defined in the paper. So the relationship between Cantor sets and their characteristic functions is of wave-set dualism; the relationship between Fuzzy sets and their membership functions is of wave-set dualism, too. Based on such wave-set dualism, **the relationship between Riemann integral of continuous functions and fuzzy sets is introduced**.

9.2 On Riemann Integral

We start to consider the Riemann integral of the unary function shown as the following:

$$f:[a,b]\to\mathbb{R},\quad x\mapsto y=f(x).$$

Firstly, the closed interval $[a,b]$ is partitioned as the following:

$$\Delta: a=x_0<x_1<\cdots<x_n=b,$$

Write

$$\begin{aligned}&\Delta_i=[x_{i-1},x_i),\quad i=1,2,\cdots,n-1,\\&\Delta_n=[x_{n-1},x_n];\\&\Delta x_i=x_i-x_{i-1},\quad i=1,2,\cdots,n\end{aligned}$$

Such partition Δ can be also denoted by $\Delta=\{\Delta_i | i=1,2,\cdots,n\}$. The set of all the partitions of $[a,b]$ is denoted by $\Xi([a,b])$.

Second we write $\|\Delta\|=\max\limits_{1\le i\le n}\{\Delta x_i\}$, which is called the norm of the partition Δ. For convenience, this natural number n is called the partition number of Δ, denoted by $n=\mathrm{par}(\Delta)$. Clearly it is true that

$$\|\Delta\|\to 0\Rightarrow n\to+\infty,$$

but not vice versa.

Thirdly, we use $C^*[a,b]$ to express the set of all almost everywhere continuous bounded functions on $[a,b]$. Based on the necessary and sufficient conditions of Riemann integrability of bounded functions, the function space $C^*[a,b]$ is just the set of all Riemann integrable functions on $[a,b]$, i.e.,

$$C^*[a,b]=R[a,b].$$

In $C^*[a,b]$, we define additive operation and scalar multiplication as the following:

$$\begin{aligned}&+:C^*[a,b]\times C^*[a,b]\to C^*[a,b]\\&\qquad\qquad (f,g)\mapsto f+g,\\&\big(\forall x\in[a,b]\big)\big((f+g)(x)=f(x)+g(x)\big);\\&\cdot:\mathbb{R}\times C^*[a,b]\to C^*[a,b]\\&\qquad (a,f)\mapsto a\cdot f,\\&\big(\forall x\in[a,b]\big)\big((a\cdot f)(x)=a\cdot f(x)\big)\end{aligned}$$

It is easy to verify that $\left(C^*[a,b],+,\cdot\right)$ is a linear space. And in this space $C^*[a,b]$, we define a norm as the following:

$$\|\cdot\|:C^*[a,b]\to[0,+\infty),\quad f\mapsto\|f\|=\sup_{x\in[a,b]}|f(x)|$$

Then we know that $\left(C^*[a,b],+,\cdot,\|\cdot\|\right)$ is a linear normed space.

Fourthly, we arbitrarily take a partition as follows:

$$\Delta=\{\Delta_i\,|\,i=1,2,\cdots,n\}\in\Xi([a,b]),$$

by using Δ, we define a group of functions on $[a,b]$ as follows:

$$\chi_{\Delta_i}:[a,b]\to\{0,1\},\quad x\mapsto\chi_{\Delta_i}(x)=\begin{cases}1, & x\in\Delta_i,\\0, & x\notin\Delta_i\end{cases}$$

$i=1,2,\cdots,n$

Apparently $\left\{\chi_{\Delta_i} \middle| i=1,2,\cdots,n\right\} \subset C^*[a,b]$, and it is easy to prove that this group of functions is linearly independent in $C^*[a,b]$. In fact, suppose that there a group of constants $a_i \in \mathbb{R}$, $i=1,2,\cdots,n$, such that

$$a_1\chi_{\Delta_1} + a_2\chi_{\Delta_2} + \cdots + a_n\chi_{\Delta_n} = 0,$$

where $0 \in C^*[a,b]$, i.e. $0(x) \equiv 0$. For any $x \in [a,b]$, there exists one and only one $i \in \{1,2,\cdots,n\}$, such that $x \in \Delta_i$; therefore we have that

$$0 = a_1\chi_{\Delta_1} + a_2\chi_{\Delta_2} + \cdots + a_n\chi_{\Delta_n} = a_i\chi_{\Delta_i}.$$

Because $\chi_{\Delta_i}(x) = 1$, $a_i = 0$. From this equation we can get the following expression:

$$(\forall i \in \{1,2,\cdots,n\})(a_i = 0);$$

so the group of functions $\left\{\chi_{\Delta_i} \middle| i=1,2,\cdots,n\right\}$ is linearly independent in the linear normed space $C^*[a,b]$. Write the following symbol:

$$G_\Delta = \text{span}\left(\left\{\chi_{\Delta_i} \middle| i=1,2,\cdots,n\right\}\right)$$

which means that it is a n dimensional linear subspace of $C^*[a,b]$ generated by $\left\{\chi_{\Delta_i} \middle| i=1,2,\cdots,n\right\}$, and $\left\{\chi_{\Delta_i} \middle| i=1,2,\cdots,n\right\}$ is just the base of the space G_Δ.

Fifthly, for any a point $\xi_i \in \Delta_i$, $i=1,2,\cdots,n$, by using f we can get n constants as the following:

$$f(\xi_i), \quad i=1,2,\cdots,n.$$

By using of the group of functions $\left\{\chi_{\Delta_i} \middle| i=1,2,\cdots,n\right\}$, we can form a linear combination as the following:

$$g_\Delta \triangleq \sum_{i=1}^{n} f(\xi_i)\cdot \chi_{\Delta_i} \in G_\Delta,$$

where it is defined as the following:

$$(\forall x \in [a,b])\left(g_\Delta(x) = \sum_{i=1}^{n} f(\xi_i)\cdot \chi_{\Delta_i}(x) \right)$$

Based on the definition of Riemann integral, if $f \in C^*[a,b]$, then we have the following expression:

$$\begin{aligned}
\lim_{\|\Delta\|\to 0} \int_a^b g_\Delta(x)\mathrm{d}x &= \lim_{\|\Delta\|\to 0} \int_a^b \sum_{i=1}^{n} f(\xi_i)\cdot \chi_{\Delta_i}(x)\mathrm{d}x \\
&= \lim_{\|\Delta\|\to 0} \sum_{i=1}^{n} f(\xi_i)\cdot \int_a^b \chi_{\Delta_i}(x)\mathrm{d}x = \lim_{\|\Delta\|\to 0} \sum_{i=1}^{n} f(\xi_i)\cdot \int_{x_{i-1}}^{x_i} \chi_{\Delta_i}(x)\mathrm{d}x \\
&= \lim_{\|\Delta\|\to 0} \sum_{i=1}^{n} f(\xi_i)\cdot \left[1\cdot m(\Delta_i)\right] = \lim_{\|\Delta\|\to 0} \sum_{i=1}^{n} f(\xi_i)\cdot (1\cdot \Delta x_i) \\
&= \lim_{\|\Delta\|\to 0} \sum_{i=1}^{n} f(\xi_i)\cdot \Delta x_i = \int_a^b f(x)\mathrm{d}x
\end{aligned}$$

Sixthly, for every number $n = 1,2,3,\cdots$, we use $\Xi^{(n)}([a,b])$ to express the set of all partitions of $[a,b]$ with partition number being n.

Thus $\left\{\Xi^{(n)}([a,b])\right\}_{n=1}^{\infty}$ forms a partition of $\Xi([a,b])$, i.e., any two of the elements in $\left\{\Xi^{(n)}([a,b])\right\}_{n=1}^{\infty}$ are disjoint and the following condition must be satisfied:

$$\Xi([a,b]) = \bigcup_{n=1}^{\infty} \Xi^{(n)}([a,b]).$$

And then, a relation of equivalence "$\sim$" defined on $\Xi([a,b])$ as the following:

$$\left(\forall \Delta_1, \Delta_2 \in \Xi([a,b])\right)\left(\Delta_1 \sim \Delta_2 \Leftrightarrow \operatorname{par}(\Delta_1) = \operatorname{par}(\Delta_2)\right)$$

So we can get the quotient set as the following:

$$\Xi([a,b])\Big/_{\sim} = \left\{[\Delta] \middle| \Delta \in \Xi([a,b])\right\},$$

where $[\Delta]$ is the equivalence class to what Δ belongs. It is not difficult to learn the expression as follows:

$$\Xi([a,b])\Big/_{\sim} = \left\{\Xi^{(n)}([a,b])\right\}_{n=1}^{\infty}.$$

Now for every $n = 1,2,3,\cdots$, in every equivalence class $\Xi^{(n)}([a,b])$, we take one representation element:

$$\Delta^{(n)} = \left\{\Delta_i^{(n)} \middle| i = 1,2,\cdots,n\right\}, \quad n = 1,2,3,\cdots$$

such that they satisfy the conditions: $\lim_{n\to\infty}\left\|\Delta^{(n)}\right\| = 0$ and the following:

$$\left(\forall n,m \in \mathbb{N}\right)\left(n > m \Rightarrow \left\|\Delta^{(n)}\right\| < \left\|\Delta^{(m)}\right\|\right).$$

Therefore we can get a sequence of linear subspaces:

$$G_{\Delta^{(n)}} = \operatorname{span}\left(\left\{\chi_{\Delta_i^{(n)}} \middle| i = 1,2,\cdots,n\right\}\right), \quad n = 1,2,3,\cdots$$

For any a point $\xi_i^{(n)} \in \Delta_i^{(n)}$, $i = 1,2,\cdots,n$, by using f, by using f we get n constants: $f\left(\xi_i^{(n)}\right), i = 1,2,\cdots,n$.

Then we can form a linear combination of $\left\{\chi_{\Delta_i^{(n)}} \middle| i = 1,2,\cdots,n\right\}$ as the following:

$$g_n \triangleq g_{\Delta^{(n)}} = \sum_{i=1}^{n} f\left(\xi_i^{(n)}\right) \cdot \chi_{\Delta_i^{(n)}} \in G_{\Delta^{(n)}},$$

where the function g_n concretely as shown as follows:

$$(\forall x \in [a,b])\left(g_n(x) = \sum_{i=1}^{n} f\left(\xi_i^{(n)}\right) \cdot \chi_{\Delta_i^{(n)}}(x) \right)$$

Thus we can get a sequence of functions coming from the space $C^*[a,b]$ shown as $\{g_n\}_{n=1}^{\infty}$. Considering the fact as the following:

$$\left\|\Delta^{(n)}\right\| \to 0 \Leftrightarrow n \to +\infty,$$

we have the following result:

$$\lim_{n\to\infty} \int_a^b g_n(x)\mathrm{d}x = \lim_{n\to\infty} \int_a^b \sum_{i=1}^{n} f\left(\xi_i^{(n)}\right) \cdot \chi_{\Delta_i^{(n)}}(x)\mathrm{d}x$$

$$= \lim_{\left\|\Delta^{(n)}\right\|\to 0} \int_a^b \sum_{i=1}^{n} f\left(\xi_i^{(n)}\right) \cdot \chi_{\Delta_i^{(n)}}(x)\mathrm{d}x$$

$$= \lim_{\left\|\Delta^{(n)}\right\|\to 0} \sum_{i=1}^{n} f\left(\xi_i^{(n)}\right) \cdot \int_a^b \chi_{\Delta_i^{(n)}}(x)\mathrm{d}x$$

$$= \lim_{\left\|\Delta^{(n)}\right\|\to 0} \sum_{i=1}^{n} f\left(\xi_i^{(n)}\right) \cdot \int_{x_{i-1}^{(n)}}^{x_i^{(n)}} \chi_{\Delta_i^{(n)}}(x)\mathrm{d}x$$

$$= \lim_{\left\|\Delta^{(n)}\right\|\to 0} \sum_{i=1}^{n} f\left(\xi_i^{(n)}\right) \cdot \left[1 \cdot m\left(\Delta_i^{(n)}\right)\right]$$

$$= \lim_{\left\|\Delta^{(n)}\right\|\to 0} \sum_{i=1}^{n} f\left(\xi_i^{(n)}\right) \cdot \left(1 \cdot \Delta^{(n)} x_i\right)$$

$$= \lim_{\left\|\Delta^{(n)}\right\|\to 0} \sum_{i=1}^{n} f\left(\xi_i^{(n)}\right) \cdot \Delta^{(n)} x_i = \int_a^b f(x)\mathrm{d}x$$

By now, we should turn to discuss the properties of the sequence of functions $\{g_n\}_{n=1}^{\infty}$ defined on $[a,b]$.

Proposition 9.2.1 If the function $f \in C[a,b]$, then the sequence of functions $\{g_n\}_{n=1}^{\infty}$ is consistently convergent to the integrand f on the integral interval $[a,b]$.

Proof. For any $\varepsilon > 0$, because f is continuous on $[a,b]$, f must be uniformly continuous on $[a,b]$. So for any two points $x, x' \in [a,b]$, there exists $\delta > 0$, such that

$$|x - x'| < \delta \Rightarrow |f(x) - f(x')| < \varepsilon .$$

We can take a natural number $N = N(\varepsilon) \in \mathbb{N}_+$, such that

$$(\forall n \in \mathbb{N}_+)\left(n > N \Rightarrow \left\|\Delta^{(n)}\right\| < \delta\right).$$

Considering the fact that there exists one and only one $i \in \{1, 2, \cdots, n\}$, such that $x \in \Delta_i^{(n)}$, $\xi_i^{(n)} \in \Delta_i^{(n)}$, and

$$\left|\xi_i^{(n)} - x\right| \le \Delta^{(n)} x_i \le \left\|\Delta^{(n)}\right\| < \delta ,$$

then when $n > N$, we must have the following inequality:

$$|g_n(x) - f(x)| = \left|f\left(\xi_i^{(n)}\right) - f(x)\right| < \varepsilon .$$

This means that $\{g_n\}_{n=1}^{\infty}$ is uniformly convergent to the integrand f on the closed interval $[a,b]$. □

From the proposition, when $f \in C[a,b]$, it is easy to know the fact as the following:

$$\lim_{n\to\infty} \int_a^b g_n(x)\,\mathrm{d}x = \int_a^b \lim_{n\to\infty} g_n(x)\mathrm{d}x = \int_a^b f(x)\mathrm{d}x .$$

Proposition 9.2.2 If $f \in C^*[a,b]$ and satisfies the following condition:

$$(\forall n \in \mathbb{N}_+)(\forall i \in \{1, 2, \cdots, n\})\left(\xi_i^{(n)} \notin A\right),$$

where A is the set of all discontinuous points of f in $[a,b]$, then the sequence of functions $\{g_n\}_{n=1}^{\infty}$ is almost everywhere convergent to the integrand f on the integral interval $[a,b]$.

Proof. First we all know the set $A \subset [a,b]$ is a zero measure set, and f is almost everywhere continuous on the set $E = [a,b] - A$. For any a point $x_0 \in E$, and for any $\varepsilon > 0$, since f is continuous on E, there must exist $\delta > 0$, such that

$$\left(\forall x \in E \cap (x_0 - \delta, x_0 + \delta)\right)\left(\left|f(x_0) - f(x)\right| < \varepsilon\right).$$

Now we can take a natural number $N = N(\varepsilon, x_0) \in \mathbb{N}_+$, such that

$$\left(\forall n \in \mathbb{N}_+\right)\left(n > N \Rightarrow \left\|\Delta^{(n)}\right\| < \delta\right).$$

Considering that there exists one and only one number $i \in \{1, 2, \cdots, n\}$, such that $x_0 \in \Delta_i^{(n)}$, $\xi_i^{(n)} \in \Delta_i^{(n)} \cap E$, and

$$\left|\xi_i^{(n)} - x_0\right| \leq \Delta^{(n)} x_i \leq \left\|\Delta^{(n)}\right\| < \delta,$$

Then when $n > N$, we surely can have the following inequality:

$$\left|g_n(x_0) - f(x_0)\right| = \left|f\left(\xi_i^{(n)}\right) - f(x_0)\right| < \varepsilon.$$

Thus $\lim\limits_{n\to+\infty} g_n(x_0) = f(x_0)$. Since $x_0 \in E$ is arbitrarily taken, we have the result: $\lim\limits_{n\to+\infty} g_n = f$, a. e. $[a,b]$. □

9.3 On Lebesgue Integral

Let $(X, \mathcal{R}, \mu)$ be a measure space and take a measurable set $E \in \mathcal{R}$ with the basic condition $\mu(E) < +\infty$. Suppose $f : E \to \mathbb{R}$ is a bounded measurable function. So we know that

$$\left(\exists c, d \in \mathbb{R}\right)\left((c < d) \wedge \left(f(E) \subset (c, d)\right)\right).$$

The set of all the partitions of $[c,d]$ is denoted by $\Xi([c,d])$. For any given partition $\Delta \in \Xi([c,d])$, where $\Delta : c = c_0 < c_1 < \cdots < c_n = d$, and

$$\Delta_k = [c_{k-1}, c_k), \quad k = 1, 2, \cdots, n-1, \quad \Delta_n = [c_{n-1}, c_n],$$

i.e., $\Delta = \{\Delta_k \mid k = 1, 2, \cdots, n\}$. Write $\|\Delta\| = \max\limits_{1\leq k\leq n}(c_k - c_{k-1})$ and

$$E_k = \{x \in E \mid f(x) \in \Delta_k\} = f^{-1}(\Delta_k),$$
$$k = 1, 2, \cdots, n$$

It is easy to know that $\{E_k | k=1,2,\cdots,n\}$ is regarded as a set partition of the measurable set E, which means that these $E_k = f^{-1}(\Delta_k)$ are mutually disjoint and satisfies the following condition:

$$\bigcup_{k=1}^{n} E_k = \bigcup_{k=1}^{n} f^{-1}(\Delta_k) = E.$$

Then we arbitrarily take a point $\eta_k \in \Delta_k$, $k=1,2,\cdots,n$, and we make a Lebesque sum as follows:

$$S(\Delta) = \sum_{k=1}^{n} \eta_k \mu(E_k).$$

If there exists a real number $s \in \mathbb{R}$, such that, for any $\varepsilon > 0$, there exists $\delta > 0$, satisfying

$$\left(\forall \Delta \in \Xi([c,d])\right)\left(\|\Delta\| < \delta \Rightarrow |S(\Delta) - s| < \varepsilon\right),$$

i.e., $s = \lim_{\|\Delta\| \to 0} S(\Delta)$, then the function f is called to be integrable on the measurable set E with respect to measure μ, and the real number s is called integral of f on E with respect to μ, denoted by

$$s = \int_E f \mathrm{d}\mu .$$

Especially, when the measure space $(X, \mathcal{R}, \mu)$ is just a Lebesgue measure space $(\mathbb{R}, \mathcal{L}, m)$, the integral $s = \int_E f \mathrm{d}\mu$ can be also denoted by the symbol $s = \int_E f \mathrm{d}m$, or by the following form:

$$s = (L)\int_E f \mathrm{d}x .$$

When $E = [a,b]$, it can be denoted by $s = (L)\int_a^b f \mathrm{d}x$. We often use the function space $L[a,b]$ to express the set of all Lebesgue integrabel functions defined on $E = [a,b]$.

Similar to the discussion about Riemann integral mentioned above, for every natural number $n = 1, 2, 3, \cdots$, we use $\Xi^{(n)}([c,d])$ to express the set of all partitions of $[c,d]$ with partition number being n. Thus $\left\{\Xi^{(n)}([c,d])\right\}_{n=1}^{\infty}$ forms a partition of $\Xi([c,d])$, i.e., any two of the elements in the sequence of sets $\left\{\Xi^{(n)}([c,d])\right\}_{n=1}^{\infty}$ are disjoint and the following condition must be satisfied:

$$\Xi([c,d]) = \bigcup_{n=1}^{\infty} \Xi^{(n)}([c,d]).$$

And then, a relation of equivalence "$\sim$" defined on $\Xi([c,d])$ as the following:

$$(\forall \Delta_1, \Delta_2 \in \Xi([c,d]))(\Delta_1 \sim \Delta_2 \Leftrightarrow \mathrm{par}(\Delta_1) = \mathrm{par}(\Delta_2))$$

So we can get the quotient set as the following:

$$\Xi([c,d])\big/_{\sim} = \left\{[\Delta] \middle| \Delta \in \Xi([c,d])\right\},$$

where $[\Delta]$ is the equivalence class to what Δ belongs. It is not difficult to learn the fact as the following:

$$\Xi([c,d])\big/_{\sim} = \left\{\Xi^{(n)}([c,d])\right\}_{n=1}^{\infty}.$$

Now for every natural number $n = 1, 2, 3, \cdots$, in every equivalence class as being $\Xi^{(n)}([c,d])$, we take one representation element:

$$\Delta^{(n)} = \left\{\Delta_k^{(n)} \middle| k = 1, 2, \cdots, n\right\}, \quad n = 1, 2, 3, \cdots$$

such that they satisfy the limit expression: $\lim\limits_{n\to\infty} \left\|\Delta^{(n)}\right\| = 0$ and the following condition:

$$(\forall n, m \in \mathbb{N})\left(n > m \Rightarrow \left\|\Delta^{(n)}\right\| < \left\|\Delta^{(m)}\right\|\right).$$

Considering that the following facts:

$$E_k^{(n)} \triangleq E\left(c_{k-1}^{(n)} \le f < c_k^{(n)}\right) \triangleq \left\{x \in [a,b] \middle| f(x) \in \left[c_{k-1}^{(n)}, c_k^{(n)}\right)\right\},$$
$$E_n^{(n)} \triangleq E\left(c_{n-1}^{(n)} \le f \le c_n^{(n)}\right) \triangleq \left\{x \in [a,b] \middle| f(x) \in \left[c_{n-1}^{(n)}, c_n^{(n)}\right]\right\},$$
$$n = 1, 2, 3, \cdots; \quad k = 1, 2, \cdots, n-1$$

The set as the following:

$$\left\{E_k^{(n)} \middle| k = 1, 2, \cdots, n\right\} = \left\{f^{-1}\left(\Delta_k^{(n)}\right) \middle| k = 1, 2, \cdots, n\right\}$$

can just form a set partition of $[a,b]$, i.e., these $E_k^{(n)}$ are mutually disjoint and satisfy the condition:

$$\bigcup_{k=1}^{n} E_k^{(n)} = [a,b].$$

Clearly $\left\{\chi_{E_k^{(n)}} \middle| k = 1, 2, \cdots, n\right\}$ is a group of linearly independent elements in $L[a,b]$. Therefore we can get a sequence of linear subspaces:

$$F_{\Delta^{(n)}} = \operatorname{span}\left(\left\{\chi_{E_k^{(n)}} \middle| k = 1, 2, \cdots, n\right\}\right),$$
$$n = 1, 2, 3, \cdots$$

For any $\eta_k^{(n)} \in \Delta_k^{(n)}$, $k = 1, 2, \cdots, n$, we can form a linear combination of the group of base functions $\left\{\chi_{E_k^{(n)}} \middle| k = 1, 2, \cdots, n\right\}$ as the following:

$$f_n \triangleq f_{\Delta^{(n)}} = \sum_{k=1}^{n} \eta_k^{(n)} \cdot \chi_{E_k^{(n)}} \in F_{\Delta^{(n)}},$$

$$(\forall x \in [a,b])\left(f_n(x) = \sum_{k=1}^{n} \eta_k^{(n)} \cdot \chi_{E_k^{(n)}}(x) \right)$$

It is worth to understand the fact as the following expression:

$$\left(\exists \xi \in E_k^{(n)}\right)\left(f(\xi) = \eta_k^{(n)}\right).$$

Thus we can get a sequence of measurable functions $\{f_n\}_{n=1}^{\infty}$ on $L[a,b]$. Seeing the fact as being: $\left\|\Delta^{(n)}\right\| \to 0 \Leftrightarrow n \to +\infty$, we surely have the following result:

$$\lim_{n\to\infty}(L)\int_a^b f_n(x)\mathrm{d}x = \lim_{n\to\infty}(L)\int_a^b \sum_{k=1}^{n} \eta_k^{(n)} \cdot \chi_{E_k^{(n)}}(x)\mathrm{d}x$$

$$= \lim_{\left\|\Delta^{(n)}\right\|\to 0}(L)\int_a^b \sum_{k=1}^{n} \eta_k^{(n)} \cdot \chi_{E_k^{(n)}}(x)\mathrm{d}x$$

$$= \lim_{\left\|\Delta^{(n)}\right\|\to 0} \sum_{k=1}^{n} \eta_k^{(n)} \cdot (L)\int_a^b \chi_{E_k^{(n)}}(x)\mathrm{d}x$$

$$= \lim_{\left\|\Delta^{(n)}\right\|\to 0} \sum_{k=1}^{n} \eta_k^{(n)} \cdot (L)\int_{E_k^{(n)}} \chi_{E_k^{(n)}}(x)\mathrm{d}x$$

$$= \lim_{\left\|\Delta^{(n)}\right\|\to 0} \sum_{k=1}^{n} \eta_k^{(n)} \cdot \left[1 \cdot m\left(E_k^{(n)}\right)\right]$$

$$= \lim_{\left\|\Delta^{(n)}\right\|\to 0} \sum_{k=1}^{n} \eta_k^{(n)} \cdot m\left(E_k^{(n)}\right) = (L)\int_a^b f(x)\mathrm{d}x$$

Proposition 9.3.1 If $f \in L[a,b]$, then the sequence of functions as being $\{f_n\}_{n=1}^{\infty}$ is in measure convergent to the integrand f on $[a,b]$.

Proof. First it is not difficulat to know the fact that, for any $\sigma > 0$, there exists a natural number $N = N(\sigma) \in \mathbb{N}_+$, such that

$$(\forall n\in \mathbb{N}_+)\left(n>N\Rightarrow \left\|\Delta^{(n)}\right\|<\sigma\right).$$

Then we have the following expression:

$$E(|f_n-f|>\sigma)\triangleq\{x\in E\,\|f_n(x)-f(x)|>\sigma\}$$

$$=\bigcup_{k=1}^{n}\{x\in E_k^{(n)}\,\|f_n(x)-f(x)|>\sigma\}$$

$$=\bigcup_{k=1}^{n}\{x\in E_k^{(n)}\,\|\eta_k^{(n)}-f(x)|>\sigma\}=\bigcup_{k=1}^{n}\varnothing=\varnothing$$

So $m\left(E\left(|f_n-f|>\sigma\right)\right)=0$, which means the following limit expression:

$$\lim_{n\to+\infty} m\left(E\left(|f_n-f|>\sigma\right)\right)=0,$$

i.e., the sequence of functions $\{f_n\}_{n=1}^{\infty}$ is in measure convergent to the integrand f on $[a,b]$. □

Because the integrand f is bounded on $[a,b]$, i.e., there exists $M>0$, such that

$$(\forall x\in[a,b])\left(|f(x)|\le M\right),$$

The sequence of functions $\{f_n\}_{n=1}^{\infty}$ must be a sequence of uniformly bounded measurable functions, which means that

$$(\forall n\in \mathbb{N}_+)(\forall x\in[a,b])\left(|f_n(x)|\le M\right).$$

Based on Lebesgue dominated convergence theorem, we get the following equation:

$$\lim_{n\to\infty}(L)\int_a^b f_n(x)\mathrm{d}x = (L)\int_a^b \lim_{n\to\infty} f_n(x)\mathrm{d}x = (L)\int_a^b f(x)\mathrm{d}x\,.$$

Remark 9.3.1 From the proof of Proposition 9.2.2, we can learn that the sequence of functions $\{g_n\}_{n=1}^{\infty}$ is continuous everywhere in the measurable set $E=[a,b]-A$ which is the set of all continuous points of f.

Let the limit function of the sequence of functions $\{g_n\}_{n=1}^{\infty}$ on E be $g=\lim\limits_{n\to\infty} g_n$. We make g extended to be a function on the whole measurable set $[a,b]$ as the following:

$$g(x)=\begin{cases}\lim\limits_{n\to\infty} g_n(x), & x\in E,\\ 0, & x\in A\end{cases}$$

Then we know the fact: $g=f$, a. e. $[a,b]$, which means that the function is Riemann integrabel, i.e. $g\in R[a,b]$. Therefore, the Riemann integral $(R)\int_a^b g(x)\mathrm{d}x$ must be meaningful. Naturally we have a question: whether the following integral equality is true:

$$(R)\int_a^b g(x)dx = (R)\int_a^b f(x)\mathrm{d}x\,.$$

Our answer is positive. In fact, based on the well-known Lebesgue integral equality:

$$(L)\int_a^b g(x)dx = (L)\int_a^b f(x)\mathrm{d}x\,,$$

By using the relationship between Lebesgue integral and Riemann integral, we immediately have the following equation:

$$(R)\int_a^b g(x)\mathrm{d}x = (L)\int_a^b g(x)\mathrm{d}x = (L)\int_a^b f(x)\mathrm{d}x = (R)\int_a^b f(x)\mathrm{d}x$$

Moreover, from the Riemann integral equality as the following:

$$(R)\int_a^b g(x)\mathrm{d}x = (R)\int_a^b f(x)\mathrm{d}x,$$

we can also find out the following result:

$$\lim_{n\to\infty}(R)\int_a^b g_n(x)\mathrm{d}x = (R)\int_a^b f(x)\mathrm{d}x$$
$$= (R)\int_a^b g(x)\mathrm{d}x = (R)\int_a^b \lim_{n\to\infty} g_n(x)\mathrm{d}x$$

This means that the limit operation of the sequence of functions $\{g_n\}_{n=1}^{\infty}$ and Riemann integral operation can be commutative without the stronger condition that $\{g_n\}_{n=1}^{\infty}$ must be uniformly convergent. □

Example 9.3.1 Now we use function approximation viewpoint to inspect the integral of Dirichlet function which is well-known function:

$$D:[0,1]\to\{0,1\}$$
$$x\mapsto D(x)=\begin{cases}1, & x\in[0,1]\cap\mathbb{Q},\\ 0, & x\in[0,1]\cap\mathbb{Q}^c\end{cases}$$

We all know that $D\notin R[0,1]$ but $D\in L[0,1]$. It is easy to know that the fact that $\Xi(\{0,1\})=\{\Delta_1,\Delta_2\}$, where $\Delta_1=\{0\}, \Delta_2=\{1\}$. Considering the following expressions:

$$E_1 = D^{-1}(\Delta_1)=[0,1]\cap\mathbb{Q}^c,$$
$$E_2 = D^{-1}(\Delta_2)=[0,1]\cap\mathbb{Q}$$

clearly $\{E_1,E_2\}$ forms a partition of $[0,1]$ and $\{\chi_{E_1},\chi_{E_2}\}$ is a group of linearly independent functions of $L[0,1]$. It can generate a two-dimension linear subspace of $L[0,1]$, denoted by

$$H \triangleq \mathrm{span}\left(\{\chi_{E_1},\chi_{E_2}\}\right).$$

Only considering the integral, the linear combination coefficients of the group of base function $\{\chi_{E_1}, \chi_{E_2}\}$ has only one way for taking, i.e.,

$$\eta_1 = 0, \quad \eta_2 = 1.$$

Therefore we get an element of the linear subspace H as the following:

$$h = \eta_1 \chi_{E_1} + \eta_2 \chi_{E_2}.$$

It is not difficult to know the fact that $D = h \in H$, and then we have the following expression:

$$\begin{aligned}
&(L)\int_{[0,1]} D\mathrm{d}m = (L)\int_0^1 D(x)\mathrm{d}x = (L)\int_0^1 h(x)\mathrm{d}x \\
&= (L)\int_0^1 \left(\eta_1\chi_{E_1}(x) + \eta_2\chi_{E_2}(x)\right)\mathrm{d}x \\
&= \eta_1 \cdot (L)\int_0^1 \chi_{E_1}(x)\mathrm{d}x + \eta_2 \cdot (L)\int_0^1 \chi_{E_2}(x)\mathrm{d}x \\
&= \eta_1 \cdot \left[1 \cdot m(E_1)\right] + \eta_2 \cdot \left[1 \cdot m(E_2)\right] \\
&= \eta_1 \cdot m(E_1) + \eta_2 \cdot m(E_2) = 0 \cdot 1 + 1 \cdot 0 = 0
\end{aligned}$$

Furthermore, if we put $(\forall n \in \mathbb{N}_+)(h_n \triangleq h)$, then we can get a sequence of functions of $L[0,1]$, i.e. $\{h_n\}_{n=1}^{\infty}$. Clearly $\{h_n\}_{n=1}^{\infty}$ can be uniformly convergent to the limit function h on $[0,1]$. Thus, in form we can learn the following equation:

$$\begin{aligned}
&\lim_{n\to\infty}(L)\int_a^b h_n(x)\mathrm{d}x = (L)\int_a^b \lim_{n\to\infty} h_n(x)\mathrm{d}x \\
&= (L)\int_a^b h(x)\mathrm{d}x = (L)\int_a^b D(x)\mathrm{d}x = 0
\end{aligned}$$

This is our well-known result. □

9.4 Unification of Riemann Integral and Lebesgue Integral

Considering the class of Riemann integrable functions $R[a,b]$, as we all known $R[a,b]=C^*[a,b]$, for any $f\in R[a,b]$, we can have a sequence of functions with discontinuity point of the first kind, which it has been denoted by $\{g_n\}_{n=1}^{\infty}$, such that

$$\lim_{n\to+\infty} g_n = f \text{ , a.e. } [a,b]$$

From the point of view of function approximation theory, every function g_n is piecewise continuous polynomial which is formed by the group of base functions $\left\{\chi_{\Delta_i^{(n)}}\middle| i=1,2,\cdots,n\right\}$. In other words, g_n is just a linear combination of $\left\{\chi_{\Delta_i^{(n)}}\middle| i=1,2,\cdots,n\right\}$ as follows:

$$g_n = f\left(\xi_1^{(n)}\right)\cdot\chi_{\Delta_1^{(n)}} + f\left(\xi_2^{(n)}\right)\cdot\chi_{\Delta_2^{(n)}} + \cdots + f\left(\xi_n^{(n)}\right)\cdot\chi_{\Delta_n^{(n)}},$$

where $f\left(\xi_1^{(n)}\right), f\left(\xi_2^{(n)}\right),\cdots, f\left(\xi_n^{(n)}\right)$ are just the linear combination coefficients.

The linear space generated by $\left\{\chi_{\Delta_i^{(n)}}\middle| i=1,2,\cdots,n\right\}$ as the following:

$$G_{\Delta^{(n)}} = \text{span}\left(\left\{\chi_{\Delta_i^{(n)}}\middle| i=1,2,\cdots,n\right\}\right)$$

is just a n dimension linear subspace of $R[a,b]$, which is closed for g_n. In other words, we can use an element g_n in the finite dimension linear space $G_{\Delta^{(n)}}$ to approximate the element f in infinite linear space in $R[a,b]$. If we write $G=\lim_{n\to+\infty} G_{\Delta^{(n)}}$, then we can have the following expression:

$$\dim(G) = \dim\left(\lim_{n\to+\infty} G_{\Delta^{(n)}}\right) = +\infty .$$

This means that it is difficult that g_n, as an element $G_{\Delta^{(n)}}$, accurately approximates f for any finite natural number $n\in\mathbb{N}_+$, where $\mathbb{N}_+$ is the set of all natural numbers. Fortunately, $G = \lim_{n\to+\infty} G_{\Delta^{(n)}}$, as a linear subspace of $R[a,b]$, is of countable base function set.

Moreover, although $\lim_{n\to+\infty} g_n = f$, a.e. $[a,b]$, this does not make it true that the limit operation and integral operation are exchangeable, i.e.,

$$\lim_{n\to\infty}(R)\int_a^b g_n(x)\mathrm{d}x = (R)\int_a^b \lim_{n\to\infty} g_n(x)\mathrm{d}x .$$

When $f \in C[a,b]$, i.e., f is a continuous function, $\lim_{n\to+\infty} g_n = f$ must be uniformly convergent in $[a,b]$; thus we have the following result:

$$\lim_{n\to\infty}(R)\int_a^b g_n(x)\mathrm{d}x = (R)\int_a^b \lim_{n\to\infty} g_n(x)\mathrm{d}x = (R)\int_a^b f(x)\mathrm{d}x .$$

On the class of Lebesgue integrable functions $L[a,b]$, for any a Lebesgue integrable function $f \in L[a,b]$, we can get a sequence of bounded measurable functions $\{f_n\}_{n=1}^{\infty}$, such that $f_n \overset{n\to+\infty}{\Rightarrow} f$. From the point of view of function approximation theory, every f_n is a generalized piecewise zero degree polynomial, and the group of base functions of structuring f_n is just the group of base functions:

$$\left\{\chi_{E_k^{(n)}} \middle| k = 1,2,\cdots,n\right\};$$

and f_n is the linear combination of $\left\{\chi_{E_k^{(n)}} \middle| k = 1,2,\cdots,n\right\}$ as the following:

$$f_n = \eta_1^{(n)} \cdot \chi_{E_1^{(n)}} + \eta_2^{(n)} \cdot \chi_{E_2^{(n)}} + \cdots + \eta_n^{(n)} \cdot \chi_{E_n^{(n)}},$$

where these real numbers $\eta_1^{(n)}, \eta_2^{(n)}, \cdots, \eta_n^{(n)}$ are regarded as the combination coefficients.

As the same as the situation about Riemann integral, the linear space generated by $\left\{\chi_{E_i^{(n)}} \middle| i=1,2,\cdots,n\right\}$ as the following:

$$F_{\Delta^{(n)}} = \mathrm{span}\left(\left\{\chi_{E_i^{(n)}} \middle| i=1,2,\cdots,n\right\}\right)$$

is just a n dimension linear subspace of $L[a,b]$, which is closed for f_n. In other words, we can use an element f_n in finite dimension linear space $F_{\Delta^{(n)}}$ to approximate the element f in infinite linear space in the function space $L[a,b]$. If we write $F = \lim_{n\to+\infty} F_{\Delta^{(n)}}$, then we have the following limit expression:

$$\dim(F) = \dim\left(\lim_{n\to+\infty} F_{\Delta^{(n)}}\right) = +\infty .$$

This means that $F = \lim_{n\to+\infty} F_{\Delta^{(n)}}$ of countable base function set.

Moreover, considering the fact that $f_n \overset{n\to+\infty}{\Rightarrow} f$, since the integrand f is bounded, $\{f_n\}_{n=1}^{\infty}$ is a sequence of uniformly. Based on Lebesgue dominated convergence theorem, we have the following result:

$$\lim_{n\to\infty}(L)\int_a^b f_n(x)\mathrm{d}x = (L)\int_a^b \lim_{n\to\infty} f_n(x)\mathrm{d}x = (L)\int_a^b f(x)\mathrm{d}x .$$

9.5 Riemann Integral of Continuous Functions

For any continuous function $f \in C[a,b]$, we have known the fact that

$$\Xi([a,b]) = \bigcup_{n=1}^{\infty} \Xi^{(n)}([a,b]).$$

For every natural number $n=1,2,3,\cdots$, we take a representative element in every equivalence class $\Xi^{(n)}([a,b])$ as the following:

$$\Delta^{(n)} = \left\{ \Delta_k^{(n)} \middle| k = 1, 2, \cdots, n \right\}, \quad n = 1, 2, 3, \cdots$$

such that they satisfy the condition: $\lim_{n\to\infty} \left\| \Delta^{(n)} \right\| = 0$ and

$$(\forall n, m \in \mathbb{N})\left(n > m \Rightarrow \left\| \Delta^{(n)} \right\| < \left\| \Delta^{(m)} \right\|\right).$$

Seeing that $\Delta^{(n)} : a = x_0^{(n)} < x_1^{(n)} < \cdots < x_n^{(n)}$, we can make the base functions that we need as follows, refer to Figure 9.5.1.

$$\mu_{A_0^{(n)}}(x) = \begin{cases} \left(x - x_1^{(n)}\right) / \left(x_0^{(n)} - x_1^{(n)}\right), & x \in \left[x_0^{(n)}, x_1^{(n)}\right); \\ 0, & \text{otherwise}, \end{cases}$$

$$\mu_{A_i^{(n)}}(x) = \begin{cases} \left(x - x_{i-1}^{(n)}\right) / \left(x_i^{(n)} - x_{i-1}^{(n)}\right), & x \in \left[x_{i-1}^{(n)}, x_i^{(n)}\right); \\ \left(x - x_{i+1}^{(n)}\right) / \left(x_i^{(n)} - x_{i+1}^{(n)}\right), & x \in \left[x_i^{(n)}, x_{i+1}^{(n)}\right); \\ 0, & \text{otherwise}; \end{cases}$$

$$i = 1, 2, \cdots, n-1,$$

$$\mu_{A_n^{(n)}}(x) = \begin{cases} \left(x - x_{n-1}^{(n)}\right) / \left(x_n^{(n)} - x_{n-1}^{(n)}\right), & x \in \left[x_{n-1}^{(n)}, x_n^{(n)}\right]; \\ 0, & \text{otherwise}, \end{cases}$$

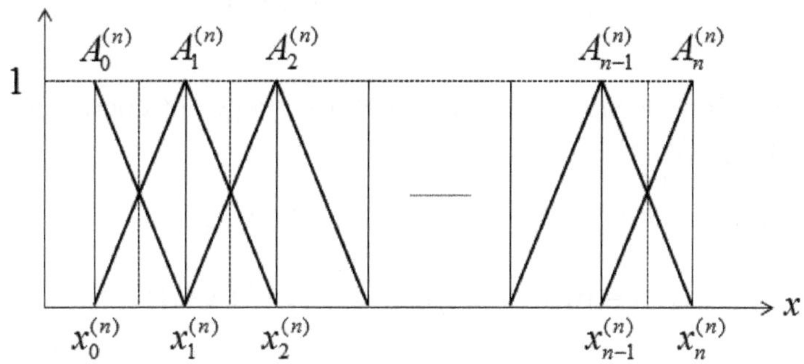

Fig. 9.5.1. Continuous base functions $A_i^{(n)}$ $(i = 0, 1, \cdots, n)$

It is easy to verify that the set $\left\{\mu_{A_0^{(n)}}, \mu_{A_1^{(n)}}, \cdots, \mu_{A_n^{(n)}}\right\}$ is a group of linearly independent functions in the function space $C[a,b]$. Then it can generate a $n+1$ dimension linear subspace of $C[a,b]$ shown as the following:

$$H_{\Delta^{(n)}} \triangleq \text{span}\left(\left\{\mu_{A_0^{(n)}}, \mu_{A_1^{(n)}}, \cdots, \mu_{A_n^{(n)}}\right\}\right).$$

So we can also have got a sequence of linear subspaces denoted by the sequence of linear subspaces $\left\{H_{\Delta^{(n)}}\right\}_{n=1}^{\infty}$, where the set as follows:

$$\left\{\mu_{A_0^{(n)}}, \mu_{A_1^{(n)}}, \cdots, \mu_{A_n^{(n)}}\right\}$$

is just the group of base elements of $H_{\Delta^{(n)}}$. By using f we can make $n+1$ constants as the following:

$$f\left(x_0^{(n)}\right), f\left(x_1^{(n)}\right), \cdots, f\left(x_n^{(n)}\right).$$

By using them, we can get a linear combination of the element coming from the set $\left\{\mu_{A_0^{(n)}}, \mu_{A_1^{(n)}}, \cdots, \mu_{A_n^{(n)}}\right\}$ as follows:

$$f_n(x) \triangleq \sum_{i=0}^{n} f\left(x_i^{(n)}\right) \mu_{A_i^{(n)}}(x).$$

This expression means that we have got a sequence of continuous functions as $\left\{f_n(x)\right\}_{n=1}^{\infty}$.

It is not difficult to verify the fact as the following:

$$(\forall i \in \{0,1,\cdots,n\})\left(f_n\left(x_i^{(n)}\right) = f\left(x_i^{(n)}\right)\right),$$

and then we know that $f_n(x)$ is a piecewise linear interpolation function about the continuous function f, where $x_0^{(n)}, x_1^{(n)}, \cdots, x_n^{(n)}$ are just its nodes of interpolation.

It is noticeable that there is an interesting fact:

$$\left(\forall i\in\{0,1,\cdots,n\}\right)\left(A_i^{(n)}\in\mathcal{F}([a,b])\right),$$

where $\mathcal{F}([a,b])$ means the set of all fuzzy sets defined on $[a,b]$, i.e., every $A_i^{(n)}$ is a fuzzy set defined on the universe $[a,b]$, and $\mu_{A_i^{(n)}}(x)$ is just the membership function of $A_i^{(n)}$. Moreover, if we define the following fuzzy sets:

$$B_i^{(n)}\triangleq\left\{f\left(x_i^{(n)}\right)\right\},\quad i=0,1,\cdots,n,$$

where every $B_i^{(n)}$ is actually a single element set, then we can get a group of **fuzzy inference rules**:

$$\left.\begin{array}{l}\text{If } x \text{ is } A_0^{(n)} \text{ then } y \text{ is } B_0^{(n)}\\ \text{If } x \text{ is } A_1^{(n)} \text{ then } y \text{ is } B_1^{(n)}\\ \cdots\cdots\\ \text{If } x \text{ is } A_n^{(n)} \text{ then } y \text{ is } B_n^{(n)}\end{array}\right\}$$

Now we return to consider the integral of continuous functions. For every number $i\in\{1,2,\cdots,n\}$, on every closed interval $\left[x_{i-1}^{(n)},x_i^{(n)}\right]$, we define a linear function $l_i^{(n)}(x)$, such that they must satisfy the following condition:

$$l_i^{(n)}\left(x_{i-1}^{(n)}\right)=f\left(x_{i-1}^{(n)}\right),\quad l_i^{(n)}\left(x_i^{(n)}\right)=f\left(x_i^{(n)}\right),$$
$$i=1,2,\cdots n$$

And then these linear function $l_i^{(n)}(x), i=1,2,\cdots n$ are extended as the following linear functions defined on $[a,b]$:

$$L_i^{(n)}(x) = \begin{cases} l_i^{(n)}(x), & x \in \left[x_{i-1}^{(n)}, x_i^{(n)}\right], \\ 0, & x \in [a,b] - \left[x_{i-1}^{(n)}, x_i^{(n)}\right] \end{cases}$$

$$i = 1, 2, \cdots n$$

It is easy to learn the following fact:

$$L_i^{(n)}(x) = f\left(x_{i-1}^{(n)}\right) + \frac{f\left(x_i^{(n)}\right) - f\left(x_{i-1}^{(n)}\right)}{x_i^{(n)} - x_{i-1}^{(n)}}\left(x - x_{i-1}^{(n)}\right),$$

where $i = 1, 2, \cdots n$, and

$$f_n(x) = \sum_{i=1}^{n} L_i^{(n)}(x).$$

Proposition 9.5.1 If $f \in C[a,b]$, then the sequence of continuous functions $\{f_n\}_{n=1}^{\infty}$ is uniformly convergent to f on $[a,b]$.

Proof. Because $f \in C[a,b]$, f is uniformly continuous on $[a,b]$. So for any $\varepsilon > 0$, and for any two points $x, x' \in [a,b]$, such that

$$(\exists \delta > 0)\left(|x - x'| < \delta \Rightarrow |f(x) - f(x')| < \varepsilon\right).$$

Now we can take a natural number $N = N(\varepsilon) \in \mathbb{N}_+$, such that

$$(\forall n \in \mathbb{N}_+)\left(n > N \Rightarrow \left\|\Delta^{(n)}\right\| < \delta\right).$$

Since $x \in [a,b]$, there must be one and only one $i \in \{1, 2, \cdots, n\}$, such that $x \in \Delta_i^{(n)}$; thus we have the following result:

$$\left|f(x)-f_n(x)\right|=\left|f(x)-L_i^{(n)}(x)\right|$$

$$=\left|f(x)-f\left(x_{i-1}^{(n)}\right)-\frac{f\left(x_i^{(n)}\right)-f\left(x_{i-1}^{(n)}\right)}{x_i^{(n)}-x_{i-1}^{(n)}}\left(x-x_{i-1}^{(n)}\right)\right|$$

$$=\left|\frac{f(x)-f\left(x_{i-1}^{(n)}\right)}{x_i^{(n)}-x_{i-1}^{(n)}}\left(x_i^{(n)}-x_{i-1}^{(n)}\right)-\frac{f\left(x_i^{(n)}\right)-f\left(x_{i-1}^{(n)}\right)}{x_i^{(n)}-x_{i-1}^{(n)}}\left(x-x_{i-1}^{(n)}\right)\right|$$

$$=\frac{\left|\left(f(x)-f\left(x_{i-1}^{(n)}\right)\right)\left(x_i^{(n)}-x_{i-1}^{(n)}\right)+\left(f\left(x_{i-1}^{(n)}\right)-f\left(x_i^{(n)}\right)\right)\left(x-x_{i-1}^{(n)}\right)\right|}{x_i^{(n)}-x_{i-1}^{(n)}}$$

$$=\frac{\left|\left(f(x)-f\left(x_{i-1}^{(n)}\right)\right)\left(x_i^{(n)}-x\right)+\left(f(x)-f\left(x_{i-1}^{(n)}\right)\right)\left(x-x_{i-1}^{(n)}\right)\right|}{x_i^{(n)}-x_{i-1}^{(n)}}$$

$$\leq\frac{\left|\left(f(x)-f\left(x_{i-1}^{(n)}\right)\right)\right|\left(x_i^{(n)}-x\right)+\left|f(x)-f\left(x_{i-1}^{(n)}\right)\right|\left(x-x_{i-1}^{(n)}\right)}{x_i^{(n)}-x_{i-1}^{(n)}}$$

$$<\varepsilon\frac{\left(x_i^{(n)}-x\right)+\left(x-x_{i-1}^{(n)}\right)}{x_i^{(n)}-x_{i-1}^{(n)}}=\varepsilon$$

Now that $x\in[a,b]$ is arbitrarily taken in $[a,b]$ by us, so the sequence of continuous functions $\{f_n\}_{n=1}^{\infty}$ is uniformly convergent to f on the integral interval $[a,b]$. □

We now take the following n points:

$$\eta_i^{(n)}\triangleq\frac{f\left(x_{i-1}^{(n)}\right)+f\left(x_i^{(n)}\right)}{2},\quad i=1,2,\cdots,n,$$

and by them we consider the integral of the continuous function f as the following:

$$\begin{aligned}
\int_a^b f(x)dx &= \int_a^b \lim_{n\to\infty} f_n(x)dx = \lim_{n\to\infty}\int_a^b f_n(x)dx \\
&= \lim_{n\to\infty}\int_a^b \sum_{i=1}^{n} L_i^{(n)}(x)dx = \lim_{n\to\infty}\sum_{i=1}^{n}\int_{x_{i-1}^{(n)}}^{x_i^{(n)}} L_i^{(n)}(x)dx \\
&= \lim_{n\to\infty}\sum_{i=1}^{n}\int_{x_{i-1}^{(n)}}^{x_i^{(n)}}\left(f\left(x_{i-1}^{(n)}\right) + \frac{f\left(x_i^{(n)}\right) - f\left(x_{i-1}^{(n)}\right)}{x_i^{(n)} - x_{i-1}^{(n)}}\left(x - x_{i-1}^{(n)}\right)\right)dx \\
&= \lim_{n\to\infty}\sum_{i=1}^{n}\frac{f\left(x_{i-1}^{(n)}\right) + f\left(x_i^{(n)}\right)}{2}\left(x_i^{(n)} - x_{i-1}^{(n)}\right) \\
&= \lim_{n\to\infty}\sum_{i=1}^{n}\frac{f\left(x_{i-1}^{(n)}\right) + f\left(x_i^{(n)}\right)}{2} m\left(\Delta_i^{(n)}\right) \\
&= \lim_{n\to\infty}\sum_{i=1}^{n}\eta_i^{(n)}\left[1\cdot m\left(\Delta_i^{(n)}\right)\right]
\end{aligned}$$

Furthermore, we write the following n real numbers as some weights:

$$w_i^{(n)} = \frac{\left|\eta_i^{(n)}\right|}{\sum_{j=1}^{n}\left|\eta_j^{(n)}\right|}, \quad i = 1, 2, \cdots, n,$$

and clearly they meet the following condition:

$$\left[\left(\forall i \in \{1, 2, \cdots, n\}\right)\left(w_i^{(n)} \in [0,1]\right)\right] \wedge \left(\sum_{i=1}^{n} w_i^{(n)} = 1\right).$$

This means that $\left(w_1^{(n)}, w_2^{(n)}, \cdots, w_n^{(n)}\right)$, $n = 1, 2, 3, \cdots$ form a sequence of weight vectors with normalization; and then we have the following expression:

$$\int_a^b f(x)dx = \lim_{n\to\infty}\sum_{i=1}^{n}\eta_i^{(n)}\left[1\cdot m\left(\Delta_i^{(n)}\right)\right]$$

$$= \lim_{n\to\infty}\sum_{i=1}^{n}\left|\eta_i^{(n)}\right|\left[\operatorname{sgn}\left(\eta_i^{(n)}\right)\cdot m\left(\Delta_i^{(n)}\right)\right]$$

$$= \lim_{n\to\infty}\sum_{i=1}^{n}w_i^{(n)}\left[\operatorname{sgn}\left(\eta_i^{(n)}\right)\cdot\left(\sum_{j=1}^{n}\left|\eta_j^{(n)}\right|\right)\cdot m\left(\Delta_i^{(n)}\right)\right]$$

where $\operatorname{sgn}\left(\eta_i^{(n)}\right)\cdot\left(\sum_{j=1}^{n}\left|\eta_j^{(n)}\right|\right)\cdot m\left(\Delta_i^{(n)}\right), i=1,2,\cdots,n$ is a group of directed areas, which they have the common height $\sum_{j=1}^{n}\left|\eta_j^{(n)}\right|$, but different widths $m\left(\Delta_i^{(n)}\right)$; and the integral $\int_a^b f(x)\mathrm{d}x$ is just the limit of the weighted summations of the group of directed areas.

Remark 9.5.1 When every partition $\Delta^{(n)}: a = x_0^{(n)} < x_1^{(n)} < \cdots < x_n^{(n)}$ is a equidistant partition, i.e.,

$$\Delta_i^{(n)}=x_i^{(n)} - x_{i-1}^{(n)} = \frac{b-a}{n}, \quad i=1,2,\cdots,n,$$

We also have the following equation:

$$\int_a^b f(x)\mathrm{d}x = \lim_{n\to\infty}\sum_{i=1}^{n}\frac{f\left(x_{i-1}^{(n)}\right)+f\left(x_i^{(n)}\right)}{2}\left(x_i^{(n)}-x_{i-1}^{(n)}\right)$$

$$=\lim_{n\to\infty}\frac{b-a}{n}\sum_{i=1}^{n}\frac{f\left(a+\frac{i-1}{n}(b-a)\right)+f\left(a+\frac{i}{n}(b-a)\right)}{2}$$

$$=\lim_{n\to\infty}\frac{b-a}{n}\left[\frac{f(a)-f(b)}{2}+\sum_{i=1}^{n}f\left(a+\frac{i}{n}(b-a)\right)\right]$$

$$=\lim_{n\to\infty}\frac{b-a}{2n}\left(f(a)-f(b)\right)+\lim_{n\to\infty}\frac{b-a}{n}\sum_{i=1}^{n}f\left(a+\frac{i}{n}(b-a)\right)$$

$$=\lim_{n\to\infty}\frac{b-a}{n}\sum_{i=1}^{n}f\left(a+\frac{i}{n}(b-a)\right)$$

$$=\lim_{n\to\infty}\frac{1}{n}\sum_{i=1}^{n}f\left(a+\frac{i}{n}(b-a)\right)(b-a)$$

where the summation $\frac{1}{n}\sum_{i=1}^{n}f\left(a+\frac{i}{n}(b-a)\right)(b-a)$ is a mean value.

However, what is the meaning of this mean value? As a matter of fact, we make a transformation as the following:

$$\int_a^b f(x)\mathrm{d}x = \lim_{n\to\infty}\frac{1}{n}\sum_{i=1}^{n}f\left(a+\frac{i}{n}(b-a)\right)(b-a)$$

$$=\lim_{n\to\infty}\frac{1}{n}\sum_{i=1}^{n}\operatorname{sgn}\left(f\left(a+\frac{i}{n}(b-a)\right)\right)\left|f\left(a+\frac{i}{n}(b-a)\right)\right|(b-a),$$

where every $\operatorname{sgn}\left(f\left(a+\frac{i}{n}(b-a)\right)\right)\left|f\left(a+\frac{i}{n}(b-a)\right)\right|(b-a)$ is a directed area. These directed areas have a common width $b-a$, but different heights $\left|f\left(a+\frac{i}{n}(b-a)\right)\right|$. Therefore the integral $\int_a^b f(x)\mathrm{d}x$ is just the limit of the mean values of the group of directed areas.

At last, we make a further transformation on the integral $\int_a^b f(x)\mathrm{d}x$ as the following:

$$\int_a^b f(x)\mathrm{d}x = \lim_{n\to\infty}\sum_{i=1}^{n} \mathrm{sgn}\left(f\left(a+\frac{i}{n}(b-a)\right)\right)\cdot\left|f\left(a+\frac{i}{n}(b-a)\right)\right|\cdot\frac{b-a}{n}$$

Then every $\left|f\left(a+\frac{i}{n}(b-a)\right)\right|\cdot\frac{b-a}{n}$ is a directed area, they have common width $\frac{b-a}{n}$, but different heights $\left|f\left(a+\frac{i}{n}(b-a)\right)\right|$, and the integral $\int_a^b f(x)\mathrm{d}x$ is just the limit of the algebraic summations of the group of directed areas. □

9.6 Conclusions

This chapter has discussed unification of Riemann integral and Lebesgue integral. The main results are as follows.

On Riemann integral, we have shown that function approximation is main tool where the group of base functions as the following:

$$\left\{\chi_{\Delta_i}\middle| i=1,2,\cdots,n\right\} \subset R[a,b]$$

plays an important role in the integral. As we all know, every Δ_i is an interval which comes from a partition on X as follows:

$$\Delta : a = x_0 < x_1 < \cdots < x_n = b\,.$$

It is worth noting the following the sequence of sets:

$$G_{\Delta^{(n)}} = \mathrm{span}\left(\left\{\chi_{\Delta_i^{(n)}}\middle| i=1,2,\cdots,n\right\}\right)$$

which is the sequence of linear subspaces in Riemann integrabel space $R[a,b]$, plays the role of its framework. This means that linear algebra plays an important role in Riemann integral.

On Lebesgue integral, we also have shown that function approximation is main tool where the group of base functions as the following:

$$\left\{\chi_{E_k^{(n)}} \middle| k=1,2,\cdots,n\right\} \subset L[a,b]$$

plays an important role in the integral. As we all know, every $E_k^{(n)}$ may not be an interval but should be measurable set which comes from the following sets:

$$E_k^{(n)} = \left\{x \in E \middle| f(x) \in \Delta_k^{(n)}\right\} = f^{-1}\left(\Delta_k^{(n)}\right),$$
$$k=1,2,\cdots,n$$

and $\left\{\Delta_k^{(n)}\right\}_{k=1}^{n}$ forms a partition on Y not on X.

In the same way, the sequence of sets as the following:

$$F_{\Delta^{(n)}} = \text{span}\left(\left\{\chi_{E_i^{(n)}} \middle| i=1,2,\cdots,n\right\}\right),$$

which is the sequence of linear subspaces in $L[a,b]$, also plays the role of its framework. This also means that linear algebra plays an important role in Lebesgue integral.

Thus, we can give the conclusion: Riemann integral and Lebesgue integral are unified under linear algebra and function approximation theory.

References

1. Zadeh L.A. (1973). Outline of a new approach to the analysis of complex systems and decision processes, IEEE Trans. SMC, 3, pp. 28–44.
2. Zadeh, L. A. (1974). The concept of a linguistic variable and its applications to approximate reasoning (I), Information Sciences, 8(2), pp. 199-249.
3. Zadeh, L. A. (1974). The concept of a linguistic variable and its applications to approximate reasoning (II), Information Sciences, 8(3), pp. 301-357.

4. Zadeh, L. A. (1975). The concept of a linguistic variable and its applications to approximate reasoning (III), Information Sciences, 9(1), pp. 43-80.
5. Li, H. X. (1998). Interpolation mechanism of fuzzy control, Science in China (Series E), 41(3), pp. 312-320.
6. Li, H. X. (1995). To see the success of fuzzy logic from mathematical essence of fuzzy control, Fuzzy Systems and Mathematics, 9(4), pp. 1-14 (in Chinese).
7. Hou, J., You, F. and Li, H. X. (2005). Some fuzzy controllers constructed by triple I method and their response capability, Progress in Natural Science, 15(1), pp. 29-37 (in Chinese).
8. Li, H. X., You, F. and Peng, J. Y. (2004). Fuzzy controllers based on some fuzzy implication operators and their response functions, Progress in Natural Science, 14(1), pp. 15-20.
9. You, F., Feng, Y. B. and Li, H. X. (2003). Fuzzy implication operators and their construction (I), Journal of Beijing Normal University, 39(5), pp. 606-611 (in Chinese).
10. You, F., Feng, Y. B., Wang, J. Y. and Li, H. X. (2004). Fuzzy implication operators and their construction (II), Journal of Beijing Normal University, 40(2), pp 168-176 (in Chinese).
11. You, F., Yang, X. Y., Li, H. X. (2004). Fuzzy implication operators and their construction (III), Journal of Beijing Normal University, 40(4), pp. 427-432 (in Chinese).
12. You, F. and Li, H. X. (2004). Fuzzy implication operators and their construction (IV), Journal of Beijing Normal University, 40(5), pp. 588-599 (in Chinese).
13. Dubois, D. and Prade, H. (1991). Fuzzy sets in approximate reasoning, Part 1: Inference with possibility distributions, Fuzzy Sets and Systems, 40(1), pp. 143-202.
14. Dubois, D. and Prade, H. (1991). Fuzzy sets in approximate reasoning, Part 2: Logical approaches, Fuzzy Sets and Systems, 40(1), pp. 203-244.
15. Li, H. X. (2006). Probability representations of fuzzy systems, Science in China (Series F), 49(3), pp. 339-363.
16. Browder, A. (1996) *Mathematical Analysis, An Introduction.* (Springer-Verlag, New York).
17. Graves, L. M. (1946) *Theory of Functions of Real Variables.* (McGraw-Hill, New York).
18. Zaanen, A. C. (1958) *An Introduction to the Theory of Integration.* (Amsterdam, North-Holland).
19. Halmos, P. K. (1950) *Measure Theory.* (D. van Nostrand, New York).
20. Bohnenblust, H. F. (1937) *Theory of Functions of Real Variables.* (Princeton University Press).
21. de Barra, G. (1981) *Measure Theory and Integration.* (Halsled Press, New York).

Chapter 10

Fuzzy Systems with a Kind of Self-adaption

10.1 Fuzzy Inference Relations with Self-adaption

Again we consider a kind of static uncertain systems with one input one output shown as in Figure 10.1.1, which it's the relation between input and output can be described by (10.1.1) as follows, where the input variable x takes its values in the universe X and the output variable y takes its values in the universe Y.

$$s: X \to Y, \quad x \mapsto y \triangleq s(x) \tag{10.1.1}$$

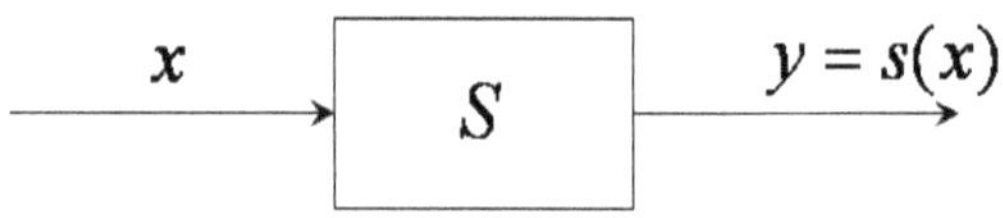

Fig. 10.1.1. Static uncertain system with one input one output

Since the system S has been supposed to be an uncertain system, based on the methods discussed in some foregoing chapters, we have no difficulty to get a group of fuzzy inference rules as the following:

$$\left.\begin{array}{l} \text{If } x \text{ is } A_i \text{ then } y \text{ is } B_i \\ i = 0, 1, \cdots, n \end{array}\right\} \tag{10.1.2}$$

where $A_i \in \mathcal{F}(X)$ and $B_i \in \mathcal{F}(Y)$, $i = 0, 1, \cdots, n$.

As we all know, the fuzzy inference relation R is fixed in CRI method. In order to enhance the ability of describing uncertain systems, we try to make the fuzzy inference relation R be having a kind of self-adaption which means that R can change with changing of the input variable of the system. So we suggest a kind of fuzzy inference with self-adaption.

Suppose input universe $X=[a,b]$ and output universe $Y=[c,d]$, and the IOD as the following:

$$\text{IOD} \triangleq \{(x_i, y_i) \in X \times Y \mid i = 0,1,\cdots,n\}$$

should meet the following conditions:

$$a = x_0 < x_1 < \cdots < x_n = b,$$
$$c = y_{k_0} \leq y_{k_1} \leq \cdots \leq y_{k_n} = d$$

where $k_i = \sigma(i)$, and σ is a $n+1$ permutation as follows:

$$\sigma = \begin{pmatrix} 0 & 1 & \cdots & n \\ k_0 & k_1 & \cdots & k_n \end{pmatrix}.$$

Thus we can get a group of fuzzy inference rules as the following:

$$\left.\begin{array}{c} \text{If } x \text{ is } A_{k_0} \text{ then } y \text{ is } B_{k_0} \\ \text{or} \\ \text{If } x \text{ is } A_{k_1} \text{ then } y \text{ is } B_{k_1} \\ \text{or} \\ \cdots\cdots \\ \text{or} \\ \text{If } x \text{ is } A_{k_n} \text{ then } y \text{ is } B_{k_n} \end{array}\right\} \tag{10.1.3}$$

In this group of rules, the inference antecedents and inference consequents are respectively as the following:

$$A_{k_i} \in \mathcal{F}(X), \quad B_{k_i} \in \mathcal{F}(Y), \quad i = 0,1,\cdots,n$$

And they can form a group of local fuzzy inference relations as follows:

$$R_{k_i}, \quad i = 0, 1, \cdots, n.$$

Then by using these R_{k_i}, $i = 0, 1, \cdots, n$, we can get the whole fuzzy inference relation $R \in \mathcal{F}(X \times Y)$. Now we take this operation: $\oplus = \Sigma w_i \langle\rangle$, and we have the following expressions:

$$\left.\begin{array}{l} R = \bigoplus_{i=0}^{n} R_{k_i} = \sum_{i=0}^{n} w_{k_i} R_{k_i} \\ \left(\forall (x,y) \in X \times Y\right) \left(R(x,y) = \sum_{i=0}^{n} w_{k_i} R_{k_i}(x,y) \right) \\ \left(\forall i \in \{0,1,\cdots,n\}\right)\left(w_i \ge 0\right), \ \sum_{i=0}^{n} w_i = 1 \end{array}\right\} \tag{10.1.4}$$

where the weight vector $W \triangleq (w_0, w_1, \cdots, w_n)$ will be confirmed. It is worth noting that the weight vector $W = (w_0, w_1, \cdots, w_n)$ is not confirmed with off-line but on-line on real time. In other words, the weight vector $W = (w_0, w_1, \cdots, w_n)$ is regarded as $n+1$ parameters which are adjusting depending on input information on-line on real time. For doing this, we rewrite $R = \sum_{i=0}^{n} w_{k_i} R_{k_i}$ as the following expressions:

$$\left.\begin{array}{l} R(W) = R(w_0, w_1, \cdots, w_n) = \sum_{i=0}^{n} w_{k_i} R_{k_i} \\ W \in [0,1]^n \\ \left(\forall i \in \{0,1,\cdots,n\}\right)\left(w_i \ge 0\right), \ \sum_{i=0}^{n} w_i = 1 \end{array}\right\} \tag{10.1.5}$$

Is it easy to understand that the weight vector $W = (w_0, w_1, \cdots, w_n)$ is a variable weight vector in essence.

How to design a variable weight vector is a very important problem. We can regard $W=(w_0, w_1, \cdots, w_n)$ as a mapping as follows:

$$\left.\begin{array}{l} W=(w_0, w_1, \cdots, w_n): \mathcal{F}(X) \to [0,1]^n \\ A \mapsto W(A)=(w_0(A), w_1(A), \cdots, w_n(A)) \end{array}\right\} \tag{10.1.6}$$

where we have the following requirements:

$$(\forall i \in \{0,1,\cdots,n\})(w_i(A) \geq 0), \quad \sum_{i=0}^{n} w_i(A)=1.$$

Clearly how to define the mapping $W=(w_0, w_1, \cdots, w_n): \mathcal{F}(X) \to \mathbb{R}^n$ is equivalent to the problem how to define the following $n+1$ functions:

$$\left.\begin{array}{l} w_i: \mathcal{F}(X) \to [0,1],\ A \mapsto w_i(A) \\ i=0,1,\cdots,n \\ (\forall i \in \{0,1,\cdots,n\})(w_i(A) \geq 0) \\ \sum_{i=0}^{n} w_i(A)=1 \end{array}\right\} \tag{10.1.7}$$

We consider two methods to solve about problem as follows.

Method 1. Function Space Method.

Suppose $\mathcal{F}(X) \subset C(X)$. Then $\mathcal{F}(X)$ can be regarded as a subspace of the linear normed space $(C(X), \|\cdot\|)$, where the norm $\|\cdot\|$ is defined as the following:

$$(\forall f \in C(X))\left(\|f\| \triangleq \max\{|f(x)| \mid x \in X\}\right).$$

Because of $(\forall A \in \mathcal{F}(X))(\|A\| \leq 1)$, we give the following definition:

$$w_i : \mathcal{F}(X) \to [0,1]$$
$$A \mapsto w_i(A) \triangleq \frac{1-\|A-A_i\|}{\sum_{i=0}^{n}\left(1-\|A-A_i\|\right)} \qquad (10.1.8)$$
$$i = 0,1,\cdots,n$$

It is easy to verify that $W = (w_0, w_1, \cdots, w_n) : \mathcal{F}(X) \to [0,1]^n$ defined by (10.1.8) must satisfy (10.1.7).We can clearly learn that (10.1.8) means the fact: the more the distance between the input fuzzy set A and the inference antecedent fuzzy set A_i, the bigger the weight corresponding to A_i; of course this is reasonable.

When $\mathcal{F}(X) \subset B(X)$, where $B(X)$ is the set of all bounded functions defined on the universe X, $\mathcal{F}(X)$ is regarded as a subspace of the linear normed space $(B(X), \|\cdot\|)$, where the norm $\|\cdot\|$ should be defined as the following:

$$(\forall f \in B(X))\left(\|f\| \triangleq \sup\{|f(x)| \mid x \in X\}\right).$$

This time, Expression (10.1.8) is also effective.

Method 2. Close Degree Method.

We first give a definition as follows.

Definition 10.1.1 The mapping $\sigma : \mathcal{F}(U) \times \mathcal{F}(U) \to [0,1]$ is called a close degree between two fuzzy sets, if it satisfies the following conditions:

1) $\sigma(A, A) = 1$;

2) $\sigma(A, B) = \sigma(B, A)$;

3) $\sigma(\varnothing, U) = 0$;

4) $A \subset B \subset C \Rightarrow \sigma(A,C) \le \sigma(A,B) \wedge \sigma(B,C)$,

where U is a universe chosen by us in advance. □

Example 10.1.1 When the universe $U \subset \mathbb{R}$, we clearly know the fact that $\mathcal{F}(U) \subset B(U)$; so $\mathcal{F}(U)$ is a linear normed subspace of the function space $\left(B(U), \|\cdot\|\right)$, denoted by $\left(\mathcal{F}(U), \|\cdot\|\right)$, and $\|\cdot\|$ has already defined in front. By means of the norm $\|\cdot\|$, we give the following mapping:

$$\begin{aligned} &\sigma: \mathcal{F}(U) \times \mathcal{F}(U) \to [0,1] \\ &(A,B) \mapsto \sigma(A,B) \triangleq 1 - \|A - B\| \end{aligned} \tag{10.1.9}$$

It is easy to verify that the mapping σ from (10.1.9) meets the conditions in Definition 10.1.1, which means it is a kind of close degree. □

Example 10.1.2 When $U = [a,b] \subset \mathbb{R}$, we let

$$F_p\left([a,b]\right) \triangleq \mathcal{F}\left([a,b]\right) \cap L^p[a,b], \quad 1 \le p < \infty.$$

Then $F_p\left([a,b]\right)$ must become a subspace of the linear normed space $\left(L^p[a,b], \|\cdot\|\right)$, as being denoted as $\left(F_p([a,b]), \|\cdot\|\right)$, where the norm $\|\cdot\|$ is defined as the following expression:

$$\left(\forall A \in L^p[a,b]\right)\left(\|A\| \triangleq \left(\int_a^b |A(u)|^p \, \mathrm{d}u \right)^{1/p} \right).$$

By means of the norm $\|\cdot\|$, we make a mapping as follows:

$$\begin{aligned} &\sigma: F_p\left([a,b]\right) \times F_p\left([a,b]\right) \to [0,1] \\ &(A,B) \mapsto \sigma(A,B) \triangleq 1 - \frac{1}{b-a} \|A - B\|^p \\ &\qquad = 1 - \frac{1}{b-a} \int_a^b |A(u) - B(u)|^p \, \mathrm{d}u. \end{aligned} \tag{10.1.10}$$

It is not difficult to verify that the mapping σ from (10.1.10) meets the conditions in Definition 10.1.1, which means it is a kind of close degree.

Especially, when $p=1$, above expression turns to be the following form:

$$\sigma(A,B)=1-\frac{1}{b-a}\int_a^b |A(u)-B(u)|\mathrm{d}u. \tag{10.1.11}$$

While $p=2$, above expression turns to be the following form:

$$\sigma(A,B)=1-\frac{1}{b-a}\int_a^b \left(A(u)-B(u)\right)^2 \mathrm{d}u. \tag{10.1.12}$$

□

After we got the tool of the close degree, we can make a kind of variable weight similar to Expression (10.1.8) as follows:

$$\begin{aligned} & w_i : \mathcal{F}(X) \to [0,1] \\ & A \mapsto w_i(A) \triangleq \frac{\sigma(A,A_i)}{\sum_{i=0}^{n}\sigma(A,A_i)}, \\ & i=0,1,\cdots,n \end{aligned} \tag{10.1.13}$$

It is easy to verify that such weight vector from Expression (10.1.13):

$$W=(w_0,w_1,\cdots,w_n): \mathcal{F}(X) \to [0,1]^n$$

can also satisfy the expression (10.1.7).

In order to show that the weight vector $W=(w_0,w_1,\cdots,w_n)$ depends on the fuzzification of the input datum $x \in X \to A \in \mathcal{F}(X)$, where A is the fuzzification of x, we denote the weight vector $W=(w_0,w_1,\cdots,w_n)$ to be the following:

$$W(A)=\left(w_0(A),w_1(A),\cdots,w_n(A)\right)$$

or simply denoted by $W(A)$.

Definition 10.1.2 The following fuzzy inference relation formed by the weight vector $W(A)=\left(w_0(A),w_1(A),\cdots,w_n(A)\right)$:

$$\left.\begin{aligned} R(W(A)) &= \sum_{i=0}^{n} w_{k_i}(A)R_{k_i}, \\ R(W(A))(u,v) &= \sum_{i=0}^{n} w_{k_i}(A)R_{k_i}(u,v) \end{aligned}\right\} \quad (10.1.14)$$

is called fuzzy inference relation with self-adaption, where $A\in\mathcal{F}(X)$ and $(u,v)\in X\times Y$ and

$$\left(\forall i\in\{0,1,\cdots,n\}\right)\left(w_i(A)\ge 0\right),\ \sum_{i=0}^{n} w_i(A)=1. \qquad \square$$

10.2 Fuzzy Systems with Self-adaption

Generally speaking, for an uncertain system S, it is difficult to build an accurate model for S only by the data set as the following:

$$\mathrm{IOD}=\left\{(x_i,y_i)\in X\times Y \,\middle|\, i=0,1,\cdots,n\right\},$$

where, by the accurate model we can get the relation between the input and the output as the following:

$$s: X\to Y,\quad x\mapsto y\triangleq s(x).$$

However, we surely can use the data set IOD to make an approximation the relation between the input and the output as the following:

$$\overline{s}_n: X\to Y,\ x\mapsto y\triangleq \overline{s}_n(x), \qquad (10.2.1)$$

such that the function $\overline{s}_n: X\to Y$ that we will make can approximate our goal function $s: X\to Y$, which means that $\|s-\overline{s}_n\|<\varepsilon$, where $\varepsilon>0$ is a kind of error number given by us in advance.

Based on the data set $X^0 \triangleq \{x_i \mid i = 0,1,\cdots,n\}$ on the universe X, we can get a group of fuzzy sets $\mathcal{A}_1 \triangleq \{A_i \mid i = 0,1,\cdots,n\}$; in the same way, by using the data set $Y^0 \triangleq \{y_i \mid i = 0,1,\cdots,n\}$ on the universe Y, we also get a group of fuzzy sets $\mathcal{B}_1 \triangleq \{B_{k_i} \mid i = 0,1,\cdots,n\}$, where the fuzzy sets A_i, B_i can be taken triangle wave membership functions.

By noting $\sigma\sigma^{-1}(i) = i$, we have $k_{\sigma^{-1}(i)} = i$; so $B_i = B_{k_{\sigma^{-1}(i)}}$. Thus, every B_i has been defined so that $\mathcal{B}_1 = \{B_i \mid i = 0,1,\cdots,n\}$.

By means of IOD, we can get a group of fuzzy inference rules as the following:

$$\left.\begin{array}{l}\text{If } x \text{ is } A_i \text{ then } y \text{ is } B_i \\ i = 0,1,\cdots,n\end{array}\right\} \tag{10.2.2}$$

Where $A_i \in \mathcal{F}(X)$ and $B_i \in \mathcal{F}(Y)$, $i = 0,1,\cdots,n$. Every fuzzy inference rule can form a local fuzzy inference relation as follows:

$$\begin{aligned}&R_i(x,y) \triangleq \theta\big(A(x), B(y)\big), \quad (x,y) \in X \times Y,\\ &i = 0,1,\cdots,n\end{aligned}$$

where $\theta : [0,1]\times[0,1] \to [0,1]$ is a kind of fuzzy implication operator. Then let $R = \bigcup_{i=0}^{n} R_i$; we get the whole fuzzy inference relation, so that we get a mapping as follows:

$$\begin{aligned}&T : \mathcal{F}(X) \to \mathcal{F}(Y), \quad A \mapsto B = T(A) \triangleq A \circ R,\\ &(\forall y \in Y)\Big(B(y) = \big(T(A)\big)(y) \triangleq \bigvee_{x\in X} \big[A(x) \wedge R(x,y)\big]\Big)\end{aligned}$$

We can use two steps to gain the following function

$$\overline{s}_n : X \to Y, \quad x \mapsto y = \overline{s}_n(x)$$

i.e., first, we will make the set to set mapping $T:\mathcal{F}(X)\to\mathcal{F}(Y)$ become a point to set mapping; second, we are going to form a point to point mapping $\overline{s}_n : X\to Y$.

Step 1. Make a point to set mapping from $T:\mathcal{F}(X)\to\mathcal{F}(Y)$.

In fact, we let

$$s_1 : X\to\mathcal{F}(Y),\quad x\mapsto s_1(x)\triangleq T\left(\{x\}\right) \tag{10.2.3}$$

So for any a point $x\in X$ and any a point $y\in Y$, we can get the following calculating form:

$$\begin{aligned}&\left(s_1(x)\right)(y)=\left(s\left(\{x\}\right)\right)(y)\\&=\bigvee_{\xi\in X}\left[\{x\}(\xi)\wedge R(\xi,y)\right]\\&=\bigvee_{\xi\in X}\left[\chi_{\{x\}}(\xi)\wedge R(\xi,y)\right]\\&=R(x,y)=\bigvee_{i=0}^{n}\left(A_i(x)\cdot B_i(y)\right)\end{aligned} \tag{10.2.4}$$

Because of $(\forall x\in X)\left(s_1(x)\in\mathcal{F}(Y)\right)$, we can let

$$\left(\forall x\in X\right)\left(B(\xi=x)\triangleq s_1(x)\right),$$

where ξ is a variable taking its value in X, and the membership function of $B(\xi=x)$ is as the following:

$$\begin{aligned}&B(y\mid\xi=x)\triangleq\left(B(\xi=x)\right)(y)=\left(s_1(x)\right)(y)\\&=R(x,y)=\bigvee_{i=0}^{n}\left(A_i(x)\cdot B_i(y)\right),\quad x\in X,\ y\in Y\end{aligned} \tag{10.2.5}$$

Step 2. Try to make the fuzzy set $B(\xi=x)=s_1(x)\in\mathcal{F}(Y)$ turn to be a point $y=\left(y(\xi)\right)_{\xi=x}=y(x)$ in the universe Y corresponding the input point $\xi=x$.

In a matter of fact, we have known the important method coming from the center of mass of the rigid body in physics. If the following conditions are satisfied:

$$\int_Y |yB(y \mid \xi = x)| \mathrm{d}y < \infty, \quad 0 < \int_Y B(y \mid \xi = x) \mathrm{d}y < \infty$$

The we can define the $y = (y(\xi))_{\xi = x} = y(x)$ as the following:

$$y = (y(\xi))_{\xi = x} = y(x) = \frac{\int_Y yB(y \mid \xi = x)\mathrm{d}y}{\int_Y B(y \mid \xi = x)\mathrm{d}y} \tag{10.2.6}$$

This means that we have got the mapping $\overline{s}_n : X \to Y$ as the following:

$$\begin{aligned} &\overline{s}_n : X \to Y \\ &x \mapsto \overline{s}_n(x) \triangleq y(x) = \frac{\int_Y yB(y \mid \xi = x)\mathrm{d}y}{\int_Y B(y \mid \xi = x)\mathrm{d}y} \end{aligned} \tag{10.2.7}$$

And then we put $B(y \mid \xi = x)$ into above expression and gain the following equation:

$$\begin{aligned} \overline{s}_n(x) &= \frac{\int_Y yB(y \mid \xi = x)\mathrm{d}y}{\int_Y B(y \mid \xi = x)\mathrm{d}y} \\ &= \frac{\int_Y y\left[\vee_{i=0}^n \left(w_i(A) \cdot A_i(x) \cdot B_i(y)\right)\right]\mathrm{d}y}{\int_Y \left[\vee_{i=0}^n \left(w_i(A) \cdot A_i(x) \cdot B_i(y)\right)\right]\mathrm{d}y} \end{aligned} \tag{10.2.8}$$

Remark 10.2.1 Since we know the following fact:

$$\left(\forall (x, y) \in X \times Y\right)\left(B(y \mid \xi = x) = R(x, y)\right),$$

Expression (10.2.7) can be written the following simpler form:

$$(\forall x \in X)\left(\overline{s}_n(x) = \frac{\int_Y yR(x,y)\mathrm{d}y}{\int_Y R(x,y)\mathrm{d}y}\right) \tag{10.2.9}$$

Because $R = \bigcup_{i=0}^{n} R_i$, actually R is formed from R_{k_i} $(i = 0,1,\cdots,n)$ by means of the operation "$\bigcup$". And except using "$\bigcup$", we have many methods to form the whole fuzzy inference relation R; so Expression (10.2.9) is of more broad meaning. □

The realizing process from Data to Formulas is called the method of fuzzy inference with self-adaptation. And the input output function

$$\overline{s}_n : X \to Y, \quad y = \overline{s}_n(x)$$

expressed by (10.2.9) is called a kind of fuzzy systems with self-adaptation.

By now, we have got the input output function $\overline{s}_n : X \to Y$ by the data set IOD, which is regarded as a kind of approximation to our goal function $s : X \to Y$. In order to simplify the calculating for the input output function $\overline{s}_n : X \to Y$, we should give a kind of calculating method. In fact, let

$$\Delta y_{k_i} = y_{k_{i+1}} - y_{k_i},\ i = 0,1,\cdots,n-1,$$

$$\Delta y_{k_n} = \frac{\sum_{i=0}^{n-1} \Delta y_{k_i}}{n} = \frac{d-c}{n}$$

Clearly $\Delta y_i = \Delta y_{k_{\sigma^{-1}(i)}}$, and then Δy_i $(i = 0,1,\cdots,n)$ have their meaning. By means of the definition definite integral, we have the following result:

$$\overline{s}_n(x) = \frac{\int_Y yB(y \mid \xi = x)\mathrm{d}y}{\int_Y B(y \mid \xi = x)\mathrm{d}y} \approx \frac{\sum_{i=0}^{n} B\left(y_i \mid \xi = x\right) y_i \Delta y_i}{\sum_{i=0}^{n} B\left(y_i \mid \xi = x\right) \Delta y_i}$$

$$= \frac{\sum_{i=0}^{n}\left[\bigvee_{j=0}^{n}\left(w_j(A)\cdot A_j(x)\cdot B_j\left(y_i\right)\right)\right] y_i \Delta y_i}{\sum_{i=0}^{n}\left[\bigvee_{j=0}^{n}\left(w_j(A)\cdot A_j(x)\cdot B_j\left(y_i\right)\right)\right] \Delta y_i} \tag{10.2.10}$$

$$= \frac{\sum_{i=0}^{n} w_i(A)\cdot A_i(x) y_i \Delta y_i}{\sum_{i=0}^{n} w_i(A)\cdot A_i(x) \Delta y_i} = \sum_{i=0}^{n} \frac{A_i^2(x)\Delta y_i}{\sum_{j=0}^{n} A_j^2(x)\Delta y_j} y_i$$

$$= \sum_{i=0}^{n} \overline{A}_i(x) y_i$$

where

$$\overline{A}_{k_i}(x) = \frac{A_{k_i}^2(x)\Delta y_{k_i}}{\sum_{j=0}^{n} A_{k_j}^2(x)\Delta y_{k_j}}, \quad i = 0, 1, \cdots, n. \tag{10.2.11}$$

It is easy to verify that the group of functions $\left\{\overline{A}_{k_i}(x)\right\}_{i=0}^{n}$ is linearly independent and is of Kronecker property:

$$\left(\forall i, j \in \{0, 1, \cdots, n\}\right)\left(\overline{A}_{k_i}\left(x_{k_j}\right) = \begin{cases} 1, & i = j, \\ 0, & i \neq j, \end{cases}\right)$$

Let

$$f_n(x) = \sum_{i=0}^{n} \overline{A}_{k_i}(x) y_{k_i}, \quad x \in X. \tag{10.2.12}$$

Then the function $f_n(x)=\sum_{i=0}^{n}\overline{A}_{k_i}(x)y_{k_i}$ is just a piecewise interpolation based on the group of base functions $\left\{\overline{A}_{k_i}(x)\right\}_{i=0}^{n}$.

Now we have known the fact that the fuzzy systems with self-adaption $\overline{s}$ is approximately a piecewise interpolation based on the group of base functions $\left\{\overline{A}_{k_i}(x)\right\}_{i=0}^{n}$, i.e., as the following:

$$\overline{s}(x)\approx f_n(x)=\sum_{i=0}^{n}\overline{A}_{k_i}(x)y_{k_i},\quad x\in X.$$

Definition 10.2.1 For the data set as the following:

$$\text{IOD}=\left\{(x_i,y_i)\in X\times Y \,\middle|\, i=0,1,\cdots,n\right\},$$

we can make a kind of fuzzy data set as follows:

$$\text{IODF}\triangleq\left\{(A_i,B_i)\in\mathcal{F}(X)\times\mathcal{F}(Y)\,\middle|\, i=0,1,\cdots,n\right\}.$$

If the fuzzy data set IODF satisfies the condition:

$$\left(\forall i\in\{0,1,\cdots,n\}\right)\left(A_i\in C(X),\, B_i\in C(Y)\right),$$

then IODF is called continuous fuzzy data set. And IODF is called a kind of two-phase fuzzy data set, if it satisfies the following conditions:

$$(\forall x\in X)\left(\sum_{i=0}^{n}A_i(x)=1\right),\quad (\forall y\in Y)\left(\sum_{i=0}^{n}B_i(y)=1\right),$$
$$(\forall x\in X)\left(\exists i\in\{0,1,\cdots,n-1\}\right)\left(A_i(x)+A_{i+1}(x)=1\right),$$
$$(\forall y\in Y)\left(\exists j\in\{0,1,\cdots,n-1\}\right)\left(B_j(y)+B_{j+1}(y)=1\right)$$

Clearly, the two-phase fuzzy data set must satisfy Kronecker property:

$$A_i\left(x_j\right)=\begin{cases}1, & i=j, \\ 0, & i\neq j,\end{cases} \quad B_i\left(y_j\right)=\begin{cases}1, & i=j, \\ 0, & i\neq j,\end{cases}$$

$$i, j\in\{0,1,\cdots,n\}.$$

□

Remark 10.2.2 When IODF is a two-phase fuzzy data set, the conclusions what we got above are also true. □

10.3 Approximation Properties of Fuzzy Systems with Self-adaption

For the data set $\mathrm{IOD}=\left\{\left(x_i, y_i\right)\in X\times Y \mid i=0,1,\cdots,n\right\}$, we denote

$$\Delta x_i \triangleq x_{i+1}-x_i, i=0,1,\cdots,n-1.$$

Clearly we have the fact that $\max_{0\le i\le n-1}\Delta x_i\to 0\Rightarrow n\to\infty$; but on the contrary, it is not true. If the following condition is true:

$$n\to\infty\Rightarrow\max_{0\le i\le n-1}\Delta x_i\to 0,$$

then the data set IOD is called harmonious; i.e., IOD is harmonious if and only if the following condition is true:

$$n\to\infty\Leftrightarrow\max_{0\le i\le n-1}\Delta x_i\to 0.$$

From now on, we always suppose the data set IOD is harmonious. Besides, for a continuous function $s\in C[a,b]$, if IOD with respect to s satisfies the interpolation condition:

$$(\forall i\in\{0,1,\cdots,n\})\left(y_i=s\left(x_i\right)\right)$$

Then it is easy to know the fact that IOD is harmonious implies the following equivalence:

$$n \to \infty \Leftrightarrow \max_{0 \le i \le n} \Delta y_{k_i} \to 0 .$$

In order to prove the following theorem, we firstly introduce what is the lattice close degree between two fuzzy sets. In practice, the following mapping is called the lattice close degree between two fuzzy sets:

$$\begin{aligned} &\sigma : \mathcal{F}(U) \times \mathcal{F}(U) \to [0,1], \\ &(A,B) \mapsto \sigma(A,B) \triangleq (A \cdot B) \wedge (A \odot B)^c \end{aligned} \tag{10.3.1}$$

where two mappings " $\cdot$ " and " $\odot$ " are defined as the following:

$$\begin{aligned} &\cdot : \mathcal{F}(U) \times \mathcal{F}(U) \to [0,1] \\ &(A,B) \mapsto \cdot(A,B) = A \cdot B \triangleq \bigvee_{u \in U} \big(A(u) \wedge B(u)\big) \\ &\odot : \mathcal{F}(U) \times \mathcal{F}(U) \to [0,1] \\ &(A,B) \mapsto \odot(A,B) = A \odot B \triangleq \bigwedge_{u \in U} \big(A(u) \vee B(u)\big) \end{aligned}$$

And the mapping " $\cdot$ " is called the inner product and the mapping " $\odot$ " is called the outer product between two fuzzy sets.

Theorem 10.3.1 For the data set of the system as the following:

$$\mathrm{IOD} = \left\{ (x_i, y_i) \in X \times Y \,\middle|\, i = 0,1,\cdots,n \right\},$$

suppose the group of fuzzy inference rules be as the following:

$$\left\{ \left(A_{k_i}, B_{k_i}\right) \in \mathcal{F}(X) \times \mathcal{F}(Y) \,\middle|\, i = 0,1,\cdots,n \right\}.$$

Fuzzy implication operator is taken as θ_{13} or θ_{14} where $\theta_{13} \triangleq \wedge$ and $\theta_{14} \triangleq \cdot$ (see [14-17]) and fuzzy inference relation is taken as $R(W(A))$ where the variable weight vector :

$$W(A) = \big(w_0(A), w_1(A), \cdots, w_n(A)\big)$$

is as follows:

$$w_i(A) = \frac{\sigma(A, A_i)}{\sum_{i=0}^{n} \sigma(A, A_i)}, \quad i = 0, 1, \cdots, n,$$

Where σ means the lattice close degree. If the input of the system is taken as a single element set, then we have the following results:

1) The fuzzy system with self-adaptation $\overline{s}$ is approximately a piecewise nonlinear interpolation function based on the group of base functions as follows:

$$\overline{A}_{k_i}(x) = \frac{A_{k_i}^2(x)\Delta y_{k_i}}{\sum_{j=0}^{n} A_{k_j}^2(x)\Delta y_{k_j}}, \quad i = 0, 1, \cdots, n. \tag{10.3.2}$$

where the interpolation function is as the following:

$$\overline{s}(x) \approx f_n(x) = \sum_{i=0}^{n} \overline{A}_{k_i}(x) y_{k_i}, \quad x \in X.$$

2) The interpolation function $f_n \in C^1[a,b]$, i.e., $f_n(x)$ is smooth on the universe $X = [a,b]$, and satisfies the following condition:

$$f_n'(x_i) = 0, \quad i = 0, 1, \cdots, n.$$

3) The interpolation function $f_n(x)$ is of universal approximation property on the universe $X = [a,b]$.

Proof. 1) For the given group of fuzzy inference rules as follows:

$$\left.\begin{array}{l}
\text{If } x \text{ is } A_{k_0} \text{ then } y \text{ is } B_{k_0} \\
\text{If } x \text{ is } A_{k_1} \text{ then } y \text{ is } B_{k_1} \\
\qquad \cdots\cdots \\
\text{If } x \text{ is } A_{k_n} \text{ then } y \text{ is } B_{k_n}
\end{array}\right\}$$

We can take the fuzzy implication operator θ_{13} or θ_{14} (e.g. we take θ_{14}) to make the following fuzzy inference relation:

$$R_{k_i} = \theta_{14}\left(A_{k_i}, B_{k_i}\right),$$
$$R_{k_i}(x,y) = \theta_{14}\left(A_{k_i}(x), B_{k_i}(y)\right) = A_{k_i}(x)\cdot B_{k_i}(y),$$
$$(x,y)\in X\times Y, \quad i = 0,1,\cdots,n.$$

By means of them we get the whole fuzzy inference relation as the following:

$$R(W(A)) = \sum_{i=0}^{n} w_{k_i}(A) R_{k_i},$$

$$R(W(A))(u,v) = \sum_{i=0}^{n} w_{k_i}(A) R_{k_i}(u,v) = \sum_{i=0}^{n} \frac{\sigma\left(A, A_{k_i}\right)}{\sum_{j=0}^{n}\sigma\left(A, A_{k_j}\right)} R_{k_i}(u,v)$$

$$= \sum_{i=0}^{n} \frac{\left(A\cdot A_{k_i}\right)\wedge\left(A\odot A_{k_i}\right)^c}{\sum_{j=0}^{n}\left(\left(A\cdot A_{k_j}\right)\wedge\left(A\odot A_{k_j}\right)^c\right)}\left(A_{k_i}(u)\cdot B_{k_i}(v)\right),$$

$$= \sum_{i=0}^{n} \frac{\left(\bigvee_{\xi\in X}\left(A(\xi)\wedge A_{k_i}(\xi)\right)\right)\wedge\left(1-\bigwedge_{\xi\in X}\left(A(\xi)\vee A_{k_i}(\xi)\right)\right)}{\sum_{j=0}^{n}\left[\left(\bigvee_{\xi\in X}\left(A(\xi)\wedge A_{k_j}(\xi)\right)\right)\wedge\left(1-\bigwedge_{\xi\in X}\left(A(\xi)\vee A_{k_j}(\xi)\right)\right)\right]}\left(A_{k_i}(u)\cdot B_{k_i}(v)\right)$$

where $A\in\mathcal{F}(X)$ and $(u,v)\in X\times Y$.

Now we arbitrarily take a point $x\in X$, which is regarded as a input value; then x is turned to be a single element set as being $A=\{x\}$. Clearly, we can learn the fact as the following:

$$A\in\mathcal{F}(X), \quad (\forall\xi\in X)\left(A(\xi) = \chi_{\{x\}}(\xi) = \{x\}(\xi)\right).$$

And for any a number $i\in\{0,1,\cdots,n\}$, we have the following expression:

$$w_i(A) = w_i\left(\{x\}\right) = \frac{\sigma\left(\{x\}, A_i\right)}{\sum_{j=0}^{n} \sigma\left(\{x\}, A_j\right)}$$

$$= \frac{\left(\{x\} \cdot A_i\right) \wedge \left(\{x\} \odot A_i\right)^c}{\sum_{j=0}^{n} \left(\left(\{x\} \cdot A_i\right) \wedge \left(\{x\} \odot A_i\right)^c\right)}$$

$$= \frac{\left(\bigvee_{\xi \in X} \left(\{x\}(\xi) \wedge A_i(\xi)\right)\right) \wedge \left(1 - \bigwedge_{\xi \in X} \left(\{x\}(\xi) \vee A_i(\xi)\right)\right)}{\sum_{j=0}^{n} \left[\left(\bigvee_{\xi \in X} \left(\{x\}(\xi) \wedge A_j(\xi)\right)\right) \wedge \left(1 - \bigwedge_{\xi \in X} \left(\{x\}(\xi) \vee A_j(\xi)\right)\right)\right]}$$

$$= \frac{A_i(x)}{\sum_{j=0}^{n} A_j(x)} = A_i(x),$$

Where we use the fact: $\sum_{j=0}^{n} A_j(x) \equiv 1$. Thus, the membership function of the fuzzy inference relation with self-adaption is as the following:

$$R\left(W(A)\right)(u,v) = R\left(W\left(\{x\}\right)\right)(u,v)$$

$$= \sum_{j=0}^{n} w_{k_j}\left(\{x\}\right) R_{k_j}(u,v) = \sum_{j=0}^{n} A_{k_j}(x)\left(A_{k_j}(u) \cdot B_{k_j}(v)\right).$$

Therefore, we have the following result:

$$\begin{aligned} B(y) &= B(y \mid \xi = x) = \left(s_4(x)\right)(y) = R(x,y) \\ &= R\left(W\left(\{x\}\right)\right)(u,v)\Big|_{(u,v)=(x,y)} = R\left(W\left(\{x\}\right)\right)(x,y) \\ &= \sum_{j=0}^{n} A_{k_j}(x)\left(A_{k_j}(x) \cdot B_{k_j}(y)\right) = \sum_{j=0}^{n} A_{k_j}^2(x) B_{k_j}(y) \end{aligned} \tag{10.3.3}$$

Finally, we have the following expression:

$$\overline{s}(x)=\frac{\int_Y yB(y\mid\xi=x)\mathrm{d}y}{\int_Y B(y\mid\xi=x)\mathrm{d}y}\approx\frac{\sum_{i=0}^{n}B\left(y_{k_i}\mid\xi=x\right)y_{k_i}\Delta y_{k_i}}{\sum_{j=0}^{n}B\left(y_{k_j}\mid\xi=x\right)\Delta y_{k_j}}$$

$$=\frac{\sum_{i=0}^{n}\left[\sum_{j=0}^{n}A_{k_j}^2(x)B_{k_j}\left(y_{k_i}\right)\right]y_{k_i}\Delta y_{k_i}}{\sum_{i=0}^{n}\left[\sum_{j=0}^{n}A_{k_j}^2(x)B_{k_j}\left(y_{k_i}\right)\right]\Delta y_{k_i}}=\frac{\sum_{i=0}^{n}A_{k_i}^2(x)y_{k_i}\Delta y_{k_i}}{\sum_{i=0}^{n}A_{k_i}^2(x)\Delta y_{k_i}}$$

$$=\sum_{i=0}^{n}\frac{A_{k_i}^2(x)\Delta y_{k_i}}{\sum_{j=0}^{n}A_{k_j}^2(x)\Delta y_{k_j}}y_{k_i}=\sum_{i=0}^{n}\overline{A}_{k_i}(x)y_{k_i}=f_n(x)$$

where we have put $f_n(x)\triangleq\sum_{i=0}^{n}\overline{A}_{k_i}(x)y_{k_i}$ and defined the following symbols:

$$\overline{A}_{k_i}(x)\triangleq\frac{A_{k_i}^2(x)\Delta y_{k_i}}{\sum_{j=0}^{n}A_{k_j}^2(x)\Delta y_{k_j}},\ i=0,1,\cdots,n. \tag{10.3.4}$$

or written as the following:

$$\overline{A}_i(x)=\frac{A_i^2(x)\Delta y_{k_{\sigma^{-1}(i)}}}{\sum_{j=0}^{n}A_j^2(x)\Delta y_{k_{\sigma^{-1}(j)}}},\quad i=0,1,\cdots,n.$$

2) Prove $f_n\in C^1[a,b]$.

In effect, for arbitrarily given a point $x\in[a,b]$, there must exist a number $i\in\{0,1,\cdots,n-1\}$, such that $x\in\left[x_i,x_{i+1}\right]$. From the structure of these fuzzy sets A_j, $j=0,1,\cdots,n$, we can know the fact:

$$\left(\forall k \in \{0,1,\cdots,n\} - \{i,i+1\}\right)\left(A_k(x) \equiv 0\right)$$

so that $f_n(x) = \overline{A}_i(x)y_i + \overline{A}_{i+1}(x)y_{i+1}$. Clearly $f_n(x)$ is continuous at everywhere in $[a,b]$. It is easy to know the fact that $\frac{\mathrm{d}f_n(x)}{\mathrm{d}x}$ is continuous at everywhere in every open interval as the following:

$$\left(x_i, x_{i+1}\right), \quad i = 0,1,\cdots,n-1.$$

Thus, we only need to prove that $\frac{\mathrm{d}f_n(x)}{\mathrm{d}x}$ is also continuous at every node x_i $(i = 0,1,\cdots,n)$ (when $i = 0$ or $i = n$, we only need to prove $\frac{\mathrm{d}f_n(x)}{\mathrm{d}x}$ is left or right continuous at x_i).

Now we can assume the number $i \notin \{0,n\}$. Let $x = x_i$. Then we have the expression: $f_n\left(x_i\right) = y_i$. In a neighborhood of the node x_i, we consider the left limit or right limit of $\frac{\mathrm{d}f_n(x)}{\mathrm{d}x}$ at x_i.

In fact, firstly, we see the left limit. At this situation, $x < x_i$, and we can have the following limit expression:

$$\begin{aligned}
\frac{\mathrm{d}f_n(x)}{\mathrm{d}x} &= \frac{\mathrm{d}}{\mathrm{d}x}\left(\overline{A}_{i-1}(x)y_{i-1} + \overline{A}_i(x)y_i\right) \\
&= \frac{\mathrm{d}}{\mathrm{d}x}\left(\frac{A_{i-1}^2(x)\Delta y_{k_{\sigma^{-1}(i-1)}} y_{i-1} + A_i^2(x)\Delta y_{k_{\sigma^{-1}(i)}} y_i}{A_{i-1}^2(x)\Delta y_{k_{\sigma^{-1}(i-1)}} + A_i^2(x)\Delta y_{k_{\sigma^{-1}(i)}}}\right) \\
&= \frac{\mathrm{d}}{\mathrm{d}x}\left(\frac{\left(\dfrac{x - x_i}{x_{i-1} - x_i}\right)^2 \Delta y_{k_{\sigma^{-1}(i-1)}} y_{i-1} + \left(\dfrac{x - x_{i-1}}{x_i - x_{i-1}}\right)^2 \Delta y_{k_{\sigma^{-1}(i)}} y_i}{\left(\dfrac{x - x_i}{x_{i-1} - x_i}\right)^2 \Delta y_{k_{\sigma^{-1}(i-1)}} + \left(\dfrac{x - x_{i-1}}{x_i - x_{i-1}}\right)^2 \Delta y_{k_{\sigma^{-1}(i)}}}\right)
\end{aligned}$$

$$= \frac{2(x-x_i)(x-x_{i-1})(x_{i-1}-x_i)(y_i-y_{i-1})\Delta y_{k_{\sigma^{-1}(i-1)}}\Delta y_{k_{\sigma^{-1}(i)}}}{\left((x-x_i)^2\Delta y_{k_{\sigma^{-1}(i-1)}}+(x-x_{i-1})^2\Delta y_{k_{\sigma^{-1}(i)}}\right)^2}$$

$$\xrightarrow{x\to x_i-0} 0.$$

Then we see the right limit. At this situation, $x > x_i$. Similarly, we have

$$\frac{\mathrm{d}f_n(x)}{\mathrm{d}x} = \frac{\mathrm{d}}{\mathrm{d}x}\left(\overline{A}_i(x)y_i + \overline{A}_{i+1}(x)y_{i+1}\right)$$

$$= \frac{\mathrm{d}}{\mathrm{d}x}\left(\frac{A_i^2(x)\Delta y_{k_{\sigma^{-1}(i)}}y_i + A_{i+1}^2(x)\Delta y_{k_{\sigma^{-1}(i+1)}}y_{i+1}}{A_i^2(x)\Delta y_{k_{\sigma^{-1}(i)}} + A_{i+1}^2(x)\Delta y_{k_{\sigma^{-1}(i+1)}}}\right)$$

$$= \frac{2(x-x_{i+1})(x-x_i)(x_i-x_{i+1})(y_{i+1}-y_i)\Delta y_{k_{\sigma^{-1}(i)}}\Delta y_{k_{\sigma^{-1}(i+1)}}}{\left((x-x_{i+1})^2\Delta y_{k_{\sigma^{-1}(i)}}+(x-x_i)^2\Delta y_{k_{\sigma^{-1}(i+1)}}\right)^2}$$

$$\xrightarrow{x\to x_i+0} 0.$$

So we have the following result:

$$\lim_{x\to x_i-0}\frac{\mathrm{d}f_n(x)}{\mathrm{d}x} = \lim_{x\to x_i+0}\frac{\mathrm{d}f_n(x)}{\mathrm{d}x} = 0$$

which means that $\frac{\mathrm{d}f_n(x)}{\mathrm{d}x}$ is continuous at every node x_i $(i = 0,1,\cdots,n)$. Thus $\frac{\mathrm{d}f_n(x)}{\mathrm{d}x}$ is continuous in $X = [a,b]$, i.e., $f_n(x)$ is smooth in the universe $X = [a,b]$.

3) It is easy to verify the fact that the group of functions $\{\overline{A}_i\}_{i=0}^n$ satisfies the conditions: this group of functions $\overline{A}_i(x)$ $(i = 0,1,\cdots,n)$ are continuous in the universe X and $\sum_{i=0}^n \overline{A}_i(x) \equiv 1$ and $\{\overline{A}_i\}_{i=0}^n$ is of two-phase property. So f_n must have the universal approximation.

For any a continuous function $s \in C[a,b]$, suppose the data set IOD satisfies the following interpolation condition with respect to $s(x)$:

$$(\forall i \in \{0,1,\cdots,n\})\left(y_i = s\left(x_i\right)\right).$$

We prove the fact that $\overline{s}_n$ converges to s according to the norm in the linear norm space $\left(C[a,b],\|\cdot\|\right)$, i.e., for arbitrarily given $\varepsilon > 0$, we have the following expression:

$$\left(\exists N \in \mathbb{N}^+\right)\left(\forall n \in \mathbb{N}^+\right)\left(n > N \Rightarrow \|s - \overline{s}_n\| < \varepsilon\right).$$

In practice, for the given $\varepsilon > 0$, we can know the following result:

$$\left(\exists N_1 \in \mathbb{N}^+\right)(\forall n \in \mathbb{N}^+)\left(n > N_1 \Rightarrow \|f_n - \overline{s}_n\| < \frac{\varepsilon}{2}\right)$$

So, when $n > N_1$, we must have the following inequality:

$$\|s - \overline{s}_n\|_\infty \le \|s - f_n\|_\infty + \|f_n - \overline{s}_n\|_\infty < \|s - f_n\|_\infty + \frac{\varepsilon}{2}.$$

Thus, we only consider to estimate $\|s - f_n\|_\infty$.

In fact, it is not difficult to know that $\left\{\overline{A}_{k_i}(x)\right\}_{i=0}^{n}$ is of two-phase property, and for any $x \in [a,b]$, there must exist a $i \in \{0,1,\cdots,n-1\}$, such that $x \in \left[x_i, x_{i+1}\right]$. Thus, we have the following equation:

$$f_n(x) = \overline{A}_{k_i}(x) y_{k_i} + \overline{A}_{k_{i+1}}(x) y_{k_{i+1}}.$$

And by means of the following expression:

$$\overline{A}_{k_i}(x) + \overline{A}_{k_{i+1}}(x) = \sum_{i=0}^{n} \overline{A}_{k_i}(x) \equiv 1,$$

we have the following inequality:

$$\begin{aligned}
|s(x)-f_n(x)| &= \left|s(x)-\left(\overline{A}_{k_i}(x)y_{k_i}+\overline{A}_{k_{i+1}}(x)y_{k_{i+1}}\right)\right| \\
&= \left|s(x)\left(\overline{A}_{k_i}(x)+\overline{A}_{k_{i+1}}(x)\right)-\left(\overline{A}_{k_i}(x)s\left(x_{k_i}\right)+\overline{A}_{k_{i+1}}(x)s\left(x_{k_{i+1}}\right)\right)\right| \\
&\le \overline{A}_{k_i}(x)\left|s(x)-s\left(x_i\right)\right|+\overline{A}_{k_{i+1}}(x)\left|s(x)-s\left(x_{i+1}\right)\right| \\
&\le \left|s(x)-s\left(x_i\right)\right|+\left|s(x)-s\left(x_{i+1}\right)\right| \le 2\max_{i\le m\le i+1}\left|s(x)-s\left(x_m\right)\right|.
\end{aligned}$$

Because $s\in C[a,b]$, $s(x)$ is uniformly continuous in $[a,b]$; for the given $\varepsilon>0$, there must exist $\delta>0$, such that

$$\left(\forall x',x''\in[a,b]\right)\left(\left|x'-x''\right|<\delta\Rightarrow\left|s\left(x'\right)-s\left(x''\right)\right|<\varepsilon/4\right).$$

Then by using the fact that IOD is harmonious, we can have the following result:

$$\left(\exists N_2\in\mathbb{N}^+\right)\left(\forall n\in\mathbb{N}^+\right)\left(n>N_2\Rightarrow\max_{0\le i\le n-1}\Delta x_i<\delta\right)$$

By noting the fact that $x\in\left[x_i,x_{i+1}\right]$, we can learn the inequality:

$$\max_{i\le m\le i+1}\left|x-x_m\right|\le\max_{i\le m\le i+1}\Delta x_m\le\max_{0\le i\le n-1}\Delta x_i<\delta,$$

so that

$$\left|s(x)-f_n(x)\right|\le 2\max_{i\le m\le i+1}\left|s(x)-s\left(x_m\right)\right|<2\frac{\varepsilon}{4}=\frac{\varepsilon}{2}.$$

Since x is arbitrarily taken in $[a,b]$, we have the following inequality:

$$\max_{x\in[a,b]}\left|s(x)-f_n(x)\right|\le\frac{\varepsilon}{2},$$

i.e. $\|s - f_n\| \leq \frac{\varepsilon}{2}$. Now we take $N \triangleq \max\{N_1, N_2\} \in \mathbb{N}^+$, we must have the following expression:

$$\left(\forall n \in \mathbb{N}^+\right)\left(n > N \Rightarrow \|s - \overline{s}_n\|_\infty < \frac{\varepsilon}{2} + \frac{\varepsilon}{2} = \varepsilon\right)$$

This means that $\overline{s}_n$ is surely of universal approximation property. □

Remark 10.3.1 We can prove the result that $f_n \notin C^2[a,b]$.

In fact, for any a node x_i $(i = 1, \cdots, n-1)$, when $x < x_i$, we have the following limit expression:

$$\frac{\mathrm{d}^2 f_n(x)}{\mathrm{d}x^2} = 2\left(x_{i-1} - x_i\right)\left(y_i - y_{i-1}\right)\Delta y_{k_{\sigma^{-1}(i-1)}} \Delta y_{k_{\sigma^{-1}(i)}} \times$$
$$\frac{\left(x - x_i\right)^2\left(x - x_i - 3\left(x - x_{i-1}\right)\right)\Delta y_{k_{\sigma^{-1}(i-1)}} + \left(x - x_{i-1}\right)^2\left(x - x_{i-1} - 3\left(x - x_i\right)\right)\Delta y_{k_{\sigma^{-1}(i)}}}{\left[\left(x - x_i\right)^2 \Delta y_{k_{\sigma^{-1}(i-1)}} + \left(x - x_{i-1}\right)^2 \Delta y_{k_{\sigma^{-1}(i)}}\right]^3}$$
$$\xrightarrow{x \to x_i - 0} \frac{\left(x_i - x_{i-1}\right)^2\left(x_i - x_{i-1}\right)\Delta y_{k_{\sigma^{-1}(i)}}}{\left[\left(x_i - x_{i-1}\right)^2 \Delta y_{k_{\sigma^{-1}(i)}}\right]^3} = \frac{1}{\left(\Delta x_{i-1}\right)^3\left(\Delta y_{k_{\sigma^{-1}(i)}}\right)^2}$$

And when $x > x_i$, we have another limit expression:

$$\frac{\mathrm{d}^2 f_n(x)}{\mathrm{d}x^2} = 2\left(x_i - x_{i+1}\right)\left(y_{i+1} - y_i\right)\Delta y_{k_{\sigma^{-1}(i)}} \Delta y_{k_{\sigma^{-1}(i+1)}} \times$$
$$\frac{\left(x - x_{i+1}\right)^2\left(x - x_{i+1} - 3\left(x - x_i\right)\right)\Delta y_{k_{\sigma^{-1}(i)}} + \left(x - x_i\right)^2\left(x - x_i - 3\left(x - x_{i+1}\right)\right)\Delta y_{k_{\sigma^{-1}(i+1)}}}{\left[\left(x - x_{i+1}\right)^2 \Delta y_{k_{\sigma^{-1}(i)}} + \left(x - x_i\right)^2 \Delta y_{k_{\sigma^{-1}(i+1)}}\right]^3}$$

$$\xrightarrow{x \to x_i + 0} \frac{\left(x - x_{i+1}\right)^2\left(x - x_{i+1}\right)\Delta y_{k_{\sigma^{-1}(i)}}}{\left[\left(x - x_{i+1}\right)^2 \Delta y_{k_{\sigma^{-1}(i)}}\right]^3} = -\frac{1}{\left(\Delta x_i\right)^3\left(\Delta y_{k_{\sigma^{-1}(i)}}\right)^2}.$$

This means that the following equation is true:

$$\lim_{x \to x_i - 0} \frac{\mathrm{d}^2 f_n(x)}{\mathrm{d}x^2} \neq \lim_{x \to x_i + 0} \frac{\mathrm{d}^2 f_n(x)}{\mathrm{d}x^2},$$

i.e. $f_n \notin C^2[a,b]$. □

Theorem 10.3.2 For the data set of the system as the following:

$$\mathrm{IOD} = \left\{ (x_i, y_i) \in X \times Y \,\middle|\, i = 0,1,\cdots,n \right\},$$

suppose the group of fuzzy inference rules is as the following:

$$\left\{ \left(\overline{A}_{k_i}, B_{k_i} \right) \in \mathcal{F}(X) \times \mathcal{F}(Y) \,\middle|\, i = 0,1,\cdots,n \right\}$$

where $\overline{A}_{k_i}$ $(i = 0,1,\cdots,n)$ are as the following:

$$\overline{A}_{k_i}(x) = \frac{A_{k_i}^2(x) \Delta y_{k_i}}{\sum_{j=0}^{n} A_{k_j}^2(x) \Delta y_{k_j}}, \quad i = 0,1,\cdots,n,$$

where A_{k_i} $(i = 0,1,\cdots,n)$ and B_{k_i} $(i = 0,1,\cdots,n)$ all can be taken as triangle wave membership functions. And the fuzzy implication operator should be taken as θ_{13} or θ_{14}, and the fuzzy inference relation is with self-adaption, i.e. $R(W(A))$, where the variable weight vector:

$$W(A) = \left(w_0(A), w_1(A), \cdots, w_n(A) \right)$$

is as the following:

$$w_i(A) = \frac{\sigma\left(A, \overline{A}_{k_i}\right)}{\sum_{j=0}^{n} \sigma\left(A, \overline{A}_{k_j}\right)}, \quad i = 0,1,\cdots,n,$$

where σ means lattice close degree. If the input value is taken as single element set, then we have the following results:

1) The fuzzy system with self-adaption $\overline{s}$ is approximately as a piecewise nonlinear interpolation as the following:

$$\overline{s}(x) \approx f_n(x) = \sum_{i=0}^{n} \overline{\overline{A}}_{k_i}(x) y_{k_i}, \quad x \in X,$$

where

$$\overline{\overline{A}}_{k_i}(x) = \frac{\left(\overline{A}_{k_i}(x)\right)^2 \Delta y_{k_i}}{\sum_{j=0}^{n}\left(\overline{A}_{k_j}(x)\right)^2 \Delta y_{k_j}} = \frac{\left(A_{k_i}(x)\right)^4 \left(\Delta y_{k_i}\right)^3}{\sum_{j=0}^{n}\left(A_{k_j}(x)\right)^4 \left(\Delta y_{k_j}\right)^3}, \tag{10.3.5}$$

$i = 0, 1, \cdots, n.$

2) The interpolation function $f_n \in C^3[a,b]$, which $f_n(x)$ is of 3 order smoothness in the universe $X = [a,b]$.

3) The interpolation function $f_n(x)$ is of universal approximation property in the universe $X = [a,b]$.

The proof of the theorem is similar to the proof of Theorem 103.1. We omit it. □

Theorem 10.3.3 For the data set of the system as the following:

$$\text{IOD} = \left\{(x_i, y_i) \in X \times Y \,\middle|\, i = 0, 1, \cdots, n\right\},$$

suppose the group of fuzzy inference rules is taken as the following:

$$\left\{\left(A_{k_i}^4, B_{k_i}\right) \in \mathcal{F}(X) \times \mathcal{F}(Y) \,\middle|\, i = 0, 1, \cdots, n\right\}$$

where A_{k_i}, B_{k_i} $(i = 0, 1, \cdots, n)$ are all triangle wave membership functions. We have the following results:

1) The fuzzy system formed by CRI method $\overline{s}$ is approximately as a piecewise nonlinear interpolation as the following:

$$\overline{s}(x) \approx f_n(x) = \sum_{i=0}^{n} A_{k_i}^{\#}(x) y_{k_i}, \quad x \in X.$$

where

$$A_{k_i}^{\#}(x) = \frac{A_{k_i}^{4}(x)\Delta y_{k_i}}{\sum_{j=0}^{n} A_{k_j}^{4}(x)\Delta y_{k_j}}, \quad i = 0,1,\cdots,n. \tag{10.3.6}$$

2) The interpolation function $f_n \in C^3[a,b]$, which $f_n(x)$ is of 3 order smoothness in $X = [a,b]$.

3) The interpolation function $f_n(x)$ is of universal approximation property in the universe $X = [a,b]$.

The proof of the theorem is omitted. □

10.4 Examples

Example 10.4.1 We consider to use a kind of fuzzy system $f_n(x)$ to approximate the well-known continuous function as follows:

$$s(x) = \sin x \in C[0,10].$$

For doing this thing, we first make an equidistant partition for the universe $X = [0,10]$ as the following:

$$h \triangleq \Delta x_i = 10/n, \quad i = 0,1,\cdots,n-1. \tag{10.4.1}$$

Second we take the fuzzy system $f_n(x)$ as the following:

$$f_n(x) = \sum_{i=0}^{n} A_{k_i}^{*}(x) y_{k_i},$$

where $A_{k_i}(x)$ are taken as triangle wave membership functions and the base functions $A^*_{k_i}(x)$ as follows:

$$A^*_{k_i}(x) = \frac{A_{k_i}(x)\Delta y_{k_i}}{\sum_{j=0}^{n} A_{k_j}(x)\Delta y_{k_j}}, \quad i = 0, 1, \cdots, n.$$

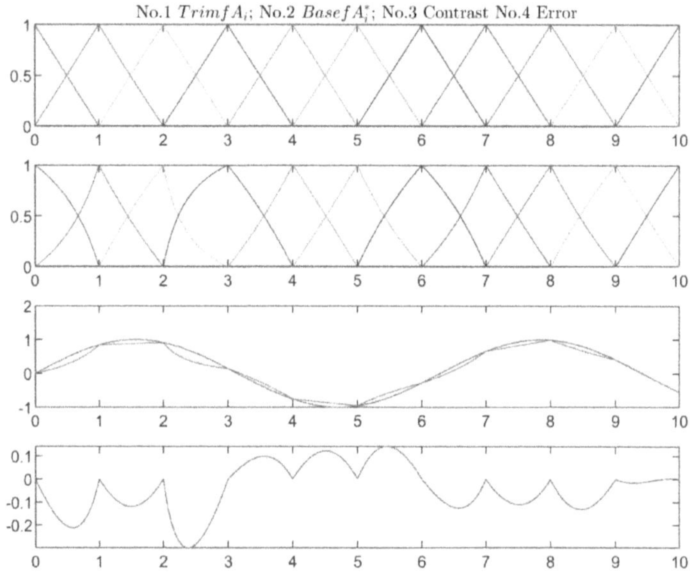

Fig. 10.4.1. Approximation situation with $n = 10$

When $n = 10$, the situation of $f_n(x)$ approximating $s(x) = \sin x$ is shown as Figure 10.4.1.

In these figures, "Trimf" means triangle wave membership functions and "Basef" does base functions.

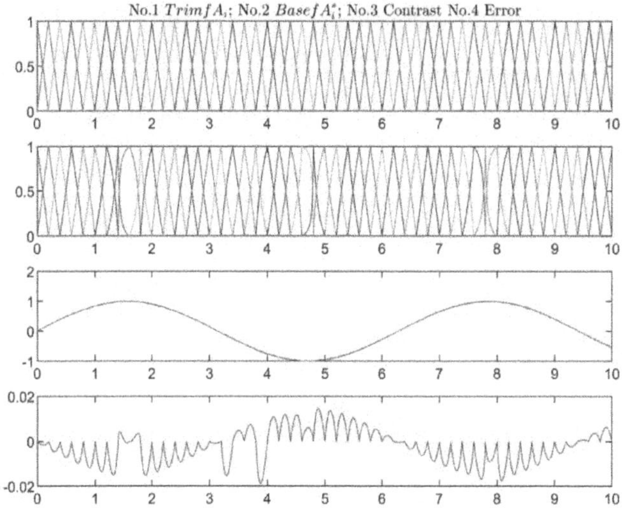

Fig. 10.4.2. Approximation situation with $n = 50$

When $n = 50$, the situation of $f_n(x)$ approximating $s(x) = \sin x$ is shown as Figure 10.4.2. □

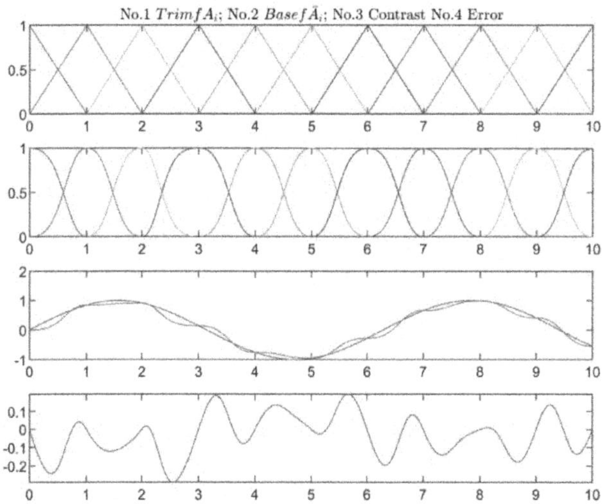

Fig. 10.4.3. Approximation situation with $n = 10$

Example 10.4.2 We also consider to use a kind of fuzzy system $f_n(x)$ to approximate $s(x) = \sin x \in C[0,10]$. First we use (10.4.1) again. Second we take the fuzzy system $f_n(x)$ as the following:

$$f_n(x) = \sum_{i=0}^{n} \overline{A}_{k_i}(x) y_{k_i},$$

where $A_{k_i}(x)$ are taken as triangle wave membership functions and the base functions $\overline{A}_{k_i}(x)$ as follows:

$$\overline{A}_{k_i}(x) = \frac{A_{k_i}^2(x)\Delta y_{k_i}}{\sum_{j=0}^{n} A_{k_j}^2(x)\Delta y_{k_j}}, \quad i = 0,1,\cdots,n.$$

When $n = 10$, the situation of $f_n(x)$ approximating $s(x) = \sin x$ is shown as Figure 10.4.3.

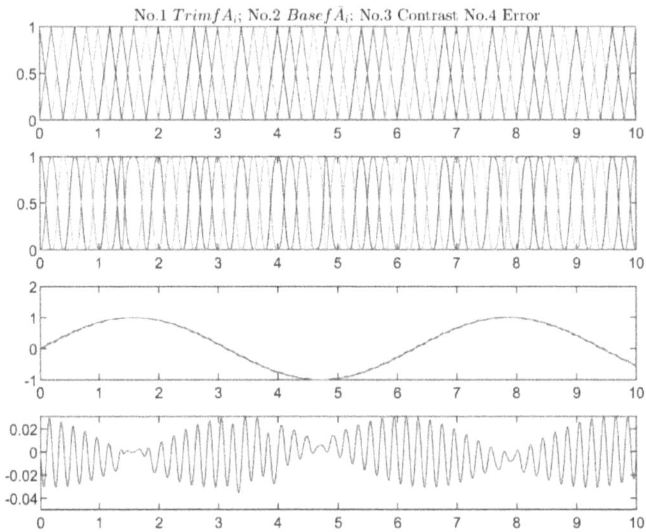

Fig. 10.4.4. Approximation situation with $n = 50$

When $n = 50$, the situation of $f_n(x)$ approximating $s(x) = \sin x$ is shown as Figure 10.4.4. □

Example 10.4.3 We again consider to use a kind of fuzzy system $f_n(x)$ to approximate $s(x) = \sin x \in C[0,10]$. First we use (10.4.1) again. Second we take the fuzzy system $f_n(x)$ as the following:

$$f_n(x) = \sum_{i=0}^{n} \overline{\overline{A}}_{k_i}(x) y_{k_i},$$

where $A_{k_i}(x)$ are taken as triangle wave membership functions and the base functions $\overline{\overline{A}}_{k_i}(x)$ as follows:

$$\overline{\overline{A}}_{k_i}(x) = \frac{\left(\overline{A}_{k_i}(x)\right)^2 \Delta y_{k_i}}{\sum_{j=0}^{n}\left(\overline{A}_{k_j}(x)\right)^2 \Delta y_{k_j}} = \frac{\left(A_{k_i}(x)\right)^4 \left(\Delta y_{k_i}\right)^3}{\sum_{j=0}^{n}\left(A_{k_j}(x)\right)^4 \left(\Delta y_{k_j}\right)^3},$$

$i = 0, 1, \cdots, n.$

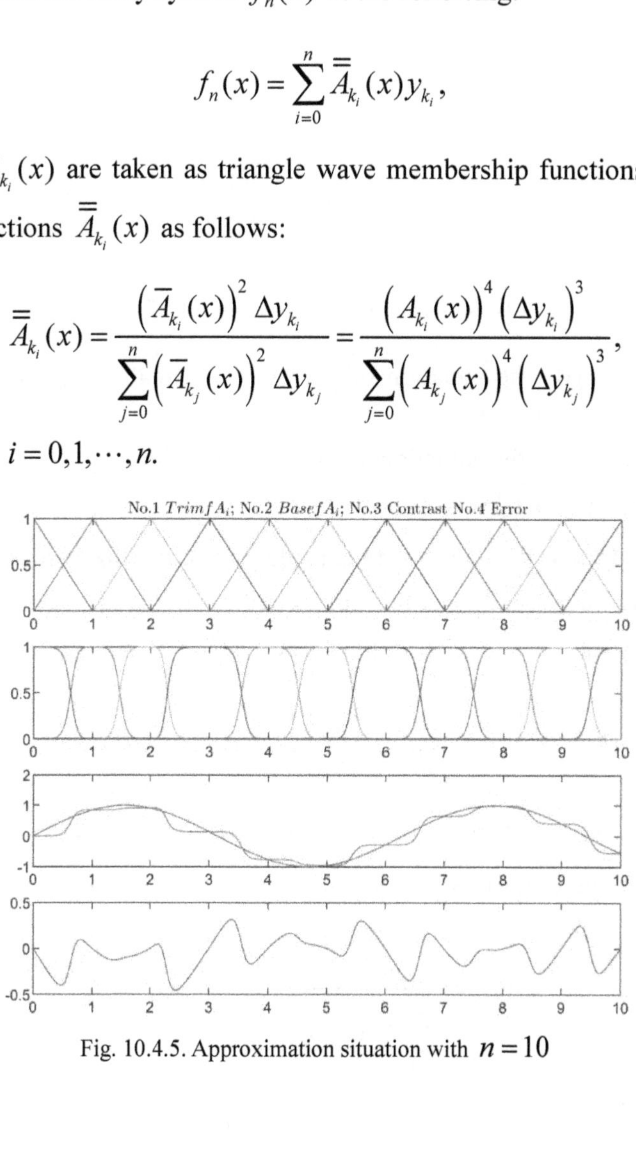

Fig. 10.4.5. Approximation situation with $n = 10$

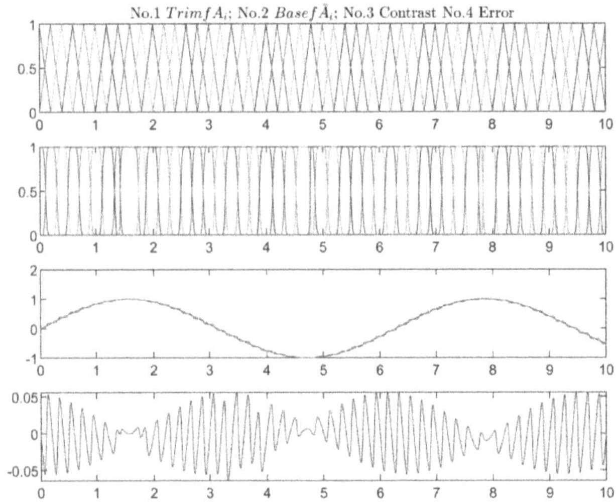

Fig. 10.4.6. Approximation situation with $n = 50$

When $n = 10$, the situation of $f_n(x)$ approximating $s(x) = \sin x$ is shown as Figure 10.4.5.

When $n = 50$, the situation of $f_n(x)$ approximating $s(x) = \sin x$ is shown as Figure 10.4.6. □

Example 10.4.4 We continue to consider to use the fuzzy system $f_n(x)$ to approximate the function $s(x) = \sin x \in C[0,10]$. First we use (10.4.1) again. Second we take the fuzzy system $f_n(x)$ as the following:

$$f_n(x) = \sum_{i=0}^{n} A_{k_i}^{\#}(x) y_{k_i},$$

where $A_{k_i}(x)$ are taken as triangle wave membership functions and the base functions $A_{k_i}^{\#}(x)$ as follows:

$$A_{k_i}^{\#}(x) = \frac{A_{k_i}^{4}(x)\Delta y_{k_i}}{\sum_{j=0}^{n} A_{k_j}^{4}(x)\Delta y_{k_j}}, \quad i = 0, 1, \cdots, n.$$

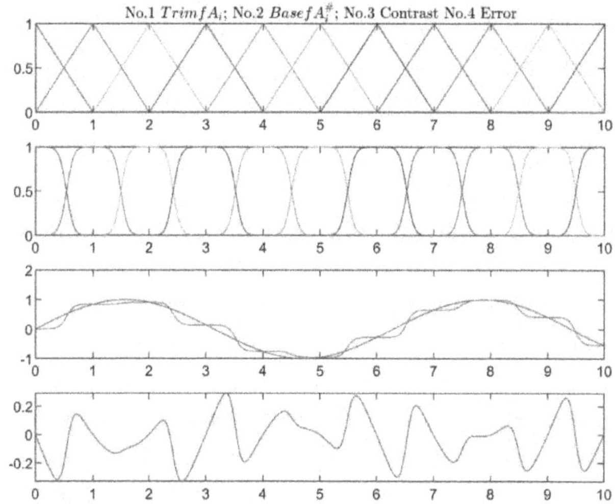

Fig. 10.4.7. Approximation situation with $n = 10$

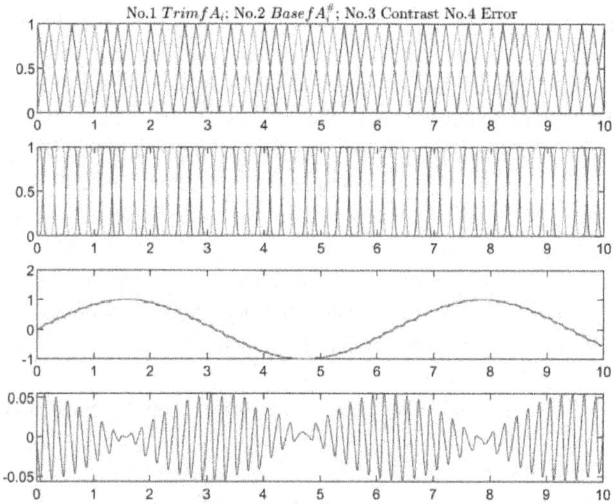

Fig. 10.4.8. Approximation situation with $n = 50$

When $n = 10$, the situation of $f_n(x)$ approximating $s(x) = \sin x$ is shown as Figure 10.4.7.

When $n = 50$, the situation of $f_n(x)$ approximating $s(x) = \sin x$ is shown as Figure 10.4.8. □

10.5 Conclusions

In this chapter, we discuss a kind of fuzzy systems with self-adaption. First, we present the self-adaptive fuzzy inference method and the construction of self-adaptive fuzzy system. Second, we prove that the self-adaptive fuzzy system not only has universal approximation but also a better smoothness. Meanwhile, we offer a method to construct fuzzy inference antecegents, such that CRI method has a general meaning. These methods will offer a lot of help for modelling on a great deal of uncertainty systems in some theory or real practice cases. At last, we give several examples to show that these methods are very effective for approximating many real continuous functions.

References

1. Zadeh, L.A. (1973). Outline of a new approach to the analysis of complex systems and decision processes, IEEE Trans. SMC, 3, pp. 28–44.
2. Zadeh, L. A. (1974). The concept of a linguistic variable and its applications to approximate reasoning (I), Information Sciences, 8(2), pp. 199-249.
3. Zadeh, L. A. (1974). The concept of a linguistic variable and its applications to approximate reasoning (II), Information Sciences, 8(3), pp. 301-357.
4. Zadeh, L. A. (1975). The concept of a linguistic variable and its applications to approximate reasoning (III), Information Sciences, 9(1), pp. 43-80.
5. Wu, W. M. (1994). *Principle and Methods of Fuzzy Reasoning*, (Guizhou Science and Technology Press, Guiyang, in Chinese).
6. Li, H. X. (1998). Interpolation mechanism of fuzzy control, Science in China (Series E), 41(3), pp. 312-320.
7. Li, H. X. (1995). To see the success of fuzzy logic from mathematical essence of fuzzy control, Fuzzy Systems and Mathematics, 9(4), pp. 1-14 (in Chinese).
8. Hou, J., You, F. and Li, H. X. (2005). Some fuzzy controllers constructed by triple I method and their response capability, Progress in Natural Science, 15(1), pp. 29-37 (in Chinese).
9. Li, H. X., You, F. and Peng, J. Y. (2004). Fuzzy controllers based on some fuzzy implication operators and their response functions, Progress in Natural Science, 14(1), pp. 15-20.

10. Wang, P. Z. and Li, H. X. (1995) *Fuzzy Systems Theory and Fuzzy Computers.* (Science Press, Beijing, in Chinese)
11. Wang, G. J. (1999). A new method for fuzzy reasoning, Fuzzy Systems and Mathematics (in Chinese), 13(3), pp. 1-10.
12. Wang, G. J. (1997). A formal deductive system of fuzzy propositional calculus, Chinese Science Bulletin, 42(10), pp. 1041-1045 (in Chinese).
13. You, F., Feng, Y. B. and Li, H. X. (2003). Fuzzy implication operators and their construction (I), Journal of Beijing Normal University, 39(5), pp. 606-611 (in Chinese).
14. You, F., Feng, Y. B., Wang, J. Y. and Li, H. X. (2004). Fuzzy implication operators and their construction (II), Journal of Beijing Normal University, 40(2), pp. 168-176 (in Chinese).
15. You, F., Yang, X. Y. and Li, H. X. (2004). Fuzzy implication operators and their construction (III), Journal of Beijing Normal University, 40(4), pp. 427-432 (in Chinese).
16. You, F. and Li, H. X. (2004). Fuzzy implication operators and their construction (IV), Journal of Beijing Normal University, 40(5), pp. 588-599 (in Chinese).
17. Dubois, D. and Prade, H. (1991). Fuzzy sets in approximate reasoning, Part 1: Inference with possibility distributions, Fuzzy Sets and Systems, 40(1), pp. 143-202.
18. Dubois, D. and Prade, H. (1991). Fuzzy sets in approximate reasoning, Part 2: Logical approaches, Fuzzy Sets and Systems, 40(1), pp. 203-244.
19. Wang, G. J. (2000) *Non-classical Mathematical Logic and Approximate Reasoning,* (Science Press, Beijing, in Chinese).
20. Wang, G. J. (1999). Full implication triple I method for fuzzy reasoning, Science in China (Series E), 29(1), pp. 43-53 (in Chinese).
21. Wang, G. J. and Song, Q. Y. (2003). A new kind of triple I method and its logical foundation, Progress in Natural Science, 13(6), pp. 575-581 (in Chinese).
22. Guo, F. F., Chen, T. Y. and Xia, Z. Q. (2003). Triple I methods for fuzzy reasoning based on maximum fuzzy entropy principle, Fuzzy Systems and Mathematics, 17(4), pp. 55-59 (in Chinese).
23. Li, H. X. (2006). Probability representations of fuzzy systems, Science in China (Series F), 49(3), pp. 339-363.

Index

Lightning Source UK Ltd.
Milton Keynes UK
UKHW020750120320
360226UK00001B/23